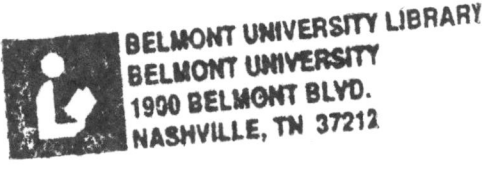

A Companion to Benjamin Franklin

BLACKWELL COMPANIONS TO AMERICAN HISTORY

This series provides essential and authoritative overviews of the scholarship that has shaped our present understanding of the American past. Edited by eminent historians, each volume tackles one of the major periods or themes of American history, with individual topics authored by key scholars who have spent considerable time in research on the questions and controversies that have sparked debate in their field of interest. The volumes are accessible for the nonspecialist, while also engaging scholars seeking a reference to the historiography or future concerns.

Published:

A Companion to the American Revolution
Edited by Jack P. Greene and J.R. Pole

A Companion to 19th-Century America
Edited by William L. Barney

A Companion to the American South
Edited by John B. Boles

A Companion to American Indian History
Edited by Philip J. Deloria and Neal Salisbury

A Companion to American Women's History
Edited by Nancy Hewitt

A Companion to Post-1945 America
Edited by Jean-Christophe Agnew and Roy Rosenzweig

A Companion to the Vietnam War
Edited by Marilyn Young and Robert Buzzanco

A Companion to Colonial America
Edited by Daniel Vickers

A Companion to 20th-Century America
Edited by Stephen J. Whitfield

A Companion to the American West
Edited by William Deverell

A Companion to American Foreign Relations
Edited by Robert Schulzinger

A Companion to the Civil War and Reconstruction
Edited by Lacy K. Ford

A Companion to American Technology
Edited by Carroll Pursell

A Companion to African-American History
Edited by Alton Hornsby

A Companion to American Immigration
Edited by Reed Ueda

A Companion to American Cultural History
Edited by Karen Halttunen

A Companion to California History
Edited by William Deverell and David Igler

A Companion to American Military History
Edited by James Bradford

A Companion Los Angeles
Edited by William Deverell and Greg Hise

A Companion to American Environmental History
Edited by Douglas Cazaux Sackman

A Companion to Benjamin Franklin
Edited by David Waldstreicher

In preparation:
A Companion to American Urban History
Edited by David Quigley

PRESIDENTIAL COMPANIONS

Published:
A Companion to Franklin D. Roosevelt
Edited by William Pederson

A Companion to Richard M. Nixon
Edited by Melvin Small

In preparation:
A Companion to Abraham Lincoln
Edited by Michael Green

A Companion to Thomas Jefferson
Edited by Francis D. Cogliano

A Companion to George Washington
Edited by Edward G. Lengel

A Companion to Harry S. Truman
Edited by Daniel S. Margolies

A Companion to Theodore Roosevelt
Edited by Serge Ricard

A Companion to Lyndon B. Johnson
Edited by Mitchell Lerner

A Companion to Andrew Jackson
Edited by Sean Patrick Adams

A Companion to Woodrow Wilson
Edited by Ross A. Kennedy

A Companion to Dwight D. Eisenhower
Edited by Chester J. Pach

A Companion to Ronald Reagan
Edited by Andrew L. Johns

A Companion to James Madison and James Monroe
Edited by Stuart Leibiger

A Companion to John Adams and John Quincy Adams
Edited by David Waldstreicher

A Companion to the Antebellum Presidents, 1837–61
Edited by Joel Silbey

A Companion to the Reconstruction Presidents, 1865–81
Edited by Edward Frantz

A COMPANION TO BENJAMIN FRANKLIN

Edited by

David Waldstreicher

A John Wiley & Sons, Ltd., Publication

This edition first published 2011
© 2011 Blackwell Publishing Limited

Blackwell Publishing was acquired by John Wiley & Sons in February 2007.
Blackwell's publishing program has been merged with Wiley's global Scientific,
Technical, and Medical business to form Wiley-Blackwell.

Registered Office
John Wiley & Sons Ltd, The Atrium, Southern Gate, Chichester, West Sussex,
PO19 8SQ, United Kingdom

Editorial Offices
350 Main Street, Malden, MA 02148-5020, USA
9600 Garsington Road, Oxford, OX4 2DQ, UK
The Atrium, Southern Gate, Chichester, West Sussex, PO19 8SQ, UK

For details of our global editorial offices, for customer services, and for information about
how to apply for permission to reuse the copyright material in this book please
see our website at www.wiley.com/wiley-blackwell.

The right of David Waldstreicher to be identified as the author of the editorial material
in this work has been asserted in accordance with the UK Copyright, Designs and
Patents Act 1988.

All rights reserved. No part of this publication may be reproduced, stored in a retrieval system,
or transmitted, in any form or by any means, electronic, mechanical, photocopying, recording or
otherwise, except as permitted by the UK Copyright, Designs and Patents Act 1988, without the
prior permission of the publisher.

Wiley also publishes its books in a variety of electronic formats. Some content that
appears in print may not be available in electronic books.

Designations used by companies to distinguish their products are often claimed as trademarks.
All brand names and product names used in this book are trade names, service marks, trademarks or
registered trademarks of their respective owners. The publisher is not associated with any product or
vendor mentioned in this book. This publication is designed to provide accurate and authoritative
information in regard to the subject matter covered. It is sold on the understanding that the publisher
is not engaged in rendering professional services. If professional advice or other expert assistance is
required, the services of a competent professional should be sought.

Library of Congress Cataloging-in-Publication Data

A companion to Benjamin Franklin / edited by David Waldstreicher.
   p. cm. – (Blackwell companions to American history)
  Includes bibliographical references and index.
  ISBN 978-1-4051-9996-4 (hardback)
1. Franklin, Benjamin, 1706-1790. 2. Statesmen–United States–Biography. 3. Scientists–United
States–Biography. 4. Inventors–United States–Biography. 5. Printers–United States–Biography.
6. United States–Intellectual life–18th century. 7. United States–History–Colonial period,
ca. 1600-1775. 8. United States–History–Revolution, 1775-1783. I. Waldstreicher, David.
  E302.6.F8C69 2011
  973.3092–dc22
  [B]
                                                          2011006753

A catalogue record for this book is available from the British Library.

This book is published in the following electronic formats: ePDFs 9781444342123;
Wiley Online Library 9781444342154; ePub 9781444342130; Mobi 9781444342147

Set in 11/13pt Galliard by SPi Publisher Services, Pondicherry, India
Printed and bound in Singapore by Markono Print Media Pte Ltd

1 2011

To the editors of
The Papers of Benjamin Franklin
1959 to the present

*But especially
Kate Ohno
Barbara Oberg
Jonathan Dull
Ellen Cohn
For being interesting
Curious
Friendly
And helpful
Like Franklin*

Contents

List of Figures	x
About the Contributors	xi
Introduction *David Waldstreicher*	1

Part I Biography   5

1 Franklin's Boston Years, 1706–1723   7
   Nian-Sheng Huang

2 The Philadelphia Years, 1723–1757   25
   George W. Boudreau

3 The Making of a Patriot, 1757–1775   46
   Sheila L. Skemp

4 Franklin Furioso, 1775–1790   65
   Jonathan R. Dull

Part II Franklin and Eighteenth-Century America   81

5 Benjamin Franklin and Colonial Society   83
   Konstantin Dierks

6 Benjamin Franklin and Pennsylvania Politics   104
   Alan Tully

7 Benjamin Franklin and Religion   129
   John Fea

8	Benjamin Franklin and the Coming of the American Revolution *Benjamin L. Carp*	146
9	Benjamin Franklin and Native Americans *Timothy J. Shannon*	164
10	The Complexion of My Country: Benjamin Franklin and the Problem of Racial Diversity *Nicholas Guyatt*	183
11	Benjamin Franklin, Capitalism, and Slavery *David Waldstreicher*	211
12	Benjamin Franklin and Women *Susan E. Klepp*	237

Part III Franklin the Writer and Thinker — 253

13	"The Manners and Situation of a Rising People": Reading Franklin's *Autobiography* *Ormond Seavey*	255
14	Poor Richard's Almanac *William Pencak*	275
15	Benjamin Franklin and Journalism *David Paul Nord*	290
16	Benjamin Franklin, the Science of Flow, and the Legacy of the Enlightenment *Laura Rigal*	308
17	Benjamin Franklin, Associations, and Civil Society *Albrecht Koschnik*	335
18	Empire and Nation *Eliga H. Gould*	359
19	Franklin's Pictorial Representations of British America *Lester C. Olson*	373

Part IV Franklin and the Categories of Inquiry — 391

20	American Literature and American Studies *Edward Cahill*	393
21	Benjamin Franklin's Material Cultures *Megan E. Walsh*	412
22	Benjamin Franklin and Political Theory *Jerry Weinberger*	430

23	Benjamin Franklin and International Relations *Leonard J. Sadosky*	463
24	Benjamin Franklin in Memory and Popular Culture *Andrew M. Schocket*	479

Bibliography 499
Index 536

List of Figures

19.1 "The Franklin Medal," 1784. Medium: silver, bronze or brass medal, maker: Augustin Dupré, size: 1 3/4" diameter. Photograph courtesy of the American Philosophical Society.   374

19.2 "JOIN, or DIE," *Pennsylvania Gazette*, May 9, 1754, p. 2, col. 2. maker: [Benjamin Franklin], publisher: Benjamin Franklin and David Hall, medium: newspaper, 2 7/8" × 2". Photograph courtesy of the Library of Congress.   375

19.3 MAGNA Britannia: her Colonies REDUC'D," Benjamin Franklin, [circa 1766]. medium: print, size: 4 1/8" × 5 7/8". Photograph courtesy of The Library Company of Philadelphia.   376

19.4 "One Sixth of a Dollar," 1776. publisher: [David] Hall and [William] Sellers, medium: colonial currency, size: 3 1/4" × 2 1/2". Photograph courtesy the Library of Congress, Thatcher Collection.   377

19.5 *Libertas Americana*, proposed and commissioned by Benjamin Franklin, executed by Augustin Dupré, 1783. Photograph courtesy of the British Museum, Department of Coins and Medals. © The Trustees of the British Museum.   377

19.6 "JOIN, or DIE," from "Copies & Extracts of Several Newspapers, printed in New England, Sept.-Nov. 1765, and referred to in Gov. Bernard's letters (108 pp.)," masthead (p. 3), February 1766. Parliamentary Archives, London.   384

About the Contributors

George W. Boudreau teaches history and humanities at Penn State's Capital College. A 1998 Ph.D. in history and American studies from Indiana University, his research explores American cultural history, ranging from readership to material culture, built environments, and public history. He was founding editor of *Early American Studies: An Interdisciplinary Journal* as well as co-editor of *Explorations in Early American Culture*. He has received numerous research fellowships, and in addition to his current teaching assignment, he directs summer research workshops for K-12 teachers from around the country, which explore the life and times of Benjamin Franklin.

Edward Cahill is an Assistant Professor of English and American Studies at Fordham University, where he teaches early American literature and culture. His essays have appeared in *American Literature, Early American Literature, Early American Studies*, and *Common-Place*. His first book, *Liberty of the Imagination: Aesthetic Theory, Literary Form, and Politics in the Early United States*, is forthcoming from the University of Pennsylvania Press.

Benjamin L. Carp is Associate Professor of History at Tufts University. He is the author of *Rebels Rising: Cities and the American Revolution* (Oxford University Press, 2007) and *Defiance of the Patriots: The Boston Tea Party and the Making of America* (Yale University Press, 2010).

Konstantin Dierks is Associate Professor of History at Indiana University, Bloomington, and author of *In My Power: Letter Writing and Communications in Early America* (University of Pennsylvania Press, 2009). He is currently working on a book on American imaginaries of the wider world from the mid-seventeenth to the mid-nineteenth century.

Jonathan R. Dull is a descendant of one of the Palatine boors about whom Franklin warned. For 31 years he served on the staff of *The Papers of Benjamin Franklin*, retiring in 2008 as Senior Associate Editor. Author of twenty articles and six books, including *Franklin the Diplomat: The French Mission* (Philadelphia, 1982), *A Diplomatic History of the American Revolution* (New Haven, 1985) and *Benjamin Franklin and the American Revolution* (Lincoln, Nebraska, 2010), he has received American, Canadian, and French literary awards.

John Fea is Associate Professor of History and Chair of the History Department at Messiah College in Grantham, Pennsylvania. He is the author of *The Way of Improvement Leads Home: Philip Vickers Fithian and the Rural Enlightenment in Early America* (Pennsylvania, 2008) and *Was America Founded as a Christian Nation: A Historical Introduction* (Westminster/John Knox, 2011). His articles on early American religion have appeared in *The Journal of American History, Explorations in Early American History and Culture, Nineteenth-Century American History*, and *Common-Place*.

Eliga H. Gould teaches history at the University of New Hampshire. He is the author most recently of *An Unfinished Peace: The American Revolution and the Legal Transformation of the European Atlantic* (2011).

Nicholas Guyatt teaches American history at the University of York in England. He is the author of *Providence and the Invention of the United States* (Cambridge, 2007), and the co-editor of *Race, Expansion and War, 1770–1830* (Palgrave, 2010). He has been a graduate fellow at the Princeton Center for Human Values and a faculty fellow at the Stanford Humanities Center, and is currently working on a book about the relationship between ideas of racial equality and schemes for racial separation in the early United States.

Nian-Sheng Huang is Professor of History at California State University Channel Islands. Working with Professor Michael Kammen, he received the doctorate in history from Cornell University in 1990. He is the author of *Benjamin Franklin in the American Thought and Culture* (1994) and *Franklin's Father Josiah* (2000), both published by the American Philosophical Society. His current research studies poverty and the poor in early Massachusetts.

Susan E. Klepp is Professor of History at Temple University and editor of the *Journal of the Early Republic*. Her recent book, *Revolutionary Conceptions: Women, Fertility and Family Limitation in America, 1760–1820* (2009) was awarded the AHA/Joan Kelly Memorial Prize in Women's History.

Albrecht Koschnik is an independent scholar living in Philadelphia, Pennsylvania. He received his Ph.D. in American History from the University of Virginia in 2000. His articles have appeared in the

William and Mary Quarterly and the collection *Beyond the Founders: New Approaches to the Political History of the Early American Republic*, among other venues, and he is the author of *"Let a Common Interest Bind Us Together": Associations, Partisanship, and Culture in Philadelphia, 1775–1840* (2007). Currently he is at work on a book manuscript describing American conceptions of civil society from the American Revolution to the Civil War.

David Paul Nord is Professor of Journalism and Adjunct Professor of History at Indiana University. He is author of *Faith in Reading: Religious Publishing and the Birth of Mass Media in America* (2004), and *Communities of Journalism: A History of American Newspapers and Their Readers* (2001), and co-editor of *A History of the Book in America, Vol. 5: The Enduring Book: Print Culture in Postwar America* (2009).

Lester C. Olson is a Professor of Communication at the University of Pittsburgh, where he specializes in public address, visual rhetoric, and human rights advocacy. His books include *Emblems of American Community in the Revolutionary Era* (1991), *Benjamin Franklin's Vision of American Community* (2004), and, with co-editors Cara A. Finnegan and Diane S. Hope, *Visual Rhetoric* (2007). His essays concerning Audre Lorde's public advocacy can be found in the *Quarterly Journal of Speech* (1997, 1998), *Philosophy & Rhetoric* (2000), *American Voices* (2005), *Queering Public Address* (2007), and *The Responsibilities of Rhetoric* (2010).

William Pencak is Professor of History and Jewish Studies at the Pennsylvania State University. He has edited the journal *Pennsylvania History* (1994–2002), founded the journal *Explorations in Early American Culture* (now *Early American Studies*) in 1997, and edited six books for Penn State Press on Pennsylvania and early American history. He is now writing a biography of William White, the first bishop of the Episcopal Church in Pennsylvania.

Laura Rigal is an Associate Professor of American Studies and English at the University of Iowa. She has published widely in the field of eighteenth and nineteenth-century American history and culture, and is the author of *The American Manufactory: Art, Labor, and the World of Things in the Early Republic* (Princeton University Press, 1998). She is presently writing a cultural history of fluid dynamics, *Rivers of Light: American Hydrodynamics and the Empire of Enlightenment, 1750–1900*, as well as an environmental history of an urban creek, *Forgetting Ralston Creek: The Environmental History of an Urban Waterway*.

Leonard J. Sadosky is an independent scholar and holds a Ph.D. from the University of Virginia (2003) and is a past fellow at both the Robert H. Smith International Center for Jefferson Studies at Monticello and Johns Hopkins

University. He is the author of *Revolutionary Negotiations: Indians, Empires, and Diplomats in the Founding of America* (2009) and co-author with Peter S. Onuf of *Jeffersonian America* (2002).

Andrew M. Schocket is Associate Professor of History and American Culture Studies at Bowling Green State University. Author of *Founding Corporate Power in Early National Philadelphia* (2007) and various articles in peer-reviewed journals, and a frequent writer for the History News Service, he is now writing a book on the American Revolution in contemporary popular culture and politics.

Timothy J. Shannon is a Professor of History at Gettysburg College in Gettysburg, Pennsylvania. He is the author of several books, including *Indians and Colonists at the Crossroads of Empire: The Albany Congress of 1754* (2000) and *Iroquois Diplomacy on the Early American Frontier* (2008).

Ormond Seavey is Professor of English at the George Washington University. He is the author of *Becoming Benjamin Franklin: the Autobiography and the Life* (1988) and the editor of Franklin, *Autobiography and Other Writings* (Oxford World's Classics, 1993).

Sheila L. Skemp is the Clare Leslie Marquette Chair of American History at the University of Mississippi, where she has taught since 1980. She is the author of *William Franklin: Son of a Patriot, Servant of a King* (Oxford, 1990) and *William and Benjamin Franklin: Patriot and Loyalist, Father and Son* (Bedford, 1994) as well as articles about Franklin in the *Pennsylvania Magazine of History and Biography*, and *Time* magazine.

Alan Tully is the Eugene C. Barker Centennial Professor of American History and Department Chair at the University of Texas at Austin. He is the author of *Pennsylvania Politics, 1746–1770. The Movement for Royal Government and Its Consequences* (1972), *William Penn's Legacy: Politics and Social Structure in Provincial Pennsylvania, 1726–1755* (1977) and *Forming American Politics: Ideas, Interests, and Institutions in Colonial New York and Pennsylvania* (1994).

David Waldstreicher is Professor of History at Temple University and the author of *In the Midst of Perpetual Fetes: The Making of American Nationalism, 1776–1820* (1997), *Runaway America: Benjamin Franklin, Slavery, and the American Revolution* (2004) and *Slavery's Constitution: From Revolution to Ratification* (2009).

Megan E. Walsh is Assistant Professor of English at the Ohio State University at Lima. She is currently working on a book about the connections between visual media, literary culture, and politics in the early republic.

Jerry Weinberger is Professor of Political Science at Michigan State University, where he is also Director of the LeFrak Forum and Co-Director of the Symposium on Science, Reason, and Modern Democracy. His latest book is *Benjamin Franklin Unmasked: On the Unity of His Moral, Religious, and Political Thought* (University Press of Kansas, 2005, paperback 2008). He is currently at work on a book on the political thought of Martin Heidegger and is an occasional contributor to *City Journal*.

Introduction

David Waldstreicher

"But do you *like* Benjamin Franklin?" It's a question I have fielded dozens of times. After writing a book about Franklin's relationship to America's original sin, slavery (Waldstreicher, 2004), I suppose I should have been prepared for it. Still the question always flummoxed me. I always answered yes, and meant it. *Of course I like Franklin. How could anyone not like Franklin?*

Not just because he was one of the most interesting people who lived in eighteenth-century America. Not just because he invented or had a hand in inventing a lot of useful things, like a stove, bifocals, and the Constitution of the United States of America. Not just because he was a shrewd, artful, sometimes hilarious writer. But because I think of myself as indebted to him in more ways that I can account for – and because I would like to build on but move beyond him in at least a few ways. Americans today *are* Benjamin Franklin. We can't help but be. *And* we are not. We can't help that, either.

Jill Lepore (2010) has recently written of the desire of some Americans to treat history as a religion, in which the founding fathers have all the answers and our job is to stay true to their words and actions. With Franklin it goes even deeper than deep politics, or religion. The fact that *The Autobiography of Benjamin Franklin* remains a classroom standard and that biographies and television series rolled off the presses for the tercentenary of his birth, makes the problem of our relationship to him rather more complicated as well as ubiquitous.

One of Franklin's great legacies to Americans was his willingness, indeed, to *run away* from home, to start something new. And one of the great

---

A Companion to Benjamin Franklin, First Edition. Edited by David Waldstreicher.
© 2011 Blackwell Publishing Ltd. Published 2011 by Blackwell Publishing Ltd.

questions in studying Franklin is to comprehend how this talented young troublemaker became the earnest artisan who became the even-tempered politician who became the sage of Philadelphia and the Western world. As one historian has remarked of another eighteenth-century New Englander, again and again Franklin seems to have been "a person with enough sense of [him]self to become someone else." (Young, 2005: 88).

The scholars in this volume do not always agree about what is important about Benjamin Franklin. But they ask the right questions, give us a cornucopia of good answers about his long career. They introduce us to what a broad swath of scholars have been saying about him and his world for the past hundred or more years. They make it clear what the difference is between hero worship and careful interpretation based on examination of the original sources. Even more, they show how good scholarship always builds on, rather than arrogantly ignoring, the work that has come before.

It is always fashionable and even expected in academia to say that scholarship on one subject or another has been advancing by leaps and bounds since, say, whoever is writing joined the enterprise. Actually, in the case of Franklin, one can detect certain lulls, but actually there have always been interesting, original books – and there have also always been derivative knockoffs and myth-building fictions. One can still pick up older biographies by Carl Van Doren (1939), Verner W. Crane (1954), Ronald Clark (1983), and even John Bach McMaster (1893), and be struck by the careful and insightful qualities, even though they did not have the modern editions of *The Papers of Benjamin Franklin* (thirty-nine volumes to date) ready at hand. These books are still a good place to start – and in some respects better than recent bestselling biographies by H.W. Brands (2000) and Walter Isaacson (2003), good writers who got a tremendous head start by standing on the shoulders of generations of scholars but who then failed to fully acknowledge their debts.

Recent brief overviews by leading scholars such as Jonathan R. Dull, Edmund S. Morgan, and Gordon S. Wood, are also fine starting points. The present volume has more to offer. By beginning with interpretive overviews of four parts of Franklin's life, it introduces the biggest issues surrounding the life of Franklin. The next section covers key aspects of Franklin's experience in the eighteenth-century world. Because Franklin was a printer who did much by writing (and much else while writing), the next group of essays deals with key aspects of his mind and his literary productions, assaying his contributions to American culture and politics. The final section addresses Franklin's place in five key interdisciplinary areas where a sense of his importance has been building as those areas of inquiry have changed in recent years. The authors in this collection have drawn on their own research and the tremendous output of several disciplines presented in the bibliography at the end of the book.

I have come up with a new answer to the question I started out with – but being a professor, I like to turn answers into new questions. Sure I *like* Franklin … but which Franklin do I like best? Sometimes I like the younger Franklin better than the senior statesman. With power comes responsibility. But in general, I like all the Franklins more all the time – because scholars keep making him more interesting.

Part I

Biography

Chapter One

Franklin's Boston Years, 1706–1723

Nian-Sheng Huang

Few Bostonians noticed the birth of Benjamin Franklin on a wintry Sunday in 1706, which has become one of the most memorialized events in history. The future printer, publisher, writer, inventor, scientist, patriot, and diplomat of international renown was the son of Abiah (Folger) and Josiah Franklin, a tallow chandler in town. The infant was baptized the same day on January 6 (Old Style; January 17, New Style) at the Old South Church, right across from the family's small tenement house in Milk Street. A growing urban center itself, colonial Boston played a crucial role in shaping the formative years of this young boy, whose energy, prodigy, ambition, and rebellion would soon make him someone to reckon with in this orthodox Puritan community. Franklin's *Autobiography* describes many major events in his childhood, the information of which modern scholars continue to rely on (unless otherwise indicated, many quotes in this chapter also came directly from part one of that book). Yet they differ in emphases. Whereas biographers from Carl Van Doren, Esmond Wright and H.W. Brands to Walter Isaacson chronicled this period, Arthur B. Tourtellot remains the one who has focused on the young Franklin in Boston. Through extensive studies of Franklin's writings in the *New-England Courant* and other contemporary publications, Perry Miller and J.A. Leo Lemay demonstrate not only how society has shaped Franklin, but also how he has fought against tradition and orthodoxy by searching for a novel voice of personal expressions at a very young age.

A Companion to Benjamin Franklin, First Edition. Edited by David Waldstreicher.
© 2011 Blackwell Publishing Ltd. Published 2011 by Blackwell Publishing Ltd.

1.1 Parents

The Franklins came from Ecton, a hamlet only a few miles outside Northampton in England, where the family had a small estate and a blacksmith shop. Born in 1657, Josiah Franklin was the youngest son of Jane White and Thomas Franklin 2nd. Their oldest son, Thomas 3rd, inherited the family estate but mistreated the father who, in 1666, moved to stay with his second son John at Banbury in the neighboring Oxfordshire. A gentle and agreeable person, John also took Josiah, then about nine years old, as apprentice in his dyeing business. Within ten years Josiah finished his apprenticeship, married Anne Child of Ecton in 1677, and had their first child Elizabeth the next year. Things then turned sour, however. Shortly after Anne gave birth to a son Samuel in 1681, Josiah's father passed away. Brother John, now thirty-nine, was finally getting married and so was another brother Benjamin, who returned to Banbury from London where his business had not gone well. All three brothers were dyers, raising their families, and trying to make it in the same town, which also had other dyers. As the youngest, Josiah wanted no competition and decided to leave. Along with Anne, five-year-old Elizabeth, two-year-old Samuel, and the infant Hannah, he left Banbury for Boston in New England in the summer of 1683.

At that time Massachusetts law (in 1651, 1662, and 1672) forbade "men or women of mean condition" to imitate the fashion of the upper class by wearing silk. A provincial town of under ten thousand souls, Boston did not have a rich clientele large enough to support newly arrived dyers until an influx of royal officials later that decade when Massachusetts became a crown colony. Not the least would it favor those dyers who were unable to establish a calender house for a heavy press to scour woolens, silk, and other delicate material. Struggling to survive but limited by resources, Josiah Franklin decided to adapt. His versatility, mechanical dexterity, and a strong personal determination, all of which were a trademark of the Franklins, helped in this transition. He tried several different businesses and finally settled as a soap boiler and candle maker, a profession he kept for the rest of his life.

After giving birth to seven children in twelve years, Anne Franklin did not survive the transatlantic migration for long and died in July 1689. In November the Reverend Samuel Willard, pastor of the Old South Church, officiated Josiah's marriage to Abiah Folger, daughter of Mary (Morrill) and Peter Folger of Nantucket. Both Abiah and Josiah later became church members and were married for more than fifty years. Fellow parishioner Samuel Sewall, in his diaries, recorded praying with them at least ten times. Josiah died in Boston in 1745 at the age of 88, and Abiah in 1752 at 85. The couple had ten children. Although never as pious as his parents,

Benjamin Franklin's childhood resembled that of his father's – both were the youngest son in the family, both were apprenticed to their older brother, both were hard-working, ingenious, multi-talented, gregarious, and public-spirited, and yet both were forced to leave and seek a new life somewhere else away from their birthplace.

1.2 Childhood and Education

The boy, who could read at the age of four or five, seemed to have promise which no loving parents would miss. They had planned to send this tenth son to serve in the ministry, and in 1714 enrolled him at the South Grammar School, which was a necessary step to prepare him for the college entrance exam. A college degree, not to mention the ability to read Latin, Greek, and Hebrew, was of course the first prerequisite for becoming a clergyman. Within a year, however, reality set in that the limited incomes from the father's trade would never be enough to feed his large family and at the same time to support his son through the grammar school, let alone a college. The boy was then withdrawn and transferred to a private writing school headed by Mr. George Brownell. Although the boy enjoyed the classes and performed reasonably well except for arithmetic, family circumstances once again resulted in his second withdrawal when he was only ten. Unlike many children from substantial families, therefore, Franklin's formal schooling ended in two years and his subsequent education was largely self-taught.

Such a serious setback must have been disappointing for anyone who had dreams to rise from an artisan background to a member of the educated community. Yet the boy did not dwell on self-pity. If he had experienced any melancholy, it was quickly replaced by a kind of upbeat self-determination which would sustain much of his adult life. If his aversion to privileges later led to a commitment to egalitarianism, the harsh realities of social divide and modest family circumstances also forced him to cultivate self-reliance, to overcome career obstacles by his own effort, to bite the tongue and not to complain about those misfortunes falling on him.

He began to develop his life-long habit of learning from commonsense wisdom, from avid reading, from personal trials and mistakes, and from close observations of human experiences. He noticed his mother's excellent dyeing skills. He learned a shorthand from his uncle Benjamin the Elder, whose interest in poetry once aroused his curiosity. He admired his father who played the violin and could "draw prettily," besides being a singer, a carpenter, and a public servant. His father's two big maps on the wall first attracted him to geography. So did the father's comments on public discourse make him realize the need to improve his own writing style. Like the father, the son relished proverbs and homely sayings. Some typified his taste, such as "Seest thou a Man diligent in his Calling, he shall stand before Kings," while others mocked those professionals whose formal training had produced no upright men, such as "God heals, and the Doctor takes the Fees" or "A countryman between 2 Lawyers, is like a fish between two cats." Simple but profound, some still would captivate his whole career, such as "The noblest question in the world is, *What Good may I do in it?*"

One thing the boy did regret was that father possessed few books beyond devout polemics. The gap was somewhat compensated later when he was able to borrow books from the tanner friend Matthew Adams. Brother James's library also helped, which consisted of works from Pliny's *Natural History*, Aristotle's *Politics*, and Herman Moll's *Geography* to an eight-volume set of *The Spectator*. The boy's perusal of books on diverse topics opened his mind to literature, history, ethics, and the natural sciences. For a while, at sixteen, Thomas Tryon's *Way to Health* converted him to a vegetarian. He enjoyed John Bunyan's *Pilgrim's Progress*, Plutarch's *Parallel Lives*, Daniel Defoe's *Essay Upon Projects*, and Cotton Mather's *Essays to Do Good*. The last two in particular had given him such a "Turn of Thinking" that he attributed his life-long commitment to public service to his early reading of them.

Franklin was not alone in his aloofness from religious services in Boston, where interest in spiritual matters did decline before the Great Awakening. He was, however, never insensitive to those good morals that anyone could demonstrate. Cotton Mather's promotion of "doing good" was one example, and his warning the young Franklin "to stoop" to avoid a head-on collision was another. From his father he learned that "nothing was useful which was not honest." From his siblings he learned the cost of his blind passion for a whistle. He would continue to learn many more similar lessons in the years to come from a series of errata, indiscretion, ignorance, and inexperience he later enumerated in the *Autobiography*. Unlike erudite writers who tended to quote classical texts by famed authorities, he was willing to share those twists and turns he had learned from his personal experiences. Whereas some critics believe that he was too earthy and self-righteous, if not downright pretentious, his habit of sharing intimate lessons must be viewed in the context of the way he had grown up and of the emphasis he had placed on how to gain knowledge not only from textbooks and classrooms but also from close observations of day-to-day activities. Thus he preferred expressions such as "God helps them that help themselves" or "'Tis hard for an empty bag to stand upright." This habit would become so proverbial that on the last day of the Constitutional Convention in 1787, delegates would hear him haranguing, at the age of eighty-one, that "the older I grow the more apt I am to doubt my own Judgment and to pay more Respect to the judgment of others" (Lemay, 1987: 1139).

1.3 Apprenticeship

Contemporary Bostonians saw crown officials wearing scarlet, wealthy men riding carriages, gentlewomen going to country estates to pick and eat cherries, and households of good fortune celebrating at the pomp of Harvard's commencement at Cambridge. The Franklins could not afford any of those luxuries. They toiled hard to make ends meet. Worse still, the smelly, hot, and extremely tedious work of a tallow chandler and soap boiler bored the boy within days. Clearly, cutting wicks, filling the mold, attending shop, and running errands would never enchant him. Even though the father was content with the trade, he quickly saw that his prodigious son was unhappy and restless. Concerned, he took the boy to visit several businesses in the hope that one of them might be to his liking, but this did not happen. The father finally decided to bind Benjamin as an apprentice to the older son James, whom he had recently helped to set up a printing shop in Queen Street.

An indenture between two kin was commonplace those days. Once bound to his own brother, the father did not see anything wrong this time. The boy, however, had an ambition as big as anyone else's. He used to have a fancy for the sea, which the father firmly disallowed – he had already lost a son going to the sea. Franklin stood out for a while and was only prevailed to sign the indentures after persuasion. Now at twelve years old, he had to serve for nine long years until twenty-one, which must have seemed eternal to this strong-minded and unfettered adolescent at the moment. The initial doubt and resistance dissipated soon after he gained great proficiency in the two basic skills of the business – typesetting and press work. He started to like the new trade, which demanded strength as well as intelligence. For one thing, he now had access to the shop's book collection. For another, he gradually became acquainted with several book sellers, stationers, and bookish customers, who took note of his interest and kindly lent books for him to read. Most of all, a wide variety of products such as sheets, broadsides, tracts, pamphlets, chapbooks, small volumes, and newspapers passed through his hand daily and he was tempted to explore whether he might write something for the printing press. Would that be ideal – a situation allowing him to combine his literary interest in reading and composition with dreary labor? Captivated by the prospect, he took steps to embrace the world of writing and print, which he thoroughly enjoyed through the rest of his life.

Franklin's expanding skills at the press, increasing knowledge of the printing business, and a growing ambition of becoming a writer boosted his ego and gradually altered his attitude toward James. Reluctant to enter the indentures in the first place, the printer's devil now gained confidence to see James as his equal, not his master. Nine years older than Franklin, James would view things differently. Perhaps feeling the threat that the junior brother might indeed be his competitor instead of his servant, he insisted on his authority as the boss. When sometimes he felt his apprentice too saucy and provocative, he was willing to use the fist to subdue him, which only led to more complaints and resentment.

The sibling crossfires caught the father in the middle. Franklin used to think that being the youngest and smartest boy in the family, he was father's favorite, which was probably true until this point. Now that the father had borrowed several hundred pounds to finance James's business, he was deeply in debt and wanted to see harmony rather than domestic quarrels that rocked the boat. Franklin sensed that father began to side with James on more occasions than before. Instinctively he felt the grip of both father and brother falling on him, a type of constraint and control he had never been comfortable with since his toddler days.

The father had his reasons to keep a balance between the two brothers. He had taken some considerable risk to help set up James's printing shop. The Franklins had produced no printers in the past. Nor was it definitively recorded where and when James had undergone standard training in the business. While acquiring the press, types, and other equipment was a considerable investment, more costly than many practical trades, success was far from guaranteed. In 1718 Boston had five printers – Bartholomew Green, John Allen, Thomas Fleet, Thomas Crump, and Samuel Kneeland. Fleet was from London. Green and Kneeland were well connected to the powerhouse of printers in the colony – they descended from Samuel Green, the second printer in Massachusetts. Although the town had developed a print culture and book trade more advanced than any other colonial center by that time, the scope of their operations remained small and limited. No one knew whether or not the local population and market demand would be large enough to support another self-proclaimed printer from the obscure family of a tallow chandler.

Since the eldest son in the family, John, had already followed the father's footsteps to become a candle maker and soap boiler, the younger ones (except for Peter who also became a candle maker) had to branch out to find their own professions. James was indeed struggling to survive in the new business for the first few years. Fortunately, both father and Uncle Benjamin the Elder were trained dyers, whose knowledge and experience helped him to add printing cloth to his business. He put this advertisement in the *Boston Gazette* in 1719 that "the Printer hereby Prints Linens, Callicoes, Silks, &c. in good Figures, very lively and durable Colours, and without the offensive Smell which commonly attends the Linens Printed here." Apparently, his special skill and technique enabled him to establish a fine reputation in this line of service. When a year later a person in Charlestown began to forge similar products by adopting his name, James was understandably outraged. He immediately published a notice which demanded an end of the practice or threatened to bring the transgressor to the court of justice.

1.4 Journalistic Debut

In fact, working for James turned out to be a blessing. According to Lemay, America's first newspaperman was not Franklin but his brother James who "made the *New-England Courant* the first literary, lively, entertaining, humorous, and proto-nationalistic American newspaper" (Lemay, 2006a: 109). The first writing in print which showed Franklin's literary talent took place in his brother's shop where he wrote a ballad called *The Lighthouse Tragedy* toward the end of 1718 (Leonard, 1999). Franklin clearly recalled that it was James who had encouraged him to write the ballad, which "sold wonderfully." Still, Franklin was indebted to his brother more than he explicitly stated in the *Autobiography*. Or as Lemay has pointed out, Franklin "learned about the printing business, running a newspaper, drumming up interest in the paper, and literary techniques from his older brother," and "learned the arts of publicity and of controversy from his brother," and that he "also imbibed his older brother's radical Whig ideology as well as his resentment of the assumption of superiority by ministers and the civil authorities" (Lemay, 2006a: 142). Working for his brother particularly suited Franklin's literary ambition, which was further stimulated by a group of friends and visitors to the shop who desired to use James's newspaper to vent their sentiments.

Two other newspapers already existed at that time, the *Boston News-Letter* and the *Boston Gazette*, which refused to publish anything critical to the established authorities, civil or religious. The *Courant* meant to be different as its title suggested. Whereas most colonial publishers printed official proceedings and copied oversea news from imported newspapers, the *Courant* sought those who could offer their individual opinions with a literary flair. It therefore attracted writers and contributors of a contrarian bent. From August 1721 to May 1722, within the first ten months of the establishment of the *New-England Courant*, at least fourteen people supported James's business by contributing ninety-four pieces of letters, essays, notes, and poems to the publication, and about a half of them contributed repeatedly. The most prolific of this group was Nathaniel Gardner, who wrote no fewer than thirty-two times for the *Courant*. He was a tanner and a partner of Matthew Adams, whom Franklin mentioned as an early friend in the *Autobiography*. He was an inventive writer and sometimes co-edited the *Courant* with James. A member of the First Church, he exposed religious abuses frequently and yet without savage mockery. In a January 1721/2 issue of the *Courant*, he sketched a character which may have made a lasting impression on Franklin, who later created his famous Poor

Richard and his wife Bridget. Gardner wrote that he was "sadly fatigu'd with a Scolding Wife, and in short she is such a *Shrew*, as I believe cannot be match'd in all Christendom." "I am such a quiet man," continued he, "(as my Neighbours can all testifie) that I willingly part with any thing for peace (the Breeches not excepted) and am afraid to say my Soul is my own in her Presence." This little gem, Lemay says, was "the best social satire to appear thus far in an American newspaper" (Lemay, 2006a: 87–89, 91).

Other contributors to the *Courant* included John Checkley, John Williams, Thomas Lane, Captain Christopher Taylor, John Eyre, Matthew Adams, and a Mrs. Staples. Born in Boston, John Checkley attended the South Grammar School. He later studied at Oxford and traveled extensively on the Continent. He wrote *Choice Dialogues between a Godly Minister & an Honest Countrymen*, which censured the Puritan doctrines of election and predestination. In this lively piece he used a country bumpkin *persona* who possessed considerable mother wit. "This incipient American posture probably delighted young Franklin." "As Franklin recognized," Lemay wrote, "Checkley imitated the first issue of the *Spectator* (which began with a description of the supposed author) but transformed it with an American flavor" (2006a: 96). Clearly, James, his unorthodox associates, and a group of opinionated contributors made the *New-England Courant* "America's first fiercely independent newspaper, a bold, antiestablishment journal that helped to create the nation's tradition of an irreverent press" (Isaacson, 2003: 22). Trained in this environment, the aspiring young Franklin was as much a creature of as an active participant in that bold, antiestablishment, and irreverent culture.

1.5 Controversy over Inoculation

From its inception, the *New-England Courant* was deeply involved in a bitter debate over the practice of inoculation following a smallpox outbreak in Boston in 1721 (Lemay, 2006a: 84). Although silent on the issue at the time (Chaplin, 2006: 23), Franklin publicly declared his belief in inoculation as "a safe and beneficial Practice" in 1736 (Van Doren, 1938: 126). Yet later generations have continued to speculate over his "true" stand, as several key players played a far more important role than he at fifteen.

Two contributors to the newspaper, Dr. William Douglass and Dr. George Steward, opposed inoculation. Dr. Steward thought that inoculated persons could spread the disease and thus insisted that only persons in excellent health might be inoculated (Lemay, 2006a: 103). Arrogant and highly opinionated, Dr. Douglass was nevertheless an independent thinker and a talented naturalist and physician. Boston's only practitioner with a medical degree from Edinburgh, he also published *A Summary, Historical and Political* (1749–1751) – an extensive two-volume account of British North

American colonies. Suspecting both the lethal nature of inoculation and its source of information, he led anti-inoculators and voiced strong opposition in July 1721 by attacking Dr. Zabdiel Boylston, who had started voluntary inoculation at the suggestion of Cotton Mather (Minardi, 2004). Yet after all facts had come in at the end of the controversy, Douglass, as a good scientist, was the first one to urge inoculation in 1730 when another epidemic threatened Boston (P. Miller, 1953: 362).

1.6 Blossoming

Franklin wrote more than a dozen pieces for his brother's journal, the first blossoming of his literary gift in print. Even though other contributors' flamboyance and antiestablishment stance stimulated him, he surpassed many of them in boldness, irony, humor, and theatrical effect, a remarkable feast for a lad at sixteen. His Silence Dogood essays, totaling fourteen in number published between April 2 and October 8, 1722, were compelling illustrations of his mind and literary imagination during this period.

Perhaps the single most remarkable accomplishment in his series was the creation of the *persona* Silence Dogood. Purported to be a minister's widow, the pseudonym itself transpired numerous inferences and mysteries. The surname mocked Cotton Mather, the running title of whose popular book *Bonifacius* was called "Essays to Do Good." The first name, "Silence," had several connotations. It derided Cotton Mather, who was a notorious busybody never silent in admonishing others. It echoed an essay signed "Rusticus" by Nathaniel Gardner, and may also have alluded to Mather's recent sermon, *Silentiarius*. These inferences became apparent as the first essay openly attacked Mather's *Magnalia Christi Americana*. As readers read the subsequent essays, however, they might think that the author could have some altruistic purpose too. In a vein similar to that of Mather's *Bonifacius*, the essayist raised schemes to improve society, such as promotion of modesty and a strong censure of waste and alcoholism. Thus, Franklin's first literary *persona* produced multiple ironies – an anonymous author who had both a penchant for privacy and an urge to talk, a member from the supposed weaker gender speaking to a powerful male audience and secretly, an under-age youngster haranguing the adult world about some of the most revered public icons and highly respected authorities.

"At the time of my Birth," Silence Dogood recalled, "my Parents were on Ship-board in their Way from *London to N. England*. My Entrance into this troublesome World was attended with the Death of my Father, a Misfortune, which tho' I was not then capable of knowing, I shall never be able to forget; for he, poor Man, stood upon the Deck rejoycing at my Birth, a merciless Wave entred the Ship, and in one Moment carry'd him beyond Reprieve. Thus was the First day which I saw, the Last that was seen by my Father; and thus was my disconsolate Mother at once made both a parent and a Widow." Such a tragic beginning was of course Franklin's strategy, which was preceded by his ridicule of Mather's account of "The Death of Mr. John Avery" in *Magnalia Christi Americana*. Franklin's masterful arrangement to maximize a dramatic effect was achieved because his witty style, clever tone, humorous reversal, and the comic situation "all burlesque the ostensible tragedy with its sentimental diction ('a merciless Wave') and religious clichés ('this troublesome World,' 'beyond Reprieve')" (Lemay, 2006a: 143–146).

Alternating between explicit biblical messages or sexual insinuations and sometimes a blunt animality, Silence Dogood continued her story. Spending her "Infancy and Childhood in Vanity and Idleness," she said, "until I was bound out Apprentice, that I might no longer be a Charge to my Indigent Mother, who was put to hard Shifts for a Living." Yet she exceeded the usual "Knowledge and Learning which is necessary for our Sex" by her interest in "reading ingenious Books," and therefore became a suitable mate for her master, the country minister. "My Reverend Master who had hitherto remained a Batchelor, (after much Meditation of the Eighteenth verse of the Second Chapter of *Genesis*) took up a Resolution to marry; and having made several unsuccessful fruitless Attempts on the more topping Sort of our Sex," said she, "he began unexpectedly to cast a loving Eye upon Me, whom he had brought up cleverly to his Hand." After laughing at his awkward proposal, she consented perhaps for "Love, or Gratitude, or Pride, or all Three."

"This unexpected Match was very astonishing to all the Country round about, and served to furnish them with Discourse for a long Time after; some approving it, others disliking it, as they were led by their various Fancies and Inclinations." After seven years of marriage, blessed with two daughters and a son, she lost her husband. She now lived in the same small town and provided lodging for the new minister. As the election season was underway, she declared her politics that she was "a mortal Enemy to arbitrary Government & Unlimited Power." "I am naturally very jealous for the Rights and Liberties of my Country," said Silence Dogood, "and the least appearance of an Incroachment on those invaluable Priviledges, is apt to make my Blood boil exceedingly" (Lemay, 2006a: 146–148).

Impressive as her life and politics may sound, she confessed that "I have likewise a natural Inclination to observe and reprove the Faults of others, at which I have an excellent Faculty." Bostonians would easily recognize that this was a parody about Puritan ministers in general and about Cotton Mather in particular. They also read, with consternation, that "the most dangerous Hypocrite in a Common-Wealth, is one who *leaves the Gospel for the sake of the Law*: A Man compounded of Law and Gospel, is able to cheat a whole Country with his Religion, and then destroy them under *Colour of*

Law." Though ostensibly a sketch of the royal governor Joseph Dudley, this vicious personal satire attacked Chief Justice Samuel Sewall, a neighbor and a fellow-parishioner with Josiah and Abiah Franklin at the Old South Church. More to come were Silence Dogood's attacks on poorly composed funeral elegies, on wealthy persons, and on those ministers who had tried to eulogize them. She suggested that the clergy were blind to the rich parishioners' oppression of the poor because the ministers "are honourably supported (as they ought to be) by their People, and see nor feel nothing of the Oppression which is obvious and burdensome to every one else" (Lemay, 2006a: 164–165). Convinced that "Publick Destruction may be easily carry'd on by *hypocritical Pretenders to Religion*," she quoted from *Cato's Letters* and insisted that "we must not judge of one another by their best Actions; since the worst Men do some Good, and all Men make fine Professions: But must judge of Men by the whole of their Conduct, and the Effects of it" (Lemay, 1987: 28).

And judge people's conduct she did. She satirized Harvard College, the temple of learning. Traveling (in a dream) over "pleasant and delightful Fields and Meadows, and thro' many small Country Towns and Villages," she found that parents were preparing to send at least one of their children to college. But these peasants "consulted their own Purses instead of the Childrens Capacities: So that I observed, a great many, yea, the most part of those who were traveling thither, were little better that Dunces and Blockheads." After entering the temple herself, she saw two sides to a high throne of learning. On the right hand sat English and on her left, "with their Faces vail'd," reclined Latin, Greek, Hebrew, etc. The latter "were very much reserv'd, and seldom or never unvail'd their Faces here, and then to few or none, tho' most of them who have in this Place acquir'd so much Learning as to distinguish them from *English*, pretended to an intimate Acquaintance with them." When asked why they were veiled, she was shown the figures of Idleness and Ignorance "who first vail'd them, and still kept them so" (Lemay, 2006a: 151–152).

She not only attacked established institutions and the upper class's hypocrisy, but also mocked pride, vanity, drunkenness, prostitution, and lavish spending among the general population. She was not reluctant to criticize those who had parted with home-spun clothing for imports and "by striving to appear rich they become really poor." Nor did she hesitate to say that all persons should serve the country they lived in. While she had not done so in the past, she resolved "to do for the future all that *lies in my Way* for the Service of my Countrymen." As she reflected on her own writing style, she realized that she could not please everyone. Yet she pursued different topics by employing many tactics – "merry and diverting", "solid and serious," "sharp and satyrical," "sober and religious" – "Thus will every one, one Time or other find some thing agreeable to his own Fancy" (Lemay, 2006a: 150).

1.7 Women

By creating the *persona* Silence Dogood and by presenting her side of views, Franklin became the first American writer who seriously pondered and commented on feminist issues of gender difference and equality. He became interested in the matter early on, shortly after he was bound to his brother in 1718, when he befriended a young man named John Collins. The two engaged in a so-called battle of sexes, debating about "the Propriety of educating the Female Sex in Learning, & their Abilities for Study." Collins took the opposing position while Franklin supported it. Even though that episode was more "for Dispute sake" than for anything else, the exercise perhaps left Franklin with some lingering questions which intrigued him to look for answers.

To be sure, Franklin was not free from the prejudices of his time. For all his affirmatives of female quality, he viewed women as the weaker and fair sex and he ridiculed the stereotyped feminine foibles (such as vanity and frivolity) as mercilessly as other human weaknesses. Yet he was far more advanced than most of his male contemporaries in recognizing women's ability and potential, even if he did not explicitly state their equality with men. Modern scholars have wondered about the sources of his ideas. Lemay pointed out the possible influences from some female members in the family. They were intelligent in many ways and Franklin long prided himself on the fact that mother Abiah and sister Jane were superb dyers who could also use New England bayberries to make a fine soap of high quality. He pointed out Franklin's boyhood teacher George Brownell who had accepted girl students. He pointed out those prominent roles Queen Elizabeth and Queen Anne had played that no contemporary English subjects dared to ignore. He further pointed out the titles by Defoe, Michael Wigglesworth, and the famous poet Anne Bradstreet, who openly expressed concerns with gender topics (Lemay, 2006a: 59–60).

It also seems, however, that the sixteen-year old apprentice was able to sympathize with females because both were under-dogs whose intelligence, talent, and potential were unrecognized and marginalized. In this sense, he and the fair sex were in the same position of being oppressed. His protest against authority and dominance was as much for Silence Dogood as for himself, while his literary devices of satires and ridicules were as much a means of self-expression as a tool in fighting that dominance. This is not to suggest that Franklin's feminism was entirely self-serving. His sensitivities, perceptive observations, and critical commentaries revealed his genuine sympathy and careful attention to issues concerning the welfare and wellbeing of women. He condemned the hoop-petticoats, a new fashion for women. He wrote: "These monstrous topsy-turvy *Mortar-Pieces*, are neither fit for the Church, the Hall, or the kitchen; and if a Number of them were well mounted on *Noddles-Island*, they would look more like Engines of War for bombarding the Town, than Ornaments of the Fair Sex" (Lemay, 2006a: 157).

Although Franklin was later known for his many projects for the public good, his first proposal (August 13 and 20, 1722), inspired by Defoe's *Essay Upon Projects*, was about forming a society for the relief of poor widows. He said that "the Country is ripe for many such *Friendly Societies*, whereby every Man might help another, without any Disservice to himself." "We have many charitable Gentlemen who Yearly give liberally to the Poor," he continued, "and where can they better bestow their Charity than on those who became so by Providence, and for ought they know on themselves." In a colony where not a few ministers' families had fallen into poverty, he asked "how many Clergymen themselves in the Country are forc'd to labour in their Fields, to keep themselves in a Condition above Want? How then shall they be able to leave any thing to their forsaken, dejected, & almost forgotten Wives and Children." Again in the voice of Silence Dogood, he concluded, "For my own Part, I have nothing left to live on, but Contentment and a few Cows; and tho' I cannot expect to be reliev'd by this Project, yet it would be no small Satisfaction to me to see it put in Practice for the benefit of others" (Lemay, 1987: 32–33).

Last but not least, Franklin openly defended women who were frequently blamed as "particularly guilty of Pride, Idleness, &c." "Men have not only as great a Share in those Vices as the Women," he wrote, "but are likewise in a great Measure the Cause of that which the Women are guilty of." Was there a peculiar female vice? Franklin wrote that "I find it a very difficult Matter to reprove Women separate from the Men; for what Vice is there in which the Men have not as great a Share as the Women? and in some have they not a far greater, as in Drunkenness, Swearing, &c? And if they have, then it follows, that a Vice is to be reproved, Men, who are most culpable, deserve the most Reprehension, and certainly therefore, ought to have it." "For notwithstanding the Men are commonly complaining how hard they are forc'd to labour," he continued, "only to maintain their Wives in Pomp and Idleness, yet if you go among the Women, you will learn, that *they have always more Work upon their Hands than they are able to do*, and that *a Woman's Work is never done, &c*." As to the charges of ignorance and folly, Franklin quickly pointed out the crux of the matter – the unequal opportunities in education. Here he expressed one of the most explicit demand for equal education for both sexes. Contrary to his usual cynical tone, he wrote with all seriousness that he "often thought of it as one of the most barbarous Customs in the World, considering us as a civiliz'd and Christian Country, that we deny the Advantages of Learning to Women. We reproach the Sex every Day with Folly and Impertinence, while I am confident, had they the Advantages of Education equal to us, they would be guilty of less than our selves." "Why did we not let her learn," he demanded, "that she might have had more Wit? Shall we upbraid Women with Folly, when 'tis only the Error of this inhuman Custom that hindred them being made wiser" (Lemay, 1987: 14–16).

1.8 Slavery

However outspoken Franklin might have been about the status of women, equally striking was his reticence on another grave injustice – the existence of slavery. For all the hypocrisy he exposed about the vanity of the clergy, superficiality in faith, falsehood in politics, and pretentiousness and wastefulness in orthodox education, he did not see any inconsistency between his personal desire for liberty and an institutionalized human bondage around him, even though he did create the first African *persona* Dingo in 1723, a case now subject to different scholarly interpretations (Waldstreicher 2004: 50–52; Lemay 2006a: 202–4). For all his attacks on well-known figures in Boston, he found no irony in the fact that whereas Samuel Sewall questioned the inhumanity of slave trade in his pamphlet *The Selling of Joseph* as early as 1700, contemporaries continued to advertise to sell slaves, including his son Samuel Jr in the *Boston News-Letter* of April 9, 1716 and his nephew Jonathan in the *Boston Gazette* of July 15 and 22 and September 30, 1728, two years before the judge's death. This sort of inconsistency was commonplace among Bostonians, who believed liberty and self-government to be their birthright as much as they tolerated holding and trading slaves to be a form of regular business transactions.

Along Union Street, where the Franklins moved to in 1712, many neighbors bought and sold slaves on a daily basis. One of them, Hugh Hall, came from the Barbados. His father and grandfather made great fortune by engaging the slave trade. Using his connections, Hall himself advertized half a dozen times every month to sell slaves and became quite wealthy in Boston. Franklin's older brother John owned a slave. Two advertisements to sell slaves appeared in 1713 in the *Boston News-Letter*. The first one read, "Three able Negro Men and three Negro Women to be sold by Messieurs Henry Dewick and William Astin, and to be seen at the House of Mr. *Josiah Franklin* at the Blue-Ball in Union Street near the Star Tavern, Boston." It seems that the father was helping Dewick and Astin to sell slaves at his residence where the three male and three female slaves might have stayed. Dewick and Astin could be passers-by traders who needed a convenient site to dispose their slaves because a month later, a female slave was sold and the second advertisement appeared without their names, "Three negro Men and two Women to be sold and seen at the House of Mr. *Josiah Franklin* at the Sign of the Blue ball in Union-Street Boston." These local events and family circumstances contributed to Franklin's insensitivity to slavery, which may in part explain why he did not see anything wrong to own household slaves himself after he achieved business success in Philadelphia, and why he only changed his views on slavery much later in life.

1.9 Crises and Runaway

Massachusetts government kept a close watch on the printing press, which had yet to fight for its freedom of expression. As the publisher of a nonconformist newspaper, James Franklin was twice censured – first in the summer of 1722 and then in January the following year. During this critical period he and Franklin made an arrangement allowing the latter to manage the newspaper while the former struggled to deal with official indictment.

The first incident took place when authorities found out a seemingly inconspicuous piece of news in James's newspaper of June 11, 1722. After reporting a quick action Rhode Island took to pursue an enemy privateer, the *New-England Courant* went on to say that "the Government of the Massachusetts are fitting out a Ship to go after the Pirates, to be commanded by Capt. Peter Papillion, and 'its thought he will sail sometime this Month, if Wind and Weather permit." This implied that Massachusetts was somehow lukewarm in its effort to catch the pirate vessel, an insinuation which infuriated authorities. The next day, the governor's council demanded the printer attend its meeting, examined him, and resolved that the paragraph "was a High affront to this Government." The House of Representatives concurred and ordered the Suffolk County sheriff to commit him to jail for a month (Lemay, 2006a: 158).

While under incarceration, James petitioned for the General Court's forgiveness by stating that he was "Truly Sensible & Heartily Sorry for the offence." He submitted that he was "Indisposed, & Suffering in his health by the Said Confinement." A certificate testified his illness, which was, ironically, signed by Dr. Zabdiel Boylston, a champion of inoculation and whom James's newspaper had attacked a year earlier. The court read James's petition and granted him the "liberty of the Prison House & Yard" only after he could post a bond. He remained in jail until July 7 (Lemay, 2006a: 158–159).

Several months later, another issue of the *Courant* on January 14, 1722/23 again angered the government. It charged that the paper "of this days [sic] date, Contains many passages, in which the Holy Scriptures are perverted and the Civil Government, Ministers & people of this Province highly reflected on." The following day, a joint committee of the Council and the House reported that "the Tendency of the Said paper is to Mock Religion, & bring it into Contempt, That the Holy Scriptures are therein prophanely abused, that the Reverend and faithful Ministers of the Gospel are Injuriously Reflected upon, his Majesties Government affronted, and the peace & Good Order of his Majesties Subjects of this Province disturbed by the Said Courant." The committee further proposed that "James Franklyn the Printer & publisher thereof be Strictly forbidden by this Court to print, or publish the New England Courant, or any Pamphlet or paper, of the like Nature, Except it be first Supervised, by the Secretary of this Providence, and the Justices of his Majesties Sessions of the peace, for the County of Suffolk, at the Next adjournment be directed to take Sufficient Bond of the Said Franklyn for his Good Behaviour, for Twelve Months." (Lemay, 2006a: 185)

To the authorities' surprise, publication of the *Courant* continued. A member on the joint committee, Samuel Sewall, noted in his diary on January 21, "The Courant comes out very impudently," perhaps referring to an indirect satire on the judge in that issue. Under local news, the *Courant* defiantly printed the General Court's deliberations and the act forbidding the proprietor to print his *Courant*. Not amused, the court took further steps to silence the printer. It ordered that a "Warrant for apprehending James Franklyn of Boston printer" be issued and that he be bound over "to answer, at the next Assizes to be held for the County of Suffolk, for his high contempt of the order of the General Assembly at the last Session." The warrant was issued on January 28, but Undersheriff John Darrell searched for him in vain. Knowing he would be arrested, James had fled Boston (Lemay, 2006a: 186).

Before his escape, James consulted his friends. Some suggested him to change the newspaper's name, which he thought inconvenient. They finally decided that the paper would be printed under the name of Benjamin Franklin who, overtly released from his indenture, would sign a clandestine contract to continue as James's subordinate for the remainder of his terms. On Monday, February 11, the *New-England Courant* did appear over the new name. A headnote explained: "The late Publisher of this Paper, finding so many Inconveniencies would arise by his carrying the Manuscripts and publick News to be supervis'd by the Secretary, as to render his carrying it on unprofitable, has intirely dropt the Undertaking. The present Publisher having receiv'd the following Piece, desires the Readers to accept of it as a Preface to what they may hereafter meet with in this Paper." This arrangement allowed James to keep his paper in the family while technically abiding by government mandate. Franklin revealed further details of the scheme in the *Autobiography*: "And to avoid the Censure of the Assembly that might fall on him, as still printing it by his Apprentice, the Contrivance was, that my old Indenture should be return'd to me with a full Discharge on the Back of it, to be shown on Occasion; but to secure to him the Benefit of my Service I was to sign new Indentures for the Remainder of the Term, which were to be kept secret" (Lemay, 2006a: 193–195).

The legal trouble dragged on through the spring and fortunately for James, a grand jury in May ruled "Ignoramus," which denied government charges a true bill for insufficient evidence. The action against James was thus dropped (Lemay, 2006a: 200–201). Just as he and friends were celebrating, an internal tension resurfaced or in Franklin's words, a "fresh Difference arising between my Brother and me, I took upon me to assert my Freedom, presuming that he would not venture to produce the new Indentures." Evidently, whereas James was struggling to protect the freedom of his press, Franklin, who had wished an escape for a long time, took advantage of his predicament to assert his personal freedom by fleeing the bondage. He correctly predicted that James could not openly challenge the claim that the old indenture had been cancelled without incriminating himself. A fraudulent cancellation and a secret indenture with the brother would expose him as the actual printer of the *Courant*, which would surely reopen all the government's charges against him.

Franklin did not immediately leave town. He attempted to find employment at other local shops. But James was apparently furious and talked to all Boston master printers to boycott and not to hire him. Franklin could have sought the father to mitigate the situation but found out, however, that he was "now siding with my Brother." As all options were then closed, "I was the rather inclin'd to leave Boston," Franklin described in the *Autobiography*, "when I reflected that I had already made myself a little obnoxious to the governing Party; and from the arbitrary Proceedings of the Assembly in my Brother's Case it was likely I might if I stay'd soon bring myself into Scrapes; and farther that my indiscrete Disputations about Religion began to make me pointed at with Horror by good People, as an Infidel or Atheist." He hid for a while, sold some books for money, and secured the help of Collins, who talked to a captain of a sloop bound for New York into taking him on board "privately." Fearing the suspicion that he was a runaway apprentice, the two friends made up a story claiming that Franklin got a girl pregnant. He must then escape under cover or the girl's family would force him to marry her. Franklin sailed sometime after mid-September, but could not find work in New York, and therefore continued his journey. He finally arrived at Philadelphia on Sunday, October 6, 1723 (Lemay, 2006a: 205–206, 224).

Still a lad at the time, Franklin was nonetheless more accomplished than most young men at the same age. Growing up with numerous siblings, he delighted the parents for his early promise. Although the family circumstances allowed but nominal schooling, his voracious reading and unorthodox self-education achieved keen insight into human nature and society. Independent minded, he left behind the parents' world of private piety and entered into one of public interest and action. Youthful diligence and intelligence quickly turned him into one of the best printers in town, while a remarkable literary talent and imagination enabled him to craft some of the most amusing and brilliant essays in colonial literature. His uncommon ability, indomitable spirit, and driving ambition propelled him to plunge into newspaper wars, in which he took great pleasure to scorn government, satirize the clergy, ridicule the powerful, and entertain the public. An obscure son of a tallow chandler when he was born in 1706, he was no doubt a highly competent craftsman and very gifted (alas insolent to some) writer by the time when he rebelled and ran away from Boston at the age of seventeen.

Further Reading

Franklin, B. (1964). *The Autobiography of Benjamin Franklin*, ed. L.W. Labaree et al. New Haven, CT.

Huang, N.S. (2000). *Franklin's Father Josiah: Life of a Colonial Boston Tallow Chandler, 1657–1745*. Philadelphia, PA.

Isaacson, W. (2003). *Benjamin Franklin: An American Life*. New York, NY.

Tourtellot, A.B. (1977). *Benjamin Franklin, The Shaping of Genius: The Boston Years*. Garden City, NY.

Chapter Two

THE PHILADELPHIA YEARS, 1723–1757

George W. Boudreau

Benjamin Franklin's Philadelphia years began on October 6, 1723. While days, years, and eras in his personal life remain cloaked in a carefully woven fabric of mystery, Franklin recalled that Sunday morning in great detail when he wrote about it almost five decades later. He had run away from his older brother's print shop, concocting a story that he "had got a naughty Girl with Child" to aid him in his journey, and traveled first to New York where he failed to find a position in a printing house. Hearing from the printer William Bradford that his son might have work for him, Franklin then walked across New Jersey to the Delaware River, got a seat on a rowboat heading downstream for Philadelphia, and took his turn at the oars as the boat made its way to the capital of Pennsylvania. (Franklin's arrival date was unknown for centuries until the discovery of his random notes on his trip to Philadelphia by Claude-Anne Lopez, a member of the Franklin Paper editorial staff, in 1980; see *Philadelphia Inquirer*, August 27, 1980).

"I have been the more particular in this Description of my Journey, and shall be so of my first Entry into that City, that you may in your Mind compare such unlikely Beginnings with the Figure I have since made there," Franklin wrote to his imagined audience – his son the royal governor of New Jersey, posterity, or others – in 1771. "I was in my Working Dress, my best Cloaths being to come round by Sea. I was dirty from my Journey; my Pockets were stuff'd out with Shirts and Stockings; I knew no Soul, nor where to look for Lodging. I was fatigu'd with Travelling, Rowing and Want of Rest. I was very hungry, and my whole Stock of Cash consisted of a Dutch Dollar and about a Shilling in Copper," he remembered. The oft-told tale that Franklin's Philadelphia life was a rags-to-riches story is belied by

---

A Companion to Benjamin Franklin, First Edition. Edited by David Waldstreicher.
© 2011 Blackwell Publishing Ltd. Published 2011 by Blackwell Publishing Ltd.

the details he provides in the *Autobiography*. He did not arrive in rags, indeed he owned enough clothes that they required shipboard transportation (and he could afford that shipping); he had a stock in cash, albeit a small one; and he had the skills that would establish him as a leader in his craft within a few years (Franklin, 1964: 75).

The image Franklin crafts of Philadelphia highlights the aspects of the city's culture that would be a part of his life in the decades to follow. Food was his first priority, and the story of his purchase of three large "puffy rolls" became a staple of Franklin lore, when the young hotheaded lad bought three times as much as he wanted for his Sunday breakfast. Arrogance or ignorance of local costs and customs were oft-posited reasons for his over-purchase; less discussed was that Franklin was actually cluing his readers into a reality of his new life: the cost of wheat in Pennsylvania's capital was a fraction of what it was in Boston. The Englishman's diet required a far smaller investment in Philadelphia, due to the natural bounty of the Delaware Valley and to the wheat blight that had affected New England for years. Pennsylvania was called "the best poor man's country in the world": it was a good place for middling people like the newly arrived Franklin, too.

Physically, Philadelphia must have been a startling departure for the native Bostonian. "I went up Market Street as far as fourth Street. ... Then I turn'd and went down Chestnut Street and part of Walnut Street, eating my Roll all the Way, and coming round found my self again at Market Street Wharff, near the Boat I came in," he wrote. The maze of colonial Boston would never have returned a wanderer to the same spot after a few simple left turns. Philadelphia had been designed by Thomas Holme, founder William Penn's surveyor for Pennsylvania, in 1681. The grid system, based perhaps on the ordered layout of military camps or more likely on a logic based in Enlightenment thought, had stretched only to Fourth Street by the 1720s, as Philadelphians ignored Penn's call for a "greene countrie towne" spanning between the Delaware and Schuylkill Rivers, and instead built a town that resembled English seaside villages, the new city's wide streets intersected with smaller alleys and lanes lined with red brick dwellings and small wooden structures all built of native Pennsylvania materials. Franklin's Sunday morning stroll took him past the Market House that sat in the center of High (Market) Street at the intersection of Second, a spot near which he would live for much of the rest of his life.

Beyond the physical and economic aspects of that Sunday morning walk, a third component affixed itself in the young printer's mind that would affect his life and career for the rest of Franklin's life. "I walk'd again up the Street, which by this time had many clean dress'd People in it who were all walking the same Way; I join'd them, and thereby was led into the great Meeting House of the Quakers near the Market. I sat down among them, and after looking round a while and hearing nothing said, being very drowzy thro' Labour and want of Rest the preceding Night, I fell fast asleep, and continu'd so till the Meeting broke up, when one was kind enough to rouse me. This was therefore the first House I was in or slept in, in Philadelphia" (Franklin, 1964: 76). Thus began Franklin's on-again, off-again relationship with the Society of Friends. Later storytellers would inaccurately call him a Quaker, a mistake he himself would feed by dressing the part of a plain-dressed Friend while in Paris in the 1770s, gaining him the sobriquet "le bon quackeur." Over the course of his first four decades in Pennsylvania, Franklin would befriend, mortify, scandalize, satirize, and support Quakers. He counted them among some of his closest friends and staunchest foes. But William Penn's religious diversity, guaranteed by the Charter of Privileges the founder signed in 1701 before his final departure for the mother country, had created a level of religious diversity by the 1720s unheard of anywhere else in the world. In Philadelphia, Quakers, Anglicans, Presbyterians, Moravians, Baptists, Catholics, Jews, German Dunkards, and Lutherans passed one another daily on the streets and met in public meetings and business dealings. One lapsed Calvinist runaway printer barely stood out among the colony's diverse, divergent population (Tolles, 1948; Bonomi, 1986; Schwartz, 1987; Moss, 2004).

2.1 Establishing a Career

Only seventeen when he arrived in Philadelphia, Franklin already had a discerning eye for others in his profession as well as a keen sense of how he might improve the print culture of his newly adopted town, it seems. Once again meeting William Bradford when he went unsuccessfully seeking work at Bradford's son Andrew's printing house, Franklin accompanied the older man to his son's rival Samuel Keimer's shop. Neither shop shined in Franklin's recollection. Bradford senior appears sly and even deceptive, priming his son's competitor with questions to learn about his plans and not revealing his identity, who Franklin thought Keimer took as an unknown townsperson who wished him well in his business. Bradford's manner left a lasting impression: Franklin remembered him as "a crafty old Sophister." But Keimer, who did offer Franklin a position, did not fare much better. Next to the plotting Bradford, he was "a mere Novice." The business was not much better: "Keimer's Printing House I found, consisted of an old shatter'd Press, and one small worn-out Fount of English, which he was then using himself, composing in it an Elegy on Aquila Rose," a recently deceased Philadelphia immigrant who had gained a reputation as a man of letters during his brief life in the city. "These two Printers I found poorly qualified for their Business. Bradford had not been bred to it, and was very illiterate; and Keimer tho' something of a Scholar, was a mere Compositor, knowing nothing of Presswork," he recalled (Franklin, 1964: 77–78).

Franklin's time in Keimer's employ provided a significant entré into Philadelphia's world of business and politics. The men with whom he worked became his first professional network in his new city, he honed skills that he had brought with him from Boston, and his reputation grew, causing a few hardships but eventual successes.

As Franklin recalled his first encounter with Pennsylvania politics, the story focused on a talented young artisan and a ne'er do well governor who made more promises than he could keep. Hearing that his missing brother-in-law might be in Philadelphia, Captain Robert Holmes wrote to the runaway from New Castle. Franklin responded to his kinsman's letter, which the captain in turn showed to Sir William Keith, proprietary lieutenant governor, who was then in that city. "The Governor read it, and seem'd surpriz'd when he was told my Age. He said I appear'd a young Man of promising Parts, and therefore should be encouraged: The Printers at Philadelphia were wretched ones, and if I would set up there, he made no doubt I should succeed; for his Part, he would procure me the publick Business, and do me every other Service in his Power." The drama played out when Sir William arrived at Keimer's print shop a short time later, ignored the master of the shop, made friendly overtures to the young journeyman, and invited Franklin to a nearby tavern "to taste ... some excellent Madeira." The oddity of the scene was not missed by either of the men working in the shop, Franklin recalled: "I was not a little surpriz'd, and Keimer star'd like a Pig poison'd" (1964: 80).

The tale that followed became one of the most famous of Franklin's autobiography. After a short acquaintance, Keith convinced Franklin to seek family funding to set up his own shop, leading Benjamin to return to Boston seeking a loan from his father, who declined to give him the funds. Franklin then returned to Philadelphia, where Keith came up with another plan: Franklin would go to London and gain business contacts and supplies and equipment, and the governor would give him the colony's printing business when he returned so he could retire the debt. The young printer left for London after attempting to meet with the governor again, secure in his belief that Keith's promised letters were in the ship's mailbag, to be opened when they reached the mother country. Finding no letters, Franklin confided the business plans to his new friend Denham, a Quaker merchant. Denham's news wasn't good: "there was not the least Probability that he had written any Letters for me, that no one who knew him had the smallest Dependance on him, and he laught at the Notion of the Governor's giving me a Letter of Credit, having as he said no Credit to give" (1964: 94).

Franklin's autobiography related a story of friendship and betrayal, a tale that revealed only part of what was going in the story of Sir William Keith. Keith had been appointed to his position by Hannah Callowhill Penn, William Penn's widow. A devout Friend herself, Hannah Penn found herself at odds with the men who controlled the annually elected Pennsylvania

Assembly, and she set about seeking an administrator for the proprietary colony who would carry out her bidding and secure the income that she and her large family now desperately needed. At first glance Keith was a strange choice to lead a Quaker colony, his baronet title as odd a fit for the supposedly democratic Friends. The sumptuous fur, armor, and wig that adorned his persona in the only contemporary portrait of him that survives must have set him apart from the broad-brimmed Quakers wearing "the best sort, but plain," as the old Quaker expression had it.

That first glance, however, showed only some of the things that made Sir William's role rocky. Franklin may have told the story as a personal betrayal, but what he was really experiencing was a contest of wills between rising political factions in 1720s Pennsylvania. Keith was attempting to break with the Penns, to become a popularly elected leader of the Assembly rather than an appointed, limited lieutenant who had to report to the proprietors back home. Keith's plan fizzled, and by the time Franklin returned to Philadelphia in 1726, his former patron was reduced to avoiding the younger man's glance (Nash, 1968; Smolenski, 2010).

Franklin told the story of his being stuck in London as one aspect of a narrative of progress and overcoming adversity. In fact, the time there would give him his first glance at many aspects of life that grew to define him, and gave him his first acquaintance with the city that was to be one of the most important relationships in his life. Franklin found lodgings in Little Britain and began a year's employment in Palmer's Printing House in Bartholomew Close. Accompanied by his friend Ralph, Franklin soaked in the cultural highlights that the Empire's capital had to offer, "going to Plays and other Places of Amusement" and spending the money he had saved for his planned business. In addition to those enjoyments, Franklin began to experience the people and ideas that London had to offer. He went to club meetings in taverns, borrowed books for a small rental fee from his neighbor John Wilcox the bookseller, and entered the emerging coffee house culture of the British capital, meeting Sir Hans Sloane and selling him curiosities for his cabinet, but missing a proposed introduction to the man at the center of the Enlightenment intellectual movement then transforming Britain: Sir Isaac Newton (1964: 96–98).

2.2 Clubs and Emerging Public Life

Each of these experiences would shape Franklin when he returned to Philadelphia in October 1726. He bid adieu to both the printing trade and London when Thomas Denham proposed to hire Franklin as his merchant's clerk and paid his passage to return to Pennsylvania. He would return to printing soon after his return to America, and to London for extended stays twice more in his lifetime. On returning to Philadelphia,

Denham opened a shop in Water Street near the Delaware River with Franklin as his clerk, and there the former printer toiled until the "Beginning of Feby. 1726/7 when I had just pass'd my 21st Year, we both were taken ill. My Distemper was a Pleurisy, which very nearly carried me off: I suffered a good deal, gave up the Point in my own mind, and was rather disappointed when I found my Self recovering; regretting in some degree that I must now some time or other have all that disagreable Work to do over again" (Franklin, 1964: 107).

After his recovery, Franklin returned to work at Keimer's printing house, and it was with some of his fellow workmen from that shop that he formed the Junto club that year. The club was the quintessential activity of the intellectual movement sweeping Anglo-America, known as the Enlightenment, and Franklin had imbibed in the ideas of "clubbable men" as he frequented the taverns and coffee houses of London during his months there. Little wonder, then, that he drew his "most ingenious acquaintances" into meetings each Friday for their mutual improvement and entertainment. He came to call the Junto "the best School of Philosophy, Morals and Politics that then existed in the Province," and its members would be some of the most important friendships that would shape the next decades of his life. The original dozen members, Joseph Brientnal, Thomas Godfrey, Nicholas Scull, William Parsons, William Maugridge, Hugh Meredith, Stephen Potts, George Webb, Robert Grace, William Coleman, and John Jones, Jr, met weekly, first in a tavern room owned by Scull, and later in a room in the home of Grace, to discuss what they had read, who they had met, and what they had observed since the previous week's meeting. A poetical account of one 1732 meeting, recorded in Scull's commonplace book, reveals the diversity of subjects members discussed, ranging from philosophy and the law to botany and archery. The Junto led Franklin to one of the watersheds of his young career (Franklin, 1964: 116–117; Boudreau, 2007: 307–317).

By early 1730, the Junto was meeting in more private quarters in Robert Grace's home, and Franklin proposed that members bring together their personal book collections so that a small library might be available to each member. "The Number was not so great as we expected; and tho' they had been of great Use, yet some Inconveniencies occurring for want of due Care of them, the Collection after about a Year was separated, and each took his Books home again." What followed would be the beginnings of Franklin's plans for civic improvement in his adopted city, and would set his course for how to do it. Writing in 1771, Franklin stated, "And now I set on foot my first Project of a public Nature, that for a Subscription Library. I drew up the Proposals, got them put into Form by our great Scrivener Brockden, and by the help of my Friends in the Junto, procur'd Fifty Subscribers of 40s. each to begin with and 10s. a Year for 50 Years, the Term our Company was to continue. ... This was the Mother of all the

N American Subscription Libraries now so numerous. It is become a great thing itself, and continually increasing" (Franklin, 1964: 130).

Evidently, writing this story led Franklin to explore the scope of what the library had meant from a distance of forty years later. "These Libraries have improv'd the general Conversation of the Americans, made the common Tradesmen and Farmers as intelligent as most Gentlemen from other Countries, and perhaps have contributed in some degree to the Stand so generally made throughout the Colonies in Defence of their Privileges," he wrote in 1771. Then, the autobiography abruptly stops. A later-added memo blames public affairs, stating "The Affairs of the Revolution occasioned the Interruption," but that was hindsight. Franklin was actually noting that his life was moving from a private to a public realm with his founding of the Library Company. Resuming the autobiography in 1784 at Passy with his "Return being uncertain, and having just now a little Leisure," Franklin made sure that the story of the Library Company's birth was included, even if he had already written the story thirteen years later "which may be struck out if found to have been already given" (Franklin, 1964: 141–142).

The added distance of time did push Franklin to further candor about the nature of public projects. "The Objections, and Reluctances I met with in Soliciting the Subscriptions, made me soon feel the Impropriety of presenting one's self as the Proposer of any useful Project that might be suppos'd to raise one's Reputation in the smallest degree above that of one's Neighbours, when one has need of their Assistance to accomplish that Project"(1964: 143). It was a lesson he would learn well and follow in the decades ahead, as he worked behind a perhaps transparent veil of anonymity to create the Union Fire Company (1736), the American Philosophical Society (1743), the Philadelphia militia (1747), the Academy and Charitable School of Philadelphia (later, the College and subsequently University of Pennsylvania, 1749), the Philadelphia Contributionship Fire Insurance Company (1751), and Pennsylvania Hospital (1752). Franklin's 1784 description of his scheme to found the Library Company – "I therefore put my self as much as I could out of sight, and stated it as a Scheme of a *Number of Friends,* who had requested me to go about and propose it" – summed up his method for calling together his fellow colonists for other means of public improvement (Franklin, 1964: 143).

2.3 Personal Life

Entry into the public sphere was not the only watershed that Franklin experienced in the early 1730s, for it was during that same time that he entered into a state of matrimony, of sorts. Franklin's common law marriage to Deborah Read Rogers Franklin, which began on September 1, 1730 is one of the more perplexing relationships of his long life, and similarly one of the most perplexing Anglo-American marriages of the eighteenth century.

The couple entered into marriage after a rocky start. Deborah had been one of the first people who saw Franklin in Philadelphia, an incident he carefully recorded in his autobiography decades later: "Thus I went up Market Street as far as fourth Street, passing by the Door of Mr Read, my future Wife's Father, when she standing at the Door saw me, & thought I made as I certainly did a most awkward ridiculous Appearance" (Franklin, 1964: 76). It was not only family lore, but also Deborah's entrance into a family narrative that she played a central role in creating, even if the autobiography gave her scant voice afterwards. Franklin soon moved into the Read household, having started work at Samuel Keimer's print shop and having received his trunk of clothing from Boston so he "made rather a more respectable Appearance in the Eyes of Miss Read," and perhaps that better appearance inspired the romantic relationship that began to blossom soon thereafter. Young love was thwarted as Franklin made plans to go to London in 1724, when Deborah's mother thought the couple should wait for marriage until he returned and the two were a bit older than their eighteen years (Franklin, 1964: 79).

As Franklin narrated the story, Deborah's life became a pathetic tale once he departed for the mother country. He admitted that he "never wrote more than one Letter, & that was to let her know I was not likely soon to return." Calling his treatment of his eventual wife "another of the great Errata of my Life, which I should wish to correct if I were to live it over again," Franklin began to enjoy the women of London, while Deborah's friends, "despairing with Reason of my Return," persuaded her to marry John Rogers, a potter. The exact nature of that couple's troubles has never been fully discovered. Franklin called his wife's first husband "a worthless Fellow tho' an excellent Workman which was Temptation of her Friends," an odd mixed compliment, to be sure. National Park Service archeologists would discover the remnant of Rogers' pottery in the mid-twentieth century, near the site of the Read house where Franklin had lodged earlier. "With him however she was never happy, and soon parted from him, refusing to cohabit with him, or bear his Name," perhaps because of the emerging rumor that Rogers had another wife in another colony. The potter disappeared from Philadelphia, eventually dying in the West Indies (Franklin, 1964: 106–107; Cotter, 1995: 93–95).

Franklin's autobiography, the most widely read text by any eighteenth-century American, clearly shows that he was neither romantic nor a Romantic, and the description he leaves of his reunion and marriage with Deborah plays a large part in that assessment. Franklin looked close to home when he began to look for a wife. After setting up his own business, he began to rent part of the house where he worked and lived to the family of Thomas Godfrey, the lackluster window glazier and brilliant mathematician who had been an original member of the Junto. Mrs Godfrey kept house for both her family and her printer landlord, and soon devised a plan for Franklin to court her relation's daughter. "The old Folks encourag'd me by continual Invitations to Supper, & by leaving us together, till at length it was time to explain." Exactly what Franklin had to "explain" during these times they were left alone together, he never said, although he did record that "that hard-to-be govern'd Passion of Youth, had hurried me frequently into Intrigues with low Women that fell in my Way, which were attended with some Expence & great Inconvenience, besides a continual risque to my Health by a Distemper which of all Things I dreaded, tho' by great good luck I escaped it" (Franklin, 1964: 127–128).

But the marriage never happened, not due to sex, but due to money. Showing a parsimony that might well have gained him the title "Father of all Yankees," Franklin refused to enter into matrimony without receiving a dowry that would "pay off my Remaining Debt for the Printing-house, about £100," he estimated. Dowry negotiations broke down as one side and then the other stood firm, the Godfreys thinking they could wait Franklin out, the printer soon displaying the hot-headedness that characterized him in his youth. In a huff, the Godfreys moved out of Franklin's rented house and shop, and Franklin "resolved to take no more Inmates." Instead, he turned his attention in earnest to finding a woman of the house, a search that exasperated him as he "soon found that the Business of a Printer being generally thought a poor one," and – his neighbors informed him – he could "not expect Money with a Wife unless with such a one, as I should not otherwise think agreeable." Exactly what these future possible Mrs Franklins lacked besides money, he never said (Franklin, 1964: 128).

Thus Deborah reentered Benjamin Franklin's narrative. He had rekindled a friendship with her family after returning from London, often went to their home on Market Street near Third, and noticed the young woman in an odd limbo between marriage and widowhood. "I pity'd poor Miss Read's unfortunate Situation, who was generally dejected, seldom cheerful, and avoided Company," Franklin wrote. He and Sarah Read jockeyed to take the blame for the relationship's earlier failure. Rogers was gone, perhaps he was dead, but his debt remained, and if Deborah remarried that debt would belong to her next husband. "We ventured however, over all these Difficulties, and I took her to wife on Sept. 1, 1730. None of the Inconveniencies happened that we had apprehended, she prov'd a good & faithful Helpmate, assisting me much by attending the Shop, we throve together, and have ever mutually endeavour'd to make each other happy. – Thus I corrected that great *Erratum* as well as I could" (Franklin, 1964: 129). And thus, Franklin summed up the beginning of the only marriage he ever had, a relationship that would span the next forty-five years of his life.

But while Franklin seemed to script Deborah into a few small and largely unnoticed parts in the narrative of his life, it would be a mistake to underplay the importance of her role in their lives to follow. The "good & faithful Helpmate" carried out work that was critical to their financial success in the years that immediately followed. Deborah tended the shop, stitched and cut pamphlets that spilled off her husband's printing presses, and the books she kept – showing a vital interaction with hundreds of customers who entered the shop over time – revealing an economic agent who knew business and the multitude of items, ideas, and actions that the people of her growing native town needed from a business that was at its heart. Indeed, it was only with J.A. Leo Lemay's transcription and web publication of Deborah's shop books that the full narrative of Deborah's economic activities became widely evident. That economic activity exasperated her husband at times. In his autobiography, Franklin told the story of being perfectly satisfied with eating breakfast every day with a pewter spoon from an earthenware bowl, but one day Deborah emerged with a silver spoon and a China bowl. "Women!" Franklin seems to shout over the centuries. He continued "she had no other Excuse or Apology to make, but that she thought *her* Husband deserv'd a Silver Spoon & China Bowl as well as any of his Neighbors" (Franklin, 1964: 145). The twenty-three shillings Deborah had decided to spend was one more action of her being an active player in the economic transformation historians have come to call the consumer revolution.

If the Franklins' courtship was unusual, that difference was quickly surpassed by their household composition. Early on in their married life, their home welcomed William, the son born out of wedlock to Franklin and a woman whose identity he never divulged. William's maternity proves to be one of the odder aspects of the gaping holes that fill Franklin's autobiography and other writings. That narrative never discusses William's birth or divulges the child's mother's name. Was it because Franklin was, in fact, writing the first section of the story for his son (as the text said) and William knew who his biological mother was? Was it because there was still reason for legal or propriety's sake to keep that secret? The text suggests many possibilities. Could William have been Deborah's son, conceived while she and Franklin were still in that strange limbo, awaiting word of the missing John Rogers? Could Franklin's protracted discussion of the hours spent "alone" with the Godfrey woman be detailing the time they conceived his child, and Franklin took the boy in when he had begun housekeeping with another woman? Was the local rumor – which persisted into the revolutionary era – that William was the son of a servant woman or slave be true? Probably the only way to end that mystery would be to conduct DNA tests on many mortal remains buried in Philadelphia and in England, an unlikely prospect. But as Jefferson scholars have learned, DNA does have a way of clearing up some controversies, even as it creates others (Skemp, 1990: 3–8; Lemay, 2006b: 23).

The Franklin family grew two years after Deborah and Benjamin began their marriage with the arrival of Francis Folger Franklin, the child whose death Franklin recalled for decades afterwards as the great tragedy of their marriage. Writing to his favorite sister Jane in 1772, he remember the child who had died in 1736 "tho' now dead 36 Years, whom I have seldom since seen equal'd in every thing, and whom to this Day I cannot think of without a Sigh" (1964: 170). But the very private tragedy that the couple experienced that fall was complicated by a rumor that spread through the town that Francis had died after being inoculated for smallpox. The cause of death had a painful irony: Franklin's brother James had stirred public controversy with his *New-England Courant* opposing inoculation in Boston. Now master of his own shop and head of his own family, and already displaying an interest in new developments in natural philosophy, Franklin supported the still-controversial medical procedure. Thus, as a man of the press, he was drawn to tell the *Pennsylvania Gazette's* readership on December 30, 1736 that "Understanding 'tis a current Report, that my Son Francis, who died lately of the Small Pox, had it by Inoculation" he wrote to assure his readers that this had never happened: "I intended to have my Child inoculated, as soon as he should have recovered sufficient Strength from a Flux with which he had been long afflicted" (Franklin, 1964: 170).

As the preeminent scholar of the Franklins' domesticity pointed out, "Deborah's greatest contribution to his future fame and glory had nothing to do with her industry and her frugality, praiseworthy as he thought them. It was an unwitting and unappreciated contribution: She did not saddle him with the numerous offspring he would have liked" (Lopez and Herbert, 1975: 33–34). Seven years would follow Francis' death before the Franklins would welcome another child. Sarah (Sally) Franklin was born August 31, 1743, more than a dozen years into her parents marriage. "Your grandaughter is the greatest lover of *her book* and *school,* of any child I ever knew, and is very dutiful to *her* mistress as well as to us," Franklin wrote to his mother on October 1, 1747, perhaps seeing more than a bit of himself in his daughter's interest in reading and education. Three years later, he wrote: "*Sally* grows a fine Girl, and is extreamly industrious with her Needle, and delights in her Book. She is of a most affectionate Temper, and perfectly Dutiful and obliging, to her Parents and to all. Perhaps I flatter my self too much; but I have Hopes that she will prove an ingenious sensible notable and worthy Woman....She goes now to the *Dancing* School," the latter reference perhaps bringing a shudder to the Puritan grandmother in far-off New England (PBF, 3: 179–180, 475).[1]

Sarah's relationship with her father would be one of the stories he would leave untold in his autobiography. Mentions of her in his surviving papers are few in her early years, though he carefully outlined the property she would inherit in the will he drafted in 1750 and in the will he wrote in 1757 added that she would receive his share in the Library Company as well as cash and property, so perhaps her love of books and reading had continued. Sarah Franklin dutifully stayed in Philadelphia with her mother when her father left for London with her older half-brother in 1757. Franklin secured a legal education and eventually a governorship for his son; he sought the same type of security for his female offspring, at least in his own mind, by trying to determine who would be a fitting husband for her. Sarah was probably more like her father than either liked to admit. She fell in love with Richard Bache, a young merchant, in the 1760s, while her father was in London and her brother was governing New Jersey. Franklin's tone to everyone involved in the courtship – potential bride, groom, and mother-of the bride – rings with more than a bit of a Puritan tone when he pushed her to break the engagement, find a more worthy prospect, or even to come to London to see the "friends" she had never met. Yet Sarah would be the child who made Franklin's international success possible. She cared for her mother when Franklin left for London and his wife refused to cross the Atlantic, she maintained his household and property for the remainder of his life, and eventually it was she – not her brother – who would support the Whig cause and actively participate in Pennsylvania's revolutionary efforts (Lopez and Herbert, 1975: 135–148, 229).

2.4 Printer, of Philadelphia

The world that Sally Franklin was born into was obviously far different than her brother's earliest years, largely due to the changing economic status of her parents. William likely did his earliest crawling on floors stained with printer's ink. The Franklins set up household within steps of Philadelphia's market sheds and town house, at the center of Philadelphia's economic and political community at Second and High streets.

Franklin returned to printing in 1727 and continued in Keimer's employ until June 1728, when his friend Hugh Meredith's father offered to bankroll the two young men opening their own shop. The early days of the business were full of problems, Franklin recalled. First, they leaked their plan to establish a newspaper to a potential employee, and when word reached Keimer, he rushed the first issue of *The Universal Instructor in all Arts and Sciences: and Pennsylvania Gazette* into print on December 24, 1728. Angered, Franklin showed that he was not above a little industrial espionage. Keimer reprinted a *Chambers' Encyclopedia* essay in his fifth issue that explained abortion. Franklin published an anonymous letter in Bradford's paper written by "Martha Careful" lambasting Franklin's foe for "Expose the Secrets of our Sex ... To be read in all *Taverns* and *Coffee-Houses*, and by the Vulgar ... I say if he Publish any more of that kind, which ought only to be in the Repositary of the Learned; my sister Molly and my Self, with some others, are Resolved to run the Hazard of taking him by the Beard, at the next Place we meet him, and make an Example of him for his Immodesty." The letter appeared on January 28, 1729; the next week, he and his close friend Joseph Breintnall began a series of essays as the "Busy Body," for Bradford's *American Weekly Mercury*. The Library Company of Philadelphia holds a collection of these original newspapers, in which someone – probably Franklin – wrote margin notes, delineating which essays he wrote, and which were penned by Breintnall, the scrivener who had helped Franklin found the Junto and Library Company. Franklin bought Keimer's failing newspaper on September 25 that year (PBF, 1: 111–138).

The months that followed saw Franklin's publishing career thrive. Franklin became Philadelphia's official printer on January 1, 1730; in July, he borrowed money from his fellow Junto members Robert Grace and William Coleman to buy out his partner Hugh Meredith, who Franklin remembered as "a Welsh-Pensilvanian, 30 Years of Age, bred to Country Work: honest, sensible, had a great deal of solid Observation, was something of a Reader," but perhaps more importantly "given to drink." Grace and Coleman convinced Franklin that Meredith was "often seen drunk in the Streets, and playing at low Games in Alehouses, much to our Discredit." Now master of his own shop, Franklin began to prosper. "I began now gradually to pay off the Debt I was under for the Printing-House. In order to secure my Credit and Character as a Tradesman, I took care not only to be in *Reality* Industrious and frugal, but to avoid all *Appearances* of the Contrary. I drest plainly; I was seen at no Places of idle Diversion; I never went out a-fishing or shooting; a Book, indeed, sometimes debauch'd me from my Work; but that was seldom, snug, and gave no Scandal: and to show that I was not above my Business, I sometimes brought home the Paper I purchas'd at the Stores, thro' the Streets on a Wheelbarrow," he wrote (Franklin, 1964: 112, 120, 122, 125).

The business success that Franklin experienced was not so much innovation as improvement on existing conditions. As historian James Green writes, "In his long career as a printer ... he was almost always second. He published the second newspaper in Pennsylvania, and the second magazine; *Poor Richard's Almanack* had to compete with two rivals when it was first published in 1732. Franklin was the second bookseller in town, the second postmaster, and the second government printer." Printer William Bradford had settled in Pennsylvania in 1685, invited by the Quakers, who dominated both the religious and political spheres at the time, to set up his shop under their watchful eye. The elder Bradford ran afoul of the Friends, and eventually moved to New York, and his son Andrew opened his Philadelphia shop in 1712. Thus, when Franklin became master of his own shop in 1730, he was going up against a competitor with decades of experience, intercolonial family connections, and the government's printing business. Franklin would acquire each of these in the years to follow (Green, 2005: 55–90).

Franklin sidestepped the print wars which had consumed Bradford and Keimer in the years before, instead aiming to produce publications that were entertaining and informative. "In the Conduct of my Newspaper I carefully excluded all Libelling and Personal Abuse, which is of late Years become so disgraceful to our Country. Whenever I was solicited to insert any thing of that kind, and the Writers pleaded as they generally did, the Liberty of the Press, and that a Newspaper was like a Stage Coach in which any one who would pay had a Right to a Place, my Answer was, that I would print the Piece separately if desired, and the Author might have as many Copies as he pleased to distribute himself, but that I would not take upon me to spread his Detraction, and that having contracted with my Subscribers to furnish them with what might be either useful or entertaining, I could not fill their Papers with private Altercation in which they had no Concern without doing them manifest Injustice" (Franklin, 1964: 165).

The success of the *Gazette* became the basis for a widening involvement in the world of print. In 1731, Franklin sponsored his former journeyman Thomas Whitemarsh to set up shop in South Carolina. That partnership would eventually lead to similar business agreements in Annapolis, New Haven, New York, and Antigua, as well as maintaining business connections with his relatives in Newport, Rhode Island, and in Boston. He also funded a German language printing office in Philadelphia from 1748 to 1758, and attempted to open a shop in the growing western town of Lancaster, Pennsylvania (Green, 2005: 84–85).

One of the chief items that these printing houses could market was *Poor Richard's Almanack*, which he began to produce in 1732. "I endeavour'd to make it both entertaining and useful, and it accordingly came to be in such Demand that I reap'd considerable Profit from it, vending annually near ten Thousand." In addition to profit, Franklin realized that "Poor Dicks" (as Deborah Franklin called it in her shop accounts) was a bully pulpit for his ideas about life, family, and community: "observing that it was generally read, scarce any Neighbourhood in the Province being without it, I consider'd it as a proper Vehicle for conveying Instruction among the common People, who bought scarce any other Books. I therefore filled all the little Spaces that occurr'd between the Remarkable Days in the Calendar, with Proverbial Sentences, chiefly such as inculcated Industry and Frugality, as the Means of procuring Wealth and thereby securing Virtue" (Franklin, 1964: 163–164).

While he attempted to avoid political controversy, Franklin did find that involvement in political affairs could benefit his business. He was chosen clerk of the Pennsylvania Assembly in October 1736, "the Place gave me a better Opportunity of keeping up an Interest among the Members, which

secu... ...ess of Printing the Votes, Laws, Paper Money, and
oth... ...for the Public, that on the whole were very profita-
bl... ...ar, Colonel Alexander Spotswood "being dissatisfied
v... ...of his Deputy at Philadelphia," Andrew Bradford,
...egligence in rendering, and Inexactitude of his Accounts
... with the Conduct of his Deputy at Philadelphia, respect-
...ligence in rendering, and Inexactitude of his Accounts" fired
...nd gave Franklin the position. Franklin was now firmly entrenched
...e political and print world in Pennsylvania. As he wrote, he "accepted it readily, and found it of great Advantage; for tho' the Salary was small, it facilitated the Corespondence that improv'd my Newspaper, encreas'd the Number demanded, as well as the Advertisements to be inserted, so that it came to afford me a very considerable Income" (Franklin, 1964: 172).

Franklin found other ways to combine his interests in politics and print. When a new member of the Pennsylvania Assembly opposed his reappointment in 1737, Franklin used his interests to get in the man's good graces. "I did not however aim at gaining his Favour by paying any servile Respect to him," Franklin cautioned, but instead "Having heard that he had in his Library a certain very scarce and curious Book, I wrote a Note to him expressing my Desire of perusing that Book, and requesting he would do me the Favour of lending it to me for a few Days. He sent it immediately; and I return'd it in about a Week, with another Note expressing strongly my Sense of the Favour. When we next met in the House he spoke to me, (which he had never done before) and with great Civility. And he ever afterwards manifested a Readiness to serve me on all Occasions, so that we became great Friends, and our Friendship continu'd to his Death" (Franklin, 1964: 171–172).

Franklin, carefully showing that the master of Philadelphia's newest printing house was not willing to play a subservient role to a politician despite the man's position, wealth, and education, was turning notions of colonial deference on their head. Deference, no, but Franklin did cultivate friendships among the colony's intellectual and governmental elite. As early as 1730, Franklin had sought the advice of James Logan, a key player in both realms. Logan had immigrated to Pennsylvania in 1699, coming with Proprietor William Penn and his family on the second (and final) voyage to Pennsylvania. Logan had stayed on when the Penns returned to England in 1701, eventually rising to wealth through the fur trade and land speculation at the same time that he held numerous offices, including chief justice and provincial secretary. But Logan's great passion was books, and his massive library filled the walls of Stenton, the country estate he built north of Philadelphia in the 1720s. It was to that country estate that Franklin and his fellow Library Company founders went for advice on their first purchases for the library. Logan became a good and useful friend in the years to follow. In 1744, Franklin published Logan's translation of Cicero's *Cato*

Major, the only original, full-sized book Franklin ever published at his own expense (and a project from which he gained no profit). No matter; the printing house's numerous other endeavors were bringing in enough to cover the expenses, and Logan lent his assistance to the man he now addressed as "My good friend B. Franklin" in numerous ways in the years before his death in 1750 (Green, 2005: 76–79; PBF, 2: 306).

Indeed, Franklin's willingness to overlook differences in ideology was perhaps most notably evident in the friendship he developed with evangelist George Whitefield, beginning in 1739. Beyond being a mere clergyman, Whitefield and the Great Awakening he inspired were a cultural phenomenon in the English-speaking world. He became the colonies' first pop star, drawing in people of diverse religious beliefs at the same time that he angered or frightened their clergymen. "The Multitudes of all Sects and Denominations that attended his Sermons were enormous, and it was matter of Speculation to me who was one of the Number, to observe the extraordinary Influence of his Oratory on his Hearers, and how much they admir'd and respected him, notwithstanding his common Abuse of them, by assuring them they were naturally *half Beasts and half Devils*," Franklin wrote. Franklin's own religious beliefs were hard to pin down by that point in his life. He had stopped regular attendance at Philadelphia's Presbyterian Church after it had ousted Rev. Samuel Hemphill, a minister Franklin supported, and Franklin does not appear to have joined Deborah in her pew at Christ Church often, if at all. Yet he gained an appreciation for Whitefield's eloquence and his mastery of communication. "It was wonderful to see the Change soon made in the Manners of our Inhabitants; from being thoughtless or indifferent about Religion, it seem'd as if all the World were growing Religious; so that one could not walk thro' the Town in an Evening without Hearing Psalms sung in different Families of every Street." Franklin became Whitefield's publisher as well as his friend, eventually becoming close enough to the famous man to offer him accommodations in his home on Market Street: "You know my House, if you can make shift with its scanty Accommodations you will be most heartily welcome," Franklin recalled in an anecdote that showed that while the two shared a friendship, they didn't necessarily also share a world view. "He reply'd, that if I made that kind Offer for Christ's sake, I should not miss of a Reward. And I return'd, *Don't let me be mistaken; it was not for Christ's sake, but for your sake*" (Franklin, 1964: 175–176; Stout, 1991; Lambert, 1993; Pencak, 2002).

2.5 Natural Philosopher

While Franklin observed the rise of the Great Awakening around him, he began to participate in the other great cultural transformation of the eighteenth century, one that would change the course of his entire life. Always curious about natural philosophy, or "science" as later generations would call it, Franklin attended Archibald Spencer's lectures on electricity while traveling on postal business in Boston in 1743. Fascinated, he purchased Spencer's electrical experimentation equipment. The months ahead would provide more leisure than the printer had ever known in his life. In 1744, David Hall arrived from London, lodged with the Franklins, and became the print shop's foreman. A journeyman from the London shop of Franklin's correspondent William Strahan, Hall gradually took over aspects of the Philadelphia shop as Benjamin Franklin's mind turned to other matters. In 1745 Peter Collinson, the London cloth merchant who had acted as the Library Company's agent since 1731 and who had prompted the colonists into observation and experimentation with his gifts of scientific texts and questions about their observation of America's natural environment, sent pamphlets about German experiments in electricity, along with a glass tube, to the members. Electricity was all the rage in natural philosophical studies around the Atlantic World at the time, and Franklin quickly felt its charge. By 1746, he found himself "immersed in electrical experiments." As in earlier studies, he drew together members of the Junto and Library Company, conducting experiments in his home and in the library's rooms, and corresponding his finding to Collinson back in London, who in 1747 began sharing the Philadelphia experiments with fellow members of the Royal Society.

The myth of Franklin during these experiments overpowers the reality. We still see him, standing alone or with small boy as an aid, in the middle of a windswept field, raising his kite into an electrical storm, just as Currier and Ives pictured it in the century after the experiments happened. The reality was slower, more complicated, and far safer. Franklin had already written up a public lecture that his friend Ebenezer Kinnersley performed in Annapolis, and his theories on electricity had already appeared in print in London when he performed his kite experiment, somewhere on Philadelphia's outskirts, sometime in mid-1752 (he never wrote down either location or date). The kite experiment would change his life. Unbeknownst to him, French natural philosophers had already used his hypothesis weeks earlier to prove his theory that lightning was just a form of the same static electricity that he and his friends had generated by rubbing a glass tube with pieces of fabric. The days and years that followed brought every form of praise the world could heap on him: honorary master's degrees from Harvard College and Yale, the Copley Medal (England's highest scientific award) and then membership in the Royal Society of London. French and German natural philosophers joined in the praise (Krider, 2005: 163–198; Chaplin, 2006: 116–159).

Franklin hoped that his "last years" could be devoted to his philosophical inquiries. He turned over control of the printing shop to Hall in 1748, developing a partnership that was lucrative enough to fund Franklin's other interests for the decades to follow. J.A. Leo Lemay, Franklin's preeminent modern biographer, estimates that the partnership, along with Franklin's real estate investments and salary as postmaster, brought in an income of £2,000 annually, the annual income of Pennsylvania's governor at the time. All of these experiments happened while Franklin was balancing a likewise increasingly busy public career that was expanding just as his interest in electricity grew. Any scholar racing against a publication deadline understands Franklin's frustration when he wrote "the Publick now considering me as a Man of Leisure, laid hold of me for their Purposes, every Part of our Civil Government, and almost at the same time, imposing some Duty upon me." That autobiographical recollection may sound like boasting – many of his memories often do – but a glimpse at Franklin's C.V. from the era shows a very busy life, indeed. On January 1, 1748, the same day he signed his partnership agreement with David Hall, Franklin refused election as the colonel of the Associators, the militia he had called for in his pamphlet *Plain Truth* the year before. Instead, Franklin would serve as a common soldier. This Cincinatus-like gesture, wise, perhaps, because Franklin indeed had no experience or expertise as a military man, was just the type of action that a man willing to accept, if not willing to seek, public power would do in Whiggish eighteenth-century politics. That October, Philadelphians elected Franklin to their Common Council. Other offices, including Justice of the Peace (1749), member of the Pennsylvania Assembly and Alderman (both 1751), and commissioner to the Albany Conference (1754), followed. During these same years, Franklin would also invest many hours founding the Academy and Charitable School of Philadelphia and Pennsylvania Hospital. Little wonder, then, that he felt that his time for experiments was being squeezed out by other activities.

2.6 Politician

Franklin's career in Pennsylvania politics began almost as early as his management of his printing house, and rose as his reputation as a man of business and civic affairs grew concomitantly with his reputation as a thinking person. That political career coincided with a transformation of the colony's political sphere being transformed. Pennsylvania had been founded as a proprietary colony, and its founder William Penn assumed the title "true and absolute Proprietor and Governor in chief" of the colony when he arrived there in 1682. Penn's stay in Pennsylvania was short, but his influence was long. Returning to England in 1684, he would only go back in 1699, having been caught up in affairs of contradictory land titles and the Glorious Revolution. His second stay, which ended in 1701, would be marked with contentious dealings with the Pennsylvania Assembly and the

Quakers who dominated it. Shortly before his final departure for Britain, Penn had signed the Charter of Privileges, a liberal government tract that would administer the colony until the revolution that granted wide franchise, annually elections, and freedom of religion. The legacy of Penn's brief administration would create the benefits, and the problems, which shaped Pennsylvania politics throughout Franklin's career.

Early on, Franklin – like other men of politics in his adopted colony – recognized Penn's importance and the level of freedom it granted them. In both his newspaper and his almanac, he celebrated Penn's contributions, the charter, and the prosperity around him. Yet Penn's departure, subsequent long illness following a stroke, and death left a political vacuum in Pennsylvania. Left to serve as regent and protector of her young sons' financial interests, Hannah Callowhill Penn sought to negotiate government policy with the increasingly independent colonial assembly. She relied on family friends such as James Logan, and sought to impose her family's will through her selection of lieutenant governors who would enforce her policies. Sir William Keith, the same governor who sent Franklin to London without the funds he needed, was one of the appointments that caused the Penn family the most problems. Others would follow.

By the time Franklin emerged into public activities, he recognized the importance of the proprietors to his plans for advancement and for civic improvement. The Library Company, Franklin's first public endeavor, received gifts from members of the Penn family and eventually a charter, and their minutes show frequent mention of the heritage that William Penn had granted the colony. When both lead proprietor John Penn and his brother arrived in 1735, the library directors made careful mention of the beneficence of the founder's family to their future success. Little wonder, perhaps, that one of the sons later grumbled within Franklin's earshot, "Then I suppose we shall hear more about our Father" (Franklin, 1905–1907).

Franklin's emergence into politics coincided with the profound transformation of Pennsylvania's land and Native American policies. In 1737, Thomas and Richard Penn, along with a group of supporters, planned and carried out the Walking Purchase, renowned now as the most egregious land grab in eighteenth-century America. The marathon team of runners which marked Pennsylvania's new boundaries that day, based on a scrap of a long-forgotten treaty William Penn had allegedly negotiated, would profoundly increase the amount of land the Penns controlled at the expense of destroying the peace and security provided by their father's Native American policy for the previous half century. It would also draw a group of land investors who owed their new wealth to Thomas and John Penn's policies, and who repaid that debt through a feudal-like belief in the policies of the proprietors. Over time, Franklin found himself in opposition to that group. As early as 1740, Andrew Bradford's *American Weekly Mercury* accused Franklin of anti-proprietary statements in the *Gazette*. As Franklin's popularity rose among his fellow citizens in the decade that follow, it obviously declined with the proprietors of his colony. In June 1748, Thomas Penn wrote to one of his supporters that Franklin "is a dangerous Man and I should be very Glad he inhabited any other Country, as I believe he is a very uneasy Spirit. However, as he is a sort of Tribune of the People, he must be treated with regard" (Jennings 1970; Harper, 2004: 167–179; Lemay, 2009: 49).

The struggle with Thomas Penn and his proprietary party followers would define Franklin's political career in the decade that followed, and that struggle would bring his Philadelphia career to an end in 1757. The issue came to a head once the French and Indian War broke out on Pennsylvania's western frontier, and the proprietors firmly refused to allow any funding bill to pass that would include taxes on their vast land holdings. "The Assembly finally, finding the Proprietaries obstinately persisted in manacling their Deputies with Instructions inconsistent not only with the Privileges of the People, but with the Service of the Crown, resolv'd to petition the King against them, and appointed me their Agent to go over to England, to present and support the Petition" (Franklin, 1964: 248).

Franklin left Philadelphia on April 4, 1757 accompanied by his son William and their slaves Peter and King, going to New York en route to the mother country (Waldstreicher, 2004: 144). Lord Loudoun, commander-in-chief of the British forces in North America, delayed permission until June 23 for the ship to sail during wartime, and Franklin used the time for reflection and writing. He created one more American persona as he composed "Father Abraham's Speech" – one of his most famous tracts – as the preface for *Poor Richard* of 1758, which would prove to be his last almanac. He addressed his "Courteous Reader", telling them that while he had been writing almanacs for a quarter century, his fellow printers seldom copied or heeded what he wrote. The elderly Father Abraham, said Poor Richard, spouted a list of maxims all quoting the almanac. Richard Saunders was vindicated. His preface statement about these fellow printers and his famous phrases rang true of the Penns and their supporters, who ignored the political tracts that had flowed from his pen in recent years. But as in life, so in his business: "the People were the best Judges of my Merit." Thus, Franklin left a long compilation of the sayings he had crafted to entertain and educate the people of the colonies as he sailed away to controversy (as well as fame) in the Old World (PBF, 7: 340).

Note

1 Labaree, Leonard W. *et al.*, eds. (1959–). *The Papers of Benjamin Franklin*. 39 vols to date. New Haven, CT: Yale University Press. Hereafter referred to as PBF.

Further Reading

Bridenbaugh, Carl and Bridenbaugh, Jessica (1942). *Rebels and Gentlemen: Philadelphia in the Age of Franklin*. New York, NY.

Boudreau, George W. (1996). " 'Highly valuable and extensively useful:' Community and readership among the eighteenth-century Philadelphia middling sort," *Pennsylvania History* 63: 302–329.

Isaacson, Walter (2003). *Benjamin Franklin: An American Life*. New York, NY.

Nash, Gary B. (1979). *The Urban Crucible: The Northern Seaports and the Origins of the American Revolution*. Cambridge, MA.

Chapter Three

THE MAKING OF A PATRIOT, 1757–1775

Sheila L. Skemp

In 1889, John T. Morse began his biography of Benjamin Franklin with an apology, as he wondered whether there was anything new to say about this famous American about whom so much had already been written. Obviously, Morse was hardly the last person to try to shed light on a man who somehow remains as enigmatic today as he probably was to his contemporaries. Historians and biographers, academics and lay people, eighteenth-century specialists, and those who focus on "modern" America all seem to think that they can capture the essence of someone who seems so accessible on the surface. Yet Franklin somehow always eludes the grasp of anyone attempting to pin him down.

Upon one thing everyone agrees. It was his long residence in England's capital that made Franklin the famous American that he became. Even his inventions and his electrical experiments would not have garnered him the attention he continues to receive had he not become identified with the fight for independence. Paradoxically, then, to understand Benjamin Franklin's commitment to America, historians must examine his time in England.

3.1 Benjamin Franklin's Political Philosophy

While historians concede that Franklin indulged in many political zigzags while he was in London, most situate him within some sort of philosophical or political context, as they attempt to explain why this particular American reacted to England the way he did. Of course not everyone agrees that

A Companion to Benjamin Franklin, First Edition. Edited by David Waldstreicher.
© 2011 Blackwell Publishing Ltd. Published 2011 by Blackwell Publishing Ltd.

Franklin even *had* a political philosophy. The most elegant and persuasive proponent of this perspective is Edmund Morgan, who sees Franklin as the ultimate pragmatist, "the least doctrinaire of men" (2002: 93). Franklin, Morgan insists, judged all policies by their efficacy, not by their theoretical purity as he sought solutions to problems that would satisfy all but the most ideological and irrational men. Thus he continually begged both England and America to avoid talking about their "rights," knowing full well that such discussions would lead to the destruction of an empire he loved. Morgan argues that Franklin was usually a man of good sense. If he trusted Parliament and king too long, it was because he expected Englishmen to be similarly sensible, thus coming to realize that their treatment of the colonies was counterproductive.

While most scholars agree that Benjamin Franklin was more pragmatic than ideological, many still insist that he had some core beliefs. For those historians, the preponderance of opinion – if not of the evidence – sees him and the colonists he represented as Whigs. Morse's work is a case in point. It paints a picture of Franklin as a thoroughgoing patriot who was above all an advocate for those simple colonial artisans, farmers, and tradesmen who fought for their rights against an aristocratic government (Morse, 1889: 101).[1] Franklin, he contends, began to support independence as early as the Stamp Act crisis. In this regard, he was in step with all colonists; he was truly a "representative man of America" (Morse, 1889: 181, 182). Similarly, Bernard Fay argues that Franklin was "born a Whig." His belief in liberty and Protestantism were central to his ability to create a "middle-class political party" in Pennsylvania (Fay, 1929: 263). He was the ultimate bourgeois, who fought an imperious and unbending aristocracy wherever he found it. Clinton Rossiter's Franklin, like Morgan's, was no ideologue but he embraced every tenet of Lockean Whiggery. He valued government based on natural law and the consent of the governed, the right to property, and equality. As early as his testimony in the House of Commons against the Stamp Act, this "great democrat of colonial America" personified values that all colonists understood (Rossiter, 1953: 290).

Whiggish portrayals of Franklin did not end in the 1950s. Francis Jennings's passionate biography, published in 1996, argues that Franklin's goal was the end of feudalism, first in Pennsylvania and then in all colonies. While he is more judicious than Jennings, Walter Isaacson also puts his subject squarely within the Whig tradition. He asserts that Franklin assiduously avoided the "Tory aristocracy." While he distrusted the rabble, his "inbred aversion to powerful establishments and idle elites" was stronger than his distaste for mob action (Isaacson, 2003: 181). If Isaacson's Franklin was a Whig, however, he was no radical, at least until 1768 when he finally "caught up" with colonial flame throwers and threw himself into the fray (Isaacson, 2003: 249).

Not everyone believes that Franklin's views were based on Lockean principles. Benjamin H. Newcomb's depiction of Franklin's enduring partnership with loyalist Joseph Galloway argues that both men were committed to colonial rights in general and assembly rights in particular. The differences between future patriot and future loyalist were minor. Their intellectual antecedents were not Locke, however, but Robert Trenchard and Thomas Gordon, those authors of *Cato's Letters* whom Bernard Bailyn has made famous. They advocated mixed government, with the balance tipped toward the legislative branch, and feared the power of a self-aggrandizing executive whose aim was to destroy liberty. Eventually, Franklin became convinced that England could not be trusted to preserve colonial liberties, while Galloway could never bring himself to turn his back on an empire that both men had once supported with equal fervor.

Paul W. Conner also maintains that Franklin had a coherent political philosophy. Rather than looking to Trenchard and Gordon, Conner portrays Franklin as a child of the enlightenment, as someone who craved order and control over his social environment. Franklin was pragmatic about means, but his commitment to an orderly, balanced, yet expanding nation of virtue never diminished. Perhaps because he lived in two port towns, his perspective was both intercolonial and transatlantic. His vision of a broad, powerful, and interconnected empire was one that few on either side of the Atlantic ever completely grasped. The same misunderstanding, argues Connor, plagues those historians who turn Franklin into an anti-government libertarian in the mold of Thomas Paine or Thomas Jefferson. He valued government, so long as it did not act arbitrarily, because it was government authority that maintained order and encouraged virtue.

Even Whig historians acknowledge – sometimes with puzzlement and faint apologies – Benjamin Franklin's early commitment to the British Empire. As early as 1898, Sydney George Fisher remarked upon the "strange confidence in the king" that was one of Franklin's enduring characteristics until the battles of Lexington and Concord led him to abandon king and country (Fisher, 1898: 225). Verner W. Crane concurs, although he sees the Tea Party as Franklin's point of no return. His abiding love of the British Empire, says Crane, blinded Franklin to the dangers of parliamentary hegemony throughout the 1750s and 1760s. As late as 1767, he admitted that since power had to reside somewhere, Parliament was as good a location for ultimate sovereignty as any other. It took Franklin even longer to blame George III for the differences dividing the empire. Equal membership in a united empire, not independence, was Franklin's goal.

Most historians, even those who clearly would prefer not to, acknowledge that Franklin was a staunch supporter of imperial unity throughout much of his adult life. If some characterize his early defenses of England as aberrations, others try to complicate without denying, the view of Franklin as an "empire man." Esmond Wright reminds readers that eighteenth-century Englishmen embraced at least four – sometimes overlapping, occasionally contradictory – perspectives on the empire. Mercantilists were intent on extracting raw materials from the colonies and regulating trade for the mother country's benefit. Administrative types dealt with a bewildering array of inefficient departments, all vying for control of the colonies. Members of the House of Commons championed parliamentary supremacy. And those interested in a large and expanding empire focused on military strategy. Franklin's views, argues Wright, were more expansive than any of these perspectives. Franklin pointed to America's rising population and the colonies' embrace of agrarian independence as evidence of the wealth and power that an unfettered but loyal America offered England. He also advocated imperial unity, and supported notions of free trade that anticipated Adam Smith. While he loved the empire, Franklin's conceptions differed from those embraced by Englishmen.

Ormond Seavey also qualifies depictions of Franklin as an uncritical admirer of king and empire. He agrees that Franklin had an "excessive and deeply emotional admiration for King George III," and that Franklin saw "no contradiction between being American and being English," (Seavey, 1988: 194, 195) but that is only part of the story. Seavey's Franklin was torn between two competing ideals. His famous essay on the *Increase of Mankind* (1751) projected an imperial vision, arguing that America was an increasingly important, even a central component of a united British Empire. But *The Way to Wealth*, which Franklin wrote en route to England in 1757, celebrated a self-sufficient society, free from European corruption. As the differences between England and America intensified, Franklin had to choose one vision; he rejected the empire in favor of independence.

Gordon Wood acknowledges no such internal conflict for Franklin, at least until the 1770s. Wood has based his career on his contention that eighteenth-century Americans were fundamentally different from their modern counterparts, arguing that the failure to understand this basic truth, distorts history. And yet, he says, most historians do just that with Franklin. They see him as the most accessible and modern member of the founding generation. They imagine him as the one colonial leader who shared the sensibilities of ordinary people because he, himself, was an "unpretentious commoner" a "Plebian in an aristocratic age"[2] (Parrington, 1927: 164). Wood disagrees. He portrays Franklin as a staunch royalist, whose profound admiration for King George III dominated his behavior. Thus he makes explicable what most historians have found puzzling and anomalous. His "missteps" were not aberrations; they reflected Franklin's very essence.[3]

Gordon Wood argues that Franklin fell helplessly in love with England in 1757 and did not fall out of love with the empire for nearly twenty years. Indeed, most of the time he was in London, Franklin "scarcely seems to have regarded himself as an American" (2004: 97). His admiration of all things English was hardly surprising. Because of his reputation as a scientist, he was wined and feted everywhere. He hobnobbed with the intellectual elite and even dined with kings. Thus, while other colonists were outraged by their shabby treatment in the capital city, Franklin failed to pick up on hints that Englishmen saw Americans as an inferior species. Supremely self-confident, he could not imagine that such barbs were aimed at him.

Nor, Gordon Wood contends, did Franklin really understand the England he loved. He never talked of the "king in Parliament." Instead he adopted "an extreme Tory position," arguing that it was to the king alone that the colonists owed allegiance (G. Wood, 2004: 122). Franklin's view ignored Parliament's victories over the Stuart kings which had limited the English monarch's power by 1688. For true Whigs, Parliament – not the king – was sovereign. But it was Parliament that most enraged Benjamin Franklin. Most historians see his advocacy of a federated empire as evidence that Franklin was a visionary supporter of the modern commonwealth system. Wood disputes this perspective, claiming that Franklin actually looked to the past, when an all-powerful king could disregard Parliament at his whim. Nevertheless, if Franklin's was an "extreme Tory" position, what are we to make of Esmond Wright's observation that the Tories were the most intransigent defenders of parliamentary supremacy?

Finally, Wood maintains that Franklin was a "courtier," – an epithet he used to condemn his loyalist son in 1774 (PBF, 1978, 21: 287).[4] Even after 1768, when he knew that his dream of making Pennsylvania a royal colony stood no chance of success, Franklin remained in England angling for a government sinecure. He clung tenaciously to his one royal office, deputy postmaster-general for the colonies. It was, Wood implies, the loss of his post office position in 1774 and his realization that no chance remained for other crown perquisites that led Franklin to embrace independence.

If Gordon Wood had had access to Brendan McConville's *The King's Three Faces,* he may have framed his argument somewhat differently. McConville insists that everyone in America – slaves and planters, yeoman farmers and merchants – was fixated on the crown until the mid-seventies. If he is correct, Franklin's adulation of the king and his antipathy to Parliament were not anomalous. Hence, Franklin was, indeed a "representative American," although the America he represented was neither republican nor democratic, but profoundly royalist.

Whig, or royalist, pragmatist or empire man, each perspective describes Benjamin Franklin at one moment or another. One way to assess the validity of the arguments historians have made over the centuries is to examine some of the turning points in Franklin's views throughout this crucial period.

3.2 The Campaign for Royal Government

In 1757, Benjamin Franklin traveled to London at the behest of the Pennsylvania Assembly, hoping to persuade the Pennsylvania proprietors to alter their most unpopular policies. The Assembly particularly despised the

Penns' use of ironclad instructions to their governors, giving executives no flexibility to negotiate with lawmakers. They also wanted the proprietors to lift the tax exemptions on their own colonial estates. At some point – historians disagree about when – Franklin concluded that the Penns would never change and thus he launched a campaign to make Pennsylvania a crown colony. Ironically, Benjamin Franklin, founding father, entered the imperial stage as an advocate for royal government. Most historians feel compelled to explain how the republican Franklin of popular myth could have embraced monarchical rule.

James H. Hutson makes a strong case for the central importance of the campaign for royal government, observing that Franklin would not have traveled to London had it not been for Pennsylvania's quarrel with Thomas Penn. And he may not have become a patriot had he remained in Philadelphia. Be that as it may, Edmund Morgan characterizes the effort as "out of character," as one of the few times when Franklin completely "lost his perspective" (2002: 102). He finds it puzzling that this shrewd political animal was unable to see that relatively few Pennsylvanians shared his goal. Nor did Franklin realize the king could be as tyrannical as the proprietors. To Gordon Wood, however, Franklin's decision makes perfect sense. His "excessive faith in the British Crown" blinded him to the dangers to colonial liberties that his pet project threatened, despite the warnings of wiser heads in England and America (G. Wood, 2006: 103).

Robert Middlekauff offers another explanation. He contends that while the plan for royal government was ill-conceived, it was not especially surprising. Middlekauff's understanding of Franklin's character differs markedly from Morgan's. He argues that the conception of a bland and equable Benjamin Franklin ignores the fact that he was a man of powerful emotions who did not invariably turn his foes away with a quip and a smile. Once he felt ill-used, he lost all sense of proportion and behaved in ways that were clearly counterproductive. Thus when Thomas Penn treated him with total disdain, sneering at the colonists' naïve assumption that their right to self-government was protected by Pennsylvania's original charter, Franklin's desire for revenge was unwavering. "Blinded by passion," he was motivated, not by political considerations but because "he wanted to hurt Penn more than anything else" (Middlekauff, 1996: 76).[5]

Whig historians do not view Franklin's campaign as either an aberration or a mistake. They see it as evidence that Franklin was obsessed by the desire for colonial self-rule. Anti-propriety sentiment, they say, had been part and parcel of Pennsylvania's political scene from the beginning, and Franklin's project simply reflecting the culture of his adopted colony. His attack on proprietary government was not, as Wood contends, a reflection of his love of the king, but of his hatred of a "one-man dictatorship" dominated by an imperious aristocrat (Burlingame, 1967: 22, 23).[6]

William S. Hanna disagrees. Hanna's Franklin – like Wood's – was ambitious, elitist, and had a profound sense of his own self-worth. Above all, he was a politician, a wheeler dealer who was always out for the main chance. Conversely, Thomas Penn was flexible, harbored "no tyrannical designs," and merely wanted to restore the balance between the Assembly and the proprietors (Hanna, 1964: 17). Moreover, Penn's view of the Pennsylvania charter was constitutionally correct while Franklin and the Assembly were "petty, unprincipled, and tyrannical" (Hanna, 1964: 133).[7] Hanna contends that getting rid of the Penns was only part of Franklin's agenda. Franklin had a "grand design in mind," as he hoped to use his influence with enlightened Englishmen to reform the empire, and to secure a position for himself in Parliament or even the ministry (Hanna, 1964: 177).

Some historians argue that Franklin planned to destroy the proprietary charter as early as 1757. Others, William Hanna, Esmond Wright, and Benjamin Newcomb most persuasively, say the decision came seven years later, after the rampaging Paxton Boys attacked "friendly" Indians with impunity and marched on Philadelphia itself. James Hutson puts the date later still. He insists that no one was serious about obtaining a royal charter until 1765. Both Franklin and the Assembly were bluffing, seeing Franklin as an intimidator who would use his influence to frighten the proprietors into concessions. Only when negotiations broke down did Franklin seriously begin pushing for royal government. In that case, neither Franklin's anger at the Penns nor his love of king and empire are necessary to explain his commitment.

Benjamin Franklin left for London in 1764. He had just suffered his first electoral defeat in the Assembly elections, but his Quaker party still controlled the lower house. It immediately asked Franklin to cross the Atlantic and to serve as the colony's agent.[8] Benjamin Newcomb maintains that despite the unpopularity of his mission, Franklin never considered the possibility that he would fail. He was sure that reasonable men would be moved by his superior arguments and powers of persuasion, and thought the connections he had made on his earlier trip to England's capital would stand him in good stead. If he was wrong, says Newcomb, his was "a pardonable delusion" (1972: 106).

Newcomb maintains that when Franklin decided to lead the push for royal government he was thinking only about the politics of the moment. He had no reason to consider the broader implications of crown control. Perhaps. There were, however, many in Pennsylvania – most notably John Dickinson – who were quite aware of those implications, and never trusted the king's men to protect Pennsylvania's liberties. Would the king respect the colony's religious diversity? What assurance was there that the crown would be more willing to recognize the Assembly's claims to autonomy than the proprietors were? Indeed, David Morgan insists that Franklin knew full well that "a royal regime might well restrict Pennsylvania's freedom of action far more than proprietary rule did." Nevertheless, he was so determined to get rid of the Penns that he did not care (D. Morgan, 1996: 122).

At the very least, there is sufficient evidence to indicate that Franklin should have known that the king's men and the proprietors agreed on the fundamentals. He had met briefly with Lord Grenville in the spring of 1759, and was shocked to hear the head of the Privy Council maintain that in the royal provinces, the king was "legislator of the colonies and when His Majesty's instructions come there, they are the law of the land" (PBF, 8: 293). Nevertheless, Franklin's eyes were firmly fixed on the prize – the royal government – when he set foot on England's shores.

3.3 The Stamp Act: 1765–1766

Although he knew about Lord Grenville's plan for a stamp tax before he left Philadelphia, Franklin seemed curiously indifferent to the impending legislation. He went through the motions, suggesting alternatives that Grenville summarily rejected. Other than that, he was silent. It did not take long before his enemies at home used his silence to argue that Franklin not only supported the tax but had actually helped write it. Franklin swiftly regained his equilibrium. He wrote extensively, lobbied members of Parliament, and eventually worked with the Rockingham ministry to secure the Stamp Act's repeal. His testimony before the House of Commons in 1766 was, as virtually everyone agrees, a tour de force. Whether or not it was instrumental in getting rid of the Stamp Act is debatable, but it revived Franklin's reputation at home.

Whig historians are especially uncomfortable explaining why Franklin was "slow to react" to the Stamp Act crisis (Brands, 2000: 368). Some deny that a problem even exists. Morse, for instance, asserts that Franklin opposed the Act from the beginning, and that his work on behalf of repeal earned him a well-deserved reputation as "representative of a disaffected people" (Morse, 1889: 101). Less colorfully, Benjamin Newcomb also contends that while both Franklin and Galloway deplored violent protests, they always saw the Act as "obviously oppressive and unjust" and as "in direct conflict with their basic principles" (1972: 107, 112). Most of Franklin's admirers, however, almost apologetically admit that their hero was temporarily caught off guard as he underestimated the depth of hostility to Parliament's first, full-blown attempt to tax the colonies. They assert that once he understood just how unpopular the Stamp Act was, he righted himself, coming out of the crisis more committed to American liberty than ever.

Still, historians find it difficult to ignore the cavalier manner in which Franklin seemed to dismiss the Stamp Act when he wrote to Pennsylvania's

Charles Thompson in July of 1765. "We might as well have hinder'd the Suns setting," he said. "But since 'tis down, my Friend, and it may be long before it rises again, Let us make as good a Night of it as we can" (PBF, 12: 207). He was so unconcerned about reaction to the Stamp Act that he secured the post of Philadelphia's Stamp Distributor for his friend John Hughes and bought some inexpensive stamped paper for his business partners.

The most obvious explanation for his tepid response is that Franklin was fixated on his campaign for royal government. As Hanna indicates, he was looking at all issues from the perspective of someone who hoped to persuade English leaders to reform the entire British Empire, drawing not just Pennsylvania but all the colonies closer to the royal orbit. Thus, the Stamp Act was "a minor matter, a necessary price" for his ultimate goal (Hanna, 1964: 174). Nevertheless, the legislation was profoundly embarrassing; it seemed to prove that his opponents were right to fear crown rule. As Hutson points out, Franklin's enemies lost no time in painting him and the Quaker Party as dupes of the very government they were trying to embrace. Ironically, it was the Proprietary party, and the Penns, themselves, who led Pennsylvania's opposition to the Stamp Act. And it was Franklin who urged his friends back home to do nothing to harm the case for royal government.

Thomas Wendel adds to the list of practical considerations that shaped Franklin's calculations. Franklin was a royal officer, as was his son, the governor of New Jersey, and thus he was legally obliged to support the king. He was an aspiring land speculator, who needed ministerial support for his schemes for western expansion. But above all his determination to avoid offending the ministry so long as his petition for a royal government remained viable inhibited his ability to speak forcefully against the Stamp Act. Once the Rockingham ministry replaced Grenville, says Wendel, Franklin was free to advocate repeal.

Bernard Fay does not stoop to such mundane explanations. Incredibly prescient, always ahead of his times, Fay's Franklin saw the Stamp Act as a blessing. He thought that because it provoked such a furor, it would force leaders on both sides of the Atlantic to discuss the relationship between England and the colonies. Such a discussion would probably result in accommodation, leading to the creation of a powerful and unified realm. More judiciously, Carl Van Doren says much the same thing. He, too, insists that Franklin always understood the opposition to the Stamp Act. "Nobody else," he avers, "had ever known so much about America" (Van Doren, 1938: 353). But even as Franklin hated the Stamp Act, he thought that violent protests would make it harder for him to work for repeal and save the empire.

Paul Conner offers a novel explanation for Franklin's mild response to parliamentary taxation. True, Franklin preferred reason to riots. More importantly, he was not blind to the salutary effects of taxation. He thought taxes made it difficult for the rich to get richer, while they encouraged frugality, industry, and republican virtue in everyone else.

If historians disagree about the reasons for Franklin's initial response to the Stamp Act, they are also at odds about the effect the controversy had on Franklin, himself. Some see it as a major turning point in his understanding of the British Empire. Verner Crane concedes that Franklin was willing to accept parliamentary taxation as late as 1765. His pet scheme for currency reform involved Parliament's establishment of a General Loan Office in America that would lend money at interest to colonists. This was, Franklin fully recognized, a form of taxation. Nevertheless, Crane insists that once he became fully aware of colonial anger, Franklin was "the early engineer of the American propaganda machine in London" (1934: 62). It was, however, the Declaratory Act that led Franklin to think systematically about the empire. Like Edmund Morgan, Crane concedes that Franklin usually avoided discussions of rights, probably because he thought they were counterproductive. Nevertheless, in private he was arriving at his own conception of Anglo–colonial relations. Crane uses the unpublished Marginalia that Franklin scribbled in pamphlets published in 1766 to argue that he was already coming to believe that Parliament was not sovereign and that the colonial legislatures were autonomous in their own realms. Still, he thought that the creation of a federation whose members were bound together by their fealty to the king would lead, not to independence, but to an enduring British Empire.

Crane's argument is suggestive but problematic. First, it is difficult, as the editors of the *Franklin Papers* observe, to know for sure just when Franklin wrote what he did. He may have jotted down his views much later than 1766. Second, Crane has a difficult time explaining Franklin's most damning testimony before the House of Commons. Edmund Morgan has correctly pointed out that Franklin misstated colonial views when he said that Americans would accept an "external" tax – essentially duties on imports – but not an "internal" tax. This ultimately led to Charles Townshend's assumption that Parliament could tax goods coming into colonial ports. Crane makes a valiant, but ultimately unsuccessful effort to explain the testimony by insisting that Franklin never said that he, himself, accepted the distinction. "Is it not," Crane asks, "quite as significant that Franklin was speaking here in the third person, not in the first?" (1934: 69). Was he not, then, simply reporting the sentiments of the colonists rather than offering his own opinion? Even if this were the case, which is doubtful, if Franklin thought that this was what Americans believed, he was surely wrong.

Cecil Currey sees Franklin's campaign for repeal as transformative. It forced him to think seriously about Anglo–colonial relations and to arrive at his view of a federated empire. But from Currey's perspective, this pointed, not to consolidation but to separatism. After 1766, Franklin worked relentlessly for independence while continuing to masquerade as a moderate. Currey dismisses Franklin's statements supporting imperial unity as propaganda designed to throw a suspicious ministry off his trail. The testimony before the House of Commons was a case in point. Franklin could not afford to give his "real" belief that Parliament had no authority over the colonies, for to do so would undercut his own influence and tip his hand. Thus he lied in public, but began to "tutor American radicals" in private (Currey, 1968: 176). David Morgan, too, sees Franklin as duplicitous and self-serving. During the early stages of the Stamp Act controversy he was all things to all people. When he finally realized that the colonies would never accept parliamentary taxation, he took "calculated steps" to mount a supremely successful publicity campaign – not, as most have it, to secure the repeal of the Stamp Act, but to salvage his own reputation (D. Morgan, 1996: 122).

Virtually alone, William Hanna argues that Franklin's stock in Pennsylvania declined due to the Stamp Act crisis. Hanna contends that Franklin became virtually irrelevant in Philadelphia politics after 1766. He tried to help Joseph Galloway and the old Quaker party, but seemed not to realize how much had changed at home. New leaders appeared, most of whom he barely knew, and imperial issues, not internecine party squabbles, dominated the political scene. In London, too, says Hanna, Franklin was more bewildered than steadfast after 1766. Nor did he have much influence there. Most leaders saw him as a major irritant or a self-interested lobbyist who could not be trusted.

William Willcox does not describe the Stamp Act crisis as a turning point for Franklin. Urging historians to take the long view, he concedes that his testimony probably enhanced Franklin's reputation, quieting the criticisms of his enemies at home and leading many Englishmen to see him as "the" colonial spokesman.[9] But while admirers praise Franklin's "fantastic" ability to "besiege" the Rockingham ministry, securing repeal almost single-handedly, Willcox judiciously insists that his testimony changed nothing, either for Anglo–American relations or Benjamin Franklin (Fay, 1929: 320).[10] Although he always supported the colonies, Franklin continued to respond to specific grievances with practical solutions that might resolve the differences dividing England and America.

3.4 Townshend and Beyond: 1767–1770

After Parliament's repeal of the Stamp Act, Benjamin Franklin assumed – or said he did – that England would never tax its colonies again. A year later, apparently taking a cue from Franklin's "grievous blunder" at the Stamp Act hearings, Townshend introduced his taxes on various luxury goods coming to America from England (V.W. Crane, 1954: 124). In response,

Pennsylvanian John Dickinson wrote a series of pamphlets known collectively as the *Farmer's Letters*, in which he argued that while Parliament had the right to regulate trade, it could not tax the colonies either internally or externally. Franklin made sure that the *Letters* appeared in the London press, although he expressed reservations about their logic. Writing to his son in 1768, he ventured his belief that Parliament either had the right both to tax and legislate for the colonies, or it could not interfere in local affairs at all. He was inclined to the latter position, saying the colonies are "so many separate states, only subject to the same King" (Willcox, 1972: 15, 76).

It is no wonder that historians argue about Franklin's political views after 1767. He espoused legislative autonomy for the colonies, but pressed for imperial unity and continued to have faith in the king. He opposed the Townshend Acts, but urged Americans to refrain from violence as they sought repeal of the hated legislation. Thus characterizations of Franklin during this period run the gamut.

David Hawke insists that in the beginning Franklin had no problem with the Townshend duties, seeing them as trade regulations rather than taxes, while Van Doren maintains that Franklin instantly "saw every sign of danger ahead" (1938: 362). Occupying the middle ground, Isaacson contends that Franklin was slow to react to the Townshend Acts although he ultimately opposed them. Indeed, he says, it was difficult for anyone – perhaps even Franklin himself – to know exactly where he stood on the issues threatening to divide his beloved empire.

Assuming, for the sake of argument, that Franklin did know what he believed and that at least by 1768 he had come to think that the Townshend Acts were unconstitutional, the question remains: Why did he remain quiet about his views, sharing them with a few confidants, while pursuing a moderate position in public? Edmund Morgan assumes that Franklin was simply too averse to the hair-splitting controversies over colonial rights to be bothered with the kind of arguments that occupied radicals at either end of the ideological spectrum. His engagement in just those kinds of arguments in private, however, would indicate that Franklin discussed the very issues that Morgan says did not much interest him. Gordon Wood, on the other hand, acknowledges that Franklin was a little taken aback by both the Stamp and Townshend Acts, but he points out that he blamed Parliament, not the king, for both pieces of legislation. Thus he continued to be a Tory. Most unpersuasively, Currey sees his silence as evidence that Franklin was already secretly working for independence.

Everyone agrees that Franklin was busy after 1767, publishing pamphlet after pamphlet, explaining the colonies to England, and England to the colonies. Nevertheless, his self-created role of mediator was strained after 1768, especially after Lord Hillsborough, already president of the Lords of Trade, assumed the newly created position of Secretary of State for the Colonies. Hillsborough was a hardliner and a stickler for details. He immediately took on Massachusetts. He thwarted Franklin's speculative schemes. And he rejected, once and for all, Pennsylvania's petition for royal government. This decision, argues Hutson, was crucial. His failure to oust the proprietors meant that Franklin was liberated, free to attack ministry and Parliament with the intensity he had once reserved for the Penns. The king's men had rejected him; thus he would reject the king. Admittedly, Franklin had known for two years that his petition was going nowhere; still the final blow to his project surely stung.

It was his acceptance of the Agency for the Massachusetts lower house in 1770, says Verner W. Crane, that was Franklin's "decisive moment" (1954: 143). Franklin had already served three colonies: Pennsylvania (1764), Georgia (1768), and New Jersey (1769). His fourth made him something akin to an ambassador at large, as he assumed responsibility for each province and spoke for the colonies as a whole.[11] But it was not simply the addition of another colony to his repertoire that made this agency so important. Massachusetts was America's most radical colony. Indeed, some of its leaders actually opposed Franklin's appointment, because he was too moderate.

David Morgan insists that Franklin "deliberately" sought the opportunity to work with men like Samuel Adams. He managed to "worm his way" into the position, amplifying his rhetoric and urging the colonies to continue their trade boycott after Parliament repealed all of the Townshend duties except for the tax on tea (D. Morgan, 1996: 161, 178).[12] Once he accepted Massachusetts's offer – that he actively sought it is unlikely – Franklin surely had to please a more demanding constituency. And it is likely that as he worked with men whose views were more extreme than his own, he became more alienated from the empire.

The Massachusetts agency was significant in another regard. It led to Franklin's nastiest confrontation with London officialdom since his quarrel with Thomas Penn nearly twenty years earlier. The appointment came from the Assembly, not from the whole government. Indeed, Governor Thomas Hutchinson refused to sign off on it. Technically, this meant that Franklin had no legal standing. Although other agents had occasionally represented the lower house alone, Hillsborough was determined to nip such irregular practice in the bud. Thus when Franklin presented his credentials to the secretary, Hillsborough refused to accept them. Franklin was furious at his treatment and determined to do no more business with the man who was most responsible for colonial affairs.

3.5 The Cockpit: 1774

The beginning of the end of Benjamin Franklin's sojourn in England came in January of 1773. He was at least partially responsible for his own fate. Virtually everyone tells the story in the same way. In 1772, someone in

England gave Franklin six letters that Thomas Hutchinson and Andrew Oliver (then lieutenant governor and secretary of Massachusetts, respectively) had written much earlier to Thomas Whately, Grenville's former secretary. The letters argued for serious imperial reform including the abridgement of some colonial rights. Franklin forwarded the letters to Speaker of the House Thomas Cushing, instructing him neither to copy nor print them. But when news of their contents spread, Cushing published the letters. Outraged by what they read, the members of the lower house asked the king to remove Governor Hutchinson from office.

Franklin tried to keep his role in sending the letters a secret. Unfortunately, Whately's brother William acted on his suspicions that John Temple was the culprit and challenged him to a duel. Whately was wounded in the affair, and when he accused his adversary of ungentlemanly behavior, Temple demanded a rematch. Determined to avoid further bloodshed, Franklin admitted that he had sent the letters to Massachusetts. After that, government leaders were out for blood, and they soon had their way.

Franklin always insisted that he sent the letters to Massachusetts in order to heal the rift between England and its colonies. He thought that by proving that the lies of a few ambitious and evil Americans were responsible for the tyrannical policies emanating from Whitehall, he would provide the colonists with a convenient scapegoat. Historians are divided about whether or not they believe Franklin. Some say he wanted to punish Hutchinson for refusing to authorize his appointment as agent. Others argue that he was still trying to prove himself to Massachusetts radicals. Currey claims that Franklin was sure the letters would stir up colonial anger, thus leading to independence. His action then was "an expression of his deep radicalism" (Currey, 1968: 310). At the other end of the spectrum, Morse simply asserts that Franklin clearly "acted according to his conscience." Unfortunately, well-placed Englishmen used the incident to "discredit the character of the representative man of America" (Morse, 1889: 181, 182).

Gordon Wood takes Franklin at his word, but he surely does not see him as a representative American. Franklin, he says, still hoped to obtain a position in the English government and was as determined as ever to hold the empire together. Consequently, he was willing to do anything, even destroy the reputation of his good friend, Thomas Hutchinson to achieve his ends. In what was a "spectacular" error in judgment, he imagined that "he and a few men of goodwill could head off the crisis" (Wood, 2004: 143). Edmund Morgan agrees that Franklin was still trying to ameliorate the differences between England and America, although he insists that Franklin would accept nothing short of colonial equality. His was not, then, an unquestioning acceptance of imperial rule. Others, perhaps most wisely, remain mystified, content to call the entire business a "serious miscalculation" (E. Morgan, 1996: 194). The fact remains that we will never really know.

Whatever his motives, the consequences were monumental. The timing could not have been worse. Franklin admitted his part in the affair on December 25, 1773. News of the Tea Party reached London on January 20, just nine days before he went before the Privy Council to support the petition for Hutchinson's removal. Already furious at Franklin's dishonorable behavior, outraged at the wanton destruction of the tea, London officialdom was eager to punish Franklin, and by proxy all colonists. Hanna argues that no one in England's capital had ever liked or trusted Franklin. This, he says, was merely the last straw. But most observers think that Franklin still enjoyed some influence and that his role in the affair of the letters dramatically reduced his power.

When Franklin appeared in a room known as the Cockpit to defend Massachusetts's petition, he underwent a ritual and very public humiliation at the hands of Solicitor General Alexander Wedderburn, an excellent orator with a flare for the dramatic. From the beginning, Wedderburn made it clear that the petition was not his real concern. He was, to the delight of an overflow crowd, determined to destroy Benjamin Franklin. He not only attacked his victim's honor, but more significantly, he argued that Franklin was "the first mover and prime conductor," the "actor and secret spring," of a small but determined cabal of Americans who aspired to nothing less than independence (Willcox, 1978, 21:57). For nearly an hour, Wedderburn heaped abuse on Franklin, who stood silently before him, enduring the catcalls from ministers whose approbation he had sought for the past decade. The Privy Council's rejection of the Massachusetts petition was both a foregone conclusion and an anti-climax. Two days later, Franklin was fired from his post office position.

Some historians do not see even his dramatic humiliation as "the" moment that led Franklin to embrace independence. William Willcox in particular argues that it was the cumulative effect of his years in England that gradually turned Franklin into a patriot. It was the process of defending the colonies, and having his arguments consistently rejected by official London, which took its toll. As one minister after another failed to listen to reason, Franklin became increasingly disillusioned.

True enough. Still, many observers agree with Jack Greene who insists that Wedderburn had alienated "the man who was perhaps the best friend they had from America" (Greene, 1976: 53). Far from being a rabble rouser, Franklin had always put the best face possible on Parliament's behavior. He deplored the Tea Party, advised Boston to pay for the ruined tea, and even offered to reimburse the company himself. Now, with the loss of his crown position and his reputation in tatters, his usefulness in London was over. Franklin had gone into the Cockpit a good Empire-man. He left as a patriot.

That puts it too strongly. More than his Cockpit experience, the Coercive Acts, which closed Boston Harbor and shut down Massachusetts government, convinced Franklin that even the king could not be trusted to protect colonial liberties. Nevertheless, Wedderburn's attack was devastating. Many historians see Franklin as supremely self-confident, even arrogant. Because they recognize his superior intellect, they assume that Franklin must have known just how intelligent and talented he was. Robert Middlekauff points out, that Franklin was a self-made man who as a result was thin-skinned and insecure. When Englishmen implied that as an American he was beneath their notice, he objected, aware enough of his own abilities to resent the disdain of men he knew were his intellectual inferiors. Unfortunately, says Middlekauff, the English government had more than its share of arrogant and mediocre men in those years.

Ormond Seavey, too, argues that historians should never ignore the personal dimension of Franklin's experience. Most colonial leaders attacked English "tyranny" from the safety of the provinces. Franklin, however, faced his enemies in person. They humiliated him publicly, ultimately expelling him from polite society, and destroying his sense of himself as a mediator between England and America. Granted, as Timothy Breen contends, most colonists suffered "humiliation" and "emotional pain" when they realized by the 1760s just how marginal their position was (Breen, 1997: 32). Still, Franklin suffered more viscerally than most.

3.6 The Final Days

Franklin did not leave for home right away. This alone convinces many scholars that neither the experience at the Cockpit nor the Coercive Acts convinced him that independence was inevitable. He was pleased when the Continental Congress met, assured that America's show of unity would make Parliament back down. He was even happier when Congress decided to quit trading with the British altogether. Remembering how effective a less thoroughgoing boycott had been in 1765, he hoped that history would repeat itself. Moreover, there was always the chance that a change in administration, would result in a more sympathetic government. Instead, when North called for parliamentary elections before the effects of the boycott could be felt, an even more hard-line Parliament assumed the reins of power.

Still, Franklin tarried. Currey suggests on the basis of exceedingly thin evidence that he remained because he was helping smuggle arms into the colonies. If Currey is right, then Wedderburn's accusations were not only fair, but actually underestimated the extent of Franklin's machinations. More likely he stayed because he was involved in a variety of backroom negotiations with those few Englishmen who saw him as the best hope they had to avoid civil war. Of course Franklin had no authority to offer anyone anything. And the people with whom he talked – Richard Howe,

Thomas Viliers, Baron Hyde, even Lord Camden, formerly William Pitt – represented no one but themselves. Franklin conceded that Pitt's attention "flattered not a little my Vanity" (Willcox, 1978, 21: 579). Camden sought his advice, and gained him entrance to the House of Lords so that he could hear for himself the "great commoner's" pleas for accommodation. But it was all a waste of time. Franklin railed at the "Hereditary Legislators" who had "scarce Discretion enough to govern a Herd of Swine" (Willcox, 1978, 21: 583). In fact, as he surely knew, even his English "friends" did not agree with him. None would consider any limitation on parliamentary sovereignty. By 1775, he was finally, however reluctantly, ready to admit defeat. It was time to go home.

Historians will never agree about when and why Franklin became a patriot. More than most founders, he remains an enigma. In part, he presents a problem because he lived so long. He was eighty-two years old at his death, and he had lived a very full life for most of those years. It would be unrealistic to assume that the Franklin of twenty-five was the same as the Franklin of fifty-five or seventy. Like all men, he was touched and changed by his experiences. Moreover, even someone of his intellectual abilities could not see into the future. Franklin was, as Morgan and others have observed, more a practical man than a theorist. He tried to solve the problems that lay before him in the present, and did not always appreciate the implications of his own actions. If conditions changed, he was willing to change with them. Consequently, many accuse him of having no core, no principles to guide him.

Not only did Franklin live so long, but he wrote so much. This was especially true from 1757 to 1775. Because he did not enjoy face-to-face relations with his colonial counterparts, he had to put pen to paper whenever he wanted to discuss his views with people at home. Franklin's paper trail is exceptionally deep. Consequently, there is always a passage somewhere to prove that Franklin was a democrat or a royalist, a Whig or a Tory. It is easy, as some historians do, to cherry pick, to quote one set of observations Franklin made about imperial affairs and to ignore others. Instead of trying to make every one of his pronouncements fit some grand overarching theme, historians might be better off, as John William Ward puts it, to "accept his variety itself as our major problem and try to understand that" (Ward, 1963: 542).

In the end, scholars should bear in mind one obvious fact. We see Franklin knowing full well that the Revolution was coming, and thus we tend to judge every statement he made as brimming with meaning and somehow having a bearing on his path to patriotism. Franklin was living in his own world, facing real problems, trying to solve those problems in a rational way. No one, not the most rabid patriot, imagined until very late in the game that America would declare independence. If Franklin was a moderate – and the preponderance of the evidence indicates that he was – so were most Americans. He may have loved England more than some – but that is a matter of degree and represents no great difference between himself and most colonials. It is unfair to demand that if he had a coherent philosophy it shaped his response to every event. To imagine that his starts and stops, his movements first in one direction and then another mean either that he had no core beliefs, or that he was a conniving conspirator who never said what he meant, is to deny that Franklin was genuinely confused and disappointed by much of what happened after 1765. In other words, it is to deny his very humanity.

Notes

1. See also Carl Van Doren's detailed biography, which contrasts a virtuous, agrarian America with a corrupt England, dependent on trade and manufacturing for its livelihood.
2. See also Cohen (1953: 27, 30) who sees Franklin as the "Horatio Alger" of the eighteenth century.
3. Only Sydney George Fisher comes close to Gordon Wood in his contention that Franklin argued from a pro-royalist stance throughout his entire sojourn in England.
4. Labaree, Leonard W. et al., eds. (1959–). *The Papers of Benjamin Franklin*. 39 vols to date. New Haven, CT: Yale University Press. Hereafter referred to as PBF.
5. Cecil Currey – less judiciously than Middlekauff – concurs. Franklin, he says, was a "proud and angry man" who launched a one-man vendetta against the Penns (Currey, 1968: 137).
6. See especially Morse, 1889: 91. Thomas Wendel and Bernard Fay also fall in this category as does William Hanna.
7. David Hawke agrees. He is, in fact, one of the few historians to give not only the Penns but also George Grenville and Lord Hillsborough high marks for being fair and judicious. He also insists that Franklin had solid reasons for urging the end of proprietary rule, even as he did not see royal government as a panacea.
8. Francis Jennings dissents from this perspective. He contends that Franklin was never really a part of the Quaker party, that in fact he was at the head of an "Anglican machine" whose members generally opposed the Friends, especially the committed pacifists among them. And they returned the favor (Jennings, 1996: 165, 166).
9. Isaacson puts the case a little more strongly. Franklin's testimony before the House of Commons saved Franklin's reputation in the colonies, he says, and led people on both sides of the Atlantic to see him as "the ambassador for America in general" (Isaacson, 2003: 229).
10. Brands's rhetoric is no less grandiose than Fay's. Grenville, he maintains, "never forgave him for single-handedly demolishing the rationale for the act" (Brands, 2000: 3).
11. David Morgan's *The Devious Dr. Franklin* is particularly useful in documenting the services, little and large, that Franklin performed for his "smaller" colonies.

12 Benjamin Newcomb (1972), too, contends that Franklin's views were in perfect harmony with those of the radical leaders in Massachusetts. But even he does not imagine that Franklin supported the means that those leaders sometimes employed.

Further Reading

Bailyn, Bernard (1974). *The Ordeal of Thomas Hutchinson*. Cambridge, MA.
Becker, Carl L. (1931). *Benjamin Franklin: A Biographical Sketch*. Ithaca, NY.
Bruce, William Cabell (1923). *Benjamin Franklin Self-Revealed*. New York, NY.
Clark, Ronald W. (1983). *Benjamin Franklin: A Biography*. New York, NY.
Fleming, Thomas (1971). *The Man Who Dared the Lightning*. New York, NY.
Gaustad, Edwin A. (2006). *Benjamin Franklin*. New York, NY.
Kammen, Michael G. (1968). *A Rope of Sand: The Colonial Agents in British Politics and the American Revolution*. Ithaca, NY.
Lopez, Claude-Anne and Eugenia W. Herbert (1975). *The Private Franklin: The Man and His Family*. New York, NY.
Nolan, J. Bennett (1956). *Benjamin Franklin in Scotland and Ireland, 1759 and 1771*. Philadelphia, PA.
Randall, Willard Sterne (1984). *A Little Revenge: Benjamin Franklin and His Son*. Boston, MA.
Skemp, Sheila L. (1990). *William Franklin: Son of a Patriot, Servant of a King*. New York, NY.
Waldstreicher, David (2004). *Runaway America: Benjamin Franklin, Slavery and the American Revolution*. New York, NY.

Chapter Four

FRANKLIN FURIOSO, 1775–1790

Jonathan R. Dull

According to his friend Joseph Priestley, Franklin shed tears as he prepared to return to America in March, 1775 (PBF, 21: 526n).[1] This display of emotion was very unusual for him. It is difficult to picture him in tears except at the death of his four-year-old son Franky (PBF, 2: 154); even the death of his wife in 1774 probably was far less wrenching, given all the years they had spent apart. It is not that he was unemotional. He was a man of strong passions such as love for his children and rage at those like Thomas Penn who crossed him, as well as other emotions he tried to keep hidden, like his pride, vanity, and fierce ambition. Instead, his outer calm was a reflection of his reserve and still more his self-control, the product of a lifetime's labor (his maxims for self-improvement are basically maxims of self-control). Such self-control was not easily attained, particularly it seems when it came to mastering anger, but it had served him well; indeed, along with his astonishing creativity and his considerable ability to charm people, it had been one of the secrets of his success. The tears he now shed speak well of him. He professed some optimism about returning to England the following autumn (PBF, 21: 534–535), but he can hardly have believed it. His departure left him open to arrest in the aftermath of the Hutchinson affair (PBF, 21: 200–201). He was leaving behind many friends whom he might never see again, as well as the country in which he had spent sixteen of the last seventeen and a half years; he feared that when he returned to America, England would seem more like home (PBF, 20: 383).

The decision of whether to leave, however, was not difficult. His loyalties had long been clear. His disgrace in the Cockpit (PBF, 21: 37–70) was not a defining moment but merely the capstone of years of frustration and

A Companion to Benjamin Franklin, First Edition. Edited by David Waldstreicher.
© 2011 Blackwell Publishing Ltd. Published 2011 by Blackwell Publishing Ltd.

humiliation. The British government earlier had made some efforts to buy his loyalty. Lord Bute had appointed his son William governor of New Jersey and Prime Minister George Grenville had named his friend John Hughes stamp distributor in Philadelphia, but this patronage on his behalf was of dubious benefit. Franklin was a very controlling father, who did not even attend the wedding when his son chose his own bride (PBF, 10: 142–143n). His son's gubernatorial appointment, in which his own role is still unclear (PBF, 10: 146–147n, 154–155), may not have been completely welcome. Worse still, his part in the selection of Hughes was a near disaster that almost led to Franklin's house in Philadelphia being sacked by a mob (PBF, 12: 271–274). Franklin retrieved his fallen reputation in America by his efforts on behalf of the American cause, such as his testimony urging repeal of the Stamp Act (PBF, 13: 124–162) and his numerous pro-American articles in the British press. It is doubtful that the British government could ever have made an offer adequate to cause Franklin to abandon his loyalty to his fellow Pennsylvanians or British-Americans. An alliance between Franklin and the British government would have required either his giving up his core beliefs (such as self-government or merit-based social mobility) or Britain's reversing the direction of its post-1750 policy toward the American colonies, a policy that involved curtailing America self-government and subordinating the colonies to an increasingly demanding central government. The question of Franklin's allegiance, however, became academic long before 1775. During his abortive 1774–1775 discussions with members of the British government on how to prevent war, Franklin was impervious to either intimidation or bribery.

On March 22, 1775, Franklin, now aboard the ship returning him to America, wrote an account of those negotiations, presumably for eventual inclusion in his autobiography (PBF, 21: 540–599). It was not published during his lifetime, but in 1786 he had it copied by his nephew Josiah Flagg (PBF, 37: 291n). Writing the journal of the negotiations may also have helped Franklin acquire some perspective on what had happened. There is no self-doubt or self-criticism in his narrative. In general it is a dispassionate, factual account; only occasionally does his anger at Parliament and the British government break through. Franklin had maintained his self-control during the discussions with various British intermediaries, claiming no authority to speak for the American colonies, but volunteering to do whatever he could to prevent the dispute over the Coercive Acts from becoming violent. He even volunteered to pay for the tea dumped into Boston harbor if the British would rescind the acts (trusting that he eventually would be repaid). He admitted that the failure of the negotiations had left him irritated and angry. His friends even had to talk him out of presenting a memorial that would have put him in danger.

He would not lose his anger at Britain for at least eight more years, perhaps for the rest of his life (see Smyth, 1905–1907, 9: 489) It would help provide the energy for his bearing a heavy workload in Philadelphia, help bolster his courage to undertake perilous missions to Montreal and Paris, and help fortify him to overcome the infirmities caused by age and illness. No patriot was more zealous, no revolutionary more dedicated to the American cause, no leader save Washington more indispensable. Beneath it all was not only his love for his country but also his rage, particularly against King George III, whom he had once idolized, but now hated. During the coming 17 months in Philadelphia he would be given additional reason to hate the king and fully become Franklin Furioso, Franklin the Enraged.

***

While Franklin was at sea, American minutemen and British regular troops fought at Lexington and Concord. He landed in Philadelphia on May 5, 1775, five days before the Continental Congress reconvened. His timing could not have been more perfect. The Pennsylvania Assembly had already picked the Pennsylvania delegation to Congress, but it quickly added him, a decision that some of its members would have reason to regret in the summer of 1776. (The conservative Pennsylvania delegation was one of the last to approve independence, whereas Franklin, hitherto outvoted by his colleagues, was one of the first members of Congress to recognize its inevitability [see PBF, 22: 288]). Some in Congress suspected Franklin at first of being a trimmer, but by deeds rather than words he convinced them otherwise. Congress functioned largely by committees. He was appointed to some 30 of them during his 17 months in Congress, including the one that drafted the Declaration of Independence (PBF, 22: xlix–liii). He also was given major responsibilities by both Philadelphia and Pennsylvania. Oddly enough, a major part of the reason Franklin was in such demand was his military expertise (Nolan, 1936). During the War of the Austrian Succession (also called as King George's War), he had organized a militia in Quaker Philadelphia to protect the city from enemy privateers. On the outbreak of the French and Indian War (later part of the Seven Years War) he had not only organized supplies for General Edward Braddock's army, but had been selected as colonel of the Pennsylvania Regiment, the same rank as was held by George Washington in Virginia. In October, 1775, he was called on to travel to Washington's headquarters in Cambridge, where he helped write regulations for the Continental Army and quite likely composed a drinking song to bolster its morale (PBF, 22: 224–241, 274–277). Franklin of course had a rather less distinguished military career than his Virginia colleague, but, accompanied by his foppish son William, he did supervise the building of forts along the Pennsylvania frontier over the winter of 1755–1756 (PBF, 6: 307–312). His not inconsiderable expertise in army administration and logistics was greatly prized during the war of 1775 against the mighty British Army and Navy. Much of his most important work was for the Pennsylvania Committee of Safety, which met daily for several hours before Congress convened. Some of the things he did were very useful, like arranging for the collection and distribution of lead, although some of his suggestions such as using pikes or bows and arrows were less so (PBF, 22: 159–161, 172–173, 175–176, 179–182, 186–187, 342–344). What it meant for Franklin was ten- or twelve-hour work days; it is little wonder that he sometimes fell asleep in his chair while attending Congress (PBF, 22: xliin, 92, 25: 78, 101–102). By now almost 70, he still made his mark as he had in the Pennsylvania Assembly – not by speeches but by the work he did behind the scenes.

What helped make his productiveness possible was the support of his family. He lived just down the street from Independence Hall in the house he had built for his late wife. Living with him were his warm, devoted, and generous daughter Sally Franklin Bache, her husband Richard Bache, and their children Benjamin (age 5 when his grandfather arrived) and William (just under age 2). A daughter, Sarah, was born during his time in Philadelphia. Franklin loved children and seems to have enjoyed his grandchildren. Quite the opposite was his relationship with his son, Governor William Franklin (Lopez and Herbert, 1975; Skemp, 1990). Soon after his arrival Franklin had several meetings with his former political disciple Joseph Galloway and with William Franklin. William insisted on fulfilling his responsibilities to the British government and Galloway supported him (PBF, 22: 32–33). Franklin broke relations with Galloway, but he could not yet break completely with his son. He had brought with him from England William's fourteen-year-old illegitimate son William Temple Franklin, who was both a link between his father and grandfather and a source of rivalry between them. When William was imprisoned for his loyalty to the king, Benjamin provided money to William's wife but no sympathy to him (PBF, 22: 551–553). Franklin had been extremely close to his social climbing son, doubtless too close for his son's good. He now saw his son's Loyalism as a personal betrayal and never forgave him; surely part of Franklin's bitterness toward King George III was the pain he felt at the loss of his adored son.

There were other reasons to hate King George. Franklin was particularly outraged by the British destruction of Charlestown, Massachusetts, during the Battle of Bunker Hill on June 17, 1775, seeing it as the beginning of a general policy of burning American ports (PBF, 22: 72, 85, 91–92, 95, 242). This was not an unreasonable fear given the brutal policies of Generals Amherst and Wolfe in the previous war (Dull, 2005: 108, 145), and the British would bear out Franklin's fears by attacking other American towns. Franklin's correspondence after the destruction of Charlestown is bitter; although he did not oppose Congressional efforts at peacefully ending the war, such as the Olive Branch Petition, he does not seem to have had any confidence in their success (PBF, 22: 72, 91, 95). Instead he involved himself in winning peace by force of arms. With the main British army trapped in Boston after its pyrrhic victory at Bunker Hill, the chief focus of American arms over the winter of 1775–1776 was Canada, a struggle in which Franklin played a part.

***

The American offensive against the British garrisons of Montreal and Quebec was motivated by a combination of pragmatic self-interest and self-glorifying idealism, much as was Franklin's own long-standing expansionism. The conquest, or, in American eyes, liberation of Canada, would have freed New England and northern New York from the danger of British attack from the north, while simultaneously spreading the virtues of American self-government. Unfortunately, the predominantly Catholic inhabitants of Canada had little interest in being liberated by Protestants from the other British colonies. The story is a common one; the armies of Revolutionary France, Napoleon in Egypt, and the United States during the War of 1812 (to say nothing of more recent examples) would share similar illusions. Montreal was easily captured, but the American attack on the city of Quebec was foiled. The American army then was forced to resort to a nearly hopeless siege, much like the French over the winter of 1759–1760. As soon as the ice melted in the St Lawrence River, a British squadron was sure to arrive to relieve Quebec. Meanwhile the American army in Montreal, almost out of money, could do little to win the hearts and minds of the suspicious inhabitants of the city.

On February 16, 1776, Congress voted to send a delegation to Montreal. Franklin and two Maryland delegates, Samuel Chase and the prominent Catholic Charles Carroll, were selected; they were accompanied by Carroll's cousin John, a Catholic priest (PBF, 22: 350–353, 367–368, 379–386). The journey, undertaken in late winter across desolate upper New York state, was so perilous that Franklin feared he might not survive it (PBF, 22: 400). The ice on Lake George was not yet melted and Franklin's party had to sleep for two nights in a pillaged house. They arrived in Montreal on April 29 to find the situation hopeless. After 12 days Franklin and Father Carroll were sent back to report to Congress (PBF, 22: 398–403, 413–421, 430n). With the arrival of British reinforcements and the outbreak of smallpox in the American army, the invasion collapsed. Franklin, however, had proved his dedication in the most impressive way possible, by risking his life.

The following summer Franklin undertook a shorter and less dangerous mission, accompanying John Adams and Edward Rutledge to Staten Island to meet with British Navy fleet commander and peace commissioner Richard Howe. The mission was largely pro forma, as Howe had no concessions to offer (PBF, 22: 518–521, 565–566, 575, 591–593, 597–608). The meeting must have been painful for Franklin, however, as Howe had been a participant in the peace discussions of 1774–1775. He and Franklin had even discussed working together to avert war (PBF, 1959: 499–500). Now

Howe was an enemy. The American delegation returned to Philadelphia having resolved nothing, not even a dispute between Franklin and his temporary roommate Adams over whether to sleep with the windows open (as the nature buff Franklin wished) or shut (as Adams, fearing catching a cold, wanted) (PBF, 22: 598; L.H. Butterfield, 1961, 3: 418).

***

By the time of the August, 1776 meeting with Howe the political situation in America was far different from the previous year. This evolution was in large part the product of America's inability to resist Britain without foreign assistance. The first step was the appointment of a committee to procure arms and ammunition for the Continental Army. This committee, called the Secret Committee, was appointed on September 19, 1775, with Franklin as one of its original nine members (PBF, 22: 204–205). Two months later Franklin was appointed to an even more important committee, the five-member Committee of Secret Correspondence, which had the duty of making contact with America's friends in Europe, mostly friends of Franklin (PBF, 22: 280–281, 287–291, 296–299). The most important contact, however, came to the committee himself. The visitor was Julien-Alexandre Achard de Bonvouloir, a young man who arrived from the West Indies. As the members of the committee guessed, he had been sent to Philadelphia by Charles Gravier, Comte de Vergennes, the French foreign minister. Meeting secretly in Carpenters' Hall, across the street from Franklin's house, the committee informed him that it wished from France two army engineers and access to French ports; Bonvouloir promised to convey their message (PBF, 22: 310–318). It would be many months before they had a response.

Foreign governments could hardly be expected to risk involvement in a simple rebellion designed to obtain address of grievances from a fellow monarch. To procure foreign assistance Congress had to proclaim American independence. As yet, however, public opinion was not ready for so dangerous and controversial a step. Opinion shifted, though, with the publication of *Common Sense* on January 10, 1776 (Fruchtman, "*Common Sense*" [1991] in Greene and Pole, eds.: 260–263). Its author, Thomas Paine, had come to Philadelphia in early 1775 with a letter of introduction from Franklin to Richard Bache (PBF, 21: 325–326, 515–518). As the public mood changed, Congress was emboldened. In March it sent Silas Deane, a delegate from Connecticut, to Paris to solicit the French government for war supplies. Probably it was Franklin who drafted his instructions (PBF, 22: 369–374). In spite of foot dragging by conservative delegations like Pennsylvania's, Congress moved toward declaring independence. Franklin was named to a committee to draft a declaration of independence; he and Adams assisted Thomas Jefferson to write it (PBF, 22: 485–486). He also helped provide material to Adams, who drafted a commercial treaty to be offered to foreign powers (L.H. Butterfield, 1961: 3, 338). Franklin and Adams then met with Howe. Upon their return in mid-September, Franklin received a long letter from his French publisher Jacques Barbeu-Dubourg, reporting that the French government was willing to assist Congress; he may also have received a short note from him reporting, erroneously, that France was preparing for war as soon as possible (PBF, 22: 453–471, 501–502). Congress reacted quickly to this encouraging news by approving the draft treaty, by selecting Franklin and Jefferson to join Deane as joint commissioners in France, and by approving instructions for them. When Jefferson declined the appointment he was replaced by former colonial agent Arthur Lee, presently in London. Franklin told a friend that having only a few years to live he would devote himself to whatever Congress wished (PBF, 22: 624–630). On October 27, 1776, he sailed from nearby Chester aboard the brig *Reprisal*. He was accompanied by two of his grandsons, fifteen-year-old William Temple Franklin and seven-year-old Benjamin Franklin Bache. Temple would serve as his grandfather's secretary, while Benny would pursue his education in Europe. The characters of the boys would be affected by their emotional distance from their grandfather. Temple became an inseparable companion to him as his father William had been, and, smothered by affection, turned into a playboy; Benny, who spent most of the next decade in Geneva being educated (as a Protestant), eventually became a printer and crusading newspaper editor (Lopez and Herbert, 1975).

***

Sailing to Europe in late autumn on a small ship like the *Reprisal* was almost as dangerous as traveling to Canada in late winter; on its return voyage the following autumn the *Reprisal* sank in a storm with only one survivor (W.B. Clark, 1932). Its voyage to France was not a pleasant one for the elderly Franklin who suffered from the diet aboard the ship, but at least it was quick. After barely a month at sea, the *Reprisal* anchored in Quiberon Bay. On December 3, Franklin and his grandsons were rowed ashore to the Breton fishing village of Auray. After a leisurely journey via Nantes and Versailles (the location of the French court for most of the year) they arrived in Paris on December 21 and quickly made contact with Deane and Lee (PBF, 23: 23–33, 47–48, 82n, 85–86n).

Franklin was a gregarious man with a need to be surrounded by friends. He had visited France in 1767 and had even dined in company with King Louis XV (PBF, 14: 252–253). More importantly for his current trip he was able to make use of two international support networks with influential branches in France. First was the Masonic movement, with which he had been affiliated for almost half a century. While in France he was welcomed into several lodges and became the venerable or titular head of one of the most prestigious among them, the Neuf Sœurs or Nine Sisters. Named after the nine muses it contained many intellectuals and members of the arts, important contacts for Franklin. Just as important was the welcome given to Franklin as a scientist. Franklin already had numerous contacts within the French scientific community and subsequently participated in the French Royal Academy of Sciences and Royal Society of Medicine. The scientific elite and the financial elite sometimes overlapped as in the case of the financier and great chemist Antoine-Laurent Lavoisier. These contacts, however, did not guarantee Franklin access to leading figures in the French government. The foreign ministry in particular was its own world; ironically Foreign Minister Vergennes and his chief assistants, the brothers Conrad-Alexandre and Joseph-Mathias Gérard, were looked down upon by the French social elite. Vergennes and his close political ally Gabriel de Sartine, the brilliant French naval minister, willingly came to Franklin's assistance, providing him with his banker Ferdinand Grand and his landlord Jacques-Donatien Leray de Chaumont (Schaeper, 1995).

Franklin's social contacts were important not because they gave him access to the seats of power but because they helped him defuse a potential threat. Through them he could use his wit, charm, and social graces to reassure members of the aristocracy that the American Revolution posed no threat to them. The Spanish court feared the contagion of revolution to its own colonies, whereas the French elite supported the American cause out of Anglophobia and a naïve assumption that France need not fear revolution (Ségur, 1824: 26). The American Revolution helped paved the way for the French Revolution by its example and, more importantly, by driving the French monarchy into eventual bankruptcy. Franklin, too, was not what he seemed. Beneath his urbane exterior Franklin was a zealous American and a hard-core supporter of the American Revolution who sent his grandson out of France for his education and who later mocked the French veterans of the American War who joined the Society of the Cincinnati (Smyth, 1905–7, 9: 161–168). In spite of personal affection for the French people and their king, he was a cold-blooded practitioner of *realpolitik* who was loyal only to the United States.

***

The first year of the American commissioners' French mission was frustrating. Vergennes was extremely anxious to see American independence and hence to weaken Britain, not out of Anglophobia, but because of British support for what he considered France's real enemy, Russia (Dull, 1975: 34–44; Dull, 2005: 249–254). He had to proceed with great caution, however, in order to avoid a premature war. Sartine was rebuilding the French Navy but it would not be ready before the end of 1777 (Dull, 1975: 49–75, 352–353). For this reason Vergennes rebuffed the commissioners' first appeal for direct assistance, although he secretly began providing them money. They had to be kept in the dark about the progress of the French Navy because Franklin laughed off warnings about the complete lack of security at the American mission (PBF, 23: 291–292, 296–299); indeed, one of Franklin and Deane's closest associates, the affable scientist Edward Bancroft, was not only playing the London stock market with inside information, but also was providing information to the British secret service. Franklin, who was reluctant to believe anything bad about his friends, was deceived completely. Because of the lack of communication with the French government, the Americans created a serious war scare in the summer of 1777, causing France to expel from French ports the *Reprisal* and two other American warships (Dull, 1975: 75–80; PBF, 24: 243–244, 472–474).

The long wait for France to announce its position proved too much for Deane. In November, 1777 he argued that the commissioners should threaten Vergennes that without more French assistance America would be forced to make peace with Britain. Franklin, with the support of Lee, successfully argued for more patience (PBF, 25: 207–208). Luckily, news arrived on December 4 of the capture of Burgoyne's army at Saratoga. This news was very opportune for Vergennes. The navy was almost ready and Vergennes had argued to Spain that their countries should decide by the following January or February to go to war with Britain (Dull, 1975: 84–87). The chief obstacle to a more aggressive policy, however, was not Spain, whose navy would not be needed for the first year of war. The real problem was King Louis XVI of France's reluctance for war. Vergennes was able to overcome it by convincing him (but not King Charles III of Spain) that war was inevitable and that France must strike first. This was much the same argument he had used in the spring of 1776 to convincible his gullible king to extend covert aid to the Americans. Franklin greatly assisted Vergennes, quite likely without realizing it, by playing along with the game. He entertained English visitors, including an emissary form Lord North and created the impression that a compromise settlement with Britain was under consideration. He used to great advantage his gift of deceiving others without having to tell a direct lie, the stock in trade of diplomats (Dull, 2010: 73–76). By now Congress and the commissioners realized that a commercial treaty would be insufficient to gain direct French participation in the war. They readily agreed to the French demand for a treaty of alliance by which neither party could make a separate peace. Both the Treaty of Amity and Commerce and the Treaty of Alliance were signed on February 6, 1778 (PBF, 25: 583–626).

***

During March France broke diplomatic relations with Britain, the commissioners were received at court, and Conrad-Alexandre Gérard was selected as France's first minister plenipotentiary to the United States. The following month a French squadron sailed for America. At the beginning of the summer, hostilities began between Britain and France. The appointment of a French minister plenipotentiary in Philadelphia dictated that Congress reciprocated; it promoted Franklin to the same rank and recalled his fellow commissioners, Lee and John Adams, who had replaced Deane (PBF, 27: 407–409). Franklin began his service as sole American representative by making a serious blunder, requesting French troops be sent to the United States, a step for which Congress was not yet ready (PBF, 27: 633–646; 28:603–606). Luckily, France did not agree to it and Franklin did not inform Congress of his mistake. Thereafter Franklin's duties were circumscribed because of his inattentiveness to security; not daring to trust him with military or diplomatic secrets, the French government chose to deal with Congress through its own representative in Philadelphia. Franklin's main duty was begging further financial assistance from the French government. Persistent yet tactful, he was very good at it, although the main reason for France's generous support was fear that the Continental Army would collapse without it, a not unreasonable concern (Buell, 1998). Much of Franklin's time was spent assisting his fellow Americans in France. With little help beyond Temple Franklin and a French secretary the American mission was overwhelmed with work. Perhaps most burdensome was the chore of checking American loan office certificates on which in a moment of madness the American commissioners had agreed to pay the interest. Although Franklin led a busy social life he took no vacations during his eight and a half years in France. The work closest to Franklin's heart was the assistance he gave the American sailors imprisoned in England or Ireland or who had escaped to France and wished assistance in returning to America. Although they were poorly treated, American prisoners in the British Isles were fortunate compared with American prisoners aboard British prison ships in New York harbor, some 10,000 of whom died from disease or neglect. Franklin was outraged at what he described as the bloodthirstiness of King George III and even the English people (PBF, 25: 653–654; 28: 461–462; 32: 119–120n; 36: 102); the obverse of those feelings was the compassion he felt for American prisoners and war victims. He invested in American loan office certificates, equivalent to war bonds, and donated his salary as American postmaster general to disabled war veterans (PBF, 22: 219; 23: 280–281n). He even attempted to capture British prisoners to exchange for Americans by fitting out French privateers under the American flag (W.B. Clark, 1956). Ironically he regarded privateering (fitting out warships privately as a business venture) as theft and eventually tried to outlaw its use (Dull, 2010: 87).

The chief consolation for his tiring duties was the friendships he made, particularly in the wealthy village of Passy between Paris and Versailles, where he lived in a wing of Chaumont's mansion. One of his best friends was the scientist Jean-Baptiste Le Roy, with whom he served on committees appointed by the Royal Academy of Sciences. He was particularly close to his neighbors, the Brillon family. He engaged in a lengthy flirtation with

Mme Brillon, which ended when she expressed her preference for having him as a surrogate father. He attempted to arrange a marriage between Temple Franklin and one of the Brillons' daughters, but they refused because Temple was not a Catholic (PBF, 34: 560–563). Another and perhaps more successful flirtation was with Mme Helvétius, the widow of a great French philosopher (Lopez, 1966). In spite of his many friends, the adulation of the French public, and the respect shown him by Vergennes, Franklin became increasingly homesick. He could not return, however, until American independence was recognized by Great Britain. The military stalemate in America finally outweighed American suspicions of French troops and the French government was invited to send an expeditionary force. It arrived in 1780 and the following year it joined with Washington to capture Cornwallis' army at Yorktown. That victory finally led to peace negotiations.

***

Congress had long prepared for peace negotiations. Initially it appointed John Adams to conduct them. Unfortunately, the well-meaning Adams, the most inept of diplomats (Hutson, 1980), rendered himself *persona non grata* to the French government. Vergennes, suspecting Adams's judgment if not his sanity, convinced Congress in 1781 to replace him with a five-member peace commission, to which Congress elected Adams, Franklin, Jefferson, Minister Designate to Spain John Jay, and Minister Designate to the Netherlands Henry Laurens. Congress instructed them to consult the French government about whatever they did (Stinchcombe, 1969).

It took several months for the news of Yorktown to bring down Lord North's government. In its desperation to survive, the North government even tried to contact Franklin and Adams, presently in the Netherlands as a replacement for Henry Laurens, who had been captured by the British and imprisoned in the Tower of London. As a sign of North's ineptitude, he selected as his emissary one of the people Franklin most hated, Thomas Digges, who had embezzled money meant for the relief of American prisoners of war (Elias and Finch, 1982). Finally, North resigned on March 20, 1782. The prime minister who replaced him was Charles Watson-Wentworth, Marques of Rockingham, who had been prime minister when the Stamp Act was repealed. Rockingham was in ill health, however, and control over the peace negotiations was in dispute between Foreign Secretary Charles James Fox and Home and Colonial Secretary William Petty, Earl of Shelburne. Franklin gave his old acquaintance Shelburne a head start by writing to congratulate him on the improved disposition of the House of Commons toward America and to thank him on behalf of their mutual friend Mme Helvétius for the gift of some gooseberry bushes; Franklin's letter was carried to Shelburne by an acquaintance of Mme Brillon (PBF, 37: 17–18, 24–25, 292–293). Shelburne immediately took the hint by sending Richard Oswald, an elderly Scots businessman, to Passy to sound out Franklin. A few weeks later Fox sent his own representative, Thomas Grenville, to meet with Vergennes and Franklin. Although Franklin summoned the other peace commissioners to join him, only Jay came and he was soon incapacitated by influenza. (Laurens was still in London, Adams was in the Netherlands negotiating a commercial treaty, and Jefferson had changed his mind about leaving America.)

Franklin was in a dream position for a diplomat. He could not only play Britain and France off against each other, but also play off Shelburne and Fox. Franklin, as subtle as he was ruthless in negotiation, made the most of his opportunity, convincing the British that he would violate congressional instructions by making a separate peace with them, while keeping his intentions secret from France. He turned down Fox's offer of an immediate acknowledgment of American independence, wisely choosing to deal instead with Shelburne (PBF, 37: 291–346). Rockingham died on July 1 and three days later Shelburne became prime minister and took full control of all the peace negotiations. Fox resigned.

Unlike Fox, Shelburne wished to make peace with France as well as the United States but he first needed an American agreement in order to put pressure on France and France's ally Spain. On July 10 Franklin verbally presented his peace conditions to Oswald, including full independence, generous borders, and fishing rights for the United States. Two weeks later Shelburne accepted Franklin's terms as a basis for negotiations (PBF, 37: 598–602, 686–687).

With peace seemingly at hand Franklin fell ill with kidney or bladder stones, leaving the negotiations in the hands of John Jay, a far less skillful and subtle negotiator, who wasted a month quibbling about Oswald's commission. Fortunately, Franklin recovered in time for the final discussions with the British, during which he and Jay were joined by John Adams. Franklin's main contribution during the final stages of the negotiations was his adamant stand against meaningful compensation to the Loyalists he so hated, particularly since his son William had become one of their leaders (Dull, 1985: 144–151). Agreement was reached on November 30. The United States was granted all of the territory east of the Mississippi, south of Canada, and north of Florida, astonishingly generous terms. As a fig leaf to cover the commissioners' disobedience of their instructions and betrayal of France, the agreement was made conditional upon France's signing its own peace agreement with Britain. The French no longer could count on active American support if the war continued; meanwhile the British withdrew an offer of Gibraltar to France's ally Spain, placing France in grave peril if the Spaniards insisted on continuing the war. Fortunately, the Spanish ambassador, Pedro Pablo Abarca de Bolea, Count de Aranda, accepted Minorca and Florida in lieu of Gibraltar, making peace possible and defusing a serious disagreement between Franklin and Vergennes (Dull,

2010: 100–101). A general preliminary agreement and armistice among all the powers at war was signed on January 20, 1783. It reaffirmed the terms already reached between Britain and the United States.

***

One of the British peace negotiators was Alleyne Fitzherbert, who was among the most astute British diplomats of the eighteenth century. He warned his superiors that Franklin was an inveterate enemy of Britain who would prevent the return of good relations if given a chance (George III agreed: Dull, 1982: 53). He was outraged that the American commissioners wished to use negotiations for a definitive peace treaty as an opportunity to introduce new articles (Dull, 2010: 101–102). Franklin and his colleagues particularly wanted Americans to enjoy the same opportunities to trade with the British West Indies that they had had before the war. Britons found this outrageous and King George III quashed American hopes by excluding American ships from the West Indies. Shelburne had been blamed for making a bad peace and driven from office. His replacement, an odd coalition between North and Fox, had no sympathy for the Americans, particularly since they were unwilling to comply with treaty terms respecting the Loyalists. The final peace treaties signed on September 3, 1783 repeated the terms of the January 20 preliminary agreements (and the November 30, 1782 conditional agreement), much to the disappointment of Franklin, Jay, and Adams.

Once the negotiations ended Franklin's health deteriorated. He was left with little to do. He did negotiate a Franco-American consular agreement with Vergennes, but it was rejected by Congress as infringing on American sovereignty. Congress refused, however, to let Franklin return home. It appointed him, Adams, and Jefferson as a new commission to negotiate commercial treaties with various European and North African countries (Franklin had negotiated such a treaty with Sweden in March, 1783, much to the displeasure of Adams and Jay, who were not allowed to participate in the negotiations: PBF, 39: 250–285). The new commission was rather unsuccessful, negotiating only a commercial treaty with Prussia that Franklin signed just before returning to America, Congress having finally relented. On the way home he stopped briefly in England where he held an icy meeting with his son William aboard ship; William signed over his property in America to his son Temple. Franklin's bitterness toward his son was unabated. Shortly after the end of the war he had written a satire in which the Loyalists were portrayed as mongrels, a singularly cruel comparison if he had in mind his illegitimate Loyalist son (PBF, 39: 232–234).

***

Franklin's services in France had not been fully appreciated by Congress, in large part because he was an infrequent correspondent compared to Jay and

Adams. It had left him in France when he wanted to return home and had denied him what he most desired, a diplomatic post for his grandson Temple (PBF, 34: 447–448).

His return to Philadelphia in the summer of 1785 was, however, a great triumph. For Pennsylvanians he was a favorite son and they honored him by electing him to three consecutive one-year terms as President of the Pennsylvania Supreme Executive Council, roughly equivalent to a governorship. He took on the task of calming party passions in the state, whose two political parties, the Constitutionalists and the Republicans, were perhaps the most highly developed in the United States. Franklin's specialty as a politician was brokering compromise agreements. His friend Benjamin Rush congratulated him on his subsequent success, comparing his accomplishments in his new position to his famous scientific experiment of calming the waves by pouring oil on them (see Smyth, 1905–1907, 9: 676; L.H. Butterfield, 1951: 1, 389–390). The respite, if such it was, proved only temporary; Franklin had perhaps inadvertently prepared the destruction of the Constitutionalist Party, many of whose positions, such as favoring a unicameral legislature, were similar to his own. Franklin's greatest political service, however, was as a member of the Constitutional Convention of 1787, where his abilities as a peacemaker helped hold the convention together (Carr, 1990). His home life, living with his daughter, son-in-law and their by now eight children, seems to have been happy. After the end of the Constitutional Convention and his final term as President of the Supreme Executive Council, he retired from public life. His hope of finishing his autobiography was frustrated, though. His health was undermined by a fall in the garden (Smyth, 1905–1907, 9: 633, 645) and his final years were painful, although his mind was still sharp until his death on April 17, 1790. He died as an international hero. The French revolutionary government even named a ship of the line after him, although ironically enough the British soon captured it. His popularity continued to grow after his death, but at a price. His image has become so sanitized as to denature him. One of his traits that has almost disappeared from view is his capacity for anger.

***

The common image of Franklin is of a kindly, amusing, tolerant, wise, and lovable avuncular figure, almost like Santa Claus. Although this picture of him is not totally false, it shows only one side of him. He could be vain, smug, self-righteous, duplicitous, and even cruel, as he was to his son William, who desperately sought and was denied reconciliation (Skemp, 1990). The price of his extraordinary self-control was repressed anger that sometime escaped his control. This anger often was justified, such as when it was directed against the selfish and greedy Thomas Penn. By 1775 his anger was directed mostly against King George III. Franklin the Enraged is more human, perhaps even more sympathetic, than the sanitized Franklin to whom we have become accustomed. The British were savage toward those who rebelled against them, whether they were Scots, Irish, British Americans or, later, French Canadians or natives of India. Franklin helped saved his fellow Americans from their revenge. We have also sanitized the American Revolution which, relative to the number of people involved, produced a very large casualty list and a phenomenal number of refugees. The rather soft Franklin of legend would have been of little use in it. Franklin Furioso was one of its most dedicated and effective leaders.

Note

1 Labaree, Leonard W. et al., eds. (1959–). *The Papers of Benjamin Franklin*. 39 vols to date. New Haven, CT: Yale University Press. Hereafter referred to as PBF.

Further Reading

Dull, Jonathan R. (1982). "Franklin the Diplomat: The French Mission," *Transactions of the American Philosophical Society* 72: 1–76.

Dull, Jonathan R. (2010). *Benjamin Franklin and the American Revolution*. Lincoln, NE.

Hutson, James (1980). *John Adams and the Diplomacy of the American Revolution*. Lexington, KY.

Labaree, Leonard W. et al., eds (1959). *The Papers of Benjamin Franklin*. Vols 22–39. New Haven, CT.

Lopez, Claude-Anne and Eugenia W. Herbert (1975). *The Private Franklin*. New Haven, CT.

Skemp, Sheila (1990). *William Franklin*. New York, NY.

Part II

Franklin and Eighteenth-Century America

Chapter Five

BENJAMIN FRANKLIN AND COLONIAL SOCIETY

Konstantin Dierks

How do we put Benjamin Franklin into the historical context of the social structures in which he lived – particularly class relations as they shifted during a lifetime that spanned almost the entirety of the eighteenth century? This might sound like a straightforward question from which one should be able to proceed rather easily, but it actually presents a significant historiographical dilemma, for two reasons. First, there has long been unsettlingly little attention paid to the analysis of class relations in the field of Early American history overall. Second, the scholarship on Benjamin Franklin – a veritable industry unto itself – has likewise tended not to consider the social structures in which he lived. The cultural category of "class" has not been animating much scholarship, and the social groups that fit under the category of "class" do not populate our leading narratives of Early American history. What is left for us is the unenviable task of explaining why reconstructing the eighteenth-century social context around Franklin is currently, in 2010, not an answerable historical problem.

We should not stop there, however. There remains the necessary task of constructing a workable image of the relationship between Franklin and his social context, based on the scholarship now available to us, whatever its limitations might be. To do so, we must reach beyond the parameters of classic scholarship on class relations, which rely upon economic production and political activism as the main measures of class experience and class consciousness. We must also reach beyond the focus of revisionist scholarship on class relations: social and cultural activities that likewise bespeak class experience and class consciousness outside the economic and political

A Companion to Benjamin Franklin, First Edition. Edited by David Waldstreicher.
© 2011 Blackwell Publishing Ltd. Published 2011 by Blackwell Publishing Ltd.

spheres. Above all, we must attend to multiplicities and hybridities – of broad class strata, of filigree status levels, of business occupations and government offices, and of social and cultural activities – which enable us to trace the shifting social solidarities and cultural horizons of a historical figure like Franklin. Given the incomplete state of current scholarship on Franklin more narrowly and on "class" more broadly, placing Franklin in relationship to his social context manages as many conceptual benefits for class analysis as historical insights into the eighteenth century. We can create a trajectory of Franklin's fluid class experience and hybrid class consciousness in his Philadelphia years and in advance of his London years, but above all we are equipped from the frustrations of this undertaking to push the conceptualization of class analysis a bit further. The gain is an appreciation of Franklin in the social context of the mid-eighteenth century, as well as an impetus for further research.

5.1 The Analytical Category of Class in Early American Historiography

On the surface, the category of "class" might seem an equal partner in the canonical triad of cultural categories – race, gender, and class – that emerged and endured from the innovations of social history as carried forward from its glory days in the 1960s and 1970s. One thinks immediately of a canonical text at the very vanguard of that social history movement: E.P. Thompson's 1963 *The Making of the English Working Class*. Yet the scholarly attention once paid to the category of class was soon overwhelmed and overshadowed by infinitely greater attention devoted to the categories of gender and race. This chronic two-leggedness of the triad can be discerned even now, decades later, in the current generation of scholarship in the field of Early American history. Perhaps the most effective way to pinpoint this imbalance in scholarship is by tracing the themes emblazoned in the titles of conference panels and papers of the Omohundro Institute of Early American History and Culture. The Institute's annual conference has, since its inaugural year in 1995, created a forum for the very cutting edge of new research in the field. Even if the innovative force of social history had by 1995 long been eclipsed by subsequent academic fashions, we can still readily see the continuing vitality of gender and race as analytical categories, and their strong primacy over class, in the programs of the Institute's sixteen annual conferences spanning from 1995 to 2010. There have been more than twice as many conference panels as well as individual papers directly addressing the categories of "gender" and "race" compared with the category of "class" (55 and 54 times, versus 26 times, respectively). Moreover, the number of panels and papers on the category of "class" has been ebbing over time, unlike the other two categories, which either have remained fairly steady (the category of "gender") or have actually been increasing (the category of "race").

These disparities become even more pronounced when one examines the various specific social categories that can fit under the umbrella of each of the three broad cultural categories. These are the social categories that have been populating research in the field of Early American history, and populating our image of the groups that constituted society in the early modern era. With respect to the cultural category of class, such social categories appeared mainly in the earlier rather than the later programs of the Institute's annual conference: the elite (10 times), the gentry (10), planters (3), merchants (14), the middling (4), artisans (2), farmers (3), labor (14), peasants (2), servants (5), and the poor (8). This list of social groups amounts, it must be remarked, to an astonishingly bare image of the class structure of Early American society. Even more problematic is that, just as with the broader cultural category of "class," these various social categories falling within it have been losing whatever limited analytical purchase they may once have had, and have been diminishing in their presence in the field. In other words, these "class" groups no longer populate our current general image of Early American society. They are effectively absent, rendering Early American society a classless one, and thereby rendering class structures and dynamics immaterial to the course of Early American history.

Meanwhile, the social categories related to gender or race have been much more prominent in the Institute's annual conference programs, sustainedly and increasingly so. Women have featured in 70 panel and paper titles, and men in 38, far outnumbering any particular class category, and together outnumbering all the sundry class categories combined. The numbers related to race are even more dramatic than the numbers related to gender. "Whites" or "Europeans" have featured 35 times, whereas Africans or blacks have featured 59 times and Native Americans 162 times. Furthermore, "slave(s)" and "slavery" have featured another 106 times, mostly related to "African" slavery although there has been a handful related to "Indian" slavery as well. Perhaps most telling is that these race categories have assumed the lion's share of full-fledged panel titles: 77 for race compared with 19 for gender and 15 for class.

What we can conclude has, under scrutiny, become plain as day. The master narrative of Early American history at the Institute's annual conferences has emphatically been a story of race first and foremost, then gender second, with class a very distant third. Compared with class, race and gender have been accorded both much greater salience as well as much greater currency in the Institute's annual conference programs. Race and gender remain, in other words, the great bequests of social history to the ongoing research and pedagogy of Early American history. Blacks, Native Americans, whites, women, and men serve as the principal social groups who have been populating our image of Early American society in the last generation of scholarship.

As would be the case if one froze any interval of historical scholarship, there are always many perfectly legitimate topics of historical inquiry not drawing attention, because they are not perceived by that particular generation of scholars as either compelling or resonant. The ebb and flow of such academic trends is precisely what invites the ongoing conceptual and empirical creativity characterizing any field of historical inquiry. Indeed, this kind of renewed creativity is what now seems to be prompting the various "geographic turns" currently affecting many historical fields, such as the Atlantic turn in early modern American history, or the imperial turn in early modern British history. It certainly must be acknowledged that the focus on race and on gender has enabled us to shatter once-obdurate and long-unproductive assumptions and narratives about the historical past – *sans* women, *sans* non-whites – and has thereby enabled us to enhance, fundamentally, both the research and the pedagogy of Early American history. Gender, race, the Atlantic world, the British Empire: these have been standing, with great creativity and great justice, at both the cutting edge and the center of the field.

Without any serious consideration of class, though. Hence, if we are aiming to situate Benjamin Franklin in the social structures and class relations of his lifetime, then the field of Early American history in its recent trajectory and current state of scholarship severely hampers that aim. We do have a helpful essay collection from 2000 edited by Larry Tise placing Franklin at least in relation to "women" if not to "gender" more holistically, i.e., including men. And we have a superb monograph by David Waldstreicher from 2004 placing Franklin at least in relation to African "slavery" if not to "race" more holistically, i.e., including Native Americans and whiteness. But we have nothing remotely comparable as these two contributions in the last generation of scholarship that places Franklin directly in relation to "class." Underlying this lacuna is a broader and deeper imbalance in the field of Early American history heavily skewed in favor of "race" and "gender" over "class."

5.2 The Analytical Category of Class in Scholarship on Franklin

This is not to say that the scholarship on Franklin has been idle. On the contrary, it has long been and continues to be irrepressibly energetic. For instance, we now eagerly await, on the strength of several recent essays, Carla Mulford's forthcoming *Benjamin Franklin and the Ends of Empire*, which is expected to situate Franklin explicitly in the context of the British Empire. Not so long ago, there was the motivation of special publishing opportunities in anticipation of the 2006 tercentenary of Franklin's birth, which drew out a spate of popular as well as academic biographies of

Franklin: by Brands (2000), Morgan (2002), Isaacson (2003), Gaustad (2006), Waldstreicher (2004), Gordon Wood (2004), and Lemay (2006a,b, 2009). These were meant to supersede the standard biographies by Carl Van Doren (1938) and Esmond Wright (1986), but for the most part they tended to follow a familiar methodology, while assuming an added burden of combing through ever more Franklin-related documents as *The Papers of Benjamin Franklin* project, begun quixotically in 1959, continues to trawl inexorably along at the Yale University Press. Given the sheer scale of Franklin's public and private writings – 39 volumes of *Papers* to date – it is easy for biographers to become lost in the vast thicket of the Franklin archive itself. To write a biography of Franklin requires exhaustive toil simply to reconstruct the ceaseless activity of Franklin's long life, never mind to factor in the social structures, cultural philosophies, political vicissitudes, and economic patterns surrounding that long life as it was spent in three metropoles: Philadelphia, London, and Paris.

Over-fortunate scholars who devote their research to Franklin as their subject can find almost any specific topic considered within the corpus of Franklin's public and private writings, enough to write a pithy essay at the least, if not an entire book. Even before the tercentenary of Franklin's birth to celebrate in 2006, there was in 1990 the bicentennial of his death to honor; these two commemorative moments bookend the last generation of outpouring scholarship on Franklin. The important 1993 essay collection *Reappraising Benjamin Franklin* unleashed a subsequent flood of topical treatments of Franklin by focusing on the journalism and printing businesses, revolutionary American politics, science, the fine arts, ethnicities, Franklin's public writing, and his public personality. What more could there be left to cover? So much more: *Benjamin Franklin and his Gods* (1999), for instance, and of course *Benjamin Franklin and Women* (2000). Now that the Franklin archive is online and searchable by keyword, scholars' capacity – and temptation perhaps – to sift through it to solve the mystery of particular topics has only magnified. Franklin and, say, the history of squirrels? Currently, that keyword search summons 29 documents with which to work. The Franklin archive is indeed the proverbial gift that keeps on giving.

Whether treated biographically or topically, Benjamin Franklin represents a scholarly industry unto himself due to his iconic status in American history of the eighteenth century. It should be of no surprise that the cultural image of Franklin has continually shifted over the course of American history since his lifetime (see Huang, 1994; and see G. Wood, 2004). It is again shifting now. Characterizations and investigations of Franklin seem to serve as windows less into Franklin as their ostensible historical subject, and more into the cultural moment of the characterization or investigation itself. With this in mind, we might speculate about the reasons why the last generation of scholarship has been so thoroughly preoccupied with one theme above all others: that of Franklin's apparently ambiguous Americanness. When did someone who was born in 1706 in Boston, a small city at the fringe of the British Empire, but who would spend nearly thirty adult years abroad in London and Paris, become an "American"? That has served as the dominant question begging explanation.

To some degree, the historical question of Franklin's Americanness has been tied closely to the question of the social structures and class relations of Franklin's time, but only, alas, in a most unhelpful, if revealing, way. It was perhaps Carl Van Doren who, in his magisterial 1938 biography, comprising 26 chapters and 845 pages, crystallized a connection between Franklin's national identity and his class status. Van Doren depicted Franklin as going through several stages of political identity development: first as a Philadelphian in Chapter 5, then as a Pennsylvanian in Chapter 7, then as an "Intercolonial" in Chapter 8, and finally as an "American" in Chapter 11. Franklin steadily widened his geographic horizons until, in 1757, on the eve of his departure to serve as colonial agent stationed in London, he plateaued not only as an "American" but also, Van Doren insisted, as a paragon of the middle class. At age 51 Franklin had become "the quintessence of provincial America." "Born of the 'middling people,' he had emerged from his class without deserting it, and he never pretended or wanted to belong to the aristocracy" (Van Doren, 1938: 260). Franklin may have thereafter spent cosmopolitan time abroad in London and Paris, including time hobnobbing with British and French aristocrats, but his middle-class Americanness was, in Van Doren's account, set firm by 1757. Even though Franklin was leaving the American colonies for a prolonged sojourn in England, he would somehow forever be an American. And even though he was transcending the middle class for whatever lay between it and the aristocracy, he would somehow forever be middle class. Van Doren did not, alas, pause to define what constituted an "American," nor what constituted a middle-class person. Leo Lemay, until his untimely death in 2008, the author of three volumes out of a projected seven-volume modern biography of Franklin, took an exceedingly long route to concurring with Van Doren's insistence upon Franklin's enduring provincial and egalitarian predilections. "Franklin's writings on America and the British Empire during the period 1748–1757 prove he had … the most outspoken Americanism of anyone at that time" (Lemay, 2009: 586). As in Van Doren's, so too in Lemay's biography was Franklin's middle-classness asserted more than analyzed, a function of a smattering of egalitarian sentiments expressed in his journalistic writing.

Because Franklin would, after 1757, spend the vast majority of the rest of his life in England and France – as an imperial official, as a cosmopolitan scientist, and as an international diplomat – he thus seemed to require some moment of "Americanization" for the sake of his iconic status in American history. At some point in his life he had to *become American*, preferably, for Van Doren, a prior experience before he spent so much time across the Atlantic. Indeed, the pithy phrase "becoming an American" has been a commonplace in biographies of Franklin (see Morgan, 2002: Ch. 7; and G. Wood, 2004: Ch. 5). Establishing the threshold when Franklin became American has likewise preoccupied other biographers (see Brands, 2000: Ch. 22; and Isaacson, 2003: Ch. 11). The answer given by most of them has not been Van Doren's and Lemay's date of 1757, but 1775 instead, the year Franklin discarded by the imperial British government that had long employed and consulted him, returned from London to Philadelphia in time to serve in the Continental Congress, and soon to sign the Declaration of Independence. What mattered foremost in these rival accounts was Franklin's political allegiance, untethered from middle-classness. If Van Doren and Lemay saw Franklin as *culturally* American by 1757, most other biographers emphasized the moment Franklin became *politically* American in 1775.

Gordon Wood stands as something of an exception among the ranks of new Franklin biographers, since he postpones Franklin's becoming an American until after his death in 1790. The posthumous publication of his autobiography in 1794 would begin to turn Franklin into a cultural symbol, a national icon, and a class archetype, all at once. He was then converted from person into myth, according to Wood, and Franklin has continued to be more mythologized than historicized ever since. Wood treats this tendency skeptically enough, but many other Franklin biographers have happily participated in the arrant mythologizing. Franklin did more than "become American," so the story goes, he seems even to have been the "first American" (see Brands, 2000). Franklin's biography is, the scholar H.W. Brands asserted in 2000, "the story of the birth of America – an America this man discovered in himself, then helped create in the world at large" (Brands, 2000: 8). In the tall order of creating America, Franklin apparently managed to create the future as well. "In his life and in his writings," insisted the biographer Walter Isaacson, Franklin was "consciously trying to create a new American archetype" (2003: 2). "Of the fathers of his country," argued the scholar Esmond Wright, Franklin was both "the most American" as well as "the most prescient of the future" (1986: 359).

What purpose are these strange futurist assertions serving? For one thing they have returned Franklin to his putative class essence, untethered from his political allegiance. Isaacson was not alone but certainly the most explicit in connecting Franklin less to his historical context, whatever it might have been, and above all to a seemingly inevitable middle-class future. Repeatedly in his biography Isaacson insisted that American society and culture would somehow someday catch up to Franklin's lead: "Franklin's blend of beliefs would become part of the outlook of much of America's middle class" (Isaacson, 2003: 425). Franklin was, simply put, "the most influential in inventing the type of society America would become" (Isaacson, 2003:

492). However exceptional a genius Franklin may have been in his own lifetime, he was destined to represent the mainstream norm in the future of American society and culture: the middle class. These accounts do not deign to explain precisely how such a cultural and social transformation would eventually occur, since their main concern is Franklin's life within its bounds, without actually reaching into the projected future to come. The assertions about Franklin's archetypal status were presented as bald presumptions, not as objects of historical analysis either with respect to Franklin in the eighteenth century, or with respect to American culture and society in some interval of the nineteenth century for however long it took "America" supposedly to become just like Franklin. To become middle class. Van Doren and Lemay located that quintessence back in the mid-eighteenth century, but Brands and Isaacson projected it forward into an opaque nineteenth-century future. For all their surface differences, both coteries of historians depicted middle-classness off stage, simply as either a presumed or an inevitable state of American society.

Again, Gordon Wood stands as an exception among Franklin biographers for providing a semblance of historical analysis of the social structures and cultural philosophies surrounding Franklin within his lifetime. It is unfortunate, though, that Wood squeezes Franklin into the pre-arranged narrative first presented, unpersuasively, in his *The Radicalism of the American Revolution* (1992). In this scheme Franklin must stand as a monarchist who became a republican, but whose lifespan did not reach a point enabling him to become a democrat. Monarchy, republic, democracy: these, according to Wood, comprised the three stages of American cultural change across the decades-long course of the "American Revolution." Wood glanced briefly back to depict a social hierarchy in early modern England as rigidly divided into gentry and commoners. While acknowledging the emergence of a middle class in England and the British Empire in the early eighteenth century, Wood did not see it as enough of a distinctive or potent social or cultural force to divert Franklin from an overriding obsession with the blessings of gentility (2004: Ch. 1). Wood saw Franklin as comprehending only a traditional social hierarchy inherited from the seventeenth century, while unable to grasp the social dynamism occurring in both Philadelphia and London early in the eighteenth century. Franklin's social aspirations and economic strivings did not, in this view, evolve as his own social position changed, nor as the social world changed around him. Instead, from the very outset, and then throughout his life, those aspirations and strivings managed to point him purely toward an end of gentility, without ever accommodating an intermediate world of the middle class. Adhering to this scheme obliges Wood to differentiate between the historically real Franklin, seen as genteel, and the retrospectively imagined Franklin, seen as middle class. Wood therefore treats Franklin's "Americanness" *within* his lifetime mainly in terms of political allegiance (i.e., that fateful year of 1775), and his

"Americanness" *after* his lifetime mainly in terms of class status (i.e., from 1794 stretching forward into the nineteenth century, and beyond).

We can conclude, without having found any consensus among Franklin biographers, that there may have been three moments when Franklin supposedly became an "American": by 1757, in 1775, or after 1794. This manner of historical question remains, it must be said, decidedly unhelpful whether one considers it in terms of either political allegiance or class allegiance. When Americanness and middle-classness are tied together, the turgid result is prone to American myth rather than American history, to historical presumption rather than historical analysis. Such a fawning question of "Americanness" has not, it must be said, been remotely salient in the conference programs of the Omohundro Institute of Early American History and Culture. Biographers' preoccupation with "Americanness" may be satisfying trade-press blinkers and choiceless public taste, but it has not advanced the subject of Franklin anywhere near the vanguard of scholarship in the field. At the Institute's annual conferences Franklin has amounted to no more than a useful instance of a particular historical question about something to which Franklin is not thought to have given "birth," nor to have "invented." Between 2001 and 2008 he has been inconspicuously embedded within five conference panels: on religious belief, revolutionary narratives, images of Florida, print media, and economic thought. Such topical – as opposed to biographical – scholarship on Franklin cannot be said to have exerted any serious influence on the field of Early American history. Outside the Institute's annual conference, the topical scholarship on Franklin has, it must be acknowledged, followed some broader trends in the field: from an older concern with international diplomacy (see Morgan, 1996; Schiff, 2005), to a newer concern with international science (see Schiffer, 2003; Dray, 2005; Chaplin, 2006), and from an older Enlightenment paradigm (see D. Anderson, 1997; Fortune and Warner, 1999), to an newer Atlantic paradigm (Chaplin, 2006; Houston, 2008). All told, the topical scholarship on Franklin might occasionally be edifying, but it certainly has not been influential, never mind cutting edge.

None of this biographical or topical scholarship helps us in any significant way to situate Franklin within the social structures and cultural philosophies of his days and years in the eighteenth century. Among topical considerations of Franklin, it is only Brandon Brame Fortune and Deborah Jean Warner who paused to analyze his scientific career in terms of class, and gender at the same time (1999: Ch. 2). They analyzed class identity as fashioned by a small, self-selecting subset of ambitious American men, not as structured on the full scale of mainstream American society and culture. For anyone hankering for class analysis of Franklin's various activities in their eighteenth-century context, Brame and Warner's engagement with class as an analytical variable was certainly a step in the right direction, but one not taken up by subsequent scholars.

Whether we look to the biographical or topical scholarship on Franklin, we remain unable to find any consensus or consistent image of Franklin's relationship to the social structures and cultural philosophies surrounding him. Even if we cannot take seriously the facile notion that Franklin "invented" either "America" or the middle class, we might conclude that Franklin was part of the middle class for some or much or all of his life, though he was initially on the poorer end of the social spectrum and ultimately on the richer end. He did not ever become an aristocrat, so what did he actually become short of that? Simply a "gentleman," without a discernible social cohort while in America, and without the country estate requisite for gentry while in England? In the face of this social opacity, we might resort to our own class terminology from the present, in lieu of the past's social terminology. Was Franklin in the end ensconced in what we might call a nebulous "upper" middle class? We still, in 2010, bicker in popular and academic culture about the ever-imprecise definition of the social classes in contemporary American life, never mind as projected back through its ever elusive place in American history. The biographical and topical scholarship on Franklin does not even begin to broach important conceptual distinctions to be made between, say, class structure, class formation, class experience, and class consciousness. Scholars have worried about the threshold when Franklin became "American," but for the most part the scholarship on Franklin has barely considered the question of when a "middle class" managed to become itself, except to project its development forward into an inevitable future beyond the eighteenth century, beyond Franklin's own lifetime.

5.3 The Analytical Category of Class in Scholarship on Eighteenth-Century Philadelphia and London

This oversight is unexpected because there has, in fact, been a pioneering and elaborated scholarship devoted to "class" in early and mid eighteenth-century Philadelphia and London, the two cities where Franklin spent almost all the formative and transformative years of his life spanning from 1723 to 1776, from age 17 to age 70. Indeed these two sites have been the focus of classic scholarship on class formation in American historiography and on middle-class formation in English historiography. On the American side, Eric Foner's *Tom Paine and Revolutionary America* (1976) and Gary B. Nash's *The Urban Crucible: Social Change, Political Consciousness, and the Origins of the American Revolution* (1979) converge on the time period after Franklin left Philadelphia for his long stint of imperial service in London. Meanwhile, Peter Earle's *The Making of the English Middle Class: Business, Society and Family Life in London, 1660–1730* (1989) plus a wave of scholarly successors stress the era before Franklin spent his time in

London. We might, in theory, use these books to reconstruct the class dynamics of Philadelphia after he left it behind in 1757, along with the class dynamics of London before he arrived there in the same year.

The American historiography cannot be straightforwardly applied to Franklin's life, it must be said. Influenced by the lead of E.P. Thompson, Foner and Nash mainly pitted working-class artisans against ruling-class merchants in their accounts of class relations in revolutionary-era Philadelphia. These two social groups may have duly sustained a tight drama of class division and conflict, but they provided an incomplete image of the working class, of the ruling class, and of the full spectrum of society. Both Foner and Nash gave relatively short shrift to the lower-class laborers beneath the level of artisans who would be the focus of Billy Smith's 1990 *The "Lower Sort": Philadelphia's Laboring People, 1750–1800*, and to the even lower status social constituencies placed in the foreground of Simon Newman's 2003 *Embodied History: The Lives of the Poor in Early Philadelphia*. Furthermore, both Foner and Nash, and Ronald Schultz (1993) following in their footsteps, overlooked the middle-class social constituencies who stood at the heart of Stuart Blumin's 1989 *The Emergence of the Middle Class: Social Experience in the American City, 1760–1900*, which featured Philadelphia as one among several urban case studies. The publication span of all these monographs – 1976 to 2003 – betrays how long it has taken scholars to accrue a reasonably three-dimensional image of the class structure in eighteenth-century Philadelphia. The old Marxian binaries – ruling class versus working class – have given way to a thicker post-Marxian spectrum of class relations: elite, middling sort, working class, and the poor (see Middleton, 2009). But the Philadelphia historiography has been premised mainly on reconstructing class strata individually, so that we must rely on a disparate, piecemeal image of class relations.

Compared with Americanist scholars, scholars of English and British history have been much more comfortable with and energetic in writing a history of class relations. Peter Earle's book on London's middle class – the "middling sort" in eighteenth-century terminology – sits within a weighty ongoing scholarship on class relations in London, in England, and in Great Britain. Its title paying unspoken homage to E.P. Thompson, Earle's book focused on middle-class formation in London, and was published in the same year (1989) as Peter Borsay's *The English Urban Renaissance: Culture and Society in the Provincial Town, 1660–1770* featuring the middling sort in the provincial cities outside London, and Paul Langford's *A Polite and Commercial People: England, 1727–1783* featuring the middling sort as a social and cultural force broadly throughout England (if not Britain or the British Empire). In contrast to Americanist scholarship, the more voluminous scholarship on class in England permits a more firmly diachronic view of the middle class and its development over time: from its emergence in the late seventeenth century, to its consolidation in the mid-eighteenth century, and ultimately to its politicization in the early nineteenth century (also see Barry and Brooks, 1994; Smail, 1994; Wahrman, 1995; Hunt, 1996). Blumin did construct something of a diachronic account of middle-class formation in America, but as a historian of the nineteenth century, he foreshortened the eighteenth century while focusing narrowly on artisans. Ultimately, the absence of a colonial American history of the middle class comes with the additional cost of making it impossible to fit Franklin within a truly Anglophone transatlantic- or British imperial-scale history of class relations. To this point our accounts are chronologically and geographically discontinuous, leaving us without the ability to construct a narrative across the Atlantic world, and across the eighteenth century. They are also conceptually incomplete, inattentive not just to multiplicity but to *multiple layers* of multiplicity in Franklin's class experience and his class consciousness.

Blumin constructed a model of the "middle class" fitting within a neat tripartite division of society that, some time in the early nineteenth century in America, began to supplant an older social order comprising numerous – far more than three – ranks. In this literalist interpretation of "class," the argument is that historians should not anachronistically apply *class* analysis to preceding social orders before the putative "emergence" of "class." One might pursue many objections to this argument, including the immediate practical one of disputing when class actually (in Blumin's words) "*emerged*," but either way it is not enough to situate a historical subject merely within a single given class strata: lower, middle, or upper. Benjamin Franklin presents an instructive case because he seems to have moved through all three class strata over the course of his life, indeed by the time he reached age 42. So who was he, truly? Once, and inescapably, of the lower sort? At the vanguard of an incipient middling sort? A wealthy gentleman, too privileged to remember his roots? How, then, do we pinpoint an essential class identity for someone like Franklin who experienced social mobility over his lifetime? Even for more ordinary colonists who experienced less dramatic social mobility than did Franklin, how do we determine the thresholds for moving from one class strata up, or down, into another? Moreover, can we ever bracket off a given class strata as a stable domain, rather than as always in a dynamic trajectory? All told, even if Franklin's class trajectory surely was exceptional in eighteenth-century American society, we can turn that exceptionality into analytical opportunities to consider broader questions of class essences, transition thresholds, and stable plateaus.

Yet even the multiplicity of three class strata does not provide sufficient nuance to capture Franklin's trajectory of upward social mobility over the course of his life. Nor do three class strata manage to encompass the complexity of the social structure in which he lived in the eighteenth century. In addition to managing to catapult himself from lower to middle to upper class by age 42, Franklin's good fortune was to make a sequence of crucial *status* transitions within these class transitions (status is deployed here in a way quite different from the pre-"class" vertical world of social *ranks* supposed by Stuart Blumin). In 1718 Franklin began his working life at age 12 as a bound apprentice to his own older brother. He managed five years later to run away to freedom, and to become a laboring journeyman and clerk, even as he remained in both cases, whether unfree apprentice or free journeyman, a member of what can be considered a "working class." This important transition from unfreedom to freedom is the central status transition highlighted by David Waldstreicher (2004: Ch. 2) because Franklin's years of unfreedom continued to haunt him for the remainder of his largely privileged life. What, though, was Franklin at birth and in childhood, before he was apprenticed and rendered unfree? He was the youngest son of a soap and candle maker – of an artisan whose livelihood situated patriarch and family in the working class. Once apprenticed Franklin became unfree, but he certainly did not fall beneath the level of the working class, into poverty. Focusing on broad class strata like the "working class" diverts us from appreciating these other crucial status transitions from freedom to unfreedom and back again to freedom. To characterize Franklin as "working class" in this early interval of his life is to describe, and to analyze, too little.

Franklin next made an important transition from dependence to independence once, in 1728, he made a transition from journeyman and clerk to master craftsman and small businessman (see Waldstreicher, 2004: Ch. 3). Did he now leave the "working class" behind, and become "middle class"? Is personal independence exclusive to the middle class, or could one be independent and working class? The class implications of this status transition from dependence to independence may be unclear, yet attaining independence was certainly important to Franklin. And this status transition was only the first of several he made in rapid succession as an enterprising young man in his twenties. He swiftly attained a status beyond mere independence to patriarchal competency as measured by his marriage to Deborah Read in 1730, and his ability to support not only himself but also a spouse and children, and soon other dependents as well. Of course, like personal independence, marriage and patrimony were not exclusive to the middle class either; he could have married and still been thoroughly working class, or even poor. Franklin did father an illegitimate son, but he seemed to have postponed marriage in prudent middle-class fashion, until having achieved a measure of economic security slightly above independence: competency. Franklin's peculiar class trajectory is less analytically helpful to us at this juncture because he was fortunate to experience only upward social mobility, without the oscillations between upward and downward mobility – opportunity and vulnerability – more typical of young men plying at the boundary between the working class and the middle class. Yet what was the precise threshold at which one moved up or moved down? Could upward mobility stay within the confines of the working class, or did it always entail a leap into the middle class? Could downward mobility stay within the confines of the middle class, or did it always entail a plunge into the working class? These are some of the elusive threshold questions exposing the rough approximation of class analysis, in contrast to the relative sharpness of status analysis. Only *relative* sharpness, it must be emphasized, since status analysis has its own arbitrariness and opacities. Marriage and patrimony could, for instance, symbolize bare patriarchy rather than actual competency.

Franklin himself did not pause to consider the class or status implications of his microeconomic achievements; he simply continued an inexorable ascent up the social ladder. In 1731 he became a business investor when he initiated the first of several long-distance printing partnerships, in this instance with Timothy Whitmarsh who was to operate a press in Charleston, South Carolina. Whitmarsh was contracted to repay Franklin's investment and to split the profits (see Frasca, 2006a: Ch. 5). This was the beginning, though emphatically not the end, of Franklin's exceptionality with respect to his ostensible peers in the Junto, the aspirational working-class male social club he helped organize in 1727. Not even many of the middle class were able to make such a transition from local businessperson to long-distance business investor. Franklin entertained such high ambitions and cast his eye on such wide horizons from a rather early moment in his own business career. Was he already then planning ahead for the life of a gentleman of the upper class, for the life of someone who invested capital rather than labored for a livelihood? In addition to the actual transitions from one class strata to another (in either direction), the tension between aspiration for oneself versus actual station in life points to further hybridities of class, since young men like Franklin were not always located in the same class strata as either their aspirations or their memories. Unsurprisingly, orbits of economic action did not necessarily match horizons of economic aspiration. Unsurprising it may be, yet hybridities such as these have not been seriously investigated by scholars of class, who tend to fence in the collective experience of a single class strata, while overlooking the dynamism of class and status transitions.

Nor did many American colonists of the middle class gain government offices with the attendant widening of horizons as did Franklin. How might we pinpoint the crucial status milestones in the various government offices he held from age 30 onward? Was one milestone his first local appointment by the colonial government, as clerk of the Pennsylvania General Assembly, in 1736? Or his first local appointment by the imperial government, as Philadelphia Postmaster, in 1737? Or his first elected political office, to the Pennsylvania General Assembly, in 1751? Or his first intercolonial appointment by the imperial government, as Deputy Postmaster General of North America, in 1753? Or his first overseas appointment by the colonial government in 1757, as agent representing the Pennsylvania General Assembly and dispatched to London? These three decades of transitions from independence to competency to business investment and finally to government service might all fit within what can be considered a "middle class," but not many members of the middle class were able to make such a transition to government service. Certainly few were able to make transitions in government service from the appointed to the elected to the commissioned, or from the local to the intercolonial to the overseas. In this case Franklin's exceptionality is analytically very useful because it enables us to discern something close to the full range of status transitions that can fall under the umbrella of a single class strata like the middle class.

Yet the problem with status transitions compared with class strata is that status transitions do not construct a coherent social group or even a cohort premised on identification, association, and mobilization. Class strata are precisely that: horizontal bands of people to some degree motivated to identify, associate, and mobilize with each other. Franklin's status transitions involved crossing horizontal thresholds, but they did not prompt, or result in, any coherent identification, association, or mobilization. A married men's club? A published writer's club? A local imperial appointee's club? No, no, and no. Franklin did, on the other hand, help start a library company seeking to empower "common tradesmen and farmers" to compete with "gentlemen" (see Franklin, *Autobiography*, 1964: 130–131). Here were avowed social solidarities – as oriented to broad class strata, not to filigree status thresholds.

So, had Franklin by his 1753 appointment as an intercolonial imperial official left the middle class behind and joined the upper class? In 1748 Franklin was financially secure enough to retire from his printing business at age 42, and to earn his income and magnify his wealth purely through capital investment and government salary. Perhaps it was at that point that he exited the middle class and became the kind of "gentleman" he and his Junto brethren had once so earnestly competed against (see G. Wood, 2004: Ch. 1). Was it the financial security to forsake laboring or was it the widening orbit of imperial service that credentialed him to be a member of the upper class? We are brought anew to the intractable problem of transition thresholds, now between the middle class and the upper class. How and when did Franklin become a "gentleman" of the upper class, and how and when did he fully secure such a position, and then plateau in it? He undoubtedly died a gentleman, in 1790, fortunate never to have experienced any downward mobility. Scholars of class relations tend to dwell discretely on one of the canonical class strata, often in tension with another strata, but without accommodating any complicating social mobility across strata, or determining precise thresholds for attaining, losing, securing, or presuming class position. Moreover, what were the brackets around, say, the middle class, when one could be considered, simply and securely, in it and of it? Alternatively, what were the hybridities as one class sensibility lingered on in another strata? How did Franklin recalibrate his social solidarities from competition against his superiors to membership among them as an equal? These are the crucial kinds of questions omitted from most of the biographical scholarship on Franklin, where he is commonly reduced to an atomized "self-made" man connected more directly to a future "America" than to his own contemporary society. We essentially learn nothing from such scholarship of the social world in which he lived, or of the social connections he cultivated and sustained (see Laird, 2006: Ch. 1). Indeed, we learn nothing of Franklin in history; we learn only of Franklin as myth.

The alternative is to be analytically alert enough to trace Franklin's long productive life through an overlapping sequence of crucial class as well as status transitions. There was unfreedom, freedom, and dependence while he was working class; independence, competency, investment, and local officialdom while he was middle class; and cosmopolitan gentility and transatlantic officialdom when he was upper class. Beyond these kinds of transitions, that productive life also involved shifting and multiplying sources of income and wealth, concomitant with multiplying work occupations and salaried positions. Compared with Franklin's class and status trajectory, it has been a more straightforward proposition for historians to examine Franklin's various discrete business careers and government offices: as journalist and artisanal printer (see Frasca, 2006a: Ch. 2; Green and Stallybrass, 2006; Lemay, 2006a), as city postmaster (see Lemay, 2006b), as entrepreneurial printer (see Waldstreicher, 2004: Ch. 5; Frasca, 2006a; Lemay, 2006b), as Pennsylvania politician (see Jennings, 1996; Waldstreicher, 2004: Ch. 6; Lemay, 2006b, 2009); as imperial postal official (see Lemay, 2009); as colonial government agent stationed in London (see Morgan, 1996; G. Wood, 2004: Ch. 2), as land speculator (see Immerman, 2010: Ch. 1), and as an American diplomat stationed in Paris (see G. Wood, 2004: Ch. 4; Schiff, 2005). This cumulation of business occupations and official positions does not, it should be noted, map so neatly onto Franklin's trajectory of class mobility and status transitions. Enough of them – for instance, his journalistic writing and his business investing – crossed over from one class strata to another, not sequential so much as overlapping. Once again we are confronted with multiplicity – this time exceeding the bounds of both class strata and status levels. And again we are confronted with Franklin's personal exceptionality which, because so spectacularly unrepresentative, affords more benefit for research agendas than insight into the historical past. Even if many colonial American men pursued more than one business occupation in order to gain and secure a competency, or simply to survive, few accumulated as prodigiously many sources of income and layers of wealth as did Franklin. Surely we cannot generalize from Franklin's astonishingly long and accomplished life itself, but we can extract crucial analytical questions from the very exceptionality of his microeconomic trajectories. In order to construct a nuanced image of the social structure and class relations surrounding any historical figure, whether as exceptional as Franklin, or entirely ordinary like many of the peers he outdid, we should be mindful of the complex interplay between multiple class strata, multiple status levels, and multiple business occupations and government offices.

We should ideally be mindful of even more: Franklin's multiple social and cultural activities which lay beyond the realms of economic productivity and personal wealth, but which nevertheless had crucial class implications. In Franklin's case these activities included his literary and political life, which enabled him to engage in public advocacy either in the voice of or on behalf of others. They also included his associational life, especially projects uncanny for their capacity to blend self, collective, and civic improvement all at once. And they included his consumer life, where the important milestone was not his 1748 retirement from business, but his 1764 design and decoration of a new townhouse in Philadelphia. To pursue a research agenda interrogating associationism beyond politics, and consumerism beyond production, has ever since E.P. Thompson's 1963 masterpiece become standard to any class analysis. We have learned to weave an appreciation of social and cultural factors – class experience outside the workplace, and class consciousness outside politics – into a vital pre-political interval of class formation, which Thompson located in the early nineteenth century for the English working class, and which Peter Earle located in the late seventeenth century for the English middle class. In other words, neither economic structures nor political activism is the sole determinant of the existence of a class strata.

This can be our cue that, beyond the various structural thresholds, transitions, and plateaus Franklin passed through in the class and status spectrum of Philadelphia society, there are also his social solidarities as well as cultural horizons to be analyzed if we are to understand more fully the social structures and class relations of Franklin's own eighteenth century. With whom did he affiliate and associate? For whom did he advocate? David Waldstreicher (2004: Ch. 4) sees Franklin as swiftly abandoning his working-class origins upon achieving freedom and independence, evident in the middle-class social solidarities expressed in his 1730s journalism. Franklin was forever haunted by his unfree origins according to Waldstreicher, but other scholars like Simon Newman see Franklin as consciously reaching back at least to certain aspects of his humbler origins as expressed in the two kinds of public advocacy – journalism and politics – he pursued in the 1730s and 1740s (2009). He may have moved up first into the middle class and then above that, and he may have wanted to bury and hide his unfree origins, but Franklin did not abandon all of his working-class social solidarities. Indeed, Gordon Wood (2004: Chs 4–5) sees Franklin's continued manipulation of his own humble origins as a way to construct a clever persona for himself when he was stationed first in London and then later in Paris, for most of the years from 1757 to 1785. Even once he had become a secure gentleman of the upper class, Franklin did not forsake his own humble origins when choosing his tactics to manipulate British and French stereotypes of American rusticity. We are confronted here again with complex hybridities which help make any precision to class analysis so elusive. If one examines his social solidarities and cultural horizons, Franklin seemed always to be embedded in more than one class strata at one time.

That was Franklin's literary and political life, haunted by his humble origins and distancing himself from them, yet also savvily manipulating those humbler origins to mesmerize and outwit his foreign hosts in London and Paris. There was also Franklin's associational life – for instance, his organization of a library company and a student academy, among numerous other institutions he helped establish back in his Philadelphia days – which seemed to reflect first his working-class and then his middle-class social solidarities in the 1730s and 1740s (see Boudreau, 1996, 2002). Yet why did Franklin not defend the struggling English-school component of his academy against the dominance of its Latin-school component (see Pollack, 2009b: 2–35)? Had he so swiftly become a traitor to the middle class, just as he once strove to leave behind the lower class? One can clearly see Franklin's social aspirations, and pretensions, reflected in the genteel male sociability guiding his scientific activities, begun in earnest in the mid-1740s (see Brame and Warner, 1999: Ch. 2). If Franklin would habitually reach back to his humble origins, he also spent early years reaching ahead toward his genteel aspirations. Social hybridities in every direction, in other words, both above and below.

Finally, there was also, beyond his productive life in gainful employ, Franklin's consumer life. We can witness Franklin exiting the working class and entering the middle class in a transitional moment chosen for its subtle drama by Franklin himself: an unexpected morning in 1731 when a "silver spoon and China bowl" appeared on his breakfast table (see Franklin, *Autobiography*, 1964: 144–145). We can witness, too, Franklin abandoning the middle class in favor of the upper class in the pompous attire he was willing to wear when sitting for a portrait by Robert Feke in 1746, just in advance of his early retirement in 1748 (G. Wood, 2004: Ch. 1). After spending nearly two decades ensconced in the middle class, Franklin moved into the upper class, where he would spend the rest of his life, if one measures by a combination of capital investment, social milieu, and cultural horizon. Yet his middle-class sensibilities endured at least up to 1764, when Franklin had a handsome townhouse built in Philadelphia in a manner which managed, with supreme ambivalence, to reflect both upper-class refinement and middle-class plainness (Cahill, 2008). Was refinement purely a function of genteel status, we might ask, attuned to ambivalence and hybridity, or could it also be a manifestation of middling status? This question is deceptively challenging because the presence and the meaning of consumer objects like a silver spoon, a porcelain bowl, a portrait, or a townhouse changed rapidly over the course of the eighteenth century.

In Franklin's Philadelphia days, the spoon and bowl bespoke middling status, and the portrait and townhouse bespoke genteel status, but commitment to and investment in consumer refinement belonged to both the middle class and the upper class. Once again we are confronted with the kind of social hybridities that require us to broaden and deepen our understanding of class analysis beyond "class" in a strict sense.

5.4 Conclusion

What can we conclude from all these layers of multiplicity and hybridity? In 1757 Franklin sailed away from a predominantly middle-class provincial city at an Atlantic periphery of the British Empire, a city increasingly riven with social conflict as a consequence of imperial warfare and its disparate effects on Pennsylvania's economy. He had moved adeptly through a trajectory of upward social mobility and reached a plateau of enviable personal wealth and public visibility, transforming himself from working-class origins into a fingers-dirty middling sort and finally into a gentleman wielding considerable economic leverage and political power. After a few weeks crossing the Atlantic Ocean, Franklin would arrive in a London whose scale of urban life, of working-class life, of middle-class life, and of genteel life were all vastly broader and deeper than what was present in Philadelphia. In London he would have to re-learn genteel attainments and middling sensibilities from the vantage of the metropole radiating outward, not from the perspective of colonies absorbing inward. Yet this was itself a measure of Franklin's exceptionality in the eighteenth century, as few of his peers from his 30 years leading the Philadelphia Junto were able to amass such liquid personal wealth or to attain such transatlantic cultural horizons. Franklin is thus in part unhelpful as an instrument for us to understand the social structures around him given his relative uniqueness: the steepness of his social mobility from working class to upper class, his experiencing only upward mobility while escaping any downward mobility, and how little time he spent navigating at the blurred boundaries between class strata.

Franklin was exceptional, moreover, not only in the trajectory of his life, but also in the vastness of his archive. That archive is certainly analytically useful for us to appreciate the multiplicity of class signifiers at work in the eighteenth century, but it is also both distractingly overwhelming and deceptively incomplete. It throws open important historical questions about social structures and class relations in the eighteenth century which it cannot answer – and which have not yet been otherwise answered in scholarship on class in Early American history. But the specific question here concerns not class analysis taken as a whole, but the relationship of a historical figure to their social context. To understand that relationship – and here is where Franklin's case is most instructive – we must add considerable nuance to class analysis, to make it ever more attentive to the interplay of social structures and individual trajectories. We must, in turn, be attentive to many layers of multiplicity: class strata and status levels, business occupations and government offices, aspirations and vulnerabilities, transitions and plateaus, social solidarities and cultural horizons, etc. If a narrow focus on class strata tends to overstate the stability of experience and consciousness, we also do not want to take the opposite tack and overstate fluidity. Instead, we must put transitions and plateaus in creative tension with each other. Above all, class analysis is key for us to appreciate much that stands outside – even if overlapping with – race and gender structures and dynamics.

As an analytical category class has faced much more theoretical challenge and conceptual instability than either race or gender. Perhaps because there was nothing comparable to the civil rights movement and the women's movement with respect to the category of class, the categories of "race" and "gender" made a more sharp contribution to the heyday of social history in the 1960s and 1970s, as well as a more seamless transition to the ascendancy of cultural history in the 1980s and 1990s. "Race" and "gender" would be applied as readily to the representational interpretive mode of cultural history, as they were applied to the experiential interpretive mode of social history. The theoretical axiom that categories like "race" and "gender" had been culturally constructed in history, and thus could and should be analytically deconstructed in scholarship, achieved hegemonic status in cultural history and licensed a confident burst of innovative scholarship. But the argument that "class" had been culturally constructed was resisted by enough scholars as a fallacy, in tenacious defense of materialism, rendering the scholarship on "class" collectively much more hesitant that the scholarship on "race" or "gender." And because class analysis has never achieved any semblance of theoretical consensus or conceptual coherence, it has been much less readily usable for histories on other subjects. Scholars' default tendency has been to deploy some brisk workable assumptions about class, but to omit any concerted class analysis. Hence, while many subjects have been related to the more usable categories of race and gender, few subjects, Benjamin Franklin among them, have been related to the category of class. It is a self-fulfilling prophecy, then, that the category of class has been rendered ever less usable. Fortunately, the Benjamin Franklin archive and the scholarship on Franklin together indicate direct and indirect ways toward a more fruitful historical analysis of social structures and class relations to be done in the future.

Further Reading

Boudreau, George W. (1996). "'Done by a tradesman': Franklin's educational proposals and the culture of eighteenth-century Pennsylvania," *Pennsylvania History* 69: 524–557.

Boudreau, George W. (2002). "'Highly valuable and extensively useful': Community and readership among the eighteenth-century Philadelphia middling sort," *Pennsylvania History* 63: 302–329.

Nash, Gary B. (1979). *The Urban Crucible: Social Change, Political Consciousness, and the Origins of the American Revolution*. Cambridge, MA.

Newman, Simon P. (2009). "Benjamin Franklin and the Leather-Apron Men: The Politics of Class in Eighteenth-Century Philadelphia," *Journal of American Studies* 43: 161–175.

Smith, Billy G. (1990). *The "Lower Sort": Philadelphia's Laboring People, 1750–1800*. Ithaca, NY.

Waldstreicher, David. (2004). *Runaway America: Benjamin Franklin, Slavery, and the American Revolution*. New York, NY.

Wood, Gordon S. (2004). *The Americanization of Benjamin Franklin*. New York, NY.

Chapter Six

BENJAMIN FRANKLIN AND PENNSYLVANIA POLITICS

Alan Tully

On June 22, 1750, Benjamin Franklin drew up and signed his initial last will and testament. In his early modern world of uncertain health and sudden mortality, a will was an instrument that demanded careful consideration and meaningful composition. "Thanks to GOD," wrote Franklin, for a life already "so long in a Land of Liberty, with a People that I love, and rais'd me, tho' a Stranger, so many Friends among them" (PBF, 3: 481; 7: 204–205).[1] These words, carefully chosen and repeated in the testamentary section of his 1757 revision, completed just as he was about to walk into a wider world, are as revealing as anything Franklin wrote. They open, in their uncluttered directness, welcome sightlines into the political world of the mature 51-year-old, Benjamin Franklin.

Three decades earlier, Franklin had found his way to a Pennsylvania, like himself quite young, but already a distinctive colonial society that would shape his life. Three principal characteristics informed the developing provinciality of Pennsylvania: the institutionalization of proprietary government, the prominence of Quakerism, and evidence of economic development. Its status as a proprietary colony originated in 1681, when King Charles II bestowed a charter for Pennsylvania on William Penn and his heirs. This foundational document included two sweeping entitlements: the power to "enact … any Laws," with the noteworthy proviso that legislation should have "the advice assent and approbation of the Freemen of the … Country … or of their Delegates," and the ownership of all lands within the specified bounds of the Pennsylvania grant (Dunn and Dunn, 1981–1987, 2: 65–66). These rights handed the proprietary family a major

---

A Companion to Benjamin Franklin, First Edition. Edited by David Waldstreicher.
© 2011 Blackwell Publishing Ltd. Published 2011 by Blackwell Publishing Ltd.

role in shaping provincial affairs. The second significant feature of the Pennsylvania colony, its Quaker character, resulted from the fact that members of the prophetic, persecuted Society of Friends had converted a young William Penn, the colony's founder, to their radical ways. During the last quarter of the seventeenth century, Penn established himself as the leading print proselytizer of Quakerism, and conceived of his Pennsylvania colony not as an escape from suffering but as an opportunity to create a Quaker world on the Delaware, a society founded on Friends' principles and sustained by a partnership between proprietor and people, illuminated by the holy guidance of the "Inner Light" (Bauman, 1983; Barbour and Frost, 1988; Braithwaite, 1912, 1919; M.M. Dunn, 1967; Endy, 1973; Dunn and Dunn, 1986, 1981–1987; Davies, 2000; Smolenski, 2010). The third characteristic that distinguished Pennsylvania, its relatively rapid pace of development, sprang from a confluence of concerted proprietorial promotion, rich lands, and a reputation for mild government that prompted strong immigration from both the British Isles and the Continent.

When 17-year-old Ben Franklin first gazed on Philadelphia in 1723, these three palpable characteristics as expressed in the political environment reflected twists and turns that William Penn had not foreseen. Subsequent to the Glorious Revolution, proprietary colonies, perceived as lax in enforcing the Navigation Acts, found themselves under attack in London. The fact that Pennsylvania Friends' notions of a "peace testimony" included both the refusal to organize a militia, and a reluctance to finance war intensified that hostility. Within the colony, a brief unsettling experience with an imposed royal government and fear of its re-imposition, a recognition that Penn's personal debts jeopardized the colony's future, and a surge of anti-proprietary sentiment occasioned by the unresponsiveness of the provincial land office prompted leading colonists to press for changes that might shelter their Quaker experiment. Reacting to pressures on both sides of the Atlantic, Penn defended many of his proprietary privileges, but at the same time demonstrated continuing support for the Quaker experiment by giving his more assertive colonials the means of self-protection. He accepted a restructuring of government in the form of the 1701 Charter of Privileges, which constituted the Assembly as a unicameral legislature and formalized a host of rights similar to those claimed by the English House of Commons. In conjunction with various subsequent statutes and assembly practices, the 1701 Frame quickly established the Assembly as the fulcrum of provincial politics. Penn's incapacitating strokes of 1712 and his death in 1718 hastened that evolution. By the time Franklin took up permanent residence in Philadelphia in 1727, a number of circumstances, including the Penn family paralysis occasioned by drawn-out litigation over the proprietary estate, a succession of governors who were either ineffective in contesting with local leaders or compliant in the face of their demands, and the extraordinarily capable leadership of a small group of popular politicians, had combined to make the Pennsylvania Assembly the most powerful popular political institution in the major Atlantic colonies (Shepherd, 1896; Root, 1912).

Quakerism, too, once planted in Pennsylvania, evolved in unexpected ways. Because many Friends had pre-immigration experiences of fellowship with other Quakers and saw Pennsylvania as an opportunity to build a transformative society, they quickly established local Quaker communities intent on fostering daily life practices of "holy conversation," built around the men's and women's meetings that George Fox and his convert spouse and co-inspiration to Friends, Margaret Fell, bequeathed to the succeeding generations (Endy, 1986; B. Levy, 1988; Mack, 1992). Some also brought minds still attuned to past prophetic voices, echoing arguments from the Old World that caused rifts in the New. Pennsylvania soon added its own Quaker schism. Prominent public Friend, George Keith, split the Society open with his disputatiousness and then, donning robes of apostasy, led some of his followers into the Church of England, while others peeled off into competing denominations (Smolenski, 2010). At the same time, political disagreements accompanying changes in the Frames of Government and the evolving proprietary situation created a factional fluidity among Quakers and Anglicans as Friends became a minority, first in Philadelphia City and County and later in large parts of Chester and Bucks Counties (Nash, 1968). Yet Quakers remained the dominant economic, cultural, social, and political presence. Friends were everywhere – not just in their many meetinghouses, but also in regional mills and stores, in prominent counting houses, and in both elected and appointed political offices. Philadelphia remained the center of a powerful Quaker cultural hearth when young Franklin came to town (Tolles, 1948; Tully, 1977, 1994; Horle, et al., 1997–2005; R. Larson, 1999; Wulf, 2000; Smolenski, 2010).

The third characteristic of Pennsylvania, its record of economic growth and development, obvious in retrospect, was not so clear in 1723 when runaway Benjamin first scuffled through Philadelphia's unpaved streets. The requisites certainly existed: extraordinarily productive soil, receptive markets within sailing distance, a developing inland economy, a noteworthy Indian trade, some access to capital and credit, and solid merchant and shopkeeper partnerships, buttressed by favorable demographics and a growing labor pool. Penn's promotional efforts among continental sectarians, in particular, attracted German and Swiss settlers sympathetic to Quakerism; capitalizing on the Pennsylvania commitment to religious toleration, his agents also appealed to other groups, including the Scotch-Irish. Young family members, indentured servants, contracted help of other kinds, and slaves filled out the ranks of a rough, hardened labor force that powered this pre-industrial society. But Pennsylvania had ups and downs (one of these downs in the early 1720s), which shaped the province's particular path toward relative prosperity. And those economic fluctuations were important to Franklin's early political life.

Classic though it is, Franklin's autobiographical narrative hardly supplies the most accurate guide to his early life. Yes, precocious beyond imagination with talents to match, and of extraordinary energy, both mentally and physically, Franklin was also an abused, angry runaway, ready for sexual adventure, and a not altogether reliable friend. Debt, misappropriation of money and spendthrift ways clearly figured more in young Ben's life than the careful accounting his *Autobiography* and *Poor Richard's Almanac* ostensibly suggest. But within the web of familial care and control that distinguished Franklin's Boston upbringing, and on his intellectual excursions and employment experiences in England during his late teens, he gained considerable education and superior skill as a printer. At about the age of 21, prompted by Quaker merchant Thomas Denham's mentoring, the dragging days of introspection on a tedious voyage back to Philadelphia, and a bout of serious illness upon landfall, Franklin grabbed his future by the neck. He realized that he wanted success and the recognition that went with it; given current life expectancies, he knew he needed to get on with it. His timing was perfect. Pennsylvania was just then entering a period of explosive economic growth that would last through the next quarter century. Franklin, and his risky business ventures, rode the wave.

Given his focus on building a successful business, it is not surprising that Franklin made the economy his entrance point for noticeable participation in Pennsylvania political affairs. In response to an economic downturn in the early 1720s, Pennsylvania had printed £45,000 in paper money, managed in a provincial loan office and funded on interest bearing mortgages, with public expenses paid in paper currency supported by mortgage interest and an excise tax. Most Pennsylvanians deemed the experiment a success and the second half of the decade saw an increasing clamor for more currency, demands met initially with strident opposition (Shepherd, 1896: 401–418). In 1729 Franklin joined the fray, with his much admired essay, "The Nature and Necessity of a Paper-Currency." Historians have often perceived this piece and an earlier, lightly circulated anonymous editorial as a brave plunge into the factionalized world of Pennsylvania politics. The timing, however, evidences a Franklin more shrewd than brave: He only entered the fray when the clamor died down. Governor Patrick Gordon had declared himself pliable on the issue; former Governor Sir William Keith, who had championed paper money as a way to cultivate popularity (after Hannah Penn, William's widow sacked him in 1726), had failed in his attempt to use the issue to gain the speakership of the Assembly; and David Lloyd, arguably the most brilliant Quaker politician of his day, who had opposed further emissions largely out of opposition to Keith, by 1728 had come around, after driving Keith back to Britain (Lokken, 1959). Opposition had shrunk to a small group, a rump of court-sanctioned proprietary "trustees," obliged to protect proprietary interests, which included keeping land prices and quit-rents at full sterling value, rather than debts payable in depreciated Pennsylvania currency. With telling perspicacity belying his youth, Franklin sized up this situation for what it offered: an opportunity to take a popular political stand, on an issue he understood and believed in, with virtually no risk of making enduring enemies.

Franklin's other significant early foray into politics was also, for the perspicacious person he was, an easy decision. Political controversy, if someone else's controversy, on an issue about which the public had some knowledge and on which there was general agreement, offered an opportunity for self-promotion. In his second issue of the *Pennsylvania Gazette* in October 1729, Franklin fired up interest with an editorial describing the Massachusetts General Court's resistance to Governor Burnett's demand for a settled annual salary, as his royal instructions dictated. Not a person in Pennsylvania would have made the case for such a practice, and precious few, in the late 1720s, would have openly argued the benefit of proprietary or royal instructions. Again, Franklin seized the opportunity to become a popular spokesperson, this time in the general terms of liberty that typified much of the era's Anglo-American political boilerplate. Franklin remarked with satisfaction that the artfully done piece brought support and encouragement from those who felt it "convenient" to have a "NewsPaper ... in the hands of one who could ... handle a Pen" (as quoted in Lemay, 2006a: 418).

Even as Franklin wrote these pieces, the political scene in Pennsylvania became more fluid, as it would remain for a decade. Clearly, Franklin recognized that. Despite occasional rash enthusiasms of the moment, Franklin played his business, civic, editorial and authorial cards so as to accumulate the chips of political relevance. As Franklin knew from his Boston experiences, the successful printer needed to avoid antagonizing the powerful. His eagerness, on first reaching Pennsylvania, to accept what proved to be the illusory goodwill of Sir William Keith, also taught him a different sort of caution: the need to take careful stock of proffered patronage from the well connected and their pretender friends. In his new environment, he quickly learned, too, that governors would come and go, bringing changes such as the reorganization of the proprietary interest when Hannah Penn turned over ownership of Pennsylvania to her three sons, and its effective management to the second of these, Thomas. From the moment of Thomas Penn's arrival in Philadelphia in 1732, through his return to England in 1741, Franklin dealt circumspectly with him. But Franklin did interact on familiar terms as a Mason, as a founding member of the Junto and the Library Company, and as a participant in other groups with men such as merchants William Allen and William Coleman, who were continuously included in the evolving circle of prominent proprietary placemen and friends.

Most importantly, Franklin maintained a solid friendship with Andrew Hamilton, whom he first met in London in 1724. As the preeminent Pennsylvania politician of the 1730s, Hamilton, though no proprietary sycophant, never lost sight of proprietary interests. Franklin watched carefully as Hamilton balanced Penn family interests against popular political appeal in his spearheading a legislative initiative to compensate the Penns for accepting pre-1732 contracted quitrents in Pennsylvania currency on par with sterling, at the same time as he stigmatized the Court of Chancery (a prerogative court that Thomas Penn dearly wanted in operation to adjudicate his property suits), as illegal under the 1701 Charter of Privileges. Both brilliant and irascible, Hamilton led the way in articulating popular political sentiment but simultaneously stirred up a succession of detractors as he strode the streets of Philadelphia. Although Hamilton was rarely free of personal controversy, and perhaps in part because of it, Franklin clearly admired the man. No other Pennsylvania politician of the day garnered more favorable press from Franklin. Later in the mid-1750s, Franklin's receptivity to Hamilton's mentoring came into full view when Franklin's public rejoinders to Governor Robert Hunter Morris echoed Hamilton's views.

In politics, personal relationships almost always have a reciprocal dimension and this one was no exception. Hamilton succeeded David Lloyd as speaker of the Assembly in 1729 and continued to hold that post, with one brief interlude, through the 1730s. His other important public posts underscored his dominance, but as speaker he threw Franklin a very important lifeline – steady income as the major contractor for government printing jobs, which included the Assembly's *Votes and Proceedings*, the provincial *Acts*, and the province's currency emissions. Most importantly, in 1736 Hamilton engineered Franklin's selection as clerk of the House of Representatives, a position he held until 1751, when son William succeeded him (Horle, *et al.*, 1997–2005, 2: 416–449).

Despite the considerable attention historians have paid to Franklin's first two decades in Philadelphia, virtually none has paid more than lip service to his politics of those years. With the notable exception of Leo Lemay, Franklin's major interpreters have focused exclusively on his business, literary, civic, socio-economic, and budding experimental interests (Wright, 1986; Brands, 2000; Morgan, 2002; Isaacson, 2003; Waldstreicher, 2004; Lemay, 2006a, b). A major reason for this is that the most telling feature of Franklin's politics of the 1730s and early 40s was its subterranean quality. When, for example, one or two individuals took runs at him in his capacity as Assembly clerk or printer of the *Votes*, he did not openly respond. His encomiums to Hamilton might seem to be outspokenly partisan but, in fact, Hamilton was a presence in both proprietary and popular politics throughout Franklin's later career. And his editorializing on the benefits of the quitrent arrears settlement, in juxtaposition to his printing of a highly inflammatory letter Governor Thomas wrote to the Board of Trade in October, 1740, distorting the issues at stake in Pennsylvania politics and maligning Quakers, were revealing expressions of Hamiltonian balancing.

As the colony's leading printer, and relying, in the face of cash flow concerns, on political patronage for regular and secure income as Assembly clerk, privy to the "in-doors" ruminations of the peoples' representatives, and as a friend, seeing his mentor Hamilton pay the price of too free a tongue, Franklin clearly came to understand the value of circumspection. However, his extreme reticence during the 1740–1742 provincial political blowup, which involved issues such as defense, pacifism, private property rights, gubernatorial and proprietary privileges, Board of Trade policies and Assembly power, and which resulted in the appearance of a hegemonic, popular Quaker Party and the reduction of proprietary political influence to an unprecedentedly low level, suggests something more, something to which Franklin's testamentary words bear witness (Tully, 1977: 24–38).

Above all else, Franklin lived with extraordinary intensity in each of his four successive environments. He was in each, in a very real sense, an outsider. In Boston, that was by choice. Despite the membership that birth and youth in that city brought, Franklin became the rebellious son and brother and a merciless social critic. In the subsequent three – Pennsylvania, Britain, and France – he arrived an ambitious outsider and strove mightily for acceptance. His affability, both genuine and studied, facilitated his success, as did, in the long course of his life, his dissociative capability: the ease with which he moved from one home to the next, slipping away from one cradle of intimate relationships to another, without entirely severing the connection. Each life he embraced with ardor and sincerity. In France, in his old age, Franklin fore-grounded his unparalleled scientific attainments to win acceptance in significant, if idiosyncratic corners of French society; he became sufficiently comfortable at Passy to contemplate remaining there for the duration of his life. In Britain, Franklin strove to enter the gentry's political world and, although he never penetrated the inner circles of the haughty eighteenth-century English political class, he managed to find enough friendship, intellectual engagement, and social comfort there to consider permanent residency.

His prime years in Pennsylvania, however, most clearly reveal the mature man and the loyalties he came to feel. He arrived in Philadelphia an outsider, "a Stranger," and by dint of his business, intellectual, experimental and civic accomplishments, by dint of his painstaking efforts to understand this unique provincial society as he helped to shape and possess it, and by dint of his willingness to take the time necessary to *belong*, he integrated with a genuineness and thoroughness that stands out against his other lived experiences. In short, as Franklin built his business, participated in the Atlantic intellectual world, improved Philadelphia, and communicated with those in the hinterland, he was performing important roles of political enablement. In the early 1740s, he was not yet where he needed to be; given the temper of the times, any attempt at greater involvement would have undone Franklin's intense quest for broad-based belonging. By the late 1740s, however, after two decades of assiduously "becoming-a-Pennsylvanian," Franklin demonstrated how thoroughly he had succeeded. He would no longer be a "Stranger" among "the People that I Love."

On November 17, 1747, Benjamin Franklin published *Plain Truth*, his extraordinary pamphlet that established him as "a man ... famous in the political world" (PBF, 4: 62). Compelling circumstances occasioned Franklin's abrupt interposition in provincial affairs. In the late spring and summer of 1747, deep into King George's War, Spanish and French enemy ships brought hostilities to the Delaware Bay. Thomas Penn had not named a gubernatorial successor to Governor Thomas, who departed Philadelphia in June. Under the 1701 Charter of Privileges and subsequent precedents, the Pennsylvania Council was virtually powerless in the absence of a governor, even in the face of imminent danger. At the same time, the Assembly, firmly in the hands of the Quaker Party, saw no reason to embrace military preparedness given Pennsylvania's history of waiting out Eurocentric conflicts, never suffering concerted seaborne attacks, avoiding Indian wars and, of course, heeding Friends' various testimonies against the practices of war. Still, council president Anthony Palmer's warnings of a planned enemy attack on a defenseless Philadelphia terrified many. What was to be done?

Franklin's answer, the opportunistic and ingenious *Plain Truth*, made the case for a citizens' initiative for defense. Within a week Franklin provided articles of association: a compact among associators to form into militia companies and choose their own company officers, who in turn would select regimental officers, all of whom would receive commissions from the provincial council. Franklin also proposed an elected military council to serve as a governing body. With public response immediate, sizeable and enthusiastic, companies formed, and Franklin and his friends encouraged their resolve with schemes to raise money for equipment, ordinance, and fortifications and appeals for support to the proprietor, the Admiralty, and neighboring colonies.

Historians' reactions to *Plain Truth* have varied. Some tend to include Franklin's appeal and the resulting Association as simply another of his successful civic initiatives (Isaacson, 2003; Pangle, 2007). Others (not necessarily mutually exclusive) see *Plain Truth* as a literary and argumentative gem, an imaginative and innovative use of the press, an expression of forward looking organizational and philosophic inventiveness, and/or a contribution to generalized discourses constructed to provide overarching coherence in a disconcertingly diverse, Atlantic world (Wright, 1986; Campbell, 1999; Brands, 2000; Lemay, 2006a,b; Houston, 2008). Persuasive and fertile, these views nevertheless miss the sense of fulfillment that the Association represented in Franklin's political maturation. He had, as it were, bided his time. A firm believer in the need to use organized military force both for defense and to achieve legitimate objectives in this less than perfect world, Franklin had previously kept these views well in hand. A close observer can see him carefully weighing where his convictions placed him relative to those around him during the 1740–1742 war-related political factionalism, and again when Pennsylvania refused military aid to Massachusetts for its Louisburg expedition in 1745. Outspoken espousal of military preparedness offered only a downside in these situations.

On the other hand, Franklin's patience and political maturity paid off handsomely in the defense crisis of 1747–1748. There was certainly risk in writing *Plain Truth*: it might have stirred up a wasp's nest. But Franklin always possessed, along with his careful calculating mind, the brass of a gambler; to miss that is to miss much of the excitement of his life. Perhaps he felt that his imminent retirement, along with the larger intellectual and scientific life he envisaged for himself, made the possible cost of public and personal ire of less moment. Most revealing of his current situation, however, was the comfortable tone of his November 28, 1747 letter to New York placeman, Cadwallader Colden. "Tho' *Plain Truth* bore somewhat hard on both Parties here, it has had the Happiness not to give much Offense to either" (PBF, 3: 213). Why? Because of Franklin's sophistication and dexterity. Franklin ostensibly upbraided both proprietary supporters and Quakers, but not surprisingly, there was a backstage story. In writing his pamphlet and drawing up his associational plans, Franklin had consulted closely with long-time friends, trusted intimates of the main proprietary spokesmen. Clearly the gentlemen, whom he derided in *Plain Truth*, knew they would take a pummeling, but accepted it in order to undermine the Quaker Party's electoral dominance by getting defense preparations on the open political agenda. They also understood that the charges Franklin made against them for inactivity in defending Pennsylvania were transparently disingenuous. There was no real stigma here.

As for the Quakers, Franklin's many years of intimate life with them gave him an understanding of the dynamics of Friends' testimonies, which modern writers tend to ignore. Most interpreters repeat the anachronistic view that Friends embraced pacifism as orthodox sometime in the late seventeenth century and that Pennsylvania Quakers overwhelmingly subscribed to that doctrine. Nothing could be further from the plain truth. Early Quakers understood "Testimonies" not as beliefs but as principles or "advices" derived from exploration of the Inner Light and subject to discussion in meeting. In the late seventeenth and early eighteenth centuries, testimonies on peace comprised ideas having to do with the degree to which individuals and groups of Friends should foreswear violence and warlike activities (Tully, 1977; Weddle, 2001). Additional complications arose in locales like Pennsylvania, where Quakers who served as magistrates understood that God placed responsibility on their shoulders to ensure order and civility (Wellenreuther, 1970; Tully, 1982, 1983). Franklin knew very well by 1747 that in Pennsylvania, what we might call thorough pacifist Quakers were few. Many Friends, while they would not enlist in the Association and would in general terms affirm the peaceful intent of the "Holy Experiment," would neither get in the way of a volunteer defense organization – they would even facilitate such an initiative, if only by avoiding opposing it.

Franklin benefited, too, from both good luck and his own sleight of hand. Rather than undertake the more customary prolonged "dealings" with a small number of Quaker merchants who had helped finance a privateer, a "stiff-rumped" Quaker meeting disowned the offenders in November 1747. This action clearly antagonized some moderates against their quick – to-discipline brethren. For his part, Franklin wrote a series of scripturally attuned pieces that cited past Quaker luminaries who had sanctioned defensive war, and then a longer essay that justified war on the strength of Biblical authority. As he expected, Quaker pacifist champions and Presbyterian war hawks soon assaulted each other, hammer and tongs, in a pamphlet war that drew attention away from Franklin's own activities (Tully, 1982).

In the wake of *Plain Truth* and the ensuing Association activities that so elevated his profile, Franklin demonstrated again his acute political sense. When friends suggested that he run for elected office, he demurred, as he had earlier when he refused election as colonel of the Association and marched with musket in the ranks. Had he stood for Assemblyman in 1748, he would have drawn the ire of the strict voices in the Quaker Party already irked by his publication of the Pennsylvania Council's June 14 resolves, which were highly critical of Quaker legislators. With Quaker Party leaders and supporters crucial segments of the broad civic constituency that Franklin wanted to hold, elected provincial office would have to wait until strict Quaker antipathy died down and the dust settled around the transition in Quaker Party leadership from the suddenly deceased John Kinsey, Jr. to Isaac Norris, Jr. Meanwhile, Franklin felt out the new strength of his proprietary connections by accepting membership in the Philadelphia Common Council, and by trying on the putative status of the "Esquire" that accompanied his appointment as judge. Already rightly identified with a number of important civic-minded groups and improvement projects, Franklin added to his accomplishments. In the early 1750s, he drove both the Academy and College of Philadelphia and the Pennsylvania Hospital from insightful inspirations to functioning institutions. These extraordinarily innovative and significant projects also had political overtones in that Franklin worked largely with proprietary supporters in the former, with the latter much more a Quaker undertaking.

This interlude, however, would not last long. *Plain Truth* – with its shrewd address to the tradesmen, artisans and farmers of Pennsylvania, and with the Association's membership as witnesses to the success of that appeal – made Franklin the undisputed hero of "middling" Pennsylvania, with accompanying flanks of support from both the "better" and "the poorer sort." For once, too, a Philadelphia man of influence seemed to clearly understand the wartime fears of those who lived closer to Hempfield,

Harris's Ferry, Easton, Reading, York, or the Delaware border than to Philadelphia. The fact that he appealed directly to English, Welsh, Scotch-Irish and German ethnics, as well as to members of various denominations, made him, in the Quaker diction of the time, a "weighty" friend indeed. As Thomas Penn remarked in one of his rare penetrating insights into Pennsylvania society, Franklin had become "a sort of Tribune of the People" (PBF, 3: 186n).

Penn's comment suggests that Franklin was a person of a different order, which during the late 1740s and 1750s the Philadelphian demonstrated beyond a doubt. His electrical experiments were attracting notice in the capacious and rarified world of natural philosophers. When the French proclaimed Franklin's genius in May of 1752 through the Paris Academy's acceptance of his hypothesis of lightning as an electrical phenomenon, and the Royal Academy joined in tardily with its bestowal of the Copley Medal in late 1753, Franklin gained deserving fame, the stuff of dreams (Chaplin, 2006).

The confidence that Franklin had in his speculations, despite occasional threads of tentativeness that accompanied his calculating self-promotion, was evident even before his public acclaim. His fertile mind delved imaginatively into other natural phenomena. If one might with diligence better comprehend the natural world as one of the major determinants of life, then might not one better understand the political and economic structures that shaped the colonial and metropolitan worlds? *Observations on the Increase of Mankind*, which Franklin drafted in 1751, began with simple observations, which led, in his articulation, to important implications and possibilities for changing the British Empire. Formerly in his life, Franklin had, on occasion, been critical of British laws and prerogative injunctions that mitigated against the efficient and responsible ordering of the extended empire. At mid-life, during these mid-century years, he became more outspokenly brash in his identification and exposure of what he considered to be narrow, counterproductive British policies and interests. And he did more than criticize. His 1751 publication of suggestions for a colonial union prefigured his well-known Albany Plan and offered the kind of fresh perspective on British and intra-colonial institutionalization that had been lacking since the late seventeenth century.

In middle age, Franklin became a dervish. His acuity, range, energy, determination, vanity, and focused angers burst forth, as they hitherto had not. That in turn opened him up to more of the personal politics of envy, dissemblance, and fear. But the vast majority of Pennsylvania influentials wanted to work with him. Most would tolerate some differences of view – even on important issues – in order to share in the sense of purpose, excitement, accomplishment and, of course, the sociability of the popular of Benjamin Franklin. For his part, by 1751, Franklin stood ready to take on the elected provincial office of Assemblyman. While various interpreters, who focus on either his civic and philosophic accomplishments or his engagement in electoral politics, see this occasion as the beginning of his political career, Assembly membership for Franklin, in fact, culminated his sustained project of political enablement (Hanna, 1964; Hutson, 1969, 1972; Brands, 2000; Pangle, 2007). In an acknowledgment of eminence earned, he easily won a Philadelphia by-election in May. In the subsequent general election he topped the poll, attracting support from both Quaker and proprietary partisans. With these votes came expectations of Franklinian political leadership.

Immediately on Franklin's election to the Assembly, Speaker Isaac Norris, Jr, put the important House business, and with it a central role in the custodianship of the Quaker Party, in the new member's hands. (For a very different view see Hanna 1964.) Franklin certainly saw this as opportunity. There were things to be done, and recently appointed Governor James Hamilton – a Pennsylvanian, son of Franklin's old mentor Andrew, a fellow Mason and an affable man – seemed a proprietary point man with whom the Assembly could work (Horle, et al., 1997–2005, 2: 449–462). Although that proved true on a small number of legislative bills, Hamilton's disingenuous and tortured rationales in refusing new currency emissions soon distinguished his governorship. Hamilton's behavior on this issue, (along with an imperious and revealing document from Thomas Penn refusing proprietary contributions for the escalating cost of Pennsylvania's native diplomacy, and Penn's initial slighting of both the Academy and College and Pennsylvania Hospital undertakings), reminded Franklin of the Penn who had been unbending in seeking what he viewed as full value for the family's pre-1732 quit-rent arrear losses, and the Penn who had attempted to convince the Board of Trade that the formation of the Association was tantamount to treason and domestic insurrection. Franklin's suspicion that Thomas Penn's instructions to his governor lay behind Hamilton's intransigence on currency bills was dead on. The chief proprietor was determined to regain long-departed prerogative privileges, the most important of which gave the governor and his appointees a hand in the appropriation of all revenue generated by the interest and excise taxes that funded Pennsylvania's paper currency. And he was equally determined to shield proprietary property from any form of taxation.

Then, in 1754, war came to Pennsylvania. And it was the circumstances of war, not civic involvement, or scientific prowess, that vaulted Franklin to a new level of prominence – just as King George's War had done in the 1740s and the Revolutionary War would do later. At a crucial juncture in Franklin's life, the French and Indian War gave him a sustained opportunity to claim unquestionable public leadership, by asserting himself as the Assembly's chief credible advocate of provincial military measures (including the provision of governmental support for both British regular and provincial troops and the adoption of Pennsylvania's first militia laws);

by galvanizing residents of southwestern Pennsylvania to provide transport and road-cutters for General Braddock's ill-fated but politically important expedition; by ranging the northwestern areas of the province in the dark days of 1756 to coordinate the defensive stockading of an exposed frontier; by becoming the cornerstone of a re-made Quaker Party that would, without equivocation, accept the onus of defending the province in wartime; by becoming the chief provincial spokesperson in the Assembly's confrontation with Thomas Penn; and by repeatedly representing the province in the extended arena of imperial/colonial affairs.

Even the most popular public servants have detractors and Franklin was no exception. At one point, for example, Philadelphia-based proprietary supporters organized their own militia unit to try to undercut the gathering public support for the Quaker Party's legislatively sanctioned version of a voluntary militia. Some provincial residents, exposed to Indian attacks, bought the proprietary line that only by ridding the Assembly of Quakers could they assure a provincial government wholeheartedly committed to defense. At the same time, the Quaker Reformation began in earnest, motivated in part by the stark choices war on the provincial doorstep had forced. Observant strict pacifists, whether Quaker, Moravian, Mennonite or others, declared themselves and peeled away from the Quaker Party (Marietta, 1984).

Despite this hemorrhaging of support, however, wartime politics clearly consolidated Franklin's popularity more than it weakened him. From the moment war arrived in Pennsylvania in May, 1754, with Washington's defeat at Fort Necessity, through June, 1757, when Franklin embarked for England as agent of the Assembly, the crux of Pennsylvania politics remained the same. On the one hand, Thomas Penn bound his governors with instructions to refuse any money bill that did not include executive participation in the appropriation of the revenue and to accept no bill that taxed proprietary estates. On the simplest level, his strategy was to use the war to strip the Assembly of its decades-old practice of controlling tax revenues and expenditures, and insofar as his agents could achieve those ends, simultaneously keep proprietary assets off provincial tax rolls. On the other hand, with the Assembly under intense pressure from provincial residents and British officials to raise money for the wartime effort – for "the King's Use" as the Quakers had long designated their grants to "Caesar" – Franklin and the Quaker Party eventually had to concede "wav[ing]" the Assembly's "Rights" regarding money bills "on this present Occasion only." The public, however, overwhelmingly agreed with their anti-proprietary views (PBF, 6: 514).

In this situation it served the interests of both Quakers and proprietary supporters to keep Franklin's goodwill. His unequivocal willingness to wage war and to carry Friends with him cleared the Quaker Party of charges of strict pacifism. For their part, proprietary supporters thought that if they could capture something of Franklin's loyalty, they could use him as a wedge to fracture the realigning Quaker oligarchy. Thus caught, Franklin clearly felt the pressure as he shouldered the burdens of war-master, political strategist, and pundit. By mid-1755, he wrote revealingly to longtime London friend and Quaker, Peter Collinson: "I am heartiely sick of our present Situation ... both Sides expect more from me than they ought, and blame me sometimes for not doing what I am not able to do, as well as for not preventing what was not in my Power to Prevent." (PBF, 6: 86). Pennsylvania politics had become a stalemate – a situation that over the years has drawn the attention of various historians eager to expose the twists and turns of the intense and ultimately prolonged conflict.

A number of interpreters who wish to explain the intense anger some of Franklin's contemporaries directed toward him in 1755–1756 posit one of two premises about his politics: prior to that time Franklin was either a proprietary supporter or an "independent." Related discussion has focused on the timing of Franklin's "turn." In both cases those who became vociferous, poisonous, and continuing critics felt that Franklin had either betrayed them or quite abruptly become a Quaker Party partisan. Franklin responded out of vanity and because of his own penchant for evening the score – whether in the short or long run (Zimmerman, 1960; Hanna, 1964; Hutson, 1969; Jennings, 1996). Similar glimpses of Franklin's character also appear in the writings of others who portray Franklin as more of an exceptional individual – in some scenarios quite principled as well as pragmatic – striving to solve the problems war brought to a Quaker Pennsylvania and consequently under attack from various ill-intentioned or simply opposing elite figures and interests (Ketcham, 1964, 1965; Hutson, 1969, 1972; Middlekauff, 1996; Morgan, 2002). Attendant argument has revolved around the question of Franklin's judgment, following the 1755–1756 crisis, in trying to oust Pennsylvania's proprietary regime and replace it with royal government (Hanna, 1964; Hutson; 1972; B.H. Newcomb, 1972; Middlekauff, 1996; Morgan, 2002; Waldstreicher, 2004). Another area of historians' concern, which has impassioned their debates as it did the polemics of the time, has to do with how to interpret the withdrawal of strict pacifist Quakers from the Assembly, Franklin's role in that watershed, and who among strict Quakers, Franklin and his supporters, and Thomas Penn and his proprietary stalwarts were primarily responsible for Native American attacks on Anglo- and Euro-American Pennsylvania residents during the early stages of the French and Indian War. On this torn-up terrain was Franklin really Franklin the good? (Thayer, 1953; Ketcham, 1963; Hanna, 1964; Hutson, 1972; B.H. Newcomb 1972; Jennings, 1996).

The situation of stalemate, however, not these later questions of interpretation, preoccupied Franklin in 1755–1756. He had not entered into the Assembly to become a eunuch; he had no tolerance for impotence in any part of his life. As he assessed his political situation during these crisis months, characteristically he saw a way of clearing away the miasma of current politics by conjuring up a British-sourced fair wind. With increasing frequency, Franklin elbowed his way into a larger political arena as war offered him numerous opportunities to cultivate British Imperial officials and senior colonial officeholders. He felt at ease with many of them. Son William's interest in a British army career and his own wartime responsibilities took Franklin into the company of senior military commanders. He found that he could manage them. His organizational capabilities in running the Pennsylvania war effort and in improving the colonial post-office widened his experience and enhanced his confidence. His draft of the Albany plan, his attendance at the conference, and his subsequent meetings and exchanges with colonists and Britons drew him further into an intellectual and practical engagement with the expansive Anglo-American world. And the siren songs of extraordinary appreciation from many of the premier philosophic minds of the Anglo/European world summoned him to join their colloquies in person.

Meanwhile, the proprietor Thomas Penn and his Pennsylvania acolytes deployed the blood-soaked stalemate they had instigated to discredit Friends among royal officials and politicians in London. Penn and his allies repeatedly represented the Quaker Party in private correspondence, personal conversation, and the press as intransigent pacifists verging on the treasonous. They portrayed Pennsylvania Friends as heirs to Quaker ancestors, who, a generation before had been castigated as a threat to order in Britain and who, along with the German voters who supported them, should be disqualified from serving in any government. With inventive tactics, Franklin won a few skirmishes with Penn's governors, but no matter. Proprietary instructions constituted a maze in which Franklin found himself trapped. The only way out seemed a voyage to England to confront Penn there, and to lobby members of the British government directly, both through the province's old friends, and, when possible, through Franklin's growing list of public figures who might now open their doors to one of the most honored philosophic minds of the Euro-American world. On January 28, 1757, the Pennsylvania Assembly resolved unanimously to send to London at least one commissioner "to solicit a Removal of the Grievances we labour under by Reason of Proprietary instructions" (PBF, 7: 109). Five months later Franklin took ship, intent on breaking the instructional chains that prevented Pennsylvania governors from negotiating on legislation and to challenge the proprietary claim of a right to exemption from provincial taxation.

Franklin achieved but limited success. After five years in Britain, he returned to Philadelphia in November 1762 with a narrow agreement between Penn and the Privy Council that allowed taxation of proprietary land, equitably assessed. A little over a year later, that was in dispute when the Indian War of 1763–1764 spread renewed violence on the frontier, again prompting demands for defense appropriations. When the Franklin-led

Assembly adopted a bill levying a land tax to fund the war effort, the new Governor, Thomas Penn's nephew John, trotted out a lawyer's reading of the proprietary/Privy Council agreement that, if applied, would result in a considerable underassessment of proprietary land.

Most historians who have focused on Franklin's political experience in colonial Pennsylvania have narrated a building of tension from the mid-1750s through the 1763–1764 years of his return, then continuing with his London sojourn, where as colonial agent he become increasingly involved in the pre-Revolutionary politics of empire (Wright, 1986; Brands, 2000; Morgan, 2002; Isaacson, 2003). In many ways, however, Franklin's role in the Pennsylvania politics of 1763–1764 seems a coda, separated from the sustained and more slowly building intensity of the early 1750s by a prolonged caesura. His return struck welcome familiar notes. Quaker Party members, who had carried the load over the preceding five years, immediately ceded leadership to him. His popularity "out of doors" had remained strong. He had been re-elected annually *in absentia*, and although narrowly defeated in Philadelphia in the 1764 election, he retained considerable popularity there (witness the crowd that turned out the following year to protect Franklin's family and property when he was rumored to be supportive of the Stamp Act), as well as in outlying areas, where community leaders acknowledged his renewed role in pressing for military measures. But the dominant progressions were the dissonant ones: the violence of war, the arguments over defense, and a dissembling governor. The intransigent Thomas Penn orchestrated the main theme by imposing his will on the province through proprietary instructions.

A few noteworthy variations, however, entered the reprise. On the frontier in 1763 a mob of rioters, the Paxton Boys, slaughtered the few remaining Conestoga Indians, which unleashed a verbal and written barrage of anti-Quaker venom. They then marched on Philadelphia to protest the province's Native policies and the underrepresentation of the backcountry in the Assembly. Uncharacteristically, Franklin added to the cacophony with his unsparing condemnation of these dissidents. His distance from the rawness of colonial society, his time in the more refined company of British acquaintances, his long-standing distaste for unyielding Presbyterianism, and his internalization of some Quaker charitableness may have played a part in triggering his uncharacteristic reaction. When Franklin's political opponents subsequently spread far and wide, his 1751 penned disparagement of German immigrants, the election campaign of 1764, which featured all these screeds, imparted a new sharpness to Franklin's views on race and ethnicity. The election also clearly demonstrated that Franklin had become, by that time, a much more broadly polarizing figure than he had been in 1755–1756. Members of the reinvigorated Proprietary faction reorganized as the "New Ticket" to oppose petitioning for royal government drew many more supporters from "middling" and "lower sort"

Pennsylvanians, who clearly had begun to share some of the opinions of Franklin's committed enemies among the provincial elite (B.H. Newcomb, 1972; Silver, 2008; Kenny, 2009).

Events of 1763–1764, thus, imparted greater clarity to the historical Franklin, but little new of note. The main theme of that short period of Franklin's Pennsylvania residency remained that which Thomas Penn orchestrated by imposing his will on the province through proprietary instructions. But this time, Franklin felt he could offer a better answer: lop off the malignancy that the proprietary family had become. With this goal in mind, Franklin turned to a chord that had intermittently been struck since William Penn's experiment had first drawn concerted criticism, and that Franklin had begun to explore in 1758: have the British ministry turn Pennsylvania into a crown colony. Franklin's electoral defeat on this issue in 1764 determined him to once more travel to England as Assembly agent to effect this end.

Historians have made much of Franklin's doggedness in pursuing the royalization of Pennsylvania in the face of irrefutable evidence of impending imperial reorganization. The standard, but also contested, explanation posits that Franklin's "thorough Contempt" for the status-conscious Thomas Penn and Penn's belittling of the vain Franklin, overcame the latter's capacity for careful appraisal (Hanna, 1964; Hutson, 1972; B.H. Newcomb, 1972; Jennings, 1996; Middlekauff, 1996; Morgan, 2002; PBF, 7: 362). However, while personal animosity played an undeniable, salient role, focus on the negative side of the politics of affection offers too confining an explanation. Franklin did display powerful feelings within the settings of his sequential homes; hatreds and aversions festered, but within larger environments of love and affection. Without Franklin's deep identification with "the People that I love" and the institutions and social relations that structured that society (which he reaffirmed in 1764 in bidding adieu a second time to "the Country I love"), Thomas Penn's disdain would not have stung as it did. So, similarly, did Franklin's variously rooted affections for Britain and the attendant empire frame the angers and sense of humiliation that he soon faced in London. Out of his identification with Pennsylvania came what to Franklin seemed the commonsense of royalization. The Crown, acting as the fount and guardian of English liberties, had granted rights and privileges, which it would not, or could not, in any practical sense emasculate, as the proprietary regime sought – with some success – to accomplish, and as some future Parliament might well consider. In Franklin's mind the successful workings of that empire clearly involved, along with differing provincial practices, widespread conjunctive authority, which he could imagine occurring in the protective shade of the royal oak (Waldstreicher, 2004: 152).

Franklin's Pennsylvania politics are only comprehensible within the context of his circles of friends, not as sequences of activities activated and controlled by the stand alone, gigantic individual, or "independent" man that so many have portrayed. Look for the Franklin "becoming-a-Pennsylvanian" and one sees not only the demanding schedule required to run a successful newspaper and printing business but also a breathtaking calendar of contact with others. Franklin's life burgeoned with group undertakings and sparkled with the joys of speculation, experimentation, irreverent questioning, literary creativity, bold advocacy, jokes and hoaxes, and the intricacies of indirection. His skeptical turn, earthiness, exuberance, the bonhomie of the artisan workplace, the obvious pleasure he took in sharing interests and occasions with a wide spectrum of the "better sort," and his nominal membership in Anglican Christ Church, all encouraged him to build and sustain firm ties to non-Quakers. These genuine friendships, so important in a whole series of Franklin's endeavors, included a few long-lived ties that spanned the 1730s to the 1770s. Just as in business and civic affairs, these relationships significantly underpinned Franklin's political career. Clearly, he enjoyed some degree of quiet political support from influential non-Quakers well into the 1750s. Even the more politically active who identified closely with the Proprietary party gave Franklin a good deal of leeway in the push and pull of mid-century Pennsylvania politics because of their enjoyment of working and socializing with him, their admiration for his acuity in his sparring with Governor Morris, their knowledge that Franklin was no Quaker, and their belief that anyone as committed to the defense of Pennsylvania as he would surely drift their way. Yet Franklin never became more than a guarded associate of the political insiders within the Proprietary coterie.

The central thread of Franklin's politics lay, not with friends, but with Friends, and with those like himself, a friend of Friends. His chief political mentor, Andrew Hamilton, a nominal Anglican, had demonstrated the importance of working with Quakers of various views. Throughout the 1740s, Assembly clerk Franklin knew intimately the popular politics of House Speaker John Kinsey, Jr, and the Quaker Party. In the 1750s, Franklin, elected with Quaker Party support, quickly became its voice, practicing a punditry that enhanced his leadership role and influencing the re-making of the Quaker Party as a number of strict Friends abandoned elected office. This profile raises the main question about Franklin's Pennsylvania politics: How did he build and sustain that long-lived Quaker confidence and support, particularly in light of his role as principal architect of Pennsylvania's wartime mobilizations? The answer lies with Franklin's values, beliefs, and concrete proposals, and with the careful way in which he articulated them, both as an expression and an amplification of a familiar, widely shared idiom of Pennsylvania politics.

Franklin's first two years of sustained residence in Pennsylvania coincided with the tail end of a generation long, often heated, public argument about the provincial constitution. A quick study – especially when exposed to creative political thinkers such as Andrew Hamilton, David Lloyd, James

Logan and Isaac Norris, Jr, and to the street and tavern conversation of the politically literate – Franklin soon realized that Pennsylvania enjoyed a unique constitution, which bestowed "singular Privileges" (PBF, 2: 35). Curiosity about the Pennsylvania past, attentive listening, and studious observation of the dynamics of government from his vantage point as Assembly clerk filled out his education. He came to understand how the combination of the Royal Charter and the 1701 Charter of Privileges gave Pennsylvania a unicameral legislature so that it might represent the "*Whole People*" in the face of the private interests that proprietors and their governors embodied (PBF, 6: 170). By the time he had matured out of his years of political apprenticeship, Franklin could expound and amplify: "The Crown ... [could] ... grant *additional* Liberties and Privileges, not used in England, but suited to the different Circumstances of different Colonies" (PBF, 6: 299). It was this view of the Pennsylvania constitution that conflated Assembly powers with popular privileges and advocated their augmentation that Franklin held tenaciously and elaborated during his days of active political leadership in Pennsylvania. Beyond that, he participated in the articulation and expansion of a set of principles and related policies that defined Pennsylvania's "singular" political culture.

Not surprisingly, one of the foremost of these was toleration. This principle lay deeply embedded in Quaker history, connected, through William Penn's writings, directly to Pennsylvania, ensconced in the colony's charters, exemplified in the hard-won practice of recognizing affirmations in an age of oaths, and expressed in immigration and related social complexities that produced at best "a medley of all Kinds of People and of all denominations" (as quoted in Tully, 1994: 292). Franklin returned to the theme of toleration repeatedly in various ruminations and expository pieces, reflecting what day-to-day life in Pennsylvania illustrated and reinforced. The most important direct expression Franklin gave to his concern for "tender consciences" appears in the scrupulous accommodation of conscientious objectors written into his various militia bills. Clearly, through 1776, he also opposed the re-imposition of oaths, and despite his Anglophilic disparagement of German immigrants at mid-century, accepted the "Mixed Multitude" that Quakers encouraged with their postulates of a common humanity (Schwartz, 1987).

Franklin also found it easy to endorse other fundamentals of the Quaker experiment: prosperity tightly tied to Quaker Pennsylvania, not only through the happenstance of its fertility, and the relatively continuous immigration of European settlers that the Holy Experiment attracted, but also because of particular policies the Assembly adopted. The most notable of these created a provincial loan office to manage the colony's paper currency and the interest payments and tax collections that supported it. Established before Franklin took up residence in Philadelphia, the loan office quickly evolved into a bulwark of Assembly and Quaker

Party power. It provided revenue for the Assembly and a variety of patronage possibilities for those who ran it. Freeholders greatly appreciated the availability of mortgages, and the absence of provincial property taxes that the loan office's revenue stream made possible. Low taxes, loans, a sound currency – all were linked to popular political power and a vision of prosperity. As a young newcomer intent on ' "becoming-a-Pennsylvanian," Franklin saw and appreciated this nexus. Years later as a leading politician, he rhetorically emphasized it as a signature Quaker Party issue, even as he occasionally reflected on the implications of such policies for a wider British colonial world.

Of various other aspects of provincial political identity that Franklin picked up on and in the light of quandaries of the day refracted in compelling ways, the most significant involved peace and war. The context of much of Franklin's political creativity resulted from the plain fact that, no matter how contested, the public face of Pennsylvania was the Quaker inspired one of peace and tranquility. However disparate the groups that gathered together under the capacious tent of popular politics – strict pacifists; a bevy of Quakers, Mennonites and others whose convictions of "tender conscience" were inchoate, untested and "unsteady"; Quaker legislators and councilors open to voting money for the "King's use" in wartime and possibly under the immediate threat of violence; and a heterogeneous population of the "Quakerized" – those individuals who had accommodated and, in some cases, acculturated to, various of Friends' practices and attitudes, projected Quaker ownership and embodied the Quaker promise to seek peace (Tully, 1994: 287–288, 297–299). Franklin certainly recognized the value of this vision. At times he embraced that vision and, at other times, accommodated it, in his various ruminations on virtue and commerce, in his involvement in civic projects, and in his understanding of the day-to-day and diplomatic dimensions of native relations. But as a realist, as he could on occasion speak of natural rights while comfortably living with their attenuation in domestic affairs, so, too, in the international context, could Franklin take the view that, while valuable peaceful enclaves such as Pennsylvania deserved continuance, they should protect themselves when predators threatened with cannon or took up tomahawk.

Arguably, Franklin's political genius appeared most vividly in his finding a way for Pennsylvania's Quaker-led Assembly and the politics of peace it espoused to accommodate rather than capitulate to the exigencies of war. The absence of a compulsory militia constituted an essential component for peaceful Pennsylvania. Yet the French and allied native advance into the Ohio country, and subsequent native attacks on Pennsylvania frontier settlers in the early months of the Great War for Empire, ignited overwhelming public demand for organized military resistance. Franklin's answer consisted of a variation of the voluntary Association of 1747-1748. In 1756, the Assembly passed a Franklin-drafted Militia Act that provided for a government-sanctioned citizen militia, led by gubernatorial-commissioned but elected officers both at the company and regimental level. It also – and this was crucial – allowed both those of tender conscience and those who disagreed with the officer-drafted articles of discipline to decline participation. Dismissed as a "Joke" by Governor Morris (who signed it, in part, to prove it so), derided and vetoed by the Board of Trade a year later, for Franklin the Militia Act fashioned a political success (Tully, 1986, 1994: 293). It brought substantial participation and encouraged the self-identification of individuals and groups willing to sign up as short-term paid, "Provincial Troops," or "rangers" who did most of the frontier fighting (PBF, 7: 52). More importantly, it squared the circle, allowing the bellicose to act out their claim of a scripture-based right to fight and the proponents of peace a way to avoid picking up arms. Along with his sponsorship of currency, excise, and direct taxation bills to finance the war, the Militia Act allowed Franklin to combine tradition, innovation, and anti-proprietary politics in a way that many provincials could construe as a commonsense extension of the Quaker approach to their custodianship of provincial Pennsylvania.

Franklin's consummate political skill clearly shows in his explications of these wartime policies in ways that elucidated the major themes of Quaker politics: guarding Pennsylvania's unique constitution; defending and extending the Assembly's powers and privileges; reinforcing the conflation of "the people" and the Assembly; dismissing the governors as agents of private interests; implying, thereby, that popular institutions were, by default, the government; advocating toleration in its multiple manifestations, such as respect for affirmations, peace testimonies, or a non-coercive militia; calling up, in visions of "Vassalage," vivid memories of lordly European tyranny – taxes, military conscription, officials beholding to the power of inherited place (PBF, 6: 162); stressing the underpinnings of Pennsylvania's prosperity – credit, low taxes, a responsible public loan office; comparing the responsibly run public loan office with the private, closed proprietary land office; and defending habits of accommodation and peace. Thus we see in the mind of mid-century, middle-aged Franklin a comprehensive understanding of Pennsylvania's past, the continuity of its political culture, and an attendant restatement, clarification, and elaboration of the politics of "civil Quakerism" (Tully, 1986, 1994: 257–309).

Identifying Franklin as a major spokesperson for civil Quakerism does not deny his familiarity with a variety of other early modern political idioms and strands of thought. But frequently the operative word in his political thinking is "use." The standard British rhetoric of rights and privileges, for example, often appears as opportunistic verbal sallies useful in making the point of the moment in relation to Franklin's encompassing articulation of provincial political dynamics. This habit of selectively appropriating what was useful and at hand manifests itself most clearly in situations in which he drew on his familiarity with Massachusetts' affairs, to give himself short run credibility while he mastered the nuances of civil Quakerism. At the same time, he was as multi-lingual metaphorically as he was in fact, and his literary talents and scientific accomplishments, exemplified in his contributions to various Euro/Atlantic intellectual circles, illustrate the multi-dimensional character of his mind. Because of this, more easily than many, Franklin may get swept up in the fashionable Atlantic World current that privileges generalized shared discourses drawn from its huge and fluid catch basin of inter-textualities. It is easy to forget that the grounding of Franklin's politics through 1765 remained, at bedrock level, intensely provincial.

To posit Franklin as a prominent articulator of civil Quakerism elicits an obvious rejoinder. Franklin was no Quaker, and certainly character, interests, beliefs, and behavior, all tell us that. *But* he was a fellow traveler of an exceptionally intimate kind. It was not one of John Adams's imaginings when, during the early Revolutionary years, he remarked, "the Friends believed him [Franklin] a wet Quaker" (as quoted in Weinberger, 2005: 10). Throughout Franklin's Pennsylvania decades, Quakers were everywhere in his life. Beginning with merchant Thomas Denham, a multitude of Friends show up in Franklin's writings, in telling vignettes; they populated many of his most vital associational civic groups; they acted as critical links in the lines of communication he established both with hinterland residents and overseas correspondents; and as Franklin increasingly absented himself from Philadelphia, they remained among his critical contacts back home. All of this the pun-loving Franklin acknowledged with the testamentary phrase "so many Friends among them."

Between 1726 and 1757, during the crucial decades in which Franklin matured from a 21-year-old runaway to a 51-year-old provincial of unparalleled stature, Quakerism pervaded Pennsylvania society. While a predisposition to incorporate the distancing habits of speculation and experimentation into his broader life formed an essential part of Franklin, that characteristic always coexisted in tension with a mind and emotions open to the immediacy of political conviction. In the Pennsylvania of his day, the political Franklin, the aspiring Franklin, and the intense, '"becoming-Pennsylvanian" Franklin *required* the working out of a comfortable cohabitation with Quakerism. Fortunately for Franklin, the second quarter of the eighteenth century made that relatively easy. During the late seventeenth and early eighteenth centuries, Pennsylvania harbored a "made in America" brand of Quakerism, which had breadth and easily merged with and reinforced the better-known years of so-called "quietism" that coincided with Franklin's Pennsylvania residency (R.M. Jones, 1921; Tully, 1977, 1994; Bronner, 1986; Vann, 1986). In these decades, the boundaries between Quakers and their many non-Quaker neighbors relating everyday practices of sociability, consumerism, and even marriage became more blurred, and more permeable than during and after the upcoming Quaker Reformation. Influence flowed both ways, but the overall tone of Pennsylvania society was, as contemporaries observed, thoroughly

"Quakerized." The Quakerization of the province, crucial to Franklin's ability to assert himself through his Quaker connections, embodied a correlate: he, like many others, was Quakerized in return. One can see the pattern occasionally in his diction: in the uses of silence that he mastered so well while sitting as clerk in the Quaker Assembly; in his various accommodations to, and inclusions of women and women's voices; in his educational emphasis on the practical and experimental; and in his aversion to sustained philosophical flights. This is not the place to sort out the relationship between Franklin and Friends in terms of influence, confluence and difference, but simply to make the point that the Quakerized character of colonial Pennsylvania created a powerful, enveloping environment that nourished Franklin's formulations and practice of the politics of civil Quakerism as well as some of his complementary habits of mind.

The heavy weight of historiography that insistently frames Franklin within the national tale of cultural and political Americanization raises the question, of course, of the relationship between his Pennsylvania political experiences and his later, London-based politics (Thayer, 1953; Hutson, 1972; Wright, 1986; Jennings, 1996; Brands, 2000; Campbell, 1999; Isaacson, 2003; Weinberger, 2005; Lemay, 2006b; Pangle, 2007). That, like Franklin's Quakerization, presents a complicated issue, ill served by sound-bite sureties. Nonetheless, one or two observations are apposite. The most repeated theme of Franklinian political literature is how his colonial politics prefigured the American Revolution, by showcasing "democratic" thought and practice, and by displaying a predilection for "independence" and "self-determination." Observers have picked out salient signifiers from as far afield as the New England of Franklin's father's generation through his second London residency to make their case. One of the most noted of these was Franklin's militia schemes of 1747–1748 and 1755–1756. These experiments are often cast as an anticipation of Revolutionary militia organizations, which sprang from the constituent power of "the People" in contradistinction to the traditional top-down organization of the militia that reflected established patterns of hierarchy, patronage, and authority, and reinforced existing royal legitimacy. To be sure contemporaries such as William Smith, Thomas Penn, and their allies saw Franklin's militias, along with Assembly appointed commissioners in charge of wartime appropriations, and the "mobocracy" of the Paxton Boys and their provincial precursors (particularly in the light of the recent "forty-five," the last in a series of Jacobite uprisings in Britain) as illustrative of a subversive, populist strand of Pennsylvania politics that if encouraged or unchallenged would foster an intolerable level of autonomy. Understandably, modern American historians, with eyes fixed on Franklin and the Revolution, tend to pick up on these Franklin contemporaries, and take their views to be an expression of prescient and credible Toryism that prove an "American" heartbeat strong in the eighteenth-century colonies.

Certainly Franklin's contemporary critics deserve to be taken seriously when they repeatedly accused him of harboring "a Republican disposition and leveling Principles," of advocating "independency," a "pure republic," or a "Common Wealth" or of aspiring to be a "CROMWELL" intent on fostering "Democracy" and "republicanism" (Ketcham, 1963: 426; Hutson, 1969: 309n; PBF, 6: 196, 3: 186n; Tully, 1994: 111). Obviously, in doing so, they were harking back to the radicalisms that the previous century's English Civil War had unleashed. Among the most successful of the wild-eyed extremists of that era were Friends, who, when they came to Pennsylvania, wove New World expressions and mutations of Friends' ethos into the socio/politico/economic fabric of *their* province. Although his occasional use of such terms as "new-modell'd" indicated Franklin could easily contend on these grounds, he was neither backward-looking nor doctrinaire (PBF, 11: 294). *But* neither was he clairvoyant. Franklin steadfastly held that, absent proprietary meddling, Pennsylvania society worked very well. As he put it, Pennsylvania was "One of the happiest Countries at this Time in the World" (PBF, 3: 305). It was an ordered world, with room to be *sui generis* under the umbrella of monarchical authority. He thought irrelevant any reservations that contemporaries might have about his version of civil Quakerism because it manifested Friends radicalism. He felt this particularly, both because of his fundamental, federalist view of the *de facto* Imperial constitution (in contradistinction to the British and various colonial constitutions) and because by mid-century, civil Quakerism had evolved into a *conservative* provincial orthodoxy – protective of its success in politics, diplomacy, economics, and religious affairs, buttressed by the well-known cultural forces of Anglicization, and protected by monarchical-based might and related standards of justice (Greene, 1986; G.S. Wood, 2004).

Franklin embodied both conservative and radical strands. His expansive conceptual creativity and openness to the tsunami of Britishness that the successes of the Seven Years War generated, and his receptiveness to the multitudinous flatteries of gentry/metropolitan inclusion, invited him to experiment with a new London home just as his visceral aversion to the provincial politics of stalemate reached its apex and provided him with an impetus to leave. At the same time, beginning in the mid-1750s, Franklin dismissed Pennsylvania "*Quakerism* (as to the matter of Defense)" out of hand as a tenable political doctrine. Once in London he also refused to cooperate with the more conscientious English Friends who represented the Yearly Meeting there and disagreed with his strategy (A. Olson, 1993; PBF, 6: 171). As the 1760s gave way to the 1770s, he found himself increasingly distanced from Friends whose public reputation came to be associated more and more, as a result of the Quaker Reformation, with that "*Quakerism*," and with their Society's growing emphasis on a related brand of court-centered, conciliatory politics. However, Franklin continued to hold fast to many of the remaining, deeply rooted, provincially conservative radicalisms of civil Quakerism. Traditional Pennsylvania, more radical in its structural accommodation and practice of "in-door" politics than any of the other major colonies, merited a constitutive place in all of the empires Franklin envisaged in later life. Committed to his Pennsylvania "love," Franklin stood as fast as he judged feasible while the British forsook reason in an amorous embrace of the goddess of sovereignty.

At heart, what made possible these complexities of later Franklinian politics was his character. Franklin's ambition, guile, and vanity are, of course, as much a given as his talents. Beyond that, what best explains his politics is the intensity of his "love" for each of his homes, the dissociative capabilities that allowed him to live his serial lives so thoroughly, and his experimentalism. The last of these guided Franklin's thought through a succession of political iterations, including the Constitution. But beneath them all through 1790, his "love" for the "People" of Pennsylvania – for his "Country" as he put it in 1764 – with its distinctive conservative radicalism, proved to be a central strand of continuity and coherence. The choices that he made and the positions that he took later in life look a little different when we give full weight to the politics of Franklin's most creative years – and to his testimony that Pennsylvania was his maiden "Land of Liberty."

Note

1 Labaree, Leonard W. *et al.*, eds. (1959–). *The Papers of Benjamin Franklin*. 39 vols to date. New Haven, CT: Yale University Press. Hereafter referred to as PBF.

Further Reading

Brands, H.W. (2000). *The First American. The Life and Times of Benjamin Franklin*. New York, NY.
Hanna, William S. (1964). *Benjamin Franklin and Pennsylvania Politics*. Stanford, CA.
Houston, Alan (2008). *Benjamin Franklin and the Politics of Improvement*. New Haven, CT.
Hutson, James H. (1972). *Pennsylvania Politics, 1746–1770. The Movement for Royal Government and Its Consequences*. Princeton, NJ.
Lemay, J.A. Leo (2006–2009). *The Life of Benjamin Franklin*, 3 vols. Philadelphia, PA.
Middlekauff, Robert (1996). *Benjamin Franklin and His Enemies*. Berkeley, CA.
Morgan, Edmund S. (2002). *Benjamin Franklin*. New Haven, CT.
Smolenski, John (2010). *Friends and Strangers: The Making of a Creole Culture in Colonial Pennsylvania*. Philadelphia, PA.
Tully, Alan (1994). *Forming American Politics. Ideals, Interests, and Institutions in Colonial New York and Pennsylvania*. Baltimore, MD.
Waldstreicher, David (2004). *Runaway America. Benjamin Franklin, Slavery and the American Revolution*. New York, NY.
Wright, Esmond (1986). *Franklin of Philadelphia*. Cambridge, MA.

Chapter Seven

BENJAMIN FRANKLIN AND RELIGION

John Fea

Benjamin Franklin's religious beliefs have been much discussed and debated, both by Franklin's contemporaries and a host of scholars and pundits who have written about him since his death in 1790. John Adams, writing in his diary in 1779, said that Franklin's beliefs placed him among "Atheists, Deists, and Libertines." In 1820, popular evangelical biographer Mason Locke Weems described Franklin as a devout Christian who died staring, presumably in adoration, at a painting of Jesus on the cross. Joseph Priestley called Franklin a deist, while a 1796 writer for the *American Annual Register* said he "believed *nothing*." In an oft-cited essay published in 1933, D.H. Lawrence accused Franklin of manipulating religion to serve his bourgeois capitalist values.

Philosopher Kerry S. Walters, whose book *Benjamin Franklin and His Gods* holds historiographical supremacy among studies of Franklin's religion, notes that Franklin "wrote both too much and too little about his religious convictions" (Walters, 1999: 1). Of all the so-called founders save Jefferson, Franklin was most fascinated with the study of religion. Yet he never condensed his thoughts on the subject into a single volume. Franklin's religious musings are scattered throughout his voluminous writings, making it difficult for scholars to bring his convictions into a coherent whole. This, of course, has not prevented them from trying.

7.1 Early Religious Influences

There is nearly universal agreement among historians that Franklin's religious beliefs grew out of his intellectual dissatisfaction with New England

Calvinism. Franklin was baptized in Boston's Old South Church and his parents – Josiah and Abiah Franklin – would remain covenanted members of the church throughout their lives. As a child of Calvinists, Franklin was well-acquainted with the Bible and the orthodox theological grid through which it should be interpreted. Josiah had planned to send his son to Harvard in preparation for a career in the ministry but, according to most biographers, he could not afford to pay for Benjamin's education. Walter Isaacson, however, has suggested that economics had little to do with Josiah's decision to redirect Franklin's vocation away from the ministry and toward candle making (and later printing). Isaacson argues that Josiah thought that his son was not suited for the ministry due to his "skeptical, puckish, curious, irreverent" nature (Isaacson, 2003: 18–19).

Historians attribute Franklin's rejection of his childhood faith to his voracious reading habits. He modeled his writing style and moral convictions after the *Spectator*, a London coffeehouse journal written by Joseph Addison and Richard Steele. Franklin's reading of his father's books in "Polemic Divinity" resulted in more questions about his Calvinist upbringing than it did answers. By the age of fifteen he had become, in the words of his *Autobiography*, "a thoroughgoing deist." According to J.A. Leo Lemay, Franklin had embraced some form of deism by the time he wrote the last of his Silence Dogood letters in October 1722 (Lemay, 2006a: 168). Walters has explored Franklin's disdain for his father's religion by employing psychologist James Fowler's "stages of faith." According to Walters, "Franklin's broad reading in the exhilarating New Learning, his angry resentment at religious and paternal authority, and his rebellious adolescent quest for identity all began to crystallize somewhere around his fifteenth year, spawning a scornful repudiation of supernaturalism and a zealous embrace of rational religion" (Walters, 1999: 34).

While Franklin turned his back on the theological tenets of his boyhood Calvinism, it is now fashionable among some scholars to argue that he may have never fully abandoned certain aspects of the cultural Calvinism in which he was raised. As we will see below, this theme runs through much of current Franklin historiography. Walters maintains that Franklin's religious skepticism was "never assimilated into his everyday existence in the same way his boyhood Calvinism was" (Walters, 1999: 39). Douglas Anderson notes that the moral flavor of the Silence Dogood letters are informed by a combination of Cotton Mather's Calvinist-informed morality (as expounded in his *Bonifacius: An Essay Upon the Good*, 1710) and the more Enlightened moral philosophy of Anthony Ashley Cooper (the Third Earl of Shaftesbury) and the *Spectator* (Anderson, 1997: 24–25). Both Walters and Anderson paint a much more nuanced picture of Franklin's thought than earlier studies, such as Alfred Owen Aldridge's 1967 work, *Benjamin Franklin and Nature's God*, that portray him as either an "infidel" or an "atheist."

7.2 A Dissertation on Liberty and Necessity, Pleasure and Pain (1725)

Because of the scattered nature of Franklin's writings on religion, scholars who are interested in the subject have tended to gravitate to his early years. It was during his teenage years and into his twenties that Franklin wrote some of his most comprehensive reflections on the subject. A natural starting point is Franklin's 1725 tract, *A Dissertation on Liberty and Necessity, Pleasure and Pain*. Published anonymously at the age of nineteen during his first visit to London, the *Dissertation* was written in response to Franklin's reading of the 1725 edition of William Wollaston's *The Religion of Nature Delineated*. According to Aldridge, Franklin found Wollaston's deistic reasoning to be "too tame" and thus set out to write a refutation. Aldridge argues that the *Dissertation* reveals Franklin's early atheism. The work treated humankind as a cog in a machine. It argued that humans have no free will, suggested that there was no difference between virtue and vice, rejected a belief in an afterlife, and described a God that is "so impersonal that it is inseparable from natural law" (Aldridge, 1967a: 17–24). Most historians agree. Lemay writes that the "materialism" of the *Dissertation* would have been "shocking" to contemporary readers (Lemay, 2006a: 289). Walters calls it an "antihumanistic manifesto" (Walters, 1999: 53).

Walters, however, is careful to note that the *Dissertation* is not as extreme of a break from Franklin's Calvinist past as some scholars might suggest. He draws comparisons between the Calvinist doctrine of predestination and the *Dissertation*'s "mechanistic determinism." There are also similarities, Walters maintains, between the *Dissertation*'s rejection of human free will and the Calvinist doctrine of the depravity of humankind, a belief that prevents men and women from "overcoming the limitations imposed by original sin." The *Dissertation* affirms the existence of an all-powerful God who wills "every event in the physical realm." This God is not unlike the Calvinist God of Franklin's youth. Though Walters is unwilling to say that Franklin wrote the *Dissertation* with Calvinism in mind, he was still influenced by certain tenets of his childhood faith (Walters, 1999: 64).

While most scholars argue, to one degree or another, that the *Dissertation* is the most radical of all Franklin's writings on religion, the real interpretive debate centers on how representative the *Dissertation* is of the religious convictions Franklin would uphold later in life. As Aldridge and other scholars are quick to point out, Franklin would come to reject nearly everything he wrote in the *Dissertation*. He tried to destroy as many of the 100 published copies of the work that he could find. Explanations abound for why Franklin rejected the *Dissertation*.

Walters calls the *Dissertation* a "false start." Franklin would eventually repudiate this work because his religious convictions changed as he grew older. Walters describes Franklin's more mature religion with the phrase "theistic perspectivism." Such a view is based on the belief that God exists, that God's nature is "inaccessible to human reason or emotion," and that humans "represent God to themselves" as a means of establishing "some sort of contact with the divine" (Walters, 1999: 10). For Walters, Franklin lived "between two worlds": the Calvinism of his upbringing and the "antihumanism" of the *Dissertation*. Franklin came to see that the God of the *Dissertation* was incapable of providing "either the emotional comfort or existential security necessary for getting through life's trials." He would thus spend the rest of his religious life looking for a middle ground between a religion informed by Enlightenment reason and a religion that allowed for a God who had the potential of being active in the affairs of humankind (Walters, 1999: 64–66).

Elizabeth Dunn also questions the idea that Franklin was a deist, although she prefers to see a relative consistency between Franklin's views in the *Dissertation* and his later religious thought. The thread of consistency that held Franklin's beliefs together was his use of the philosophical argument from "design" to prove the existence of God. In the *Dissertation*, she argues, Franklin asserted that there is a "First Mover, who is called God, Maker of the Universe." Such a God is omniscient, omnipotent, benevolent, and has sovereign control over his creation. In an argument similar to Walters' view that Franklin maintained some of his childhood Calvinism, Dunn suggests that Franklin's rejection of the doctrine of free will is fitting with a creator-God who controls everything and holds the universe in place by his providence. Franklin's assertion that there is no distinction between good and evil should be interpreted in light of the theological presupposition that even evil could serve God's ultimate plan, "obliterating the difference between good and bad." Like other historians of Franklin's religion, Dunn concludes that the only reason Franklin turned his back on the *Dissertation* was because he was disturbed by the way some readers might interpret his argument, particularly as it relates to moral behavior and ethics (1987: 501–509).

Others, however, see a definite consistency between Franklin's views in the *Dissertation* and the religious convictions he would carry with him for the rest of his life. Lemay has argued that Franklin never gave up the nihilism of the *Dissertation*. The reference in the *Autobiography* to his attempt to destroy the existing copies did not mean that he abandoned the idea of the *Dissertation*, but rather became wiser and more prudent "about revealing his private opinions" to friends and family members who might be disappointed by his lack of faith. If anything, Franklin learned from writing the *Dissertation* that he was no longer interested in "metaphysics," preferring instead to focus his thinking on religion's practical use to society (Lemay, 2006a: 289–290).

Jerry Weinberger makes a more forceful argument along these lines. He challenges the notion, which is a popular interpretive strain in the works of

Aldridge, Walters and (to some degree) Lemay, as well as in the works of popular biographers such as Gordon Wood, Edmund Morgan, and Isaacson, that the Franklin who penned the *Dissertation* softened his atheism in favor of a more pragmatic religion that would benefit the moral climate of society. Scholars, Weinberger maintains, have been duped by Franklin's rejection of the *Dissertation* in his autobiography. Franklin never turned his back on the extreme skepticism of the *Dissertation* and, in fact, lied to the readers of his *Autobiography* whenever he discussed his "religious principles." Franklin was a man of many masks, but Weinberger claims to have "unmasked" him by showing the consistency of his religious thought (Weinberger, 2005: x–xix, 48–50).

7.3 Articles of Belief and Acts of Religion

Most historians agree that Franklin's next major piece of writing about religion, the "Articles of Belief and Acts of Religion" (1728), is distinguished from the *Dissertation on Liberty and Necessity* by the fact that it is, as Walters notes, a "private memorandum" meant to be used by Franklin during acts of personal devotion (Walters, 1999: 75). The Articles are a deeply worshipful piece meant to offer praise and adoration. They reflect "the alienation of a soul infinitely distant from God" (Walters, 1999: 75–78). Donald Meyer maintains that the Articles show that Franklin was less concerned with "the workings of an enormous machine than with seeing himself emotionally in some kind of relationship with a vastness that seems beyond human conceptualization." This piece is "less one of curiosity than of awe and wonder" (Meyer, 1987: 156). Dunn writes that Articles were written to "celebrate the goodness of God and the joy of worship." They capture Franklin's lifelong use of the argument from design to prove the existence of a First Cause that created the universe (E.E. Dunn, 1987: 509). Weinberger calls the Articles "bizarre," concluding that they were meant to be "deliberately funny" and "tongue in cheek" (Weinberger, 2005: 162, 164). Lemay suggests that we should take the Articles seriously as a legitimate attempt by Franklin to write a liturgy and practice it, even though it was not something in which he could find any certainty about God (Lemay, 2006a: 370).

Anderson argues that the Articles were informed by Franklin's reading of the seventeenth-century Puritan poet John Milton. Franklin quotes directly from Milton's doxological hymn in book 5 of *Paradise Lost*. His sections on "Adoration," "Petition," and "Thanks," and his quoting of the Eighteenth Psalm, suggests that Franklin used the Articles enhance his spiritual life. But unlike the Puritans, who had no problem with worshipping and adoring God in their private lives solely for the purpose of drawing closer to the Divine, Franklin's devotional thoughts were always connected to how the worship of God might prompt him "to become a social agent." For

Anderson, even Franklin's most personal reflection on the relationship between humans and their Creator was understood within a framework of social utility (D. Anderson, 1997: 65–70).

Most scholarship on Franklin's religion uses the Articles to discuss whether or not Franklin was a polytheist. Franklin writes that "the Infinite has created many Gods, vastly superior to Man, who can better conceive his Perfections than we, and return him a more rational and glorious Praise." Franklin adds that these Gods are immortal and rule over their own planets and solar systems. Interpretations on Franklin's supposed polytheism abound. Aldridge maintains that Franklin's understanding of a plurality of Gods, presiding over a plurality of worlds, reflects his belief in the classical idea of the "Great Chain of Being." He insists that Franklin never abandoned the polytheistic thought of the Articles (Aldridge, 1967: 25–27). Lemay describes Franklin's musings on multiple Gods as a "surprise," but in the end agrees with Aldridge. Lemay's Franklin was influenced by a belief in the "Great Chain of Being," which he may have learned from his reading of any number of eighteenth-century writers, including Locke, Addison and Steele, and Pope (Lemay, 2006a: 361).

Some scholars try to construct links between the doxological nature of the Articles and Franklin's reference to a plurality of gods. For Meyer, Franklin's gods were essential to the devotional nature of the Articles. Since the God who created the world was so distant to human beings, Franklin needed intermediate gods to connect with this "Great Mystery of Being" on a deeper level (Meyer, 1987: 157). Elizabeth Dunn makes a similar argument: "Intermediary gods resolved the discontinuity between an unfathomable Creator and the innate desire to know and worship a higher being" (1987: 511). Walters takes aim at Aldridge by arguing that Franklin was not a polytheist. He concludes that there is no evidence to suggest that Franklin carried these polytheistic ideas with him throughout his life. Polytheism was out of character for Franklin. Moreover, it is difficult, Walters notes, to trace the intellectual origins of this view in the books that Franklin read. Instead, like Meyer and Dunn, Walters concludes that Franklin used polytheistic language to help him make sense of God's remoteness. It was a "metaphorical attempt to talk about a distant God." Franklin's belief in subordinate gods was an attempt to make the one true God (Franklin's "First Cause") more "accessible to the mind and comforting to the heart than the mostly abstract Supreme Architect" (Walters, 1999: 79–87).

7.4 On the Providence of God in the Government of the World (1732)

In 1732, Franklin delivered a paper before the Junto, an intellectual circle of friends who met together in Philadelphia for the purpose of promoting mutual improvement, entitled "On the Providence of God in the

Government of the World." In this essay, one of the few Junto lectures that was not published, Franklin argued that humans did not need Christian theology or Biblical revelation to understand God. Instead, he assumed that there was a God who was the creator of the universe and then devoted his lecture to proving that God is providentially active in the affairs of human beings. Scholars have paid careful attention to the similarities and differences between "On the Providence of God" and the *Dissertation on Liberty and Necessity*. Elizabeth Dunn concludes that the "methodology" of both works is identical in the sense that they argue for the existence of God using natural theology or the argument from design (1987: 513). Owen Aldridge argues that "On Providence" moves "to the opposite extreme" of the *Dissertation* in the sense that Franklin affirms human beings have free will (Aldridge, 1967: 34). Similar arguments are made by Walters (1999: 97) and Lemay (2006a: 345). Weinberger cannot let the differing views on free will in these two texts go without commentary. He calls "On the Providence of God" a "comically absurd" essay that is an "insult to human reason." It is the "mirror image" of the *Dissertation* and thus cannot conceivably represent Franklin's true thoughts on the matter. He adds: "We would have to take Franklin for a dunce to think he ever took this argument seriously" (Weinberger, 2005: 166–170). Similarly, but with less bravado, Lemay concludes that "On the Providence of God" does not make sense. Franklin's attempts at reconciling free will and divine sovereignty are filled with logical contradictions (Lemay, 2006a: 355).

Scholars agree that "On the Providence of God" is also a significant departure from Franklin's previous religious writings because it affirms a belief in an active God. Donald Meyer maintains that "Franklin wanted to believe in both the efficacy of prayer and the afterlife." Such an interest in prayer and the intervention of the divine into human affairs would remain a part of Franklin's belief system for the rest of his life. This kind of divine activism was evident, among other places, in his request for prayer at the Constitutional Convention in 1787 (1987: 159). Aldridge makes a similar argument, but claims that Franklin's belief in prayer and an active God was "a position from which he later more than once retreated when beset by doubt." He also suggests that since "On the Providence of God" was written for the Junto, Franklin could not reveal his true religious convictions in the way that he had in the anonymous *Dissertation* because his reputation as a Philadelphia citizen and businessman was at stake. In a remark that seems to completely ignore the dominance of Christian orthodox religion in colonial America, Aldridge concludes that Franklin's belief in an active and providential God was "extremely rare in the eighteenth-century, except in the works of a few orthodox Christian theologians" (Aldridge, 1967: 34–38).

Kerry Walters departs from the scholarly consensus when he makes the case that "On the Providence of God" is a defense of a "very orthodox doctrine of Calvinism." Franklin's doctrine of providence was more than just a synonym for "natural design." Rather, by embracing the belief that

God "sometimes interferes by his particular Providence," Franklin was turning "away from deism's insistence that the doctrine of special providences insults the deity and destroys the immutability of the natural order" (Walters, 1999: 97–104). Indeed, even Aldridge admits that Franklin's view of Providence was not common among contemporary deists (Aldridge, 1967: 38). For Walters, "On the Providence of God" was just another example of Franklin's life-long wavering between Enlightenment religion and Calvinism.

"On the Providence of God" was one of the first Franklin writings to explicitly argue for the social usefulness of religious belief. Nearly all scholars are in agreement on this point. With free will, Franklin argued, comes civic responsibility. If Franklin's God was willing to set aside his control over the universe in order to give human beings free will, then such a sacrificial act should serve as a model for humans to set aside their own interests for the good of others (D. Anderson, 1997: 79). When men and women express their love for God, give him thanks, and make petitions to him, such religious practice would become a regulator of human action resulting in benevolence to others (Lemay, 2006a: 354). Franklin's defense of the afterlife in "On the Providence of God," and his belief in the efficacy of prayer, were meant to serve moral and social purposes (D. Meyer, 1987: 159).

7.5 The Hemphill Affair (1735) and the "Zealous Presbyterians"

In the wake of "On the Providence of God," Franklin turned his attention to the social utility of religion. Though scholars such as Lemay, Aldridge, and Weinberger have argued that Franklin never gave up the skepticism of the *Dissertation on Liberty and Necessity*, he did not stop dabbling in questions of "metaphysics." From this point forward his religious writings focus almost entirely on the role that religion might play in the Enlightenment quest for moral and social improvement. This new emphasis is seen clearly in his decision to come to the aid of Presbyterian clergyman Samuel Hemphill.

In 1734, the Presbyterian Church in Philadelphia – a church that Franklin often attended – installed Samuel Hemphill, a minister from Ireland, to assist its aging minister, Jedidiah Andrews. Franklin had never liked Andrews' preaching. He thought the veteran minister was more concerned about turning his congregation into good Presbyterians than he was in leading them along the path of public virtue. Hemphill, who was popular among the congregation and, at least according to Franklin, a better preacher than Andrews, taught a moral message that was more akin to Franklin's convictions about the usefulness of religion to society. Hemphill's moral sermons, however, got him in trouble with the Synod. Andrews and others accused him of preaching unorthodox sermons that placed too much emphasis on human works as a means of salvation. When Andrews reported Hemphill to the Synod, claiming that he was a heretic, Franklin came to the new minister's defense. He used his newspaper, *The Pennsylvania Gazette,* and his printing press to publish articles and pamphlets arguing that it was Hemphill, not Andrews or the Synod, who was practicing true Christianity. Edmund Morgan has called Franklin's articles in defense of Hemphill "the clearest statement he ever made about Christianity as he thought it ought to be" (2002: 21).

Melvin Buxbaum emphasizes Franklin's anger during the course of the Hemphill Affair. Franklin was "different from the kindly friend to all religion created in the *Autobiography*" and his attacks on Andrews and the Philadelphia Synod go "far beyond the 'rubs' Silence Dogood gave the Boston Establishment." Buxbaum portrays Franklin as a man who wanted to convince the world of the injustice shown to Hemphill. In order to do so he expanded his argument to attack not only Andrews and the members of the Synod, but all Protestant clergy. Buxbaum accuses Franklin of engaging in the "fussy nit-picking and long-winded logic chopping he often claimed to despise." Generally, Buxbaum agrees with most scholars that Franklin despised Presbyterians because of their failure to transfer their theological beliefs into a system of morality that would benefit society (Buxbaum, 1975: 97–111). Jerry Weinberger utilizes much of Buxbaum's argument, implying that Franklin's true colors – a distrust of Calvinist dogma and a hatred of Presbyterians – came through clearly in his defense of Hemphill (Weinberger, 2005: 279–281).

Walters sees Franklin's attack on Andrews, the Presbyterians, and the clergy in general as partly autobiographical. The failure of traditional churches to provide a liturgy untainted by dogma had prompted him to write his own private liturgy in the form of the "Articles of Belief and Acts of Religion" in 1728. Franklin had staked out his own religious path and now, in his support of Hemphill, "defended the right of others to do likewise" (D. Anderson makes a similar argument (1997: 81)). For Walters, Franklin's involvement in the Hemphill Affair was an attempt to defend his belief in liberty of conscience in matters of religion. Franklin believed that the Presbyterian Church's stand in the Hemphill undermined the possibility of religious dialogue, a practice that he believed to be the key to religious pluralism. A kind of pluralism rooted in vigorous conversation and civil discussion was replaced by dogmatism and "sectarian disagreement." Walters sees the Hemphill Affair as another turning point in Franklin's religious life. From this point forward Franklin would avoid religious controversy. He would also leave the Presbyterian Church and become a pewholder in Christ Church, an Anglican congregation that emphasized the moral contributions that religion made to society and took a more latitudinarian approach to religious differences (Walters, 1999: 138–141).

Lemay has offered the most thorough treatment to date of Franklin's role in the Hemphill Affair. First, he sees Franklin's involvement in this ecclesiastical trial as "among his errors as a young man" and suggests that Franklin "foolishly opposed public opinion" by supporting the controversial clergyman. Second, Lemay argues that the Hemphill Affair reveals the persistence of Franklin's skepticism that he first revealed in the *Dissertation on Liberty and Necessity*. Finally, Lemay offers several interesting interpretive suggestions for why Franklin got involved in this case in the first place. He suggests that Franklin's defense of Hemphill was linked to an illness he was suffering around the time of the trial. This illness may have led Franklin to see the Hemphill case as a last chance before he died to share his views about religious toleration and the importance of religion to the moral improvement of society. Lemay also suggests that the illness may have clouded Franklin's judgment, thus explaining why he was "impatient and irritable with the others' opinions" (Lemay, 2006b: 234, 238, 262).

Lemay also proposes that Franklin wrote his pamphlets defending Hemphill with his recently deceased brother in mind. James Franklin, the Boston printer who Benjamin was apprenticed to as a boy, had built a reputation in Boston as a staunch critic of the New England clergy. Despite their differences, which have been well covered by historians, Franklin kept in touch with his brother in Boston and maintained an affection for him after he left New England for Philadelphia. The Hemphill essays, Lemay suggests, may have been written to memorialize James. Another reason Franklin took up Hemphill's case may have been related to the fact that the moderator of the Philadelphia Synod's commission appointed to preside over the Hemphill heresy trial was Ebenezer Pemberton Jr, the son of Franklin's childhood minister in Boston. Franklin went to grammar school with Pemberton Jr, but following graduation their paths diverged dramatically. Pemberton went to Harvard, while Franklin went to work as an apprentice. According to Lemay, "thinking of Ebenezer Pemberton as Hemphill's judge may have brought back all the old resentments that Franklin felt when his father took him out of grammar school" and made him an artisan (Lemay, 2006b: 262–263).

Franklin would never get over his hostility to the Presbyterians of colonial Pennsylvania. As Buxbaum has shown most clearly, Franklin would continue to wage battles against Presbyterians over the leadership of the College of Philadelphia, the control of the Pennsylvania government, and the protection of Philadelphia against the rebellious Scots-Irish, particularly the famed Paxton Boys (Buxbaum, 1975: 153–219). While Buxbaum's *Benjamin Franklin and the Zealous Presbyterians* has held up quite well, a new treatment of Franklin and his relationship with colonial and revolutionary-era Presbyterians (and the role of Presbyterians in the American Revolution in the mid-Atlantic) is long overdue.

7.6 Franklin, George Whitefield, and Eighteenth-Century Evangelicalism

Much as has been made of Benjamin Franklin's relationship with evangelical revivalist George Whitefield, the man who historian Harry Stout has dubbed "Anglo-America's first modern celebrity" (Stout, 1991: xiii). Franklin first preached in Philadelphia in November 1739 and Franklin heard him two days later, noting the "extraordinary Influence of his Oratory on his hearers." This was not the last time Franklin would be attracted to a Whitefield sermon. Whitefield would eventually contract Franklin to print his journals and Franklin would prove to be a supporter of Whitefield's evangelistic efforts in Philadelphia. Despite their fundamental differences on the subject of religion, they would strike up a friendship that would last until Whitefield's death in 1770. As Stout puts it, "Franklin forever encouraged Whitefield to look after the state of his badly deteriorating health, while Whitefield continually encouraged Franklin to look after the state of his badly deteriorating soul" (Stout, 1991: 222). Whitefield was a regular guest in the Franklin home. They worked together in the founding of the Philadelphia Academy and even discussed the possibility of establishing a colony in Ohio.

What inspired this friendship between two of the most popular public figures in the British-American colonies? Walter Isaacson suggests that Franklin was attracted to Whitefield because of the revivalist's practice of "shaking up the local establishment." Franklin enjoyed watching local clergyman squirm when Whitefield came into town and challenged their commitment to the gospel (Isaacson, 2003: 111). Aldridge and Stout suggest in passing that Whitefield, who was shy, awkward, and looking for wife, may have been attracted to the ease in which Franklin behaved among female company (Aldridge, 1967: 106; Stout, 1991: 221). Stout argues that Franklin and Whitefield's friendship was based on a mutual love and common life experiences. Both were self-made men who would eventually have their share of marital problems and both had a sense of how to succeed in the culture of mid-eighteenth-century America (Stout, 1991: 222–233).

Buxbaum claims that the *Autobiography*[8] in which Franklin speaks of Whitefield in very positive terms, has skewed our understanding of the Franklin–Whitefield relationship. Though Franklin supported Whitefield during his earliest tours of Philadelphia, he eventually withdrew his support. According to Buxbaum, Whitefield's beliefs about original sin "galled" Franklin, both "intellectually and morally." Moreover, Whitefield upheld the same Calvinist beliefs that Franklin had openly rejected in his 1735 defense of Samuel Hemphill. Buxbaum also suggests that Franklin grew tired of Whitefield's arrogant personality. In other words, the more the evangelical (New Side) wing of the Presbyterian Church embraced

Whitefield, the less Franklin felt comfortable supporting him. Franklin and Whitefield kept up a correspondence and continued to work together on projects that would be mutually beneficial, but their theological and personality differences were just too strong to merit any kind of deep or lasting friendship (Buxbaum, 1975: 138–145).

Frank Lambert offers a more economic view of the Franklin–Whitefield friendship. As he suggests, Franklin saw Whitefield as "good business as well as good news." Franklin knew the power of print in eighteenth-century America, but so did Whitefield. Rather than focusing entirely on Whitefield's oratory skills, Lambert calls our attention to the way Whitefield used print to promote himself and his message. Franklin, who never shied away from self-promotion, would have certainly been impressed with Whitefield's skill at selling himself. The two men worked together, with the help of Whitefield's assistant William Seward, to stage the greatest public relations campaign in the history of the British-American colonies. Lambert concludes that "any explanation of the friendship must begin with Whitefield's impact on Franklin's printing business." Though Lambert does not deny the fact that Franklin and Whitefield developed a real friendship based on mutual affection, their relationship was born and sustained through their business relationship: "Franklin made money, Whitefield gained souls, and the two men became friends" (Lambert, 1993: 529–554).

Other scholars argue that Franklin and Whitefield became close friends because they both championed moral reform and religious ecumenism. Walters notes that Whitefield's commitment to building schools, caring for orphans, and criticizing slaveholders for their cruel treatment of slaves, merged very well with Franklin's convictions on the social utility of religion. They both believed, according to Walters, "that the marrow of true religion is in doing good and pursing one's own god with courage and sincerity…" Franklin could "ignore Whitefield's enthusiasm and conventional religious language while applauding his good work" (Walters, 1999: 142–145). Aldridge, Landsman, Lemay, and Stout make identical arguments. But Walters, more than any other writer on the Franklin–Whitefield friendship, reminds us that both men were eager to "promote an ecumenical spirit of religious tolerance." Franklin may not have accepted Whitefield's evangelicalism, but he did admire the preacher's message for its simplicity and its lack of "arcane theology." The Grand Itinerant's message transcended denominational differences (Walters, 1999: 143–145).

7.7 Franklin and the Quakers

Most of Franklin's writings about the Society of Friends, the religious sect that came to his aid when he first arrived in Philadelphia as a runaway apprentice from Boston, were more reflections on Quaker political power than they were statements of Quaker religious belief. Franklin's career in Pennsylvania politics was marked by long-standing arguments against Friends because their pacifism prevented them from contributing to the military defense of the colony. Two of Philadelphia's leading Quakers – James Logan and Isaac Norris Jr. – served as unofficial political mentors to Franklin. He would maintain lifelong friendships with Quaker politicians, merchants, and scientists. Some historians have even suggested that Franklin's success as a businessman and his proto-capitalism was informed entirely by his embrace of Quaker business principles such as industry and frugality. Franklin even passed himself off as a Quakers during his stint as an American diplomat in Paris.

Franklin did, however, occasionally write about Quaker religion. He visited a Quaker meeting once and promptly fell asleep during the silence that was so characteristic of Quaker worship. Jacquelyn Miller suggests that Franklin "disliked" Quakerism because it upheld sectarianism principles such as pacifism that were not conductive to the public good of Pennsylvania (1990: 327–331). Aldridge argues that Franklin admired Quakerism because of its affirmation of simplicity, frugality, anti-slavery, and humanitarianism (Aldridge, 1967: 145). Walters concurs. Franklin liked Quakerism because it rejected complicated creeds, championed equality, and did not preach dogmatism. David Waldstreicher notes that Franklin developed close relationships with anti-slavery Quakers such Anthony Benezet and Benjamin Lay despite the fact that his printing business benefited from slave labor (2004: 79–83).

7.8 Moral Perfection and the Art of Virtue

As we have seen, in the years following the *Dissertation on Liberty and Necessity*, Franklin's religious beliefs always took a backseat to the quest for moral improvement or, as Douglas Anderson writes, "the transformation of pure belief into active principle." In fact, most historians have concluded that the pursuit of virtue and "moral perfection" *was* Franklin's religion. Scholarly treatment of the relationship between religion and morality in Franklin's thought and life focuses almost entirely upon the prologue (the only portion that remains extant) of the "Plan of Conduct" and his *Autobiographical* reflections on the "Art of Virtue," including his "bold and arduous Project of arriving at moral Perfection" (Franklin 1987a: 1383). Franklin wrote the Plan in 1726 during the return voyage of his first trip to London. Historians agree that it was written because Franklin was experiencing guilty feelings about his personal behavior in London and had grown disgusted over the immoral acts of his friends. Sometime around 1731 or 1732 he proposed his moral perfection project. Readers of the *Autobiography* recall that Franklin strove to reach this state of perfection by habitually applying thirteen virtues – temperance, silence, order, resolution, frugality, industry, sincerity, justice, moderation, cleanliness, tranquility, chastity, and humility – to his daily behavior. The *Autobiography* also described Franklin's interest in composing a small book, "The Art of Virtue," to serve as a handy guide for anyone interested in pursuing a moral life. Though Franklin apparently spent considerable time working on this proposed volume, he would never complete it.

Walters suggests that Franklin's "Plan of Conduct," which focused on the virtues of frugality, sincerity, and charity, was influenced by Daniel Defoe's *An Essay upon Projects* (1697) and Cotton Mather's *Bonifacius* (1710). Both books were part of his father's personal library. *An Essay upon Projects* extolled Enlightenment beliefs in self-improvement by focusing on the way that public and private morality is informed by sociability and community. Like *An Essay upon Projects*, Mather's *Bonifacius* also connected the moral advancement of society to institutions such as voluntary societies, the family, and the church. According to Walters, the "Plan of Conduct," which was informed by Defoe and Mather, would shape Franklin's future civic projects in Philadelphia (Walters, 1999: 114–115).

Although Franklin believed that reason was essential to scientific advancement, Walters argues that he did not feel the same way about the role of reason in the science of morals. More than any other scholar of Franklin's religious and moral thought, Walters stressed Franklin's pessimistic view of human nature and the inability of human reason to arrive at moral precepts. Because Franklin rejected strongly the Christian doctrine of original sin, he was forced to explain his dour understanding of human nature without relying upon theology. According to Walters, Franklin turned to Hobbes's *Leviathan* and Mandeville's *Fable of the Bees* to explain humankind's natural propensity for viciousness and self-interest. Much of Franklin's moral writings were thus written to "tame" or "redeem" human nature. Parting ways with D.H. Lawrence's assault on Franklin's religious and moral writings, Walters argues that Franklin was not as much concerned with religion and virtue because it helped him pursue ambition and wealth, but instead thought it was the only way of providing an antidote to the inherent self-interest of human beings. In this sense, Franklin's moral thought was a sort of secular Calvinism (Walters, 1999: 117–125). Religion scholar David Holmes takes a similar, though much less developed, view of Franklin's pessimism about human nature (Holmes, 2006: 54–55).

Alan Houston takes a slightly different approach. Instead of drawing on Defoe, New England Calvinists, or a host of other eighteenth-century moral philosophers, Houston argues that the moral thought of Franklin's moral writings are based on John Locke's idea that morality depends on an individual's capacity to suspend acting upon the inherent desires and passions that all human beings possess. In addition to Franklin's moral writings referenced above, Houston explains Franklin's understanding of virtue through two letters he wrote to his parents in 1738. In response to his parents' concern about his rejection of Calvinist orthodoxy, Franklin once again defended the moral usefulness of a generic religion that transcended theological and denominational differences (this is the same kind of religion and morality that he extolled three years earlier in his defense of Reverend Samuel Hemphill). Houston references the latitudinarian religious principles of Freemasonry as just one example of the kind of religion he espoused (Houston, 2008: 33–39).

Douglas Anderson's discussion of Franklin's ethical beliefs is geared heavily toward the moral maxims of *Poor Richard's Almanac*, a work that he claims is preoccupied with moral reform. For Anderson, Franklin's views, both in the *Almanac* and generally, are informed by British moral philosophers such as Shaftesbury and Francis Hutcheson. He describes the *Almanac* as a work in sympathy with Shaftesbury's "home spun" model of ethical and spiritual self-examination. Franklin was even influenced by Shaftesbury's belief in the "therapeutic effect of good humor." Anderson also situates the character or "poor" Richard Saunders in the moral world of the Junto, a club with a common goal of moral improvement, as evidenced in some of Franklin's private writings such as the "Plan of Conduct" and the "Art of Virtue." In one of the more innovative interpretations of *Poor Richard's Almanac*, Anderson suggests that the almanac is a "moral discourse with the calendar," particularly the religious calendar (1997: 103–109).

Ned Landsman connects the intellectual, moral, and religious dimensions of Franklin's thought to the eighteenth-century "tradesman's Enlightenment." This version of the Enlightenment, which influenced many artisans in search of self-improvement and gentility, was defined by a blend of religious skepticism and moral striving. As part of this movement, Franklin preached economic success as a means of bettering society. Virtues such as diligence, thrift, industry, and sobriety were related to the values of eighteenth-century tradesmen. The Junto – a gathering of artisans concerned with their own moral and economic development – was the primary intellectual environment where Franklin's moral thinking merged with his vocation as a printer. Tradesmen societies, both in Great Britain and America, had a reputation for independent thinking and theological heterodoxy. Although few of these societies promoted Deism or unbelief, they did place the practice of moral behavior over the tenets of religious creedalism (Landsman, 1997: 143–147).

Leo Lemay focused his attention on the Aristotelian nature of Franklin's moral thinking. One of the primary ways in which Franklin distinguished himself from the ethical system of his Calvinist upbringing was by teaching that virtue was achieved through "discipline and the gradual formation of habits." Parting ways with his Puritan ancestors (and, I might add, his contemporary, Jonathan Edwards), Franklin believed that a conversion experience or special infusion of divine grace was not necessary for one to live a moral life. Yet, like Walters, Lemay maintains that the faith instilled in young Franklin by his parents may have had some influence on Franklin in the sense that his understanding of moral progress was not unlike the ethical striving found in the Puritan idea of Christian holiness or sanctification. Lemay also reminds us that Franklin was influenced by the idea that morality is often shaped by environment. On numerous occasions Franklin mentioned how his religious upbringing, his schooling in the morality of the Bible, and his belief in God provided him with a "tolerable Character" (Lemay, 2006b: 95–96).

7.9 Conclusion

Elizabeth Dunn has noted that Franklin's references to religion in his writing and in the *Autobiography* "reveal a religious system" that is "remarkable for its consistency through the upheavals of the eighteenth century" (1987: 521). Franklin took on many projects to try to make traditional creeds and prayers more accessible to people of all faiths. His generic religion was evident in several of his minor religious writings. *The Speech of Polly Baker* (1746) was written, according to Aldridge, as a deistical attack on the dogmatism of the clergy (Aldridge, 1967: 133–134). Sometime around 1760 Franklin revised the Lord's Prayer so that it could be presented to the public in a style void of antiquated language. Walters argues that his "more concise" and "equally expressive" version of the prayer reflected Franklin's generic brand of religion. Franklin wanted to show that no sect or denomination "has a monopoly on God talk" (Walters, 1999: 146). Similarly, in 1765 Franklin and Lord Le Despencer rewrote the Book of Common Prayer because they believed it was too long and filled with obscure theological references. Aldridge understands their edits of the text, especially their decision to omit or abbreviate long Old Testament passages (especially the Psalms), as a form of "deistical anti-Biblicism." Yet it should also be interpreted as a legitimate attempt to improve Anglican worship and is representative of Franklin's belief, as first put forth in the "Article of Belief and Acts of Worship," that a religious service should focus more on prayer and adoration than on sermons and the pronouncement of theological dogma (Aldridge, 1967: 170–174). According to Henry May, Franklin was most attracted to Anglicanism for these very reasons (May, 1976: 127).

In his "Dialogue Between Two Presbyterians," published in 1735 as part of his defense of Reverend Samuel Hemphill, Franklin wrote that "Morality and Virtue is the End ... and if the end be obtained it is no matter by what means." Whether Franklin was a deist, an adherent of "theistic perspectivism," an atheist, or a polytheist, historians all agree that he was ultimately a moralist who saw religion as essential to the promotion of societal virtue.

In this sense he was, as Henry May has described him, a "student of comparative religion" (May, 1976: 127).

Five weeks before his death, Franklin summarized his religious beliefs in an oft-quoted letter to Ezra Stiles. The pertinent part of that letter is worth citing below:

> Here is my Creed. I believe in one God, Creator of the Universe: That he governs the World by his Providence. That he ought to be worshipped. That the most acceptable Service we can render him, is doing good to his other Children. That the Soul of Man is immortal, and will be treated with Justice in another Life, respect(ing) its Conduct in this. These I take to be the fundamental Principles of all sound Religion, and I regard them as you do, in whatever Sect I meet with them.
>
> As to Jesus of Nazareth, my Opinion of whom you particularly desire, I think the System of Morals and his Religion, as he left them to us, the best the World ever saw or it likely to see; but I apprehend it has received various corrupting Changes, and I have, with most of the present Dissenters in England, some Doubts as to his Divinity; tho' it is a question I do not dogmatize upon, have never studied it, and think it needless to busy myself with it now, when I expect soon an Opportunity of knowing the Truth with less trouble.

The response, of course, was classic Franklin. As the historiography of his religion makes clear, Franklin does not easily conform to any eighteenth-century religious system. Future historians who attempt to label or pigeonhole him will have their work cut out for them.

Further Reading

Aldridge, Alfred Owen (1967). *Benjamin Franklin and Nature's God*. Durham, NC.
Anderson, Douglas (1997). *The Radical Enlightenments of Benjamin Franklin*. Baltimore, MD.
Buxbaum, Melvin H. (1975). *Benjamin Franklin and the Zealous Presbyterians*. University Park, PA.
Dunn, Elizabeth E. (1987). "From a Bold Youth to a Reflective Sage: A Reevaluation of Benjamin Franklin's Religion," *Pennsylvania Magazine of History and Biography* 111: 501–524.
Lemay, J.A. Leo (2006a). *The Life of Benjamin Franklin, Volume 1: Journalist, 1706–1730*. Philadelphia, PA.
Lemay, J.A. Leo (2006b). *The Life of Benjamin Franklin, Volume 2: Printer and Publisher, 1730–1747*. Philadelphia, PA.
Walters, Kerry S. (1999). *Benjamin Franklin and His Gods*. Urbana, IL.

Chapter Eight

BENJAMIN FRANKLIN AND THE COMING OF THE AMERICAN REVOLUTION

Benjamin L. Carp

Benjamin Franklin was an unlikely founding father. In the early 1760s, he seriously considered settling in Great Britain permanently. He returned to London in 1764 to beg the British ministry to impose a royal government on his home colony in Pennsylvania. He recommended a friend, John Hughes, to serve as an executor of the Stamp Act in Philadelphia, and, as a result, local crowds menaced both their houses. Indeed, not long before Bostonians were hanging effigies of Lord Bute (an adviser to the king) from the Liberty Tree, Franklin was hanging an engraved portrait of Bute in his home, and bragging about his connections to the man. Franklin held imperial office as a deputy postmaster, maneuvered to have his son William appointed a royal governor of New Jersey, and was on close terms with such anti-radicals as Massachusetts governor Thomas Hutchinson (until the 1770s) and Pennsylvania legislator Joseph Galloway. He spent the crucial pre-revolutionary decade of 1765 to 1775, not agitating in the colonies, but hobnobbing with British noblemen and bureaucrats in England. We find him, for most of this decade, fighting for reconciliation and greater authority rather than radical dissent, much less separation. Partly because Franklin's connections to Great Britain were so strong, from his time in the Second Continental Congress, through much of his diplomatic mission to France, to the signing of the Treaty of Paris in 1783, fellow Americans accused him of incompetence, laziness, disloyalty, and even espionage.

Yet Franklin not only became a founding father, but a full-throated one, between the crucial years of 1774 and 1776. In his belated acceptance of American grievances against the British Empire, he was not so different from many of the "reluctant revolutionaries" who eventually turned against

A Companion to Benjamin Franklin, First Edition. Edited by David Waldstreicher.
© 2011 Blackwell Publishing Ltd. Published 2011 by Blackwell Publishing Ltd.

Great Britain. While the popular understanding of Franklin has often distorted his reputation, historians have come to starkly different (and often opposing) conclusions about the nature of Franklin's importance to the American Revolution. Franklin was not, properly speaking, an ideologue, a revolutionary, or a resistance leader. He was instead possessed of an imperial vision for America. He had a knack for sociability and self-fashioning, but he exaggerated his ability to keep his emotions in check, particularly when it came to betrayal. And he was a consummate communicator, who could use his influence to mediate or meddle, agitate or antagonize. The themes of empire, identity, and communication are key to understanding Franklin's revolutionary movements.

8.1 Franklin's Reputation as a Revolutionary

Franklin owes his popular reputation as a revolutionary to four principal characteristics of his life: his uncanny timing, his relationship to Philadelphia, his fame as the American self-made man, and his legacy as a scientist and Enlightenment thinker. This is clear from various forms of public commemoration as well as the standard biographical treatments – the early sections of Clinton Rossiter's profile (1953) are a typical example.

In hindsight, Franklin really does seem to have had a knack for cementing his place in the history of the American Revolution. He was the only person present at the three most crucial events of the broader Revolutionary Era: the signing of the Declaration of Independence in 1776, the signing of the Treaty of Paris in 1783, and the drafting of the Constitution in 1787. Although, after 1757, he was only present in Philadelphia for about eight out of the last forty-three years of his life, he managed to witness personally both the dissolution of the British colonies in America and the establishment of the United States. In many respects this was because Franklin's peers often found him indispensable: he was needed in the Continental Congress and in the peace commission, and his elderly presence at the Constitutional Convention lent it a certain prestige (though his actual participation was minimal). Americans have long held their founding documents sacred, and Franklin's imprimatur on both the Declaration and the Constitution automatically confirms his Revolutionary reputation. Many readers make the mistake of reading Franklin backwards from his post-1776 efforts on behalf of the United States onto the earlier years of resistance.

Franklin's relationship to Philadelphia, the "First City," also helps determine his Revolutionary legacy (Nash, 2002). He was a printer when newspaper polemics were considered crucial to revolutionary mobilization. He was a civic organizer – a founder of libraries, fire companies, and philosophical societies – in an age when voluntarism became a crucial republican virtue. He was a public servant who journeyed to London in service of Pennsylvania. Although he remained absent from Philadelphia for much of the pre-Revolutionary decade, Franklin's mark on the city was indelible. Many Americans, in their visits to the Liberty Bell and Independence Hall, came to consider Philadelphia to be the birthplace of America. Despite having torn down his Market Street home, Philadelphians came to embrace Franklin as one of the city's most prominent sons. If Philadelphia was the preeminent Revolutionary city and Franklin was the preeminent Philadelphian, then by association, Dr Franklin acquired the reputation as the obstetrician who helped bring America to life. A consensus historian such as Clinton Rossiter could crow, "the city pushed upward, thanks to men like Franklin, toward new levels of communal co-operation" (1956: 157).

The problems with this syllogism are manifold. First, Philadelphia was in many ways a latecomer to the Revolutionary movement (Ryerson, 1978). It was relatively peaceful during the Stamp Act crisis, compared to other, more turbulent seaport cities. Philadelphians were the last to sign on to the nonimportation agreements of 1768–1770 – these were boycotts designed to force the repeal of the Townshend duties on tea, lead, paper, and glass. Throughout the imperial crisis, the oligarchic Pennsylvania Assembly tried to maintain a conservative consensus, and it never shut down over disputes about prerogative, as did those of South Carolina or Massachusetts. The Whig leaders who mobilized Philadelphia during the years of resistance to Parliament did so in Benjamin Franklin's absence: a pamphleteer such as John Dickinson, a crowd organizer like Timothy Matlack, an activist merchant like George Clymer, or an outsider like Thomas Paine. Until he returned to America in 1775, Franklin was hardly the most important actor in Pennsylvania politics or Philadelphia's agitation (Hanna, 1964: chap. 12).

Third, Franklin acquired his Revolutionary reputation because he was a self-made entrepreneur. As the youngest son of a tallow chandler who achieved his fortune as an ink-stained printer, he collected the aphorisms of Poor Richard, the striver, and he authored *The Way to Wealth* in 1758. By the 1750s, Franklin found himself accepted as a gentleman and a scholar, and later as a diplomat and statesman. During his lifetime, Franklin benefited from his reputation as an artisan made good. As Marc Egnal (1988: 202) writes, "Party chieftain Benjamin Franklin, the model of the successful artisan, remained a particular object of veneration among the lower classes." At the same time, as Ronald Schultz points out, Franklin dismayed these loyal followers and split Philadelphia's working community by associating himself a bit too closely with the British ministry during the passage of the Stamp Act (1993: 31). Nevertheless, by the end of his life, Franklin still cultivated the identity of a mechanic (Olton, 1975: 11).

While most of the people of eighteenth-century Europe and Asia suffered under tyrants and rigid caste systems, Franklin helped show the world that

America might be the "best poor man's country in the world," a place where an ordinary white person had every opportunity to advance in the world, so long as he or she was frugal and industrious (Lemon, 1972). T.H. Breen (2004) highlights the ways in which Poor Richard's virtues became harnessed to nonimportation movements that protested against the Stamp Act of 1765, the Townshend Act of 1767, the Tea Act of 1773, and the Coercive Acts of 1774. Indeed, Franklin often argued, "nothing can contribute to increase more rapidly the Wealth and Prosperity of our Country, than a total Forbearing of those Luxuries, or Providing them within ourselves" (Franklin to Joseph Galloway, March 21, 1770, PBF, 17: 118).[1] Franklin's *Autobiography* was designed to show a man who had risen by dint of his own self-abnegation and hard work.

Partly as a result of Franklin's self-fashioning, his career and life became, to later generations, a testament to America's revolutionary potential as a place of social mobility rather than hereditary nobility (Fliegelman, 1982; G. Wood, 1992: 283, 342, 351; Mulford, 1996). Gordon Wood (1992: 369) argues that America "would discover its greatness by creating a prosperous free society belonging to ... common people with their common interests in making money and getting ahead." If this was what had made America revolutionary, then Franklin looked (especially to nineteenth-century audiences) like an exemplar of this trend.

Historians have shown that Franklin's unique rise also owed a great deal to the monarchical system of patronage (Bushman, 1985: 57; G. Wood, 1992: 76–77). In other words, most middle-class men on the make in the eighteenth century relied upon the favors of wealthy patrons. Furthermore, Gary B. Nash (1977) and Billy G. Smith (1984) demonstrate that Franklin's career was the exception rather than the rule – economic mobility was decreasing, rather than increasing, as the Revolution approached. Franklin was not only unable to stand in for the striving poor of Early America, but, as David Waldstreicher (2004) argues, he actively worked against them in many cases – as a cut-throat businessman, as a printer of advertisements for runaways, and as a politician who helped compromise away the hopes of the enslaved.

Finally, Franklin's scientific reputation contributed to his reputation as a revolutionary. During the controversies of the 1760s and 1770s, many Britons professed their low esteem of Americans as a *"republican race, mixed rabble of Scotch, Irish and foreign vagabonds, descendants of convicts, ungrateful rebels* &c." (Franklin, Invectives Against the Americans, 1765, quoted in G. Wood, 2004: 115). In response, Americans came to think of themselves as defiant underdogs fighting back against the powerful British Empire; they saw America as an adolescent breaking free from the bonds of its parent country. In this climate of debate, Franklin's scientific accomplishments and inventions helped refute Comte de Buffon's notion that the New World was a place of degeneration, and that, by implication,

Americans were inferior. Though he was merely a colonial American, Franklin found himself honored by English and Scottish universities, invited to join the Royal Society, and feted by foreign noblemen and scholars. For subsequent generations of Americans, who prided themselves on American ingenuity and technological superiority, Franklin's contributions to the scientific revolution and its advances for humankind made him a figure who uniquely transcended the American Revolution. As Carla Mulford writes: Franklin after World War II "became a supreme representative of the greatness of American possibilities in the frenzy of publicity about the proverbial American way" (2009b: 8). Ironically, Franklin himself later prioritized his public service over scientific inquiry, though he continued to trade on his scientific reputation for political ends.

Since the historical study of the American Revolution has become more Atlantic and global in scope, Franklin's scientific contributions have become even more salient in the twenty-first century. This is no accident: while much recent scholarship shuns the nationalist aspects of Franklin's career and life, scholars can still find much to admire and analyze in his universalist achievements. Franklin's particular position as a man on both sides of the Atlantic opens him up, not just to imperial perspectives on the American Revolution, but Atlantic and transnational perspectives. His cosmopolitanism led historians to track Franklin along the global threads of science, slavery, and empire (Cohen, 1995; Waldstreicher, 2004; Dray, 2005; Chaplin, 2006). William Appleman Williams was the rare voice who dismissed Franklin's achievements in the sphere of science, calling him "only a lucky, albeit clever, amateur," and criticizing the later American conflation of "technological facility" with "scientific spirit" (1961: 92), an argument that I. Bernard Cohen (1956: 1990) vigorously disputes.

Franklin, then, acquired his reputation as the revolutionary signer of great documents, the favorite son of Revolutionary Philadelphia, the self-made refutation of hereditary aristocracy, and a man of the transatlantic Enlightenment. Historians have concluded that he deserved most of these accolades, even if some of them proved to be exaggerations. Yet Franklin's journey from a subject of the British Empire to an American citizen was far more interesting than these demigod-like stereotypes would suggest. A more careful understanding of Franklin's identity, worldview, actions, and decisions will help to reshape scholarly interpretations of the origins of the American Revolution.

8.2 The Imperial Franklin

Historians have long understood that the story of the American Revolution is not a simple nationalist narrative that unfolded only on American shores – not merely a Philadelphia story, a story of American sacred documents, or a story of American greatness. Instead, scholars of the revolution locate the American colonies within the context of the wider British Empire. As Jack P. Greene notes, Franklin's own explanation of the Revolution "focused primarily on developments not in America but in Britain" (1995b: 45). Franklin's observations and actions during the turbulent years of 1763–1776, when he was mostly in London, bespeak his importance to a broader narrative about the coming of the Revolution. From Lawrence Henry Gipson (1954), Jack Sosin (1965), and Michael Kammen (1968) to Marc Egnal (1988), Jack P. Greene (1986), and Theodore Draper (1996), scholars have examined the coming of the Revolution as an imperial crisis or a struggle for provincial power, and Franklin has played a significant role in their discussions. Whether they have been critical or friendly toward Franklin's actions, these imperial and neo-imperial scholars have engaged with Franklin more directly than historians from other schools of thought.

Franklin scholars such as Gerald Stourzh (1954, 1969) and Paul W. Conner (1965) emphasized Franklin's expansionism. Walter LaFeber (1972), a student of William Appleman Williams, characterizes Franklin as an "empire builder" (11) who, as early as 1751, envisioned the westward expansion of the Anglo-Saxon race. Similarly, Marc Egnal (1988), another scholar trained at the University of Wisconsin, described Franklin as one of America's most important expansionists, by which he meant an elite colonial leader dedicated to fostering America's rise. In his *Observations Concerning the Increase of Mankind* (1751), Franklin raved about the fertility of North America and the explosion of its white population, and predicted great things. Franklin decided that European powers and Native American opponents could not be allowed to interfere with America's potential, and Great Britain had a responsibility to foster rather than restrict American growth.

Before his disillusionment in the late 1760s, Franklin largely interpreted American greatness as a component part of British greatness. He was a budding neo-mercantilist with significant new ideas about how the American colonies would contribute to British power. Drew McCoy (1978: 606) writes that Franklin was "committed to maintaining America as a predominantly agricultural society," while Conner (1965: 71) argues, "Franklin's originality lay in his belief that the expansion of the colonial population and market, to the greater glory of the British mercantile system, would be facilitated by permitting manufacturing in the colonies." Britons, Conner argues, were unconvinced by his arguments that the colonies would not, free of restrictions on manufacturing, become a competitor to Great Britain. And Franklin, given his notions of a virtuous citizenry, envisioned that Americans would manufacture only necessities rather than luxuries. Yet Jack Crowley argues that the Americans did not initially intend to break free of a dependent commercial relationship with Great Britain, because they found it so beneficial: "Franklin did not refer to denials of economic opportunity as grievances," and seldom condemned British trade regulations (1993: 8–9). Only later did Franklin, as a neo-mercantilist, seek "an independent, integrated, and inclusive nation capable of standing up to the commercial empire from which it sprang" (Ben-Atar, 1998: 114).

Franklin never became the most eloquent spokesman for American rights, but he seems to have outshone many native English people in his praise for Great Britain. Gordon Wood called him "a thoroughgoing imperialist and royalist," and it is not hard to find evidence of this in Franklin's own writings (2004: 91). The "little Island" of Britain, he wrote, enjoyed "in almost every Neighbourhood, more sensible, virtuous and elegant Minds, than we can collect in ranging 100 Leagues of our vast Forests" (BF to Mary Stevenson, March 25, 1763, PBF, 10: 232). Franklin loved London, and he venerated British liberty, British commerce, and British institutions – including both the Crown and Parliament (Greene, 1995a: 253–256). As late as 1787, Franklin wrote of "a natural inclination in mankind to Kingly Government" (cited in G. Wood, 1992: 28). Until the middle of the 1770s Franklin was a firm supporter of the king.

At the same time, Franklin was aware of the British system's faults. He had seen corruption at various levels of government, he complained about the transportation of convicts to America, and he noted that ignorance of American affairs (and prejudice toward Americans themselves) was common in Great Britain (Greene, 1995a: 256–257). In the 1750s, Franklin became livid at arbitrary power in one particular guise – the proprietors of Pennsylvania. James H. Hutson (1972) and Francis Jennings (1996) both emphasized Franklin's fight against the Penn family (and their supporters in the Proprietary party) as a precursor to the fight waged by the Sons of Liberty against prerogative power. It was during this struggle that Franklin first wrote, "Those who would give up essential Liberty, to purchase a little temporary Safety, deserve neither Liberty nor Safety" (Pennsylvania Assembly: Reply to Governor [November 11, 1755], in PBF, 6: 242). Franklin long believed that the British Empire was the best protector of American security and liberty. As a result, in the 1750s and 1760s, Franklin's quest for better governance (and partisan advantage) in Pennsylvania led him to seek royal government for the colony.

Although Franklin later criticized the British imperial system and introduced proposals for reform, many historians have stressed that, prior to the 1770s, his overarching goal was to improve the British Empire and America's place within it. Greene described Benjamin Franklin, prior to 1774, as "the best friend" the British had from America. "Franklin, far from being a plotter of sedition and rebellion, had been a consistent exponent of imperial harmony and union" (1995a: 249). In 1760, Franklin warned readers that "grievous tyranny and oppression" might be enough to drive the colonies to unite, but this possibility seemed remote to Franklin at the time (Franklin, *Interest of Great Britain Considered*, in PBF, 9: 90, cited by Greene, 1992b: 304). In the midst of imperial turmoil, Franklin cultivated the image of a humble, prudent, and restrained man – in doing so, Greene argues, he became a "classic public-spirited Trimmer" who favored systemic equilibrium and pragmatic solutions over radical zealotry and government overreach (1995a: 251).

8.3 Briton to American

Franklin's absence from America during the years 1764 to early 1775 has made him a poor fit for historians exploring how Americans became politically mobilized to resist the acts of Parliament. Pauline Maier (1972), John Shy (1976, 1990), Richard Alan Ryerson (1978), Gary B. Nash (1979), and Benjamin L. Carp (2007), as they analyzed the Sons of Liberty, the militia, the radical committees, and urban political movements, could only bring Franklin into their narratives tangentially.

Franklin was hardly a champion of popular action before the late 1760s. In 1759, he took to the *London Chronicle* to assure readers that New Englanders, rather than being infused with "*a levelling spirit,*" were protective of property (PBF, 8: 341–342, quoted in Greene, 1992a: 243). In the 1760s, as dissidents took to the streets to protest British taxation and took up arms to protest restrictive western land policies (and reaffirm their aggressive stance toward Native Americans), Franklin took the field against a Pennsylvania "Country Mob" so as to assert the authority of the Pennsylvania legislature (Franklin to John Fothergill, March 14, 1764, PBF, 11: 101–105). As Pennsylvania prepared for its annual elections in October 1764, Franklin tried to limit the proliferation of taverns as sites of political mobilization, largely because he saw the taverns as helping his enemies – the colony's proprietors had granted their licenses (P.J. Thompson, 1999: 135–139). Franklin could be disdainful towards dissenters; when his enemies in the Pennsylvania Assembly objected to his appointment as an agent to go to London, he wrote, "This mode of *Protesting* by the Minority ... is quite new among us" (Franklin, *Remarks on a Late Protest*, November 7, 1764, in PBF, 11: 430, quoted in Carp, 2007: 188–189). During his famous appearance before the House of Commons in 1766, Franklin urged the prosecution of American crowd leaders (Egnal, 1988: 201).[2] As Conner concludes, Franklin "had spent most of his life strengthening the hand of political authority, not weakening it" (1965: 140).

Even as he disdained popular mobilization, Franklin took decidedly *un*popular stances on British taxation in America during the mid-1760s. He told a friend in Parliament in January 1764, "I am not much alarm'd about your Schemes of raising Money on us." In fact, he suggested not just a duty on tea (which Parliament would impose three years later), but on all East India Company goods (Franklin to Richard Jackson, February 11, 1764,

PBF, 11: 76). His reaction to the Molasses Act, Currency Act, and Stamp Act of 1764–1765 were muted (Egnal, 1988: 196–202). This was partly because Franklin was angling for a new charter for Pennsylvania, and partly because at the time he was still deeply respectful of Parliament's authority (Greene, 1995a: 261). After arguing against its imposition, Franklin grudgingly accepted the Stamp Act, which imposed taxes on a variety of legal and printed documents in America. In doing so, Franklin compounded his unpopularity back in Pennsylvania: Benjamin Rush, the young Philadelphia physician, cried, "*O Franklin, Franklin*, thou curse to Pennsylvania and America, may the most accumulated vengeance burst speedily on thy guilty head!" (quoted in G. Wood, 2004: 111). Even when Franklin did finally mount a defense of American rights, he argued (at first) to suspend rather than repeal the Stamp Act, called for American representation in Parliament, and urged a different tax on currency (Egnal, 1988: 201).

Yet, in Greene's interpretation, Franklin quickly realized that his initial optimism about Parliament's good intentions was misplaced; as a result, he pivoted away from his conciliatory stance and began mounting a vigorous defense of America in the London newspapers (1990: 73; 1995a: 261; V.W. Crane, 1950). When Franklin famously testified before the House of Commons in February 1766, he made it as clear as possible to the assembled members of Parliament that Americans would never submit to a stamp tax or pay any similar tax. When asked whether Americans denied Parliament's power to levy any tax whatsoever, Franklin (at the prompting of the Rockingham Administration) tied his contemporaries – and future historians – in knots with the singular idea that Americans would accept duties to regulate commerce (external taxes), but not internal taxes such as the stamp tax. Edmund and Helen Morgan dispelled the notion that Americans would have accepted these external taxes. "Though Franklin must have known that the American objections to taxation were more sweeping, he was anxious to assist in the repeal, and he knew that the American claims of exemption [from taxation] were a stumbling block" (Morgan and Morgan, 1962: 9, 345–346). In any event, Franklin's sometime enemy, John Dickinson, was soon to scrap the entire distinction between the two types of taxation in the *Letters from a Farmer in Pennsylvania* of 1767–1768, and argue instead that Parliament could impose regulations but not levy taxes. In the meantime, Franklin's remarks to Parliament were published throughout the colonies, and Franklin received credit for helping to usher in the repeal of the Stamp Act. Was Franklin mistaken or deluded in his initial grudging acceptance of the Stamp Act? Was he hamstrung by Pennsylvania's quest for royal government? Was he opportunistically tacking to the political winds? Was he trying to strike the best possible deal for the American colonies, in accordance with his neo-mercantilist ideas? Scholars continue to debate these questions.

Once Parliament passed the repeal, Franklin embraced a renewed optimism about future relations between Great Britain and the American colonies. While Greene (1990) and other historians stress that Franklin was privately calling for colonial autonomy before most other Americans, others argue that Franklin played down the brinksmanship that arose from American rhetoric and Parliament's passage of the Declaratory Act. As a man comfortable with both the British and American mindset, he cast himself as the indispensable negotiator who could work out a compromise between extremists on both sides. Meanwhile, Progressive historians like Appleman Williams (1961), Jensen (1968: 232–237, 391, 400), and Cecil Currey (1978) argue that Franklin's own interests in western lands had motivated his disagreements with the British government all along. Currey (1978) argues that Franklin's image as a moderate has been exaggerated; instead, Franklin was radicalized as early as the Stamp Act crisis, and his motives were, rather than "public-spirited" (in Greene's formulation) often self-interested. "Only his broad mercantilist vision and his opportunism," William Appleman Williams writes, "kept him from becoming a Loyalist" (1961: 93). Richard W. Van Alstyne (1965: 44) makes a slightly different argument about the nature of Franklin's opportunism; in 1773, he writes, "[c]learly Franklin looked forward to the next war as the opportunity for completing the conquests which the British government had foregone in 1763." Franklin was a pragmatist, a builder of sociable networks, a printer, and a land speculator rather than a person who worried about rigorous intellectual consistency. To the extent that he was an ideologue, it was in his vision for America as the spearhead of an expanding empire. To protect this vision, he counseled Britons not to be too harsh, and Americans not to be too rash. He urged people to avoid discussions of first principles, of conspiracy fears, of abstract concepts such as sovereignty, of hostile language that might alienate the other side.

Franklin kept trying to ingratiate himself with the ministry by condemning smuggling and the "rash Proceedings" in America in 1767 (Franklin to Joseph Galloway, August 8, 1767, PBF, 14: 230). Only when Hillsborough finally dismissed Franklin's quest for royal government in 1768 (and with it, perhaps, Franklin's dreams of high office), did Franklin fully embrace the cause of American resistance to Parliament (Egnal, 1988: 207). By 1769 and 1770, Franklin could be found denying parliamentary authority and calling for boycotts of British goods. Even so, in the aftermath of the Boston Tea Party he urged the town of Boston to make reparations for the East India Company's destroyed tea so as to prevent a further escalation of the crisis.

Historians will no doubt continue to argue about the degree and sincerity of Franklin's radicalism, and the exact moment when his affections for the British Empire deteriorated. These questions are not solely important for understanding Franklin as an individual; Greene argues that Franklin was a "surrogate for the vast majority of American colonists," who were deeply affectionate toward the mother country but became reluctantly estranged by British hostility, jealousy, and rigidity (Greene, 1995a: 284). Clinton Rossiter argues that Franklin was paying himself a high compliment when he wrote, "it has often happened to me, that while I have been thought here [in London] too much of an American, I have in America been deem'd too much of an Englishman" (1953: 298). But Franklin's statement only teases the scholar who is given the task of parsing out Franklin's true motivations, the way he fashioned different masks for different audiences, and his own conflicted identity.

8.4 The Political and the Personal

In thinking about Greene's notion of Franklin as a surrogate for the American colonists, it is important to remember that for eighteenth-century members of the elite, the concepts of personal honor and political reputation were almost inextricably mixed. As Larzer Ziff writes, Franklin well understood "the inseparability of the individual and society, the dependence of private character upon public perception, and the need to associate if one were to succeed" (1991: 84). William Hanna argues that for Franklin, "differences of opinion became personal threats to his position and honor," but in this Franklin was little different from his contemporaries among the elite (1964: 199). While Progressive historians have often stressed that the self-interest of American politicians motivated their political decisions, historians of the Revolution's ideological origins have also explored the ways in which broader threats to liberty and autonomy pricked at the psyches of American pamphleteers and leaders. For this reason, Greene called for a closer look at the "emotional dimensions" of the revolution's causes, and like many other historians, he found Franklin a fruitful subject (1995b: 47).

These scholars have often linked the developments of the Revolutionary Era to questions of *identity*. In trying to determine how the American colonists identified themselves, historians have compared Benjamin Franklin to a variety of figures. William Appleman Williams writes that Thomas Pownall (governor of Massachusetts) and Franklin were both land speculators with the outlook of "the nabob" (1961: 78). Such nabobs – provincial *arrivistes* – assumed they would inherit the empire, and sought to further their own interests by allying themselves with important British figures. Gordon Wood argues that in 1760 there was little difference between Franklin and Thomas Hutchinson (another governor of Massachusetts), both prudent imperial officials dedicated to the empire (2004: 10), and Bernard Bailyn (1974) made similar comparisons. David Waldstreicher calls the Irish-born William Knox, a Georgia planter who eventually became an undersecretary in the American department, Franklin's "imperial alter ego" (2004: 186). Where Knox insisted upon Parliamentary sovereignty over the colonies, Franklin insisted that colonial assemblies had an exclusive right over internal legislation, which would better allow the colonists to protect their own property (including slave property). In the 1760s, Knox and Hutchinson were both in a position to provide fellow colonists with a bulwark against imperial encroachment – instead they threw in their lot with imperial officials aiming to consolidate metropolitan control. Franklin was close to making some of the same choices, but he did not.

Caustic interpretations stress that Franklin's opinions on the empire were grounded in what was good for Franklin. Thus Marc Egnal's: "Franklin's quest for a new [Pennsylvania] charter, which triggered the struggles of 1764, had the earmarks of a personal campaign whose ultimate goal was a royal governorship for Franklin" (1988: 195). William Hanna writes that Franklin was optimistic about the empire so long as British officials treated him favorably (1964: 197). Cecil Currey argues that Franklin belatedly fought the Stamp Act "in an attempt to strengthen his weak political position in Pennsylvania" (1978: 391) and continued to protest against the British government out of bitterness over his frustrated land speculation schemes. Franklin's disagreements with the Earl of Hillsborough had stemmed at least in part from their disagreements over western policy – Franklin and a group of associates wanted to settle new lands under the auspices of the Vandalia Company. In 1771, the Earl of Hillsborough rejected Franklin's credentials as colonial agent "with something between a Smile and a Sneer," and given him "*a mix'd Look of Anger and Contempt*" (Franklin, Account of Audience with Hillsborough, January 16, 1771, in PBF, 18: 12,14). Franklin, finding that he was on bad terms with Hillsborough and the rest of the British ministry, saw his speculative interests, policy aims, and ambitions simultaneously thwarted.

And so Franklin took the final plunge into the arms of the American radicals. Franklin completed this process of fashioning himself anew by committing one of the most duplicitous acts of his life, an "unsavory attack" on the top two officials of Massachusetts (Sosin, 1965: 143). By a means that still elude historians, he obtained letters that Hutchinson and Andrew Oliver had written to Great Britain between 1767 and 1769, complaining about the actions of Boston radicals. Franklin transmitted them to Thomas Cushing, speaker of the Massachusetts House of Representatives. The Massachusetts Sons of Liberty, who were looking for any excuse to overthrow their governor and lieutenant governor, seized upon the letters' content and shouted for the removal of Hutchinson and Oliver. Franklin justified his action by saying that he hoped the letters would demonstrate that "friends of government" like Hutchinson were traducing the reputation of American agitators. Therefore, Franklin hoped to argue, the friends of government bore the responsibility for stirring up the imperial crisis.

In London the affair caused a scandal, leading to a duel, to Alexander Wedderburn excoriating Franklin in the Cockpit, and to Franklin being fired from his position as postmaster – and it might have eventually led to Franklin's conviction and arrest. In trying to make Hutchinson and Oliver the scapegoats for the rebellion in Massachusetts, Franklin became a scapegoat himself – he had affirmed the suspicions of British officials that he was treacherous meddler, and he was a convenient target as London reacted angrily to news of the Boston Tea Party. Fittingly, Franklin sustained a personal attack for his political actions (and those of his allies), after having made his own personal attack for political purposes.

If Franklin had behaved in a duplicitous fashion, then this was because he had learned early that humans were prone to using secrecy and deception against one another, but print – since it represented a broad political community – could conquer the world of secrecy (Ziff, 1991: 87, 106). As a result, Franklin defended his conduct during the Hutchinson–Oliver letters affair: "he regarded all writing as public property" (102), and the only true scapegoat was miscommunication (Looby, 1996: 71). After pointing out the irony of a postmaster being fired for circulating stolen mail, Christopher Looby highlights "an obvious analogy between the tactics of the committees of correspondence – which sought to exclude the British third party from the circuit of colonial communications – and those of Franklin, as he sought to exclude the royal officials from the chain of communication between colony and crown" (76–77). This suggests a new narrative of the revolution: one that saw the colonists establishing their own networks of communication while excluding the British officials who were attempting to encroach upon American aims.

Franklin's break from the empire, while it was underpinned by ideology and a keen sense of holding the British government accountable, also left behind a trail of personal disagreements and petty acts of betrayal. As Gordon Wood writes, "The Revolution was a very personal matter for Franklin, more personal perhaps than it was for any other Revolutionary leader" (2004: 158). As Franklin's opportunities for economic and political advancement dribbled away, he threw in his lot with the Americans: as a Quaker had asked an acquaintance long before, "didst thee ever know Dr. Franklin to be in a minority?" (Bruce, 1917, 2: 98 n1). And although he does not mention Franklin specifically, Arthur M. Schlesinger writes, "What great issue in history has not been scarred by sordid motives, personal antagonisms, and unintelligent decisions?" (1922: 178–179). By the time Franklin joined the Second Continental Congress in 1775, John Adams was writing, "He does not hesitate at our boldest Measures, but rather seems to think us, too irresolute, and backward" (John Adams to Abigail Adams, July 23, 1775, Butterfield, 1963, 1: 253). Franklin had become radicalized.

In addition to his accumulated disappointments with the British Empire in the years since the Stamp Act, three British actions appear to have particularly angered Franklin and affirmed his dedication to the American cause. The first was the burning of American towns. On hearing the news of the Battle of Bunker Hill, Franklin wrote to a British correspondent, "without the least Necessity, they ['the Ministerial Troops']... burnt a fine, undefended Town, opposite to Boston, called Charlestown." He continued, "In all our Wars, from our first settlement in America, to the present time, we never received so much damage from the Indian *Savages*, as in this one day from these." This letter also mentions Franklin's second and third new grievances: "exciting an Insurrection among the Blacks" and "hiring the Indian savages to assassinate our Planters in the Back-Settlements" (Franklin to Jonathan Shipley, July 7, 1775, PBF, 22: 93–98). These three acts, he wrote to David Hartley, a Member of Parliament, "are by no means Acts of a legitimate Government: they are of barbarous Tyranny and dissolve all Allegiance" (Franklin to David Hartley, September 12, 1775, PBF, 22: 196). When Franklin worked with the Marquis de Lafayette in 1779 on a list of prints to illustrate British cruelties, a few of the proposed images portrayed typical violations of the laws of war – mistreatment of prisoners and civilians – but the most prominent themes were the British government's incitement of blacks and Indians and the destruction of American towns (Franklin and Lafayette's List of Prints to Illustrate British Cruelties, [*c.* May 1779], PBF, 29: 590–593). When Franklin was negotiating the Treaty of Paris, he was still demanding reparations for the towns that had suffered at the hands of the British.

Looby (1996: 125–128) suggests that the revolution was actually quite traumatic for Franklin. One of the few times that Franklin mentions the revolution in his *Autobiography* is to lament that his advice for keeping the colonies in the empire was ignored. "How," Looby therefore asks, "could he identify himself with America if he held that its founding act, the Revolution, was an avoidable mistake?"

8.5 Franklin's Revolutionary Role

Historians appear to have valued Franklin less for the originality of his revolutionary ideas or for any sort of rock-ribbed idealism than for his pragmatic and perceptive views on the structure and dynamics of the British Empire. Franklin appears sporadically in Bernard Bailyn's *The Ideological Origins of the American Revolution* (1967, 1992), less often than John Adams, John Dickinson, or Thomas Jefferson; both Bailyn (1974: 238) and Gordon Wood (2004: 125) think of him as too rational and pragmatic (though sometimes lacking in judgment) to be as ideological as other American leaders. Temperamentally, Franklin does not seem to have been much of a rebel – William Appleman Williams writes that he was "in no sense a revolutionary" (1961: 92). According to many historians, and to

Franklin himself, he preferred instead to achieve his ends through discussion, compromise, and moderation. Bailyn and other students of revolutionary ideology do credit him as a critic of self-interested imperial governors (Bailyn, 1967: 102), primogeniture (G. Wood, 1992: 182), and the exercise of arbitrary power (Rossiter, 1953: 289; Morgan, 2002: 163–164), and as a proponent of free speech and a free press (Rossiter, 1953: 298–301) as well as the right of local legislative representation (Hutson, 1972). In the 1750s, Franklin was aware of corruption in Great Britain, and he was optimistic that American and British subjects could be vigilant about combating it together; but by 1775, he was no longer so confident, and feared that British corruption was about to envelop Americans (Bailyn, 1967, 1992: 88–89, 136).

Historians have noted some ideas of Franklin's that were unusual for his time – in some cases these were radical ideas that he embraced at before other Revolutionary leaders; in other cases they were ideas too conservative or archaic for his peers. Greene (1990: 113–120) and Gordon Wood highlight Franklin's vision of "an empire in which all the colonies were tied to Great Britain solely through the king" (2004: 123), an idea that was radical from Parliament's perspective, but one that in hindsight appears decidedly monarchist in the context of Americans' radical republicanism. Conner (1965: x) emphasizes that Franklin sought a "New American Order – virtuous, evolving, and harmonious."

Franklin supported unicameralism for the state of Pennsylvania in 1776, a concept that the United States Constitution, and most states, rejected as too democratic (G. Wood, 2004: 164–166, 218–220). During the debates on the Constitution, he opposed the executive's absolute veto and fought the attempt to impose property qualifications on suffrage (Beard, 1913: 197). He argued, also unsuccessfully, that government officials should draw no salary – an idea not so much radical as a throwback to more aristocratic times (G. Wood, 1992: 291–292). Edmund Morgan points to Franklin's long-held belief that property was not a natural right, but rather a "Creature of Society and is subject to the Calls of that Society whenever its Necessities shall require it, even to its last Farthing" (Franklin, Queries and Remarks on "Hints for the Members of the Pennsylvania Convention," quoted in Morgan, 2002: 307). This idea, implying that excess property belonged to the republican state rather than the citizen, was out of step with most of the elite Founders' beliefs, but not with those of "radical Dissenters" and perhaps many other Americans. Staughton Lynd traces Franklin's attraction to such radical ideas to his artisan origins as a printer (1968: 36, 69–71).

Like many Britons of the time, Franklin believed that a government's authority rested on voluntary consent rather than coercion by force. He supported David Hume's belief in the importance of public opinion (Greene, 1995b: 22–23; Morgan, 2002). American affection toward Great Britain was not based on its financial or military dependence, but on their faith in a just, benevolent, equitable British Empire, and their nationalist pride in British prowess and liberty. By custom and previous agreement, Americans retained their rights to representative government, and of taxing and legislating for themselves. Beginning in 1764, Americans perceived threats to these rights, and in displaying their "British Spirit of Liberty," they angered British statesmen further. The distance across the Atlantic Ocean contributed to British ignorance and misrepresentations on the part of civil officers. In short, like subsequent historians, Franklin emphasized British folly, British corruption, and British malicious intention. Unlike Bailyn's pamphleteers, however, Franklin did not emphasize a conspiracy of men corrupted by power (Bailyn, 1967: 37–38).

If Bailyn had little to say about Franklin, his emphasis on the world of print led other scholars to link Franklin to republican ideals. In Michael Warner's telling, "an emerging political language – republicanism – and a new set of ground rules for discourse – the public sphere – jointly made each other intelligible. ... Print discourse made it possible to imagine a people that could act as a people and in distinction from the state" (1990: xiii). Franklin, as a printer and deputy postmaster, was at the "center of communication and public life" at a time when "Newspaper readerships ... became among the most important forms of political organization in the colonies" (68). Across great distances of time and place, power could best be exercised through language (Looby, 1996: 67). Franklin and other Americans came to believe that print, rather than speech, was "the ideal and idealized guardian of civic liberty, as print discourse exposes corruption in its lurking holes but does so without occupying a lurking hole of its own" (82). Public life had to be "uncontaminated by particular aspirations, party affiliations, dependencies on governments and ministers, influences of powerful men, and the like" (90). Ziff (1991: 191) and Looby (1996: 132–133, 143–144) argue that representative government and the world of print had allowed American men to move from the world of hereditary aristocracy and patriarchal authority, where they were undistinguished, to a place of distinction, while still avoiding mob rule.

Historians, as they continue to regard Franklin with a critical eye, must be careful to remember that Franklin *was* something of a meddler and schemer. He was, after all, "very much aware that he was mediating between opinion in the two countries" (V.W. Crane, 1950: xviii), and he "saw that print's capacity to diffuse information, thought, and sentiment beyond the limits of place and moment" meant that it could transcend boundaries and reach a "common reader" (Ziff, 1991: 91, 93). As Conner points out, Franklin's loss of the deputy postmastership, and his attendant reputation, in 1774, "ended Franklin's double life as mediator-agitator" (1965: 160). Like most people, Franklin presented different sides of himself to different people, and his opinion on the American resistance to Britain was often shaped by his audience or correspondent. Franklin's enemies often noted "the connection between his self-concealing designs and his manipulation of letters" (Warner, 1990: 90). Furthermore, Franklin could be as preeningly self-justifying as John Adams or any of the other so-called "Founding Fathers," and so we cannot always take him at his word.

Given his predilections, how accurate were his perceptions? Scholars ought to pay greater attention to Franklin's role as a vessel for communication, as a printer, a writer, and a correspondent. It has become a cliché to observe that the distance across the Atlantic played a large role in fostering miscommunications and misunderstandings between Great Britain and the colonies – in the case of the Hutchinson–Oliver affair, Franklin deliberately took advantage of the gaps in communication with the intention of enhancing the reputation of the Massachusetts Sons of Liberty and destroying that of the Massachusetts friends of government. Franklin's role as a mediator and communicator during the crucial years of 1764–1776 raises an analytical problem: was Franklin communicating British sentiments accurately to the Americans, and vice versa? We know Franklin valued the importance of public opinion in government; yet we also need to look past some of his more disingenuous statements and evaluate him as a *shaper* of public opinion. Scholars need to explore these questions, in order to test the arguments of Greene and other historians of the Revolution who have relied on Franklin's perceptions to explain his imperial vision and the self-fashioning of his identity. Otherwise, it will be difficult for us to expect Franklin, who was largely absent from America and exceptional in so many other ways, to be a "surrogate" for the views of American colonists. Indeed, Looby (1996: 128) wonders how Franklin could present himself as an American surrogate when he had such significant doubts about the necessity and wisdom of the revolution. Franklin, the unlikely founding father, played a key role in the mobilization of the American colonists toward rebellion and independence. What is less clear is whether Franklin intended this outcome or not.

Notes

1. Labaree, Leonard W. et al., eds. (1959–). *The Papers of Benjamin Franklin*. 39 vols to date. New Haven, CT: Yale University Press. Hereafter referred to as PBF.
2. A call for prosecutions was a disingenuous tactic often used by Whig leaders, which allowed them to appear in favor of proper authority while knowing that successful prosecution was either unlikely, or would be inconsequential.

Further Reading

Conner, P.W. (1965). *Poor Richard's Politicks: Benjamin Franklin and His New American Order*. New York, NY.

Currey, C.B. (1978). *Road to Revolution: Benjamin Franklin in England, 1765–1775*, 2nd edn. Gloucester, MA.

Draper, T. (1996). *A Struggle for Power: The American Revolution*. New York, NY.

Egnal, M. (1988). *A Mighty Empire: The Origins of the American Revolution*. Ithaca, NY.

Greene, J.P. (1995a). "The Alienation of Benjamin Franklin, British American," in *Understanding the American Revolution: Issues and Actors*. Charlottesville, VA., pp. 247–284.

Kammen, M.G. (1968). *A Rope of Sand: The Colonial Agents, British Politics, and the American Revolution*. Ithaca, NY.

Moran, D.T. (1996). *The Devious Dr. Franklin, Colonial Agent: Benjamin Franklin's Years in London*. Macon, GA.

Sosin, J.M. (1965). *Agents and Merchants: British Colonial Policy and the Origins of the American Revolution, 1763–1775*. Lincoln, NE.

Waldstreicher, D. (2004). *Runaway America: Benjamin Franklin, Slavery, and the American Revolution*. New York, NY.

Wood, G. (2004). *The Americanization of Benjamin Franklin*. New York, NY.

Chapter Nine

BENJAMIN FRANKLIN AND NATIVE AMERICANS

Timothy J. Shannon

Benjamin Franklin knew two Indians. More precisely, he knew two types of Indians. The first were flesh-and-blood Indians he encountered as a printer and politician working in Pennsylvania. Mostly of the Iroquois, Delaware, and Shawnee nations, these Indians played a central role in Pennsylvania's frontier security, fur trade, and diplomatic relations. The idioms and customs of their diplomacy fascinated Franklin, and he printed editions of their treaties with colonial governments. As a Pennsylvania assemblyman, Franklin participated in some of these negotiations and helped conduct Pennsylvania's Indian affairs. Franklin recognized in these Indians a shared humanity, and he genuinely engaged with the issues and problems they raised in such diplomatic encounters. He wrote about them sympathetically and on some occasions even assumed their point of view to illustrate the foibles and prejudices of the supposedly more civilized Europeans.

The second kind of Indians Franklin knew were the metaphorical ones who populated the works of Enlightenment thinkers in America and Europe. Identified neither by individual name or tribal affiliation, these were the faceless hunter-gatherers of the American forests who lived in the state of nature and whose habits illustrated both the unspoiled virtues and inherent savagery of primitive man. Franklin most often wrote about these Indians when he was addressing a European audience, while working as a colonial agent in Britain or as an American diplomat in France. These Indians became a convenient trope for him as he promoted the patriot cause or Western expansion. From Franklin's vantage point in London and Paris, the two cities where he spent most of his life after 1757, these Indians were the marauding horde on the American frontier, manipulated by

A Companion to Benjamin Franklin, First Edition. Edited by David Waldstreicher.
© 2011 Blackwell Publishing Ltd. Published 2011 by Blackwell Publishing Ltd.

European allies, crippled by their addiction to alcohol, and doomed to extinction by the rise of the United States.

Historians, when they have written about Franklin's relationship with Native Americans, have not always taken care to separate these two types of Indians, but like Walt Whitman, Franklin was large enough to contain multitudes. Over the course of his lifetime, he thought and wrote about Indians on many occasions and contradicted himself in his opinions about them just as frequently. Depending on the purpose with which he wrote, Franklin could describe Indians as eloquent diplomats or bloodthirsty killers, as the embodiment of American virtues or as impediments along the path to America's future. To understand Franklin's relationship with Native Americans, it is necessary to draw the line between these real and imagined Indians and to understand the contexts in which he wrote about each.

Franklin's interactions and thoughts on Native Americans are spread throughout a lifetime of personal correspondence, political pamphlets, newspaper editorials, and essays. Among the founding fathers, he left the most significant archive of materials related to the subject. George Washington, in his work as a soldier, surveyor, and land speculator, had more extensive encounters with Indians than Franklin, but was not inclined to *think* about them – their culture and society, their language and politics, their past and their future – in the same way. Thomas Jefferson shared Franklin's predilection for such inquiries but did not have the same opportunities as Franklin to observe Indians firsthand. Of other Enlightenment figures who wrote about Native Americans – John Locke, Jean Jacques Rousseau, the Abbé Raynal, Comte de Buffon – only Cadwallader Colden, the Scottish polymath and royal officeholder in New York, and Hector St Jean de Creveceour, the French émigré to and exile from British North America – rivaled Franklin's experience with Indians, but neither matched his multifaceted interest in them. Among his contemporaries, Franklin stands apart for the influence he has had, for better and worse, on our modern ideas and attitudes about Native Americans and their place in the American nation.

9.1 "Doing Business with those Barbarians"

Franklin's interest in Native Americans first became apparent when he printed Indian treaties conducted by the Pennsylvania government. As his engagement in Pennsylvania's politics deepened, he participated in those diplomatic negotiations himself, most famously at the Albany Congress of 1754. In letters from this same era, he shared ideas with correspondents about such practical matters as regulating the fur trade, securing Pennsylvania's frontier from hostile Indians, and managing intercolonial Indian relations more effectively. In the long span of his career, Franklin's full-bore immersion in such matters was relatively brief, falling between his election to the Pennsylvania Assembly in 1751 and his departure for his first mission as a colonial agent in London in 1757. Nevertheless, these experiences were formative in how he thought and wrote about Indians for the rest of his life, and some scholars have gone so far as to claim that his encounters with Indians during this period shaped his political beliefs about democracy and federalism.

Franklin was not the first colonial printer to publish Indian treaties, but he was the most prolific. Between 1736 and 1762, Franklin (and beginning in 1753 with his partner David Hall) published fourteen Indian treaties in thirteen imprints, roughly twenty-five percent of the Indian treaties published during the colonial era. Printers in Massachusetts and New York had published earlier Indian treaties, some dating to the late seventeenth century, and Philadelphia printer Andrew Bradford had published two Pennsylvania treaties during the 1720s, but Franklin's output came to define the genre for scholars of early American literature. J.A. Leo Lemay identified Franklin's treaties, printed in folio in generously-spaced type, as "the most aesthetically pleasing products of his press," (2006–2009, 2: 379) and bibliographer Lawrence C. Wroth described Franklin's output as the definitive examples of the Indian treaty genre (1927–1928). In the modern era, Franklin's treaties have been collected and reprinted twice, in 1938 and 2006 (Boyd, 1938; Kalter, 2006).

Franklin probably initially printed Indian treaties because he was paid to do so by the Pennsylvania government, which would have wanted copies to circulate among government officials in the colonies and London. The first two treaties he published, in 1736 and 1742, convened in Philadelphia, and it is likely he attended them in his capacity as clerk of the Assembly. Even if he had no official role, Franklin could have attended the proceedings as a curious onlooker; colonial officials took pains to convene such councils before large audiences, to impress their Indian guests with their power, and to lend an air of legitimacy to the negotiations. These two treaties were Franklin's first exposure to the particular customs of Iroquois diplomacy. The Iroquois confederacy, known to Franklin and his contemporaries as the Six Nations, occupied strategic ground between French Canada and the northern British colonies, and its chiefs were the most significant native power brokers in Pennsylvania's Indian relations, laying claim to authority over the Delawares, Shawnees, and a number of other native groups living along the Delaware, Susquehanna, and Ohio frontiers. When a delegation of Iroquois came to Philadelphia in 1736 to conduct a treaty, Franklin reported the occasion in the *Pennsylvania Gazette*, adopting the Indians' own metaphor to explain the purpose of the meeting ("to brighten the Chain of Friendship") and explaining how their speakers used a "Handful of little Sticks" to serve as "Memorandums of the Points" they made during their speeches (*Pennsylvania Gazette*, October 14, 1736). In the treaties he published, Franklin assumed a similar editorial role, adding glosses and footnotes to help the reader decipher the Indians' words and actions.

By the mid-1740s, Franklin was marketing Indian treaties to a broader readership. *A Treaty, Held at the Town of Lancaster ... In June, 1744* (1745) had a print run of about 1,000 copies. Franklin advertised it for sale in the *Pennsylvania Gazette* and distributed copies beyond Philadelphia via agents in Maryland, New York, Virginia, and New England (Lemay, 2006–2009, 2: 394). He shipped 200 copies to William Strahan, his London bookseller, hoping that the treaty would find an audience there. Apologizing to Strahan for the smallness of American affairs when compared with the great wars, politics, and events of Europe, Franklin nevertheless recommended the Lancaster treaty to him, "as the Method of doing Business with those Barbarians may perhaps afford you some Amusement" (PBF, 2: 411, 416).[1] Despite this ungracious characterization, Franklin clearly appreciated the ethnographic glimpse that treaty-making provided into native life and customs. By conveying the majesty of Indian oratory, explaining the protocol that governed their diplomacy, and detailing the process by which they mediated their differences with colonists, Franklin's Indian treaties provided *prima facie* evidence of Indian humanity and cultural integrity.

Franklin participated in treaties in an official capacity three times, each time as a commissioner appointed by the Pennsylvania Assembly. In 1753, he attended a treaty conference convened in the frontier town of Carlisle, Pennsylvania with pro-British Indians from the Forks of the Ohio (modern Pittsburgh). A year later, he attended the Albany Congress, a treaty conference famous for the plan of intercolonial union Franklin presented there. In November 1756, he served as a commissioner at a treaty in Easton, Pennsylvania, convened to conduct peace negotiations with French-allied Delaware Indians from the Susquehanna Valley. At the Carlisle Treaty, Franklin heard the Ohio Indians' complaints about Pennsylvania's failure to arm its Indian allies against the French or to control its Western fur traders. Concerned that the pacifist principles of Pennsylvania's Quaker party and the avarice of its fur traders were compromising the colony's security, Franklin pushed for greater intercolonial cooperation on such matters and sought advice from James Bowdoin in Massachusetts on that colony's regulation of the fur trade. A year later, Franklin made intercolonial cooperation in Indian affairs a central component of the plan of union he presented in Albany. At the Easton treaty in November 1756, he and the other commissioners from the Assembly listened to the Delawares' complaints about the Walking Purchase, a shady land deal conducted by William Penn's heirs twenty years earlier. Franklin sailed for London not long afterward to serve as the Assembly's advocate against the Penns before the Crown; had he stayed in Philadelphia, he would have doubtlessly attended the subsequent Easton treaties that tried to undo the damage done by the Walking Purchase.

Some scholars have interpreted Franklin's interest in treaty-making and his advocacy of intercolonial union as evidence that his ideas about American union were influenced by native statecraft. The so-called Iroquois Influence Thesis maintains that Franklin considered the Iroquois confederacy a suitable model for the British colonies to imitate in balancing self-government and mutual interests, and that during his later career, he introduced these ideas to the Articles of Confederation and the Constitution of the United States. Although the Iroquois Influence Thesis has been dismissed by the leading scholars of the eighteenth-century Iroquois, it remains current in grade school curricula and popular media. It merits mention here because it illustrates the disjuncture between Franklin's encounters with flesh-and-blood Indians and his use of metaphorical ones in his writings.

Franklin's first ideas about intercolonial union grew out of his correspondence with Archibald Kennedy and Cadwallader Colden, two royal officials in New York who shared his scientific and political interests. After reading a manuscript draft of Kennedy's *The Importance of Gaining and Preserving the Friendship of the Indians to the British Interest, Considered* in 1751, Franklin wrote an endorsement of the pamphlet's proposal to create a royal superintendent of Indian affairs and added his own thoughts on forming a "general Council" composed of representatives from each colony and funded by an intercolonial tax on liquor. Franklin compared his proposed union to the Iroquois confederacy: "It would be a very strange Thing, if six Nations of ignorant Savages should be capable of forming a Scheme for such an Union, and be able to execute it in such a Manner, as that it has subsisted Ages, and appears indissoluble; and yet that a like Union should be impracticable for ten or a Dozen English Colonies, to whom it is more necessary, and must be more advantageous; and who cannot be supposed to want an equal Understanding of their Interests" (PBF, 4: 118–119). This was a backhanded compliment indeed, aimed at chiding his fellow colonists for being so dilatory in acting on their own best interests when "ignorant Savages" were obviously capable of doing so.

Supporters of the Iroquois Influence Thesis cite this passage alongside a speech by the Onondaga chief Canasatego delivered at the Lancaster treaty of 1744, in which he urged his colonial counterparts to follow the Iroquois example: "Our wise Forefathers established Union and Amity between the *Five Nations*; this had made us formidable; this has given us great Weight and Authority with our neighbouring Nations. We are a powerful Confederacy; and by your observing the same Methods our wise Forefathers have taken, you will acquire fresh Strength and Power; therefore, whatever befals you, never fall one with another" (cited in Kalter, 2006: 118). According to the Iroquois Influence Thesis, Franklin took Canasatego's advice to heart and borrowed from the Iroquois when drafting the Albany Plan and contributing to subsequent blueprints for American federalism.

There is one major problem with connecting the dots between Canasatego's speech, Franklin's interest in intercolonial union, and his participation in the Albany Congress, Second Continental Congress, and Constitutional Convention: Franklin himself never did so. In all of his writings, he never showed evidence of being familiar with the nature of the Iroquois confederacy in any depth greater than that exhibited in his letter to Kennedy. He knew the Iroquois were joined in a native confederacy that apparently pre-dated the European colonization of North America, but he never inquired with any of his correspondents about how the Iroquois confederacy worked as a form of intramural government. Colden, one of Franklin's regular correspondents and the author of a history of the Iroquois, would have been the logical choice for doing so, but even the well-informed Colden knew the Iroquois confederacy only in the same way Franklin did, as a diplomatic entity encountered at treaty conferences. Furthermore, there is a consistency between Franklin's references to the Iroquois in his letter to Strahan and his letter to Kennedy. In both instances, Franklin condescends to them, referring to them as "Barbarians" and "Savages," respectively. Franklin found Iroquois diplomatic customs intriguing and he admired the united front they presented to outsiders, but there is no evidence that he ever considered them possessed of a form of government he thought worthy of study or imitation. By definition, barbarians and savages had no government.

Despite this lack of textual evidence, proponents of the Iroquois Influence Thesis cling to the notion that Franklin and his colonial contemporaries somehow imbibed native ideas about democracy and federalism by listening to Indian speeches at treaty conferences or perhaps by engaging their native counterparts in private conversations on such occasions. The image of Franklin sitting cross-legged at a council fire and sharing a pipe with Canasatego is an appealing one, but it has no basis in the sources. Although Franklin did not keep a private journal during any of the treaty conferences he attended, several of his peers did. These sources indicate that colonial commissioners engaged in highly ritualized behavior with Indian participants at treaty conferences, toasting each other, exchanging presents, and engaging in polite small talk, but on no recorded occasion did they ever discuss the nature of Iroquois governance. The absence of this kind of intellectual cross-pollination, so necessary to sustain the Iroquois Influence Thesis, is perhaps best illustrated by Franklin's own summation of the colonial commissioners' interaction with the Indians at the Albany Congress. Writing to Colden shortly after that meeting ended. Franklin complained of the Indians' late arrival, when "after all, nothing of much Importance was transacted with them: at least nothing equal to the Expence and Trouble" (PBF, 5: 392–393) the commissioners had gone through to be there. These are hardly the words of someone inspired by his encounters with the Iroquois to imitate their example in his designs for American federalism.

As a Pennsylvania commissioner at Indian treaties, Franklin dealt with real problems presented by real Indians: trading abuses, diplomatic neglect, and land frauds. In the fraught atmosphere of colonial-Indian relations during the 1750s, there was little time at treaty conferences for joint seminars on political theory or indigenous forms of government. When Franklin did refer to Indians as political creatures, he described them in derogatory terms that placed them well below Europeans on the scale of civilization. The flesh-and-blood Indian was a neighbor who needed to be understood and placated for the sake of colonial security and prosperity; the metaphorical Indian was merely a benighted savage who could be used to illustrate the colonists' own shortcomings.

9.2 "Different Tribes, Nations and Languages"

The nature of Pennsylvania's Indian relations changed drastically after General Edward Braddock's defeat on the banks of the Monongahela River in July 1755. The destruction of Braddock's army by a combined force of Indian warriors and French soldiers from Fort Duquesne cemented the French hold on the Forks of the Ohio and exposed the defenseless nature of Pennsylvania's frontier. Although allied with the Quaker party in its struggles against the Penn family, Franklin had never embraced pacifism as a principle or policy. When an invasion scare gripped Philadelphia in 1747 during King George's War, Franklin promoted his idea for a volunteer militia by raising the specter of the Iroquois shifting their allegiance to the French and attacking Pennsylvania's unprotected frontier (PBF, 3: 194–195). Eight years later, as Delaware war parties raided settlements along the Susquehanna corridor, he organized another volunteer militia and supervised the construction of forts in Northampton County. As a military man, Franklin did not blanch at the use of brutal methods for fighting the Indian enemy. He inquired with Governor Robert Hunter Morris about encouragement (i.e. bounties) that might be given to "Volunteer Scalping Parties" (PBF, 6: 360). In a letter to Indian interpreter Conrad Weiser, a fellow veteran of Pennsylvania's treaty conferences, Franklin proposed using dogs to flush out and run down enemy Indians, as "was the Spanish method of guarding their marches" (Nolan, 1936: 37). In recommending such measures, Franklin showed himself to be of the same mind as his contemporaries when it came to fighting Indians: a savage enemy who attacked civilians, tortured captives, and mutilated corpses did not merit the mercies of the rules of war, but rather response in kind.

By the time Franklin returned from his first London mission in 1762, the Seven Years War had torn the fabric of Pennsylvania's Indian relations beyond repair. At the Easton treaty of 1758, the Delawares and colonial agents had finally hammered out workable peace terms, and the successful completion of General John Forbes' campaign against Fort Duquesne shortly thereafter restored security for frontier settlers. But William Penn's vision of a peaceable kingdom had been shattered by three years of carnage. In that time, the language that Pennsylvania's inhabitants used to describe intercultural relations had become racialized, as ethnically and religiously diverse colonists united under their identification as "white people" suffering at the hands of "our Savage neighbours" (Silver, 2008: vii). The Pennsylvania government's endorsement of scalp bounties gave tacit approval to vigilantism that erased the line between hostile and peaceful Indians.

Franklin witnessed the intensity of this violence during the Paxton Boys crisis of 1763–1764. In two separate attacks in December 1763, a band of Scottish-Irish colonists murdered the twenty inhabitants of Conestoga, the remnant of a once-populous Indian town in the lower Susquehanna Valley. A threat to no one in the region, the Conestogas had lived meagerly but peacefully by peddling brooms and baskets and seeking charity among their colonial neighbors. The ferocity of the Paxton Boys' attacks on them – marked by the execution and mutilation of unarmed men, women, and children – shocked Franklin, who became even more concerned when the Paxton Boys, swelling in number to several hundred, marched eastward, announcing their intention to kill Christian Indians who were being sheltered in Philadelphia by sympathetic Quakers and Moravians. Franklin's *Narrative of the Late Massacres in Lancaster County*, published in January 1764, was the opening salvo in a pamphlet war between the Paxton Boys' detractors and supporters that raged as Franklin worked with other prominent Philadelphians to protect the city from mob violence.

The *Narrative of the Late Massacres* was in many respects the culmination of Franklin's involvement in Pennsylvania's Indian affairs. Although he wrote it in response to a particular crisis and to discredit the actions of fellow colonists, Franklin argued his case with a clarity that distilled what his first-hand experiences with Indians had taught him: that they were individuals possessed of the same humanity as himself; that they lived in communities as culturally and politically distinct from each other as the colonists were; and that Indians held no monopoly on the savagery evident on the American frontier.

In the pamphlet's opening pages, Franklin humanizes the victims of the Paxton Boys by identifying them by name and their filial relationships to each other. Having established them as individuals and families, he then relates the history of "this little Society" (PBF, 11: 50), invoking their treaty relationship with the Pennsylvania government that dated back to the days of William Penn. Turning his attention to the Paxton Boys, Franklin dismissed the argument that their murderous treatment of the Conestogas was justified by the violence visited upon the frontier by other Indians during Pontiac's War: "If an Indian injures me, does it follow that I may revenge that Injury on all Indians? It is well known that Indians are of different Tribes, Nations and Languages, as well as the White People"

(PBF, 11: 55). Challenging the racial rhetoric that had come to define anti-Indian sentiment during the war years, Franklin observed:

> The only Crime of these poor Wretches seems to have been, that they have a reddish brown Skin, and black Hair; and some People of that Sort, it seems, had murdered some of our Relations. If it be right to kill Men for such a Reason, then, should any Man, with a freckled Face and red Hair, kill a Wife or Child of mine, it would be right for me to revenge it, by killing all the freckled red-haired Men, Women and Children, I could afterwards any where meet with. (PBF, 11:55)

Franklin took care to distance himself from the non-violence preached by the Quakers and Moravians: "I beg that I may not be understood as framing Apologies for *all* Indians." Instead, he invoked the fidelity with which the Conestogas and Iroquois (with whom the Conestogas were affiliated) had kept their treaty obligations "ever since we knew them." The Paxton Boys, on the other hand, had acted on a "brutal undistinguishing Resentment against *all* Indians, Friends as well as Foes," proving themselves to be "CHRISTIANS WHITE SAVAGES" (PBF, 11: 66).

By way of timely cooperation with his political enemy Governor John Penn, Franklin was able to raise Philadelphia's defenses and turn back peaceably the Paxton Boys' advance on the city. Nevertheless, his defense of the Conestogas and the Indian refugees in Philadelphia made him unpopular among many of his fellow Pennsylvanians, and in the election of 1764, he lost his Assembly seat. Not long after, he returned to London on his second mission as a colonial agent, no doubt pleased to leave the rancor of Pennsylvania's politics behind him. As he crossed the Atlantic, he took with him perhaps the most nuanced view of Native Americans that any colonist had ever carried to Britain. Franklin had an intimate knowledge of the methods and issues involved in Indian diplomacy; he knew that Indians could be fierce and unforgiving enemies in war, but also steadfast allies and reliable partners in peace; he knew that some Indians nations were powerful and independent enough to swing the balance of power between French and British interests in North America, and that others had been so diminished by their encounter with Europeans that they needed protection from their vicious colonial neighbors. Most of all, Franklin knew that while Indians were different from Europeans, they were fellow human beings knit together by kin and community, as deserving of justice, liberty, and security as any Christian or white person.

9.3 "Merciless Indian Savages"

Once back in London, Franklin quickly became embroiled in the Anglo-American crisis that blossomed after the passage of the Stamp Act. As the most famous and voluble American living in Britain, he became the *de facto* spokesman for the patriot cause, and the original purpose of his mission – to represent the Pennsylvania Assembly's case against the proprietary government of the Penns – took a backseat to that new role. Accordingly, his writings about Indians during this period shifted away from the specific matters of war and diplomacy in Pennsylvania toward more general considerations about the Indians' place in Britain's North American empire. As Franklin made the patriots' case before the British government and public, he constructed a narrative about British interests in North America in which Indians played two roles, as customers for the fur trade and as the chief impediment to the colonists' western expansion.

Faceless and nameless Indian warriors, armed by their European allies and let loose on backcountry settlers, became stock characters in the narrative Franklin constructed about the origins and aftermath of the Seven Years War during his London years. In *The Interest of Great Britain Considered* (1760), the first political pamphlet he published in London, Franklin described the Indians' method of warfare as an extension of the skills and practices they acquired in their hunting. Raiding parties, ranging from five to fifty warriors, used stealth and surprise to attack unsuspecting civilians, leaving families "murder'd and scalp'd" (PBF, 9: 67) in their beds, livestock slaughtered and homesteads burned, and the unlucky survivors dragged into captivity. These Indians, corrupted and supplied by French priests and traders, prevented colonists from settling new land west of the Appalachians. Policymakers who thought "our present colonies are large enough and numerous enough" realized this and so believed that "the French ought to be left in North America to prevent their [the colonists'] increase, lest they become not only *useless* but *dangerous* to Britain" (PBF, 9: 77).

Arguing against the restoration of Canada to France, Franklin emphasized that the engrossment of the French fur trade was a boon for British manufacturers and a primary reason why Britain went to war with France in 1754. He listed first among his "Humorous Reasons for Restoring Canada" this point: "We should restore Canada; because an uninterrupted trade with the Indians throughout a vast country, where the communication by water is so easy, would encrease our commerce, *already too great*, and occasion a large additional demand for our manufactures, already too dear" (PBF, 8: 449–450). Answering Stamp Act supporters who argued that the Seven Years War had been fought at British expense to defend American interests, Franklin again raised the issue of the fur trade. "The last war was begun, *not* 'for the immediate protection' of all Americans," Franklin answered one editorialist, "but for the protection of *British trade*, carried on with *British manufactures* among the Indians in America" (PBF, 12: 411). When examined before Parliament to explain the American opposition to the Stamp Act, he claimed that the Crown had sent Braddock's army to America "to protect your trade," and that the "trade with the Indians, though carried on in America, is not an American interest." The colonists were "chiefly farmers and planters" who produced not a single "article of commerce with the Indians" and who had always defended themselves against hostile Indians "without any troops sent to their assistance from this country" (PBF, 13: 151–152). The war had been fought to open new markets for British manufacturers and merchants, and they should rightfully bear the costs of maintaining the army that now occupied this conquered territory.

As the Anglo-American crisis intensified, Franklin resorted to describing the British as he had once described the French: the puppet-masters of savage minions who could be used to keep the colonists confined to the eastern seaboard. In "Rules by Which a Great Empire May be Reduced to a Small One" (1773), one of his last satirical pieces for the London press, Franklin assigned sinister motives to the Crown's decision to withdraw troops from frontier garrisons in favor of quartering them in eastern cities: "Send Armies into their [the colonists'] Country under Pretence of protecting the Inhabitants; but instead of garrisoning the Forts on their Frontiers with those Troops, to prevent Incursions, demolish those Forts, and order the Troops into the Heart of the Country, that the Savages may be encouraged to attack the Frontiers, and that the Troops may be protected by the Inhabitants" (PBF, 20: 399). This line of argument found its most enduring expression in the founding document of the United States of America. In the litany of grievances contained in the Declaration of Independence, the final one indicts King George III for having "endeavoured to bring on the Inhabitants of our Frontiers, the merciless Indian Savages, whose known Rule of Warfare, is an undistinguished Destruction, of all Ages, Sexes and Conditions" (Armitage, 2007: 169).

Those words were of course primarily Thomas Jefferson's, but Franklin served on the committee that edited the document, and of its five members he had the longest track record of writing about Indians in this manner, as the storm troopers of empire on the American frontier. Serving as a peace commissioner in 1777, Franklin voiced a similar sentiment in a letter to the British prime minister Lord North, expressing dismay that North's government had yet to disavow its "invitation to the Indian savages, [made] at a public treaty, to drink the blood, and feast upon the body of those whom you called your subjects" (PBF, 25: 274). Five years later Franklin was still railing against the king for unleashing the Indians on his own countrymen: "It is he who has furnished the Savages with Hatchets and Scalping Knives, and engages them to fall upon our defenceless Farmers, and murder them with their Wives and Children paying for their Scalps, of which the Account kept already amounts as I have heard, to near *two Thousand*" (PBF, 37: 586–587). Scalp bounties and other inducements offered by the British to their Indian allies were to Franklin the ultimate violation of the bonds of civility and consanguinity that had once held the Anglo-American empire together.

9.4 "Savages We Call them, Because their Manners Differ from Ours"

When Franklin wrote about Indians as merciless savages, he was using them as proxies to attack European enemies of the American colonists. When his topic did not concern such wartime grievances, he was more inclined to describe Indian savagery not so much as a Hobbesian world of perpetual violence and brutality, but as a Lockean state of nature in which Native Americans lived in relative peace, liberty, and ease compared with their European contemporaries. This view of Native Americans had a long and distinguished lineage in European letters, and Franklin's contributions to it were not especially original, but by distilling the ideas of previous writers, he helped cement the Native American's reputation as a noble savage in Enlightenment thought.

Franklin's most significant articulation of the noble savage idea came in "Remarks Concerning the Savages of North-America" (1783), one of the brief unpublished essays he wrote for his salon associates during his Paris years. "Remarks" owes an obvious debt to Michel de Montaigne's "Des Cannibales" (1580), perhaps the most influential depiction of the noble savage in Renaissance literature. Montaigne's cultural relativism was evident in his definition of barbarism – "Each man calls barbarism whatever is not his own practice" (Montaigne, 1943: 77) – and his positive comparison of Indian cannibalism to European methods of execution – "there is more barbarity in eating a man alive than in eating him dead, in tearing by tortures and the rack a body still full of feeling, in roasting him bit by bit, having him bitten and mangled by dogs and swine ... than in roasting him and eating him dead" (Montaigne, 1943: 85).

Franklin aped Montaigne's definition of barbarism in the opening sentence of "Remarks": "Savages we call them, because their manners differ from ours, which we think the Perfection of Civility; they think the same of theirs" (Franklin, 1987: 969). He also borrowed from Montaigne the rhetorical device of critiquing civilized society through the eyes of an Indian observer. In Montaigne's case, the perspective was provided by three Indian visitors to Rouen, who when asked to report what they found "most amazing" about France named two things: first, "they thought it very strange that so many grown men, bearded, strong, and armed" submitted to the rule of a child-king, and secondly, that "they had noticed that there were among us men full and gorged with all sorts of good things, and that their other halves were beggars at their doors, emaciated with hunger and poverty" (Montaigne, 1943: 91).

In "Remarks," Franklin twice used Canasatego, the Iroquois chief whose speeches Franklin had published in the Lancaster Treaty of 1744, in the same capacity, as a stranger in a strange land whose insights exposed the contradictions and hypocrisies in European society. In the first instance, Franklin embellished on an incident that had occurred at the Lancaster treaty. During their closing speech, the Virginian delegation offered to enroll some Iroquois children *gratis* at a mission school in Williamsburg. At the treaty, Canastego politely declined the offer, stating:

> We ... love our Children too well to send them so great a Way, and the *Indians* are not inclined to give their Children Learning. We allow it to be good, and we thank you for your Invitation but our Customs differing from yours, you will be so good as to excuse us. (Kalter, 2006: 117–118)

In Franklin's retelling of this exchange, he changed Canasatego's response to emphasize the Indians' disgust with European education. The chief explained that the Iroquois had previously sent some of their children to similar schools in the northern colonies, "but when they came back to us, they were bad Runners, ignorant of every means of living in the Woods, unable to bear either Cold or Hunger, and knew neither how to build a Cabin, take a Deer, or kill an Enemy; spoke our Language imperfectly; were fit therefore neither for Hunters, Warriors, or Counsellors; they were totally good for nothing." Instead, Canasatego recommended, "if The Gentlemen of Virginia will send us a dozen of their Sons, we will take great Care of their Education, instruct them in all we know, and make *Men* of them" (Franklin, 1987: 969–970).

Having undercut the European presumption that Indians would naturally want to learn and emulate European ways, Franklin returned to Canasatego at the end of the essay to take a swipe at the Europeans' supposedly Christian virtues. This time he fabricated a story he claimed to have heard from the Indian interpreter Conrad Weiser. One day, while sharing a pipe with Weiser, Canasatego asked his old friend to explain something to him. The Indian chief had often been to Albany and noticed that once a week, the Dutch traders there closed their shops and "assemble all in the great House." What did they do inside that great house? "They meet there," Weiser explained, "to hear & learn *good things*." Canasatego expressed doubts about that explanation. Instead, he thought "the real Purpose" of the weekly meeting "was to consult, how to cheat Indians in the Price of Beaver." Canasatego reminded Weiser of the reception that any white person received when visiting an Indian village: "we all treat him as I treat you; we dry him if he is wet, we warm him if he is cold, and given him Meat & Drink that he may allay his Thirst & Hunger, & we spread soft Furs for him to rest & sleep on." But when Indians visit "a white Man's House in Albany, and ask for Victuals & Drink, they say, where is your Money? And if I have none, they say, get out, you Indian dog" (Franklin, 1987: 973–974).

Montaigne and Franklin shared the assumption that Indians possessed a natural politeness – as exhibited in their hospitality, sympathy, and generosity – because they still lived in the state of nature. Montaigne explained this by reversing the supposed connection between nature and barbarism. "Wild" people exhibited greater civility because their lives were closer to nature's original perfection, uncluttered by artificial distinctions and divisions imposed by religion and society: "it is those that we have changed artificially and led astray from the common order, that we should rather call wild" (Montaigne, 1943: 77).

Franklin also believed that the state of nature more accurately reflected human nature than did civilized society. Writing to his London correspondent Peter Collinson in 1753, Franklin attributed the lack of success in "every attempt to civilize our American Indians" to human nature's preference for "a life of ease, of freedom from care and labour." Indians had "almost all their Wants ... supplied by the spontaneous Productions of Nature, with the addition of very little labour" (PBF, 4: 481). As proof that this was in fact the natural order of things, Franklin offered his observations about Indian and colonial children exposed to each other's cultures. Indian children enrolled in mission schools or bound out to colonial families took their first chance to run away home, never to return. Colonial children ransomed out of Indian captivity, on the other hand, "tho' ... treated with all imaginable tenderness to prevail with them to stay among the English, yet in a Short time they become disgusted with our manner of life, and the care and pains that are necessary to support it, and take the first good Opportunity of escaping again into the Woods, from whence there is no reclaiming them" (PBF, 4: 481–482).

But in Franklin's reasoning, life in the state of nature also retarded the Indians' economic and political development. The American landscape, with its plentiful hunting and fishing, enabled Indians to live in their nomadic manner and earn their living with little effort. "They visit us frequently, and see the advantages that Arts, Sciences, and compact Society procure us," Franklin wrote to Collinson, "... yet they have never shewn any Inclination to change their manner of life for ours, or to learn any of our Arts." Reflecting on this reluctance, Franklin posited that humans first embraced labor and technological innovation "not from choice, but from necessity," when population growth, warfare, or geography forced them "into some narrow Territories, which without labour would not afford them Food" (PBF, 4: 482). With little need to labor and no arts and sciences to create in them a desire for artificial wants, Indians developed no notions of property or wealth, and hence, created no laws or governments to protect them. Indians were naturally hospitable because they had so little to share. They were neither possessive nor grasping because their few wants were so easily met.

This absence of material wealth meant that Indians lived without social inequality, but it also meant that they possessed no government or laws, that they had yet to enter into the social contract that was the foundation of civil society. In "Remarks Concerning the Savages of North-America," Franklin described Indian society as held together by persuasion rather than coercion: "all their Government is by Counsel or Advice of the Sages; there is no Force, there are no Prisons, no Officers to compel Obedience, or inflict Punishment" (Franklin, 1987: 969). Although Franklin admired Indian oratory, he could find in it no model for government worthy of imitation by people who had already entered into a social contract.

Franklin also used the noble savage to question and poke fun at the doctrinal certainties of Christianity. In describing Native American spiritual beliefs, he tended to present Indians as fellow deists who acknowledged an all-powerful creator but doubted the veracity of scriptural stories and Christianity's monopoly on truth. In "The Captivity of William Henry" (1768), a satire he wrote for the *London Chronicle*, Franklin fabricated the story of a New England captive living among the Iroquois, who took it upon himself to catechize his captors, including the old chief Canasatego (who, it should be apparent by now, was Franklin's go-to Indian for such tales). After the earnest captive related the Genesis creation story, his Indian listeners returned the favor by relating first the Oneida creation story and then the Seneca. When the captive claimed that only the Genesis story was true because it was "written down by direction of the great spirit himself," Canasatego chastised him for his impoliteness: "You see I always believed your stories, why do you not believe mine?" The other Indians agreed and told their would-be catechist that "my stories indeed might be best for white people, but Indian stories were undoubtedly best for Indians" (PBF, 15: 151–157).

Franklin revisited this theme fifteen years later in "Remarks Concerning the Savages of North-America." This time he related the experience of a Swedish missionary who preached at Conestoga, taking care to relate "the principal historical Facts on which our Religion is founded, such as the Fall of our first Parents by Eating the Apple, the Coming of Christ to repair the Mischief, his Miracles and Suffering, &c." After this sermon ended, an Indian rose and thanked the missionary for the valuable lesson: "It is indeed bad to eat Apples. It is better to make them all into Cyder." The native orator then related his people's creation story. The missionary, "disgusted with this idle Tale," told the Indians that he had imparted "sacred Truths" to them to replace such "mere Fable, Fiction & Falsehood." As in "The Captivity of William Henry," his audience politely but firmly corrected him: "we ... believed all your Stories; why do you refuse to believe ours?" (Franklin, 1987: 971–972).

As was the case with his opinions on Indian government, Franklin's descriptions of Indian religion did not exhibit great depth or subtlety. He liked retelling native creation stories, but mostly as a device for challenging the authority of Genesis. The skeptical but polite Indian auditors he wrote about in these instances mimicked Franklin's own impatience with overzealous preachers and Christian evangelicals. In particular, Canasatego – a flesh-and-blood Indian diplomat from Franklin's early career – became during his London and Paris years a convenient one-Indian chorus whose wry dismissals of Christian scripture and doctrine proved the superior moral sensibilities of natural man. This presentation of the noble savage in Franklin's writings owed more to Montaigne than any actual Indians Franklin may have met in his lifetime.

9.5 "The Lovely White and Red"

Franklin's writings about Indians, especially after he left the Pennsylvania Assembly in 1757, rarely engaged concrete issues related to colonial-Indian relations. Instead, he dealt mostly in metaphorical Indians, using them to symbolize the savagery of frontier warfare, the perfidy of the British Crown, or the merits of deism over Christianity. Unlike Washington and Jefferson, Franklin never served as President of the United States and therefore never confronted the challenge of developing a coherent Indian policy for the new nation. It is difficult, then, to speak definitively about the future Franklin envisioned for Indians in the American nation, but his most significant utterances on the matter did not bode well for the land's native inhabitants.

In "Observations Concerning the Increase of Mankind" (1751), Franklin marveled at the rate of population growth in the colonies and predicted the day when more of the king's subjects would live in America than Britain. In the closing paragraph, he recommended "excluding all Blacks and Tawneys" from America, so that "the lovely White and Red" (PBF, 4: 234) might define the continent's complexion. Franklin did not, however, expect "the lovely White and Red" to intermingle. Nowhere in this essay or elsewhere in his writings did he endorse intermarriage or predict the creation of a mestizo population similar to that in Spanish America. On the contrary, Franklin tended to describe colonial population growth in North America as a demographic juggernaut that native peoples would be unable to withstand.

In "Observations," Franklin explained the dynamics of population growth in terms of political economy and social evolution. As hunters, Indians required large expanses of land to support their comparatively meager populations. European colonists, as farmers and husbandmen, were capable of supporting much larger populations on the small tracts of land Indians readily sold to them in exchange for manufactured goods. This exchange would continue so long as Indians preferred their life of ease in the state of nature to a life of labor spent on the farms and in the workshops of colonial society. As fur-bearing animals became scarcer, Indians would retire further into the wilderness to pursue their game, melting away before the demographic tide of the colonists.

Franklin did not expect this process of dispossession to be particularly violent or even difficult. Rather, it would unfold with its own logic, the natural consequence of the Indians' inferior position on the ladder of civilization. Franklin recognized their right to the land as its first occupants and in a 1773 editorial lampooned the claims European powers made to American soil based on the right of discovery. Such "Parchment Right," he conjectured, would be rejected out of hand by any Indian as "directly contrary to the Nature of Things and to Common-sense" (PBF, 20: 119). Instead, legitimate title to Indian land came by way of either purchase or conquest. Writing to John Sevier, a land speculator on the southern frontier in 1787, Franklin advised that purchase was always the preferred option: "It is indeed extreamly imprudent in us to quarrel with them [Indians] for their Lands, as they are generally willing to sell, and sell such good Bargains ... it is much cheaper as well as honester, to buy their Lands than to take them by Force" (*The Papers of Benjamin Franklin, Digital Edition*).

In his letter to Sevier, Franklin anticipated the federal Indian policy that would emerge during the next twenty years. As President, George Washington rejected the right of conquest that the federal and state governments had made to Indian lands during the 1780s in favor of negotiating purchases for lands in the trans-Appalachian frontier. Jefferson refined this approach by making the fur trade a tool of Indian dispossession. Jefferson advised the federal agents in charge of frontier trading posts to extend liberal credit to their Indian customers because land sales would be the only way to relieve themselves of such debts. Franklin did not live to see his suggestions to Sevier implemented by the federal government, but they did become the cornerstone of federal Indian policy well into the nineteenth century.

Franklin's most famous pronouncement about the fate of the Indians comes from his *Autobiography*, in a passage written in 1788, recalling his service as a commissioner at the Carlisle treaty thirty-five years earlier. Noting the Indians' proclivity for consuming alcohol at such meetings, Franklin related in a self-congratulatory tone how he and his fellow commissioners had managed to keep their native guests on task by refusing to serve them any rum until their business was over. When finally they delivered the promised rum to the one hundred or so Indians in attendance, Franklin was shocked by the scene at ensued: "We found they had made a great Bonfire in the Middle of the Square. They were all drunk, Men and Women, quarrelling and fighting. Their dark-color'd Bodies, half naked, seen only in the gloomy Light of the Bonfire, running after and beating one another with Firebrands, accompanied by their horrid Yellings, form'd a Scene the most resembling our Ideas of Hell that could well be imagin'd." The following day, an unnamed Indian chief explained their behavior: "The Orator acknowledg'd the Fault, but laid it upon the Rum, by saying, '*The great Spirit who made all things made every thing for some*

Use, and whatever Use he design'd any thing for, that Use it should always be put to; Now, when he made Rum, he said, LET THIS BE FOR INDIANS TO GET DRUNK WITH. And it must be so.'" Franklin did not disagree. Reflecting on the Indians' explanation of their indulgence, he concluded, "indeed if it be the Design of Providence to extirpate these Savages in order to make room for Cultivators of the Earth, it seems not improbable that Rum may be the appointed Means" (Franklin, 1986a: 135–136).

Written late in his life, many years after his public service in Pennsylvania had brought him into direct contact with Indians, this passage succinctly ties together the themes that had come to dominate Franklin's opinions about Indians. Their way of life could not be sustained in the face of colonization. The fur trade, which had lured them into contact and exchange with Europeans, would prove to be their undoing, introducing them to alcohol and forcing them to sell their land from under their feet. Furthermore, this process was preordained. Providence and history were on the side of the "Cultivators of the Earth," who would displace the Indians and multiply endlessly on their former hunting grounds.

Franklin's opinions about Indians could be insightful and prejudicial, sympathetic and condescending. He was one of the rare Anglo-Americans of the colonial and Revolutionary eras to assume an Indian perspective in his writings or to describe positively their character, manners, customs, and spiritual beliefs. At times, he exhibited an anthropologist's fascination with Indian society and embraced a preternaturally modern cultural relativism. Among his colonial and European contemporaries, his interest in Indians as independent peoples – distinct from each other and their colonial neighbors and possessing customs and beliefs with their own cultural integrity – was unparalleled. Yet, as his career took him beyond Pennsylvania, Franklin grew just as guilty as his contemporaries of reducing Indians to stereotypical savages, whether noble or not. He could not foresee a place for Indians in the future of America because he condemned them to its past. Like the primeval forest they occupied, they would be unable to sustain themselves in the face of the progress of American civilization.

For many of Franklin's peers, Indians were condemned to extinction because they lacked and were uninterested in acquiring the trappings of Christian civility. For Franklin, it was never an issue of convincing Indians to convert spiritually; in his eyes, they were already deists and therefore more attuned to the animating force behind Creation than the Christian sectarians who presumed to instruct them. Rather, their crippling liability was their reliance on hunting and gathering as their means of subsistence. Time and again, Franklin referred to Indians in these terms, as economic savages who ranged over the landscape, plucking from it as necessary the resources they needed to sustain their simple way of life. It was this image of the lazy and improvident Indian hunter, the antithesis of Franklin's self-presentation in his *Autobiography*, that enabled him to justify their dispossession as merely the unfolding of the natural order of providential design. Jefferson and practically every significant white advocate of the Indian in the early national period shared this opinion. Indian hunters could not coexist alongside white farmers; westward migration offered their only means of cultural and physical survival. In this manner, Franklin's Enlightenment tolerance provided an intellectual foundation for the Indian removal policies of Andrew Jackson.

NOTE

1 Labaree, Leonard W. *et al.*, eds. (1959–). *The Papers of Benjamin Franklin.* 39 vols to date. New Haven, CT: Yale University Press. Hereafter referred to as PBF.

FURTHER READING

Anderson, Fred (2000). *Crucible of War: The Seven Years' War and the Fate of Empire in British North America, 1754–1766.* New York, NY: Knopf, 2000.

Jennings, Francis (1984). *The Ambiguous Iroquois Empire: The Covenant Chain Confederation of Indian Tribes with English Colonies from its beginnings to the Lancaster Treaty of 1744.* New York, NY: Norton.

Jennings, Francis (1996). *Benjamin Franklin, Politician.* New York, NY: Norton.

Kenny, Kevin (2009). *Peaceable Kingdom Lost: The Paxton Boys and the Destruction of William Penn's Holy Experiment.* New York, NY: Oxford University Press.

Levy, Philip A., Samuel B. Payne Jr, Donald A. Grinde Jr, Bruce E. Johansen (1996). "Forum: The 'Iroquois influence thesis' – con and pro," *William and Mary Quarterly,* 3rd ser. 53: 587–636.

Merrell, James H. (1999). *Into the American Woods: Negotiators on the Pennsylvania Frontier.* New York, NY: Norton.

Merrell, James H. (2006). "'I desire all that I have said … may be taken down aright': Revisiting Teedyuscung's 1756 Treaty Council Speeches," *William and Mary Quarterly,* 3rd ser. 63: 777–826.

Merritt, Jane T. (2003). *At the Crossroads: Indians and Empires on a Mid-Atlantic Frontier, 1700–1763.* Chapel Hill, NC: University of North Carolina Press.

Middlekauff, Robert (1996). *Benjamin Franklin and His Enemies.* Berkeley, CA: University of California Press.

Shannon, Timothy J. (2000). *Indians and Colonists at the Crossroads of Empire: The Albany Congress of 1754.* Ithaca, NY: Cornell University Press.

Shannon, Timothy J. (2008). *Iroquois Diplomacy on the Early American Frontier.* New York, NY: Penguin.

Wallace, Anthony F.C. (1999). *Jefferson and the Indians: The Tragic Fate of the First Americans.* Cambridge, MA: Harvard University Press.

Ward, Matthew C. (2003). *Breaking the Backcountry: The Seven Years' War in Virginia and Pennsylvania, 1754–1765.* Pittsburgh, PA: University of Pittsburgh Press.

Chapter Ten

The Complexion of My Country: Benjamin Franklin and the Problem of Racial Diversity

Nicholas Guyatt

When Franklin moved to Philadelphia in 1723, William Penn's colony was home to only 6,000 white people. By 1790, the year in which Franklin died and the United States government conducted its first census, Pennsylvania had nearly half a million inhabitants and was one of the most diverse places on earth. Although Franklin spent long sojourns in Britain and France, and played an important role on the national and international stage in his last thirty years, the work of his life was managing the social and political consequences of Pennsylvania's rapid expansion. As a printer, Franklin published Indian treaties, antislavery tracts, anti-German rants, and runaway slave advertisements. As a colonial official and eventually a national celebrity, Franklin wrote widely about Indian policy, the role of slavery in the British Empire and the connections between race, immigration, and citizenship. He corresponded with pioneering abolitionists like Granville Sharp and Jacques-Pierre Brissot, befriended leading race theorists like Comte de Buffon and Lord Kames, and worked out his ideas about race with a close personal stake in the moral and practical consequences: he owned slaves, dealt directly with Native American leaders, and bought land on the distant frontier. If, as many scholars have argued, modern racial thinking began in earnest in the eighteenth century, Franklin was well placed to observe and even to shape new assumptions about physical difference and social potential.

Franklin frequently encountered the intellectual and social challenges of human diversity, and he labored to meet these challenges against a dramatic and shifting political backdrop. He approached questions of race and belonging as a colonial politician, an imperial strategist, an ardent nationalist,

A Companion to Benjamin Franklin, First Edition. Edited by David Waldstreicher.
© 2011 Blackwell Publishing Ltd. Published 2011 by Blackwell Publishing Ltd.

and an international reformer. He provides a window on the emergence of eighteenth-century race thinking as a practical process: Franklin's views on race emerged mostly from direct experience rather than from reading. But his career also provides an unusually clear vantage on how the American racial landscape was shaped by questions of imperialism, nationalism, and internationalism.

10.1 Making "Good Subjects"

Most histories of European and American racial thinking argue that, at some point in the eighteenth or nineteenth century, white thinkers embraced a system of racial classification that defined fixed and permanent differences between human beings; with this system in place, it was relatively easy to conclude that some races had a higher capacity and potential than others (Jordan, 1968; Wheeler, 2000). But when did racism become an orthodoxy in the Atlantic world? David Hume argued for permanent black inferiority in a footnote to an essay he wrote in 1753. Lord Kames, the Scottish jurist, hinted in a 1774 study that the different peoples of the world had been created separately and had different capacities. And Thomas Jefferson, during his diplomatic mission to France in the mid-1780s, infamously argued that Africans might be permanently inferior to whites in the "scale of beings" (Hume, 1753: 291; Kames, 1774, vol. 1: 35–39; Jefferson, 1785, 252–263).

At first glance, Benjamin Franklin would seem to have reached a similar conclusion ahead of this illustrious company. In 1751, in his "Observations Concerning the Increase of Mankind," he projected a further increase in Pennsylvania's population and candidly described the people he would like as fellow colonists:

> [T]he Number of purely white People in the World is proportionably very small. All Africa is black or tawny. Asia chiefly tawny. America (exclusive of the new Comers) wholly so. And in Europe, the Spaniards, Italians, French, Russians and Swedes, are generally of what we call a swarthy Complexion; as are the Germans also, the Saxons only excepted, who with the English, make the principal Body of White People on the Face of the Earth. I could wish their Numbers were increased. And while we are, as I may call it, *Scouring* our planet, by clearing America of Woods, and so making this Side of our Globe reflect a brighter Light to the Eyes of Inhabitants in Mars or Venus, why should we in the Sight of Superior Beings, darken its People? Why increase the Sons of Africa, by Planting them in America, where we have so fair an Opportunity, by excluding all Blacks and Tawneys, of increasing the lovely White and Red?

In his final prescription Franklin had not glimpsed an Anglo-Indian utopia in which Native Americans and colonists would fill up the continent: the "white and red" referred to the two shades of the British complexion, which clearly contrasted with the "wholly tawny" Native Americans (PBF, 4: 225–234).[1]

It was not unusual for eighteenth-century thinkers to write inconsistently on the subject of race, though we tend to assume that ideas about universalism and the unity of the human race were gradually eroded by pseudo-scientific arguments for fixed difference and racial hierarchy. But after this florid paean to whiteness in 1751, Franklin seemed to move in the opposite direction. He became more insistent on non-white potential and on the human rights that were vouchsafed by universalism. Instead of seeing Franklin as swimming against the tide, we should question our assumption of a linear shift from a loose body of ideas about human variety to a fixed scheme of racial difference. On the question of race, eighteenth-century thinkers were carried on a number of intellectual currents – not all of them moving in the same direction.

Franklin and his correspondents used the word "race" promiscuously: at various points, it could refer to the people of a particular country – the "British race," for example – or the entire human species. Franklin and his friends applied the term to blacks and Indians on occasion, but could also write about "the race of youth," "the whole race of womankind," or even "the present Race of young Printers." The term was much too slippery to act as a foundation for a coherent scheme of discrimination. But, just as Franklin's views about race were influenced less by his reading than by his experience, so the practices of enslavement, dispossession, or marginalization did not always depend on a well-developed racism. Franklin's fate was to discover the limits of liberal thinking in the varied racial landscape of the eighteenth century mid-Atlantic (PBF, 3: 188–204, 10: 395–396, 1: 243–248, 4: 225–234, 11: 413–417, 35: 592–593).

***

As Franklin made his way in the 1730s and 1740s, establishing his fortune as a printer and making forays into Philadelphia and Pennsylvania politics, he soon perceived the gulf between William Penn's original vision for the colony and the messy reality that had ensued. Penn had imagined a Quaker settlement with a pacific attitude towards Native Americans; Franklin saw a jumbled and sprawling population, poorly equipped to defend itself from the French and their Indian allies. When Franklin had amassed enough money to retire from his printing duties in 1748, he became still more involved in debates about the makeup and security of Pennsylvania. In doing so, he thought about a simple question: Who would make a good colonist?

This led him to consider the vibrant settlements of German-speaking people that were clustered around Philadelphia. In 1747, as the French bore down on the colony, Franklin published a pamphlet (in English and

German) urging Pennsylvanians to repel the advance. Franklin flattered the "brave and steady Germans," and expected them to defend their new home (PBF, 3: 203). But he was unimpressed with their response, and over the next few years he developed serious doubts about their suitability as colonists. The immediate source of Franklin's unease was language. As a man who had tied his career to the proliferating influence of cheap print, he was frustrated by the barrier between himself and a prospective German readership. (Although he printed a number of German books, he never mastered the language himself.) Franklin originally expressed these doubts in letters to friends, though his views trickled into print in 1751 as a postscript to a pamphlet on Indian relations. Pennsylvania would soon become a German colony, Franklin warned, unless the tide of emigration could be held back. English settlers should learn German, he added bitterly, or they would find themselves living "as in a foreign Country" (PBF, 4: 117–122).

It was at this moment that Franklin developed two important ideas about the colonies: that emigration to America would not depopulate the British Isles (which allayed the fears of some British commentators); and that a combination of prudent emigration and natural increase would lead to a doubling of the American population every generation. But he remained anxious about the current crop of European arrivals. In the eighteenth century, two of the largest populations to arrive in Pennsylvania were convicts and Germans. The former were "human serpents," Franklin insisted, and it was unlikely that their transplantation to America would spark a reform of their morals. (If British officials believed that a new climate could have this renovating effect, perhaps Pennsylvania should export its rattlesnakes to Britain and distribute them "in the gardens of the Prime Ministers, the Lords of Trade and Members of Parliament" [PBF, 4: 131–133].) Germans were only a little better:

> Why should the Palatine Boors be suffered to swarm into our Settlements, and by herding together establish their Language and Manners to the Exclusion of ours? Why should Pennsylvania, founded by the English, become a Colony of *Aliens*, who will shortly be so numerous as to Germanize us instead of our Anglifying them, and will never adopt our Language or Customs, any more than they can acquire our Complexion. (PBF, 4: 234)

Franklin was unimpressed both by the contribution of German settlers to the defense of the colony and by the response to his previous appeals (in German, no less) to their loyalty. His insistence that the Germans looked physically different from English settlers, meanwhile, gives some sense of the unsettled racial landscape of the mid-eighteenth century. Were the Germans white? Plainly Franklin thought they were not, in this essay at least, and he grouped them with the black, tawny, and swarthy peoples against whom Britain (and British America) had become a redoubt.

Other local commentators were more optimistic about the contribution of Germans to the colony's future, suggesting that the amalgamation of Germans and Anglos would solve the problem (PBF, 5: 206–214). Franklin stood his ground. In response to a letter from an English friend, Peter Collinson, he insisted that intermarriage would "either cost too much, or have no Effect." (Franklin envisaged, unromantically, that the authorities would have to offer Anglos land grants to marry Germans.) "The German Women are generally so disagreeable to an English Eye, that it wou'd require great Portions to induce Englishmen to marry them." The Germans, meanwhile, were so enamored with "thick and strong" women that the slender beauty of English girls would go unappreciated (PBF, 5: 18–20, 5: 158–160).

While Franklin used the argument about beauty to cast doubt on the prospects of intermarriage, this was a retreat from his earlier insistence that Germans were racially distinct from Britons. It now seemed that culture rather than nature had produced any differences between them. Moreover, cultural distinctions did not always flatter the British. In another letter to Collinson, also written in 1753, Franklin praised the "habitual industry and frugality" of many German settlers, which contrasted with the laziness of some "poor English Manufacturers and day Labourers" who had come to the American colonies. Again, culture rather than race seemed the key to understanding the difference:

> When I consider, that the English are the Offspring of Germans, that the Climate they live in is much of the same Temperature, when I can see nothing in Nature that should create this Difference, I am apt to suspect it must arise from Institution, and I have sometimes doubted, whether the Laws peculiar to England which compel the Rich to maintain the poor, have not given the latter, a Dependance that very much lessens the care of providing against the wants of old Age. (PBF, 4: 479–480)

This was classic environmentalism: institutions shaped people as surely as climate could, a point that Comte de Buffon made to great acclaim in the first volumes of his *Natural History*. (Franklin had been acquainted with Buffon's work since 1747, and received a copy of the *Natural History* from a Paris friend in 1754 [PBF, 3: 110–112, 5: 253–254, 6: 97–101].) Throughout the 1750s, Franklin presented a public face of accommodation and encouragement on the German issue. He followed his own suggestion that a "tender" policy be pursued with the existing German immigrants, and he served as trustee of a charity that taught English to Germans in the hope that they would become "good Subjects to his Majesty King George" (PBF, 6: 532–535). But his prevailing doubts about their citizenship potential remained a time bomb beneath his political ambitions in Pennsylvania.

By the early 1760s, Franklin had tired of the power of the Penn family, which continued to appoint the colony's governor. In 1764 he proposed that the Proprietor's man be replaced by a royal governor who might be more responsive to the wishes of the entire colony (Wood, 2004: 99–101; PBF, 11: 157–173). Ironically, given what happened just a decade later, Franklin pitched this as a populist campaign. But his appeal for support from the German community was wrecked when the defenders of proprietary government dug up those intemperate words from 1751 about "Palatine Boors" and the German threat to British settlement. Franklin tried to deflect the criticism – when he had said "boors," he insisted, he had simply meant "farmers" – but he was thoroughly embarrassed by the affair (Silver, 2008: 218–221). Franklin lost the royalization campaign and his seat in the colonial assembly. Soon after, he moved to England and effectively abdicated from popular politics in Pennsylvania. He spent the next two decades in Europe, leaving the business of courting Germans at the ballot box to his enterprising rivals.

***

When Franklin thought about Germans, he immediately fretted about integration. He did not experience the same anxiety about Native Americans. This had less to do with perceived racial differences than with the distinctive place of indigenous people in the colonial system (Pencak and Richter, 2004; Harper, 2006; Silver, 2008). Many of the most powerful white voices in that system had a stake in Indians living apart from whites. Merchants in London and Philadelphia supplied Indians with finished goods and sold their furs and pelts; colonial officials on both sides of the Atlantic supported the trade as the primary means of exchange between whites and Indians, and the system seemed stable and even mutually beneficial (at least until the slump in fur prices that began in the late 1750s). Franklin, like many civic-minded colonists, was a firm supporter of Christian missions and Indian schools. He had also profited from printing the colony's Indian treaties, which he distributed to curious European readers as well as to Pennsylvanians (Kalter, 2006). But the dynamics of the colonial system meant that there were few calls for the Indians to be assimilated into Anglo-American life and politics, in the way that Franklin and others were demanding for the Germans.

The problem, however, was the French; or, rather, the perception on the part of Franklin and other prominent Pennsylvanians that the French were desperate to disrupt the equilibrium of Indian trade and modest British settlement. The French were never very successful at persuading large numbers of colonists to settle in Canada, but officials in London and Philadelphia nevertheless feared that prospect. In the mid-1740s, during another French-British war, Franklin warned colonists about the dangers of abandoning the interior to the French (PBF, 3: 188–204). Indians would be particularly liable to switch allegiances if they had been unjustly treated by the British, and terrible results would follow: "Deserting of Plantations,

Ruin, Bloodshed and Confusion!" When French troops began to move south from Canada into the Ohio country – building a series of forts between Lake Erie and what is now Pittsburgh in the early 1750s – Franklin and his allies were convinced that the future of British America was at stake. If the French succeeded in taking this area, "our debtors, and loose English people, our German servants, and slaves, will probably desert to them." The settling of "a great people behind us" would doom the British colonies (PBF, 5: 457–463).

The solution to this dilemma had two components. First, Franklin sought to streamline and harmonize white-Indian relations, which looked hopelessly uncoordinated even as the French threat increased: colonies competed for land claims and trading rights; white settlers spilled over treaty lines and started wars with offended Indian nations; London officials had trouble keeping track of what was happening, even though much of this activity was conducted in the name of the King. Franklin's solution was the Albany Plan of 1754, which envisaged a single governing structure for the American colonies and for Indian relations in particular (PBF, 5: 387–392, 399–417). The Six Nations had recognized the benefits of a confederacy, Franklin noted. That the British colonies, with much greater claims to civilized status, had failed to reach the same conclusion was an embarrassment.

Franklin's other proposal was to settle two new British colonies between Lake Erie and the Ohio River, thereby forcing open what he called the "dreaded junction" between Pennsylvania and the western land that would guarantee its eventual expansion (PBF, 5: 457–463). Franklin discussed this idea with the Miami Indians during treaty negotiations in the fall of 1753; he believed that both the Six Nations and the Indians of the Northwest were willing to sell large parcels of land in return for goods and secure access to British markets. Needless to say, the new colonies would benefit from the implementation of the Albany Plan, which would offer them collective security and the benefits of a coordinated Indian policy throughout British America.

Franklin built these ambitious plans on a selective and not altogether consistent view of Indian intentions and ability. He shared William Penn's view that British colonies could be established and expanded without injustice to Native Americans: if whites ensured that they did not "much interfere" with Indian hunting grounds, paid fair prices for land, and supplied Indians with "many things they wanted," a happy balance could be struck between the demands of an expanding settler population and the lifeways of indigenous people (PBF, 4: 225–226). Until the 1770s, when the political context of colonial-Indian relations changed dramatically, Franklin rejected suggestions that Native Americans were innately untrustworthy or aggressive, and he critiqued the aggression and intransigence of backcountry settlers. But this critique was rooted in the same questionable proposition: that Indians would happily part with lands – and at a bargain price – if they were approached in friendship rather than at gunpoint.

Neither of Franklin's proposals was adopted. Commercial and political rivalries both within and between the colonies worked against an acceptance of the Albany Plan and Franklin's preemptive settlements, while London officials blanched at the prospect of closer coordination between the King's distant subjects. Instead, war with France broke out in 1755 in the "dreaded junction," just as Franklin had predicted. In a letter in the summer of 1756 to his friend George Whitefield, the celebrated evangelist, Franklin daydreamed that they had been employed by the King to oversee one of the projected western colonies and to "settle in that fine Country a large Strong Body of Religious and Industrious People" (PBF, 6: 468–469). This would have strengthened the greater British nation and advanced the cause of religion among Native Americans. "Might it not greatly facilitate the Introduction of pure Religion among the Heathen," Franklin asked, "if we could, by such a Colony, show them a better Sample of Christians than they commonly see in our Indian Traders, the most vicious and abandoned Wretches of our Nation?"

Although Franklin was supportive of missionary efforts among the Indians, he noted that even those who had spent time in eastern towns and cities seemed nonplussed by "the advantages that Arts, Sciences, and compact Society procure us." Native Americans were "not deficient in natural understanding," he told his friend Peter Collinson, and seemed aware of the tradeoffs between their way of life and the "civilized" path followed by British colonists (PBF, 4: 479–486). Theorists like Buffon had explained Native American "backwardness" in environmental terms: America abounded with game, the Native American population was relatively small, so there was no pressure on the indigenous population to advance to the pastoralist or agriculturalist stages of human development. Franklin shared this view but, unlike Buffon, he had had the unsettling experience of watching Native Americans encounter Philadelphia and shrug their shoulders. Where was the expected epiphany at the glory of civilization?

This could not be a racial phenomenon because white colonists who had become Indian captives as children could never be reconciled to civilized society after their rescue: "They become disgusted with our manner of life, and the care and pains that are necessary to support it, and take the first good Opportunity of escaping again into the Woods, from whence there is no reclaiming them." Even the rich would bolt for the forests if exposed to the attractions of savage life. One wealthy Pennsylvania captive had been returned to his family "to possess a good Estate"; on realizing the work required to maintain it, he fled back to the wilderness "reserving to himself nothing but a gun and a match-Coat."

Franklin here approached the conclusions of Jean Jacques-Rousseau, who used Native Americans both to satirize the pretensions of commercial society and to outline the natural rights of men. Perhaps the Indian way of life was a rebuke to modern civilization, and more closely approximated a human ideal that had been lost amidst the bustle and bombast of European "progress." Franklin wryly noted that Onondaga Indians had, at a recent treaty negotiation, politely declined the British offer to supply school places in colonial towns for their children. They had already tried this, and had been presented with hopelessly maladjusted graduates who did not know how to catch beaver, hunt deer, or surprise an enemy. The Onondagas appreciated the gesture, though, and offered instead to take "a dozen or two" of the best British children back with them, and to "bring them up in really what was the best manner and make men of them" (see also Chapter 9). Stories like this appealed greatly to Franklin's mischievous side, but the structure of the colonial trading system shielded him from the question of Indian integration. He could indulge a relativism or even a romanticism about Indians in the 1750s and 1760s, although the American Revolution would eventually force him to choose sides (PBF, 17: 380–400, 18: 208–211).

* * *

Compared with the last two decades of his life, Franklin said relatively little about slavery and black ability in the years before the imperial crisis of the late 1760s. But slaves were a ubiquitous presence in his household, his professional life, and in the city at large. As a printer, Franklin ran advertisements for runaways in the *Pennsylvania Gazette*, but also agreed to publish some of the first antislavery tracts to appear in the colony. In the early 1730s he purchased a number of slaves to work in his print shop or as domestic servants. There was nothing unusual about this. Even the Quaker establishment was protective of slavery in the 1730s, and one of the early antislavery writers published by Franklin – Ralph Sandiford – was banished from the sect for attacking slavery without the approval of the yearly Quaker meeting. But Franklin freely opted to become a slaveholder despite his familiarity with the nascent abolitionist argument. He continued to own slaves for fifty years, even after he became immersed in the international antislavery movement that developed in the 1770s. When his final slave left his service in 1781, it was through death rather than manumission (Waldstreicher, 2004).

Philadelphia in the eighteenth century was a city of overlapping hierarchies: gender, race, religion, social standing and, of course, money determined one's place and the limits of advancement. Although his ascent through American society would eventually become a cliché, one of Franklin's early satirical essays suggests both his disregard for the socially ambitious and his sense that the color line – whatever its physical origin – was a foundational marker of difference. Writing in the *Pennsylvania Gazette* in 1733, Franklin's ostensible target was that species of social snobbery which gripped the city's multiplying arrivistes (Lemay, 1987: 218–220). Contempt for servants and condescension toward one's purported inferiors were the hallmarks of the nouveau riche. In religion, politics and even romance, bumptious people crossed boundaries and then attempted to erase their origins. Franklin, on the other hand, preferred "to know my self and my Station." He presented the striking example of Philadelphia's small mixed-race population to clinch the argument. Mulattoes looked down on blacks and aspired to the status of whites, but earned the opprobrium of both. Blacks resented the new-found hauteur of the mulatto; whites resented the mulattoes' assumptions of equality, especially since mixed-race Philadelphians were "but just above" black people. Franklin's strange positioning here – mulattoes not equidistant from whites and blacks, but one rung above the black population – suggests an operational racism within Philadelphia that was both casual and deep-seated. It is tempting to see in the essay – and in Franklin's playful assumption of the pseudonym "BLACKAMORE" – an affinity between all who were marginalized by colonial America's many versions of inequality. But Franklin's employment of race as proverbially indelible is jarring.

Over the years, Franklin worked out his ideas about slavery and black ability against the backdrop of personal, even intimate experience. Although slavery and blackness had clearly become synonymous in the American colonies by the middle of the eighteenth century, Franklin's first pointed antislavery comments – in his 1751 "Observations concerning the Increase of Mankind" – were cast in economic terms (PBF, 4: 224–234). Slaves were undesirable because their condition made them natural thieves. They made free people lazy by undermining the connection between hard work and material reward. And they diminished the opportunities for poor (white) people by depriving them of jobs and by concentrating land in the hands of wealthy planters.

Franklin exhibited a casual prejudice about black ability. In the same essay, he regretted that Africans (along with the Germans) had "blacken'd half America" with their presence. In a letter to his mother in 1750, he alluded vaguely to problems he'd been having with his slaves at home, and declared that "we do not like Negro Servants" (PBF, 1: 474–475). Franklin did not theorize his apparent distaste towards black people, and his antislavery feelings advanced even as he retained doubts about black ability. In April 1757, on the verge of his departure for London in his new capacity as agent of the Pennsylvania Assembly, Franklin added a manumission clause to his will (PBF, 7: 199–205). (Although, again, his unusual longevity meant that the slaves in question died in his service regardless of the clause.)

Around this time, Franklin was contacted by the London clergyman John Waring with a proposal for the establishment of a "Negro School" in Philadelphia (PBF, 7: 98–101). Waring was a member of the Bray Society, a group of clergymen and philanthropists who hoped to evangelize the American slave population. As with similar efforts to introduce Christianity among the slaves of the British West Indies, Waring's plan carefully avoided any criticism of slavery: in fact, blacks who had been educated and brought to Christ would become "more faithful and honest in their Master's Service," or so Waring claimed. (The plan would depend upon masters agreeing to pay for the education of their slaves.) Franklin supported the idea, and provided Waring with a field guide to the sensitivities of Philadelphia slaveholders (PBF, 7: 356, 377–379).

While Franklin was in London, Waring and his associates kept him closely informed of the progress of their Philadelphia school. Franklin's wife Deborah wrote him in 1759 to say that the enterprise was a great success, and that she intended to enroll their slave Othello as a pupil (PBF, 8: 425). When Franklin returned to America in 1762, he agreed to help with the planning of new schools in New York, Rhode Island, and Virginia (PBF, 10: 298–300). Meanwhile, his visit to the flagship school in Philadelphia forced him to reevaluate his unhappy experiences with his own slaves. In another letter to Waring in December 1763, Franklin admitted that he had been surprised by the quality of the students.

> I was on the whole much pleas'd, and from what I then saw, have conceiv'd a higher Opinion of the natural Capacities of the black Race, than I had ever before entertained. Their Apprehension seems as quick, their Memory as strong, and their Docility in every Respect equal to that of white Children. You will wonder perhaps that I should ever doubt it, and I will not undertake to justify all my Prejudices, nor to account for them. (PBF, 10: 395–396)

Franklin had traveled to Europe in 1757 with at least two slaves in his entourage – one belonging to him, one to his son William – and had been irritated when William's slave King fled their service "while we were absent in the Country." King had ended up with a "Lady who was very fond of the Merit of making him a Christian," and the Franklins were content to indulge her in the improvement project and to postpone a decision on whether they would reclaim or offload their unruly property (PBF, 9: 173–177). If Franklin sounded acerbic on this point, and felt that the British were much too indulgent of their servants (black and white), the Bray schools seem to have altered his thinking. In the years that followed, he was less willing to dismiss black ability. He was also forced to adapt to a new political and moral framework, as both the imperial crisis and the emergence of an Atlantic abolitionist movement challenged him to clarify his views about slavery.

10.2 Between Empire and Nation

During the period from 1757 to 1785, Franklin spent only three years in America. His perspective on Indian relations and slavery was principally international and imperial, even as he retained an interest in the local ramifications of these issues in Pennsylvania. When Franklin returned to America in 1762, the Seven Years War had already been decided in favor of Britain. To some of the military commanders who had secured the victory – most notoriously, General Jeffrey Amherst – this meant that the old methods of diplomacy were anachronistic. There was no longer any need to purchase the Indians' friendship with lavish gifts, or to sit through the interminable theater of treaty negotiations to secure British claims (F. Anderson, 2000: 469–471).

Franklin, who continued to hope for a slow colonization of the trans-Appalachian region, was considerably more astute. In a letter to an MP in March 1763, he recommended that Britain "should let the Indians feel as little as possible, the Superiority we have acquired" (PBF, 10: 208–215). A ribbon of French settlers and traders from Lake Erie to the Mississippi River would remain even after French troops were withdrawn. Franklin had personal experience of Indian diplomacy, and believed that land cessions could be more easily secured through negotiation (however elaborate and costly) than through imperial fiat. Amherst's haughty behavior quickly produced a reaction from the Indians: during the spring of 1763, the Ottawa leader Pontiac launched a rebellion that spread throughout the old Northwest (Calloway, 2006: 66–76).

Franklin also realized the danger posed by his fellow colonists. Assemblies were keen to send surveyors and traders beyond the Appalachians, as if the western regions were the spoils of the war with France, and backcountry settlers spilled onto native lands and attacked Indians without fear of the consequences. He soon witnessed these problems at first hand. In December 1763, as Pontiac's Rebellion wound down, a group of colonists from Paxton Township in central Pennsylvania waged an extraordinary vigilante campaign against Conestoga Indians living in Lancaster, a town that was closer to Philadelphia than to the colony's western frontier. Having massacred nearly two dozen Indians – including a group that had taken refuge in the local jail – the rioters chased down another group of Indians who were hiding in Philadelphia itself. In a rare move of solidarity with the governor, Franklin met with the rioters to defuse the situation. Although the "Paxton Boys" returned home without any further violence, they won concessions from the Assembly and were never tried for the murders (Kenny, 2009).

Franklin quickly produced a pamphlet disparaging those who would wage race war in Pennsylvania. The Indians who had been targeted by the Paxton rioters had nothing to do with Pontiac's Rebellion or with attacks on the frontier. They were mostly converts to Christianity who had been living among white people for years or had fled to the east as refugees. Whatever outrages the rioters had themselves suffered, it was folly for them to revenge themselves in this way:

If an Indian injures me, does it follow that I may revenge that Injury on all Indians? It is well known that Indians are of different Tribes, Nations and Languages, as well as the White People. In Europe, if the French, who are White People, should injure the Dutch, are they to revenge it on the English, because they too are White People? The only Crime of these poor Wretches seems to have been, that they had a reddish brown Skin, and black Hair; and some People of that Sort, it seems, had murdered some of our Relations. (PBF, 11: 47–69)

Franklin continued the analogy: If his wife were killed by a man with red hair, would he be entitled to vengeance upon all "red-haired Men, Women and Children, I could afterwards anywhere meet with"? The proposition was absurd, and the rioters had acted "to the eternal Disgrace of their Country and Colour."

When he returned to London in 1764, acting again as an agent for Pennsylvania, Franklin argued that Indian relations should be managed directly by Britain and treated as an imperial priority. He supported the British decisions to restrict colonial settlement beyond the Appalachians and to create Crown-appointed superintendents who would enjoy exclusive control over trade and diplomacy. He continued to believe that the thin line of backcountry settlement amounted to a tripwire for Indian wars, and that a well-managed and compact western colony would be a better option. But he still envisaged an empire of commerce rather than settlement in which the old subtleties of white–Indian relations might be restored. He also strengthened his personal and professional ties to Philadelphia merchants who profited from the Indian trade (PBF, 12: 403–406, 13: 416, 13: 395–402).

Two developments in the mid-1760s upset Franklin's balance. First, British bureaucrats proved lackadaisical in their handling of Native American relations. Franklin was alarmed to hear that Sir William Johnson, British superintendent for Indian affairs in the northern colonies, had sent proposals and treaty outlines to London and had not received a response. In the febrile mood after Pontiac's Rebellion, Franklin and Johnson agreed on the need for decisiveness: the Six Nations were willing to cede their claims to land to the south and west of Lake Erie, and a group of Delawares and Shawnees had even offered to make land grants to compensate Philadelphia traders for the losses they had experienced during the 1763 uprising (PBF, 11: 326–330, 13: 416, 14: 257–260). But Johnson spent nearly two years waiting for Lord Shelburne and the Board of Trade to reply to his report outlining a revised boundary for western settlement. When Franklin eventually confronted Shelburne at a dinner in November 1767, Shelburne admitted that he had never seen the documents (PBF, 14: 322–326). With many British officials skeptical of the strategy of expanding western settlements, Franklin came to doubt Britain's competence and commitment.

The other challenge to an imperial Indian machinery was more subtle. In 1765, Franklin was drawn into the crisis surrounding American protests against the Stamp Act. Franklin, ensconced in London society once again, did not realize the inflammatory potential of the Act. When news of his relaxed outlook trickled across the Atlantic, some Americans imagined that he might even be the Act's author. As angry crowds in America's largest cities began to mass against tax collectors and other officials – briefly threatening Franklin's grand house in Philadelphia – he struggled furiously to overturn the impression that he now favored Britain over America (Wood, 2006; 107–113).

During a high-wire appearance before a Westminster committee in February 1766, Franklin rehearsed arguments that had been circulating in America over the previous months (PBF, 13: 129–159). The Stamp Act rested on the assumption that Britain was effectively subsidizing America's prosperity through its military presence, and that colonists should remunerate the mother country accordingly. Indian affairs presented an obvious point of tension. Many American settlers chafed at the restrictions on settlement imposed in 1763, and saw the Crown's effort to coordinate Indian policy and security after the Seven Years War as belated and self-interested. Although Franklin had been an advocate of centralization and imperial control, he now told MPs what his American audience wanted to hear: the Indian trade operated principally to the advantage of Britain, rather than America; the colonists were "chiefly farmers and planters" who had little interest in commerce with indigenous people; the Seven Years War had been "really a British war," rather than an American one; and American settlers had always shown themselves able to manage Indian diplomacy and even war without Britain's assistance.

Franklin had been a frequent critic of backcountry settlers; even after the Stamp Act crisis, he shared the view that "our Frontier People are yet greater Barbarians than the Indians" (PBF, 13: 416). But as the imperial crisis deepened in the years before 1775, he began to embrace a more emotional version of American history in which colonists had always practiced a heroic self-sufficiency. He also became anxious that the British ministry actually craved an Indian conflict. Would not this weaken the colonies and bolster the case for a British military presence (PBF, 15: 80–82)? By the outbreak of the Revolution, Franklin had inverted his earlier position: Indians were now British-sponsored murderers who threatened the peaceful farming families of the frontier – "the poorest and most innocent people." On his return to America in 1775, Franklin quietly sought to bring Indian relations under the authority of the Continental Congress (PBF, 22: 120–125). But in public he poured fuel on the frontier conflicts he had earlier hoped to avert. As British commanders on the eve of the Revolution looked to secure alliances with Indian nations from Georgia to Canada, Franklin tore up his plans for intricate imperial diplomacy and fell in with the "innocent outsettlers" (PBF, 22: 93–98, 22: 199–201).

***

The breakdown in relations between America and Britain also shaped Franklin's response to the emerging British antislavery movement. American opponents of the Stamp Act were quick to present the new tax as a form of slavery. British commentators accused the colonists of hypocrisy, since Americans seemed quite happy to enslave Africans. Beyond these charges and counter-charges, a number of British and American voices began to make a concerted case against the institution of slavery itself. This placed Franklin in an awkward position. He had admitted that slavery was corrosive and undesirable, but had taken no steps to free his own slaves. Now he struggled to separate a nascent antislavery movement from the cynical jibes of imperial propagandists.

Even committed British antislavery writers recognized the potential of America-bashing to advance their agenda. The visionary campaigner Granville Sharp loaded his 1769 book on the *Dangerous Tendency of Tolerating Slavery* with salvoes against American hypocrisy: "Men who do not scruple to detain others in Slavery have but a very partial and unjust claim to the protection of the laws of liberty" (Sharp, 1796: 81). Franklin responded with an anonymous pamphlet insisting that many slaveholders behaved "with great Humanity," that the condition of poor white workers in Britain "seems something a little like Slavery," and that the majority of black slaves were "dark, sullen, malicious, revengeful and cruel in the highest Degree" (PBF, 17: 37–44). These claims were later mainstays of the proslavery argument.

Franklin came close to a racialized defense of slavery in this essay (He even speculated that Britons must have enslaved their colliers for "having black faces," forgetting that "under the Smut their Skin is *white*, that they are *honest good People*"). But his attack on the character of African slaves was grounded principally on the notion that they were "mischievous Villains in their own Country." The African leaders who sustained the slave trade used America as a safety valve for their own undesirable subjects, an argument that precisely followed Franklin's complaint about the transportation of British convicts to America. He also insisted that the British commercial interest – and especially the Royal African Company – was the serpent that had tempted Americans into the slave economy. Even now, colonists who wanted to curb the trade were frustrated by an alliance of proslavery merchants and politicians in Britain and the Caribbean.

At this point, Franklin seemed vulnerable to the call of a purely nationalist and proslavery racism. His personal acquaintance with abolitionists in Britain and America seems to have pulled him from the brink. He received encouraging reports from the Philadelphia reformer Anthony Benezet, who insisted that the mood in the northern colonies (and even in the upper South) had turned decisively against the slave trade (PBF, 19: 112–116, 22: 254–260). In London, Franklin befriended Granville Sharp and the other members of his antislavery network. Franklin's first public attack on slavery was published just after the decision in the Somerset case in the spring of 1772, which implied that slavery could not be legally enforced within the British Isles. In an editorial in the *London Chronicle*, Franklin argued for the abolition of the slave trade and suggested that existing slaves in America should be freed "after they become of age" (PBF, 19: 187–188). He even pasted a few lines from Benezet's most recent letter into this essay. Franklin, it seemed, had become a mouthpiece for abolitionists.

In reality, Franklin was caught between two understandings of abolitionism's relationship to the imperial breakdown. Sharp, Benezet, and other antislavery reformers believed that abolition might reconcile the colonies and the mother country. Although this seems a fanciful idea, British reformers imagined that Lord North's government would soon collapse under the pressure of its own repressive policy, and that the opposition would coalesce around a comprehensive system of imperial reform in which conceptions of liberty would be harmonized and universalized. In the fall of 1775, British MP David Hartley sought Franklin's support for an effort to give slaves the right of jury trials in America, hoping both to curb slavery and to gather up the broken pieces of the empire: "Let us all be reunited in this as a foundation to extirpate slavery from the face of the earth" (PBF, 22: 257). Granville Sharp and his associates abandoned their efforts to score points for abolition by exposing American hypocrisy. Sharp resigned his position at the Ordnance office in protest at the war, and quietly sided with the Americans in the hope that political and moral reform might overwhelm both sides of the empire

Franklin appreciated the support of his progressive friends in Britain, and led them to believe that he looked forward to the triumph of antislavery. But the imperatives of an international antislavery effort fought for their place with the competing concerns of American nationalism – in particular, Franklin argued that Britain had behaved with unusual savagery in encouraging American slaves to desert their masters and fight for the king (PBF, 22: 93–98, 23: 69–79). The dilemma remained even after the United States had secured its independence.

10.3 Revolutionary Legacies

In the early summer of 1782, as Franklin worked on the draft of a peace treaty in Paris, he received news that history had repeated itself: Another group of friendly Indians in central Pennsylvania had been massacred by white vigilantes, this time on a much larger scale than in 1763. Nearly 100

Moravian Christian Indians – men, women, and children, most of them refugees – had been executed by a posse of white assailants at the settlement of Gnadenhutten that spring. A group of local whites descended on their temporary refuge, huddling them into huts before beginning the slaughter. While the Moravian Indians sang hymns and hoped for divine intervention, their attackers worked slowly, with a cooper's mallet, until they had all been bludgeoned to death (Silver, 2008: 265–276).

Franklin was horrified. He wrote immediately to James Hutton, a British Moravian, to convey his "infinite Pain and Vexation". But while in 1763 he had bemoaned the iniquity of white settlers in the Lancaster killings, now he identified a different culprit (PBF, 37: 586–588):

> Some of the Indians may be suppos'd to have committed Sins, but one cannot think the little Children had committed any worthy of Death. Why has a single Man in England, who happens to love Blood, and to hate Americans; been permitted to gratify that bad Temper, by hiring German Murderers, and joining them with his own, to destroy in a continued Course of bloody Years, near 100,000 human Creatures[?]. ... It is he who has furnished the Savages with Hatchets and Scalping Knives, and engages them to fall upon our defenceless Farmers, and murder them with their Wives and Children paying for their Scalps, of which the Account kept already amounts as I have heard, to near *two Thousand*. Perhaps the People of the Frontier exasperated by the Cruelties of the Indians have ... been induced to kill all Indians that fall into their Hands, without Distinction, so that even these horrid Murders of our poor Moravians may be laid to his Charge

Urging his friend to keep an open mind about what had really happened, Franklin attached a clipping from a Philadelphia newspaper alleging that the killers had acted in self-defense. In his patient and dignified reply, Hutton urged Franklin first to use his influence with the "Pens. Govt. to take effectual Care to protect & save the Remainder of those unhappy People". The newspaper smear on the Moravian Indians was tasteless and patently false. Hutton thought it absurd to blame the king for the massacres, and he objected to Franklin's effort to impute savage tendencies to any nation. "The Germans are not more murtherers than your French allies, all is murther if you please." He told a story from his schooldays in which another boy had punched him and he had retaliated: "He was punishd for striking me and I for returning the Blow for, said the master, the second Blow, the returnd Blow began the Battle." Hutton struggled to see any right after the war's beginning, or to attribute its myriad wrongs to any individual (PBF, 37: 666–667).

Hutton was on the defeated side in the war but, after the Gnadenhutten massacre, it was Franklin who seemed defensive. He had been reminded, in the most unpleasant fashion, that his personal effort to remake white–Indian relations in Pennsylvania had been a failure. The American victory enabled the Confederation Congress to play a more central role in white–Indian relations, but this hardly helped Native Americans. Congress dreaded the interference of Britain and Spain in the area between the Appalachians and the Mississippi, and politicians argued for a more aggressive settlement policy to check these imperial rivals. Confederation politicians saw western land sales as the chief source of revenue by which the new nation might repay its war debts, and pushed hard in the 1780s for a new set of treaties and land concessions. Indian policy was again shaped by the rhetoric of conquest rather than diplomacy, as it had been in the months before Pontiac's Rebellion (Prucha, 1984, vol. 1: 42–50; Wallace, 1999: 161–165).

According to the English writer George Grieve, Franklin had said on many occasions in Paris that the United States would "shortly find herself using violence against the savages" in spite of "reason, philosophy and eloquence" (Chastellux, 1789, 1: 404). (Franklin blamed the British, of course.) He could not see a way to avoid the "horrid extremity" of a race war in America and, on his return to the United States, Franklin was mostly a bystander. In 1786, after a request from the Marquis de Lafayette in Paris, he asked General Josiah Harmar (who commanded the U.S. Army in the Northwest) to collect vocabularies from the Shawnee and Delaware Indians (Lafayette to BF, Feb 10, 1786, FDE).[2] Like Thomas Jefferson, Franklin and Lafayette had already begun to refigure the Indians as objects of fascination and benevolence (BF to Lafayette, April 17, 1787, FDE). This may have been premature, given the drubbings handed out by the Northwestern Indians to Harmar and his fellow commanders in the early 1790s. But this romantic view was already spreading through the intellectual circles of America and Europe. (Lafayette told Franklin that the vocabularies had been requested personally by Catherine the Great.)

As the reality of a new wave of Indian dispossession became clear, Franklin's views came full circle. In 1787 and 1788, he corresponded with John Sevier, a soldier and settler who had become governor of the breakaway state of Franklin in what is now northeastern Tennessee. Franklin gave Sevier a basic lesson in Indian relations: The settlers should avoid war by "preventing Encroachments on their Lands." He acknowledged that "the strongest governments are hardly able to restrain the disorderly People who are generally on the Frontiers"; the challenges facing authorities in a new state far from the seaboard must be nearly insurmountable. But his underlying message was clear. If Sevier's fellow settlers encroached on Indian land, with or without the support of the Governor of Franklin, "Congress will not justifie them in the Breach of a solemn Treaty. ... If they bring upon themselves an Indian War, they will not be supported in it" (BF to Sevier, June 30, 1787, FDE).

Sevier's replies insisted that he and his fellow settlers had enjoyed peace with the Indians to this point (Sevier to BF, September 12 and November 2,

1787, FDE). Franklin, who had recently heard of an impending war between the Creeks and the state of Georgia, was not convinced. He repeated his advice in another letter that captures the limits of his vision:

> During the Course of a long Life in which I have made Observations on public Affairs, it has appear'd to me that almost every War between the Indians and Whites has been occasion'd by some Injustice of the latter towards the former. It is indeed extreamly imprudent in us to quarrel with them for their Lands, as they are generally willing to sell, and sell such good Bargains: And a War with them is so mischievous to us, in unsettling frequently a great Part of our Frontier, and reducing the Inhabitants to Poverty and Distress, and is besides so expensive that it is much cheaper as well as honester, to buy their Lands than to take them by Force. (BF to Sevier, December 16, 1787 (FDE))

Franklin retained his exasperation at the cycle of violence on the frontier, and his sense that backcountry settlers were to blame for much of the trouble. But even after decades of experience, he retained a conviction that there was no fundamental incompatibility between justice for the Indians and white expansion into their territory.

***

In June 1781, the death of Franklin's servant George in Philadelphia ended his fifty-year career as a slaveholder. Franklin was in Paris, and it is hard to know whether he gave serious thought to this milestone (PBF, 35: 184–185). But the years between George's death and Franklin's passing in 1790 saw a flurry of activity on the question of slavery, culminating in the famous Pennsylvania Abolition Society petition to the House of Representatives. Franklin's recent admirers have seen his signature on this petition as confirmation of his visionary status: While his countrymen dithered or dug in on the issue of slavery, Franklin realized both the dangers presented by its persistence and the radical measures required to remove it from American life. But this story has it backwards. The petition was the culmination of an international effort against slavery, and it seems less exceptional when restored to this context.

Franklin was well positioned to note the mixed impact of the revolutionary war on American slavery. He had decried the British for encouraging slave revolts, and had included black soldiers in his rogues' gallery of enemies to the patriot cause (along with savage Indians). But he had also cheered the efforts of Granville Sharp and Anthony Benezet, and had rejoiced in the news that Pennsylvania and other northern colonies had edged towards abolishing slavery. The American victory hardly removed the many contradictions surrounding slavery's persistence in the United States. In 1782 and 1783, Congress ordered Franklin and his fellow peace commissioners to demand that the British return "plunder" taken during the war: this was a euphemism for the reenslavement of thousands of people who had deserted Patriot masters during the Revolution to seek freedom from the British (PBF, 38: 413). While Franklin faithfully followed his orders, he began to think more boldly about slavery and its origins.

In his letters and in his rough drafts of essays, Franklin recalled that slavery had initially been justified as a humane alternative to death for prisoners of war. Most societies had now adopted prisoner exchanges rather than permanent servitude, and Franklin hoped that the laws of war might become more enlightened in the coming years. (After the carnage of the Revolution, Franklin suggested the exemption of all "cultivators of the earth" from combatant status.) Slavery seemed an anachronism against this evolutionary narrative, and Franklin suggested in a 1782 draft essay that the moment had arrived for general abolition (PBF, 37: 617–620). He was more specific about the fate of the sugar islands than the mainland colonies: Britain and France would do better to "let them govern themselves and put them under the Protection of all the Powers of Europe as neutral Countries open to the Commerce of all." But if Franklin's thoughts on the Caribbean had a self-interested dimension, they were hardly likely to assure slaveholders at home.

During his last years in France, when the Revolution had been all but secured, Franklin took stock of how Europeans viewed the promise of America. He was deluged by questions from potential immigrants, and a little alarmed by the common assumption that Americans (and their slaves) lived in seigneurial ease. Only hard work could secure success in the United States, Franklin maintained. If the young nobility from the southern states had given a different impression, as they slouched around Europe wasting their ill-gotten inheritances, no one should be fooled ("Information To Those Who Would Remove to America," March 1784, FDE). Meanwhile, Franklin received nagging letters from Anthony Benezet about the work still to be done in the United States on the slavery question: Benezet thought it "sorrowfully astonishing" that, in spite of the rhetoric of liberty on which the new nation had been founded, slavery was still legal in nearly all the states. He also wondered if Franklin, who had "the ear of the King of France," might try to advance the fledging French campaign against the slave trade before leaving for home (Benezet to BF, May 5 and May 8, 1783, FDE).

For a few nervous weeks, Franklin's homecoming seemed in doubt. A rumor circulated in the summer of 1785 that his ship had been seized off the coast of France by Algerian raiders. The British newspapers delighted in the prospect that Franklin himself might have been "carried into slavery," as his friend Richard Price later reported (Price to BF, November 5, 1783, FDE). A group of Americans on another ship suffered this fate but Franklin, with his usual good fortune, dodged the pirates and returned to a hero's welcome in Philadelphia. As he settled back into American life, he agreed to become president of the Pennsylvania Abolition Society (PAS) and continued to correspond with leading figures in the international abolitionist movement. Granville Sharp, the guiding light of the Society for the Abolition of the Slave Trade, was his principal contact in Britain. In France, he helped to guide Jacques-Pierre Brissot, who founded the Société des Amis des Noirs in 1788 and paid a visit to Philadelphia soon afterwards.

The Quaker activists who had revived the PAS in 1784 viewed Franklin as a key recruit. They were conscious of the need to diversify their ranks and broaden their argument beyond religion, and keen to trade on Franklin's celebrity. Benezet had already mapped out a political strategy: The PAS should ground the fight for black liberty in the Declaration of Independence and its ringing defense of equality. The Society's constitution, revised with Franklin's help in the spring of 1787, outlined three core arguments for abolition: the religious injunction of the golden rule; an insistence on the unity of mankind, in keeping with the scientific and religious orthodoxy of the 1780s; and the promotion of "the blessing of freedom" to "every part of the human race," as implied by the universalist rhetoric of the American Revolution (Constitution of the PAS, April 23, 1783, FDE). In early 1788, the Society sent letters to state governors from Delaware to New Hampshire insisting that slavery was "repugnant" to the "political principles and forms of government" that now prevailed in America. To Franklin's delight, he received a series of positive replies suggesting that slavery's days were numbered (John Collins to BF, May 12, 1788, and Samuel Huntington to BF, May 2, 1788, FDE).

After the death of Anthony Benezet in 1784, Granville Sharp became Franklin's closest confidant on the slavery question. Sharp had high hopes for the new United States. He believed that Americans would recognize the iniquity of slaveholding now that they had personal experience of "the horrid effects and unlawfulness of arbitrary power" (Woods, 1967: 10). He also expected that the abolition of slavery would be only one of a number of progressive measures in a new society dedicated to fairness and equality. Sharp's mind raced at the possibilities. Americans might adopt a new currency based on labor rather than silver or gold; this would ensure that every person retained a connection to the real work on which prosperity was based. The American republic would also need a new form of politics in which the views of every citizen could be channeled into decision making; Sharp politely advanced the system of Frankpledge, an amalgam of Biblical and medieval government (Sharp to BF, May 9, June 17 and July 5, 1785, August 13, 1786, FDE). Back in the 1770s, Sharp had envisaged a form of sharecropping for freed slaves in America, cheerfully insisting that blacks would form a "new and useful order of men" lodged somewhere between slavery and full freedom. In the mid-1780s, he moved beyond this and imagined a radical overhaul of the entire fabric of American society (Woods, 1967: 15–16).

Sharp conceded that his proposals might seem visionary, especially when applied to the established states of the seaboard. Perhaps they could be applied first to the new western settlements? Sharp waited patiently for Franklin to introduce these ideas at the Constitutional Convention in Philadelphia (Sharp to BF, August 13, 1786, FDE). In the meantime, he adapted them to a different context. In the winter of 1786/1787, Sharp helped to persuade around 400 people, mostly black loyalists from the revolutionary war who had taken refuge in London, to found a new colony in West Africa that would be governed by the experimental principles he had shared with Franklin (Hochschild, 2005: 145–147, 174–177). As these migrants left England in the spring of 1787, Sharp imagined that he had placed two bets on the political transformation promised by revolution and abolition. Either his small band of colonists would establish Frankpledge and social justice in Sierra Leone, or the wise men gathering in Philadelphia would breathe the same principles into the new forms of government in the United States.

Sharp was disappointed on both fronts. Sierra Leone was a disaster. The colonists arrived as the rainy season was beginning, and the colony's organizers had done a poor job of reconciling local leaders to the new arrivals (Hochschild, 2005: 177–180). Sharp, anxious that Franklin would blame the colony's travails on its eccentric political principles, bemoaned "the wickedness and *gross intemperance* of the Settlers themselves, both White and Black!" (Sharp to BF, January 10, 1787 (1788), FDE.) The news from Philadelphia was not much better. Sharp was bruised to hear that Frankpledge had not received serious discussion at the Constitutional Convention, even after he had briefed Franklin on its potential. The American obsession with "balance of power" was misplaced, Sharp insisted, since Europe's rulers had frequently demonstrated how one could easily "juggl[e] all the political weight and power into *one* of the Scales." And there were at least two massive concessions to slavery in the draft Constitution: the restrictions on any effort to curb the slave trade until 1808, and the guarantees to return fugitive slaves across state lines (Waldstreicher, 2009). Franklin may have flattered himself with the thought that the Constitution was neutral on the question of slavery, or that the 1808 provision was a form of gradual abolition. Sharp, at least, would not indulge Franklin's vanity: the clauses on the trade and on fugitive slaves "are so clearly *null and void* by their *iniquity*, that it would be even *a crime* to regard them as law!" (Sharp to BF, January 10, 1788, FDE).

The compromises at the Constitutional Convention should have dented Franklin's confidence that the cause of antislavery was moving forward. But in the letters from sympathetic state governors, or in the updates and embassies from British and French activists, or in the renewed assault on West Indian slavery after the publication of Thomas Clarkson's *Essay* in 1786, Franklin had enough data to plot the course of antislavery on an upward vector. Richard Price, the British reformer, assured Franklin in 1787 that the antislavery campaign had unleashed a new concern for the cause of "human rights" more generally (Price to BF, September 26, 1787, FDE). The London Society reported that the "hand of providence" was clearly evident in the "disinterested zeal ... discovering itself in different countries" on the slavery issue (Society for the Abolition of the Slave Trade to the PAS, July 30, 1788, FDE). In August 1789, Franklin even received a letter from David Hartley, the British MP who had insisted in 1775 that the cause of antislavery could heal the rift in the empire. Hartley congratulated Franklin on the French Revolution, the latest happy effect of the American triumph, and hoped that Britain and America could yet be united "in perpetual friendship and intercourse" by the "universal emancipation of mankind from every species of tyranny" (Hartley to BF, August 1789, FDE.) A few months later, Franklin signed the PAS petition to the House of Representatives demanding the immediate abolition of slavery in America (PAS to Congress, February 3, 1790, FDE).

In the spring of 1790, Franklin was the leader of the PAS in name only; it was the Quaker merchant who James Pemberton piloted the Society towards its collision with the first federal Congress. But Franklin's correspondence suggests that he was hardly a figurehead or puppet for more radical thinkers. Although he had helped to broker the compromises that protected slavery during the Constitutional Convention, the cause of international antislavery had advanced even during the two and a half years since those secret meetings in Philadelphia. There is no reason to suspect that his views in 1789 and 1790 were anything other than sincerely held.

Franklin's final words on slavery were directed against the Georgia representative James Jackson. During the House debates on the PAS petition, even many speakers from the deep South looked to cut off the discussion or to bury their purpose in euphemisms. The Constitution, after all, had demonstrated that it was possible to bolster slavery without bringing its claims and moral standing into public view. (Or without even mentioning the word "slavery," for that matter.) James Jackson, tiring of the petitioners and his lily-livered colleagues, bluntly made the case for slavery as a positive good. It had been "commended" in the scriptures, and who were the Quakers to dispute this authority? In a brutish aside, Jackson suggested that any federal judge who found slavery to be illegal would struggle to impose his decision in Georgia; "perhaps even the existence of such a Judge might be in danger" (U.S. Congress, 1834: 1242). Here was a glimpse of a very different future than the one that Franklin, Sharp, Brissot, and the antislavery international had been touting. Was it reasonable for Franklin to recognize Jackson as a better guide to the republic's future? Perhaps not. It was by no means clear that Georgia and South Carolina could make good on any threat to leave the Union over abolition, or that those states could rely on even the rest of the South to toe the proslavery line (Nash, 2006a: 75–85, 96–106). Nearly all of the Virginia delegation had voted to admit the Quaker petitions into the House record, against Jackson's vituperative opposition, and many prominent Virginia slaveholders admitted in the early 1790s that slavery was a doomed institution.

With Jackson in his sights, Franklin took up his pen to write one last satire for the *Federal Gazette*. Under the pseudonym "Historicus," he claimed to have unearthed a speech by an Algerian official writing in defense of slavery in 1687. This proslavery "African" sounded a lot like the representative from Georgia: The African climate was so hot that white slaves rather than African freemen would have to work the land; white slaves would be subjected to terrible conditions in their own countries if they were freed and repatriated, and they could not remain as free citizens in Africa because "our people will not pollute themselves by intermarrying with them"; if they were "planted in the wilderness" they would be overrun by "wild Arabs" who would "molest and destroy or again enslave them." The only option was to maintain slavery forever (March 23, 1790, FDE).

Franklin must have known that James Madison was already laying the charges that would scuttle the PAS petition, but the immediate prospects of Congressional abolition were not his only concern. After the conclusion of the Algerian speech, Historicus told readers of the *Gazette* that the British parliament would presumably reject the petitions that had recently been submitted in London against the slave trade, since "like motives are apt to produce in the minds of men like opinions and resolutions" (March 23, 1790, FDE). His British friends were telling him precisely the opposite. William Wilberforce was lobbying the British Prime Minister on a weekly basis, two separate parliamentary investigations were compiling evidence of the cruelties of the Middle Passage, and the price of human beings in the slave markets of the British West Indies was soaring as merchants and slaveholders feared that the game was up. Franklin lived long enough to see the defeat of the PAS petition, but there was reason to think that the antislavery millennium was just around the corner.

10.4 Conclusion

Thomas Jefferson lived too long for the good of his reputation. By the mid-1820s, the emerging sectional conflict had highlighted his fecklessness on the issue of slavery, while the rapid expansion of white settlers to the Mississippi River (and beyond) had embarrassed his pieties about Native Americans. Franklin, on the other hand, left the stage with impeccable timing. He had taken tentative steps to establish the new republic's Indian relations on a more durable basis, reprising his calls from the 1760s for careful regulation of Indian trade and a hard line against squatters and settler violence. His own longevity had relieved him of the moral stain of slavery, and in his last decade he kept company with the international movement to curb the institution.

Within a few months of his death, things began to unravel. In October 1790, Franklin's acquaintance Josiah Harmar clumsily began the first major Indian war of the new federal era. Initially the Miamis and Shawnees triumphed over Harmar's forces, but Washington and his Cabinet poured troops into what is now Ohio and Indiana until Native Americans were forced to accept another coercive treaty in 1795 (Prucha, 1984, 1: 61–67; Wallace, 1999: 170–174). This was not the end of the line for armed resistance to U.S. expansion in the old Northwest, but it dealt a sobering rebuke to Franklin's suggestion that white settlement and Indian commerce might be happily balanced by an enlightened central government.

At the same time, the antislavery international that Franklin and his friends had built was coming apart. Tensions between Britain and France over the direction of the French Revolution distracted leaders like Jacques-Pierre Brissot and tarnished the idea of universal human rights. In 1791, Brissot shuttered the Société des Amis des Noirs and took up a seat in the National Assembly, arguing for war with Britain and France's other neighbors (Rossignol, 2010). That same year, French legislators helped to set off the slave uprising in Saint-Domingue, the world's most profitable colony. Although the resulting Haitian Revolution was the largest and most successful emancipation in modern history, it owed considerably more to the slaves themselves than to the hesitations and the bickering of officials in France. By the end of the 1790s, the French government was doing everything in its power to re-impose slavery in Haiti by force.

The political chaos in France and the Caribbean was a godsend to the British sugar lobby, which somberly insisted that the regicide, Thermidor and the burning plantations of Saint-Domingue illuminated the true character of radical reform. This relieved the immediate pressure on Parliament to abolish the trade, but the disappointment of these years had a deeper effect. For some stalwarts of the abolitionist struggle, it depressed the hope that sweeping change was imminent or even possible. In 1799, Franklin's old friend Benjamin Rush wrote Granville Sharp a sad letter from Philadelphia, which was itself consumed by bitter political fighting over the European wars (Woods, 1967: 33). "Since the year 1790," Rush declared, "I have taken no part in the disputes or parties of our country." Rush had come to think that "disorder would reign every where until the coming of the Messiah." Or even that "this disorder is perhaps necessary to form a contrast to his divine and peaceful government." Here was another argument that, in unscrupulous hands, would bolster Southern slavery in the decades ahead (Guyatt, 2007: 241–244).

***

In debates about the future of Indians, blacks, and German immigrants, Franklin was both hypocritical and inconsistent. In the case of the Germans of Pennsylvania, this caught up with him in his own lifetime. In the matter of slavery and the fate of Native Americans, he had more room for maneuver. It is hard to account for his willingness to keep his slaves in bondage even as he ingratiated himself with abolitionists on both sides of the Atlantic. Thomas Jefferson, who spent decades as an antislavery slaveholder, glossed this paradox by speculating that blacks were inferior to whites and likely to be vengeful freemen. Franklin did not follow this line, though he imagined himself to be an unusually kind master. (Jefferson did the same.)

Franklin's inconsistencies towards Native Americans made less of an impression on his contemporaries – partly because they were shared by many other liberal Americans, and partly because the social and political landscape of the American interior was in a state of perpetual crisis for much of his life. Franklin's ideal for Indian relations envisaged a profitable commerce organized under a strong central government, and a slow and orderly process of white expansion. He championed this model in the early 1750s, and it still seemed the key to peace and prosperity nearly forty years later. The problem was that the conditions required to implement the plan never materialized. Franklin might, perhaps, have realized that the troubles he held to be exceptional – war with France, squabbles between western settlers and eastern legislatures, war with Britain, more squabbles between settlers and eastern politicians – had actually become normative. But this would have challenged his central assumption that white expansion and justice for Native Americans were harmonious objectives. Jefferson, who consigned blacks to an lower place in the scale of beings, had trouble seeing the Indians as inferiors. Franklin, for his part, could never quite understand why their extraordinary love of liberty – which made them such vibrant symbols of the American future – was shackled to a vast apathy toward private property (PBF, 13: 433–441). He didn't look for an answer to this conundrum in the emerging language of race. Instead, he dug in his heels and kept hoping that the peaceful equilibrium he had envisaged in 1750 would eventually be established.

I do not mean to excuse Franklin for these moments of doublespeak and inconsistency. Franklin's scant recourse to the certainties of race suggests that he was fully aware of the moral dilemmas bound up with American diversity in the eighteenth century. But an accounting of his career demands some acknowledgment of the role of international frameworks in defining political and moral possibilities. In his approach to Native Americans and to slavery, Franklin's looked to harness the hydraulics of empire and nation. He wrote often and at length about how power might be extended across vast distances. And yet his efforts to rationalize Pennsylvanian and British Indian policy were complicated by events and processes beyond his control: French attacks, turf wars between the different colonies and states, the lassitude or self-interest of bureaucrats. Franklin clearly saw backcountry settlers as a destabilizing influence. They repeatedly upset the protocols and promises of British and American officials. But the symbolic and practical role of those settlers was itself hostage to imperial and national fortune, as Franklin discovered in his patriotic writing of the mid-1770s and, more unhappily, when he tried to explain the Gnadenhutten massacre in 1782.

The same was true of the antislavery movement, which gained momentum in the 1780s not because the patriots triumphed in the American Revolution but because antislavery activists appropriated that outcome as a victory for their cause. Franklin's halting abolitionism took flight in an international context. Granville Sharp, David Hartley, Richard Price, the Marquis de Lafayette, and many other European friends urged Franklin to imagine an American future without slavery, and reassured him that their nations would come together to support the abolition effort. But by the 1790s, it was nearly impossible to hold together this international coalition, to the detriment of the cause in America.

This international context helps to explain Franklin's last stand against slavery, and qualifies the assumption that he was unusually prophetic in aligning himself with the abolitionist cause in the first federal Congress. But it is still worth saying that Franklin's encounters with blacks, Indians and immigrants brought him into early contact with debates and dilemmas that were central to the history of the United States before 1900.

In his own way, Franklin was an American pioneer in the field of race just as he was in so many other areas of enquiry. But it was in the limits of his thinking rather than his emancipated vision that he proved to be a pathfinder. Franklin ran into the thickets and dead-ends of the American racial landscape before almost everyone else, and he was better at covering his tracks than finding a way out.

Notes

1 Labaree, Leonard W. et al., eds. (1959–). *The Papers of Benjamin Franklin*. 39 vols to date. New Haven, CT: Yale University Press. Hereafter referred to as PBF.
2 Franklin, Benjamin (2006). *The Papers of Benjamin Franklin: Digital Edition*. Los Altos, CA. Available at: http://franklinpapers.org/franklin/ Hereafter referred to as FDE.

Further Reading

Harper, Steven Craig (2006). *Promised Land: Penn's Holy Experiment, The Walking Purchase, and the Dispossession of Delawares, 1600–1763*. Bethlehem, PA.
Jordan, Winthrop D. (1968). *White Over Black: American Attitudes Toward the Negro, 1550–1812*. Chapel Hill, NC.
Kenny, Kevin (2009). *Peaceable Kingdom Lost: The Paxton Boys and the Destruction of William Penn's Holy Experiment*. New York, NY.

Pencak William A., Daniel K. Richter (2004). *Friends and Enemies in Penn's Woods: Indians, Colonists and the Racial Construction of Pennsylvania*. University Park, PA.

Silver, Peter (2008). *Our Savage Neighbors: How Indian War Transformed Early America*. New York, NY.

Waldstreicher, D. (2004). *Runaway America: Benjamin Franklin, Slavery, and the American Revolution*. New York, NY.

Chapter Eleven

BENJAMIN FRANKLIN, CAPITALISM, AND SLAVERY

David Waldstreicher

In *Capitalism and Slavery* (1944), Eric Williams described the rise of the American north, and ultimately the revolution and the United States itself, as an outgrowth of the rise of the West Indian sugar colonies. To Williams, the origins of capitalism and the conditions for the American Revolution lay within, not outside or against, slavery. Leading economic historian Russell R. Menard concurs, arguing that we get a more realistic picture of American colonial development from Williams than we do from recent synthetic treatments (Menard, 2001). Indeed, the centrality of slavery to the development of New England has been stressed by Bernard Bailyn, who has never been accused of economic determinism or of putting too great a stress on slavery (Bailyn, 2000).

Perhaps the relative neglect of Williams' work by scholars of early America and the American Revolution derives from Williams' focus, in the rest of his book, on the British colonies that did not rebel, as well as more famous argument that the revolution encouraged industrial capitalism and thus, ultimately, worked against the slave system. The emphasis shifts from causes to consequences, from slavery to antislavery; the revolution becomes mainly a pivot in explaining how, in Williams' later much-debated terms, slavery declined because, after sugar provided start-up capital, British capitalism no longer had use for the institution. Williams' own transition from the subject of the revolution to the economic causes for slavery's decline turns on a quotation from Adam Smith, for whom English colonial policy amounted to "a manifest violation of the most sacred rights of mankind … impertinent badges of slavery imposed upon [colonists], without sufficient reason, by the groundless jealousy of the merchants and manufacturers of the

A Companion to Benjamin Franklin, First Edition. Edited by David Waldstreicher.
© 2011 Blackwell Publishing Ltd. Published 2011 by Blackwell Publishing Ltd.

mother country." In 1776, according to Williams, Smith had captured a fundamental meaning and ultimate effect of the American Revolution: its rejection of one form of capitalism (merchant, colonial, and slave-based) and its embrace of another (free trade, industrial, and free labor). But slavery created the conditions that Smith and the American revolutionaries wanted to credit to freedom (E. Williams, 1944: 107, 120, 1984: 217).

Smith's adoption of the rhetoric of British enslavement of the colonists is especially striking in light of his evasion of the subject of slave-produced wealth in the British nation. Where did this key argument from the founder of modern pro-capitalist economic thinking come from? There is every reason to believe it came from Smith's dialogue with Benjamin Franklin.

Students of Adam Smith and Franklin have weighed the evidence for their meeting of the minds and Franklin's particular influence on Smith. The evidence for influence includes their common attraction to physiocracy, their similar "provincial cosmopolitanism," Smith's possession of copies of Franklin's *Observations on the Increase of Mankind* (printed in 1755, 1760, and 1769), their meeting in Scotland in 1759, and a remembrance by Deborah Norris Logan of the two conferring, and even passing drafts of manuscript, during the years Franklin resided in London (Eliot, 1924; L. Carey, 1928: 36, 59, 106–131; Nolan, 1938: 200; Dorfman, 1971: 6, 9, 18–19; Muller, 1993: 22; Winch, 1996: 3; Lemay, 2009: 606–608). Michael Perelman has argued that Smith derived his rose-colored view of the North American economy, including his limited ability to factor in slavery or unfree labor generally, from Franklin. That influence itself became invisible because of the revolution. Smith agreed with Franklin on the folly of coercion, and much of *The Wealth of Nations* (1776) can be seen as a brief against British policy toward the colonies up to 1776. But by the time Smith was ready to publish, Franklin was anathema in England and could not be cited or credited as an authority (Perelman, 2000: 237–247, 254–279).

Leading historians of the revolution emphasize its antislavery effects, not its slave-owning roots. Gordon S. Wood describes conditions of freedom and entrepreneurship already present before the revolution and credits the revolution for further unleashing free enterprise. The founding generation may have unleashed an ultimately crass form of democratic capitalism, but it is nothing short of perverse to suggest that slavery played much of a role in that process or that they could have done anything more about slavery, because they were not talking about slavery. For Joyce Appleby, the persistence of slavery was a function of southern backwardness and resistance to the rise of capitalism (though even she now describes eighteenth-century capitalism as having "two faces"). For both scholars, Franklin epitomizes the capitalist, democratic, and antislavery thrust of the early United States. Franklin's America was hardworking, independent, proudly middle class, and ultimately antislavery (G.S. Wood, 1992, 2004; Appleby, 1996, 2001, 2009: 121–162).

Such interpretations surely have something to do with Franklin's popularity in recent years. To call Franklin "the first American" is to identify America and its colonial origins with freedom rather than slavery (Brands, 2000; Taylor, 2003). The identification of Franklin with freedom and with opposition to slavery has been reinforced during the past fifteen years by founding fathers historians and biographers. For Joseph J. Ellis and others, Franklin's antislavery credentials stand as the jewel in the founders' crown, particularly at a time when other revolutionary leaders have come under renewed scrutiny for their slaveholding (E.S. Morgan, 1991: 46; West, 1998: 5, 8; Ellis, 2000: 108–113). Even those who believe that the founding of the republic solidified rather than undermined slavery find Franklin useful as a foil. Building the case for Thomas Jefferson's hypocrisy, Paul Finkelman contrasts him with Franklin, "who, unlike Jefferson, believed in racial equality" (Finkelman, 2001: 174).

Like Jefferson, Franklin had an extremely long career in public life, which tempts us to take his late statements and actions as the most significant, authentic, and wise positions of "the founders." In part because he retired early from business, in part because he went to Europe and escaped his own Pennsylvania house, which continued to he home to slaves, he evaded the gaps between principle, policy, and practice that seem to condemn other founders to retrospective judgment. Franklin even lived long enough for his slaves to run away or die off – he did not have to actually free them in order to feel like, and seem, an emancipator. Yet only when antislavery became politically safe in his home state, after he returned from France, did he make fighting slavery part of his public identity. A longer view must confront the particular as well as belated nature of Franklin's criticisms of American slavery. The accepted view of an enlightened Franklin moving from a proslavery or indifferent position to active antislavery in his late years (Lopez, 2000a: 196–205; Nash, 2006a; Houston, 2008: 222) underestimates his engagement with slavery as a crucial aspect of his own and the colonies' political economy. Instead of considering Franklin as a northern or Yankee savior, and Jefferson as a southern sinner, it might be more realistic to consider Jefferson as an upper-south trimmer and Franklin as a lower-north mediator of eighteenth-century American political economy. Franklin's careful rhetoric and diplomacy helped Jefferson and other slaveholders resolve the contradiction between their fight against English tyranny and their ownership of slaves. He played a crucial mediating role between those who came to believe that the revolution should end slavery and those who hoped the revolution would do away with disturbing threats to slavery.

Celebrants of Franklin as our capitalist antislavery founder are correct, however, in assuming that Franklin's perspective on African slavery reflected his understanding and experience of the early American economy. His disillusionment with imperial political economy turned first and repeatedly on the colonists' investments in labor as commodity and as capital. For this reason Franklin's interest in slavery also provides a useful window on the labor question, and capitalism more generally, in the making of the American Revolution. The intensification of market relations in early eighteenth-century New England and mid-eighteenth century Philadelphia and its environs may have led Franklin to become the very incarnation of the spirit of capitalism. But the same relations spelled the rise of unfree labor markets (Waldstreicher, 1999, 2004). The freedom of some white men in a booming Atlantic economy depended on the bondage of others, some distant and some quite near (Solow, 1987, 1991b; D. Richardson, 1991; Jones, 1998; Eltis, 1999; Linebaugh and Rediker, 2000; Bézis-Selfa, 2004; Inikori, 2002; Tomlins, 2010).

During the eighteenth century, capitalism broke down many of the constraints of family and tradition, and did so with a particularly poignant if not tragic unevenness in regions on the periphery of both the economy and traditional institutions. The peripheral nature of the New World is precisely what led the old institution of slavery to become central to new imperial economies (Blackburn, 1997; Eltis, 1999). Therefore it is especially important to define capitalism, as I will do here, not only in terms of its freedoms but also in terms of its constraints. As recent Marxian accounts emphasize, capitalism coerced more and more people into dependence on the international labor market during the eighteenth century. Capitalism began to commodify everything, beginning with the colonies' most scarce commodity: people (Wallerstein, 1985; McNally, 1988; Linebaugh and Rediker, 2000; E. Wood, 2002; Tomlins, 2010).

Franklin puzzled over the changes involved in turning intimate relationships with reciprocal obligations – such as the apprenticeship to his brother that he escaped by running away – into something else. It mattered greatly that he came from New England, where a family labor system lay at the basis of economy and society but was experiencing severe strains by the time of his youth (Levy, 2009). Starting with the larger American scarcity of labor, in his popular early writings Franklin experimented with *people as capital*, a rhetoric that could address the freeing of some and the enslavement of others in the marketplace. He championed personal freedom within the bounds of one's station in life, while finessing the fact that rising men in colonial America had to prevent others from seizing their freedom. His role as a printer and proponent of paper money in the 1730s and 1740s inspired him to craft playful but revealing commentaries on the simultaneous rise of capitalism and unfree labor. The ironic distance he kept from his middling personae, such as Poor Richard Saunders, attests to their nature as marketed products. Paper money, and other products of his press, not only reflected but also helped regulate the conditions of freedom and unfreedom during capitalism's mid-Atlantic takeoff. Franklin's experience and his writings tell the optimistic side of the story, in which there seemed to be little difference between the coercion of servants and slaves and the other healthy workings of the expanding market. If it produced wealth and stability, the regulation of persons and laborers by the press could even stand as a model form of public service.

Only later, from the late 1740s to the early 1760s, did Franklin develop a merchant capitalist critique of slavery, arguing that slavery was inefficient compared to free labor, its encouragement an example of bad imperial regulation. He explicitly distanced white colonists from their slaves, from the natives, and from racialized European immigrants, all of whom threatened to dilute Anglo-American equality and the profits of property-owning colonists. But because his analysis of slavery's unprofitability seemed counterintuitive in the age of staple-driven colonization and economic growth (McCusker and Menard, 1985), he began to experiment with racism to supplement his attack on the institutions of slavery and convict labor. When this strategy proved ineffective, Franklin began to compare the unwillingness of the English to allow the Americans to regulate their own trade – especially the trade in laborers – to a kind of enslavement of the white colonists, an enslavement that left British Americans awash in a sea of undesirable nonwhites. Eventually, the critique of metaphorical or political "slavery" (and real or African slavery, blamed on the British) became a critique of empire itself, as Franklin helped forge a historically crucial combination of revolutionary American nationalism, capitalism, antislavery, and racism.

In the process, Franklin projected criticisms of colonial slavery back across the ocean, turning them into the very mark or essence of anti-Americanism. It was in this geopolitical context, during the 1770s, that Franklin developed the myth of colonial north America as the land of the free, a myth into which he literally wrote his own life in the famous first part of the *Autobiography*. This politically useful myth of early American freedom required Franklin to mislead his readers, and perhaps himself, about the economic impact of unfree labor on his life and world. It still prevents us from seeing the extent to which Franklin and America's independence depended first on slavery and later on the denial of slavery's importance to a nascent American capitalism (Rockman, 2006).

In 1723 Benjamin Franklin broke the terms of his apprenticeship to James Franklin and ran away from Boston to New York. Failing to find freeman's wages there, he proceeded to Philadelphia. Writing his autobiography some forty-eight years later, Franklin took special pleasure in narrating that moment when, after various nautical mishaps, he finally strolled off the Philadelphia wharf in his sodden, dirty clothes. Twice, he informs us, he was "suspected to be some runaway Servant, and in danger of being taken up on that Suspicion" (1990: 23, 26). Such scenes, narrated with humor and not a little irony, have the remarkable effect of drawing our attention to Franklin's rise from obscure origins and away from the fact that he in fact *was* a runaway servant – a criminal – and could well have been arrested.

That he faced such a potential diversion from his eventual rise was due to a structuring fact of life in his mid-Atlantic world: the trade in laborers.

Production for export, the settling of new lands, and the "consumer revolution" created a huge demand for labor in the mid-Atlantic colonies that was filled alternately, depending largely on supply and price, by indentured immigrant servants from the margins of the newly named "Great Britain," and slaves from Africa, the West Indies, and other mainland colonies. While in the long run slave labor per se may have been less efficient for the mixed needs of mid-Atlantic property owners, in the meantime a remarkably flexible labor system emerged, wherein slaves and servants were regularly rented as well as sold. Pennsylvanians "regarded black labor as just another commodity," to be bought or sold as profit dictated (Salinger, 1987: 81). In Pennsylvania as elsewhere this workforce was clearly multiracial – white and black and mixed-blood; foreign, Creole, and native – as well as free, indentured, and slave. It was not at all clear that either slavery or servitude was on the decline at any time before the revolution. If anything, the profusion of both sorts of alienated "others" warranted concern, but not enough to warrant any consistent official action, such as import duties, because the availability of both servants and slaves depressed the prices for both, thereby alleviating the "problem" (for employers) of high wages for freemen.

The mixed labor market spelled contradictory extremes of freedom and bondage. On the one hand, there were occasional opportunities to earn freedom, choose one's master, or steal oneself by running away, as Franklin did. On the other hand, the risks to masters involved in this flexible labor market encouraged them to invest more heavily in bound labor and look for ways to promote security in their labor investments, to reduce turnover cost. This was particularly true in the mid-Atlantic hinterlands of New York and Philadelphia, areas that, not surprisingly, saw the most creative and extensive use of new methods for importing, selling, renting, and recapturing bound labor, such as the advertisements that underwrote Franklin's newspaper (Waldstreicher, 1999).

In the world of Benjamin Franklin, slavery, servitude, and freedom worked together and provided a flexible basis for American expansion. In a set of queries written for the Junto, the club he founded in 1727 (see also Chapter 2), Franklin revealed this open-endedness by asking, "Does the importation of Servants increase or Advance the Wealth of our Country?" Franklin was thinking of the wealth *in* servants as well as the wealth that servants produced. The importation of not-yet-free people would certainly increase their own and the polity's wealth if all servants were destined to become wealth-producing freemen, but even when Franklin asked this question in 1732, he knew this proposition to be uncertain and that his own experience was as much an exception as the rule (Lemon, 1972; Schweitzer, 1987; Moraley, 2006). Nor, on the other hand, could servants always be counted on as a good investment for their masters, especially if they ran away as Franklin had. Consequently, Franklin's next question for the Junto was, "Would not an Office of Insurance for Servants be of Service, and what Methods are proper for erecting such an Office?" (1987: 209) Masters might, in other words, leverage the capital invested in servants to share the risks associated with buying potential runaways. Since masters also often acted individualistically, in an entrepreneurial fashion, by hiring for wages men who might turn out to be to be runaway servants, an insurance scheme could save employers from their own competition as well as from the expropriations of their self-stealing bondsmen.

Franklin identified the wealth of masters with that of "our Country," a logical extension of his daily practice as editor-printer of the *Pennsylvania Gazette*, for the newspaper has emerged as an important venue for the sale and recovery of unfree workers. When Samuel Keimer started the paper in 1728, he offered each subscriber a free advertisement every six months. The first three advertisements to appear in the paper were for land, a runaway servant, and the sale of a Negro man: "enquire of the Printer, and know further" (*Pennsylvania Gazette*, October 1, November 2, 1728; Smith and Wojtowicz, 1989; Meaders, 1993). The *Gazette* carried runaway and servant and slave-for-sale advertisement in every issue until, by the 1750s, when Franklin received a silent partner's share averaging £467 a year, each issue carried more than a dozen fugitive and sale advertisements (Van Doren, 1938: 123, 129; Waldstreicher, 1999: 250).

Franklin not only ran local advertisements, he also participated in the local slave and servant trade by selling goods and persons, and acting as an agent for their sale. In 1732 he offered sugar, soap, goose feathers, coffee, servants, and slaves, sometimes in the same advertisement: "TO BE SOLD, A Dutch Servant Man and his Wife, for Two Years and Eight Months, a genteel riding Chair, almost new, a Ten Cord Flat with new Sails and Rigging, a Fishing Boat, and sundry sorts of Household Goods." The language was the same whether the commodity was sundry or genteel, indentured like the German couple or enslaved like the "Two likely young Negroes, one a Lad about 19. The other a Girl of 15, to be sold. Inquire of the printer." Clothes, tea, servants, or slaves: all were advertised as "parcels," as a divisible number of mutually exchangeable commodities. Franklin also acted as an agent for masters seeking to recapture their absconded property. The material ramifications of print, despite its creation of disembodied community, were nowhere more evident than when masters arrived at Franklin's shop to get more information about a worker who had been put on sale, or to pick up fugitives who had been caught and delivered. And the reach of print was nowhere more telling than in its creation of a network of printers and readers who bought and sold workers or garnered cash rewards for information about them. This network, which Franklin extended and developed more effectively than any other contemporary printer, stood in direct opposition to the attempts of the indentured and enslaved to use their mobility to their own advantage (Waldstreicher, 1999: 268–272).

How can we square such facts with the venerable interpretive tradition that stresses Franklin's almost single-handed invention of the market-oriented free individual? (Breitwieser, 1984: 171–305; Patterson, 1988: 3–33; Wilson, 1989: 21–65; Zuckerman, 1993a: 152–170; Rice, 1997: 3–6, 45–69) Or with the literature on Franklin as an innovator of a particularly republican print culture? (Seavey, 1988; Warner, 1990; Ziff, 1992: 83–106) Republican print culture embodied communal good while easing the path of commerce; newspapers were, after all, a "metacommodity": a commodity about commodities (B. Anderson, 1991: Ch. 2). In this context, especially early in the century, the worthy editor straddled a delicate position between old and new understandings of individuality and the common good in market culture. The printer as public servant performed a balancing act between promoting trade and curbing its excesses. In a 1731 "Petition to the Pennsylvania Assembly regarding Fairs," Franklin complained that fairs were not real or serious commerce, but rather were run for "a Concourse of Rude people." At fairs, youths found themselves "in mix'd Companies of vicious Servants and Negroes. That Servants who think by Custom they have a Right to Liberty of going out at those Times, commonly disorder themselves so as to be unfit for Business in some Time after; and what is worse, having perhaps done some Mischief in their liquor, and afraid of Correction, or getting ill among Companions, they combine to run away more than at any other Time" (PBF, 1: 111–112).[1] The fair's traditional disorders, and the middling and gentry sorts' push back against "customs in common," here take on a distinctively colonial town flavor (E.P. Thompson, 1991). One of the excesses of the colonial American marketplace was the uncontrolled circulation of human commodities (including fugitives), which if unchecked could undermine the wealth and improvement the marketplace was supposed to create.

Another, related excess quickly emerging as a central theme in Franklin's public writing, was improper, counterproductive consumption, especially by the lower orders. In the first *Poor Richard's Almanack* (1733), Franklin invented the persona of the sensible if eccentric Richard Saunders, whose "excessive proud" wife threatened to keep him "excessive poor." The next year, public patronage of the *Almanack* created an embarrassment of riches explicitly addressed in the *Almanack*'s own introduction: while Richard bought only a secondhand coat, his wife has purchased shoes, two new shifts, and a petticoat. In part by constructing women as the hyperconsuming other. Franklin invented a poor yet virtuous male persona, and claimed print culture (via the almanac) and the marketplace (via the virtues of thrift) for ordinary free men (PBF, 1: 288, 311, 349; Pencak, 1992). Gender differences symbolize the order of class here, an order that participation in the market and in print could and sometimes did obscure. Franklin celebrated the market's ability to reduce everything to relative value, to enable people to pretend theatrically to be other than what they are, only to shore up, in statements that could be read either as parodies of the lower orders or as satires on elite pretensions, the need for a rational, calculating approach to behavior in order to conserve the opportunities the marketplace offered.

Franklin's populism was real enough, but it was tempered by political realism, a counting of the cost of drawing large numbers into the marketplace without excessively offending the wealthy or overexciting the indigent and unfree. His first published writing on the subject of race, a short essay signed "Blackamore" that appeared in the *Gazette* just before the publication of the first *Almanack*, also diminished a social distinction in the service of a market ethos. In the voice of a self-described "mechanick," Franklin satirized a "*Mollato* gentleman" – but not for the purpose of decrying racial intermixing, which he revealingly takes for granted as a social reality, or satirizing racism. Franklin's target, instead, was the irrational, self-destructive, would-be gentleman. Mulattoes are a metaphor for those of intermediate or mutating status: people putting on airs or missing their cues. They are no exception but rather the rule about modesty and the proper limitation of self-fashioning in a world of two classes – the ordinary and the gentle.

> Their Approach towards Whiteness, makes them look back with some kind of Scorn upon the Colour they seem to have left, while the Negroes, who do not think them better than themselves, return their Contempt with Interest: And the Whites, who respect them no Whit the more for their nearer Affinity in Colour, are apt to regard their Behaviour as too bold and assuming, and bordering upon Impudence. As they are next to Negroes, and but just above 'em, they are terribly afraid of being thought Negroes, and therefore avoid as much as possible their Company or Commerce and Whitefolks are as little fond of the company of *Molattoes*. (Franklin, 1987: 218–220)

Where association is conceived of as "commerce," reputation is a competitive marketplace, and resentment can be likened to social capital, ironically lent out with "interest." As the rest of the essay is devoted to the social (not racial) "Mungrel" (one of whom us compared to "a Monkey that climbs a Tree, the higher he goes, the more he shows his Arse"), the overall effect is to relativize race as another form of social distinction, perhaps no less but certainly no more real than gentility. Indeed, by suggesting that "there are perhaps *Molattoes* in religion, in Politicks, in Love, and in several other Things," and that "none appear to me so monstrously ridiculous as the '*Molatto Gentleman*,'" Franklin leaves open the possibility that racial prejudice is wholly arbitrary, at least compared with the real yardstick of class. Race is only a version of class – a cheap substitute in fact. In this view, blacks, though lowest on the social scale, can contribute to the common good, and in fact might do so by providing a lesson of humility to their upwardly mobile betters. The "mechanick" author suggests as much by making his own racial status ambiguous in signing himself "BLACKAMORE" – possibly a black man, possibly a white man passing as black.

Franklin's combination of sympathy for and ridicule of those who strove for wealth and distinction is as striking as his willingness to employ racial categories to relativize social difference. The Molatto Gentleman essay provides important clues into Franklin's perspective at the defining moment of his emergence as a social commentator. Together with his other writings and what we know of his early history, it suggests that Benjamin Franklin of the early 1730s, a promising young artisan and former runaway, found himself suspended between gentility and the "Atlantic working class" (Linebaugh and Rediker, 2000). To describe him as middle class would be anachronistic for an age when the "middling sorts" were only just emerging; to emphasize solely his critique of undeserving elites, or his seizure of gentility, would be to tell only parts of his complex story, to account for only fractions of his complex process of reinvention and appropriation (Blumin, 1989; Howe, 1997: 8; G.S. Wood, 2004). He resolved, or rather worked with, the contradictions of this position through astounding uses of irony, in fictive criticisms of the high and low, through the successive invention and publication of imaginary selves (Silence Dogood, Richard Saunders) who were then deconstructed in turn.

There is reason to believe that many people were working through these ambiguities in an expanding marketplace. And yet Franklin's position was already a privileged one. We cannot ignore the distances created by his printing and his personae or the fact that he began to profit so handsomely from them. His invention of imaginary people, disembodied abstractions of the self who worked in the marketplace for him and for the public, reflected efforts at mastery more than they told about the lives of the unfree. However picaresque and creative many of the unfree were, they represented themselves, in the flesh. The successful practice of anonymous authorship and the deft editorial hand, by contrast, were lessons in surrogacy (Roach, 1996): They showed that it is possible to invent or project other persons who act, under one's control, in one's stead. As Grantland Rice and Michael Warner have argued, the process commodified the self and authorship and created a new kind of authority as well as authorship in the process (Warner, 1990: 72–96; 1993: 75–87; Rice, 1997: 45–69). This was a lesson Franklin learned early, when, as he tells us in the *Autobiography*, his first broadside poems and serious essays moved people more when they did not know the actual (and unfree) identity of the indentured servant who wrote them. He learned in again when his brother, James Franklin, slapped with a special edict that he "*should no longer print the Paper called the New England Courant,*" (Van Doren, 1939: 31) came up with the idea that it could be printed under the name of his apprentice and brother Benjamin, whose unfreedom would be renounced – temporarily, for the occasion. Under pressure from his betters, James Franklin's freedom, his ability to act, increased greatly insofar as he could manipulate the terms of his brother's legal status. This incident, however, enabled young Ben to do him one better, claiming to be a freeman because his new, secretly signed indentures could not be publicly acknowledged. The logics of property and "representative personality" (Breitwieser, 1984) freed the owned Franklin to become an owner.

For Franklin, then, there were compelling parallels between writing for print, the printing trade, and the actions of the people and property one owned in the marketplace. His attitude toward paper money, a very controversial subject at the time (Newell, Chs 7–11), typifies this emerging set of relationships. Franklin took many occasions to sing the praises of paper currency, even as it arguably sped the process of turning labor, and laborers, into commodities. The money problem provided the first occasion for Franklin's expression of a labor theory of value – but from the perspective not just of laborers, as Ronald Schultz has argued (1993: 25), but of the consumers, the owners, of labor. "The riches of a country are to be valued by the quantity of labor its inhabitants are ale to purchase, and not by the quantity of silver and gold they possess," he wrote in *A Modest Inquiry into the Nature and Necessity of a Paper Currency* (1726). The particularities of the colonial economy required paper money, to encourage free men to hope to see the results of their labor, to decrease the consumption of European goods, and ultimately to spur the immigration of "labouring men." Thus, for Franklin, not only can money be seen as "Coined Land," as the land bankers of the era had begun to describe it: money is also coined labor. Since labor is nothing if not human time, if the circulation of a currency saves money, it actually creates real – not just paper – wealth (Van Doren, 1939: 102; Franklin, 1987: 119–135).

Of course, Franklin did not believe that people were literally equivalent to money. Rather, he demonstrated, and would continue to demonstrate in his widely distributed writings, that paper and people were usefully analogous. *What* people were like money? This question led to another: *What kind of people* performed labor that saved more money than investments in their time and tools cost?

To say that paper money would solve the distinctively American problem of scarce labor was actually to say more than that money facilitated exchange by turning "labor value" into "exchange value," as Karl Marx put it in his own critical gloss on Franklin. (Marx simultaneously celebrated and denigrated Franklin for offering "the first conscious, clear, and almost trite analysis of exchange value into labor value," stressing that he did so in a fundamentally bourgeois vein that "abstracted" and "alienated" labor [L. Carey, 1928: 16–44; Marx, 1972: 18–19; Marx 1977: I, 142n18]).

Money was not just coined labor: in its ideal form it was coined unfree labor – implicitly and innovatively in the form of the servant or slave, but metaphorically in the form of the unpaid work of women and children. In *Advice to a Young Tradesman, Written by an Old One* (1748), a compendium and elaboration of the advice in *Poor Richard's Almanack*, we find that not only "Time is Money" and "Credit is Money," but "Money is of a prolifick generating Nature. Money can beget Money, and its offspring can beget more, and so on." If the creation of capital is a blessing on the order of human reproduction, its destruction can be a metaphor for true evil: "he that murders a Crown, destroys all it might have produc'd, even Scores of Pounds." This understanding of people and money, and people *as* money, could even, in the famous "Speech of Miss Polly Baker" (1747), get an unwed mother off the legal hook, because she produced wealth in persons, thus adding to the commonwealth. The radical potential of Franklin's sexual politics relied on the logic of the production and commodification of persons as capital. Debates about women and their children might even be resolved by considering people as the ultimate form of capital (Franklin, 1987: 320–322, 305–308).

In this context, the famous prefaces and sayings in *Poor Richard's Almanack* (written by Franklin annually from 1733 to 1756) addressed free men with and without servants, urging them ultimately to come to grips with and naturalize a cash economy dependent upon unfree as well as wage labor. As Poor Richard Saunders, Franklin gave low-priced lessons about the relationship between labor, property, and money – even when conducting an intermittent monologue over whether he (Poor Richard) or the printer (Franklin) actually made a profit in doing so. Franklin even played with the idea that he, the printer, exploited Richard, apprenticing him to the public. By splitting himself in this manner, Franklin made it possible to speak simultaneously to various constituencies of freemen, a task his maxims, in aggregate, repeatedly accomplished. For every encomium to simple self-reliance – without servants – in the almanacs ("If you'd have a Servant that you like, serve your self"), there is a suggestion that people, especially those that work with their hands, should not "forget their proper Station," a directive about keeping servants in their place ("Never intreat a servant to dwell with thee"), and advice on how to recognize, and generalize, good surrogates. ("There are three faithful friends, an old wife, an old dog, and ready money") (PBF, 2: 5, 165, 261; 3: 170, 192, 196).

In a context in which bound servitude was a structure for the repayment of what immigrants, bankrupts, and those without capital owed for their maintenance, Poor Richard glorified the independent farmer or artisan and urged him not to fall into debt. Where freedom was literally the absence of debt, and servitude its presence, it made all the more sense to equate capital with freedom and with command over others' labor. Thus the advice Richard Saunders gave, for all his protestations of poverty, applied to masters and those who aspired to be masters, artisans and small farmers who could ill afford to offend elite patrons and ordinary customers. While Poor Richard continued to trumpet a labor theory of value, and thus the claims of artisans, in the 1740s, the almanacs staked out a precarious middle ground between the advocacy of wealth and warnings against the dangers of wealth seeking by working folk. This middle ground is the only way, it seems to me, to account for the Old Tradesman's serious advice, its comic overabundance, and the ridicule he finally faces in the marketplace from the people, who ignore him and go about their commercial business. These delightful theatricalities should not obscure its meanings for labor, which can be summarized as: work hard –and make your servants do the same or more. The ambivalences, even contradictions about work in the almanacs – who does it and under what circumstances – reflect the mixed labor system of Franklin's America, his attempts to rationalize the system through the trope of people as capital. These were the ambivalences of the master classes in early America, who were driven simultaneously to value their dearly bought laborers and to insist that the same unskilled menials were undeserving of freedom. For example, in 1748, Poor Richard entreated a husband to keep working, "Tho' his collected Rent his Bags supply,/Or honest, careful Slaves scarce need his eye." Three years later he wrote, "Not to oversee Workmen, is to leave them your Purse open." Franklin particularly addressed the kind of masters like himself, who had to work and who also worried about whether their surrogates were working as hard, and who needed to squeeze the most out of their sometimes recalcitrant subordinates in order to succeed (PBF, 2: 218; 3: 260; 4: 85–86, 94, 97; 5: 181, 473, 475).

Franklin continued to devote significant intellectual energy to the problem of surrogates, especially as he amassed enough capital to retire from his Philadelphia shop in 1748 but remained invested in several printing establishments, from Newport to Antigua. Because others recognized the potential of treating circulating labor like capital, and because servants themselves learned to take advantage of such a situation, Franklin became quite interested in the problem of runaway servants – especially those who enlisted in the British service or were impressed during wartime. The tendency for slaves and servants to run away seems to have led Franklin to think about what sorts of servants were really most valuable because they were least likely to suddenly take their full value into their own hands. The trade in slaves and contract labor seemed, at mid-century, to undermine security in that labor. Much as there were limits to the ability of paper money to stimulate labor and thus wealth, there were limits to the profitable circulation of labor itself. The roots of Franklin's antislavery, then, lay in the same place as his acceptance of slavery: his understanding of labor and capital, a major aspect of his own success and his much-celebrated ideas about America. The fundamental, yet enabling, contradiction at work became manifest in the wake of increasing slave importation, slave resistance, and imperial regulation. By 1750 it led him to articulate a form of racism – and a kind of antislavery – previously absent in his writing and practice.

Colonial growth led directly to imperial wars that joined metropolitans and colonists in a common enterprise but also put special strains on colonial societies, exposing the fault lines of race and bondage as well as differing assumptions about economic regulation and governance (Gipson, 1937–1970, 13: 181–184; Greene, 1973). In *Plain Truth* (1747), Franklin advocated wartime defense measures as Quaker-dominated Philadelphia faced potential raiding. If people did not take up arms, "your Persons, Fortunes, Wives and Daughters, shall be subject to the wanton and unbridled Rage, Rapine, and Lust of Negroes, Molattoes, and others, the vilest and most abandoned of mankind." People of color are again a metaphor, as in the "Blackamore" essay, but here with a much surer sense of the whiteness of a community of "we, the middling People." For the ordinary "Tradesmen, Shopkeepers, and farmers of this Province and City," mulatto seamen symbolize a world turned upside down, literally embodying (while racializing and sexualizing) the problem of war itself. Having divided the city rhetorically between rich and middling sorts, Franklin rested his call to arms upon the common, cross-class characteristics of the "BRITISH RACE ... BRITONS, tho' a Hundred Years transplanted, and to the remotest part of the Earth, may yet retain ... that *Zeal* for the *Publick Good*, that *military Prowess*, that *undaunted Spirit*, which has in every Age distinguished their Nation." Adding some praise for "Brave Irish protestants" and "brave and steady Germans," Franklin, writing anonymously as "a Tradesman of Philadelphia," sought a racial and imperial nationhood that would counter domestic religious divisions and the risks to profits, safety, and the interdependence of ranks brought on by the wars of the trading empire (PBF, 3: 198–199, 202–204).

Three years later Franklin penned his "Observations concerning the Increase of Mankind," an effort to reimagine the political economy of the mid-Atlantic, and the American future generally, without slaves or a permanent class of servants (PBF, 4: 225–234). The essay is often pointed to as an early formulation of the safety-valve or frontier thesis of American history, whereby the lower classes shake off the dust and move to unclaimed land rather than remaining where they are and becoming an exploited urban proletariat. Upward mobility and earlier marriage, Franklin argued, had already spurred a rapid rise in population: "our People must at least be doubled every 20 Years." The population boom would in turn create a market for consumer goods made in England. Both colonies and metropolis would thrive in these circumstances, absent conquerable Indians, ill-advised imperial taxation (the immediate spur to the essay was the Iron Act of 1750), and the overconsumption of luxury goods.

Even if industrious colonists began to manufacture, the high cost of labor in the colonies would make it impossible for colonial manufacturers to compete with British imports in a way that harmed the empire. The only remaining problem the mistaken idea that "by the Labour of Slaves, *America* may possibly vie in Cheapness of Manufactures with *Britain*." It was mistaken because slavery was actually a bad investment in the colonies when interest rates were high there, wages for manufacturing were low in England, and "every Slave being *by Nature a thief.*" Indeed, only the tendency of whites to graduate from servitude or run away beforehand had lured masters to buy slaves – a strategy which, Franklin insisted, only stunted the economy and, like other colonial initiatives (such as ironworks), could be taxed or legislated out of existence. The number of whites in a nation, whose labor was equivalent to true wealth, actually diminished in proportion to the number of slaves. Counterintuitively (as far as the imperial view from London was concerned), Franklin argued that the slave societies cultivating the Caribbean and the mainland south did not represent the future of the empire and America, because their white populations remained stagnant. Slaves and their owners did not exhibit "frugality and Industry": they were wasteful, unlike the infinitely compounding free people-commodities of Pennsylvania.

Dismissing the wealth-producing capacities of slaves while bringing the issues of policy and peopling together enabled Franklin boldly to address the slavery question – which, the wars of the 1740s had taught him, was also a question of imperial policy. This was even more the case in 1750, when a treaty with Spain awarded the *asiento*, or right to supply slaves to Spanish colonies, to the British. He turned slavery into a question of the overall trade in people, in which it could look like a bad bargain at the macroeconomic level. Slaves were taking up spaces that could be occupied by white immigrants, who would in the long run would add more wealth to an expanding empire. If the English thought correctly about their common interest with their fellow Britons across the water they would actually free the trade in people from a narrowly conceived mercantilist policy, which put the rights and interests of Englishmen over colonists and everyone else, and instead use *race* as a benchmark in economic policy. In "Observations" Franklinian industry and frugality require race in order to bring the seemingly divergent interests of the colonists and the metropolis back together. Colonists and Englishmen were white Britons; they deserved preferment over all darker races – a capacious category constructed more politically than phenotypically. This is why "Observations" concludes with its now-famous passage pleading for the whitening of America and the Americanization of whiteness:

[T]he Number of purely white People in the World is proportionably [*sic*] very small. All Africa is black or tawny. Asia chiefly tawny. America (exclusive of the new Comers) wholly so. And in Europe, the Spaniards, Italians, French,

Russians and Swedes, are generally of what we call a swarthy Complexion; as are the Germans also, the Saxons only excepted, who with the English, make the principal Body of White People on the Face of the Earth. I could wish their Numbers were increased. And while we are, as I may call it, *Scouring* our Planet, by clearing America of Woods, and so making this Side of our Globe reflect a brighter Light to the Eyes of Inhabitants in Mars or Venus, why should we in the Sight of Superior Beings, darken its People? why increase the Sons of Africa, by Planting them in America, where we have so fair an Opportunity, by excluding all Blacks and Tawneys, of increasing the lovely White and Red? But perhaps I am partial to the Complexion of my Country, for such Kind of Partiality is natural to Mankind.

The problem was that to anyone not on Mars or Venus but still on the ground in North America or Europe, it was obvious that America still belonged to the black, the tawny (Indians), and the swarthy. But not for long. Franklin concluded by turning the looking glass on himself, and in doing so depicted the real Anglo-American as white, with the turn of a phrase: "But perhaps I am partial to the Complexion of my Country, for such Kind of Partiality is natural to Mankind." If "race" prejudice is irrational, it is a "natural" irrationality. The darker races might not be inferior, but they do not have to be if racism can be naturalized and identified with a true realization of industrious America –Europe's enlightened future.

Since at least the time of William Appelman Williams (1959), Franklin's "Observations" have become an important text in the history of American "white liberal" race thinking and imperialism. Paul Conner and Timothy Shannon place the essay at the center of Franklin's thinking (Conner, 1965: 75–84; Shannon, 2000: 98–101). So does J. A. Leo Lemay, but in a celebratory vein, as "the fundamental document of the American Revolution." Lemay recognizes the nationalist themes but soft-plays the more disturbing accompaniments, calling them ethnocentric and racist, and leaving it at that (Lemay, 2009: xiii, 240–264). The more sophisticated attempts to mitigate the racism or to see through it to something higher than imperial politics or neo-nationalism take the form of an argument that Franklin is being ironic, or even satirical, about racism in the service of a true pluralism (D. Anderson, 1997: 158–167; Weinberger, 2005: 263–266, 323; Houston, 2008: 136). The irony is present, but it does not detract from the nationalist politics in Franklin; rather, it allows Franklin to have it both ways – to say that the imperial nationalism under construction is simply more important than the question of where ironic play with race prejudice may lead "us." If Franklin is too modern to be racist, in other words, he's also modern enough to use race as a political tool, winking at those who know better along the way.

Franklin was quite up to date in pairing enlightenment with racism but against slavery. During the late 1740s David Hume began to argue that slavery had spoiled the ancient republics while also maintaining that Africa's lack of poets and scientists proved its inferiority (Porter, 2000: 200; Hume, 1994: 86, 123). Hume and Franklin later became good friends; eventually Hume singled out Franklin as the first genius of the New World, precisely the kind he contrasted to Africans (Van Doren, 1939: 290; Waldstreicher, 2004: 182–183): Like Hume, Smith, and the other thinkers of Scottish Enlightenment, Franklin had special reason to write the provinces into the history of British imperial progress. He had more reason, though, to keep slaves and their economic contributions out of the picture of "my Country." And he had still more reason to preserve racial distinctions, intellectually defensible or not, if this would advance white colonists' claims to equality in an empire its theorists associated with commerce and progress.

During the 1750s Franklin became the foremost provincial theorist of British colonialism and nationalism, in an era when colonists and other Britons repeatedly disagreed about how they should view and treat each other (Crane, 1936; Stourzh, 1969: 33–112; Seavey, 1993: 19–37). Far more than historians have acknowledged, these controversies included debates about the supply of labor, especially in the wake of King George's War and the Seven Years War, when disrupted trading patterns forced colonial masters to compete with imperial armies for the bodies of free and unfree men. In light of subsequent developments, it is striking how early and consistently Franklin employed his adept vocabulary of people, labor, and capital to improve upon what became the patriots' most consistent and internally unifying protest rhetoric: their complaint against being treated like "slaves."

Franklin's earliest complaints concerned the sale of British convicts in America as indentured servants, which the administration in London forbade colonial assemblies to regulate. The forced transportation of convicts put into practice the idea of the colonies as a satellite for inferiors, turned into, at best, half-citizens and, at worst, objects laboring for the benefit of the home country. (Franklin also saw the impressment of seamen as a contravention of the rights of Britons and compared it to slavery as early as 1762; PBF, 35: 497). If the premise of convict labor dumping was that the colonies were inferior to the metropole, the subject forced Franklin to engage in a different rhetorical strategy than the unifying British nationalism of *Plain Truth* and the "Observations Concerning the Increase of Mankind." Indeed, in articulating his opposition to the flood of English, Scottish, and Irish reprobates he saw arriving in the colonies, Franklin for the first time took on a distinctive American identity, signing a 1751 *Pennsylvania Gazette* article "AMERICANUS."

In the editorial that set up "Americanus," Franklin has retailed news about the venal activities of convicts, the epitome of which was a Maryland servant who, poised to stab his mistress, cut off his hand instead, only to add, "*Now make me work, if you can.*" A work world in which "hands" not only ran away with their limbs but cut them off to spite their masters was a seriously deranged world, in which virtuous natural increase was replaced by sin, disease, and filth.

> what good *Mother* ever sent *Thieves* and *Villains* to accompany her *Children*; to corrupt some with their infectious Vices, and murder the rest? What *Father* ever endeavour'd to spread the *Plague* in his *Family!* – We do not ask Fish, but thou givest us *Serpents*, and worse than Serpents! – In what can *Britain* show a more Sovereign Contempt for us, than by emptying their *Jails* into our Settlements; unless their would likewise empty their *Jakes* on our Tables?

The "Americanus" essay developed the symbol of the snake as a figure for this unnatural, yet original and sexual, sin of empire. Franklin insisted that America's native rattlesnakes, "Felons-convict from the Beginning of the World," should be sentenced not to death but to transportation – to England! Perhaps the change of climate would change their nature, he remarked in a satirical reversal of both continental speculation about the effects of New World weather and English justifications for exporting felons (to reform them). He further questioned where empire's original sin lay – in the garden or with the master planters? – by adding that some Parliament courtiers were already all too reptilian in their venal, seducing habits. Franklin had taken a symbol of British insult and thrown in back. The snakes came from England (Franklin, 1987: 357–359, 359–361, 377).

Yet it was not long before the threat of Indian depredations, and the uneven integration of American into imperial priorities and strategies during wartime, inspired Franklin to make the snake the symbol of American unity (Lemay, 1987: 465–499; Norton, 1988: 88–91; L.C. Olson, 1991: 24–74). Protesting against being lumped with the dregs of empire (convicts, outlanders like the Irish and Scots, Indians, and Africans), Franklin and the colonial master classes could not but seek to invert the stereotypes. In the process they not only engaged with but also began to appropriate the charges of inequality and exploitation being leveled by, and on behalf of, the empire's truly oppressed peoples. Franklin, in other words, was pioneering a distinctly Creole perspective akin to those of other "subordinant and dominant" people in the British Empire (Canny and Pagden, 1987; B. Anderson, 1991: 47–66; Daunton and Halpern, 1999: 5). Writing to Massachusetts Governor William Shirley of his plan of union in 1754, Franklin asked whether colonists had, "by hazarding their Lives and Fortunes in subduing and settling new Countries, extending the Dominion and increasing the Commerce of their Mother Nation," "forfeited the native Rights of Britons, which they think ought rather to have been given them, as due to such Merit, if they had been before in a State of Slavery" (PBF, 5: 447). Even if the colonists had once had more in common with American slaves than with Britons, they possessed natural rights and produced wealth. They should not be taxed like a conquered people.

What did the "Rights of Britons" have to do with actual slaves and servants? Nothing – and everything. The rights of the empire to impress labor into the navy would "intirely destroy the Trade of bringing servants to the colonies," Franklin complained in a letter to another colonial official in 1756. Taking one servant from a household or business could make others useless, as he had found in his printing house. Even voluntary enlistment was the end of colonists' wealth rather than the glory of empire, for servants could multiply themselves and their own capital by collecting bounties and then running away: "he may repeat the Frolick as often as he pleases." The loss of freedom of the American owning classes to manipulate their property in persons was nothing less than a form of enslavement that would create more (African) enslavement and a decline in white freedom: "Upon the whole I see clearly, that the Consequence will be, the Introduction of slaves, and thereby weakening the Colonies, and preventing their increase in White Inhabitants" (PBF, 6: 396–400, 472–475).

It was Franklin's innovation, then, to tie the discourse of liberty and slavery not merely to abstract rights or to the a demand for inclusion in the materially thriving British Empire but also to the specific problems of labor, population, and colonial profits, understood as questions of capital (and thus later, logically as well as viscerally, of taxation). After traveling to England in 1757 as a colonial agent, he evinced what in retrospect appears to be a contradictory position on slavery itself, one explicable only when we accept that he was playing a representative role in which his own views on slavery were less relevant than the desire for the debate over real and metaphorical slavery to strengthen rather than weaken the colonists' position. The continuing search for his true beliefs or feeling about race and slavery misses his more important *political* stances, which reveal his understanding (and sympathetic commentators' lack of interest in) of slavery's complex relationship with changing economic and political institutions. His "Observations" (reprinted, for example, in 1760 with his pamphlet on keeping Canada rather than Guadeloupe in the empire after the Seven Years War) certainly suggested that he opposed slave labor. He began to work with the associates of Dr Bray, early proponents of philanthropic antislavery, in setting up schools for young blacks. He engaged intermittently in a dialogue with a coterie of British thinkers who attempted to theorize empire without slavery during the 1760s (PBF, 10: 395–396; Van Doren, 1939: 288; Cohen, 1995: 191–192; Van Horne, 1993; Brown, 2002). Yet at the same time Franklin, as the official agent of Georgia, pushed that colony's new charter, complete with a slave code, through Parliament.

Did these contradictions disturb Franklin? He had already maintained publicly (and there is no evidence to suggest he did not believe) that the slave and the convict servant trade existed more for the benefit of British investors than for American colonists. Slavery's persistence and growth were the result of imperial policy, an example of what went wrong when the colonists' economic ventures were unfairly regulated. In this context, and with the imperial controversy heating up after the Seven Years War ended, the critique of slavery could be aligned with a defense of America's British rights – not just because slavery was the opposite of liberty, or because chattel slavery was the particular "nightmare" of slaveholding American patriots (Bailyn, 1967: 232–246; Okoye, 1980), but also because of the special importance of the labor supply in the colonies. For Franklin, the inability of the colonies to regulate their own labor supply contributed to Americans' self-identification as slaves in the protest movement.

Their lack of control over labor (for Franklin, the source of wealth; for masters, a crucial repository of capital) made colonists slaves of the metropole. The struggle against changing conditions of labor recruitment – not just trade and taxes, but also the trade in workers – lay at the precise overlap of economic, political, and ideological concerns, as the inefficacy of colonial protest against new regulations could be seen as itself a form of political "slavery." Franklin zeroed in on this theme for a transatlantic audience, with characteristic humor and devastating clarity. In "Invectives Against the Americans" (1765), a typically pseudonymous piece for the English press, he adopted an English voice to observe that the Americans are called a *"republican race, a mixed rabble of Scotch, Irish, and foreign vagabonds, descendants of convicts"*: "Our slaves, they may be thought: But every master of slaves ought to know, that though all the slave possesses is the property of the master, his *goodwill* is his own, he bestows it where he pleases; and it is *some importance* to the master's *profit*, if he can obtain that *good-will* at the cheap rate of a few kind words, with fair and gentle usage." It is striking that here, almost for the first time in his voluminous writings, Franklin looked at exploitative labor relations from the point of view of the laborer. He returned also to the theme of personality and self-representation as commodities in the marketplace, but in a newly satiric vein. It was as if talk, "the cheap rate of a few kind words," had been devalued now that Americans were the objects, not the subjects, of capitalist ventures. But not permanently. "These people [the colonists], however, are not, never were, nor ever will be our slaves." The world is still divided in two, but the real Americans are on the free, property-owning side: "The first settlers of New England particularly, were English gentlemen of fortune." English descent is the source of freedom, the justification for the colonists' political agency (Crane, 1950: xli-liii; Franklin, 1987: 562–564).

How, then, might colonists account for such treatment by the English themselves? The "Mother Country," Franklin wrote in a song, might well act like an old woman who cannot accept that her children are grown, "But still an old Mother should have due Respect, / *which nobody can deny, &c.*" It was the "Abuse of [from] her Man" that was truly intolerable to the innocent young colonists and need not be borne, because as legitimate children the colonies were not to be subjected to corporal punishment.

Unlike such children, "when Servants make mischief, they earn the Rattan" (Franklin, 1987: 565–566). Franklin chose to develop the trope of the colonies as children in order to object to the alternative: the colonies as servants and slaves. The familial discourse of British national politics allowed colonial protest to develop within recently revised, sentimentalized notions of monarchy in particular and patriarchy in general (Fliegelman, 1982; Bushman, 1985; Colley, 1992: 195–236). Franklin had written in 1754 that "Instructions from the Crown to the Colonies ... should be plainly just and reasonable, and rather savour of Fatherly Tenderness and Affection, than of Masterly harshness and Severity" (PBF, 5: 332). Questioning an inferior status as Britain's surrogate while implying, at the end of the "Mother Country" song, that only time (the Mother's death) would eventually solve the generational conundrum, Franklin was at the forefront of colonists' efforts to spin the familial language of politics in such a way as to wiggle the Creole sons out of a servile position.

Unfortunately for Franklin and the other patriot leaders, the objection to being treated like slaves could, in the absence of racism, all too easily be inverted in the name of the servants and slaves themselves. The English political context was of crucial importance here. The rhetoric of American innocence and enslavement moved some Britons at home – after all, it improved on some domestic struggles for liberty – but not enough of them, and not in sympathy with white colonists alone. Some abolitionists used the mounting protest of the colonies to amplify their arguments against slavery, but anti-Americanism proved just as useful to those who wanted to point out what they understandably saw as a more severe case of oppression. Opponents of American protest, in turn, did not hesitate to use antislavery rhetoric against the Americans. In the deft hands of a Samuel Johnson, anti-Americanism and antislavery reinforced each other (Joy, 1998: 60–81; Gould, 2000: 106–147; C.L. Brown, 2006).

By 1770 it had become all too clear to antislavery agitators that the colonists cared much more about "slavery" when they – not their slaves – were seen as its victims. Franklin addressed the contradiction between antislavery theory and colonial protest that year in the form of "A Conversation Between an Englishman, a Scotchman, and an American, on the Subject of Slavery." That he had been backed into a corner is apparent from the beginning, for the Englishman gets the first, Johnsonian word, accusing the Americans of hypocrisy and recommending that they read "*Granville Sharpe's* book upon Slavery." The American responds that it is indeed a good book, but that the hypocrisy lies with the English, since the larger effect of this attack on the Americans is "to render us odious, and to encourage those who would oppress us, by representing us as unworthy of the Liberty we are now contending for" (Franklin, 1987: 646–647).

The antislavery complaint against the Americans, Franklin insists, is too "general" because the "Foundation" of slavery in America is not general.

New England has few slaves, mostly "Footmen": the same is true for New York, New Jersey, and Pennsylvania. Even in Virginia and South Carolina, slavery is a vestige of privilege for the few, the "old rich Inhabitants." The real Americans – ninety-nine out of a hundred families – do not own a slave. What is more, the poor in England, far more than in America, are regulated like slaves. England, in fact, began the slave trade, which continues only because "You bring the Slaves to us, and tempt us to purchase them."

When the English interlocutor cites the harshness of slave laws, the Americans responds by asserting that they are less harsh when there are fewer slaves. He chides the abolitionist for sentimentalism concerning blacks: "Perhaps you may imagine the Negroes to be a mild, tempered tractable Kind of People. Some of them are indeed so. But the Majority are of a plotting Disposition, dark, sullen, malicious, revengeful, and cruel in the highest Degree. ... Indeed many of them, being mischievous Villains in their own Country, are sold off by their Princes by way of Punishment by Exile and Slavery, as you here ship off your Convicts." As in the "Observations" two decades earlier, Franklin undermines slavery mainly to make Americans look better and in the process confirms negative views of Africans in America. The blame for the evils of the unfree labor system can then be fixed on prior historical and natural facts. In this case, it also serves to buttress an argument about "the Villains you transport" and why they "must be Ruled with a Rod of Iron." When the Scotsman objects that the Americans willingly buy both slaves and felons, the American refuses to budge on the question of responsibility. With low prices, "you force upon us the Convicts as well as the Slaves." Anticipating the arguments of later (Southern) defenders of slavery, Franklin goes so far as to call up the image of white slavery in the coalmines of Scotland. Finally the American, transformed into the defender of all liberties, redefines slavery as all unfree, bought labor, accusing the English of founding their great empire on the slavery of soldiers and sailors who not only experience social death but cause the death of others (Franklin, 1987: 648–653).

By 1772 Franklin had explicitly placed himself on the side of antislavery in private letters to Anthony Benezet and Granville Sharp. Yet a close examination of his public writings and correspondence on the subject shows how carefully he exculpated the colonists from any responsibility for the institution. In April 1773 he wrote the Dublin cleric Richard Woodward of hearing that "a Disposition to abolish Slavery prevails in North America, that many of the Pennsylvanians have set their slaves at liberty, that even the Virginia Assembly have petitioned the King to make a Law for preventing the Importation of more Slaves into the Colony." But he predicted (rightly) that the King would disallow this law, as with anti-convict importation measures: "the Interest of a few Merchants here [in London] has more Weight with Government than that of Thousands at a Distance." Antislavery proved the case for English corruption, which suggested the virtues of

American self-government. Thus antislavery sentiment itself, for Franklin, needed to be recast as sympathy for the colonists whenever it suggested the reverse. In response to the Somerset decision, which seemed to declare slavery illegal on English soil, Franklin ridiculed the liberation of one slave by a nation that still jealously guarded the slave trade. It did not help, doubtless, that Lord Mansfield, the presiding judge, was a consistent critic of colonial resistance to parliamentary legislation (PBF, 19: 113–117, 269; 20: 41, 193, 155–156, 296).

Soon the matter of Franklin's own loyalty, amid his blistering attacks on British man-trading as the epitome of the government's oppressive tendencies, got intertwined with the slavery issue. Franklin's decisive alienation from Great Britain probably occurred in January, 1774, when he was called on the carpet before the Privy Council's Committee on Plantation Affairs and called a thief by Solicitor General Alexander Wedderburn. The alienation, though, was deeper than psychological, and had been building for some time, for Wedderburn's otherwise inexplicably harsh denunciation of Franklin in the "Cockpit" responded explicitly to Franklin's published rhetorical projections of the theft of persons onto the British. In this context, it is rather less surprising that Wedderburn compared Franklin, "the wily American," so publicly to a "bloody African" slave trader, a character in a contemporary play. The experience only confirmed what Franklin had been warning against: arrogant Englishmen who could not tell the difference between a fellow Briton and a slave-trading African chieftain (Carey, 1928: 72–73; Van Doren, 1938: 470, 519; R. Clark, 1983: 243–244; Greene, 1995a: 248; PBF, 20: 390; 21: 50).

In response, Franklin wrote more letters for the press depicting the British as intentional man traders, developing and dramatizing the notion of Britain's enslavement of the colonies. He depicted a British ruling class literally ready to sell the colonists "to the best Bidder." In ventriloquized English voices, he described the Americans in these pieces as runaways, convicts, and chattel, to be ruled by "the method made use of by the Planters in the West Indies ... who appoint what they call a Negro Driver, who is chosen from among the Slaves." He took on the role of a "FREEHOLDER OF OLD SARUM" (the ultimate rotten borough and a symbol of aristocratic corruption) to propose castration as "the most feasible Method of humbling our rebellious Vassals of North America," lest they "slip their Necks out of the Collar, and from being Slaves set up for Masters." The same essay suggested that oppressing the Americans would prevent excess migration to the colonies and an ensuing loss of English wealth. America was the land of opportunity and freedom, Britain the home of tyranny and human commodification. In such a context, singling out American mainland slavery would make little sense, except for those wishing to advance Britain's privileges of enslavement. Franklin's rhetorical inflations comparing colonial relations to unfree labor – as in a fake bill disallowing Britons from emigrating for more than seven years – drew attention to the servant and slave trades and away from the everyday aspects of labor in North America. At a time when the nascent antislavery movement in England focused on the evils of the trade, this was a potent appropriation, to say the least (PBF, 21: 183–186, 221–222, 485, 605, 608).

In Franklin's rhetoric, colonial contradictions were equated with slavery and foisted upon England. What remained American were the positive aspects of merchant capitalism: free labor, imperial wealth, and neo-mercantlist economic independence (McCoy, 1980: 51–69; Crowley, 1993; Ben-Atar, 1998: 108–112). While minister to France, Franklin followed the logic of the virtuous free labor of Americans to the level of myth. America was a "manufactory of men" – free men, not slaves. Luxury goods, he insisted, were not a significant source of wealth or of debt in America, though they were the source of England's corruption as a navigating, privateering nation (Van Doren, 1938: 711, 747–751, 770; Franklin, 1987: 992–994). In *Information to Those Who Would Remove to America* (1782; also printed on his own press at Passy in 1784), Franklin depicted the quintessential American as a freeholder who worked for himself, with his own hands: "America is the land of Labour," where wages turned into property, as "Multitudes of poor People from England, Ireland, Scotland, and Germany, have by this means in a few Years become wealthy Farmers" (Franklin, 1987: 976–977).

During the late 1780s, recent biographers maintain, Franklin emerged as a true antislavery hero. Nicholas Guyatt's essay in this volume suggests there was some real heft to Franklin's antislavery during the earlier 1780s as well. But it matters how he got there. Franklin's perceptions of emergent capitalism, his criticisms of slavery, and his skillful deployment of racism made him the perfect person to justify America – slavery and all – in the crucible of the revolution. Combined with his other arguments about British national identity, the labor market, and imperial political economy, antislavery actually became integral to Franklin's vision once he turned it on the British. But it was an antislavery compromised by its projection of blame for slavery – the other face of capitalism – onto the metropole, and an antislavery that racialized the emerging American identity in such a way as to reinforce the assumption that Africans were not and could not be members of the new national polity.

Capitalism has been given credit, by some, for the rise of antislavery; for others, antislavery helped legitimize wage labor, and thus industrial capitalism, in the same historical epoch (Bender, 1993). In the North American case, the story of capitalism and slavery is longer than this, more complicated, and certainly more disturbing for those who would like to see capitalism as meaning, essentially, progress alone (Rockman, 2006; Tomlins, 2010). The appropriation of antislavery by one of America's premier theorists and innovators of capitalism in practice may have helped delegitimize slavery, but it first deflected attention away from African slavery while also advancing the racially exclusive dimension of revolutionary nationalism. Only by disregarding the importance of slavery to the rise of Franklin and his North can we understand the revolution as having had antislavery effects but no proslavery causes – or Franklin as having made the nation and helped end slavery at once.

In 1759, the year he met Franklin, Adam Smith attacked America – North and South, mainland and islands – as a moral world turned upside down, thanks in large measure to slavery. By 1776 and *The Wealth of Nations*, Smith accepted the Franklinian view that slavery neither amounted to much on the mainland nor accounted for capitalist wealth (Smith, 1976: 206–207; Perelman, 2002: 229–253; Drescher, 2002: 19–33, 247n41). The change is fraught with implications for understanding both the American Revolution and Franklin. As elsewhere, reality was one thing, ideology another. Franklin and the revolutionary movement he led depended on forgetting the roots of capitalist growth, most of all the economic role of New England and the middle colonies in the world economy. The American Revolution surely set in motion a chain of events that changed capitalism and undermined slavery in some places. But it also mystified the late colonial past. Franklin was central to both processes. The tendency for Americans and their historians to take Franklin's ideological arguments, and even his autobiography, as a starting point for explaining the meaning of the revolution or capitalism practically guarantees that the role of slavery in the making of the nation will be fundamentally understated, if not completely misunderstood.

Note

1 Labaree, Leonard W. *et al.*, eds. (1959–). *The Papers of Benjamin Franklin*. 39 vols to date. New Haven, CT: Yale University Press. Hereafter referred to as PBF.

Further Reading

Brown, Christopher Leslie (2006). *Moral Capital: Foundations of British Abolitionism*. Chapel Hill, NC.

Carey, Lewis (1928). *Franklin's Economic Views*. New York, NY.

Conner, Paul W. (1965). *Poor Richard's Politicks: Benjamin Franklin and his New American Order*. New York, NY.

Crowley, John E. (1993). *The Privileges of Independence: Neomercantilism and the American Revolution*. Baltimore, MD.

Eliot, Thomas D. (1924). "The relations between Adam Smith and Benjamin Franklin before 1776," *Political Science Quarterly* 39: 67–96.

Matson, Cathy D., ed. (2006). *The Economy of Early America: Historical Perspectives and New Directions.* University Park.

McCoy, Drew R. (1978). "Benjamin Franklin's vision of a republican political economy for America," *William and Mary Quarterly* 35: 605–628.

Nash, Gary B. (2006), "Franklin and Slavery," *American Philosophical Society Proceedings* 150: 620–637.

Newman, Simon P. (2009). "Benjamin Franklin and the leather-apron men: The politics of class in eighteenth-century Philadelphia," *Journal of American Studies* 43 (2): 161–175.

Perelman, Michael (2002). *The Invention of Capitalism: Classical Political Economy and the Secret History of Primitive Accumulation.* Durham, NC.

Waldstreicher, David (2004). *Runaway America: Benjamin Franklin, Slavery, and the American Revolution.* New York, NY.

Chapter Twelve

BENJAMIN FRANKLIN AND WOMEN

Susan E. Klepp

The current cult of the "founding fathers" – a vague term that variously encompasses members of the late colonial legislatures, the Continental Congresses, the continental army's officer corps, the Annapolis Convention, the Constitutional Convention, the state ratifying conventions, and the first few administrations or sometimes even every voter and soldier in America – allows little room for women. It is true that Abigail Smith Adams has achieved a rare prominence in recent biographies, histories, and television series so that she sometimes outshines her husband, John Adams. And Thomas Jefferson has become firmly linked to Sally Hemings in recent historiography just as he was in his private life and in the vitriolic political campaigns of the early republic. But the stories of most founders rattle on without any substantive discussion of women.

The exception is Benjamin Franklin (BF). He left both personal and published works addressed to particular women correspondents or thoughts about women in general. Female kin and acquaintances kept his letters for posterity. He was unusually open about at least some of his "errata" with women. He formed temporary families of wives and, particularly, of daughters, throughout his life. He recorded many of his flirtations. He sometimes laughed at gendered conventions. And occasionally he wrote as a female character. There is a large body of scholarship on his female relatives, correspondents, business partners, and friendships. There are articles on his feminine personas, his views on female education, his feminist ideas, or his misogyny. His popular image at the turn of the twenty-first century is as a "babe magnet," a "skirt-chaser," a philanderer, and the progenitor of a line of bastards – a lively trickster

---

A Companion to Benjamin Franklin, First Edition. Edited by David Waldstreicher.
© 2011 Blackwell Publishing Ltd. Published 2011 by Blackwell Publishing Ltd.

god in a pantheon of mummified heroes (Anon, 1939; Block, 1975; Middlekauff, 1996: 115; Lopez, 2003; Rettig, 2009).

It was not always thus. One of the first Franklin biographies respectfully devoted five lines to the "Miss Read" who became BF's "valuable and affectionate wife." His daughter's existence was acknowledged, although she was not named. That's it for BF and women at the dawn of the nineteenth century (Hardie, 1805: II, 386–410). The scholarly image of BF in the nineteenth century was of the elder statesman, Dr Franklin, who apparently had no private or social life (for example, Bancroft, 1875: X, 554). Meanwhile, the popular image of BF for much of the nineteenth century was of the young boy called Ben (not Benjamin, and certainly not Doctor) who achieved success by working hard, seizing opportunity, and doing good. He was an American Dick Whittington, or the industrious apprentice of Hogarth's visual imagining, or a real-life precursor to the fictional "Ragged Dick" character created by Horatio Alger. This Ben was too young or too hardworking to concern himself with women. "Ben was born in 1706," wrote Nathaniel Hawthorne in a cloying children's book, and soon "Ben was a bright boy at his book" while "filled with schemes for the public benefit!" (Hawthorne, 1851: 273, 276). BF was a youthful template for upward mobility through economic success.

This properly Victorian and industrially useful Franklin began to disappear in the last year of the century as two publications highlighting his relationships with women brought new interpretations of BF, ones perhaps more appealing to a reading public tired of Comstockery and bowdlerism. Copies of BF's 1745 letter known as the "Old Mistresses Apologue" had been circulating privately from the 1880s with the original locked first in the State Department's vault and later in the Library of Congress as too indecent to be read (except by librarians). The "Apologue" was a letter to a young man advising marriage, but also advocating, as a second best option, taking an experienced, discrete, and grateful post-menopausal woman as a lover. Sydney George Fisher, one of the first American social historians, published most of the letter in 1899 (pp. 126–128). Paul Leicester Ford, who had privately and anonymously printed a copy of the letter, did not include it in his article on Franklin and women, but published other slightly risqué writings from later in BF's life (1899b, 58: 3, 410–427). Larry Tise provides a full history of the publication history of the "Old Mistresses Apologue" (2000b: 6–10), while Carla Mulford situates the interpretations of BF in their cultural contexts (2000: 103–128; also Huang, 1994: 158–162). The recovery of this letter and its open publication in 1926 charted the rapid changes in American attitudes toward sexuality in the early decades of the twentieth century. Given the insulting treatment that Deborah Franklin (DF) was about to receive in twentieth-century accounts, the new interpretation was perhaps accompanied by a backlash against women's increasing engagement in politics, the economy, and society.

As BF's apparent approval of extramarital sex became well known, biographers sought reasons for his profligacy. The overwhelming consensus was that the problem was less with Benjamin and more with Deborah Franklin. Fisher began the drumbeat in a modest way. DF was "not a congenial companion for Franklin," he wrote, although she had "homely, housewifely virtues, [a] handsome figure, good health, and wholesome common sense" (Fisher, 1898: 118). Ford went further: DF was a "potential drag on her husband's public and social life." She was "wholly unfit for the duties" of a diplomat's wife because "she was a woman wholly lacking in cultivation." Nor was this only in London and Paris, for supposedly "even in Philadelphia she was not received socially, and this seems to have made her jealous of Franklin's public career." She was a "turbulent" character, according to a single contemporary source (Ford, 1899a: 415). That there was no evidence of her being snubbed and plenty of evidence of her social interactions with a wide range of Philadelphians did not prevent the accusation from being repeated by one biographer after another for more than a century.

In 1911, DF was accused of being a bastard-bearer, the low woman who was the real mother of BF's illegitimate son, William (Hart, 1911, 35: 308–314). For earlier speculation that it was a servant remaining in the household who was the mother (see Ford, 1889). This now improbable charge was widely accepted, although usually with a grain or two of salt (Van Doren, 1938: 91–93). Why BF and DF would have saddled their son with the label of bastard when colonial clergymen were often quite willing to alter inconvenient birthdates is not explained by this theory of William's parenthood. That William sometimes referred to DF as his mother simply means that she filled that role in his life. His biological mother remains unknown.

With the singular exceptions of two 1950s pieces on DF by the librarian at the American Philosophical Society, the negative assessments of BF's wife continued and even intensified into the first decade of the twenty-first century (Riley, 1951, 1953; the tenor of the times can be seen in Becker, 1931, 3: 144). For example, biographer Walter Isaacson found DF to be "rather plain" even in her twenties while BF had "husky good looks and genial charm." Their marriage was supposedly loveless, so much so that Isaacson speculates that the reason they had just two children was that they "lacked abundant intimacy or found conceiving not always easy." The latter suggestion is far more likely than the first. BF may have had experiential reasons to dread the possibility of a "continual Risk to [his] Health by a distemper" acquired from his visits to prostitutes. Poorly treated sexually transmitted diseases can leave scars that block sperm. Besides, what BF remembered about his reasons for marrying forty years after the event was the sexual outlet that it had provided. It may be that BF and DF were not physiologically infertile, but that they were adept at practicing birth control. Her mother was a pharmacist and also had a small family (Isaacson, 2003: 43, 120).

Gordon Wood recycled these old demeaning comments in his 2004 biography of BF. DF was, in his telling, "loud and lowly and scarcely literate." She was "an embarrassment." And like other biographers, Wood found that the other women in BF's life were far more attractive. Margaret Stevenson, his London landlady and companion, represented the sophistication of the English metropolis so that BF supposedly "would not have been comfortable with the loud and plain Mrs. Franklin accompanying him." Polly Stevenson, Margaret Stevenson's daughter, "was more lively and intelligent than [his Philadelphia daughter] Sally Franklin." No wonder then that Franklin later became enamored with Anne-Catherine Helvétius and her "warm and bantering cheekiness" when his wife and daughter were such disappointments (Wood, 2004: 32–34, 90, 132, 209). Wood's biography appears to be among the last gasps of a century's flood of snide comments about DF. For a revolution in scholarship about BF and women was occurring as this biography was being published, one that would examine the many reiterations of Paul Leicester Ford's demeaning assumptions about DF and her place in history. The maturing of the field of women's history, a fresh reading of the usual sources and the discovery of new evidence were the factors leading to a reinterpretation of women and Franklin.

Historians stopped denigrating the Franklin women – or at least some did. As late as 2004 Leo Lemay actually "add[ed] a bit of disingenuousness and officiousness to what we know of Deborah's character"; that character was, to use his words, rash, brazen, presumptuous, full of herself, too proud, and not egalitarian (Lemay, 2004, 67: 607–621). But even he began to back off in the third volume of his life of BF, published in 2009 (Lemay, 2009: 267–273; see also Fry, 2003). The old interpretations could not stand. DF, Jane Mecom, Sally Franklin, and others emerged from BF's shadow to be considered as individuals whose lives not only intersected with BF's but who had interests, beliefs, and activities of their own, even if remaining under the considerable educational, cultural, and legal liabilities of the times. In these most recent studies there was no longer a need to categorize the women in BF's life as of two types only – as either suitable or unsuitable for the Great Man. If BF could be a multifaceted human being, then so too could these women.

A symposium in 1994 led to *Benjamin Franklin and Women*, edited by Larry Tise and published in 2000. It began the process of revision. The significant economic contributions of DF, the rebellion of Sally Franklin, the distinctive personalities of three of his female correspondents, and the gendered cultural milieu in which he operated were discussed (Tise, 2000a). But even more radical departures were in the works.

The twentieth-century image of DF as intellectually incurious, home-bound and rather stupid was countered by two historians, David Waldstreicher and Joyce E. Chaplin, who independently noticed her engagement with both antislavery ameliorists, like the Bray Associates, and activists among the Anglicans and Quakers, including the radical abolitionist, Benjamin Lay. While the Franklins owned enslaved men, women, and children at various points in their lives, and aided in the buying and selling of enslaved individuals through their newspaper, they both came to have doubts about the morality of keeping slaves. BF may have had doubts, but he found it impolitic to act on those doubts in the 1750s and 1760s. DF supported the activities of the Bray Associates and sent her young servant Othello to one of the schools the Associates maintained. At DF's urging, BF visited the school and altered his opinion about the intellectual capacity of Africans, but his views were kept private until the very end of his life. DF hung a portrait of radical antislavery activist Benjamin Lay in the house while he was in England. They had, in Chaplin's analysis, a marriage in which they agreed to disagree, at least on some topics and open support for antislavery was one of those points (Waldstreicher, 2004: 194; Chaplin, 2006: 180–181, 223, quote on 156).

More sustained analyses of DF's independent life came from Jennifer Reed Fry in 2003 and Vivian Bruce Conger in 2009. In these essays, DF is discovered to be a vibrant, politically astute supporter of her husband's career, and certainly not a "drag." She stayed in Philadelphia of her own free will and not because she was left behind as an "embarrassment." Her management of BF's affairs made his extended stays overseas financially and politically possible. DF created an office for herself in their new house where she kept her books (many on theology) and family pictures. She was quite sociable, entertaining their friends and associates at the typically feminine tea table and at the traditionally masculine dinner table. She supervised the operations of the post office, she protected the postal system from criticism by a lord, and she protected their house from an angry mob. She promoted her daughter's interests. Her relationship with her husband was one of give and take, more companionate than patriarchal (Fry, 2006; Conger, 2009, 2010; see also Skemp, 2000 for a less-independent DF. Some of these interpretive breakthroughs were anticipated by Lopez and Herbert [1975], although relationships are somewhat romanticized in their account. BF is the focus, the active and superior partner, while DF is presented as largely passive.) If their marriage is seen as more equitable, even loving, then BF has become less of an uncontrolled womanizer, and more playful than profligate. Still, he was no plaster saint and the one "snapshot" of Franklin among the many formal, posed portraits is a 1767 sketch of the doubly married man with neither Mrs Franklin nor Mrs Stevenson, but with an unknown "young Lady on his knee" with their hands and mouths "in amorous reciprocation" (Sellers, 1962: 80–81, catalogue 28). The relationship of DF and BF has undergone the wildest interpretive swings, but attention to the tensions and stresses and transgressions in contemporary understandings of gender relations and an appreciation for the whole lives of women can inform other aspects of Benjamin Franklin and women.

The question is whether this new interpretive model will alter the popular image of BF as a skirt-chaser. It will no doubt be difficult since the randy image of BF is embedded in popular musicals like *1776*, a staple of high-school productions, and even more pervasively in the enormously popular movie and television series *M*A*S*H*, where the smart, playful, subversive and womanizing main character is named Benjamin Franklin Pierce. These caricatures and many others of the historical BF are simple, somewhat titillating, and serve to enliven those distant founding fathers. They also serve to exclude the women in BF's life from the popular understanding of American history. But there is at least one sign of change. A one-woman show produced at Temple University incorporates many of the recent findings of historians in entertaining and often gripping narrative (Sloan and Moritz, 2010).

12.1 What is to be Done?

Now that DF has been lifted out of the dustbin of history, at least partially, and some of the cobwebs cleared away, what other subjects related to the women in BF's life and thought could use another look? What follows are some areas of interest.

Ancestry. BF never questioned patrilineal descent and the privileges that accompanied that religious, legal, and cultural construction of male primacy. Men were paterfamilias, heads of their households. Wives, children, and apprentices "belonged" to the master of the household by law and custom. The family's home and its contents were his property alone, and even DF usually referred to the house she had constructed, furnished, and lived in while he was abroad as his, not theirs. Late in life BF wrote to a friend urging that his son marry because the "Wheel of Life ... has roll'd down to him from Adam without Interruption [and] should not stop with him" (PBF, 38, 667).[1] Women, starting with the unmentioned and invisible foremother Eve, did not count as family, and the generations could be numbered, genealogies created, and kinship celebrated without including female names, experiences, or contributions. It was a viewpoint that shaped the *Autobiography*. The third through the seventh paragraphs give extensive details of the males in the Franklin line. In paragraph eight, there is a brief mention of his mother's marriage. The rest of that long paragraph concerns his mother's father (Lemay, 1986a: 2–6). Even BF's suggestion that girls be taught accounting was not meant for women's benefit, but so that widows might manage "till a son is grown up" and "can go on with [the family enterprise], to the lasting advantage and enriching of the family," that is, the male line (Lemay, 1986a: 81).

It is not as though BF was ignorant of his mother's or wife's ancestry. In 1758, for example, he wrote a lengthy letter to DF on his visit to her relatives in Birmingham (PBF, 8: 166). It is just that his wife's family was of only passing interest. Of course, women were not the only ones belittled by these conventional attitudes; the tracing of the Franklin heritage in 1771 also served to humiliate BF's estranged illegitimate son, whose base-born birth made him the equivalent of a female, a mere footnote in the family tree. Later historians and genealogists have compensated for the patriarchal genealogy recorded by BF. (See the major biographers plus Cowell, 1884; Baldwin, 1941; Dallett, 1960. Look for the forthcoming work by Karin A. Wulf on genealogy in colonial America.)

Still, BF was perversely complex and when it came to naming his legitimate children, the emphasis was on maternal lines. Son Francis Folger Franklin's alliterative name memorialized BF's mother's family while daughter Sarah was named for her maternal grandmother. This was unusual – the common naming practice in early Philadelphia was to name the first-born male after the father or the paternal grandparent, and the first daughter after the paternal grandmother. Only later children's names would honor the distaff side. Perhaps these two cases of maternal names grafted on to the paternal line are instances of DF's influence rather than a willingness on BF's part to include women's lineages.

Mother. Little is known of BF's mother, Abiah Folger Franklin. There are a few surviving letters to and from mother and son plus a few comments in the *Autobiography*. The mentions of Abiah reflect contemporary standards of strict propriety and seem formulaic and stilted rather than heartfelt. BF noted that she had "an excellent constitution," which no doubt helped her get through her ten pregnancies. She "suckled all 10 children." This was high praise when written in 1771 (Lemay, 1986a: 8). It meant that she rejected vanity and fashionable indulgence by refusing to send her newborn offspring to wet nurses, even though her figure would consequently sag and stretch from childbearing and breastfeeding. She chose not to turn over responsibility for her tender infants and instead accepted the laborious task of rearing them herself. This self-abnegation was considered the highest of womanly virtues and was part of a contemporary medical and moral campaign to encourage European and colonial women to breastfeed. The absence of detail on Abiah Franklin was intended as a compliment: she was, as BF recorded on her tombstone, "discreet and virtuous." BF treated her in his autobiography with the same formal discretion that he praised on her memorial. Whether she concurred in the appropriateness of feminine humility and reticence is unknown. The lack of documentation has discouraged scholarly investigation although Matthew Garrett has uncovered a possible portrait and gives a detailed literary analysis of the *Autobiography* (Garrett, 2008).

Sister. BF frequently embraced new acquaintances as companions and as frequently discarded them when no longer useful. Death and distance frequently intervened. There was one friendship, however, that survived during his whole life and that was his relationship with his youngest sister, Jane Franklin Mecom. As the youngest son in the family, perhaps he particularly enjoyed playing the role of big brother. He could be insufferable in that role: he wrote to her when she was fourteen that "I had almost determined on a tea table [as a gift to her] but when I considered that the character of a housewife was far preferable to that of being only a pretty gentlewoman, I concluded to send you a *spinning wheel*" (BF to Jane, 1727, FDE),[2] Fortunately, their relationship matured over time and they wrote as near equals. She kept him informed of family and of New England politics. He wrote her of politics and his other activities. She at times depended on his financial support, while the survival of many of his writings was the consequence of her collection and stewardship of many of those papers. The best study of Mecom is the most recent (Stern, 2006). Earlier accounts tend to be patronizing and assume that Mecom was apolitical and emotional, unlike her older brother. She was portrayed as a victim of her circumstances, rather than an actor. Stern carefully refutes those stereotypical assumptions. She was not afraid to question his actions and opinions, especially during the Stamp Act crisis and regarding BF's apparent lack of religious beliefs. She had a mind and life of her own.

The collection and annotation of their correspondence by Carl Van Doren remains valuable (see Van Doren, 1950a,b; Sellers, 1955, is a discussion of a miniature of BF in Mecom's possession; Lopez and Herbert, 1975, esp. 104–105, 114–115).

Mother-in-Law. DF's mother, Sarah Read, has received little attention in the scholarship on the Franklins. Stanley Finger is the only biographer to recognize her state-of-the art knowledge of pharmaceuticals – most writers have simply dismissed her as a kind of a quack peddling her homemade salves and ointments (Finger, 2006: 23–26). Her generous gift of real estate to her daughter and son-in-law is meticulously detailed in the work of Hannah Benner Roach (Roach, 1960).

Daughter. Sarah (Sally) Franklin Bache was better treated by twentieth-century historians than her mother. One of her first biographers was a descendant (Duane, 1848). Not surprisingly this was a very positive portrayal. Yet she was labeled as less intelligent than Englishwomen and as ungrateful for selling the 408 diamonds embedded in a broach given to her father by Louis XVI of France. Larry Tise finds it a declaration of independence (2000c). Her work in the Ladies Association of 1780, an early women's political organization, has been overshadowed by discussions of her co-director, Esther DeBerdt Reed. Her letters, at the American Philosophical Society, have been little used. There has been a recent revival of interest, partly because of the attention given to her mother. (Baetier, 2003, traces the many copies of her portrait that family members had painted; Lopez and Herbert, 1975.)

Other Female Relatives. BF's cousin, Kezia Folger Coffin, an outspoken Loyalist during the American Revolution, is discussed in Chambers and Norling (2008). His daughter-in-law has received scant attention (Streumph, 1970). Even less attention has been paid to other kin.

Landladies. Margaret Stevenson surely deserves some scholarly attention, although the Benjamin Franklin House Museum in Craven Street, London offers a multimedia presentation of the household with a film that includes actors portraying BF and Mrs Stevenson. There are brief mentions of other landladies in the *Autobiography* (Lemay, 1986a: 37–38; see also Roach, 1960).

Younger Women and Substitute Families. Landladies often became substitute families, but Franklin had varied relationships with younger women: some fatherly, some playful, some sexually charged. Lopez in "Three Women, Three Styles," rightfully points out BF's capacity for treating women as unique individuals (Lopez, 2000b). Jan Lewis reminds readers of the inequities that prevailed in these exchanges (Lewis, 2000; see also S.M. Harris, 1995b).

Many of the letters between BF and particular women have been published with valuable introductions, but there is a need for a fresh reading, more sophisticated gendered analysis and wider angle of vision (de Ternant, 1928; Matthews, 1928; Roelker and Greene, 1948, 1949; Bell, 1956; Stifler, 1927).

Teacher. There is a long tradition, but no evidence, that BF learned penmanship at the writing school maintained by Madam Sarah Knight in Boston (See Felks, 1969; Bush, 1990).

Business Associates. These articles on women printers who operated within BF's printing network stress the pathbreaking careers of these often heroic women. The eighteenth-century economy, the print market or the financial liabilities involved in being part of this network are little explored (Baker, 1977; Henry, 1977; C.J. Young, 2001; Waldstreicher, 2004; Frasca, 2006).

French Aristocratic Women. This was an area of particular interest to twentieth-century biographers of BF. As much as they denigrated DF, they exalted the women of the Second Estate. The whole subject could be revisited to incorporate recent feminist scholarship from both France and the United States (Fay, 1928; Lopez, 1966; Slessarev, 1966; Medlin, 1977, 1980; Aldridge, 1972; Lipowski, 1984; Gustafson, 1987; Prince, 2006; Schiff, 2009).

Invisible Women. Only a small portion of the women BF knew actually appear in his writings. Infants and toddlers were generally absent, while enslaved women and serving women, shopkeepers and nurses, midwives, and laundresses were all invisible or nearly so. Prostitutes got only a passing mention. He treated Cherokee women with disdain, ignoring their contributions to diplomatic negotiations and attempting to buy them off with cheap trinkets. He found German women unattractive (*Pennsylvania*

Archives, 1787, Ser. 1, XI: 181–183). David Waldstreicher has observed that "In his *Almanack*, he did not so much forget or deny the importance of servants, slaves, and wives as conflate them all together in the fungible mix of money-producing people" (2004: 108). Those working people, free, enslaved or femes covert had their own ideas and the simplistic homilies of the Almanacs were read differently and often countered with more or less success in real life.

Sex, Sexuality, the Emotions. There has been comparatively little serious study of sex, sexuality, or the body considering the subject was supposed babe magnet and skirt-chaser (see Hoefnagel, 1989; Royot, 1993; Erkkila, 2000; Hadlak, 2000; Lewis, 2000). There has been more attention paid to Franklin, heterosexual love, and the expression of emotions. The historical context is often underdeveloped (Fay, 1928; Van Gastel, 1990; Bloch, 1993; Lemay, 2001; Carton, 2002; Chaves, 2007).

Female Personas. BF was unusual in frequently assuming a female character in his writings. Scholars have looked at the Silence Dogood essays of his adolescence and the famous Polly Baker essay of 1747 but have not explored the totality of his feminine personas, nor explained the temporal pattern of these pretended female authors. Some of the most significant of these impersonations are Mrs Silence Dogood and Margaret Aftercast in 1722, Martha Careful, Caelia Shortface, and Patience in 1729, Betty Diligent in 1730, Alice Addertongue and Celia Single in 1732, Bridget Saunders in 1734 and 1738, Miss Polly Baker in 1747, and then a long hiatus until "The Left Hand" was written in 1785. Adopting a female voice allowed him to present an outsider's view of issues, events, or personalities. But what else might be going on here? Leo Lemay assumes that these fictive females prove that BF had a rare ability to empathize with women – if so, it had pretty much disappeared by 1750. More research is needed (Smeall, 1959, 1960; Lemay, 1965, 1976, 2006b: 125–126, 136, 144, 147–148, 166–169, 548–549; Aldridge, 1972; Lipper, 1980; M. Hall, 1990 [1960]).

Female Readership. Women readers were fans of Franklin's publications as well as men. This is something of a surprise since the aphorisms in *Poor Richard's Almanac* reprise many of the commonplace stereotypes of female irrationality, deviousness, shrewishness, irresponsibility, and more that filled the press and popular discourse. Yet in New York City in 1735, Abigail Franks quoted some of Franklin's "Raillery" on newlyweds who when they have "marrid att Leissure they doe repent in haste" from the previous year's almanac. In 1759, Hannah Callender copied into her diary an example of "Ben: Franklins droll humour" which was circulating in a copy of his recent letter to his sister. Fourteen years later, Sally Eve's "Mama [lamented that] we have no such almanacks as what his was." And twenty-seven years after that, Elizabeth Drinker found the two volumes of his collected works to be "entertaining." Quaker Milcah Martha Moore included both examples of his wit and celebrations of his inventions in an anthology destined for classroom use (although there was a critique of his prorevolutionary politics) (Herskowitz and Meyer, 1968: 47; Eve, 1773: 30; Crane, 1991, 2: 1368; La Courreye Blecki and Wulf, 1997, 217–220, 280–281; Klepp and Wulf, 2010: 86).

Women give as well as get in the battles of the sexes that fill *Poor Richard's Almanac*. According to the first almanac in 1733, "my spouse and I could not agree/Striving about superiority." There's "Nothing more like a Fool, than a drunken Man," but then "our times *drink* all away./ Never mind it, she'l be sober after the Holidays." And in 1734, "all you Men that have good Wives, respect their Virtues equal with your Lives." There were many messages that might have appealed to men or to women or to both. Still, this was mockery, not reform and the dominant advice was for self-controlled men to rule, for women to be meek and mild and productive, and servants to serve (Willis, 1868; Smeall, 1960; Stabile, 2000; Waldstreicher, 2004: 101–110; but see Lyons, 2006: 37–42).

Philosophy, Science, Politics, Policy. BF promoted early marriage and high birth rates on the colonial or national level, but he married at about the average age and he and DF had an unusually small family of two legitimate children. Philadelphians in the colonial era who had long-lasting marriages like the Franklins' produced an average of eight children. BF advocated the social, economic, and imperial advantages of large families in several essays. He collected statistics on births and family size to bolster his arguments. He never considered the physical tax on women from constant childbearing.

Why did the Franklins not have a larger number of children? Perhaps there was a health issue involved in the low fertility of BF and DF. But the Franklins' small family might have been purposeful. BF's writings tended to categorize childrearing as an consumer expense that precluded other choices. As Claude-Anne Lopez notes, their small family contributed to the wealth that made it possible for BF to retire from business and engage in public service and scientific experiments. Lopez finds this to have been accidental and attributes the infertility to DF, but it may have been planned. BF criticized his nephew for having too large a family and on those grounds refused to help him financially. The assumption was that the nephew's large family was due to carelessness and irresponsibility. Births could be and should be limited. So how to reconcile his public pronouncements on the advantages of rapid population growth with his private, much more restrained behavior? (Lopez and Herbert, 1975: 33–34; Hodgson, 1991; Waldstreicher, 2004: 171; Klepp, 2009; Lopez, 2010).

BF also seems to have been inconsistent in his assessment of the marriage ways of the Pennsylvania Germans, writing privately that English men would never be attracted to hardworking German women, yet the highest praise he could find for his own wife was her industry and frugality, a "plain Country Joan." A design to hasten the assimilation of the Germans into the British Empire by encouraging intermarriage was answered by BF as follows: the "Proposal of Encouraging Intermarriages between the English and Germans, by Donations, &c. I think would either cost too much, or have no Effect. The German Women are generally so disagreable to an English Eye, that it wou'd require great Portions to induce Englishmen to marry them. Nor would the German Ideas of Beauty generally agree with our Women; *dick und starcke,* that is, *thick and strong,* always enters into their Description of a pretty Girl: for the value of a Wife with them consists much in the Work she is able to do. So that it would require a round Sum with an English Wife to make up to a Dutch Man the difference in Labour and Frugality. This Matter therefore I think had better be left to itself." By denigrating their opposites among the Germans, BF emphasized beauty, slenderness, leisure, and discretionary spending in the wives of Englishmen, characteristics much more difficult to achieve with numerous children (PBF, "To Peter Collinson" [1753?]; Weaver, 1957).

Religion. BF was raised in the Calvinist tradition and on occasion attended the Presbyterian church in Philadelphia. As a young man, he openly toyed with deism. BF even speculated privately about the possible existence of multiple, finite gods under a distant dominant deity in his "Articles of Belief" of 1728. His highest professed values were truth, sincerity, and integrity, while his much publicized thirteen virtues in the *Autobiography* made good business sense but omit such generous traits as friendship, love, sympathy, and charity (Lemay, 2006a: 360–371, 2006b: 23–25). For the most part BF was a secularist. His attention to any religious system was fitful and seems to have been influenced primarily by its political utility.

While BF is considered to have preferred abstract science and reason to supernatural beliefs, at least in his surviving writings, many of the women in his family embraced a religious orientation grounded both in church ritual and faith. His mother, his younger sister, his wife, and daughter were all more devout than he. Still, when his daughter wished to leave Christ Church because she did not like the minister, BF wrote a stinging response: "Go constantly to Church," he ordered his twenty-year-old daughter (Lopez and Herbert, 1975: 122). What was sauce for this young adult goose, was decidedly not sauce for papa gander. It was as if BF wanted to enforce separate mental universes for men and women – an ideology of separation and opposition that anticipates the idealized nineteenth century separate spheres of private, pious females and public, secular men.

DF was a life-long member of the Church of England and, as the evidence strongly suggests, a supporter of the teachings of William Law. She owned two of his books, lent them out, and asked for their return through an advertisement in the *Pennsylvania Gazette.* She was in good company in her choice of reading material: Edward Gibbon, Samuel Johnson, John and Charles Wesley, George Whitefield, and William Wilberforce all admired Law's popular works as well. Law found little benefit in attending church, but urged his followers to pray privately. However, the greatest emphasis in his popular works was on charity. True Christians should devote their lives to the poor, the downtrodden, and the enslaved to mitigate their suffering. It was a message of tolerance for other cultures, social outreach to the impoverished, and gradual societal reformation. DF's interest in education and her qualms about slavery may have been strengthened by reading Law. BF's commitment to civic improvement, to the founding of the Pennsylvania Hospital, the Library Company, the Academy, and more would probably have met with DF's approval, even if they had different justifications for their creation, with BF focused on self-improvement and civic advancement and DF on faith and service.

In some respects DF and BF agreed to disagree on religion and religious observation. The children were raised as Anglicans, BF paid the family's pew rent at Christ Church and he was buried next to DF and their son in the Christ Church burying ground. Yet he never became a member himself.

Domestic Spheres and Places. According to most historians there were no separate, gendered spheres in Franklin's Philadelphia houses, even when he was off in Europe and DF was in Philadelphia supervising the construction of what both called "his" house. BF's home was his castle, and his alone, even when he was not there. Therefore Vivian Bruce Conger's recent article is like a breath of fresh air in uncovering the ways in which DF asserted herself and her interests during the building process (Riley, 1953; Roach, 1960; Lopez, 1981; Talbott, 2005b; Cahill, 2008; Conger, 2009).

As Feminist. It is anachronistic to attempt to locate BF as a feminist or anti-feminist, as if these were simple, self-evident terms that can be transported across time and space without definition or appreciation of the historical context. He did promote women's education in general, but women's education was for the family's benefit, not the woman's, and higher education was strictly for boys. He treated female business associates as he treated men (this was not necessarily a good thing since these partnerships were unequal). He seems never to have considered expanding women's legal rights, but Mary Wollstonecraft's influential book on the rights of women was only published two years after BF's death. He did treat many women as individuals, but could discard them when they were no longer useful. And he treated his own daughter rather shabbily, giving her many fewer advantages than her half-brother, William. It is not known whether BF supported his son William's biological mother or how he took custody of the baby. He took pride in being a founder of the Pennsylvania Hospital, but the hospital did not initially take obstetrical or gynecological cases and treated far more men than women.

BF as a young runaway could collude with a friend to explain his sneaking around the docks – they blamed a woman, a "naughty girl" whose parents were supposedly threatening a shotgun marriage. They assumed that men would present a united front against a forward female and that their elders would be impressed with BF's virility in getting the woman "with Child." They were right. BF was not turned over to authorities by the ship's captain. The absconding apprentice sailed off to Philadelphia (Lemay, 1986a: 17).

There is one sentence from the *Pennsylvania Gazette* and an abbreviated version of it in the *Autobiography* that might meet some of the expectations of some twenty-first-century feminists. The slightly longer version comes at the end of a short article describing the devices and mottoes adopted by the voluntary militia companies created in 1747 for the defense of Pennsylvania. BF writes: "Most of the above Colours, together with the Officers Half-Pikes and Spontons [spontoon, a type of half-pike or blade], and even the Halberts, Drums, &c. have been given by the good Ladies of this City, who raised Money by Subscription among themselves for that Purpose" (article reproduced in Lemay, 1986a: 92; Lemay, 2009: 40–41). BF had been the driving force behind the creation of the Association, the militia companies, but it seems that he – or, more likely, DF – also mobilized large numbers of women. (It would have been unseemly for a man to go around recruiting other men's wives.) The women raised funds on their own, painted the silk flags that were to be carried into battle, publicly presented the flags to the troops, and provided funds for other equipment. So this effort presumed that wives could control cash, that they could be politically and militarily engaged, and that they were necessary to the creation public opinion. Almost nothing else is known of these women's activities, but in 1755 DF headed a delegation of women who welcomed Charlotte Brown, Matron of the British Army Hospital, to Philadelphia. Then in 1780, Sarah Franklin Bache and Ester DeBerdt Reed formed the Ladies Association, which also raised subscriptions among women for the benefit of the troops. And during the Civil War, another descendent, Elizabeth Duane Gillespie, would likewise organize women to provide for northern soldiers. Perhaps we can discern the development of a feminine political tradition passed from mother to daughter over the course of the eighteenth and nineteenth centuries.

Still, the women were primarily cheerleaders on the sidelines of men's military activities, for all that they undertook public roles in raising money. Later, BF commended the Moravians for their comprehensive preparation for attack in 1757: guns and ammunition for the men, and stones for the women to drop on their enemies' heads. Even in dire emergencies men and women were unequal (Lemay, 1986a: 124).

Leo Lemay's first two volumes of biography extol BF's pioneering proto-feminism based on BF's call for women's improvement through education, his use of feminine personas, and his advocacy of companionate marriages (Lemay, 2006a,b: *passim*). All but two of the chapters in Larry Tise's collection paint a substantially darker view of BF's relationships with women. By the time the third volume of Lemay's biography appeared, the references to proto-feminism were absent, BF was certainly not a modern feminist and it is doubtful that he was even a proto-feminist in most aspects of his life. He was willing to grant some women unusual opportunities in education or in shaping public opinion as long as these were useful. He did think that women's upbringing exaggerated their faults, but this does not mean that he thought women could become men's equals or equivalents. He avowed companionate marriages, but did not support his daughter's choice of a husband. His aphorisms and other writings were popular with women as well as men, but often dealt in stereotypes. It seems that he was inconsistent, muddled, and contradictory on the subject of women – like many men and women of his day (Wages, 1973; Lerat, 1993; Kelley, 2000).

Individuals and family, carnality and intimacy, play and exploitation, advocacy and practice, virtue and practicality, girls and boys, women and men: there is much more to explore in tracing the many relationships of BF, gender, sexuality, and power.

Notes

1 Labaree, Leonard W. et al., eds. (1959–). *The Papers of Benjamin Franklin.* 39 vols to date. New Haven, CT: Yale University Press. Hereafter referred to as PBF.
2 Franklin, Benjamin (2006). *The Papers of Benjamin Franklin: Digital Edition.* Los Altos, CA. http://franklinpapers.org/franklin/. Hereafter referred to as FDE.

Further Reading

Bloch, Ruth A. (1993). "Women, love and virtue in the thought of Edwards and Franklin," in *Benjamin Franklin, Jonathon Edwards and the Representation of American Culture*, B. Barbara, ed. New York, NY: Oberg and Harry S. Stout, pp. 134–151.

Conger, Vivian Bruce (2009). "'There is grate odds between a mans being at home and a broad:' Deborah Read Franklin and the eighteenth-century home," *Gender and History* 21: 592–607.

Fry, Jennifer Reed (2006). "'Extraordinary freedom and great humility:' A reinterpretation of Deborah Franklin," *Pennsylvania Magazine of History and Biography* 127: 167–196.

Lemay, J.A. Leo (2004). "Deborah Franklin, Lord Loudoun, and Franklin's 'Autobiography'," *Huntington Library Quarterly* 67: 607–621.

Lopez, Claude-Anne (1966). *Mon Cher Papa: Franklin and the Ladies of Paris* New Haven, CT.

Lopez, Claude-Anne and Eugenia W. Herbert (1975). *The Private Franklin: The Man and His Family.* New York, NY.

Tise, Larry, ed. (2000). *Benjamin Franklin and Women.* University Park, PA.

Part III

Franklin the Writer and Thinker

Chapter Thirteen

"The Manners and Situation of a Rising People": Reading Franklin's *Autobiography*

Ormond Seavey

It is clear that Benjamin Franklin is unrecognizable without consideration of his *Autobiography*. That central work, a preoccupation of his intermittently from 1771 until his death in 1790 defines him as a certain kind of person. To a great extent his achievement was to have become that person. The seal of that person is the record of the *Autobiography*. That he engaged in noteworthy experimenting and theorizing in various areas of technology and natural science, that he managed the rupture that turned the American colonies into an independent nation and engineered the financial and military support necessary to the success of the American Revolution, that he set his hand to all the most important early declarations and compacts – these and other accomplishments all relate to the record of his life he himself set down.

Other noteworthy figures manifest themselves as ideas, as in the case of Plato, Frederick Douglass, Mary Wollstonecraft, Jonathan Edwards, and Voltaire. It is possible to consider Franklin in terms of his ideas, but such efforts miss something. Even early reactions to him characteristically take the form not of responses to ideas or political positions so much as responses to a certain personality. As early as 1757, a Pennsylvanian admirer of Franklin recorded his enthusiasm in poetry, after referring to the creation of the defense establishment for the colony and the foundation of the Academy at Philadelphia, later to be known as the University of Pennsylvania:

> Great thy rewards for all thy Labours done,
> And at the great Tribunal will be known.
> There will thy Genius other worlds survey,

A Companion to Benjamin Franklin, First Edition. Edited by David Waldstreicher.
© 2011 Blackwell Publishing Ltd. Published 2011 by Blackwell Publishing Ltd.

> And there adore the glorious God of day.
> There Bacon Newton will our F——lin greet.
> And place him in his Electrisic seat.
> 'Ore Uurope, Asia, Africk's, scienc'd Fame,
> The Royal Medal will exalt thy name;
> Transfer the Palm by thy great genius won
> And proudly own America's great son.
> If then thy sphere, to Electrise above,
> Dart me one ray in pitty and in love
> Oh! Send thy influence, if permitted, send,
> To guide my soul to my beloved Friend."
> "Musing Near a Cool Spring (PBF, 7: 74)[1]

The admirer's verses anticipate many of the subsequent terms of collective endearment that would develop from the *Autobiography,* but years before its composition. The anonymous author knows only enough about Franklin's electrical career to see it as quasi-magical or spiritual in character. Franklin's achievement is simultaneously individual and representative of America. A somewhat conventional piety is subsumed into hero worship so that an eventually angelic or divine Franklin has powers of intervention in the sublunar world.

By contrast, as the proprietors of Pennsylvania anticipate the arrival of Franklin in England later in the same year, they do not fear him, regardless of his scientific prowess, reasoning that a disparity exists between those people who count in the realms of science and the decision-making set. Richard Peters, the proprietors' *consigliere* in Philadelphia, writes to Thomas Penn to warn of the potential that Franklin might exercise his scientific and personal leverage in London to relieve the Penns of their power in the colony after he arrives in London. In a May 14, 1757 letter to Peters, Penn replies that such concerns exaggerate the effects a colonist with scientific credentials might have on colonial policy: "I think I wrote you before that Mr. Franklin's popularity is nothing here, and that he will be looked very coldly upon by the great People, there are very few of any consequence that have heard of his Electrical Experiments, those matters being attended to by a particular Sort of People, many of whom of the greatest consequence I know well, but it is quite another sort of People, who are to determine the Dispute between us" (quoted in PBF, 7: 111n). Clearly Thomas Penn anticipates in Franklin nothing more formidable than an inspired tinkerer. For a while Penn's confidence that the caste of policy-makers – the great People – did not mostly include the scientific elite proved sound, as Franklin's English negotiations to unseat the proprietary family staggered in the late 1750s, but overall Penn's perception of Franklin's insufficiency must stand as one of the noteworthy miscalculations in early American history.

John Adams had no opportunity to read the *Autobiography* but did know its author well enough to recognize how potent he had been as a historical figure. Writing in 1811 in one of various efforts at vindicating his reputation, Adams says: "His reputation was more universal than that of Leibnitz or Newton, Frederick or Voltaire, and his character more beloved and esteemed than any or all of them. ... Franklin's fame was universal. His name was familiar to government and people, to kings, courtiers, nobility, clergy, and philosophers, as well as to plebeians, to such a degree that there was scarcely a peasant or a citizen, a *valet de chambre*, coachman or footman, a lady's chambermaid or a scullion in a kichen, who was not familiar with it, and who did not consider him as a friend to human kind." Such a eulogy would seem effusive coming from one of Franklin's admirers, but Adams writes out of anger and indignation and had come to hate him passionately. "To develop that complication of causes, which conspired to produce so singular a phenomenon, is far beyond my means or forces. Perhaps it can never be done without a complete history of the philosophy and politics of the eighteenth century. Such a work would be one of the most important that ever was written; more interesting to this and future ages than the 'Decline and Fall of the Roman Empire,' splendid and useful as that is ..." (Adams, 1850–1856: 660). For Adams, Franklin represented the Eighteenth Century. A figure prone to deep self-criticism himself, Adams knew that it had been his own century as well, a time for which he had been out of joint. Still, Franklin's perfect adaptation to his times displayed for Adams how limited his adversary finally was.

The Franklin who had maneuvered Adams out of the line of communication with the French ministry in 1780 – the particular source of Adams's grievance – had not done so by some display of superior statecraft or ideas, but by the force of a powerful personality. Grasping that personality Adams confesses to be "far beyond my means or forces" (1850–1856: **xxx**). That is the personality presented in the *Autobiography*.

Perhaps the present moment in critical theory is one most favorable to appropriate responses to Franklin and to the *Autobiography* because Franklin recognized early that he himself was a text. This is just the perception of material which most naturally occurs to literary critics of the present moment. As early as 1728 in his well-known comic epitaph he characterizes himself as "an old Book ... [awaiting] a new & more perfect Edition" (PBF, 1: 111).

That preoccupation with textuality would eventually be incorporated into the *Autobiography* with all its references to *errata* and to passages in his life that might or might not be revised, but it also manifests itself readily in his writings over the intervening four decades. The books we value require close, even microscopic examination. The recognition of what microscopes reveal is set forth for the readers of *Poor Richard Improved* for 1751 in a passage whose paradoxes are insistent. What appears to us from common observation proves on microscopic survey to be something else, with analogies quite unexpected: "The human Skin, by the Help of the

Microscope, is found to be covered over with an infinite Number of Scales lying over one another, as in fishes; and it is probably the same in other Animals" (PBF, 4: 90). These observations are not merely the arcana of inaccessible virtuosi. The almanac readers are able to decipher the hidden nature of things by virtue of reading the marginal passages extending from April through October of 1751 (PBF, 4: 90n). Franklin does not assume that readers come to texts or to any experience lacking curiosity or capacities for subtle interpretation.

Also in the 1740s and 1750s when Franklin considered the phenomenon of the great field preacher George Whitefield – a figure so unlike himself that he seemed to exist almost exclusively not as text but as sound – the same sorts of alterations of perspective based on distance and scale occur. Near the time when Whitefield was preaching in Philadelphia, Franklin was noting how the distance from the source of that sound affected the power of its message. The *Autobiography* replicates an observation earlier made in *Poor Richard* for 1749 about how many tens of thousands could hear an orator speaking outdoors. The message can disperse itself to as many as 45,000 closely packed hearers (PBF, 3: 336). But along with his calculation about how many could hear Whitefield in the *Autobiography* comes his story of how an acquaintance of his had been nearly persuaded by the power of Whitefield's voice into borrowing money to contribute to a charitable cause of dubious soundness except that the prospective lender to whom he had turned "had the firmness not to be affected by the Preacher. His Answer was, '*At any other time, Friend Hopkinson, I would lend to thee freely: but not now; for thee seems to be out of thy right Senses.–*" (Franklin, 1981: 1408).

Before describing his friend's vulnerability to Whitefield's spoken words, the *Autobiography* reports Franklin's own excessive contribution to the collector's dish, but overall Franklin does not share Whitefield's views, seeing them as contrary to an acceptance of the general views of people as a whole, the sort of general public who might be instructed by Poor Richard about microscopes. Just as noteworthy as Whitefield's temporary success in "assuring them they were naturally *half Beasts and half Devils*" (Franklin, 1981: 1406) is the longer-term awareness that this view came and went, producing only a temporary shift of public behavior.

The refuser of generosity toward the clamor of public acceptance reminds us of the value of the resisting critique, just the sort of critique which is too seldom applied to Franklin's *Autobiography*. The serious study of Franklin's *Autobiography* has suffered from the refusal to subject Franklin's text to the close scrutiny that it really invites. As a result much of the criticism of the *Autobiography* has the qualities of the gentle and effusive applause of Jane Austen fans to her novels or the gaga plaudits of Thoreau from self-conscious environmentalists or congenital New Englanders. As in those cases, an aura of piety suffuses the supposed criticism. What the criticism of Franklin's *Autobiography* needs most is a figure like the acquaintance of friend Hopkinson, someone free of awe but also attentive to what is to be read. Too many supposed critical treatments of Franklin fall short of the critic's essential responsibility, to be critical.

Hence the continuing value – routinely denied or overlooked by Franklin's devotees but still acknowledged outside of their own coven – of D.H. Lawrence's provocative essay on Franklin in *Studies in Classic American Literature*. In fact Lawrence is far more respectful of Franklin's importance than those who dismiss the essay seem to think, but Franklin represents a mode of consciousness deeply alien to that mode which Lawrence spent his life championing. Franklin's supposed friends who dismiss Lawrence confuse him with far more lightweight adversaries, who would align Franklin with Babbittry or see him as an English spy during the Revolution – just to cite the looniest negative claims.

Always conscious of nuances about social class and the impenetrability of the upper class to someone like himself or Franklin, who can only cite great talents as credentials, Lawrence even aligns himself with Franklin. Lawrence could see that upper-class Philadelphia, the old families controlling its politics all his life, would see Franklin as an upstart. Fame abroad – or even in the newly developed nation – did not translate into anything more than conditional acceptance by families such as the Biddles, Norrises, and Ingersolls. In his turn, Lawrence felt that Bertrand Russell or Lady Ottoline Morrell knew him to be an indifferently educated child of the collieries rather than their peer. What he saw in Franklin was another socially anxious striver like himself. Except that Franklin's strivings somehow took the wrong course, in their aim at a deliberate and conscious mastery of the self.

It is quite likely that the readers of this volume will find an acknowledgment of Lawrence's importance to be at best an act of irreverence and at worst a betrayal of the seriousness of the study of Franklin. But the greater danger to that study is an unwillingness to pursue it in a spirit of disinterested criticism, as if Franklin is a holy icon to be protected from any but the eyes of the believers, who serve as protectors of the icon's special powers. Franklin in our time does not require imitation or adulation. Those of us who regularly teach his work in the classroom know that some students see Franklin as an exemplar of the self-determined individual they seek to become while other students wonder how he could be so casual about personal connections to particular others as he cruises past such detritus along his way as John Collins, James Ralph, Samuel Keimer, or probably Deborah Read. Both the admirers and the detractors among our students have seen something genuinely present in the *Autobiography*. A text generating such divergent responses requires a nuanced and flexible criticism. By now it has been over two centuries since Franklin stopped writing the *Autobiography*. No one imagines the direct imitation of Franklin's thirteen-week program of moral improvement, so the Society of the Free and Easy has no more a chance of existing in the twenty-first century than it did in the eighteenth. In fact much of the criticism of Franklin's *Autobiography* suffers from a spirit of reverence.

At present the study of American literature is properly cautious about claims of American exceptionalism, as such claims prove to carry so much suspect political baggage – and those making such claims prove to be oblivious to the contexts of international literature where counterparts to the supposedly uniquely American phenomena exist. But despite the risks of considering these questions, abandonment of the consideration would render much of the writing of the late eighteenth and nineteenth centuries unintelligible. If the category of a distinctively American literature does not really exist, what were Brackenridge and Freneau, Royal Tyler, Charles Brockden Brown, Emerson, Margaret Fuller, Melville or a variety of others fretting about, when they made their claims for American literature? Lawrence admits to some unclarity about whether there is an American literature really distinct from English literature. Writing in 1923 just before the emergence of the noteworthy American writers of that decade, Lawrence offers the reaction of the contemporary American to the supposed national literary heritage: "'The old American literature! Franklin, Cooper, Hawthorne & Co.? All that mass of words! all so unreal!' cries the live American" (Lawrence, 1964: vii). But in fact Lawrence sees in those earlier writers a vitality that he fails to see in the active American writers of 1923. Though he will seem to heap abuse on Franklin, that critique appears in the context of a sophisticated and well-informed revaluation and appreciation of early American writing – a category which for Lawrence extends through the first half of the nineteenth century. That there is a distinctive American literature is clear to Lawrence, even though he finds some of its features to be deplorable and unconsciously dependent upon the English source.

Those who ignore or avoid Lawrence's essay sometimes class it with other British denigrations of American literature and culture from a perspective of superiority. But Lawrence was not part of the British literary establishment, a precinct then as closed to him as it is to Whitman or Melville. A later critique would admit him posthumously into the company of Dickens and George Eliot, as F.R. Leavis does, but in 1923 and earlier Lawrence struggled in the British literary scene with the reputation as an interloper lacking high seriousness. For Lawrence American literature and America do not constitute bad or ungrateful children. Like Lawrence himself American literature had broken from the established English pattern. Lawrence finally feels akin to what he calls the classic American writers, in particular Melville and Whitman. "Classic" American literature provides Lawrence a sort of fulcrum by which he can seek to shift English writing away from patterns he feels are no longer vital, for example the vestiges of Victorian writing still active in English literary life.

In Lawrence's rendition of "Classic American" literature, Franklin occupies a special and honored place in his overall schema. Before Franklin there had been the Puritans and Pilgrims, who had merely fled England for negative reasons without envisioning what sort of new life might exist in this alien place.

> What did the Pilgrim Fathers come for, then, when they came so gruesomely over the black sea? Oh, it was in a black spirit. A black revulsion from Europe, from the old authority of Europe, from kings and bishops and popes. And more. When you look into it, more. They were black, masterful men, they wanted something else. No kings, no bishops maybe. Even no God Almighty. But also, no more of this new 'humanity' which followed the Renaissance. None of this new liberty which was to be so pretty in Europe. Something grimmer, by no means free-and-easy. (Lawrence, 1964: 5)

There is a frenzied and impressionistic quality in Lawrence's prose that those who insist on precision can bridle at. But most reflecting historians will acknowledge that there exists an inner significance to the events of the past. Lawrence intuits that significance and his observations of these masterful men with their horror of kings, bishops, and religious ceremonies reminds us of real historical figures such as John Endecott, Thomas Dudley, John Milton, and Roger Williams. (Whether intentional or not, Lawrence's emphasis on the expression "masterless men," a category associated in his mind with the Puritans, echoes the concern Hobbes expresses in Leviathan for what he calls masterless men – ex-soldiers, vagabonds, runaways – a group who disrupt all efforts to bring society under rational control. Puritans in both old and New England also felt anxieties about the masterless, but they themselves were also conducting their own resistance to civil control such as they experienced it. See Michael Walzer's still provocative consideration of this issue in *The Revolution of the Saints*.) Franklin represents for Lawrence an important development beyond what he sees as the merely negative and reactive impulses of the Puritans. Franklin turns the Puritan effort at social control inward and makes the self its own warden. It is Franklin's success at that self-mastery that represents his immense importance and, for Lawrence, his great danger. Franklin had perfected a system of bringing the self under conscious control, and the record of how that control could be exercised is his *Autobiography*. But it had not been merely a personal achievement. Franklin's model for the self had turned into the national preoccupation.

Lawrence could recognize the power of that self-control. It also carries for him social class associations – specifically with his working-class father. "I can remember, when I was a little boy, my father used to buy a scrubby yearly almanac with the sun and moon and stars on the cover. And it used to prophesy bloodshed and famine. But also crammed in corners it had little anecdotes and humorisms, with a moral tag. And I used to have my little priggish laugh at the woman who counted her chickens before they hatched and so forth, and I was convinced that honesty was the best policy, also a little priggishly. The author of these bits was Poor Richard, and Poor Richard was Benjamin Franklin, writing in Philadelphia well over a hundred years before" (Lawrence, 1964: 14). Few memories could be more painful to recall for Lawrence than these. He had not always been the jaunty Paul Morel, strutting about the world with a fine insouciance. He had been his father's priggish little boy, reading almanacs for hints about lower class survival.

Those Franklin scholars who squint over their shoulders at Lawrence typically accuse him of missing Franklin's sense of humor, as if Lawrence lacked a sense of humor. It is certainly true that there exists in Lawrence's fiction an overall fierce intensity of exposition that might seem to preclude any comic perception of the world. But Lawrence could also see the humorous aspect of himself as the bad boy thumbing his nose at the great American icon. After offering Franklin's all-purpose creed and then proposing his own reversed version in a seemingly manic riff, Lawrence observes, "It is rather fun to play at Benjamin" (Lawrence, 1964: 16). Even the exultant defier of "old daddy Franklin" is a comic exaggeration, carefully positioned. Lawrence finally recognizes, as many Franklin adherents do not, that Franklin's characteristic humor operates above all as a further exercise of the self's control over experience. When he describes how he abandons vegetarianism off Block Island, Franklin asserts a further exercise of self-management. He will not be superseded as merely another young impractical idealist. That young idealist is overtaken by the rationalist who sees that "when the Fish were opened, I saw smaller Fish taken out of their Stomachs:– Then, thought I, if you eat one another, I don't see why we mayn't eat you. So I din'd upon Cod very heartily and continu'd to eat with other People, returning only now & then occasionally to a vegetable Diet. So convenient a thing it is to be a *reasonable Creature*, since it enables one to find or make a Reason for every thing one has a mind to do." (Franklin, 1981: 1339) As told, the situation reflects his perceptions of the time, not merely a later self's justifications. Even as a boy Franklin could mobilize humor to attain control over a situation. The other characteristic mistake Franklin scholars make about Lawrence's essay is to accept at face value its manic surface, believing it to be a momentary outburst. The plain facts of the essay's genesis, which I laid out some years ago, indicate just the opposite. Rather than some immediate irritant, Franklin constituted a long-term adversary to all that Lawrence valued most essentially. In a 1916 letter to Catherine Carswell, Lawrence declared that he planned to move to America regardless of what he felt he knew about Americans: "Because there, I know, the *skies* are not so old, the air is newer, the earth is not tired. Don't think I have any illusions about the people, the life" (Lawrence, 1984: 25). There are numerous references in this period to anticipations that Lawrence would exchange his impoverished exile in rural Cornwall for a projected life in America. In 1918–1919 he published in the *English Review* a version of *Studies in Classic American Literature*. He had written to Amy Lowell earlier that he had been at work on the essays for five years. The *English Review* version of *Studies* is rather more conventional in its presentation than the eventual book version would be, though the ideas there are closely akin to those in the final version. Evidently Lawrence found the periodical version of *Studies* an inadequate expression of his ideas. In 1918 he and Frieda left England traveling around the world, and tinkering with the essays along the way, eventually stopping for a while in Taos, New Mexico, where they lived on the ranch of Mabel Dodge Luhan. The *English Review* essay on Franklin hardly focuses on Franklin, concerning itself rather with a theory of artistic creation utterly at odds with Franklin's disposition to manage and control experience. That theory is latent rather than explicit in the final Franklin essay, I think that the explicitness of his theorizing about creation in the earlier version may have struck him as inartistic, so the theory needed to be embedded in a more articulated critique. Thus there is nothing madcap or spontaneous about Lawrence's view of Franklin or of American literature, except that an appropriate articulation of his views required the appearance of spontaneity because spontaneity – a quality never much valued by Franklin – struck Lawrence as the essential access of the creative mind to experience. So Lawrence carefully crafts the wild rant about Franklin.

That Lawrence rightly recognizes Franklin's disregard for spontaneity can be easily confirmed by considering those occasions in the *Autobiography* where surprise and spontaneity might have been dramatized. Every reader recognizes that the central scene in the narrative is the one where young Franklin first enters Philadelphia. Much is unexpected in the new city: the bread is different from what he had known in Boston, where a port city featured something closer to hardtack. In this scene, the most elaborately rendered one in the entire narration, Franklin does acknowledge surprise. But in general Franklin subordinates perceptions of surprise or spontaneity, replacing them with extended calculation. One of the great disturbing events in his young life occurs as he discovers that the promises of support from Governor Keith in the form of financial support for the printing press he would presumably acquire on a trip to England had come to nothing, eventually leaving him stranded in London without any support beyond what his own wits could supply. Rather than describe his first emotional state upon discovering the governor's cheat, he remonstrates at the unfairness of his behavior, while acknowledging the governor's virtues as a writer, administrator, and drafter of legislation (Franklin, 1981: 1345). But Franklin's neglect of spontaneity is nowhere more clearly demonstrated than in his relations with women, beginning with Deborah Read, his eventual wife. She appears first of all as the laughing spectator of his first awkward walk along the streets of Philadelphia. His early attraction to her is credited to proximity. He leaves her in Philadelphia as he goes off to London, writing her one letter explaining that he will not be returning. Discarded, she marries on the rebound unwisely to a likely bigamist. While in London Franklin had "attempted Familiarities [with James Ralph's girl friend], (another Erratum) which she repuls'd with a proper Resentment" (Franklin, 1981: 1347). There is no pause between the event and its critique. After returning to Philadelphia, Franklin turns to casual sexual contacts ("that hard-to-be-govern'd Passion of Youth, had hurried me into Intrigues with low Women that fell in my Way ..." [Franklin, 1981: 1371]). Eventually he goes back to Deborah as the best option he has in a marriage. Everything about what might in another person be described as his emotional or passionate life is depicted in terms of calculation.

Franklin's *Autobiography* has been available to readers in one form or other since the 1790s, so it has experienced a somewhat varied history of reactions. In the nineteenth century, reactions to Franklin were responses to someone not so long gone. Joseph Dennie, who was like Franklin a New Englander transplanted to Philadelphia but one with deeply conservative views, saw Franklin as a dangerous radical – mostly a negative example. At the point where he writes, Dennie could not have had access to the *Autobiography*, but these sentiments express his vitriolic views: "From a diligent review of his character, conduct, and writings, the author of this article has acquired the right to affirm, that this pseudo philosopher has been a mischief to his country. He was the founder of that Grub-street sect, who have professedly attempted to degrade literature to the level of vulgar capacities, and debase the polished and current language of books, by the vile alloy of provincial idioms and colloquial barbarism, the shame of grammar, and akin to any language, rather than English. He was one of our first Jacobins, the first to lay his head in the lap of French harlotry; and prostrate the Christianity and honour of his country to the deism and democracies of Paris" (quoted in Leary, 1948: 243). By contrast Horace Greeley some years later would see Franklin as embodying a rise to greatness that appears almost inevitable. "The salient feature of his career is its uniformity. ... You cannot say when he ceased to be poor, or unknown, or powerless; he steps into each new and higher position as if he had been born just for that; you know that his newspaper, his almanac, his electrical researches, his parliamentary service, his diplomacy, were the best of that time; but who can say that he was more admirable in one field of useful effort than another?" (quoted in Parton 1866, II: 678) By the beginning of the twentieth century in particular, Franklin comes to seem superhuman, not a political figure with a scientific side or a scientist who also participated in politics, but in Carl Van Doren's ringing words in his 1938 biography "a harmonious human multitude" (Van Doren, 1938: 782). Dwarfed by this spectacle, the scholars of the past hundred years vie with one another for the most extravagant claims to make for him. The great critical problem must be how to acknowledge Franklin's genuine accomplishments while also recognizing the human who did them. The *Autobiography* succeeds in converting admissions of deficiency – in particular the "errata" – into marks of superiority.

Unfortunately for critics of the *Autobiography,* recourse to literary traditions of autobiography have limited value in understanding what Franklin is doing. It ought to be stressed that every author of autobiography is aware above all of how distinctive this life has been. It is not surprising that Franklin should see his life as lacking the sort of pattern that other lives before his had followed. Various critics, among them William Spengemann and Daniel Shea, have located the *Autobiography* in contexts of spiritual autobiography that can be traced back to Augustine, but aside from his acquaintance with Bunyan, it is not easy to discover in Franklin an awareness of that tradition. As Leo Lemay pointed out back in 1976 in an essay lamentably buried away in a research library publication, "The fictive world of Franklin's Autobiography portrays the first completely modern world that I know in Western literature: nonfeudal, nonaristocratic, and nonreligious" (Lemay, 1978: 25). Half a century earlier Lawrence had also recognized Franklin's essential modernity, aligning him with the Ford car and Charley Chaplin – like Lawrence himself a figure suspended between English origins and a current American setting. For Lawrence the modern had an American cast to it, for better or worse. To note Franklin's modernity is also to open up the real access to a valuable critique of the *Autobiography* because only the most fatuous reader could consider modernity to be a domain free of complication. Lawrence, who is himself one of the heralds of modernism, could see its terrible cost to the self. Franklin does not have to be merely the poor boy who makes good. In that role he merely joins Cardinal Wolsey or Dick Whittington, the one with the cat in the nursery rhyme, thrice lord mayor of London-town.

I think there is evidence of the modernity of the *Autobiography* in the letters which Franklin incorporates between the first and second parts. These letters, from Abel James and Benjamin Vaughan, appear to be incorporated to account for why Franklin resumes the writing in France after leaving the project since 1771. James, a Philadelphia merchant who has come upon the manuscript and notes for the first part; with a passing pious reference to Ecclesiastes on the brevity of life, writes to encourage Franklin to resume the project, sending along a copy of Franklin's Notes. For James the principal value to the life would be the model of industry and temperance. Franklin then forwards James's letter to Vaughan, his English editor, for comment. Vaughan envisions the life in larger, more extensive terms. For one thing, Vaughan worries that the life might be otherwise rendered by less competent hands. Among other considerations, Vaughan refers to three previous traditions of autobiography which this life will contrast with, the Newgate memoir, the spiritual autobiography, and the literary apologia: "the lives of various public cut-throats and intriguers, and with absurd monastic self-tormentors, or with vain literary triflers" (Franklin, 1981: 1377). Vaughan's reference to absurd monastic self-tormentors responds to Abel James's reference to the Preacher in his letter (Ecclesiastes, 12: 1–8). For young Vaughan as he anticipates the resumption of the autobiography the great question is the organization and conduct of life. Vaughan relates the record of the life to a long-promised Franklin writing project several times referred to in letters to his friends, a treatise on what he calls *The Art of Virtue*. When the composition of this treatise had been first mentioned back as early as 1760, it had been a freestanding self-help project, based on his own experiences. Here is his description of the piece in a letter to Lord Kames, the Scottish intellectual he had come to know in Great Britain: "I purpose, likewise, a little Work for the Benefit of Youth, to be called "The Art of Virtue." From the Title you will hardly conjecture what the Nature of such a Book may be. I must therefore explain a little. Many People lead bad Lives that would gladly lead good ones, but know not *how* to make the Change. They have frequently *resolv'd* and *endeavour'd* it; but in vain, because their Endeavours have not been properly conducted. To exhort People to be good, to be just, to be temperate, &c. without *shewing* them *how* to be just, to be temperate, &c. seems like the ineffectual Charity mention'd by the Apostle, which consisted in saying to the Hungry, the Cold, and the Naked, *be ye fed, be ye warmed, be ye clothed,* without shewing them how they should get Food, Fire, or Clothing" (Franklin, 1987: 765–766). Franklin's insistent underlinings in the letter indicate his engagement with the project, but the press of public business over the next several decades prevented him from composing it. Vaughan's letter incorporated into the *Autobiography* brought up the projected text again, linking the record of his life in the memoirs to this free-standing but not yet composed treatise: "the chance which your life will give for the forming of future great men; and in conjunction with your *Art of Virtue*, (which you design to publish) of improving the features of private character, and consequently of aiding all happiness both public and domestic" (Franklin, 1981: 1374).

The upshot of Vaughan's reminder of the uncompleted "Art of Virtue" appears as Franklin incorporates what must be assumed to be the substance of that project into the second part of the *Autobiography*. A project such as the "Art of Virtue" might appear to connect the *Autobiography* with a long-standing tradition in religious writing focusing on prudential guidance – a tradition certainly discoverable in the Bible. It has long been recognized that the border between the eighteenth-century old-light quasi-Arminian divines and Franklin was fairly blurred. Mitchell Breitwieser has usefully spelled out the connections between the effort to correct the self in its inveterate willfulness and limitation and the celebration of the self as the site of value, the one project undertaken by Cotton Mather and the succeeding effort the legacy of Franklin. But Benjamin Vaughan, the English protégé, wishes to align the "Art of Virtue" not to some post-religious accommodation but to the future of new states for whom such accommodations might be irrelevant. By 1784 when Franklin undertook to continue the *Autobiography* beyond Part One, he was no longer interested in composing a separate treatise on the art of virtue, perhaps recognizing some of the problems of exposition that project would entail, so rather than abandoning it he incorporates what appear to be its central features into the second part of the *Autobiography*.

Nothing could be more distinctly modern than the subordination of religion that Franklin accomplishes in the *Autobiography*, always accomplished by suggestion and rhetorical arrangement. In keeping with Vaughan's encouragement, he turns to the project directly after describing his disappointment with the preaching of Philadelphia Presbyterians. As he sets up the presentation of the art of virtue, his "great and arduous Project of achieving moral Perfection," (Franklin, 1981: 1383) he first discusses his separation from the public practice of Presbyterian worship in Philadelphia.

It is the distinction between private and public that creates the context for his project. So preoccupied with that distinction is he that as he embarks on his critique of public worship that he incorporates his articles of belief in an oddly huddled package embedded within a paragraph, unlike the careful exposition to those articles that he would fit into the beginning of the third part three years later while writing in Philadelphia. Religion, as he frames it, is a purely personal matter, and his experience of its forays into the public sphere had been disappointing. He describes how he had once attended a Presbyterian service where the sermon's text from Philippians had seemed to require an exposition of public responsibilities, but instead the sermon stressed only individual duties such as the duties to attend public worship, partake of the sacrament, and respect ministers (Franklin, 1981: 1382–1383). Raised in the Boston of the Mathers, Franklin is quite aware that his own priorities, which relegate religion to the domain of personal tastes, defy an earlier orthodoxy which had insisted that religion should contain and inflect everything else. Having set aside religion's claims to centrality Franklin actually pushes the "Art of Virtue" beyond the more modest claims that he had articulated in the 1760 letter describing the project to Lord Kames. In that letter Franklin had stipulated some of its grounds by reference to allusions to the Bible. By 1784 he sets up this effort at self-perfection as a replacement to anything biblically grounded.

One critical challenge in reading the *Autobiography* is that Franklin presents something different from the narrative of life experiences together with reflections on those experiences that is more characteristic of autobiographies, like those of John Woolman or John Stuart Mill. In some sense, regardless of the acknowledgement of errata, the *Autobiography* is itself the superior model for experience in a way comparable to the way Aristotle takes the tragedies of Sophocles as his model in the *Poetics*. Franklin's life, together with the proposed organizing principles in the "Art of Virtue," is the model life for anyone.

On the other hand in the details it includes, Franklin does specify the ways that his life cannot be imitated. He arrives in Philadelphia when many of its needed civic institutions remain to be established – such as a public library, a college, a hospital, appropriate city lighting, fire protection. All of these institutions come to be established, in large part through Franklin's management. As Benjamin Vaughan had anticipated: "All that has happened to you is also connected with the detail of the manners and situation of *a rising* people, and in this respect I do not think that the writings of Caesar and Tacitus can be more interesting to a true judge of human nature and society" (Franklin, 1981: 1374). In Vaughan's mind Franklin's experiences in America can be related to Caesar's *de Bello Gallico* or Tacitus's *Germania* as works of ethnographic examination. But by incorporating the "Art of Virtue" into his text Franklin alters the way the text must be read. As Lawrence demonstrates with raucous force, it is the project of arriving at moral perfection that remains at the heart of how Franklin must be remembered.

To say all of this is to suggest beginnings for an adequate critique of the *Autobiography*, which is one of those texts where a simplicity of surface leads readers in a hurry to accept that they have picked up everything. But what Mitchell Breitwieser observed in 1984 remains true today. "Franklin criticism has in general failed to achieve the level of intellectual appraisal to be found in recent work on [Cotton] Mather: Franklin is still treated largely as a benign and open sensibility rather than as a coherent and deliberate rhetorical project" (1984: 173). I would suggest that the problematic aspects of Mather have generated the resisting critique which has eluded Franklin. No one without the exercise of a sophisticated critical practice has landed Mather as a harbinger of the modernity that appears too easily to be Franklin's milieu.

One basis for the complications that can be considered in the *Autobiography* is its strange composition history, which can be briefly sketched. Certainly the history of its composition points to some of the complications of the text. Alfred Owen Aldridge has depicted that complication at one point with a vividness of expression uncharacteristic of so careful a scholar: "In form, Franklin's work is a virtual disaster. First of all, it is composed of four separate parts, written during four widely separated periods. Although there is no need of going into the elaborate history of Franklin's text, which has been covered in a number of recent books, some attention should be given to the aesthetic effects of its having been composed in stages. Franklin, for example, had in mind a set of readers for the first part completely different from those he had in mind for the other three. The first part was presumably written for the benefit of his family; the three others for the world at large. For this reason, I am unable to accept the theory that there is any kind of conscious art in Franklin's over-all structure as opposed to the separate parts..." (1967: 48). It might appear that Aldridge finds Franklin's *Autobiography* inartistic, but the real message is that the text developed according to some marvelous organic principle of its own, growing like an oak or a willow – Franklin scholars can sometimes prove as elusive and subtle as their material.

A few basic points can be made about the text's composition. Franklin began writing at Twyford, the country house of Joseph Shipley, the Bishop of Saint Asaph, a political ally who had provided Franklin with a pleasant rural retreat from the business of serving as colonial agent for Pennsylvania in the summer of 1771. The text makes it clear that he began the writing without any preliminary notes or outline but that he creates an outline for himself, the so-called "Notes" after a few pages of writing. After several pages composed with his characteristic lucidity, he pauses with the following self-conscious observation: "By my rambling Digressions I perceive my self to be grown old. I us'd to write more methodically,–But one does not dress for private Company as for a publick Ball. 'Tis perhaps only Negligence" (Franklin, 1981: 1316). We know from his letters that Franklin spent only fifteen days at Twyford in late July and early August 1771. It has been my own speculation that only the beginning of the first part was composed at Twyford and not the entire narrative taking him from birth to 1731. It strikes me as unlikely that so sociable a person as Franklin could have spent the entire time at Twyford holed up in his room writing (Seavey, 1988: 245–246). On the other hand, so eminent and knowledgeable a scholar as Carl Van Doren has described how he envisioned Franklin at work at Twyford: "With his swift, powerful ease, Franklin in his week or so wrote nearly a half of the Autobiography; on the whole the best part" (Van Doren, 1938: 415). For myself I can offer no textual evidence that the composition of Part I lasted beyond August 13, 1771. In their definitive consideration of the text of the *Autobiography*, J.A. Leo Lemay and P.M. Zall are unwilling to go beyond the heading "Twyford, at the Bishop of St. Asaph's" and their judgment is certainly well-informed on more consequential matters (Lemay and Zall, 1981: xx–xxi). In any case, Franklin paused in the composition, set the project aside, and focused on the complicated task of representing several colonies or legislative bodies to the British government until 1775 when circumstances obliged him to decamp for America bringing along with him a trunk of manuscripts which would be eventually stowed for supposed safe-keeping at the point when he had to leave America for France as the U.S. minister.

The text of the *Autobiography* languished for over a decade until Franklin picked it up in Paris (to be more exact, Passy, the suburb where the U.S. mission was located) in 1784 after he had done the most important work of his time there as U.S. minister, negotiating a treaty with the French and eventually joining with other American envoys in reaching the peace treaty with Britain that ended the Revolutionary War. By this time Franklin's importance had greatly expanded beyond its standing in 1771. At that point he had been the most significant American then living. By 1784 Franklin had become the formidable cultural presence that Adams would later describe. "His reputation was more universal than that of Leibnitz or Newton, Frederick or Voltaire, and his character more beloved and esteemed than any or all of them." Peter Shaw in a text introduction to Franklin's writings points out that "his name was made known to more contemporaries than had probably been aware of the existence of Alexander the Great, Jesus Christ, or Charlemagne in their own times" (1982: vii). This figure was not going to be concerning himself about "little family Anecdotes of no Importance to others" (Franklin, 1981: 1372) in the quite misleading words of the memorandum appended to the first part as he commences the second. From this point onward the *Autobiography* purports to deal with larger human issues.

On the other hand Franklin sticks with the outline he had drawn up at Twyford adding little more than a sketchy summary of what materials might go into a description of his time in London until 1775, material he would not live to incorporate into the narrative. Moreover his attention to details is not overtaken by the grand expectations imposed by Abel James or Benjamin Vaughan. As a writer who had composed mostly for publication since the 1720s he seems, as Hugh Dawson points out, to have framed the combination of the first two parts into a version that might be published in its own right (1977/8: 289–290).

Despite the appearance of a conclusion to the *Autobiography* at the end of the second part, Franklin anticipated further work on the project when he returned to Philadelphia in 1785 when he could have access to his dispersed and disorganized personal papers. Just as he sees his life as a text, he came to see the text of his *Autobiography* as a kind of companion, something whose completion had to be prolonged just as his own life was being so prolonged. Despite having access to his papers in Philadelphia, he found himself again pulled back into public life. The new post-revolutionary American state governments took in some cases rather idiosyncratic forms. In lieu of a single responsible chief executive, Pennsylvania had created for itself a Supreme Executive Council, to which Franklin was immediately elected and shortly named the president of that body, so the 79-year-old Franklin would begin to serve for three years as in effect the governor of Pennsylvania. By the end of his time in that office he would serve also as a delegate to the Constitutional Convention. A year later as the Constitution was being ratified, he took up the writing of the *Autobiography* yet again, this time promising Benjamin Vaughan that he would move expeditiously forward, promising to "omit all facts and transactions that may not have a tendency to benefit the young reader" (Franklin, 1987: 1168). It is a promise Franklin was unable to keep. The third part of the *Autobiography* comes to be enmeshed in matters which access to his papers offered him, considerations which he continued to feel important like the Albany Congress or the list of provisions for officers in Braddock's army. Franklin finds himself mired in details which his papers had provided, much to the benefit of subsequent historians who could mine his text for the materials of monographs, but not always contributing to the distinction of his text as a whole. There is no real separation between the third and fourth parts of the *Autobiography*. Franklin remained actively working on the project, not even pausing as he arranged to have copies of the first three parts sent off to two European friends, Vaughan and Louis-Guillaume Le Veillard, his friend and Passy landlord, whose reactions were solicited. Probably Franklin made stylistic changes in the versions sent off to Vaughan and Le Veillard, copied by his grandson Benjamin Franklin Bache. Letters from Franklin in the early months of 1790 indicate he was at work on the writing although slowed by physical pain from gout and kidney stones. In April 1790 he died leaving the project uncompleted but with the expectation that William Temple Franklin, his other grandson, would arrange for its publication together with his other works. Never very reliable or industrious, Temple Franklin made his way back to France with the copy of the *Autobiography* on which his grandfather had been working and apparently traded that copy with Le Veillard to secure a version easier to print from. At some point over the next decades, Temple Franklin contributed some revised wording to the text, and eventually he steered it to publication in 1817.

From this brief history of the text's composition it is possible to derive various conclusions relevant to the interpretation of the *Autobiography*. First of all, for a text so continually hailed as ultimately American, much of it is composed in England and France and reflective of the views of someone who has adapted successfully to those settings. Franklin has absorbed ideas that distinguish him from Americans of his own time. It is clear from Franklin's text of the *Autobiography* that the density of detail included in the description of his first arrival into Philadelphia reflects his awareness of the narrative possibilities in the novel. A few pages before that arrival he describes his rescue of a drunken Dutchman from New York harbor who happens to have in his pocket a Dutch (or German) edition of Bunyan's *Pilgrim's Progress*, Franklin observes about Bunyan: "Honest John was the first that I know of who mix'd Narration & Dialogue, a Method of Writing very engaging to the Reader, who in the most interesting Parts finds himself as it were brought into the Company, & present at the Discourse. De foe in his Cruso, his Moll Flanders, Religious Courtship, Family Instructor, & other Pieces, has imitated it with Success. And Richardson has done the same in his Pamela, &c. – " (Franklin, 1981: 1326). A time would come when observations of this sort, locating Bunyan, Defoe, and Richardson together as originators of a new genre, would be widely shared, but that perception was not yet common. It would be some years before a writer born in America would venture to write a novel on his or her own, but Franklin in 1771 can recognize what possibilities for audience engagement the new genre entailed, so the arrival into Philadelphia is rendered with the narrative fidelity to detail and timing that characterize the eighteenth-century novel. As for the influences on Franklin in France in 1784 the disposition to defy religion and the clergy that helped to frame the introduction of the "Art of Virtue" represent an adaptation of attitudes common among advanced French thinkers of the 1780s. At work as a printer in Philadelphia in the early part of the century Franklin had been careful not to alienate the more religiously oriented people who might be his customers or collaborators, but in Passy he can recall the Presbyterian minister as a failure to inspire civic energies. My own earlier work on the *Autobiography* sought to set the work in an Enlightenment context, but there is more to be done by early American literary scholars who are also conversant with literary and intellectual developments across the Atlantic.

Another corollary of this examination of the textual history indicates that not all published texts of the *Autobiography* can be relied on. In the 1860s the American diplomat and man of letters John Bigelow, then the U.S. minister to France, located and purchased the manuscript version of the *Autobiography* in Franklin's own hands, recovering that text through a remarkable and serendipitous effort of detective work. Bigelow would then go on to edit and publish that text in 1868, preliminary to his eventual editing of Franklin's writings (1887–1889). A comparison of that text with versions then in circulation made it clear that William Temple Franklin had altered his grandfather's wording in the edition of 1817. In 1949 Max Farrand accomplished the next step in reconstructing Franklin's *Autobiography* by editing his Parallel Text Edition in which three versions of the text appeared side by side: the version in Franklin's own hand, William Temple Franklin's edition, and a French translation possibly of the version sent to Le Veillard. Having thus advanced the understanding of the text's history, Farrand then took an unfortunate next step by seeking to reconstruct what he called the fair copy of the *Autobiography*, the version Benjamin Bache sent to Le Veillard, presumably overseen by Franklin himself and including changes in wording made in late 1789. The basis for Farrand's supposed reconstruction of the fair copy was a comparison with the French translation. But what Farrand generated is itself nothing other than series of personal conjectures about what the English version might have been. It is thus lacking in any authority beyond conjecture. That version is still in print in various paperback editions. It is a version to be avoided by anyone seriously interested in what Franklin wrote in his life story. The only versions of value are those which make use of the definitive edition of the only version available in Franklin's own hand, *The Autobiography of Benjamin Franklin: A Genetic Text*, edited by J.A. Leo Lemay and P.M. Zall. In addition those texts which presume to modernize

Franklin's spelling or punctuation violate his own sense as a printer that the practice of restricting capital letters to the beginnings of sentences reduces the possibilities for emphasis that an author is entitled to.

Note

1 Labaree, Leonard W. *et al.*, eds. (1959–). *The Papers of Benjamin Franklin*. 39 vols to date. New Haven, CT: Yale University Press. Hereafter referred to as PBF.

Further Reading

Adams, John (1850–1856). *The Works of John Adams, Second President of the United States*, Charles Francis Adams, ed. Boston, MA: Little, Brown.

Aldridge, Alfred Owen (1967). "Form and substance in Franklin's autobiography" in *Essays on American Literature in Honor of Jay B. Hubbell*, Clarence Ghodes, ed. Durham, NC: Duke University Press.

Baker, Jennifer Jordan (2000). "Benjamin Franklin's *Autobiography* and the credibility of personality," *Early American Literature* 35: 274–375.

Breitwieser, Mitchell Robert (1984). *Cotton Mather and Benjamin Franklin: The Price of Representative Personality*. Cambridge: Cambridge University Press.

Crane, Verner W. (1949). "Review of the restoration of a 'Fair Copy,'" *Modern Philology* 47: 127–134.

Dawson, Hugh (1977/8). "Franklin's 'Memoirs' in 1784: The Design of the *Autobiography*, Parts I and II ...," *Early American Literature* 12:286–93.

Franklin, Benjamin (1949). *Benjamin Franklin's Memoirs: Parallel Text Edition*, Max Farrand, ed. Berkeley, CA: University of California Press.

Franklin, Benjamin (1949). *Benjamin Franklin's Memoirs: The Restoration of a "Fair Copy,"* Max Farrand, ed. Berkeley, CA: University of California Press.

Leonard W. Labaree, William Willcox, Barbara Oberg *et al.*, eds. (1959–). *The Papers of Benjamin Franklin*, New Haven, CT: Yale University Press.

Franklin, Benjamin (1981). *The Autobiography of Benjamin Franklin: A Genetic Text*, J.A. Leo Lemay, and P.M. Zall, eds. Knoxville, TN: University of Tennessee Press.

Franklin, Benjamin (1987). *Autobiography* in *Writings*, J.A. Leo Lemay, ed. New York, NY: Library of America.

Franklin, Benjamin (1987). *Writings*, J.A. Leo Lemay, ed. New York, NY: Library of America.

Lawrence, D.H. (1964). *Studies in Classic American Literature* [1923]. New York, NY: Viking.

Lawrence, D.H. (1984). *The Letters of D.H. Lawrence*, James T. Boulton, and Andrew Robertson, ed. Cambridge: Cambridge University Press.

Leary, Lewis (1948). "Joseph Dennie on Benjamin Franklin," *Pennsylvania Magazine of History and Biography* 72: 240–246.

Lemay, J.A. Leo (1978). "Benjamin Franklin, universal genius" in *The Renaissance Man in the Eighteenth Century: Papers read at a Clark Library Seminar 9 October 1976*. Los Angeles, CA: William Andrews Clark Memorial Library, UCLA.

Parton, James (1866). *Life and Times of Benjamin Franklin*, 2 vols. Boston, MA: Houghton Mifflin.

Seavey, Ormond (1985). "D.H. Lawrence and 'The first dummy American,'" *Georgia Review* 39: 113–128.

Seavey, Ormond (1987). "Benjamin Franklin and D.H. Lawrence as conflicting modes of consciousness" in *Critical Essays on Benjamin Franklin*, Melvin H. Buxbaum, ed. Boston, MA: G.K. Hall.

Seavey, Ormond (1988). *Becoming Benjamin Franklin: The Autobiography and the Life*. University Park, PA: Pennsylvania State University Press.

Shaw, Peter (1982). "*Introduction*" to Franklin, *The Autobiography and Other Writings*. New York, NY: Bantam.

Shea, Daniel B. (1968). *Spiritual Autobiography in Early America*. Madison, WI: University of Wisconsin Press.

Spengemann, William (1980). *The Forms of Autobiography*. New Haven, CT: Yale University Press.

Van Doren, Carl (1938). *Benjamin Franklin*. New York, NY: Viking.

Walzer, Michael (1973). *The Revolution of the Saints: A Study of the Origins of Radical Politics*. New York, NY: Atheneuem.

Zall, P.M. (1989). *Franklin's Autobiography: A Model Life*. Boston, MA: G.K. Hall.

Zuckerman, Michael (1993). "Doing good while doing well: Benevolence and self-interest in Franklin's Autobiography" in *Reappraising Benjamin Franklin: A Bicentennial Perspective*, J.A. Leo Lemay, ed. Newark, DE: University of Delaware Press, 441–451.

Chapter Fourteen

Poor Richard's Almanac

William Pencak

At least in print, Benjamin Franklin was usually not himself. At the age of sixteen, he made his entry on the public stage as "Silence Dogood," an elderly woman, criticizing the pretensions of Harvard College and the hypocrisy of Massachusetts' lapsed puritanical elite. At eighty-four, he took his final bow as Sidi Mehemet Ibrahim, a North African Muslim, fallaciously arguing for the enslavement of Christians using the arguments offered by proslavery advocates in the United States to keep Africans in bondage. In between, he appeared as a "Blackamoor" castigating the idle rich, Polly Baker, a pregnant unmarried woman, Obadiah Plainman, the King of Prussia, and many more guises, including an enigmatic character in his autobiography known as "I" (Pencak, 2007). But by far the most famous of Franklin's fictional personae was "Poor Richard," the author of the best-known early American almanac, which appeared from 1732 to 1757 for the years 1733 to 1758 – as today, colonial almanacs were published late in the year preceding that for which their information was intended.

In 1732, the twenty-six-year-old Franklin began publishing an almanac in Philadelphia. Franklin had proven himself the most successful of the three printers in Philadelphia – the others being Andrew Bradford and his former employer Samuel Keimer. In 1729 he and his partner William Meredith began to print Pennsylvania's paper currency – shortly after he had urged that it do so in "The Busybody" Essays Nos. 8 and 9 and "A Modest Inquiry into the Nature and Necessity of a Paper Currency." The following year they replaced Andrew Bradford as the official government printers of Pennsylvania, which included publishing laws, documents, and proclamations as well as money (Lemay, 2006a: 36, 215). Also in 1729,

---

A Companion to Benjamin Franklin, First Edition. Edited by David Waldstreicher.
© 2011 Blackwell Publishing Ltd. Published 2011 by Blackwell Publishing Ltd.

Franklin and Meredith purchased the *Pennsylvania Gazette*, the province's only newspaper, from Keimer. Franklin and Meredith also began to publish other writers' almanacs that year – Thomas Godfrey's *Pennsylvania Almanac* in 1729 and John Jerman's *American Almanac* in 1730[1] – that Bradford had previously printed. However, in 1732, both Godfrey and Jerman returned to Bradford, who was publishing three other almanacs as well. These were written by Titan Leeds, who had taken over his father Daniel's almanac, published since 1687, in 1715 and retitled it *An American Almanack*; Jacob Taylor, who began publishing his almanac in 1700; and William Birkett who entered the lists in 1728. Left without an almanac, Franklin hastily produced *Poor Richard* for 1733 at almost the last possible moment, on December 28, 1732 (Sappenfield, 1973: 57, 58 125, 126).

Almanacs appeared regularly in England after the late sixteenth century. Although they were also published in France and elsewhere on the European continent, they were especially important in a nation where perhaps half the population was literate, although many barely so (Capp, 1979). Except for the Bible and (perhaps) a few well-known religious books, they became the most widely distributed form of popular literature. Tables of sunrise, phases of the moons, lists of fairs, distances between cities, important historical dates, remedies for various diseases, commonsense advice, and suggestions for better crops filled most almanacs. Some added jokes, stories of monsters, giants, and far-off lands, while versions with sophisticated essays, puzzles, and scientific information appealed to the elite (Stowell, 1977).

Thanks to his visit to England in 1726, Franklin had experienced at least some of the numerous almanacs of various sorts that were regularly published. Franklin could thus enter a crowded field in Philadelphia confident that quality would prevail, as it had in his securing the government's printing trade and the *Pennsylvania Gazette*. Franklin's choice of a pseudonym, Richard Saunders, simply added a "s" to the name of the real Richard Saunder, who published *Apollo Anglicanus*, the most serious and intellectual of all English almanacs. Saunder brought to his readers the latest scientific developments, treatises on how weather really occurred, and discussions of the physical properties of clouds, rainbows, and the cosmos (Lemay, 2006a: 172). He did not allow the ethnic jokes, British jingoism, coarse humor, and astrology-based prophecies of doom or success that characterized most British almanacs to compromise his integrity.

Franklin's use of "Saunders" suggests that in part he intended that his almanac would go beyond the sort of basic information contained in most almanacs (Nickels, 1976). He would add political, scientific, moral, and philosophical observations and essays that some almanacs in America, such as those of Leeds and Birkett, were already including. *Poor Richard* had 24 pages until it "improved" with 36 as of 1748 – many almanacs had only 8 or 16. In this light, *Poor Richard* can be seen as the third in a trinity of educational projects Franklin had begun shortly after he returned from

England in 1726. In 1727, Franklin started the Junto, where young tradesmen such as himself would explore philosophical, political, and scientific questions on their own, thereby providing an education approximating the college experience – there was no college in Philadelphia – Franklin's poverty had denied him in Massachusetts (Boudreau, 2002). Franklin had observed that many discussion groups flourished in England, for instance, in coffee-houses (M. Ellis, 2006). Similarly, five years after he returned, he founded the Library Company of Philadelphia, where subscribers contributed to the cost of purchasing books that they could borrow (Boudreau, 1996). Colleges (one in Massachusetts, one in Connecticut, and one in Virginia) and personal libraries, the only other kind in early America, did not in general allow borrowing, although the Reverend Cotton Mather had permitted young Franklin to borrow from his several-hundred-volume collection. In England, however, parish libraries were allowing local residents to take books home (Kelly, 1966: 68). *Poor Richard's Almanac*, the name of its fictional author suggested, would be yet another of Franklin's educational projects. From the start, too, it was an intercolonial project: Franklin sent 500 of the first *Poor Richards* to his partner Thomas Whitemarsh in Charleston, and in 1733 shipped 300 and 200, respectively, to his brother James in Newport, Rhode Island, and Thomas Fleet of Boston (C.W. Miller, 1961: 97).

Yet even at this early age, Franklin realized the learning that would most appeal to his readers needed to be sugar-coated with stories, humor, and anecdotes: "The single greatest reason for the success of the *Poor Richards* was Franklin's ability to spice the prosaic matter of the ordinary almanac with more engaging commentary than his competitors could write" (C.W. Miller, 1961: 111). Hence his title *Poor Richard* may be seen as a tribute to *Poor Robin*, by far the most humorous of the English almanacs. *Poor Robin* mocked the high and mighty, including Parliament in 1725: "We cannot expect much state matters will be debated except in plays and puppet shows, where Harlequin can strut and talk as great as Julius Caesar." The same year, he declared his patriotism by printing two calendars "the good, old-fashioned English Honest Protestant account; and the foreign maggoty Jacobite account" – until 1752 the English still used the Julian calendar, rather than the Gregorian adopted by the Catholic Church. *Robin* also published a mock-guide of the road to poverty that Franklin would reverse as "The Way to Wealth" in his final *Poor Richard*: "From Riches to Covetousness; from Covetousness to Ambition; from Ambition to Infatuation; from Infatuation to Stock-Jobbing of Bubbles; from Stock-Jobbing of Bubbles to Scarps of Paper; and from thence to Poverty" (*Poor Robin* 1725).

Yet there was another *Poor Robin* almanac – published by Franklin's brother James (1697–1735), to whom he had been apprenticed in Boston. Readers of Franklin's *Autobiography* only get the negative side of their relationship (although if they read between the lines they would realize there was another side). Franklin included his brother in his circle of almanac distributers: James had relocated to Newport, Rhode Island, to escape prosecution for his criticisms of the Massachusetts elite in what was the first protest newspaper in the North American colonies, *The New-England Courant*, where Benjamin's "Silence Dogood" published her letters. Franklin's own career shows he admired his brother's identification with the underdog and willingness to subvert satirically the powers-that-be. The similarity of *Poor Richard* and *Poor Robin* also suggests a way of thanking the man who taught him printing, the road to his success (Sappenfield, 1973: 128; Lemay, 2006b: 172).

And a success *Poor Richard* was: by 1736 Franklin was selling nearly 10,000 copies a year (Lemay, 2006b: 378) not only in both Lancaster and Philadelphia, Pennsylvania, but in New England and the American South. Besides Newport, Boston, and Charleston, Annapolis, Williamsburg, and New York were other sites of distribution – for which Franklin printed slightly revised almanacs listing different fairs, roads, mileages, and court dates – in short, all of the major cities on the mainland of British North America (C.W. Miller, 1961: 111). Franklin's sales never approached the 60,000 credited to Nathanael Ames of Dedham, Massachusetts, but his were the only almanacs in North America with significant continent-wide distribution (Horrocks, 2006: 42, 44). Especially following the deaths of Samuel Keimer in 1739 and Andrew Bradford in 1742, Franklin profited as well from publishing his competitors' almanacs: all-in-all, he published 89 issues of 12 different almanacs, including several in German (Winkler, 1977: 36).

Whatever his own scientific views, Franklin satisfied his readers' predilections for astrology, printing "the man of signs" and predictions of various events (humorously, in the first *Poor Richard*, foretelling the death on October 17, 1733, of his best competitor Titan Leeds), including comets, eclipses, and the weather. By the mid-eighteenth century many colonials, learning about Newtonian astronomy, had abandoned the belief that comets or earthquakes were signs of God's displeasure or that people could read the stars to predict the future (Eisenstadt, 1998; Gromin, 2007). Franklin thus included the expected elements of popular, traditional pseudo-science (such as predicting the weather, which he wrote in 1739 was as easy "as pissing abed") much as newspapers today print astrology columns. But as his humorous preface to *Poor Richard's* 1751 edition shows, his allegiance was clearly with science:

> Astrology is one of the most ancient Sciences, had in high Esteem of old, by the Wise and Great. Formerly, no Prince would make War or Peace, nor any General fight a Battle, in short, no important Affair was taken without first consulting an *Astrologer*, who examined the Aspects and Configurations of

the heavenly bodies, and mark'd the *lucky hour*. Now the noble Art (more Shame to the Age we live in!) is dwindled into contempt; the Great neglect us [Astrologers], Empires make Leagues, and Parliaments Laws, without advising with us; and scarce any other Use is made of our learned Labors, than to find the best time [for] cutting Corns, or gelding Pigs, – this Mischief we owe in a great Measure to ourselves: The ignorant Herd of Mankind: had they not been encourag'd to it by some of us, would never have dared to deprecate our sacred Dictates; but *Urania* has been betray'd by her own Sons: those whom she had favored with the greatest skill in her divine art, the most eminent astronomers among the Moderns, the *Newtons, Helleys*, [Haleys], and *Whistons* have wantonly condem'd and abus'd her, contrary to the Light of their own Consciouses [sic].

Or, in *Poor Richard* 1756:

> Astronomy hail! Science Heavenly, born!
> Thy Schemes the Life assist, the Mind adorn,
> Newton! vast Mind! whose piercying Powers Applyed
> The Secret Cause of Motion first described;...

Franklin also eschewed discussions or depictions of dwarves, giants, fabulous monsters, and miraculous cures that his contemporaries found useful for almanac sales whether or not they believed them. Instead, he offered clear, reasonable explanations of natural phenomena.

As was the eighteenth-century practice in a world without copyright, Franklin borrowed his ingredients freely from others, but mixed them all in an appealing casserole of his own. He used an English poem lauding astronomer Sir Isaac Newton by Moses Browne and borrowed one from John Hughes to applaud his fellow-almanac maker Jacob Taylor of Philadelphia (McKillop, 1948: 383–385). The hoax of Titan Leeds' death was similar to Jonathan Swift's Bickerstaff deception (Ross, 1940: 785–794). The 1752 edition included 21 sayings from Samuel Richardson's novel *Clarissa*, published in England in 1748 (M.J. Shaw, 2007: 29). Between 1753 and 1757, 32 of *Poor Richard's* proverbs were lifted, with only slight changes if any, from the *Political, Moral, Miscellaneous Thoughts and Reflections* of George Savile, the First Marques of Halifax (R. Newcomb, 1955: 535–539).[2] Franklin was also influenced by William Penn's *Some Fruits of Solitude*, a collection of 407 maxims published in 1693 and expanded to 855 in 1702, Penn's "most enduring work, reprinted and read far more widely than any of his other tracts" (Dunn and Dunn, 1986: 364). Penn's stress on brotherhood and societal harmony appears in *Poor Richard* many times, as would befit a colony that adored its founder and his ideals posthumously (the settlers had given Penn a hard time when he was alive). Echoing Penn, *Poor Richard* enjoined his readers: "Hear no ill of a Friend, nor speak any of an Enemy" (1739); "A quarrelsome Man has no good Neighbours" (1746);

"A little well-gotten will do us more good,/Than lordships and scepters by Rapine and Blood" (1743).

Another source for Franklin's thought was eighteenth-century British political theory. His almanacs incorporated and helped to spread the "New Whig" ideology of the English political opposition. John Trenchard and William Gordon first published "Cato's Letters" in the *Independent Whig* between 1719 and 723. No fewer than nine collections of their contents were reprinted before the first *Poor Richard* appeared, so Franklin could have read them in either England or America. The authors took to task the monarchs and governments of the world for squandering their peoples' blood in wars and for oppressing them in peace. They criticized the extravagance and corruption of aristocrats, hinting that English liberty itself was threatened by venal and power-hungry rulers who comprised most of Parliament. Trenchard and Gordon contrasted the sorry fate of most nations with the prosperity and enjoyment of people who had the public-spirited virtue to keep their societies free of such parasites and govern themselves.

Trenchard and Gordon greatly influenced the "country" ideology of resistance which led to the American Revolution (Bailyn, 1968) and Franklin himself (Jacobson, 1965: xxxi, 1–11). While historians have looked primarily at the colonies' pamphlets and newspapers to prove their point, *Poor Richard* (and other almanacs) ought not to be ignored. Sixteen-year-old Franklin was already quoting from *Cato's Letters* in his 1722 "Silence Dogood Letters." In *Poor Richard* Franklin only mentioned Cato twice explicitly: "Think Cato sees thee," he wrote in 1741, calling attention to the noble Roman who lived simply and put the preservation of Roman republican liberty above all else. In 1756, also praised Cato's willingness to share his soldiers' hardships. His readers were probably not conversant with the Roman classics, and Franklin realized that an exaggerated show of learning would only alienate them.

So Franklin used modern far more than classical figures to illustrate his points. Franklin contrasted William Penn as his principal virtuous statesman as opposed to contemporary villains such as Kings Louis XIV and XV of France (never contemporary British monarchs). In 1748, the first and expanded edition of *Poor Richard Improved* (Franklin retired from printing that year) he praised Penn as "the great founder of this Province; who prudently and benevolently sought success to himself by no other means, than securing the *liberty*, and endeavoring the *happiness* of his people." Louis XIV, on the contrary, "Paid Learned Men for Writing/And valiant men for Righting," although he "Himself could neither write nor fight." (1735). Louis XV "called his most christian majesty … bids fair to be as great a mischief-maker as his [great]grandfather; or in the language of poets and orators, a *Hero*." There are three great destroyers of mankind, *Plague, Famine, and Hero* (1748).

But even great men such as William Penn are not the real "heroes" of *Poor Richard's Almanac*. These are none other than common people whom are intelligent, work hard and peacefully attend to their business – that is, people who resemble Poor Richard/Benjamin Franklin himself. In 1752, as he wrote a poem in praise of Pennsylvania:

> But who her Sons, that to her Int'rest true,
> Still plan with Wisdom, and with Zeal pursue?
> These found most frequently in Life's *Middle State*,
> Rich without God, and without Titles great: ...
> When Gifts like these conferr'd by bounteous Heav'n,
> Talents and Will to the same Person giv'n,
> That man ennobled doth an HERO rise,
> Fame and his Virtues lift him to the Skies. ...
> O! were I form'd to share his heavn'ly Fire,
> In Parts and Pow'rs strong as in Desire;
> Moses, Lycurgus, Numa I revere,
> Their Wisdom great, their Love to Man sincere;
> By *publick spirit* rank'd the first of Men,
> Yet I'd not enby them, not even P[enn].

In this remarkable poem, Franklin calls attention to both Pennsylvania and himself, for the "Middle State" can mean either the province that has avoided the wars of its southern and northern neighbors – or his own status as a member of the middle class. Further, given that historians such as Richard D. Brown (1990) and Michael Warner (1990) – borrowing on Jürgen Habermas's insights for Europe (1989) – have detailed the rise of the "public sphere" in eighteenth-century America, it is significant that Franklin uses the phrase "publick sp[ir/here]it" to describe this "Middle State" man – himself – as a HERO, outranking the great lawgivers of antiquity and even the revered Penn. No longer did who make an argument count – a clergyman, a monarch – but the content of the argument exposed to a much larger, more literate public through print, discussion clubs, and political participation made its validity a matter of debate. Franklin made a remarkably similar point in a piece he wrote in the *Pennsylvania Gazette* on October 20, 1737, "Upon the Talents Requisite in an Almanack Writer." He satirically observed that the first qualification was that "he should be descended of a great family, and bear a Coat of Arms," which "gives Lustre and Authority to what a man writes, and makes the common People to believe, that certainly *this is a great man.*" Simply by asserting what would have been accepted throughout most of the English-speaking world a century earlier, Franklin provoked snickers and signed the death warrant of a more restrictive public world.

Franklin by 1752 had become famous as the inventor and organizer of associations such as the fire company, college, library, and street paving societies of Philadelphia – the HERO of public spirit. In this he represented the common *man* (a term I deliberately use instead of person) that he considered the most important component of a good society. Franklin had frequently stressed this point in *Poor Richard* previously, but never with such obvious reference to himself. "Bucephalus the Horse of Alexand[er], hath as lasting fame as his Master" and "an innocent Plowman is more worthy than a vicious Prince" appeared in 1735. "Thou hadst better eat salt with the Philosophers of Greece, than sugar with the Courtiers of Italy" (1740). A 1741 poem expressed this "labor theory of value" with respect to human beings:

> The Monarch, when his Table's spread,
> To th'farmer is oblig'd for Bread;
> And when in all his Glory drest,
> Owest to the Loom his royal Vest:
> Do not the Mason's Toil and Care
> Protect him from th'inclement Air?
> Does not the Cutler's Art supply,
> The Ornament that guards his thigh?

Yet for all its attractiveness, Franklin's public sphere was limited. Franklin did not laud common folk indiscriminately. The good man was diligent in his calling, and after prospering but put his wealth and intelligence at the service of his community as did Franklin himself. The almanac abounds with proverbs such as "*All* things are easy to Industry, *All* things difficult to Sloth" (1734) and "The diligent Spinner has a large shrift" (1756). Other proverbs warn against greed and ostentation. "A wise Man will desire no more, than what he may get justly, use soverly, distribute cheerfully, and leave contentedly" (1756); "The D___l wipes is B___h with poor Folks' Pride" (1743).

The "good life" belonged to those who applied themselves, but many refused. And Franklin found an ethnic and racial dimension in this refusal. In other writings, he condemns "Palatine boors" (Pennsylvania Germans), "white, Christian savages" (Scottish-Irish frontiersmen), Indians (he wonders in the *Autobiography* if liquor was the means "of Providence to extirpate these Savages in order to make room for the Cultivators of the Earth") and blacks ("Why increase the sons of Africa by planting them in America, where we have so fair an opportunity, by excluding all blacks and tawnys, of increasing the lovely red and white?") To be sure, he also expressed sympathy for some of these groups – especially Indians persecuted by frontiersmen – and became an opponent of slavery and founder of the Franklin Academy (later Franklin and Marshall College) in Lancaster that had a curriculum for German-speakers late in life. This shows he was capable of expanding his vision, although during the years he wrote *Poor Richard* there is no sign he regarded such people in general as worthy of participation in his virtuous commonwealth (Van Doren, 1938: 218, 244–245, 310, 315, 774).

As *Poor Richard* articulated a public sphere open to men of ability and civic spirit, he was closing it to the vast majority of the population of North America. The voluntary associations he helped to establish and which gave form to the newly emergent society were in theory open to everyone, but in fact drew their membership primarily from well-educated, middle-to-upper class white males, of English descent, and primarily from the Philadelphia area rather than the countryside. Still, it must be stressed, this was a far wider public sphere than found anywhere else in the world at the time. He can hardly be blamed for failing to incorporate blacks, Indians, or men without property (who did not receive the right to vote until after the Revolution) into the commonwealth.

Still, an important element of Franklin's thought was that the poor, for the most part, deserved to be poor, and this could encompass racial and ethnic groups as a whole. While it is easy enough to applaud Franklin's denunciations of pernicious kings, shyster lawyers, quack doctors, hypocritical preachers, and rich wastrels, the other side of his economic theory was that unlike the traditional Old World public sphere of ecclesiastical, aristocratical, monarchical authority, Franklin's new order attached a moral stigma to those who could not "earn" the right to participate, supposedly in fair competition with their fellow inhabitants. They failed to take advantage of the opportunities that *Poor Richard*'s career, and Franklin's own, demonstrated were available to those who applied themselves.

The apotheosis of *Poor Richard's* philosophy that the deserving will win out is "The Way to Wealth," written for Franklin's final *Poor Richard*. Here, as "Father Abraham," Franklin assumed the quasi-biblical persona and authority of the patriarch who led his people to the land flowing with milk and honey. Nor should the occasion for his advice be overlooked. Father Abraham is rebuking people who are buying merchandise they do not need at an auction while complaining about the heavy taxes that, they contend, are ruining both themselves and the country. Recapitulating a quarter-century of *Poor Richard's* wisdom, Father Abraham retorts that "we are taxed twice as much by our Idleness, three times as much by our Pride, and four times as much by our Folly," and he urges people to stop buying luxuries and stay out of debt. Totally absent is any sense that the provincial taxation required by the French and Indian War was a real hardship – a case Franklin made before Parliament when he was questioned about the Stamp Act riots in 1765 (Cobbett, 1813: 138) – or that declining economic opportunity in Pennsylvania was hardening class lines and rendering the path Franklin had ascended earlier in the century much steeper (Smith, 1981; Simler, 1986).

The absence of injunctions to be charitable – traditional in English almanacs – for the month of December in *Poor Richard* before the mid-1750s, when they began to appear, is good evidence that general prosperity reigned in Pennsylvania until that time, but then the French and Indian War was accompanied by much personal suffering. Franklin first terms charity to the poor a duty in 1754, a precept he repeats in 1757 and at the end of "The Way to Wealth." Yet he does not view poverty as a serious social problem: rather, the poor provide an opportunity for the successful yet virtuous person to obtain "the Blessing of Heaven." In 1757, *Poor Richard* writes that "at the Day of Judgment ... it will more avail us, that we have thrown a Handful of Flour or Chaff in Charity to a Nest of contemptible pismires, than that we could master all the Hosts of Heaven, and call every Star by its proper Name." It is hard not to read this passage to mean that all a successful man need do is toss a bone to the poor, "contemptible though they are." Franklin's own charitable efforts in Philadelphia, for instance, did not include anything like a general welfare fund for the impoverished, who were cared for either by family, churches, or the almshouse.

Similarly, in "The Way to Wealth," charity is an afterthought, meriting exactly one sentence near the very end, and bestowed more for the welfare of the giver than the recipient:

> Do not depend too much upon you own *Industry*, and *Frugality*, and *Prudence*, though excellent things, for they may all be blasted without the Blessing of Heaven. ... Therefore ask that Blessing humbly, and be not uncharitable to those that at present seem to want it, but comfort and help them. Remember *Job* suffered, and was afterwards prosperous.

Franklin comes close to saying that poverty is only a temporary problem for the deserving and that we ought to help the *worthy* poor as we, too, might suffer provisional misfortunes.

Women, of course, were another group Franklin could not include in the public sphere, although his fictional characters beginning with Silence Dogood and including Bridget Saunders, Poor Richard's wife, showed that he indeed imagined women as articulate beings who would have much to contribute were they permitted to do so. In the eighteenth-century world in which he lived, however, the best women could do was to find fulfillment as honored helpmates of their husbands. "A good Wife and Health, is a Man's best Wealth," Poor Richard wrote in 1746. That year's preface praised his own spouse: "Thanks to kind Readers and a careful Wife,/ With Plenty bless'd, I lead an easy Life/My Business Writing,/ Hers to drain the Mead." Although Franklin and Poor Richard are not always identical, it is easy to see that here he was honoring his own wife, Deborah Read Franklin, who ran the shop in which she sold the items he printed in addition to salves, ointments, soaps, materials for dress-making, and imported books. Her assistance and business acumen – he entrusted his affairs to her when he left town, including during his protracted agency in Britain – helped him eliminate the debt he had acquired for going into business between the time they affirmed their union in September, 1730, and the publication of the first *Poor Richard's Almanac* two years later (Mulford, 2009c: 112).[3]

Conversely, none was more miserable than a woman without a husband, such as "Doris a Widow, past her Prime ... How should the helpless Woman rest?/One's gone; nor can she get another" [husband]. Doris exemplified Franklin's belief that if a man needed a woman for a satisfying existence, the reverse was even more true. Women who failed to become helpful homemakers merited the same scorn as did men who lacked industry, thrift, and public spirit.

In his very first almanac, *Poor Richard* listed the signs of a good-for-nothing female:

> She that will eat her Breakfast in Her Bed
> And spend the Morn in dressing of her Head,
> And sit at Dinner like a maiden Bride
> And talk of nothing all Day but of Pride.

Franklin's main point, however, is that such a woman, who was obviously enjoying herself, hurt her husband: "What a case is he that shall have her."

Franklin not only respected women who kept to their place and performed their duties faithfully, condemning husbands who failed to honor them, but by giving what was perhaps the most interesting preface of the all the almanacs to Bridget Saunders, Richard's fictional wife, he became the voice of women who were not appreciated by their husbands or allowed to express themselves or enjoy life within their means. In 1738, Bridget Saunders intervenes to replace the preface planned by her absent husband, and criticizes him for the fact he was planning to tell the world about her "little Fault or two" including that she was "proud ... loud ... and ... got a new Petticoat, and abundance of such kind of stuff... [and] has lately taken a fancy to drink a little Tea now and then." Franklin was here alluding to the case of Pennsylvania as a whole, characterized by skyrocketing imports from Britain symbolized by the ability of even middle-class women to purchase attractive tea sets (Breen, 1988). But here he was not referring to Deborah Franklin, whose industry and frugality he praised elsewhere as equal to his own (Fry, 2003). Earlier, Poor Richard had referred to Bridget as his "viceroy" (1733) and "duchess" (1734).

Despite her indispensable domestic duties, a woman could not enter the public sphere. Franklin inadvertently confirmed this by mentioning women only three times when the almanacs took a more political turn between 1748 and 1758, after *Poor Richard* became *Poor Richard Improved*: "An undutiful Daughter, will prove an unmanageable Wife" (1750), "A Man without a Wife, is but Half a Man" (1755), and "Dally not with other Folks' Women or Money" (1757). From 1733 to 1737, Franklin had frequently discussed wives, good and otherwise. But the 1748 issue marked a significant rejection of the social and domestic emphasis of the earlier almanacs and a turning toward issues such as science and politics (Pencak,

1992). Nowhere is this more apparent than in the prefaces. The early introductions are light literary masterpieces: at times Franklin pretends his competitors are dead, he mocks their predictions, he pokes fun at astrology, he lets Bridget Saunders speak for women. But in 1748, the prefaces cease being humorous short squibs designed to sell copies and become lengthier instructional essays in science, morals, national self-defense, and history. Salability was replaced in the almanac by public service announcements as money-making gave way to public service in Franklin's own life: he retired from printing that year as he believed, correctly, that he had made enough.

Politics was an important part of the new Franklin and the new *Poor Richard*. He had remained largely apolitical until late 1747, when he organized a volunteer defense force in Pennsylvania in case privateers who had appeared in the Delaware River during a war with Spain and France threatened the province. But such a move drew him into politics: many of the Quakers who dominated Pennsylvania were opposed even to a voluntary force of non-Quakers, believing that preparation for war would draw down the wrath of God on people who had won divine favor for their policy of peace (Gannon, 1998).

Much of *Poor Richard's* content for the 1750s concerns defense, which became an issue as hitherto pacifist Pennsylvania was drawn into the French and Indian War. As early as 1750, Franklin drew an implicit parallel between Pennsylvania and the 1453 conquest of Constantinople by the Turks:

> When it was beseig'd, the Emperor made most earnest Application to his People, that they Would contribute Money to enable him to pay his Troops, and defray the expence of defending it; but they, through Covetousness refused, pretending Poverty. Yet the Turks in pillaging it found so much wealth among them, that even their common Soldiers were enriched.

In 1750, it seemed Franklin was more critical of Pennsylvania's assembly and people, but by the middle of the decade his anger was directed mostly against proprietor Thomas Penn, who was unwilling to let his lands be taxed even though the assembly was willing (given this condition) to donate money "for the King's use" that went to defense.

An entry for 1756 specifically attacked "officers" who were unwilling to share their people's sufferings:

> When an Army is to march thro' a Wilderness, where the Conveniences of life are scarce to be obtain'd even for Money, many Hardships, Wants, and Difficulties must necessarily be borne by the Soldiers; which nothing tends more to make tolerable, than the Example of their Officers, If these Riot in plenty, while those suffer Hunger and Thirst, Respect and Obedience are in Danger of being lost, and Mutiny or Desertion taking their places.

Franklin's rise to political prominence in the 1750s, along with his scientific experiments that led to his election to Britain's Royal Society and honorary doctorates from Harvard and Yale in 1753, also gave him a heightened sense of his own destiny, which is easy to read in *Poor Richard*. In July 1756, after he mused on biblical figures called by God from humble stations to perform great deeds including Saul, David, the shepherds who visited Jesus, and the twelve Apostles, Franklin concluded that "God never encourages idleness, and despises not persons in the meanest employments" who "have been busy in the honest Employment of their Vocation." The following year, he tried to convince (or congratulate) himself that his own spectacular rise was indeed destined to do good for his fellow countrymen:

> *Ambition* to be greater and richer, merely that a Man may have it in his Power to do more Service to his Friends and the Publick, is of a quiet, orderly Kind, pleased if it succeeds, resigned if it fails. But the *Ambition* that has *itself* only in View, is restless, turbulent, regardless of public Peace or general Interest, and the secret Maker of most Mischiefs, between nations, Parties, Friends, and Neighbours.

As in his *Autobiography*, where Franklin mentioned his struggle to remain humble after he was criticized for seeming proud, Franklin was using *Poor Richard* to come to terms with the fact that he was now faced at this stage of his life with the temptations of wealth and high office. In 1757 he would go to Britain as Pennsylvania's agent in an attempt to replace the Penn family proprietors with a royal governor – for which, given his fame as a scientist and writer as well as the Pennsylvanian on the spot – he would be a logical candidate. Indeed, his son William, whose principal qualification was that he was Benjamin's son, became Governor of New Jersey in 1763.

It is interesting to speculate whether on his journey to London, Franklin remembered a bit of advice he had included in *Poor Richard* for 1734, perhaps in remembrance of his trip to England as a youth in which the expected recommendations from Pennsylvania's Governor William Keith failed to materialize and he was forced to struggle and survive on his own:

> Some of our Sparks to London town do go,
> Fashions to see, and yearn the World to know;
> Who at Return have nought but these to show,
> New wig above, and new Disease below.
> Thus the Jack Ass a Traveler once would be ...

But Franklin made good use on his second trip overseas (in June and July) to write the preface to his final almanac for 1758. "The Way to Wealth" is a compendium of many of the proverbs he included over the years, and the author is no longer Poor Richard, but Father Abraham. Unfortunately for Franklin's reputation, this has been the most read and quoted of all parts of the almanacs. Since it deals almost exclusively with the acquisition and preservation of wealth through industrious hard work Franklin himself has frequently been mistaken for a selfish capitalist – most famously in D.H. Lawrence's *Studies in Classic American Literature* (1923) and Max Weber's *The Protestant Ethic and the Spirit of Capitalism* (1930) – rather than the man who made good to do good. But here we are not once (through Poor Richard alone) but twice removed from Franklin himself, and while there are of course elements of the real Franklin in *Poor Richard,* the almanacs need to be read in tandem with what we know about his life. Franklin did not work as a printer past the age of 42, when he turned exclusively to public service and – what he undoubtedly considered identical with it – advancing his own career in science, literature, and politics (Zuckerman, 1993b). Weber's and Lawrence's interpretations of Franklin derive from the 1920s, the very era when capitalists were being blamed for World War I and a society that embraced "The Way to Wealth" had driven Europe and the United States to wars (both class and international), depressions, extremes of wealth and poverty, and a restrictive middle-class morality from which the "Roaring Twenties" had provided a welcome respite. Closer to Franklin's own time, the eighteenth-century French revolutionaries realized that "The Way to Wealth" and Franklin's own exemplary life were in fact proclaiming a new, better society, where ability and hard work rather than birth or inherited wealth would dominate. Aside from the *Autobiography,* it is the "Way to Wealth" by which Franklin, for better or worse, has been best known. It was translated into almost every European language and has circulated as a pamphlet until the present time (Lemay, 2009: 574–584).

The real significance of Poor Richard's almanac is not that it proclaims the virtues of capitalism, but rather than it linked high and popular culture in early America, communicating the virtues of the common man to the elite and the benefits of scientific, literary, and historical knowledge to ordinary folk. Colonial America and its cities were sufficiently small-scaled, and poverty and wealth on a European scale sufficiently absent, that there was no real separation of high and popular literature in the eighteenth-century colonies (D.D. Hall, 1979). Franklin did more than anyone in eighteenth-century British America to create the public sphere where ordinary inhabitants (granted, mostly middle- and upper-class white men, but not only them) discussed politics, science, and philosophy among themselves and made their discussions effective through participation in elections, crowds, associations to promote learning and ultimately revolution. Such a public sphere was only beginning to appear in the 1710s and 1720s (Warner, 1990: 58–96), when publications not sanctioned by the various provincial governments appeared, such as Franklin's own "Silence Dogood" letters and his brother's subversive newspaper, *The New-England Courant.*

Franklin brought his Boston (and soon London) experience to Pennsylvania, expanding its public sphere by taking over its newspaper, writing numerous essays in it and published separately, forming the Library Company and Junto, and creating *Poor Richard*, in what must be considered one of the most extensive educational endeavors in human history – all by the age of twenty-seven! Given the wide circulation of Franklin's almanac, the claim can be made that it played an important role in the international Enlightenment's questioning of traditional institutions. It thus emerges as the perfect symbol for his own career, in which the apolitical Philadelphian was transformed into an actor on the stage of world history. It is therefore appropriate that King Louis XVI of France would rename the *Serapis*, the British warship captured by John Paul Jones, the "Bonhomme Richard," in honor of the man who was now America's minister to France.[4] For Franklin had first used *Poor Richard's* voice to express the ideals for which Jones and his fellow revolutionaries were fighting.

Notes

1. *Poor Richard's Almanack*, and other almanacs, are spelled without the "k" at the end of "Almanack" usual in the colonial era. All references to almanacs in this chapter are for the year on the title page – almanacs then as now were published late in the preceding year.
2. For example for 1753, Franklin only omitted two words and changed one from a maxim of Halifax: "The Good deeds of the Governed will be starved if [it is] not fed by the good Deeds [Conduct] of the Governors." Franklin's changes are in brackets.
3. Mulford also stresses that Franklin believed women should receive a more substantive education in the liberal arts and sciences than was common at the time.
4. "Richard" in French is an infrequently used term for "rich man," and thus it would have made no sense to name the ship "Poor Rich Man." "Bonhomme" means good fellow.

Further Reading

Drake, M. (1962). *Almanacs of the United States*. 2 vols. New York, NY.

Frasca, R. (1997). "To rescue the Germans out of Sauer's hands: Benjamin Franklin's German language printing partnerships," *Pennsylvania Magazine of History and Biography* 121: 329–350.

Frasca, R. (2006). "The partnership at Carolina having succeeded was encouraged to engage in others: The genesis of Benjamin Franklin's printing network," *Southern Studies* 13: 1–23.

Green, J.N., and Stallybrass, P. (2006). *Benjamin Franklin: Writer and Printer*. New Castle, DE.

Wilson, R.J. (1989). *Figures of Speech: American Writers and the Literary Marketplace*. New York, NY.

Wroth, L.D. (1942). "Benjamin Franklin: The printer at work," *Journal of the Franklin Institute* 234: 105–132.

Chapter Fifteen

BENJAMIN FRANKLIN AND JOURNALISM

David Paul Nord

In 1855 the popular writer James Parton brought out a biography of Horace Greeley, the famous editor of the *New York Tribune*, one of the country's leading daily newspapers. Parton's book is a classic success story of that era: a rustic, penniless New England youth goes to the big city and through hard work and determination rises to prominence and power. In an early chapter, Parton describes young Greeley's unpromising arrival in New York in 1831, a "sorry figure" with all his possessions in a bundle tied to a stick over his shoulder. Had the New York grandees he passed near the Battery noticed him, they never could have imagined his future success. This was a scene that Parton knew would resonate with his readers: "Nor did Miss Reed [sic], of Philadelphia, when she saw Benjamin Franklin pass her father's house, eating a large roll and carrying two others under his arms, see in that poor wanderer any likeness to her future husband, the husband that made her a proud and immortal wife" (1855: 123).

Parton's reference was drawn from one of the most popular books of the era, the autobiography of Benjamin Franklin. By the 1850s, Franklin's account of his early life had established the archetype of the rags-to-riches narrative. Successful men routinely credited the *Autobiography* as a model for their own rise. Horace Greeley himself, in a lecture titled "Self-Made Men," declared Franklin "the consummate type and flowering of human nature under the skies in colonial America" (1864: 678). For Greeley and other newspaper publishers of his generation, Franklin was a compelling model of self-fashioning because he was a printer and journalist as well as a civic leader, scientist, diplomat, and patriot. He was one of them, their own patron saint, their own founder. By the time of Greeley's death in 1872,

---

A Companion to Benjamin Franklin, First Edition. Edited by David Waldstreicher.
© 2011 Blackwell Publishing Ltd. Published 2011 by Blackwell Publishing Ltd.

however, Franklin's central role in the history of journalism had begun to fade, as journalism itself entered a new era of self-conscious professionalism and commercial independence. For more than a century after the Civil War, journalism historiography was dominated by journalists and former journalists whose subject was the origin of the modern metropolitan daily newspaper. Only gradually in the latter half of the twentieth century did Franklin's role as a major figure in American journalism history reappear in a new edition, corrected and amended by academic historians and literary biographers.

This chapter charts the ebb and flow of Benjamin Franklin's reputation among journalists and in the historiography of journalism, with some attention as well to literary criticism and biography. My story unfolds in five parts plus an epilogue. In Part 1, during the antebellum era, Franklin embodied for journalists the poor printer/tradesman who raised himself to civic and literary prominence. In Part 2, during the half-century after the Civil War, Franklin represented an ancient regime of American journalism that had been eclipsed by a modern journalism born in the nineteenth century. In Part 3, in the early twentieth century, Franklin-the-journalist reemerged in literary studies, as the definition of what counts as literature was expanded. In Part 4, in the late twentieth century, academic historians of journalism rediscovered Franklin as a business entrepreneur and as an exponent of press liberty. In Part 5, in the early twenty-first century, Franklin's journalism took on an important role in a new wave of biographical literature that marked the tricentennial of Franklin's birth. In each era the reputation of Franklin-the-journalist turned on authors' understanding of what journalism and literature are or should be. In the epilogue, I will suggest that it might be time for yet another take on Franklin-the-journalist, as the meaning of journalism is changing yet again in our own era, the era of the Internet.

15.1 Printers and Self-Made Newspapermen

In the early nineteenth century, newspapermen revered the memory of Benjamin Franklin because he had been a printer. In his *History of Printing in America*, Isaiah Thomas set the pattern for how Franklin would be portrayed in the early historiography of American journalism (Thomas, 1810). Thomas acknowledged Franklin's fame in Europe and the United States as statesman and scientist, but the Franklin story he tells focuses almost entirely on Franklin's early career as writer, printer, publisher, and bookseller in Boston and Philadelphia before 1748. It is a story split into five brief sections: Franklin's apprenticeship in Boston; his early writings for his brother's newspaper, the *New-England Courant*; his rise to master printer and businessman in Philadelphia; his successful development of the

Pennsylvania Gazette after 1729; and his failed attempt to launch a magazine in 1741. Thomas's chief source is Franklin's autobiography, specifically the first London edition of 1793, which included only "part one" on his early life. Like many popular nineteenth-century Franklin biographers, Thomas simply quotes Franklin's own account. He includes many of the soon-to-be-famous anecdotes, including Franklin's self-composed epitaph ("The Body of Benjamin Franklin, Printer ..."), and the scene of Franklin's unpromising arrival in Philadelphia, strolling past the house of his future wife, Deborah Read, with a bread roll under each arm. Thomas says he included accounts of Franklin's early life because they illustrate his rise from inauspicious beginnings to worldwide fame (Thomas, 1810, 1: 314–315). Not coincidentally, Thomas's own career had followed almost exactly this same Franklinesque trajectory (Rorabaugh, 1986).

Though *History of Printing* covers the full range of the printing business, Thomas devotes more space to newspapers than to any other product of the press. That is because most eighteenth-century printers published newspapers and sank a great deal of time and effort into them. And this was a business strategy that continued well into the nineteenth century. For Thomas and the generation of printers that followed him, journalism history was printing history, and Franklin was the American archetype. As editions of the autobiography and popular biographies based on the autobiography proliferated, printers began to formalize their homage to their patron saint in annual banquets on his birthday, January 17. These celebrations produced a series of historical lectures and proceedings, which are explored by Nian-Sheng Huang in his excellent study of the image of Franklin in American culture (1994: 81–87). What Huang does not note is that most of these celebrants were no longer hands-on printers. They were newspaper publishers and civic boosters who had, like Franklin, risen out of the print shop. For example, at a printers' festival in Rochester on Franklin's birthday in 1847, several of the speakers had been the first printers in their towns in western New York, and now they were substantial newspapermen. Their history of printing was largely a history of newspapers. Like Franklin and Isaiah Thomas, these men were editors, publishers, and civic leaders who had begun their working lives as poor apprentices, self-educated at the typecases of newspaper offices (Follett, 1847; Brenton, 1850; Weed, 1851; Buckingham, 1852).

By mid-century Horace Greeley – a printer's apprentice in East Poultney, Vermont, who had risen to the editorship of one of the world's great newspapers – was often considered the best representative of this Franklinian model of journalism history. Though the historian Richard D. Miles finds the Greeley–Franklin comparison absurd, many nineteenth-century Americans did not – doubtless because the comparison was not about philosophy, writing style, or service to country but simply about the rise of poor apprentice to learned, self-made man (R.D. Miles, 1957: 133; Huang,

1994: 49–50). As late as 1872, when Greeley made his quixotic run for the presidency, his supporters trumpeted him as "the modern Franklin" (Clay, 1872: ix). A campaign biographer wrote that "it is common to hear Franklin cited as the greatest of all self-made men this country has produced. But it is questionable whether HORACE GREELEY is not in the main, the equal, if not the superior of Franklin. … Young men of America! the two truest and greatest examples of self-made men which your country has produced are Benjamin Franklin and HORACE GREELEY" (Reavis, 1872: 502).

15.2 Modern Journalism: Independent and Professional

Horace Greeley lost the 1872 presidential election in a landslide, and before the electoral votes were even counted he was dead. Greeley's passing marked the end of an era in American journalism and the end of the rags-to-riches, apprentice-to-publisher model of journalism history. Greeley was the last "modern Franklin" – at least the last of that version of Franklin, the Franklin of the autobiography, "B. Franklin, Printer." Beginning in the 1870s, a new journalism historiography emerged whose origin story lay in the 1830s, not in the colonial era. The subject of interest was the rise of the modern metropolitan daily newspaper. Greeley was a major contributor to the modern newspaper, but the more emblematic figure was Greeley's flamboyant, megalomanical nemesis, James Gordon Bennett, founder of the *New York Herald*. Bennett was never a printer. As a boy he had read Franklin's autobiography, but he was inspired as well by the career of a very different sort of self-made man: Napoleon (Pray, 1855: 32).

The first major work of this new journalism historiography – indeed, the first comprehensive history of American journalism – was Frederic Hudson's *Journalism in the United States*, which appeared in 1873. For many years Hudson had been managing editor on the *New York Herald*. In his book, he has little to say about Benjamin Franklin but much to say about his late boss, James Gordon Bennett, who had died a few months before Greeley in 1872. The few stories about Franklin that Hudson does include are the usual ones. Like Isaiah Thomas, Hudson simply quotes the autobiography verbatim. Mainly he hurries through the eighteenth century on his way to the more important nineteenth. He downplays the self-made-man theme, and he scoffs at the cult of Franklin among printers and newspapermen (Hudson, 1873: xxxi). Hudson's only reference to Franklin's public career beyond the printing office is sly criticism for neglecting his newspaper: "In spite of what he says in his autobiography, it has been asserted that Franklin wrote but little for the *Gazette*. He dabbled in politics and electricity, and set up printing-offices in other places, so that his time was pretty well occupied" (Hudson, 1873: 78).

Benjamin Franklin "dabbled" in politics? Hudson's choice of verb is revealing. For him, direct involvement in government and politics was the cardinal sin of journalism. (Greeley was the cardinal sinner.) The "revolution" in journalism that began in the 1830s and culminated in the 1870s was, in Hudson's view, the rise of the modern professional, even "scientific," newspaper editor, who was entirely independent of party. "With the death of the founder of the *Tribune* [Greeley]," Hudson writes, "party journalism pure and simple, managed by accomplished and experienced editors, inaugurated by Jefferson and Hamilton, aided by such writers as Fenno, Bache, Duane, Freneau, Coleman, Cheetham, Ritchie, and Croswell, has ceased to exist, and Independent Journalism becomes a fact impressed on the minds of the people" (Hudson, 1873: 778). This is not to say that the modern newspaperman was apolitical or even nonpartisan. Independent editors eschewed party enthrallment, not necessarily party ideology or advocacy. The master of this revolutionary change, according to Hudson, was Bennett. "He never wanted political office, and would never accept of any nomination," Hudson writes. "He always looked upon the Press as superior to the Party. Hence the success of the *Herald* as an independent journal" (1873: 778).

Other newspaper editors of the 1870s, though much less enamored of Bennett, agreed with Hudson's storyline. For example, Whitelaw Reid, Greeley's successor as editor of the *Tribune*, described a series of technological improvements that had revolutionized the newspaper industry in the nineteenth century: the type-revolving cylinder press, the steam railroad, the electric telegraph, the transoceanic submarine cable, the cylindrical stereotype plate, and so on. Reid also identified "another revolution as startling as any":

> The conduct of newspapers ceased to be the work of journeymen printers, of propagandists, needy politicians, starveling lawyers, or adventurers. Its new developments compelled the use of large capital, and thus the modern metropolitan daily journal became a great business enterprise, as legitimate as a railroad or a line of steamships, and as rigidly demanding the best business management." (Reid, 1879: 6)

Reid acknowledged the great editors of the past, including Ben Franklin and Horace Greeley. But he declared that newspapers of the 1870s were better written, better edited, more widely read, and therefore more influential than ever before (1879: 69–70).

This historical perspective ran through much popular writing on journalism at that time. In 1875 in a wide-ranging collection of commentaries by and about leading newspaper editors, the unifying theme is suggested by the opening sentence of the introduction: "During the last twenty years journalism has become prominent, if not re-eminent, as a profession"

(Wingate, 1875: 7). By "profession" the contributors often meant college education, sometimes even specialized training for journalism. They also meant rigorous business practices. And they meant fast, complete, accurate, and impartial reporting of the news. As Whitelaw Reid put it, "The essence, the life-blood of the daily paper of to-day is the *news*" (1875: 25).

There was not much room for Benjamin Franklin in this new historiography of journalism. Editors in the 1870s mention Franklin from time to time in their commentaries; he pops up in the 1875 collection in the chapter on Horace Greeley, naturally. But usually even newspaper editors mention him as an exemplar of virtue, not of journalism. The satirical essays that Franklin describes in the autobiography, such as his Silence Dogood pieces for the *Courant*, were not hard news and were therefore not the kind of journalism these men valued. For example, in his popular U.S. history, William Cullen Bryant, long-time editor of the *New York Evening Post*, pays little attention to Franklin's journalism (1873: 173, 1881, 3: 189–191). Bryant's literary editor on the *Evening Post*, John Bigelow, was an avid Franklin student and an important editor of the autobiography. Bigelow celebrates Franklin as a great moralist and self-made man and as an appropriate sage for the difficult era of Reconstruction. But Bigelow says little about Franklin's journalism (Bigelow, 1868). The literary biographer and critic F.B. Sanborn, in a historical essay prompted by the publication of Hudson's book, praises Franklin's *Pennsylvania Gazette* as "the first really good newspaper in America." But Franklin was too responsive to majority opinion for Sanborn, a former abolitionist. He was too comfortable, too cautious, and not independent enough (Sanborn, 1874: 58, 62). The most famous piece on Franklin from the 1870s was Mark Twain's comic take on the *Autobiography*, which he said had made life miserable for several generations of American boys, with nothing there about journalism (Twain, 1875).

This late nineteenth-century perspective, especially Hudson's influential book, left a lasting legacy for American journalism historiography. In particular, two aspects of Hudson's *Journalism in the United States* shaped historical writing throughout the twentieth century. The first is *presentism*. Journalism historians have tended to use history to shed light on the present; the era of greatest interest is always *now*. For example, the most important mid-twentieth-century historian of journalism, Frank Luther Mott, declares in the first paragraph of *American Journalism* that he will "look to history mainly for help in understanding present problems and for guidance in facing the future" (Mott, 1941: v). The second aspect is *periodization*. Hudson's division of journalism history into what might be called the Old and New Testaments – before and after the advent of the "penny press" of the 1830s – had a powerful and permanent influence. In the major syntheses written in the early twentieth century, the tables of contents are nearly identical: The key moment is the birth of the modern, independent daily newspaper in New York City in the decade after 1833

(Lee, 1917; Payne, 1920; Bleyer, 1927; Nerone, 1987). In this periodization of journalism historiography – which lives on in the standard textbooks – no colonial journalist, even the illustrious Ben Franklin, has a pivotal role to play (Emery et al., 2000; Sloan, 2008; Folkerts et al., 2009).

15.3 Literary Canon

Much like journalism history, literary studies in the late nineteenth century scorned the colonial era in favor of the recent past. If the golden age of journalism emerged in the decades after 1830, so did the golden age of American literature. In 1887 Charles Richardson of Dartmouth College dismissed most eighteenth-century American writing from literary studies by definition. It was too "practical" to be literature (C.F. Richardson, 1887: 1). In 1901 Barrett Wendell of Harvard categorically declared that "we can instantly perceive that only the last, the Americans of the nineteenth century, have produced literature of any importance" (1901: 9). This was literary history devoted to the construction of a literary renaissance in the age of Poe, Emerson, and Hawthorne, and there was little room in the canon for the writer of Silence Dogood, *Poor Richard*, or the autobiography (R.D. Miles, 1957: 141). In late-nineteenth-century literary history, as in journalism history, Franklin appears only fleetingly, along the dark road of the past that leads to a brighter present.

This crabbed academic view of literature began to fade in the early years of the twentieth century. The editors of the three-volume *Cambridge History of American Literature*, published in 1917, explicitly rejected the aesthetic straitjacket of Richardson, Wendell, and others, proclaiming an inclusive definition of literature as one of the main goals of their book: "It will be a survey of the life of the American people as expressed in their writings rather than a history of *belles-lettres* alone" (Trent et al., 1917, 3: viii–x). Lead editor William Peterfield Trent of Columbia University had already put one of his graduate students, Elizabeth Christine Cook, to work on a study of colonial newspapers. Cook's dissertation, published in 1912, launched a trend in literary studies of taking more seriously the literature of early American newspapers. Central to Cook's study are the early Boston literary newspapers, the *New-England Courant* and the *New England Weekly Journal* (Cook, 1912: Chs 1, 2). Founded by Benjamin Franklin's brother James in 1721 and written by a club of local wits and would-be litterateurs, the *Courant* took on a foundational role in twentieth-century American literary historiography. In journalism historiography the *Courant* is remembered mainly for its political role in the controversy over smallpox inoculation in Boston in 1721–1722, but in literary studies it is remembered as the first publication to import and adapt for an American audience the style of the British literary journalists Joseph Addison, Richard Steele, and Daniel Defoe (Cook, 1912: 15–18, 1917: 112–113; Mott, 1941: 15–17; P. Miller, 1953: 333–334). The heightened interest among literary historians in James Franklin and his club of contributors placed the young Ben Franklin's earliest writings in the *Courant* (his Silence Dogood essays) into a richer literary context (Shields, 1997: 266–269). Though he ran away to Philadelphia at age seventeen, Benjamin Franklin's journalistic writing for the *Courant* found a place in the expanded literary canon of New England and early America (Sappenfield, 1973: Ch. 2).

Meanwhile, the compilers of Franklin's papers were casting their nets more widely into other periodical literature as well – especially the *Pennsylvania Gazette* – to snare more of Franklin's anonymous, ephemeral writings. Cook drew on the ten-volume edition of Franklin's papers compiled by Albert Henry Smyth for her 1912 dissertation, which included the first serious study of Franklin's work in the *Gazette* (Smyth, 1905–1907; Cook, 1912: Ch. 4). "The brilliant little pieces Franklin wrote for his *Pennsylvania Gazette* have an imperishable place in American literature," she declared in a chapter for the *Cambridge History*. "It is none the less true that they belong to colonial journalism" (Cook, 1917: 115). For literary scholars the interest in Franklin's journalism, encouraged by the canon-expanding example of the *Cambridge History*, continued to grow throughout the twentieth century. Indeed, one of the great biographies of Franklin was written by one of the editors of the *Cambridge History*, Carl Van Doren (1938).

Van Doren, whose massive biography appeared in 1938, drew more on Franklin's ephemeral writings than had any previous biographer. He lauds Smyth's copious edition of Franklin's papers, but by 1938 even more Franklin material had been identified, including many anonymous periodical pieces, both serious and light (Van Doren, 1938: vi, 785). Van Doren's Pulitzer Prize-winning work encouraged a flood of Franklin scholarship in the twentieth century, the most important of which was the *Papers of Benjamin Franklin* project, launched in 1959 and running to thirty-nine volumes by 2008 (Larabee *et al.*, 1959–). On the journalistic writings of Franklin – especially his newspaper and magazine pieces written in London after he left the *Gazette* – a key source is Verner Crane's *Benjamin Franklin's Letters to the Press, 1758–1775* (V.W. Crane, 1950; Lemay, 1986b: 16). Though the book is now sixty years old, Crane's introduction remains one of the best accounts we have of Franklin's role in the system of Anglo-American political journalism in the crucial decades leading up to the American Revolution.

This rising interest among literary scholars in Franklin's journalistic writing had some impact on mainstream journalism history, but not much – for two reasons. First, journalism historians of the late twentieth century, like their forebears, continued to neglect the colonial press. For example, over the last two decades the principal scholarly journals in the field, *Journalism*

History and *American Journalism*, have published hundreds of articles but only a handful on the seventeenth and eighteenth centuries and only two on Franklin specifically, both by Ralph Frasca (Frasca, 1988, 1996). As usual for journalism historians, the recent past has been more compelling. Second, when journalism historians have produced substantial studies of eighteenth-century journalism, Franklin plays an important but pretty traditional role. Mainly the stories are the usual ones: Franklin's work on the *New-England Courant* and the *Pennsylvania Gazette* before his retirement from printing in 1748. When Franklin-the-writer has appeared in mainstream journalism history he is typically the Franklin of the autobiography (Kobre, 1960; Sloan and Williams, 1994). An important, but lonely, exception to this pattern of neglect is David Copeland's *Colonial American Newspapers*. In this detailed study of the content of eighteenth-century newspapers – including the *Pennsylvania Gazette* – Copeland gives Franklin a great deal of credit for promoting the growth of local and regional *news* in American papers after 1730 (Copeland, 1997: 72, 265, 272–273).

15.4 Freedom of the Press and History of the Book

Though the expansion of the Franklin literary canon did not have broad impact on journalism historiography, Franklin did come into play in two new subfields of journalism history: studies of freedom of the press and studies of the business practices of eighteenth-century newspapers. These subfields were seeded from outside the mainstream of journalism historiography. The first came from the history of constitutional law, which in the decades after World War I developed an intense interest in the First Amendment. The second came from the history of printing and publishing, which in the 1970s and 1980s developed into a more contextualized history of print culture, now often called the "history of the book."

In the wake of World War I, the issue of freedom of speech and press exploded in the streets, in the courts, and in the work of legal scholars. For the first time, the U.S. Supreme Court took up First Amendment cases and wrote into the vocabulary of jurisprudence such soon-to-be-famous phrases as "clear and present danger." For lawyers and scholars, a crucial historical question presented itself: What was the original intent of the framers of the First Amendment? By mid-century a scholarly consensus had emerged that the American framers had sought not only to prevent censorship (prior restraint), a position already then established in English law, but also to repudiate the common law of seditious libel, which made words that promoted sedition seditious in themselves. This libertarian history of the origins of the First Amendment was spelled out most vividly in 1941 by Harvard law professor Zechariah Chafee, Jr (1941: 21–22).

Twenty years later a young legal historian named Leonard Levy turned this liberal orthodoxy on its head with the publication of *Legacy of Suppression* (1960). In *Legacy* Levy argues that the framers of the First Amendment did not intend to abolish the common law of seditious libel; only after the tumultuous experience of the Sedition Act of 1798 did a genuinely libertarian understanding of freedom of the press appear in America. Levy's revisionist history rattled civil libertarians, who feared it would seep into the courts and reverse the trend toward broader press freedom. Though some legal scholars rejected Levy's history, most were persuaded. Then in the 1970s the Levy thesis, as it came to be called, sparked the interest of journalism historians in the legal history of the colonial press. What struck these scholars was the utter disconnect between the narrow understanding of press freedom that Levy had supposedly identified and the actual performance of American newspapers, which were loaded with scurrilous and seditious journalism throughout the eighteenth century (Baldasty, 1976; Smith and Baldasty, 1979; D.A. Anderson, 1983).

Though he never backed away from his central argument, Levy was impressed – and perplexed – by this new historiography of press practice. In a revised edition of *Legacy* published in 1985, Levy wrote (1985: xvi):

> I ... maintain that the law of seditious libel, which was not superseded by either the Revolution or the First Amendment, made political discussion in this country dependent upon government sufferance. I find it difficult to believe that meaningful freedom of the press could exist in that condition. That so many courageous and irresponsible editors daily risked imprisonment amazes me.

Despite that nod to actual newspaper practice, Levy conceded nothing to his critics in the realms of legal theory or the history of original intent. And the debate raged on through the 1980s, injecting new life into journalism historiography of the colonial press (Chamberlin and Brown, 1982; Rabban, 1985, 1997; Copeland, 2006). One of Levy's most ardent critics was Jeffery A. Smith, who argued not only that newspaper journalism was free-wheeling and frequently seditious but that colonial printers often held to a libertarian ideology as well (J.A. Smith, 1988).

Benjamin Franklin crops up on both sides of the debate. For Levy, Franklin exemplifies early Americans' constricted view of press liberty. Franklin's two most explicit statements on freedom of the press were his "Apology for Printers," first published in the *Pennsylvania Gazette* in 1731 (Labaree, 1959, 1: 194–199), and a newspaper article on the "Court of the Press" published in 1789 (Smyth, 1905–1907, 10: 36–40). In both pieces, Franklin supports a press open to all opinions but seems to draw the line at content that would do real personal injury or break the law. In Levy's view, the "Apology for Printers" is a pathetically weak brief for press freedom. "If his statement was as influential and representative as it has been reputed," Levy writes, "it simply shows the superficiality of American thinking on this subject" (1985: 121). Levy adds: "During a lifetime in politics and publishing, Franklin never went on record as criticizing the concept of seditious libel" (192). The journalism historians, especially Jeffery Smith, used Franklin against Levy. Smith argues that the totality of Franklin's career clearly reveals a libertarian understanding of the role of a free press in self-government (1988, 1990, 1993). In Smith's view, Levy's position is anachronistic – that is, it judges the past by a twentieth-century theory of press freedom. Smith and others argue that the framers drew a distinction between public officials as agents of government and as private parties. In the 1789 article, Smith says, Franklin "thought press freedom meant a right to express opinions on public matters, but should not mean a liberty to make false statements damaging to an individual's reputation" (2008: 180).

The best work in the anti-Levy historiography of colonial journalism is by Robert W.T. Martin, who deftly unpacks and historicizes the eighteenth-century phrase "free and open press" (1994, 2001). Though politicians and publishers routinely used "free and open" together, the two words actually meant different things and had roots in different political theories, according to Martin. "Free" was a civic republican concept that idealized the press as a defender of the public good and as a bulwark against corrupt, tyrannical government. "Open" was a liberal (libertarian) concept that idealized the press as a common carrier open to all voices and opinions. During the crisis of the Revolution, the two traditions clashed, split apart, and produced the kind of contradictory press behavior that Levy found so puzzling – that is, the criers for press freedom just as crying loudly for the suppression of loyalist publications. As Arthur Schlesinger, Sr, had put it (quoted approvingly by Leonard Levy): "Liberty of speech belonged solely to those who spoke the speech of liberty" (Levy, 1985: 173). For Martin, this inconsistency was not the result of political hypocrisy or of a lingering commitment to the law of seditious libel. It was instead a case of the "free press" ideal momentarily trumping the "open press" ideal in the heat of Revolution. Like Smith, Robert W.T. Martin sees in Benjamin Franklin – as theorist as well as practitioner – the fascinating complexity of the eighteenth-century notion of the "free and open press" (1994: 514, 2001: 55–56; Copeland, 2006: 211–214).

Another historian of the eighteenth-century American press, Stephen Botein, saw in Franklin's "Apology for Printers" something different: not political theory but merely the "trade habits of neutrality" (1975: 191). In an important article published in 1975, Botein argued that the business organization and environment of the print shop shaped the political strategies of the colonial printer. Botein was an early exponent of what has come to be called the "history of the book." A key insight of this new cultural history of print is the idea that the physical object in historical context – its form, its creation, its distribution, and especially its use – is as important as its content (Warner, 1990; Chartier, 1994; Amory and Hall, 2000; Nord, 2008a). Botein, who died too young in 1985, was involved with the American Antiquarian Society, a research library in Massachusetts that became an important incubator of print culture history. By setting colonial newspapers into their material and business contexts, Botein helped to link journalism history with legal and political history and with the emerging "history of the book."

The most ambitious effort to follow Botein's lead is *The Public Prints* by Charles Clark, another denizen of the American Antiquarian Society. In his book, Clark traces the history of American newspapers from their roots in handwritten newsletters in the seventeenth century to their maturity as major cultural institutions by the 1740s (C.E. Clark, 1994, 2000). *The Public Prints* is a masterwork of contextualization. Clark sets the newspaper into the histories of literature, politics, business, religion, technology, urban life, government policy, English journalism, and readership. The last context – the history of readers and reading – is an important one, for it is central to the "history of the book" project. To understand the cultural work of printed materials, we need to understand how those materials were actually used in the daily lives of people in the past (R.D. Brown, 1989; D.D. Hall, 1996). In *The Public Prints*, Clark includes a chapter titled "The Ritual: the Reader's World." In this chapter he draws on a variety of manuscript materials, such as letters and diaries, to catch a glimpse of how readers used newspapers in the early eighteenth century. Furthermore, with the word "ritual," Clark links his study to the work of communication scholar James W. Carey, who challenged journalism historians to pay attention to the *ritual uses* of journalism as well to its *transmission* (production and distribution) (1989; Nord, 2006).

In Clark's study, Benjamin Franklin plays a significant role, but it is a role set into the context of the colonial newspaper business in general. In a chapter on the *New-England Courant*, Clark mentions Franklin only in passing. He devotes more attention to the community of writers that gathered around the newspaper – the "Couranteers" – the most important of whom was Ben's "less appreciated" brother James (Clark, 1994: 128). Clark covers Benjamin Franklin's own newspaper, the *Pennsylvania Gazette*, in rich detail but as one of several newspapers that nicely illustrate how the newspaper fit into the business practices of the eighteenth-century printer/publisher. "No one would think of denying that Franklin's talents were exceptional," Clark writes. "He was not, however, the only printer in the Anglo-American world who was able to publish what would be by his definition a 'good News-Paper'" (Clark, 1994: 194). But no matter how representative Franklin was, he was more than just the first among equals. In an article written with Charles Wetherell, Clark presents an especially detailed study of the journalism in the most important colonial newspaper. The paper? Franklin's *Pennsylvania Gazette* (Clark and Wetherell, 1989).

In other studies in the history-of-the-book style, Franklin plays a similar role: representative exemplar of common business strategies, yet exceptional and innovative as well. Perhaps better than any other historian of the book, James Green uses Franklin to illustrate how the colonial American printer built a successful business. Green explores the range of Franklin's Philadelphia work, including government printing; job printing; newspaper, magazine, and almanac printing; book and pamphlet printing; book and stationery sales; and postmastership. Other printer/publisher/booksellers followed a similar path, but none so adeptly as Benjamin Franklin (Green, 2000: 257–271, 2005). Similarly, Thomas Leonard explores the "synergy" of the colonial printing business – that is, how printers moved journalistic content across different print formats to spark reader interest and boost sales. Young Ben learned these lessons from his brother James in Boston. Leonard writes, "The scene of a shop, anchored by a newspaper, issuing a variety of printed fare is so familiar to us that we may have difficulty appreciating just how innovative the Franklins were" (Leonard, 1999: 454). In another example, Ralph Frasca describes the intercolonial networks that linked the businesses of printers. Frasca's book is the first business history of colonial journalism that is hemispheric in scope. And who created the most extensive network of this type? Benjamin Franklin, of course (Frasca, 2006a). Finally, when historians of the book have turned to the study of how the physicality of print – "printedness" – interacted with the public sphere in eighteenth-century America, there is Franklin yet again, as an illustrative case study of how the political print culture worked and also as an inventor of that culture (Warner, 1990: Ch. 3).

15.5 Biography and Journalism

The expanded Franklin literary canon, the heightened interest in free-press theory and history, and the emergent "history of the book" have not prompted much specialized work on Benjamin Franklin in mainstream journalism historiography. But this does not mean that Franklin-the-journalist has been neglected. Indeed, a 550-page volume appeared in 2006 titled *The Life of Benjamin Franklin: Journalist, 1706–1730*. This is the first volume of J.A. Leo Lemay's monumental biography (Lemay, 2006a). The fact that Lemay chose the word "journalist" to identify this volume on Franklin's early career suggests how important Franklin's journalism has become in literary and biographical studies, if not in the specialized historiography of journalism. Though Lemay's is the most important, it is just one of several Franklin biographies that have appeared in recent years. For a century, biographers have taken Franklin's early journalism seriously, but recent biographies have done something more: They have suggested that Franklin's style of thought was – though they do not say this explicitly – journalistic.

Leo Lemay died in 2008, having brought out three volumes of the projected seven-volume biography (Lemay, 2006a,b, 2009). Despite the work's prodigious size, scope, and attention to quotidian detail, Lemay did not imagine that it would say everything that could be said about Franklin. Like all biographies, it has a certain bent. "It is a literary biography," Lemay says, "with more discussions of Franklin's writings than any previous life" (Lemay, 2006a: xiii–xiv). Lemay's fascination with Franklin's literary style and his journalism grew from a career-long hobby of sleuthing out Franklin's anonymous and pseudonymous writings. Though the *Papers of Benjamin Franklin* project has been impressively thorough, Lemay was always lurking nearby, listing in his *Canon of Benjamin Franklin* and in each of his biographical volumes "new attributions" that the *Papers* editors had overlooked or excluded (Lemay, 1986). It is the amazing range and diversity of Franklin's writing, from serious treatises to scandalous satires, that Lemay seems to like best. By age 40, Franklin had become one of the best and most prolific American writers of his day, according to Lemay: "His style was more accessible and yet more densely packed with possible meaning than any American contemporary. Not until Edgar Allan Poe did America produce a writer who was both as popular and as subtle as Franklin. By 1748 he had become a major writer" (2006b: 554).

Much of Franklin's fugitive, ephemeral writing – throughout his life – was newspaper journalism (Aldridge, 1962; Bosco, 1987; Lemay, 1986). And Lemay devotes a great deal of attention to it in his biography. He also explores in more detail than any other biographer the business and design side of the *Pennsylvania Gazette*. Under Franklin the *Gazette* was an innovator – a very successful one – in news, advertising, typographical design, and subscription sales and distribution. By the mid-1730s, according to Lemay, Franklin's newspaper work had laid the foundation for his later public career and international fame: "Litterateurs throughout the colonies were beginning to recognize that the editor-printer of the *Pennsylvania Gazette* was a gifted man of letters" (Lemay, 2006b: 153). Lemay's conclusion is simple and unequivocal: "He was the best journalist of colonial America" (Lemay, 2006a: xiv). And what made Franklin a great journalist? Lemay declares (2006a: 455):

> It was not mainly … the kind or amount of news that really distinguished Franklin's paper but the excellent writing. No other crime reporter or political reporter of the day matched the quality or the interest of Franklin's reporting. And no other journalist of his time wrote such interesting hoaxes, skits, essays, and satires.

For Lemay, Benjamin Franklin was a great journalist in part because he wrote interesting hoaxes, skits, essays, and satires. Frederic Hudson or Whitelaw Reid or any other prominent journalist of the 1870s would have been horrified by such a judgment. For them, the essence of good journalism was *news* – not hoaxes, skits, essays, and satires. Hudson believed that the progress of journalism was progress in news gathering and distribution, and it could be measured in locomotive and ocean steamer speeds, telegraph and submarine cable capacities, and revolutions-per-minute of a Hoe cylinder press (Hudson, 1873: 774–776). Getting the news fast and first was the standard, not only for modern journalism itself but for the historians who chronicled its rise. By the early twentieth century, hoaxes in particular, no matter how innocent or entertaining, had fallen far out of favor (Nord, 2008b). But in literary studies the twentieth century was an era of canon-busting, with scholars scorning *belles-lettres* in favor of folk art, pop culture, and commercial kitsch. Leo Lemay arrived at just the right time to see in Benjamin Franklin's ephemeral newspaper writings real – and really good – journalism. His Chapter 18 in Volume 1, titled simply "Journalist," is one of the best accounts we have of the American colonial newspaper (Lemay, 2006a).

Do journalists today see Franklin's journalism as Lemay sees it? Not quite. One of the most popular of the recent biographies of Franklin was written by a journalist, Walter Isaacson, former editor and executive at CNN and *Time Magazine* (Isaacson, 2003). Isaacson loves Franklin as much as Lemay does, and he finds Franklin's journalism just as appealing. Like Lemay, he is happy to define as journalism the full range of Franklin's ephemeral writing, including the hoaxes. But Isaacson is much less interested in the literary quality of the journalism than in its public purpose. He is more impressed by Franklin's style of thought than by his style of writing. And what was that style of thought? It was "experimental," "pragmatic," "tolerant," "practical," "egalitarian," and "willing to compromise" (Isaacson, 2003: 145, 468, 487, 491–492). Franklin used journalism to promote "public-private partnerships" (Isaacson, 2003: 148). In an compact summary of Franklin's style of thought, Isaacson writes (2003: 149):

> In his political philosophy, as in his religion and science, Franklin was generally non-ideological, indeed allergic to anything smacking of dogma. Instead, he was, in most aspects of his life, interested in finding out what worked.... He had an empirical temperament that was generally averse to sweeping passions, and he espoused a kindly humanism that emphasized the somewhat sentimental (but still quite real) earthly goal of 'doing good' for his fellow man.

This is a style of thought that might be called *journalistic*. By that I mean that these are the values of a mainstream, working journalist like Walter Isaacson. They are about the civic function of writing, not about its specific form or content (Isaacson, 2005). Even Franklin's more specialized economic and scientific writings, according to other recent biographers, illustrate the link between writing and pragmatic public service (E.S. Morgan, 2002: 304; Chaplin, 2006: 8; Houston, 2008: 16). In the end, for Isaacson the values of Franklin are the values of America (2003: 492):

> The roots of much of what distinguishes the nation can be found in Franklin: its cracker-barrel humor and wisdom; its technological ingenuity; its pluralistic tolerance; its ability to weave together individualism and community cooperation; its philosophical pragmatism; its celebration of meritocratic mobility; the idealistic streak ingrained in its foreign policy; and the Main Street (or Market Street) virtues that serve as the foundation for its civic values.

And, not coincidentally, these are the values, now rather wistfully espoused, of American journalism.

15.6 Epilogue: Mash-Up

In 1887 the literary critic Charles Richardson held Franklin's journalism up to the standards of eighteenth-century English literature and found it wanting. Of his Boston and Philadelphia years, Richardson writes (1887: 158–159):

> Franklin had already begun his voluminous and miscellaneous contributions to printed matter, but not as an author. His 'works' fill a goodly row of octavos, but how miscellaneous is their character! ... The truth about Franklin as a miscellaneous writer – a truth which any one may verify by a day's reading in his collected works – is that most of his productions, while respectable, of wide range, well-written, sensible, and telling, are not of the highest rank, and that, measured by the tests of English literature between 1725 and 1775, they are commonplace.

A revealing phrase in Richardson's assessment is: "not as an author." In a recent study of Franklin as writer and printer, James Green and Peter Stallybrass make a similar point about authorship. Only with his scientific writings and later with the autobiography did Franklin become "an author" – that is, a writer whose name was bound up in permanent form with his work. "From this perspective," they write, "Franklin was never an author when he was active as a printer in Boston, London, and Philadelphia. During that time, he wrote short, fugitive pieces in newspapers, almanacs, and pamphlets that lasted only as long as the perishable and disposable material forms on which they were printed" (Green and Stallybrass, 2006: 171). Like Lemay, but contra Richardson, Green and Stallybrass find this one of the most interesting and significant aspects of Franklin's career. Perhaps better than any other American, Benjamin Franklin illustrates what it meant to be a writer in the print culture and manuscript culture of the eighteenth-century Atlantic world.

But Green and Stallybrass go a step farther than Lemay in their appreciation of Franklin. For Lemay it is always about the writing: Even when Franklin borrowed and reprinted content, such as the aphorisms in *Poor Richard's Almanac*, he always added and improved. Green and Stallybrass, on the other hand, are fascinated by the borrowing and reprinting process itself, which was such an important part of a writer's life and a printer's trade in that era. Not only did Franklin publish nearly all of his newspaper writing anonymously or pseudonymously, he also was pleased to imitate, borrow, revise, and reuse the writings of others. In this way, he operated in the "long Renaissance tradition of commonplacing" – that is, collecting and reworking the wisdom of the ages. Green and Stallybrass argue that Franklin did not believe in patents or in the concept of plagiarism because he did not believe in the private ownership of knowledge:

> For Franklin, ideas were a common treasury to be shared by all. It was not imitation or even plagiarism that was the problem; it was the claim to intellectual property, a claim that justifies itself by *producing* 'plagiarism' (i.e., the possibility of shared knowledge) as its moral (and later, legal) antithesis. Franklin argued that the immorality lay in the fences that intellectual property erected that preserved knowledge for the rich and powerful and prevented its free circulation. (Green and Stallybrass, 2006: 23)

Green and Stallybrass's interest is historical, so they rarely stray into the digital world of the twenty-first century. But they could. Their Benjamin Franklin sounds a lot like Lawrence Lessig, Kembrew McLeod, or any of the other gurus of the "free culture" movement today (Lessig, 2004; McLeod, 2005). These Internet activists are not opposed in principle to intellectual property, but they resist what they see as the ever-tightening control of copyright by the rich and powerful of our time: media corporations. They see in the digital world, especially the Internet, a wonderful public space for creativity, but only if creators have access to the materials of our common culture. Just as Franklin-the-journalist collected, revised, reworked, and reprinted the commonplace materials of his culture, so today do bloggers, new media designers, and news Web site entrepreneurs gather cultural materials and reshape them into something new. Like Franklin, they copy, aggregate, link, sample, mash-up, remix, digest, repost, and retweet. So was Benjamin Franklin a retweeter? No one has said that yet, but some contributor to the next wave of Franklin biographies might. Biographers and historians always see past lives through the lens of their own present. And to see Franklin as a kind of Internet progenitor might actually make some sense.

Further Reading

Clark, C.E. (1994). *The Public Prints: The Newspaper in Anglo-American Culture, 1665–1740*. New York, NY.

Copeland, D.A. (1997). *Colonial American Newspapers: Character and Content*. Newark, DE.

Crane, V.W. (1950). *Benjamin Franklin's Letters to the Press, 1758–1775*. Chapel Hill, NC.

Frasca, R. (2006). *Benjamin Franklin's Printing Network: Disseminating Virtue in Early America*. Columbia, MO.

Green, J.N. and Stallybrass, P. (2006). *Benjamin Franklin: Writer and Printer*. New Castle, DE.

Isaacson, W. (2003). *Benjamin Franklin: An American Life*. New York, NY.

Lemay, J.A.L. (2006a). *The Life of Benjamin Franklin, vol. 1: Journalist, 1706–1730*. Philadelphia, PA.

Lemay, J.A.L. (2006b). *The Life of Benjamin Franklin, vol. 2: Printer and Publisher, 1730–1747*. Philadelphia, PA.

Martin, R.W.T. (2001). *The Free and Open Press: The Founding of American Democratic Press Liberty, 1640–1800*. New York, NY.

Smith, J.A. (1990). *Franklin and Bache: Envisioning the Enlightened Republic*. New York, NY.

Chapter Sixteen

Benjamin Franklin, the Science of Flow, and the Legacy of the Enlightenment

Laura Rigal

In the opening pages of the 1798 Gothic novel *Wieland, or the Transformation*, the Protestant father of a young family named Wieland is praying on his estate outside Philadelphia when suddenly, with a loud explosion, he bursts into flame. A doctor rushes to the scene, only to find the man sprawled beneath a luminous cloud, his clothes reduced to ashes, but hair and slippers untouched. Carried delirious into the house, his skin "throughout the greater part of his body scorched and bruised," Wieland dies within two hours, emitting "insupportable exhalations and crawling putrefaction" (C.B. Brown, 1798: 19–20).

Who, or what was the source of this event? A "bolt of lightning" from the clear night sky? A murderous intruder bearing "a pistol" or an explosive device "like a mine"? (1798: 18, 21) Before his death, Wieland reported being struck on the right arm, as if by a club. But the clue does little to explain his appalling combustion. Eventually, his well-educated children begin to wonder if, perhaps, the cause was supernatural, "fresh proof that the Divine Ruler interferes in human affairs, … enforcing submission to his will." Wieland's highly intelligent daughter Clara, however, introduces a more up-to-date hypothesis. If the cause was not divine, she speculates, perhaps it was "merely the irregular expansion of the fluid that imparts warmth to our hearts and our blood, caused by the fatigue of the preceding day, or flowing, by established laws, from the condition of his thoughts?" (1798: 20–21)

Clara's theory condenses a number of eighteenth-century Newtonian sciences that analyzed physical and physiological processes from the point

---

A Companion to Benjamin Franklin, First Edition. Edited by David Waldstreicher.
© 2011 Blackwell Publishing Ltd. Published 2011 by Blackwell Publishing Ltd.

of view of fluid dynamics. Such investigations – into hemodynamics (blood flow), heat, respiration, electricity, and "the nervous fluid" – were deeply indebted to "the established laws" of Newtonian physics governing bodies in motion. In the second half of the eighteenth century, natural philosophers in Europe and the Americas, including Benjamin Franklin, focused intently upon the dynamics of, and relations among, fluid systems. Between his first electrical experiments in the late 1740s and his death in 1790, Franklin himself experimented in most of the fields implicated in Wieland's death: lightning and electrical shock, explosives, hydrology, body heat, respiration, fermentation, and the inflammable fluid known as "phlogiston" (today's oxygen). Within the world of the novel, Wieland's dark death is never solved. But, one thing is clear: It is no accident that the novelist Charles Brockden Brown set Wieland's uncanny (*unheimlich*) combustion outside Philadelphia, the longtime home of Benjamin Franklin, inventor of lightning rods, founder of the American Philosophical Society, and ambassador of Enlightenment in the eighteenth-century Atlantic world. Franklin is often characterized as the representative of a uniquely American scientific and political Enlightenment. In fact, he crossed the Atlantic Ocean eight times during his career, and spent 29 years of the last 33 years of his life in Europe. Franklin's Enlightenment was irreducibly international – and spontaneous combustion a circum-Atlantic as well as American problem.

As if to underline the international as well as Enlightenment origins of Clara's hypothesis, Brown notes that, in fact, Wieland's (fictional) death is a *bona fide* case of spontaneous human combustion, similar to others documented in French, Italian, and British medical literature: "A case, in its symptoms exactly parallel to this," Brown writes, "is published in one of the Journals of Florence." Similar cases are "reported by Messrs. Merille and Muraire, in the *Journal de Medicine*, for February and May, 1783," while the "researches of Maffei and Fontana have thrown some light upon this subject" (C.B. Brown, 1798: 21n). Like Clara, the novelist opens the door to scientific explanations. But, rather than exposing the cause, medical discourse redoubles the mystery. Like present-day accounts of flying saucers, ghosts, and conversations with the dead, spontaneous human combustion evoked multiple explanations: physical, physiological, and theological. It also introduced the possibility of magic, or human agents such as witches or sorcerers, deploying supernatural means. In the matter of inexplicable explosions, magic was the darkness through which Enlightenment physics and philosophy defined itself. As the philosopher Voltaire writes in *L'Encyclopédie*, the famous French compendium of Enlightenment theory and practice, a modern man of letters (*gens de letters*) no longer pores over Greek and Latin texts. Instead, "with the aid of a sound philosophy," his criticism "destroys all the prejudices with which society was afflicted: astrologers' predictions, false prodigies, false marvels, and superstitious customs" (Sutton, 1981: 375).

In Brown's novel, Wieland's weird death challenges the structural binary of reason versus superstition that continues to define the "Enlightenment" as the dawn of modern empirical science. In fact, Wieland's spontaneous combustion suggests that nothing was more *typical* of the Age of Reason than such "freaks" or anomalies of nature, which stood at the limits of Enlightenment taxonomies and epistemologies, as fascinating problems on which experimental science could deploy its apparatus. In fact, marvels and prodigies were the everyday business of Newtonian experimentalists such as Franklin. Many everyday phenomena – lightning strikes, shooting stars, static electricity, fires, volcanic eruptions, earthquakes, the randomness of birth and death – lacked any single, definitive, causal explanation. Being epistemologically unstable, such events were resonant with mystery, danger, and dread. Their power accrued to the Enlightenment philosopher who could narrate their genesis, or diminish their effects. Ultimately, then, the eighteenth-century Enlightenment was not a victory of light over the darkness, or of scientific truth over the reign of error. Rather, it was an intense struggle over social dominance and natural resources, in which a new order of things, and a new dynamic of cultural power, were being asserted in the name of human progress.

Philosophers of science and technology Bruno Latour and Michel Foucault, make a similar argument when they ask historians to reconsider the dichotomies of fact versus "fetish," reason versus madness, and freedom versus tyranny, that continue to shape histories of the Enlightenment. Like other Gothic novels of the late-eighteenth century, *Wieland* highlights the ambiguous legacy of the Enlightenment's dawning faith in the light of Reason, and in social improvement through science and technology. Although Franklin himself does not appear in *Wieland*, the novel's gloomy anxiety about the limits of human knowledge is an unmistakable commentary on the forces marshaled by the Newtonian public sphere in which Franklin played such a significant role. It has been somewhat difficult for American historians to situate Franklin clearly against the bright lights of European science and philosophy, among whom he appeared as a first American "genius" (in Thomas Jefferson's words (1785: 126)) or, as historian Joyce Chaplin puts it, "the first scientific American" (2006: 66). In popular and scholarly mythology, as in Jefferson's account, Franklin's life continues to be identified with the revolutionary birth of the United States which, like Franklin himself, seemed to emerge *ex nihilo* from provincial obscurity onto the stage of world history. This is the Franklin of the "radical," or truly revolutionary, American Enlightenment as Gordon Wood and Douglas Anderson define it, in which the thirteen colonies definitively altered the politically repressive and economically static trajectories of European class society and mercantilist policies.

This is also the Enlightenment of the small flood of Franklin biographies that emerged between 2001 and 2009 in celebration of the tricentennial of Franklin's birth. Gordon Wood has commented positively, but wryly, on the uncritical bias of many of these otherwise excellent studies, such as *CNN* Chairman and *TIME* managing editor Walter Isaacson's *Benjamin Franklin: An American Life* (2003). In popular mythology, Franklin has long been viewed as the "most accessible and ... democratic," humorous and plain-spoken of the eighteenth-century "Founders." But scholars as well associate Franklin with what is uniquely "American." Surprisingly, as Wood observes, even historians who "tend not to believe anymore in the notion of an American character," make an exception for Franklin: "[I]f there is such a thing, then Franklin seems to exemplify it" (G.S. Wood, 2004: 1). In popular and scholarly studies, Franklin tends to be viewed on his own terms, as a cosmopolitan man of letters who arose, virtually self-created, from the Delaware River valley to stand "before kings ... [and not] before mean men," through his own efforts as a workman, writer and man of science "diligent in his calling" (Franklin, 1986a: 88).

Cultural historian Robert A. Ferguson, by contrast, offers a more nuanced view of Franklin's Enlightenment when he argues in *The American Enlightenment, 1750–1820*, that its brilliant accomplishments and utopian hopes must be evaluated in relationship to their unforeseen consequences in the nineteenth and especially the twentieth centuries. In fact, he points out, the Revolutionary Enlightenment is more accurately, because more dialectically, defined by a group of twentieth-century European philosophers who were compelled to revisit its legacy in the wake of the military and political catastrophes of the twentieth and twenty-first centuries (1997: 22–25). In the decades following World War II, Jurgen Habermas (1989), Max Horkheimer and Theodore Adorno (1972), and Hannah Arendt (1959) (and, more recently, Giorgio Agamben (2005)), among others, focused on several persistent and disturbing questions. How could the explosive disasters of the twentieth and twenty-first centuries have arisen among the liberal, secular, and scientific nations of modern Europe? What are the limits of modern science, technology, and empirical "reason?" What does European fascism, militarism, colonialism, and the Cold War nightmare of nuclear holocaust have to do, if anything, with the Enlightenment origins of liberal governments in Europe and the Americas? Here, Ferguson makes a crucial point, arguing that many Americans have had a difficult time acknowledging the more painful legacies of the Revolutionary Enlightenment because, continuing to operate within it, they distinguish too sharply between the ideology of the Enlightenment in America, and the history of Enlightenment in Europe. This tendency obscures both the mixed historical legacy of the eighteenth-century Enlightenment, and its relationship the globalized economic and techno-scientific systems of the twentieth and twenty-first centuries. As his multinational network of correspondents reveal, the Enlightenment embraced Newtonian philosophers (*philosophes, illuminati, philosophen, filosofo*) in Germany, Italy, the Netherlands, Scandinavia, Russia, Austria, Spain, Spanish-America, and the Caribbean.

Ferguson's argument encourages a more careful, less "American," and less selective reading of Franklin and the Enlightenment, one that perceives the connections among his scientific, financial, social, and political pursuits by attending closely to his investment in the dynamics of flow – or fluid systems. Scholarly and popular admiration of Franklin's ingenious inventions, sly humor, and rhetorical skills have left readers too much in the dark regarding Franklin's investment in bio-power: the interplay of political power, social hygienics, and Newtonian hydrodynamics that structured his career. While Franklin was a brilliant prose stylist, social performer, and creative natural philosopher, both Franklin and the Enlightenment will be useless to us if their political, social, and techno-scientific legacies are viewed in isolation from the darker currents of the Atlantic world that Franklin claimed to illuminate, but which, in fact, he rode, right into the present.

In American literary and cultural studies, scholars frequently identify early American Enlightenment science with natural history, or the collection and descriptive taxonomies of animal, vegetable, and mineral resources. This is understandable since, as Mary Louise Pratt (1992) demonstrates, European and Euro-American imperial expansion relied directly on inventories of natural and human resources. Further, the assembly of data was crucial to all inductive (Baconian, Lockean, Linnaean, and Newtonian) sciences. However, it was not natural history, but the Newtonian focus on hydrodynamic systems – the mechanics and management of fluids in motion – that justifies defining the Enlightenment as a radical, even explosive, transformation of "Man's" ability to model, measure, and manipulate previously incomprehensible physiological and physical processes. Moreover, because it undergirded investigations across wildly disparate fields, fluid dynamics help to explain why Enlightenment philosophers such as Franklin felt they could range freely and fluidly among and within virtually any field of human inquiry, be it historical, political, economic, physical, or physiological. From this point of view, the physics of flow defines the hydrodynamic structure of the international Enlightenment as an epistemic shift in the history of communication through the emergence of "the bourgeois public sphere."

Since the early 1990s, definitions of the Enlightenment have taken into account not only Immanuel Kant's classic 1784 essay "What is Enlightenment?" but also Jurgen Habermas' 1962 *The Structural Transformation of the Public Sphere: An Inquiry Into A Category of Bourgeois Society*. Habermas encourages historians to view the eighteenth-century Enlightenment as a transformation in the means of communication through the emergence of heterogeneous networks for circulating argument and information. Such networks were "public" in that they were distinct from (but still engaged with) monarchical, dynastic, and religious, spatio-temporal imaginaries against which, as Benedict Anderson argues, modern "print nationalisms" had begun to assert themselves. But the Enlightenment "public sphere" went beyond print media, taking shape (outside governments proper) in widely dispersed local environments dominated by face-to-face contact: taverns, clubs, coffee houses, salons, tea-tables, theaters, ships, and shops. Such sites were penetrated and connected by various genres of communication: lectures, scientific demonstrations, conversations, hand-written letters, manuscript documents, printed pamphlets, as well as magazines, newspapers, and books of all kinds, bound in paper or animal skin. It was, then, through the media and meeting places of the bourgeois public sphere, that, in a storm-tossed and war-torn Atlantic world, Franklin embarked upon his brilliant electrical career.

16.1 The Spirits of Marshes and Bogs

In 1789, A.M. Vassali-Eandi, an Italian student of electricity described Benjamin Franklin admiringly as a "physico-politician" (Pace, 1958: 61). Translated from Italian, the phrase neatly defines the place Franklin generated for himself within the communication networks of the international Enlightenment in the second half of the eighteenth century. After 1750, many of Franklin's most appreciative admirers were leading figures of the Italian Enlightenment who drew directly on his electrical experiments. Giovanni Beccaria, Allessandro Volta, Lazzaro Spallanzani, Luigi Galvani and, earlier, Felice Fontana and Scipio Maffei had followed Franklin's career since the early 1750s, when his name began to circulate beyond British colonial circles as the inventor of a lightning rod and author of a charming collection of letters titled *New Experiments in Electricity, By Benjamin Franklin, of Philadelphia, in America* (London, 1751; Paris, 1752; Leipzig, 1758). In his notes to *Wieland* on the subject of spontaneous human combustion, Brown cites "Maffei and Fontana," early admirers of Franklin among the Italian *Illuminati*. In Verona, Francesco Scipione, Marquis de Maffei (1675–1755) had engaged in the flurry of mid-century lightning-rod experiments in which Franklin had participated. The author of "*Della formazione dei fulmini (On the Formation of Lightning)*," Maffei was nominated in 1747, together with Franklin, for election to the British Royal Society. Maffei had suggested that lightning could be generated within human bodies, causing them to spontaneously ignite and burn. Thus, an anonymous New York reviewer (probably Brown, or William Dunlap) writes of Wieland's combustion: "If Maffei, were still alive … he would take advantage of [these fatal accidents] to support an opinion which he entertained that lightning is sometimes kindled within the human body, and destroys it" (*American Review and Literary Journal for the Year 1801*, 338).

Felice Fontana (1730–1805) was an Italian physicist who investigated the relationship among fluidity, respiration, and combustion in animal bodies. The author of *Principi generali della soliditàe della fluidità dé corpi*, (1783), Fontana traveled through Europe in the late 1770s, investigating military technologies for the Duke of Tuscany. Like Franklin's friend, the Newtonian psychologist David Hartley, Fontana was a pioneer in the biomechanics of cognition, specializing in "irritability" and "the nervous fluid." In January, 1783 he was elected to the American Philosophical Society (Philadelphia's version of the British Royal Society) of which Franklin was president. The two men belonged to the same "physico-political" networks, and in 1779 had met in London, where they had an opportunity to inspect a newly invented "Electrical Pistol" that, as their mutual friend Jan Ingenhousz recalled, "discharged inflam[m]able air with great Force and Explosion ... and was Supposed to answer the Purpose of Gunn-Powder" (Pace, 1958: 37; PBF, 12: 44).[1]

Spontaneous combustion indirectly lights up the scientific networks and studies of "aetherial" fluids in which Franklin was enmeshed. In the 1770s and 1780s, phlogiston was championed by Franklin's philosophical friend Joseph Priestley as the invisible fluid that not only generated oxidation (rust) but constituted the fire of life itself through respiration. At the dawn of modern chemistry, fluid "fires" such as phlogiston underwrote a variety of seemingly unrelated bio-mechanical hypotheses, including theories of spontaneous combustion implicating the combustible properties of "phlogiston," fermentation, and alcoholic "spirits." For instance, the 1801 review of *Wieland* in Brown's *American Review and Literary Journal* notes the cases of the "unfortunate countess Cornelia Bandi" and an Italian Priest named Bertholi, who perished by apparent spontaneous combustion in 1731 and 1776, respectively. But the more common cases involve isolated, dissipated women, "advanced in years, remarkably fat, and much addicted to the use of spirituous liquors." In such instances, Brown explains, "the phlogiston of the animal humours" in the "epigastric viscera" is "called forth by that of the spirituous liquors," with which it combines. When their remains were discovered, the women's bodies had virtually evaporated "by their whole substance spontaneously taking fire," leaving only greasy ashes, scattered body parts, and a hideous odor (*American Review and Literary Journal for the Year 1801*, 339).

Such mysterious and unhygienic matters were at the center of overlapping investigations by Franklin, Priestley, and their Newtonian correspondents, including Italian electricians Beccaria and Volta, Austrian plant physiologist Ingenhousz, and Franklin's friend the Scots military doctor John Pringle, President of the Royal Society and author of *Diseases of the Army* (1776). Like Franklin, Pringle was the humanitarian enemy of putrid wetlands, and a committed advocate of draining Britain's bogs and lowlands in the interests of saving soldiers, who died regularly of dysentery and "effluvial fevers" before they could be killed in battle. While Franklin's interest in phlogiston was an outgrowth of his experiments in combustion and electricity, it was equally fired by his dislike of marshes. As cultural studies theorists Peter Stallybrass and Allon White have shown, the eighteenth-century drive to drain British bogs and marshes went hand in hand with the effort to eliminate medieval fairs, festivals, and holy-days (holidays) from the European calendar. According to Stallybrass and White, these Enlightenment social reforms were of a piece with the emergence of modern authorship which (viewed in relationship to supressing fairs and draining swamps) was established as a kind of "dry ground," where bourgeois scientific, social, and literary authority could be cultivated. The elevation of authors as the generators and owners of their own mental products depended, in turn, upon the circulatory flows of the bourgeois public sphere, where magazines, journals, and newspapers, salons, clubs, and voluminous personal correspondence were actively generating a new kind of social identity: the media celebrity, of which Franklin was an early edition.

Franklin's contributions to Priestley's *Experiments and Observations on Different Kinds of Air* (1774–1777) include experiments on the inflammable air of stagnant or muddy water. In the 1760s, several reports had surfaced across from Philadelphia, on the New Jersey side of the Delaware River, of mysterious cases of creeks, ponds, and river water whose surfaces were observed ablaze, "like inflamed spirits." By "spirits" Franklin specifically meant alcoholic spirits. Eighteenth-century Newtonians such as Franklin, Priestley, and Volta repeatedly entertained readers and audiences with combustible glasses of wine and other "spirituous liquors," warmed, and ignited by the "electrical fire," or the application of a candle. From England, then, Franklin wrote to Priestley that he had tried to reproduce the fiery waters of New Jersey. Somewhere in London he attempted to ignite the "stagnant water of deep ditches" by holding a candle to the surface and stirring the bottom with a stick. Nothing happened – but Franklin ended up in bed with an "intermitting fever" due to "my breathing too much of the foul" and inflammable "air" (Priestley, 1774–1777, 1: 323).

Like Pringle, Franklin was the enemy of mud and marshland, as inconvenient, potentially explosive environments. He frequently advocated draining smelly, swampy soils which, like many hard-working European-Americans, he regarded as so much wasted land, useless for farming, and an obstacle to travel and communication. The unimproved wetlands of urban rivers, creeks, and ditches for instance, not only generated unexplained fires, their effluvial miasma, or bad air ("mal-aria") was thought to cause putrid or intermitting fevers, such as today's cholera, yellow fever, typhoid, and other mosquito- and water-borne illnesses. But disease and inflammable air were not the only risks associated with marshes. Their unreformed muck represented socioeconomic stasis and something worse – dirt, danger, regression, and potential humiliation. In a letter sent in 1780 to Priestley from Passy, France, on the occasion of Priestley's desire to quit his position as a tutor, Franklin narrates another anecdote of the Delaware River. Priestley found his job onerous, but Franklin advised him to stay on board, at the risk of experiencing an even more instable and inconvenient situation. In his youth, Franklin writes, he was descending the Delaware in a sloop on a hot day, with a group of "not very Agreeable" strangers, when their boat was becalmed between tides. On the river bank, Franklin spied a "pleasant green meadow in the middle of which was a large shady tree." Having a book to read, and wishing to pass the time more "agreeably," he persuaded the sloop's captain to put him ashore. "Being landed," however, he was unpleasantly surprised:

> I found the greatest part of my Meadow was really a Marsh, in crossing which, to come at my Tree, I was up to my knees in Mire; and I had not placed myself under its Shade five Minutes, before the Muskitoes in Swarms found me out, attack'd my Legs, Hands, and Face, and made my Reading and my Rest impossible; so that I return'd to the Beach, and call'd for the Boat to come and take me aboard again, where I was oblig'd to bear the Heat I had strove to quit, and also the Laughter of the Company. (Franklin to Priestley, February 8, 1780; PBF, 31: 455–56)

Franklin's message to Priestley is, of course, "the grass is always greener" on the riverbank. But the point is framed by "the Laughter of the Company" – and the experience of shame. Intimately tied to rage and its consequences (including further humiliation), shame motivates several defining episodes in Franklin's autobiography. In Boston, Franklin smothers his wish to be a poet when his father "ridicule[s]" his "Performance ... telling me Verse-makers were always Beggars" (Franklin, 1986a: 14). He runs away from Boston to Philadelphia to escape his tyrant brother, who "demean'd me too much," and "often beat me." Ten years later, a successful printer, he abruptly quits Samuel Keimer's printing establishment when Keimer publically "demeans" him. Hearing a commotion in the street, Franklin had put his head out a window to take a look, when Keimer, "being in the street look'd up and saw me, call'd out to me in a loud voice and angry Tone to mind my Business, adding some reproachful Words that nettled me the more for the Publicity, all the Neighbors who were looking out on the same Occasion being Witnesses how I was treated" (Franklin, 1986a: 21, 60).

Such moments reference an intensely face-to-face, early modern community, structured by rank, patronage, and deference, in which public dishonor is socially momentous. Such experiences of humiliation and anger would become internationally and geo-politically significant in 1774 when, after years of conciliatory diplomacy in London on behalf of the colonies, Franklin was publically upbraided in the British House of Lords. In response, he decided, abruptly and irrevocably, to support the American Revolution, and returned to Philadelphia for the first time in fifteen years.

As Ferguson observes, one of Franklin's strategies to avoid humiliation was a technique of calculated silence, which effectively masked and rechanneled rage (1997: 16). Like phlogiston and fermenting spirits, anger was a combustible that generated resentment among friends and family: "A Positive assuming Manner," Franklin concludes, "seldom fails to disgust and tends to create Opposition" (1986a: 19). Skillfully managed, however, resentment was the fiery fuel of industry and social mobility. Channeled, it enabled Franklin to avoid being dragged down in perilous times by people whose stability or allegiance was uncertain.

Completed in the last decade of his life, Franklin's autobiography is, above all, a manual of techniques for pulling oneself out of the social swamp of "mean" (small, inferior, as well as tyrannical or violent) persons and places. "Having emerged from the poverty and obscurity in which I was born and bred," Franklin writes (1986a: 3):

> and having gone so far through life with a considerable share of felicity, the conducing means I made use of, ... [my posterity] may find some of them suitable to their own situations, and therefore fit to be imitated.

While Franklin offers instructions for avoiding conflict and rising in the world, he does so by contrasting his "conducing means" with the stories of friends and family who go under. The benign opening of the autobiography belies the dark undercurrent of people dragged down into obscurity by the monsters of their own "idleness, thoughtlessness, imprudence" (George Webb); rigid religious fundamentalism (Samuel Keimer); static and affixed socio-cultural identities (the "wild Irishmen," black slaves, and Indians of Pennsylvania); and alcoholism or debt (John Collins, Hugh Meredith, and the beer-guzzling pressmen of Watt's English printing house). The differences of rank, education, or talent separating success from failure are relatively slight. What distinguishes the men and boys who sink or fail to keep their heads above water (the alcoholic Collins, who retires to Barbados, or the "wild Irishman" who flees Franklin's print shop) is that they did not, or could not, generate the dynamic of social self-creation that floated Franklin's boat in the communication and commercial networks of the bourgeois public sphere.

As horizontal as it was vertical, Franklin's upward mobility was a social physics of movement generated at the line (+/−) between attraction/repulsion, connection/separation. It was not Franklin's unique gifts, in other words, but his fluency in the marks of social difference that kept him afloat and in motion. His enduring significance is traceable to his canny exploitation of the fluid dynamism inherent in the structural dichotomies through which the Newtonian Enlightenment dawned: movement versus stasis, expansion versus contraction, channeled versus "wild" flows. Here lies the sociopolitical significance of Franklin's unique contribution to electrical science: his theory of bipolar, or positive and negative (+/−) electrical charges, and his argument that electricity was "a single fluid," whose effects of attraction/repulsion were hydrodynamically structured – as the accumulation, drainage, channeling, or obstruction of flow.

People without the skills of self-management go under in Franklin's book, even if they can literally swim, as both Franklin and Collins could.

Where others are sunk by alcohol, idleness, or simply the failure to concentrate, Franklin passes through, or around, all obstacles to dynamic self-conduction. In the end, the positive (+) valence of his survival unfolds against the negative (−) background of floundering or "stuck" persons whose nonappearance and disappearance lift his success into the foreground, by dint of contrast. Franklin's primary relationship to the dark and the light, the pluses and minuses (+/−), of the international Enlightenment was his extraordinary ability to ride the waves, as well as the deeper currents, of a divided world. The beer-drinking pressmen at Watts' printing house made an astute observation when they dubbed Franklin "the water-American" for his avoidance of alcohol. While his career proceeded "swimmingly," a black and fermenting marshland awaited all drunk and undisciplined – as well as overly rigid or fixed – characters (Franklin, 1986a: 33, 76). In fact, excessive social and economic fixity, as well as too much fluidity, could cause a man to sink. Instead of overconsuming, on one hand, or utterly rejecting "spirits," therefore, Franklin ignited them, converting the energy of the difference into instructive entertainment.

16.2 The Fire Within

Franklin first began to experiment with electricity in Philadelphia in 1745, when he received a Leyden jar, or "phial," from friends in London. An apparatus for holding and applying electrical charges, a Leyden jar is a lead-covered glass jar filled with water or metal, with a wire passed into the interior and protruding from a cork at the top. When the wire is charged positively, the lead exterior of the jar is charged negatively. When Franklin began to publicize electrical experiments with the jar, he entered a highly politicized world of European electrical investigation in which British, French, Dutch, and German experimenters played a leading role. As Simon Shaeffer demonstrates, Franklin's electrical experiments were fully in keeping with the showman spirit of the Newtonian public sphere. Somewhere between a university lecture and a dime museum, eighteenth-century shows were spaces for individuals to display the marvels of nature, and to make a place for themselves in a difficult crowd. Many of Franklin's most entertaining experiments were inspired by European electrical exhibitions. In Britain, for instance, the celebrated William Watson was already igniting glasses of wine, directing shocks through the bodies of ladies and gentlemen, and mysteriously sending electricity across rivers. Like Watson, Franklin would exploit the Newtonian doctrine of "active fluids," sometimes called "aether," elaborated by Newton, and by natural philosophers such as Wilhelm Homberg and Herman Boerhaave (Schaffer, 1993: 496).

Franklin used various metaphors to describe the flow of electricity, labelling it variously a "fluid," a "fire," or an "aether" consisting of "particles extremely subtile [*sic*] that can permeate common matter, even the densest metals, with ... ease and freedom" (Cohen, 1941: 171). Franklin's central contribution to electrical science was his theory that electricity was a single fluid with a bipolar or binary charge by means of which it could be evoked, rather like spring water, and then channelized, "pumped," or drained: "We know that the electrical fluid is in common matter, because we can pump it *out* by the [Leyden jar] or [glass] tube" (Cohen, 1941: 214). Most of his experiments are extended demonstrations of the conservation of charges, according to which "any production of a positive charge in one body (a net gain in electrical fluid) is always accompanied by an equal and opposite negative charge (a net loss in electrical fluid) in one or more other bodies." The shocking or entertaining effects of plus (+) and minus (−) charges were embedded in the underlying "sameness" of a fluid that "is equally diffused in our walls, floors, earth, and the whole mass of common matter." The electrical scientist generates the electrical fire as a "build-up" or, conversely, a debit of charge, "not by creating, but collecting it" (Cohen, 1941: 202). The terms plus and minus simply indicate the directional flows through which electrical fluid was accumulated or subtracted via conduction. When set in motion by the electrician, it circulates, creating wonderful effects in the process of "electrising" or "de-electrising" the bodies brought into contact with the system, until it reaches equilibrium or finds "original equality" (Cohen, 1941: 175).

Many readers of Franklin's theory of charges have noticed its resemblance to debits and credits in the ledger-book method of account-keeping used by eighteenth-century merchants and tradesmen. The pluses and minuses of book-keeping mark a connection between the seemingly unrelated domains of commerce, physics, and communication within the heterogeneous sites of communicative exchange that constituted the Enlightenment public sphere. The commercial and hydrodynamic exchanges marked by +/− indicate the historical emergence of modern "communication" itself as an analytic category and a structural necessity (or "spirit-fact") of Enlightenment self-definition.

Under the hands of the electrical philosopher, electricity ebbed and flowed like a tidal river. Its flow could be consciously controlled, as if by dams, or channeled through "canals" designed and maintained by the Newtonian engineer. Indeed, as Franklin emphasized over and over again, the first principle of electricity was the fact that as fire, or "aether," it penetrates all matter, existing "quite calmly in all particulate objects, prior to any operation. In its original state it is better described, in fact, as a kind of *aether*-net" (Cohen, 208–209). In its uncanny forecast of twentieth-century digital communications, Franklin's Newtonian formulation – "*aether*-net" – points to the historical co-emergence of eighteenth-century hydrodynamics with the modern (geo-) science of communication. Moreover, as a circulatory system, this aether-net was not merely external to, but already inherent within organic and inorganic bodies.

Franklin's electrical principles are neatly illustrated by one of his early experiments: "the electric spider." The goal is to "animate" a spider made of linen thread and a burnt cork, "with a grain or two of lead stuck in him, to give him more weight." The spider is suspended on a thread between two wires, and one of the wires is given a negative charge by application of the Leyden jar. The inequality of charges in the two wires is evidenced by the motion of the spider, who must perform the labor of "fetching and carrying" the electrical charge, until the Leyden jar runs out of current. In this simple experiment, Franklin identifies the hydrodynamics of electricity with the self-moving character that defines animal life. The electrical spider is not only testimony to the scientific magic of the electrician, who generates animated "life" from "dead" materials. Its oscillation also suggests that organic life itself is bio-mechanical: "Then, we animate him [by applying the Leyden jar to one of the wires] ... He will immediately fly to the wire of the Phial, bend his legs in touching it; then spring off, and fly to the wire on the table: thence again to the wire of the phial, playing with his legs against both, in a very entertaining manner [and appearing] perfectly alive to persons unacquainted" (Cohen, 1941: 177, 178n, 183).

Along with his glass tube and Leyden jar, which arrived from Peter Collinson in 1745, Franklin also received a copy of the April issue of the London *Gentleman's Magazine*, which contained an essay by Albrecht von Haller describing German experiments with electricity. Haller's essay emphasized performances involving human bodies and the firing of alcoholic spirits, declaring that tricks with static electricity had "taken the place of quadrille in the fashionable world" (Heilbron, 1979: 326). Haller recounts one experiment called "the hanging boy," in which a small boy is suspended from ropes and sparks of fire evoked from his face and hands by rubbing an electrified glass tube from his feet, to prove that "fire is diffus'd through all Space, and may be produced from all "Bodies." Franklin and his co-experimenters in Philadelphia reproduced another of Haller's fashionable experiments, the "*Venus electrificata*" or "the electrical kiss," of which they claimed to have "encreased vastly the force" (Cohen, 1941: 170). Franklin explains: "Let A and B stand on wax ... give one of them the electrised phial in hand; let the other take hold of the wire; there will be a small spark; but when their lips approach, they will be struck and shock'd ..." (Cohen, 1941: 177).

Communicating his results in the form of familiar letters describing American versions of French, German, or British electrical entertainments, Franklin's *New Experiments* instructed but also amused European audiences. What characterized the editions of the *New Experiments* (five English, three French, one each in German and Italian) was their simple and modest, yet manly, plain style – as well as exotically provincial details. The rhetorical art of Franklin's letters on electricity is well illustrated by an "electrical party" organized along the "*Skuylkill* River," which included a feast of "electrocuted turkey" roasted on an electrical "jack." Franklin closed the "electrical season" of 1748 with "a party of pleasure on the banks of *Skuylkil[l]*." The entertainment begins with the "firing of spirits [glasses of wine] by means of a spark sent [from one side of the river to the other] without any conductor than the water." Next a turkey is "killed for our dinner by the electrical shock, and roasted by the electrical jack, before a fire kindled by the electrified bottle: when the healths of all the famous electricians in England, Holland, France, and German [are] drunk in electrified bumpers, under the discharge of guns from the electrical battery" (Cohen, 1941: 199–200).

It was not his electrical parties, however, but his theory of lightning that established Franklin's reputation among the European *gens de lettres*. As a matter of science, Franklin used lightning rods to prove that lightning was an electrical phenomenon. Metal rods, erected on roofs or steeples, were simply a more spectacular demonstration of the circulation of electrical fluid in the form of flows, discharged through oppositely charged conductors. Lighting could be "channeled," then, by metal rods erected on roofs and grounded in the earth. Advertised and tested throughout the Newtonian public sphere of the 1750s, the lightning rod fully emerged as a political symbol during the American Revolution against British commercial domination. Franklin was the Revolution's representative in France, living in Passy, outside Paris, when his advocacy of pointed lightning rods became a grounding symbol of the Enlightenment's faith in republican political reform. By 1778, with the treaty of alliance between France and the colonies, Franklin's lightning rod signified a physico-political alliance between the French and American Enlightenments. Arriving in Paris in December 1776, Franklin, then in his late seventies, crippled by gout, the "stone" and an annoying skin condition (perhaps eczema), quickly emerged as an icon of revolution and hero of the international Enlightenment. Pictured in portraits, busts, and engravings, and praised by philosophers-Voltaire and Turgot, Franklin's French admirers declared (in Latin) *Eripuit coelo fulmen sceptrumque tyrannis*: "He seized lightning from the heavens and the scepter from tyrants."

Technically, of course, Franklin did not have to seize lightning from heaven: it already existed in all matter, everywhere on earth. As philosophical readers of the *New Experiments* would know, Franklin's electrical aether inhered in all things as, in effect, the power of the bio-political and techno-scientific Enlightenment, waiting to be tapped. As techno-science, Franklin's lightning rod was a water-witching instrument presaging the dams, canals, and hydroelectrical projects of industrial modernization. As both a universal resource and the tool of its extraction, electricity simply awaited Enlightened Newtonian "husbandmen" to collect and channelize it through commerce, education, and social engineering – or to release it more explosively in fiery wars against tyranny, magic, and "rigid" fundamentalisms. Throughout the eighteenth century, wars between the European imperial powers sent periodic shock waves through the commercial and political networks of the Atlantic world. Particularly memorable in this regard, the Seven Years or French and Indian War (1756–1763) – sometimes called the first "world war" – fomented violence throughout the North American interior, deployed American Indian warriors as military allies on both sides, and generated economic upheaval in urban seaports. During the Seven Years War, Franklin became personally immersed in the military and economic facts of British colonial policy – provisioning the British army, procuring gunpowder, building forts, making Indian treaties, and speculating in Ohio lands with Pennsylvania trader Samuel Wharton.

A surprising number of Franklin's experiments involve military ordinance, deployed to test the conducting properties of metals, and the ignition of gunpowder. If electricity was entertaining, it was also dangerous. On one hand, Franklin's lightning rod and his knowledge of military matters, including explosives, were valuable to the members of the British government who consulted with him about defending gunpowder supplies from lightning. On the other hand, however, Franklin's electrical skills, like his experience in the American French and Indian War, were also something of a worry. As J.L. Heilbron recalls, a rumor agitated London in the early days of the American Revolution that Franklin had invented an infernal bomb "the size of a toothpick case," that could reduce St Paul's Cathedral to ashes (2007: 353). In another instance, the British worried that Franklin was plotting to incinerate the British fleet by erecting a series of deflecting mirrors along the coast of France, which was then allied with the Revolutionary colonies (Chaplin, 2006: 256).

Despite its dangers, however, lightning rod experiments encouraged imitators across Europe. Predictably, the Newtonian fad produced collateral damage, including a freak accident in St Petersburg that reminded readers that lightning was still a marvel and a mystery, even for Newtonian weathermen. In 1752, a natural philosopher in St Petersburg named Georg Wilhelm Richmann planned to replicate the Euro-American experiments with lightening. Undertaken in virtually every European capital in the 1750s, the idea was to both prove the efficacy of the lighting rod to one's national community, and seize enough power from heaven to circulate one's name in the Newtonian public sphere. Richmann set up his electrical apparatus in the summer of 1752, and awaited a thunder storm. When clouds appeared on the horizon, he hurried home in the company of one Sokolov, his engraver from the Russian Imperial Academy.

Reaching home, Richmann went directly to his electrical apparatus at the window. The storm was far away and the sky relatively clear, the darkest clouds in the distance. Approaching the lightning rod, and leaning over the electrical indicator, Richmann was standing a foot away from the iron rod, when "a palish blue ball of fire, as big as a fist, came out of the rod without any contact whatsoever. It went right to the forehead of the professor, who in that instant fell back without uttering a sound" (Stenhoff, 1999: 75). Engraved prints of the disaster as witnessed by Sokolov circulated in magazines and books through the eighteenth and even nineteenth centuries. Medical details follow, mingling empirical transparency with graphic horror: "There appeared a red spot from the forehead from which spurted some drops of blood through the pores, without wounding the surrounding skin. The shoe belonging to the left foot was burst open. Uncovering the foot at that place they found a blue mark, by which it is concluded that the electrical force of the thunder, having forced into the head, made its way out again at the foot" (Stenhoff, 1999: 75). Accounts of Richmann's death dramatize the "fist of fire," a detail that suggests supernatural agency, in an episode reminiscent of Wieland's fictional combustion, and of the curious 1776 case of the Italian Priest Bertholi, who ignited while kneeling at prayer. Indeed, Richmann's death continues to be referenced today as an early account of a still-unexplained phenomenon known as ball lightning.

From the eighteenth through the twentieth century, reports of ball lightning describe luminous "balls" of lightning, large and small, tumbling from mountains, or stormy skies, to strike their victims with an unexpected, fatal shock. Like spontaneous combustion, ball lightning was an eighteenth-century marvel, emerging between fact and faith. Both underline the epistemological strangeness of Newtonian experiments with the fiery fluids of life (and death) imagined as flows, inherent in all "particulate matter" – organic, animate, or inanimate. Richmann's electrocution is another possible source for Wieland's death in Brown's novel, in which Wieland's doctor, rushing to his aid, witnesses a strange "cloud" of light above the victim (1798: 19). Like Wieland's combustion, Richmann's electrocution raises questions of causality that are rife with anxiety, paranoia, and even conspiracy. What power is it, these stories ask, that the international Enlightenment not only evokes from, but channels into and through, the systems of living organisms?

16.3 Fire, Water, and Fur

Crucially, electricity did not generate combustion by means of momentum. On the contrary, it operated as a form of internal combustion, by engaging the +/− "currents" within every body. The electrical fluid did not penetrate from outside, through the force of momentum, like a bullet or a fist. Consider, for example, in the small town of Cremona, Italy, where, in 1777, the weather vane of a church was struck by lightning and perforated with eighteen holes. Following the lightning strike, Italian scientist Carlo Barletti suggested in *Analisi d'un nuovo Fenomeno del Fulmine*, that the vane, made of hammered copper and tin, had been perforated by two separate streams, made up of multiple threads of lightning, striking each side of the vane at the same instant. Barletti believed, erroneously as Franklin notes, that the perforations were occasion'd (if I understand him rightly) by Streams or Threads of Electric Matter, of different and contrary kinds,

> rushing violently towards each other, and meeting with the Vane, so accidentally placed, as to be found precisely in the Place of their Meeting, where it was pierc'd by all of them, they all striking on both its Sides at the same Instant. This however is so extraordinary an Accident as to be in the Author's own Opinion almost miraculous. (Franklin to Ingenhousz, June 21, 1782; PBF, 37: 504)

In fact, the miracle lay in Barletti's failure to distinguish between momentum and the more "subtle" operation of electricity. Barletti defined electricity as streams of liquid or projectiles with momentum, rather than as a dynamic (+/−) evoking the electrical fluid already within the hammered metal – the particulate aether-net – of the weather vane itself. Barletti imagined lightning arriving with the force of momentum from outside, perforating the metal from two sides at once, like fists of fire, or bullets trailing streams of light from the sky. In fact, Franklin politely explains, the perforations were not caused "by the Force of a Projectile passing thro'," but rather by the Explosion or the Dilation in passing, of a single, "subtil Line of Fluid." No experiments in electricity, he continues, have yet "proved that the electric Fluid in its violent Passage thro' the Air … has what we call a Momentum." Instead it, in effect, channels itself through bodies (called conductors) by engaging dynamically with the fire within: it is not "a Force capable of pushing forward, or overthrowing the objects it strikes against, even tho' it sometimes pierces them" (PBF, 37: 50). Yet as other experiments reveal, electricity *was* somehow connected with heat.

If electricity lacked momentum, however, it was allied with heat. Both, when unobstructed, would burn, explode, ignite, and kill. "When the electrical fire," Franklin writes, "strikes through a body, it acts upon the common fire contained in it, and puts that fire in motion; and if there be sufficient quantity of each kind of fire, the body will be inflamed" (Cohen, 1941: 210). Because heat was cooperative with electricity, Franklin's *Experiments* focus repeatedly on how moisture, temperature, and fermentation affect the conduction versus nonconduction of electricity. Like his colleagues Fontana, Priestley, and Ingenhausz, Franklin attended closely to phase transitions marked by the contraction versus expansion, separation, and dissipation of matter. During combustion, they noted, both heat and electricity acted to separate the "parts" of solid materials by melting, dissolving, or shattering, as well as emitting light. In such cases, Franklin theorizes, the electrical fire either meets or becomes the fire of heat. Following experiments on rats, turkeys, gunpowder, hammered gold leaf, and coal, he concludes, "Common fire, is in all bodies more or less, as well as electrical fire. Perhaps they may be different modifications of the same element; or they may be different elements" (Cohen, 1941: 210).

Evidence of the relationship between heat and electricity lay in the pain caused by the mutual repulsion or internal fissuring of "parts" when either electricity or heat is applied to a human or animal body. Gunpowder explodes, marshes blaze, spirits fire, steeples collapse, trees shatter, and dissipated women burst into flame because "the fire" already existed in them:

> There is a certain Quantity of this Fluid, called Fire, in every living human Body, which Fluid, being in due Proportion, keeps the Parts of the Flesh and Blood at such a just Distance from each other, as that the Flesh and Nerves are suple, and the Blood fit for Circulation. ... if too much of this Fluid be communicated to the Flesh, the Parts are separated too far, and Pain ensues as when they are separated by a Pin or Lancet. The Sensation that the Separation by Fire occasions, we call Heat, or Burning ... (Franklin to Ebenezer Kinnersley, February 20, 1762; PBF, 12: 232)

In Franklin's *New Experiments*, 'fire' is an all-purpose word for any phase-changing "fluid" (sometime called "*menstrua*" by eighteenth-century metal-smiths) that "separates," liquifies, or dissipates matter – as when wine is heated, gold melts, or lightning strikes a human or animal body. In applications of electrical current and/or heat, gunpowder explodes, spirits ignite, marshes blaze, steeples collapse, trees shatter, foundations explode, and dissipated women burst into flame because the fire already existed in them "in a solid State, being only discovered when separating." Coal, for instance, "contain[s] a great deal of solid Fire," while "Gunpowder is almost all solid Fire" (PBF, 12: 232).

In animals, however, the separating action of heat or lightning could be affected by water and other "juices." If the physics of fire had applications, in industry, military affairs, and public safety, it was also essential to the maintenance of organic life. Like his Austrian friend Ingenhousz, Franklin hypothesized that the conversion of the life-giving heat of plants into the "fire" of animal and human life was accomplished by the "juices" of digestion Franklin's own attention to the physiology of juicy or "watry" fluids was an extension of his work on the fires of heat and electricity. For instance, he writes in 1757, "I imagine that Animal Heat arises by or from a Kind of Fermentation in the Juices of the Body, in the same Manner as Heat arises in the Liquors preparing for Distillation; wherein there is a separation of the spirituous from the watry and earthy parts" (Franklin to John Lining, April 14, 1757; PBF, 7: 184).

If heat and fermentation were necessary to animal life, the juices of living bodies also made them excellent conductors Given the conducting capacity of fluid systems, therefore, it was wiser to stand in an open field, rather than under a sap-filled tree, during an electrical storm:

> [W]hen the cloaths are wet, if a flash in its way to the ground should strike your head, it may run in the water over the surface of your body; whereas, if your cloathes were dry, it would go through the body, because the blood and other humours, containing so much water, are more ready conductors. Hence a wet rat cannot be killed by the exploding electrical bottle, when a dry rat may. (Cohen, 1941: 209–210)

Unlike the turkeys of Franklin's electrical party, rats stand in for human bodies in this "wet fur" experiment. Franklin experimented repeatedly with rats and small animals. Further animal research would suggest to him, in fact, that a larger glass Leyden jar might have killed the rat "though wet" (Cohen, 1941: 210n). Like fur or feathers, human skin (wet or dry) affected conduction as well as maintaining or communicating body heat.

In "Electric Body Manipulation as Performance Art" (2009) Arthur Elsenaar and Remko Scha point out that the Leyden jar was deployed to electrocute an unknown number of small animals in Europe and the Americas during the late eighteenth century. Experiments performed by Franklin and Priestley alone (along with Daniel Gralath of Danzig, who experimented on insects) sacrificed a virtual barnyard of beetles, rats, shrews, dogs, cats, geese, guinea fowls, chickens, and turkeys. Eighteenth-century Leyden jars simply could not generate enough charge to electrocute a human being, however, although they were powerful enough "to violate the integrity" of the body "and cause major or minor damage," such as nose-bleeds, unconsciousness, and mild amnesia (Elsenaaar and Scha, 2002: 19). Franklin's experiments with electrocution were limited to animals; but, as Elsenaar and Scha rightly conclude, "We all know where this would lead. The deadly experiments with animals presage the deliberate electrocution of humans" (3). The electric chair would not be invented until 1890, following the construction of New York City's first central electric generating plants by the Edison Company. Like the guillotine of revolutionary Paris in 1793, the electric chair was conceived as a humane form of execution. Unfortunately, things did not go as smoothly as planned when the first man to die in the chair (William Kemmler) was electrocuted. He required two separate applications of the fire: his body smoked and his skin burned unevenly. Spectators fled the acrid odor and putrid exhalations. The electrocution of animals, meanwhile, continued apace, as documented by Thomas Edison's silent film of 1903, *Electrocuting an Elephant*, in which Topsy, an elephant deemed dangerous at Coney Island's Luna Park, is executed with cyanide and an AC current measuring 6,600 volts (the 'voltaic' measurement being named after the Italian Newtonian Alessandro Volta). Coney Island had initially considered hanging the elephant but after protests by the New York Humane Society, electrocution was deemed more humanitarian, having been used to execute human criminals since 1890.

If bodies burned and smoked during electrocution, "spirits" were more readily fired. Like other early industrialists, Franklin viewed alcoholic spirits from a medico-moral point of view, as an obstacle to progress and sign of socioeconomic regression, forged in the fiery hell of the devil himself. Franklin made precisely these connections in his humorous description of a 1750 treaty meeting at Carlisle with Iroquois, Delaware, and other "Ohio Indians." Franklin was a Pennsylvania commissioner at the Carlisle treaty, which was also attended by the German/American translator Conrad Weiser and the Iroquois leader Half-King, or Tanaghrisson. But, recalling the event in his autobiography, Franklin's most vivid recollection is of a hellish scene of Indians wild with "spirits." Faced with some 100 Algonquian and Iroquoian Indians drunk with rum at the end of the treaty negotiations, Franklin interprets the scene as a Providential sign that the Iroquois, Mingo, Delaware, and Shawnee would eventually be extirpated from the Ohio country, to make way for the "Cultivators of the earth."

> They were all drunk Men and Women, quarreling and fighting. Their darkcolor'd Bodies, half naked, seen only by the gloomy Light of the Bonfire, running after and beating one another with Firebrands, accompanied by their horrid Yellings, form'd a Scene the most resembling our ideas of Hell that could well be imagin'd. At Midnight a Number of them came thundering at our Door, demanding more Rum; of which we took no Notice. (Franklin, 1986a: 135)

This demonic scene immediately follows Franklin's account of his experiences during the Great Awakening revivalism of the 1740s, when he was able to find universal principles of moral duty in virtually every Protestant sect of Pennsylvania, from the evangelical theologies of George Whitfield and Gilbert Tennant to the Moravian followers of Zinzendorf. When it comes to Native American beliefs and customs, however, the only element Franklin seems to recognize in his memoirs (apart from "the Great Spirit") are alcoholic spirits. Franklin casts the drunken Indians as un-Enlightened, nonmodern peoples, by setting their "dark bodies" against the light of combustion, while signaling his own detachment from their dissipated "thundering." "And indeed," Franklin writes, "if it be the Design of Providence to extirpate these Savages to make way for the Cultivators of the Earth, it seems not improbable that Rum may be the appointed means. It has already annihilated all the Tribes who formerly inhabited the Seacoast" (Franklin, 1986a: 135–136). Franklin offsets this grim forecast, however, with a parody of Indian oratory, in the humorous style of his Parisian "bagatelles." When an old Indian "counselor" arrives to apologize for the debauchery, his words both mock and support Franklin's views: "*The Great Spirit, who made all things, made everything for some use, and whatever use he designed anything for, that use it should always be put to. Now, when he made rum, he said, 'Let this be for the Indians to get drunk with,' and it must be so*" (Franklin, 1986a: 135).

When Franklin penned this reductive philosophizing, his words reflected his financial involvement in an ultimately unsuccessful land speculation scheme in western Pennsylvania. Franklin's interest in Ohio Indian lands began in 1768, with the first treaty at Fort Stanwix, called to address the geopolitical consequences of French defeat in the Seven Years (or the French and Indian) War. With the British victorious in North America, the attention of colonial investors, settlers, and land speculators had begun to turn west. While the Fort Stanwix treaty was organized to adjudicate the boundary line separating the colonies from British-managed Indian territory, a group of land speculators, including Franklin, his son William, Samuel Wharton, and William Trent used the opportunity to obtain an enormous grant of land, roughly one-fourth the size of present day West Virginia, from the Iroquois confederacy, in direct violation of British laws limiting white settlement to the east side of the Allegheny River. The goal of Franklin's group, known later as the Grand Ohio Company, was to found the fourteenth American colony, to be named "Vandalia" or, less arcanely, "Westsylvania."

Franklin's cartoonish depiction of Indians "fired up" with liquor justifies both his own financial investment in Indian land, and the +/− social dynamics of rising and failing set forth elsewhere in his autobiography. Like disorganized debtors, spongy wetlands, and belief in magic, Native Americans who abused fermented spirits would naturally take fire and fade from the landscape of Enlightened commerce and cultivation. Historians rarely connect Franklin's darkly humorous political anecdotes with his electrical papers, or with the structure of the Newtonian public sphere. But Franklin's satiric and scientific discourses are not disjunctive. They are connected by the dynamics of structural difference (plus/minus, attraction/repulsion, contraction/expansion) deployed as a social and economic as well as Newtonian analytic. The physics of plus and minus (+/−) functioned as a universal system of accounting, a global grade book for recording flows of peoples, commodities, money, and information on the model of hydraulic exchanges.

As might be expected, given his interest in Indian lands, and his sensitivity to stasis, decay, and nonconduction, Franklin was an avid proponent of free, or privately managed, trade. In 1766, his protests against the British mercantilist regulation of American commerce included a series of reflections on British laws regulating the North American fur trade. Written "at the Request of Lord Shelburne," Franklin's analysis of British trade policy draws an explicit parallel between the impossibility of regulating the vast American interior and the absurdity of trying to control colonial commerce with taxes, tariffs, and regulations which unjustly strengthened the British economy at the expense of her colonies.

With the defeat of France and the acquisition of Canada in 1763, the Board of Trade under William Petty, Lord Shelburne, had begun to draft new regulations for the far-flung American commercial networks connecting the Native peoples of the continental interior with the restive colonies and, through them, with the markets and manufactories of Europe. Like the French before them, the British fur trade employed Native peoples as harvesters, hunters, slaughterers, and processers of animal skin. These skins included deerskin as well as beaver, otter, marten, and fox fur, with which the eastern half of North America was still extraordinarily rich, even after decades of harvesting for international markets. In return for valuable pelts and skins obtained by Indian labor, British manufacturers shipped "Indian trade" goods (textiles, beads, axes, mirrors, pots, pans, sugar, tea and, unofficially, guns, gunpowder, and alcohol) over the Atlantic to be exchanged for furs by Anglo-American and/or *metis* middlemen, scattered through the interior from Newfoundland to the Gulf of Mexico. Remarkably, the British administered the vast Indian trade, and managed the contested Proclamation Line separating the Indians from the colonies, by means of two American "Superintendants" and their agencies, one for the sprawling Northern and another for the Southern district.

By 1766, however, the colonies had begun to actively protest British trade regulations of all kinds, including regulation of the Indian trade. In London, their diplomatic mouthpiece was Franklin. In a series of impressively astute comments on Shelburne's forty-four proposed regulations of the Indian trade, Franklin waxed eloquent on the "unnaturalness" of British efforts to regulate commerce in the vast forests of North America. Responding to the thirty-third regulation in Shelburne's list – that "all trade will be carried on by tariffs set by the commissaries at the … truckhouses" – Franklin seizes the chance to make a point about the British obstruction of colonial commerce as well as the Indian trade. The British colonial government must allow a free flow of transactions in a trade network conducted by buyer and seller alone (September 13, 1766; PBF, 13: 433):

> It seems contrary to the Nature of Commerce for Government to interferc in the Prices of Commodities. Trade is a voluntary Thing between Buyer and Seller, in every Article of which each exercises his own Judgment and is to please himself. Suppose either trader or Indian is dissatisfied with the Tariff, and refuses to barter on those Terms: Are the Refusers to be compell'd? If not, Why should an Indian be forbidden to take more Goods for his Skins that your Tariff allows if the Trader is willing to give them; or a Trader more Skins for his Goods if the Indian is willing to give them? … the separate Desire of each to get most Custom will operate in bringing their Goods down to a reasonable Price. It therefore seems to me, that Trade will best find and make its own Rates. And that Government cannot well interfere, unless it would take the whole Trade into its own Hands, as in some Colonies it does, and manage it by its own Servants at its own Risque.

When he wrote these lines, Franklin was in London arguing the case against British mercantilist constraints on the thirteen colonies. In addition to taxes on paper, tea, or sugar, the British had forbidden Americans to manufacture or export goods within certain sectors of the American consumer economy monopolized by British manufactures or trade goods. By the early 1770s, after more than ten years of conciliatory diplomatic efforts, Franklin had come to recognize that, despite the support of pro-American statesmen such as William Pitt, the British would accept neither the principles of free trade and equal representation, nor the legitimacy of colonial economic interests on a par with British commerce and manufactures. Especially onerous to Franklin were British laws forbidding not only the export of American manufactures but the restriction of free use of North American resources, including, in particular, the trading, selling, and processing of beaver, marten, otter, or fox skins. Motivated by resentment over economic subordination, the American Revolution was a sharp commercial rejection of British trade regulations. Laws such as the Navigation Act, Hatters Act, Steel, Hammer and Slit Iron Acts, levied by a distant, prejudicial, and rigid British political hierarchy, were experienced by many American tradesmen and legislators as damaging, demeaning attempts to subordinate them. British regulations had turned the colonies into a market for British commodities (textiles, hats, metal goods) while exploiting lucrative American natural resources (furs, lumber, ore) at the expense of colonial craftsmen.

The Hatters Act was a particularly egregious policy, of considerable symbolic significance to both the colonists and the French, who had once dominated the North American fur trade. This Act forbade American hatters to make use the furs and skins harvested "in their own backyard" or to manufacture hats for export or domestic use. Among other repressive British regulations, Franklin had complained for years about the Hatters Act, forbidding American hatters to manufacture hats of beaver, marten, and other indigenous furs, while enforcing the export of American furs to Britain for use by British hatters. Writing as "Benevolus" in 1767 Franklin confronted claims that the British had a right to tax the colonies simply because the British army had protected them from the French and Indians during the Seven Years War. On the contrary, Franklin declared, it was the British interests in the fur trade that had motivated the war in America. The British had fought to maintain control "of the Ohio trade with the Indians, a trade carried on chiefly for account of British merchants ... [and for] the manufactures of Britain, which had also all the skins and furs produced by that trade ..." (PBF, 14: 110).

In his 1768 "Causes of the American Discontents" Franklin complained that "the Hatters of England have prevailed to obtain an Act in their own favor, restraining that manufacture in America, in order to oblige the Americans to send their beaver to England to be manufactured, and purchase back the hats, loaded with the charges of a double transportation" (January 5, 1768; PBF, 15: 3). In his 1766 responses to Sherburne's regulations of the Indian trade, in which Sherburne proposed to tax all furs exported (to Britain), as a way of financing British administration of the trade, Franklin responded, tight-lipped (PBF, 15: 3):

> As the Goods for the Indian Trade all go from England, and the Peltry is chiefly brought to England perhaps is will be best to lay the Duty [on England for] the Exportation of [Peltry], and the importation of 'Trade Goods' and avoid meddling with the Question of Right to lay Duties in America by Parliament here.

Privately, in angry marginalia to a British pamphlet supporting British commercial policies toward the colonies, Franklin summarized his views in a tone he ordinarily repressed (PBF, 17: 348):

> I am sick of these forced Obligations. As to the great Kindness of these 558 Parliamentary Guardians of American Privileges, who can forbear smiling that has seen the Navigation Act, the Hatters Act, the Steel, Hammer and Slit Iron Acts, and numberless others restraining our Trade, obstructing our Manufactures, and forbidding us the Use of the Gifts of God and Nature? Hopeful Guardians truly!

With the Hatters Act, then, both France and the American colonies had, in effect, lost the Seven Years War for commercial dominance in North America. Subordinated within the British mercantile system, the colonists of 1766 could suddenly identify with France's defeat and humiliation in 1763. In the decade prior to the Revolutionary War, the thirteen colonies, with access to the most bountiful fur resources in the eighteenth-century world east of Siberia, were required to buy hats from British or Dutch hat-makers. Intolerably, North American hatters and furriers were forced to watch while American beaver, fox, otter, and pine marten pelts were shipped across the Atlantic to be made into hats in Europe, and returned for sale in the colonies at high cost. It was within this fur-trading matrix of British, Euro-American, French, and Native American interests that Franklin appeared in Paris in the winter of 1776, wearing a soft hat made of pine marten fur, or "American sable" (Buskirk *et al.*). In January of 1777, he described the appearance of his "cap" among the "Powder'd Heads of Paris," in an affectionate letter to Mary (Polly) Hewson, the daughter of his London landlady:

> My dear Polley Figure to yourself an old Man with grey Hair appearing under a Martin Fur Cap, among the Powder'd heads of Paris. It is this odd Figure that salutes you; with Handfuls of Blessings on you and your dear little ones. (Franklin to Mary Hewson, January 12, 1777; PBF, 23: 155)

Suffering from a skin condition, and likely needing a soft hat to cover his scalp (and protect it from cold), Franklin's "Martin Fur" cap also signaled the rapacious commercial dynamics of international geopolitics in the age of Enlightenment. Among other things it implied that both the French, expelled from the fur fields of North America, and the colonies, restrained by British trade policies, were equally oppressed by the same imperial enemy. Signaling their joint interest in the vast Indian trade, where control of land meant control of the fur trade, Franklin's pine marten cap heralded the Franco-American military alliance he had arrived in Paris to achieve. French and American interests were one in their resentment of British commercial tyranny in North America. Geopolitically, a pine marten hat (unlike the more commonplace and business-like "beaver") signaled control of the continental interior and the Indian trade from the Ohio country to the Great Lakes and beyond. If gold and silver had fueled Spanish colonialism in South America, deerskin and fine furs were a privileged currency of empire in eighteenth century North America.

The pine marten, harvested throughout the Northeastern woodlands, was a recognized North American commodity. Sometimes referred to as "American sable," marten fur was a North American answer to Russian sable, worn by tsars and princes for centuries and by British royalty since the reign of Henry VIII. A royal trophy of great value, sable had been harvested in Siberia almost as long as memory has served. A "Sable Road" intersected the Spice Road at Tobolsk, Siberia's capital, from which the Russians ran the eighteenth-century sable trade. During Franklin's lifetime the pine marten was abundant in the woods of eastern Canada and the northern colonies, its soft fur valued by Europeans for its warmth and silky, luxurious texture. Some fifty years after the American Revolution, the pine martin verged on extinction – like the once vast beaver populations of the northeastern and middle colonies. On Franklin's head, however, it substituted for hair, both his own, and the powdered wig ordinarily worn on diplomatic occasions as a matter of fashion, or mark of privilege and statesmanship, in most European capitals. From the perspective of hemostatics and heat flow, of course, marten fur also kept the heat from pouring from his head, as from a chimney. Most important of all, perhaps, being silky and soft, it encouraged petting from the French women who reportedly showed such an interest in him in the philosophical/republican circles of Enlightenment Paris.

As luxurious "natural" commodities, pine marten, beaver, fox, mink, and otter furs had enriched France prior to the Seven Years War. On Franklin's head, the fur of the American sable charmingly displayed American resistance to British trade regulations, British Parliament, and the "royal brute" himself, George III, excoriated in Tom Paine's *Common Sense* and demonized in the *Declaration of Independence*. Franklin hoped to seduce the French into supporting the American Revolution, because, without French assistance, the war was likely doomed. Wearing the marten pelt as a "native" American wig, Franklin signaled to a fashion-sensitive French audience that, from the point of view of commerce, fashion, and love, their alliance would serve both colonial and French interests. As recently proved by the colonies' unsuccessful 1775 invasion of Quebec City, Franklin's headgear suggested that, by supporting the American war, the French might directly or indirectly regain control of their lost American empire. In diplomacy, then, as in electrical entertainments, flirting involved negotiating a matrix of underlying interests, and a fine line between attraction and repulsion. Franklin's "Martin fur" cap was not, in other words, a Davy Crocket-style pelt of raccoon hair, with a tail. It was a complex sign of the British-dominated Indian trade and of French humiliation in the French and Indian War, a republican political statement within the bourgeois public sphere, and a signal of violence (and alliance) in yet another war of empire.

Franklin's own lightness as a humorist and rhetorician has long deflected attention from the Enlightenment's historical emergence against a background of oppression, catastrophe, and war. As a result, his relationship to the Enlightenment has been rather poorly understood. What is the connection between the bright hopes of the Revolutionary Enlightenment, -including Franklin's faith in secular, rational self-determination- and an eighteenth-century marked by poverty, ecocide, slavery, epidemic illness, and war? In the final decades of the eighteenth century, the international Enlightenment proclaimed the Rights of Man and the Age of Reason, freedom from tyranny, and improved conditions for the suffering poor. In the process, the bourgeois public sphere carried messages of abolition and women's "equality," as well as revolution. By the 1790s, after Franklin's death, the public sphere conveyed news of almost apocalyptic significance – for those with ears to hear. A *novus ordo seclorum* or "new order of the ages" was dawning, to be governed by the universal rights of Man and the laws of nature – including Newtonian fluid systems theory. But such declarations put a brave face on dark times. Viewed from the perspective of fluid dynamics, or the philosophies of flow, the bourgeois Enlightenment resembles a boat fueled ingeniously by its own internal combustion- or a self-reflecting mirror, raised like a shield against the organic chaos of what appears to be, by contrast, a Gothic night of death by drowning. For this reason, it is easy to understand why modern scholars, operating within the enduring educational, economic, and technological apparatuses of the international Enlightenment, have had difficulty locating Franklin's face against the brightness of the light he did so much to generate.

Note

1 Labaree, Leonard W., Willcox William, Oberg Barbara, *et al.*, eds. (1959–). *The Papers of Benjamin Franklin*. 39 vols to date. New Haven, CT: Yale University Press. Hereafter referred to as PBF.

Further Reading

Anderson, Fred, and Andrew Cayton (2005). *The Dominion of War: Empire and Liberty in North America*. New York, NY.

Carlos, Ann Marina (2010). *Commerce by a Frozen Sea: Native Americans and the European Fur Trade*. Philadelphia, PA.

Cohen, I. Bernard (1956). *Franklin and Newton: An Inquiry into Speculative Newtonian Experimental Science and Franklin's Work in Electricity as an Example Thereof*. Memoirs of the American Philosophical Society 43. Philadelphia, PA.

Ferguson, Robert A (1997). *The American Enlightenment, 1750–1820*. Cambridge, MA.

Foucault, Michel (1977). *The History of Sexuality, Volume One: An Introduction*, translated by Robert Hurley. New York: Vintage Books.

Foucault, Michel (1984). "What is Enlightenment?" ("Qu'est-ce que les Lumières?"), in *The Foucault Reader*, Paul Rabinow, ed. New York, NY: Pantheon, pp. 32–50.

Godineau, Dominique (1998). *The Women of Paris and Their French Revolution*. Translated by Katherine Streip. Berkeley, CA.

Kafer, Peter (2004). *Charles Brockden Brown's Revolution and the Birth of the American Gothic*. Philadelphia, PA.

Latour, Bruno (1993). *We Have Never Been Modern*. Translated by Catherine Porter. Cambridge, MA.

Linebaugh, Peter (2000). *The Many-headed Hydra: Sailors, Slaves, Commoners, and the Hidden History of the Revolutionary Atlantic*. Boston, MA.

Mah, Harold (2004). *Enlightenment Phantasies: Cultural Identity in France and Germany, 1750–1914*. Ithaca, NY.

Milburn, Colin (2008). *Nanovision: Engineering the Future*. Durham, NC.

Noble, David F. (1998). *The Religion of Technology: The Divinity of Man and The Spirit of Invention*. New York, NY.

Pace, Antonio (1958). *Benjamin Franklin and Italy*. Philadelphia, PA.

Pancaldi, Giuliano (2005). *Volta, Science and Culture in the Age of Enlightenment*. Princeton, NJ.

Schmidt, Leigh Eric (2000). *Hearing Things: Religion, Illusion, and the American Enlightenment*. Cambridge, MA.

Chapter Seventeen

Benjamin Franklin, Associations, and Civil Society

Albrecht Koschnik

Eighteenth-century Anglo-Americans embraced the increasing opportunities for "projecting" new civic institutions and new forms of voluntary association to advance science, literature, and education, to address the numerous problems created by emerging urban spaces, and to answer public needs where government would not act (see P. Clark, 2000; M. Novak, 2008). Benjamin Franklin was the leading builder of civic institutions in colonial British North America, joining private initiative to achieve public ends in an unprecedentedly broad range of fields. His efforts included the creation of the first subscription library, the first fire company, the first scientific organization, Pennsylvania's first militia, as well as a host of other civic initiatives. And his associational connections furthered his own advancement. At a time when the opportunities for even the most enterprising skilled artisans were limited, Franklin became a major writer, scientist, and public figure even before he retired from his printing business and devoted his time to study and public office. Any account of Franklin's civic activism runs the danger of naturalizing his actions: He is seen as the archetypical associator, "the first American" (Brands), whose life reveals unchanging features of American middle-class culture (Isaacson, 2003). But the task of the historian is to explain in what specific ways and for what specific reasons Franklin chose to spearhead the creation of civic institutions. Conflict and contradictions are not discernible in his *Autobiography*, whose reinvention of his life obscures rather than illuminates the context and sources of his civic activism.

Franklin figures prominently in the scholarly literature on the eighteenth-century public sphere (see especially Warner), but goes largely unnoticed in

A Companion to Benjamin Franklin, First Edition. Edited by David Waldstreicher.
© 2011 Blackwell Publishing Ltd. Published 2011 by Blackwell Publishing Ltd.

the recent work on the history of civil society in the United States, with the exception of Kathleen McCarthy's *American Creed*. Civil society is here understood as the space between the family and the state occupied by institutions grounding social and political movements, economic activity, community building, as well as a broad range of public debate and inquiry. Franklin's absence from the civil-society literature can be easily explained by the distinct disciplinary contexts in which work on these issues has been done. The public sphere has been of particular interest to early Americanists, not the least in American literature and American studies, and most of the influential work has focused on the eighteenth century. In contrast, the concept of civil society has been most fruitfully explored in political science and historical sociology, which are primarily concerned with the nineteenth and twentieth centuries. Historians of early America are now in the process of charting the development of civil society in colonial America and the early national United States (among others, Ryan, 1999; W.J. Novak, 2001; Brooke, 2004; M. Harris, 2005; Neem, 2008; K. Butterfield, 2009). Indeed, the diversity of Franklin's endeavors to create voluntary associations and civic institutions is better represented by the term civil society. Jürgen Habermas's original formulation – "the public sphere of civil society" – points to the public sphere as one dimension of civil society (1989: 85), primarily concerned with communication and publicity and the institutions facilitating them, whereas civil society encompasses the full range of associations and institutions.

Though Franklin wrote no single, comprehensive treatise on building civil society, his various writings, including calls for civic action and the proposals and constitutions for specific institutions, constitute a summation of his thinking on these matters. In the intellectual histories describing the evolution of the concept of civil society other eighteenth-century figures, such as Adam Ferguson, Adam Smith, Jean-Jacques Rousseau, and Edmund Burke, play a central role, whereas Franklin goes unmentioned (representative: Ehrenberg). To the extent that general histories of civil society refer to developments in North America, Alexis de Tocqueville's *Democracy in America* acts as a representative account of American conceptions of civil society. This essay concentrates on Franklin's years in Philadelphia and London, 1723 to 1757, and on his own writings and the recent literature on his civic efforts and involvement in the scientific, literary, and philanthropic worlds of the eighteenth century, and applies them to an exploration of the civil-society dimensions of his life. Inevitably, a consideration of Franklin's civic endeavors becomes an engagement with contemporary debates about the status of American civil society, of questions about self-interest and altruism, and communitarianism versus individualism. In this regard Franklin stands at the center of some of the most salient questions in American social and intellectual history.

When Franklin arrived in Philadelphia in 1723 the town had no civic institutions. On the eve of the American Revolution, Charleston, Boston,

New York, and Philadelphia possessed libraries, scientific and learned societies, fire and insurance companies, as well as ethnic and fraternal societies in a diversity and sophistication unimaginable at the beginning of the eighteenth century. Franklin played a central role in the emergence of this new associational world in the colonies. Emulation and innovation fused in his conception and realization of civic activism. During his first stay in London, December 1724 to July 1726, he frequented coffeehouses and taverns. There he immersed himself in talk about books and magazines that developed a new civic sensibility, such as Richard Steele and Joseph Addison's *Tatler* (1709–1711) and *Spectator* (1711–1712) (which Franklin had already seen in Boston and copied and memorized), John Trenchard and Thomas Gordon's *Cato's Letters* (1720–1723), and the Third Earl of Shaftesbury's "Sensus Communis, an Essay on the Freedom of Wit and Humor" (in *Characteristics of Men, Manners, Opinions, Times,* 1711). After his return to Philadelphia Franklin drew on the interests and skills he had honed in London. As a writer and as the printer and editor of the *Pennsylvania Gazette* he contributed to the emergence of a print public sphere in the colonies, primarily carried by newspapers. Following Michael Warner, Franklin became "the first American to fashion a career entirely of letters" – at a time when religious and political authorities gained and exercised authority and influence primarily as speakers and preachers. Franklin's anonymously published newspaper essays took advantage of the print public sphere's modalities to favor general authority over personal opinion. His various pseudonyms and personas allowed him to express views "without reference to himself" (1990: 76, 84). Preserving his anonymity – and gaining the authority of a generalized anonymity – was a major accomplishment for a printer's apprentice in a world where knowing something about an author carried particular weight in determining the truth and significance of a statement.

As David Shields notes, Franklin aspired to join the "republic of letters." The term emerged in the late seventeenth-century "to designate an imagined community made up of authors and readers who recognized neither national boundaries nor religious affiliations for the free exchange of ideas, beliefs, and convictions" (2008: 50). Republics could be face-to-face gatherings, such as clubs and coffeehouses, others combined personal interaction with formal correspondence networks. Thus they were not synonymous with print, but encompassed print communication as well as all types of learned and conversational formal and informal gatherings. Whereas Michael Warner focuses on the effects of print communication, Shields points to the institutions – associations, libraries, learned societies – that shaped Franklin's conception of the republic of letters and facilitated his rise among men of letters in the British Empire. Here Franklin's preference for sociability and conversation over the public rhetoric of the pulpit and the state assembly dovetailed with the predominant form of exchange in the clubs of the republic of letters. He placed conversation over oratory, as it implied "communicative partnership and exchange," rather than authority and hierarchy (53).

For his first Philadelphia association, the Junto, Franklin found inspiration in several texts he found in his father's library and also encountered while in London that combined self-improvement with civic improvement. Daniel Defoe's *An Essay upon Projects* (1697), Cotton Mather's *Essays to do Good* (1710), and John Locke's "Rules of a Society, which met once a Week, for the Improvement of useful Knowledge, and for the promoting of Christian Truth and Charity" (in *A Collection of Several Pieces*, 1720) provided blueprints for benevolent and mutual-improvement societies. Already in the third Silence Dogood essay (1722) did Franklin note that "it is undoubtedly the Duty of all Persons to serve the Country they live in" (PBF, 1: 13).[1] Defoe suggested civic improvements similar to those Franklin later offered for Philadelphia: fire insurance, a pension fund for seamen, welfare for widows and the elderly, and academies for the children of middling parents. Mather and Defoe both emphasized the importance of cooperation to do good. Where Mather aimed to encourage piety and suppress vice, Defoe embraced self-interest and connected the pursuit of private wellbeing to advancing the public good – exactly what Franklin would present as "doing well by doing good," as the interdependent impulses of self-interest and selflessness, utilitarianism and empathy. Franklin embraced Mather's brief for doing good, and quoted him in the *Poor Richard's Almanac* for 1737 ("The noblest question in the world is *What Good may I do in it?*"; PBF, 2: 171), but separated serving humanity as a principle from its religious underpinnings (achieving salvation). Esmond Wright, however, insists that Puritanism's social conscience remained a lasting part of Franklin's outlook (see the discussion of these matters in Wright, 1986: 23–28, and Lemay, 2006a: 145–147, including reference to a likely Quaker influence – honoring God and doing good were inextricably connected). Leo Lemay points out that Franklin did not reference Mather in the first part of his autobiography, written in 1771, but revised himself in 1788, apparently more willing to acknowledge Mather's impact late in life (Leemay, 2006a: 47). In 1784 Franklin wrote Samuel Mather that his father's essays had given him "such a turn of thinking, as to have an influence on my conduct through life, for I have always set a greater value on the character of a *doer of good*, than on any other kind of reputation; and if I have been, as you seem to think, a useful citizen, the public owes the advantage of it to that book" (May 12, 1784; Franklin, 1987: 1092).

In the Junto Franklin wanted to recreate the sociability, wit, and disputation he had observed in London clubs. Founded in the fall of 1727 the Junto – the name derived from the Latin "juncta," meaning joined together – was among the first mutual-help societies in the colonies. Its members were young men, aspirational artisans and early-career professionals, who were attracted by the promise of self-improvement and social advancement – Franklin would judge it "the best School of Philosophy, Morals and Politics that then existed in the Province" (Franklin, 1964: 118). Though the discussion of divisive religious and political questions was discouraged, debating topics combined philosophy, science, self-discipline, commerce, local and imperial news, and philanthropy and civic matters. Meetings of the Junto constituted the framework for discussing many of Franklin's most important civic projects, including the library, fire fighting and fire insurance, paving the city's streets, the town watch, and the militia association. Members met every Friday evening (Lemay estimates that Franklin attended regularly until he left Philadelphia in 1757; 2006a: 355–356); they required of themselves to regularly write essays and propose discussion topics. Franklin devised a set of twenty-four "standing queries" intended to guide the members in generating fruitful subjects for discussion, not the least concerning public policy (see PBF, 1: 255–269; discussed in Lemay, 2006a: 339–342; Grimm, 1956: 441–444, notes the strong similarities between Locke's "Rules" and Franklin's queries). The proceedings of the Junto were private – effectively, it aimed, though not successfully, to be a secret society – to allow the conversation to be candid and provocative. Initially the association was called the Leather Apron Club. This led outsiders to assume that the members were the political tools of Governor Keith and parroted his opinions, since tradesmen could not have found the time and incentive to read and debate on their own. "The allegation represented quite well the contemporary assumption that reading, reflection, and debate belonged to propertied men, the only men capable of forming ideas that were not beholden to the support of others," Joyce Chaplin points out. "That seems to have been precisely the prejudice that Franklin and his friends were trying to escape. They read to improve themselves and make themselves independent gentlemen" – thus the change to Junto (2006: 41).

Kathleen McCarthy employs a central interpretive category of the recent civil-society scholarship to describe the work of the Junto. As a means for the social advancement and public service of its members the Junto created "social capital," understood as "the trust that enables individuals to work collaboratively to benefit themselves and the larger society" (2003: 18). Junto members offered Franklin contacts and information, and the meetings provided material for his newspaper columns. He received his first major printing job through a member, and two members loaned him the money to buy out his first business partner and operate the *Pennsylvania Gazette* under his sole proprietorship. Franklin also noted attempts by the original members to form additional Juntos to gather information and create more opportunities for business connections and the exercise of public influence (Franklin, 1964: 170–171). Social capital emphasizes how individuals coming together generate the goodwill and the power to transform combined personal interest into a force advancing the public good. "Self-improvement led inevitably to the improvement of city and state," concludes Esmond Wright. "What the Philadelphia Junto inculcated was the art of civic virtue, a code of municipal improvement for Philadelphia" (1986: 39).

The mutually constitutive impulses of self-improvement, social advancement, and civic improvement – the creation of social capital – and the combination of private virtue and public service ran through Franklin's entire adult life. Emphasizing his multidimensional relationships with institutions, individuals, and ideas goes against persistent misconceptions, beginning with the nineteenth-century adoption of Franklin as a "spokesman for capitalism" and the unbridled pursuit of wealth, which see him as the quintessential self-made man and entrepreneur and the first and best exhibit for the prevalence of acquisitive individualism in American culture (G.S. Wood, 2004: 13, see 246; for example, Weber, 1990; Bellah et al., 1985). But Franklin mocked "the general Foible of Mankind, in the Pursuit of Wealth to no End." He wanted people to say about him that "*He lived usefully*, [rather] than, *He died rich*" (BF to Wm. Strahan, June 2, 1750, BF to Abiah Franklin, April 12, 1750, PBF, 3: 479, 475). Further, such a view also ignores that he was the most conspicuous associator in eighteenth-century North America, all of whose civic improvement projects were cooperative ventures. Franklin's advancement and social mobility not the least depended on the patronage and encouragement of the genteel and powerful who supported him financially and eased his way into appointive offices. "He could never have made it in the way he did in that hierarchical society," concludes Gordon Wood, "if he had not been helped by men of influence and supported at crucial points" (2004: 26, see 25–27, also Zuckerman, 1993a: 154).

Franklin knew that he lived in a world of patronage and mutual obligations in which no man could act alone. At the same time, he recognized the prevalence of self-interest. In 1731 he noted that the "great Affairs of the World" were "carried on and effected by Parties," propelled by "their present general Interest," in addition to each man's "particular private Interest." "[A]s soon as a Party has gain'd its general Point, each Member becomes intent upon his particular Interest," as "few in Public Affairs act from a meer View of the Good of their Country, whatever they may pretend" (PBF, 1: 192–193). As Michael Zuckerman points out, benevolence and interest were always connected in Franklin's mind: "Even in his more self-seeking aspects, the Philadelphian did not set any sharp distinction between private pursuits and a self-conscious consideration of the public welfare" (1993b: 443). Already in the Junto did Franklin place a particular emphasis on benevolence: New members had to affirm that they "loved mankind in general," and one of the standing queries asked members was "do you think of any thing at present, in which the Junto may be serviceable to *mankind?*" (PBF, 1: 257, 259). As a newspaper editor, Michael Warner notes, political conflict led Franklin to appeal to "a neutral and rational ground of public representation, where citizens were called on to exercise civic virtue by placing the common good over personal interest" (1990: 76). In the *Proposals Relating to the Education of Youth in Pennsylvania* (1749) Franklin posited as the objective of all education the inculcation of "public spirit," rather than religion, to foster "an *Inclination* join'd with an *Ability* to serve Mankind, one's Country, Friends and Family" (PBF, 3: 412, 419). Franklin's public career offered evidence that he adhered to these principles: He did not use his postmastership to gain an advantage over his competitors in the newspaper business (unlike his predecessor William Bradford); he did not patent his stove design or the lightning rod; and he printed his advice manual concerning smallpox inoculation as well as his proposals for the militia association and the Academy at his own expense. Zuckerman sees such behavior as evidence for an "abhorrence of monopolistic exploitation of innovations" and an "attachment to open exchange of information that might better the human condition" (1993b: 446).

John C. Van Horne, much more explicitly than other commentators, points to the religious dimensions of Franklin's philanthropic appeals. Though he does not disagree with Esmond Wright that Franklin could separate civic duty from religious impulses, Van Horne focuses on the evidence that shows Franklin connecting benevolence with "pleasing God." In "On the Providence of God in the Government of the World" (1730) he noted that a belief in providence would "render us Benevolent, Useful and Beneficial to others" (PBF, 1: 269). In the following year Franklin identified charity as "that Virtue which most of all recommends us to the Deity" (*Pennsylvania Gazette*, March 25, 1731). Public appeals, such as support for the hospital, referenced charity as a Christian duty. And in the autobiography Franklin concluded that "the most acceptable Service of God was the doing Good to Man" (Franklin, 1964: 146). According to Van Horne, Franklin "held that doing good for humanity was the highest good and the act most valued and appreciated by the Creator. Thus in meeting society's needs, Franklin not only served the common good but also brought a kind of divine benediction on himself as well" (431). Van Horne also emphasizes the collective nature of Franklin's benevolence. Individual acts of charity might help on occasion, but Franklin recognized that realizing civic projects required cooperation: in his "Appeal for the Hospital" (1751) he pointed out that "the Good particular Men may do separately ... is small, compared with what they may do collectively, or by joint Endeavor and Interest" (PBF, 4: 150).

In contrast, Alan Houston argues that cooperation, mutual trust, and civic improvement grew out of commercial relations. Unlike the fellow feeling and shared values urged by Christian moralists, or the fear of social disorder that led Machiavellians to turn to the security of the "well-ordered state," eighteenth-century thinkers preoccupied with the nature and consequences of commerce, epitomized by Adam Smith, "sought to explain the emergence of cooperative social relations through the power of needs and interests. At base, they argued, humans joined together because they were useful to each other. Through the reciprocal exchange of goods and services, men and women acquired the skills and habits needed to sustain social order" (Houston, 2008: 12–13). Classical republicanism posited virtue and commerce as antithetical, with the latter corrupting all civic sentiment. But Franklin embraced a conception of civic virtue that was not at odds with commerce. Writing as "a TRADESMAN of Philadelphia," in his appeal for support of the militia association in 1747 Franklin "explicitly appealed to trade as a bond of union and motive for valor. The Association itself was funded through a lottery, making the virtuous activity of citizen-soldiers dependent on a frivolous game of chance" (63). In western political thought the body politic was often represented as a human body, which implied hierarchy (a royal head, for example), whereas Franklin, whose "touchstone was the tightly woven world of commerce," focused on interdependence and worked to convince Philadelphians that their interests coincided in defending the city. "The body politic was a commercial society, its bonding force the mutual satisfaction of needs and interests" generated by a commercial economy (79).

With the Junto meetings generating a regular stream of information and inspiration, Franklin turned to Freemasonry, which offered him a different model of associating in the pursuit of civic virtue and personal improvement. He probably observed or heard about Masonic lodges in London. Joining a lodge "represented his initial attempt at a cosmopolitan status" (Chaplin, 2006: 51). Franklin was elected a member of Philadelphia's St John's Lodge in January 1731, the earliest known lodge in the colonies, and Grand Master in June 1734. He reprinted James Anderson's *Constitutions of the Free Masons* (1734), the basic text on masonry and in demand in the colonies (there also were lodges in Boston and Charleston, and possibly in Newport and Lancaster, Pennsylvania). Franklin attended lodge meetings in Philadelphia until 1757, also on his travels in other colonies and abroad, and served as master of a French lodge in the early 1780s. Being a Mason connoted upward social mobility and promised continental and international connections and a framework for civic-mindedness that transcended colonial and imperial boundaries. Membership in a colonial lodge indeed became a marker of gentility: gentlemen could join, commoners could not. (When he joined St John's, most members were artisans, but in the course of the 1730s the new inductees were primarily merchants and professionals.) In 1731 Franklin jotted down that even the most civic-minded individuals "primarily consider'd that their own and their Country's Interest was united," rather than to act "with a View to the Good of Mankind."

Though Franklin did not reference Masonry explicitly, at the time that he joined St John's, as Gordon Wood emphasizes, he also pondered "raising a united Party for Virtue" – as a balance against "self-interested men" – by forming the "Virtuous and good Men of all nations into a regular Body, to be govern'd by suitable good and wise Rules, which good and wise Men may probably be more unanimous in their Obedience to, than common People are to common Laws." Franklin inserted these notes into his autobiography, where he added that the party – initially limited to "young and single Men only" and kept secret to "prevent the Solicitation for Admission of Improper Persons – would offer members "their Advice Assistance and Support to each other in promoting one another's Interest, Business, and Advancement in Life" ("Observations on my Reading History in Library," PBF, 1: 193; Franklin, 1964: 161–163; G.S. Wood, 2004: 42–43; see Bullock, 1996: 50–52). However, the Junto performed these tasks rather well: it met more frequently, discussed a wider range of subjects, and forced its members to actively engage in matters of civic improvement. His hope for an international civic institution remained largely unrealized.

Franklin's continuous insistence on the public usefulness of his associational activities distinguished them from other eighteenth-century ventures. Franklin's sociability and carefully-wrought literary productions made him an ideal-typical citizen of the republic of letters, and his associations aimed to facilitate the entry of colonial savants into the transatlantic republic of letters. Some of the colonial clubs and private circles described by David Shields (1997), for example, dedicated to fostering polite conversation and the literary productions of their members, often circulated in manuscript, also belonged to that republic. Dr Alexander Hamilton's Tuesday Club in Annapolis focused on burlesque, satire, and parody, and uneasily straddled matters of religion and state (Somerville). Other clubs concentrated on fellowship and competitive recreation, often in a distinctly genteel setting, such as Philadelphia's Fishing Company of the Colony in Schuylkill (which shared members with the Junto). But Franklin suffused even his most private circles such as the Junto with the insistence on the public usefulness of the members' associational endeavors, and this set them apart from the world of other colonial clubs. While at least some of the latter engaged with public matters, and offered their members the liberty to discuss controversial subjects within the confines of a private assembly (though many forbade discussing divisive religious and political questions outright), they did not possess as consistently a civic dimension as Franklin's projects, and did not aim to influence and improve the lives of their neighbors.

The Library Company of Philadelphia was the first Anglo-American subscription library and the first successful public lending library in the colonies. There was no British model for a subscription library, and Franklin devoted more time to library business than to any other civic project, as founder, director, librarian, secretary, and book agent while in London. Attempts to create a Junto library – effectively, pooling the books owned by Junto members – had failed, but they subscribed to library shares heavily, and solicited further subscriptions. At least nine of the twelve original library directors were Junto members. In 1731 all the first subscribers were young men, and most were artisans, but a few years later new subscribers were primarily professionals and merchants, and by 1740 the price of a share had risen from forty shillings to six pounds and ten shillings (by way of adding the annual dues of ten shillings to the share price every year), pricing the convenient access to knowledge out of the reach of most artisans. Nonshareholders, though, could check out books for a cash deposit and weekly fee – and this provision turned the Library Company into a public lending library. In 1768, when five subscription and commercial circulation libraries competed with the Library Company, and all libraries faced growing difficulties attracting new subscribers, the directors reduced share prices, now at twenty-one pounds, to a fixed ten pounds (Lemay, 2006b: 95, 104, 111, 119; Green, 2007). When the directors of the Library Company solicited the support of proprietor Thomas Penn – the library would receive a corporate charter in 1742 – they pointed to the advantageous "climate and situation" of his colony and praised its government and the "native genius of its people," who were "capable of every kind of improvement." But they also offered an explanation for the inevitably slow development of civic institutions in new settlements, an account that Franklin would repeat in his proposals for the American Philosophical Society and the Academy. "When colonies are in their infancy, the refinements of life, it seems, cannot be much attended to. To encourage agriculture, promote trade, and establish good laws must be the principal care of the first founders; while other arts and sciences, less immediately necessary, how excellent and useful soever, are left to the care and cultivation of posterity" (May 16, 1733, PBF, 1: 320; see "A Proposal for Promoting Useful Knowledge …," PBF, May 14, 1743; 2: 380; "On the Need for an Academy", August 24, 1749; PBF, 3: 385–386).

The Library Company's acquisition policies reflected Franklin's preference for usefulness and education over mere entertainment. The first printed catalogue (1741) shows the holdings, depending almost entirely upon purchases from London, to be half literature and science and one-third history, but comparatively little theology. For Carl Bridenbaugh this is clear proof of an Enlightenment influence (1977: 77). At the same time, libraries connected the quest for promoting useful knowledge and civic improvement to concerns over social advancement and status maintenance. James Raven stresses that Franklin's conception of libraries – "a purported democracy of understanding and egalitarian improvement" – quickly gave way to libraries that formed elite institutions, markers of gentility and politeness and outposts of European high culture, catering to men who possessed both the material resources and the leisure necessary for intellectual pursuits (2007: 49–50). But in his *Autobiography* Franklin chose to emphasize how the Library Company, and the numerous libraries patterned after it, appealed to and transformed their middling patrons. Libraries "have improv'd the general Conversation of the Americans, [and] made the common Tradesmen and Farmers as intelligent as most Gentlemen from other Countries." He also suggested that the holdings – heavy on English Whig writers – "have contributed in some degree to the Stand so generally made throughout the Colonies in Defence of their Privileges" (1964: 130–131, similarly 142).

Franklin's "projecting public Spirit" extended over virtually every dimension of urban life (Franklin, 1964: 54). Michael McMahon, Edmund Morgan, and John Van Horne emphasize that his civic leadership occurred in a specific time and place. Philadelphia was rapidly growing in the early eighteenth century, but the municipal corporation remained unresponsive to the demands created by a changing urban landscape, and its ineffectiveness opened up a space for civic action. Franklin closely observed Philadelphia's expansion and the associated administrative challenges (what McMahon conceptualizes as the transition from town to city). The lack of a developed civic infrastructure forced Franklin to consider how Philadelphians could address a plethora of problems, and his response assumed two interrelated forms: publications, not the least essays in the *Pennsylvania Gazette*, outlining a problem and making the case for joint action as the best means to provide a solution, and the creation of institutions to implement that response. He lobbied for the creation of a night watch, paid for by a progressive tax on property, but succeeded only in 1756, after he had served as alderman and councilman for eight years. He also advocated for street cleaning, paving, and lighting, smallpox inoculation, and fire protection. The town's houses were mostly built of wood and stood in close proximity to each other, and the frequent fires were the urban hazard most frightening to residents and property owners. Beginning in 1730 Franklin recommended the acquisition of engines, buckets, and other tools, and celebrated the civic virtue of men who turned out to fight fires: "here are brave Men, Men of Spirit and Humanity, good Citizens, or Neighbours, capably and worthy of civil Society, and the Enjoyment of a happy Government" ("Pennsylvanus," *Pennsylvania Gazette*, December 20, 1733). In 1736 Franklin, joined by Junto members and Library Company subscribers, formed the Union Fire Company, Philadelphia's first fire-fighting association.

McMahon (1992) notes that Franklin's proposals were closely interrelated, though not always easily accomplished and on occasion outright failures. Recommendations for the regulation of bakeries aimed at preventing fires, and the proposed night watch would also be on the lookout for fires, not just preventing crime. In 1739 Franklin began a campaign against the pollution caused by tanners and similar businesses around Dock Street, thus pitting concerns for public safety against the claims of propertyholders. He unsuccessfully argued that the tanners' property rights could be satisfied by relocating the tanneries to spaces outside of the city limits (*Pennsylvania Gazette*, August 30, 1739). Making these proposals in the face of governmental inaction, effectively advocating the "constraining [of] private commercial interests" (McMahon, 1992: 166), pitted private economic liberty favored by the men who sat on the city corporation and in the colonial assembly against public responsibility and a concern for the common good, and clearly demonstrated the limited influence of the latter. During Franklin's service on the city council (1748–1755) a lack of public funds also defeated similar efforts, such as bridge building and dock renovation.

Cooperative action required that the public had to be prepared for accepting Franklin's premises. He had to convince Philadelphians that the problems he identified were serious, the solutions feasible and frugal, and that an overwhelming majority of residents agreed with his proposals. (Relying on a series of carefully prepared written statements also helped him to avoid public speaking, never one of his strengths.) Thus the rhetorical strategies Franklin employed to advance his causes stood at the center of his entire civic project. According to David Larson, "Franklin presented himself as an independent, interested in the good of the community as a whole rather than devoted to a particular religious or political group" (1986: 199). In condemning particularism and making universal claims about the character of the polity and civil society of Pennsylvania, specifically the unity and interdependence of all interests, he followed common rhetorical strategies (see Smolenski [2005]), an unavoidable course of action given the tensions and mistrust between religious and political constituencies. Before 1755, at least, Franklin placed principle over faction in his public pronouncements and succeeded in styling himself as an independent and pragmatic civil-society actor, adopting "the persona of the fair-minded, rational, good citizen" (Larson, 1986: 216). Larson describes Franklin's various pitches for public efforts as acts of persuasion, balancing pleas for altruism and fellowship with appeals to self-interest. His strategy was "founded upon his dual view of human nature. Convinced that mankind is neither so blatantly selfish as to be moved solely by appeals to self-interest, nor so wholly altruistic as to act simply through sympathy for others, Franklin develops techniques which appeal to both sides of human nature. With increasing subtlety and skill, Franklin argues in the philanthropic papers that acts which appear only to help a few, such as establishing an educational academy or a charitable hospital, will ultimately benefit almost every member of the community. In his development of persuasive strategies which unite appeals to altruism and self-interest, Franklin succeeds in grounding the public welfare in private acts of justice and generosity" (216–217). In emphasizing the general usefulness of the Academy, for example, he pointed to the contribution it would make to "the Cultivation and Improvement of a Country, [and] the Wisdom, Riches, and Strength, Virtue and Piety, the Welfare and Happiness of a People" (PBF, 3: 422).

The success of Franklin's civic ventures also required that he carefully incorporated all constituencies into the process of formulating and implementing proposals, accounted for their specific concerns, and downplayed his own role in the proceedings. To generate support for the militia association Franklin held three meetings over the course of four days in November 1747, the first specifically for the middling sort, whom he addressed, according to Richard Peters, as "the first Movers in every useful undertaking that had been projected for the good of the City." When the attendees offered to sign the plan of association on the spot, he urged them to wait, suggesting "to offer it at least to the Gentlemen and if they come into it, well and good, we shall be the better able to carry it into Execution" (Richard Peters to Thomas Penn, November 29, 1747, PBF, 3: 216). Indeed, a second meeting, specifically gathering "gentlemen" and "merchants," also approved the plan; and a third, now open meeting collected over 1,000 signatures and united and "diffuse[d] credit among a large number of citizens" (S.F. Griffith, 1992: 137). Finding support also meant accommodating wishes Franklin did not necessarily consider germane to an institution's mission. Edmund Morgan calls this Franklin's "pragmatism": "a willingness not to insist on some abstract principle in transactions with other people, a willingness to make concessions" (2005: 299). For example, his original proposal for the curriculum of the Academy omitted Latin and Greek as not relevant to future merchants and tradesmen, but he discovered that the potential sponsors of the institution, wealthy Philadelphians, favored instruction in those subjects; consequently, the Academy's constitution provided for a Greek and Latin school. Another crucial strategy, much emphasized in the autobiography, evolved out of Franklin's recognition that his projects had the greatest chance of success if they appeared to originate with other men and his central involvement was not readily visible. Franklin learned, in Morgan's words, "to lead from the rear" (2005: 300), and such self-effacement grew out of experience. Concerning the creation of the Library Company Franklin recalled that "the Objections, and Reluctances I met with in Soliciting the Subscriptions, made me soon feel the Impropriety of presenting one's self as the Proposer of any useful Project that might be suppos'd to raise one's Reputation in the smallest degree above that of one's Neighbours, when one has need of their Assistance to accomplish that Project. I therefore put myself as much as I could out of sight, and stated it as a Scheme of a *Number of Friends*, who had requested me to go about and propose it to such as they thought Lovers of Reading. In this way my Affair went on more smoothly, and I ever after practis'd it on such Occasions; and from my frequent Successes, can heartily recommend it" (Franklin, 1964: 143; see a virtually identical statement concerning the Academy on 193).

Franklin maintained a life-long interest in improving the opportunities and life chances of the middling sorts (see Smith). Following the Junto and the Library Company, the Academy belonged to the line of Franklin's civic projects intended to provide easier access to education and knowledge for the sons of middling parents. Other members of the revolutionary generation, such as John Adams and Thomas Jefferson, believed in the existence of a natural aristocracy, but Franklin again and again returned to the egalitarian potential of a wide distribution of knowledge. His plans for the academy represented his attempt to offer young Philadelphians the education he had wanted for himself yet could not obtain, given his father's reduced circumstances. Josiah Franklin had sent him to a Boston grammar school as a preparation for going to college; Franklin had done well there – he rose to the head of his class – but after a year he had to transfer to a school with a curriculum limited to writing and arithmetic, and then assisted in his father's soap-making shop. He proudly noted that the Library Company "afforded me the means of Improvement by constant Study … and thus repair'd in some Degree the Loss of the Learned Education my Father once intended for me" (Franklin, 1964: 143; see Boudreau, 1996).

In his proposals for the Academy Franklin departed from the predominant educational philosophies (learning for its own sake or for the glory of God) to emphasize instruction immediately applicable to the likely occupations of middling men. Subjects included modern history, geography, comparative religion and culture, morality, oratory and print, political science, rhetoric and composition, agriculture, trade and commerce, technology, and science (see detailed survey in Lemay, 2009: 183–189). In Franklin's plan the "English School," a division of the Academy, focused on instruction based on English-language works, such as *Cato's Letters* and *The Spectator*, that he himself had used to improve his English. The graduates would "come out of this School fitted for learning any Business, Calling, or Profession, except such wherein Languages are required; and tho' unacquainted with any ancient or foreign Tongue, they will be Masters of their own, which is of more immediate and general Use" (PBF, 4: 107–108). Other languages would be offered tailored to specific future vocations: Latin and Greek for ministers, French, German, and Spanish for merchants. This was not an education for gentlemen, as taught in the colonial colleges, but for the professions (see Boudreau, 2002). The Academy was to be governed by a board of trustees, not the state or a church, and Franklin carefully steered the curriculum into a secular direction, not the least to keep the school out of the snares of denominational controversy. Eventually, the Academy's provost, the Anglican minister William Smith, redefined its mission and focused on educating the sons of wealthy Anglicans, the source of bitter divisions between him and Franklin.

Most contentious were those projects that challenged the authority of the state. In the fall of 1747, Philadelphia seemed to be threatened by

French and Spanish privateers coming up the Delaware River. Pennsylvania was the only colony without a compulsory militia, but the proprietary rulers and the colonial assembly, dominated by pacifist Quakers, hesitated to take any defensive measures – and as secretary of the assembly Franklin was in the ideal position to observe governmental inaction. Thus private initiative had to lead the way in organizing the defense of the city and colony. In November Franklin published *Plain Truth; or, Serious Considerations on the Present State of the City of Philadelphia, and Province of Pennsylvania*. In it he emphasized the vulnerability of the colony, the inaction of its government, the crippling pacifism of most Quakers, and the obliviousness of people in the city and the interior to the approaching threat. His authorship was publicly known, and his condemnation of both the Quaker and Proprietary parties let him appear independent and gained him the support of men in both parties (Lemay, 2009: 11). Franklin had tailored his pitch carefully: before the publication of *Plain Truth*, the *Pennsylvania Gazette* carried articles appealing to moderate Quakers, who were open to supporting defensive measures, such as James Logan, and later delegated Richard Peters, the provincial secretary and clerk of the governor's council, to defend the proceedings before the proprietors. He pitched the pamphlet's content and language to middling readers – it was addressed to "the middling People, the Farmers, Shopkeepers and Tradesmen of this city and country," who were ignored by "those Great and rich Men" – and who were especially affected by the impending raids, as they could not flee like wealthier residents and stood to lose their possessions (PBF, 3: 201). "*Plain Truth* was Franklin's first overtly political statement," argues Joyce Chaplin, as it "indicted the colony's leaders for abdicating their duty to defend Pennsylvania." Franklin's signature – "A TRADESMAN of Philadelphia" – made it "clear that he stood apart – socially and morally – from Pennsylvania's genteel elite" (2006: 101). But he also emphasized "interdependence and unity" to "undercut the divisiveness of his criticism of the elites," employing organic metaphors and likening Pennsylvania to the human body (Griffith, 1992: 144, see 141–144). (Despite the signature, as Richard Peters reported to Thomas Penn [November 24, 1747; PBF, 3: 214–215], Franklin composed *Plain Truth* together with Tench Francis, attorney general of the province; William Coleman, a member of Philadelphia's Common Council and clerk of the city court; and Thomas Hopkinson, admiralty judge and member of the Provincial Council – thus he worked with three high-ranking officeholders, a collaboration not revealed in the autobiography.) Over the course of three public meetings Franklin circulated and discussed his "Form of Association" and gathered the signatures of volunteer militiamen, eventually collecting 10,000 names in the colony by the spring of 1748. Philadelphia's common council approved the association and a lottery to raise funds for arms and supplies, especially cannons and batteries for fortifications on the Delaware River, as did the governor's council. Franklin declined the election to colonel and instead served as a private, as he thought it wise to deemphasize his role in the proceedings as much as possible. This was also due, perhaps, to the recognition of his tenuous genteel status that made serving as an officer look presumptuous, as Gordon Wood suggests (2004: 60).

It was important to Franklin that the Association would not reify social hierarchy. The volunteers elected their officers directly, hopefully based on merit and military skills (the limited evidence suggests that the officers were professionals, merchants, and skilled craftsmen). Companies were formed by location, for strictly practical reasons but also to, in Franklin's words, "prevent People's sorting themselves into Companies, according to their Ranks in Life, their Quality or Station. 'Tis designed to mix the Great and Small together, for the sake of Union and Encouragement" ("Form of Association," PBF, 3: 209.) What united men of different wealth, and made them citizens of equal status, was their "shared vulnerability" to foreign assault – mobilizing and joining together for self-protection justified the Association (Houston, 2008: 91). Alan Houston points to the larger import of decoupling social and cultural allegiances from the work of a voluntary association. "What looks like a principle of equality from a philosophical point of view can also be seen as a characteristic of associational life from a sociological point of view. Recall that toleration was meant to separate religion and politics, so that the beliefs and practices of faith did not directly map onto the rights and obligations of citizenship. Religious association and civic life were (or ought to be) distinct." In this way "equality within an association was preserved by carefully separating membership in it from other roles and identities," a circumstance that helps to account for the success of the militia association.

The Association not only engaged but challenged the government of Pennsylvania, a stance all other voluntary associations avoided carefully. Sally Griffith considers this as a radical break with the past, propelled by unprecedented governmental inaction and abdication of responsibility in the face of a major crisis. By later standards of voluntary action the efforts of the Association seem highly conventional – a public call to action, public meetings, a subscription drive, the portrayal of the project as "the spontaneous outpouring of community spirit" – but in 1747 "only the extremity of the situation … made the formation of an extra-governmental militia acceptable" (1992: 137, 138). The Association gave a public voice to artisans and tradesmen and associated them with a critique of proprietor and ruling Quakers, whose neglect of their civic duties opened the door for a wider circle of citizens to play a decisive role in public affairs (150). *Plain Truth* indeed suggested that the inaction of proprietor and assembly had severed the bond between governors and governed: "*Protection* is as truly due from the Government to the People, as *Obedience* from the People to the Government" (PBF, 3: 199). And the preamble to the "Form of

Association" identified "a breach in the larger social fabric," according to Douglas Anderson. It "make[s] the case for a neglect of governmental obligation that frees the 'subject' to form new arrangements with his 'Fellow Subjects' for the safety of the commonwealth." The Association was organized like a "substitute government for Pennsylvania, with a written constitution, a system of elections, assemblies, laws, and taxes" (191, 192; see PBF, 2: 205–206). Indeed, nothing could disguise the fact that the association constituted Franklin's "first exercise in state-making," as Edmund Morgan notes. "Franklin recognized that his military organization of the colony posed a direct challenge to the authority of [the colony's] government. ... His association had the look of the social contract that eighteenth-century thinkers envisaged as the origin of all government. So Franklin was careful not only to keep his place in the back seat but also to keep the militia from appearing to rival the existing government" (2002: 67, 69). Thomas Penn, however, could not accept that the allegiance of the colony's residents to the proprietary government was conditional: "the people of America are too often ready to act in defiance of the Government." The creation of the Association expressed a "Contempt to Government, and cannot end in anything but Anarchy and Confusion." The Association constituted a distinct "Military Common Wealth" within the colonial government – a challenge to the constituted authorities – that amounted to a "little less than Treason" (Penn to Lynford Lardner, March 29, 1748, Penn to Richard Peters, March 30, 1748; PBF, 3: 186). Franklin had hoped to preempt the appearance of questioning the proprietors' prerogatives, by having the elected officers also receive a commission from the Governor's Council, for example, but Penn noted that the subscribers to the Association pledged themselves to obey its own council rather than the governor's (PBF, 3: 187).

It is important, though, not to overstate the novelty of the militia association. In Jessica Choppin Roney's assessment, it first and foremost formed an extension of already existing associational practices, such as membership appeals or financial strategies. By 1747 Philadelphians could look back on a quarter century of associating. The Association was "predicated on the experience and work of the organizations that came before it," and operated in the "civic space" between government and private citizens that the older organizations had carved out. Its leading members, such as the lottery managers, heavily drew on their organizational expertise. "Operating in a context of hands-off provincial government, weak local government, and quarrelsome provincial factions, Philadelphia's clubs and organizations offered a unique venue through which to work on community aims, bridge distinct religious and ethnic subcommunities, and manifest individual civic commitment and public virtue" (Roney, 2010: 361). In pitching *Plain Truth* primarily to the middling sorts Franklin addressed the keenest associators, the men who had created the Library

Company and the fire companies. At the same time, the Association united men across ethnic, social, and religious lines: from his previous ventures Franklin had learned that involving leading men and gaining their support was vital to success. The Association went beyond customary procedures of Philadelphia club life, though, by soliciting funds from non-members, which in turn led to appeals to residents outside of the circle of mid-eighteenth-century joiners (who had to have sufficient discretionary funds in order to join). Public debates concerning the association revolved around the question "whether self-defense was compatible with Christian religion," not about its legitimacy in assuming governmental functions; its right to exist was "implicitly accepted by promoters and critics alike" (380; see Gannon, 1998: 51–58). Thomas Penn, as the absentee proprietor, had the leisure to consider the Association's potential impact on constituted authority; the residents of Pennsylvania worried primarily about defending the colony. And Roney emphasizes that Penn effectively stood alone in condemning it. The city corporation donated to the Association, and the governor and his council resolved "to give all due Protection and Encouragement to the Members of the Association" and did not interfere in its administration or the deployment of its resources (PBF, 3: 185).

Civil society and the state could cooperate fruitfully. The Pennsylvania Assembly granted charters to the academy and the Pennsylvania Hospital. "The commonwealth ideal," notes Kathleen McCarthy, "the notion that public and private interests were blended under the sanction of a charter, infused Franklin's associational work, providing legal authority and support for a variety of privately initiated civic improvement schemes" (2003: 21). The assembly also granted money to the academy, and Franklin organized a petition drive urging it, successfully, to provide funds for the erection of the hospital building. In his autobiography Franklin delighted in describing his ingenious scheme of soliciting private donations with the promise of matching money from the assembly, and coaxing the promise of a matching grant out of reluctant assemblymen by pointing to the up-front private financing in the hospital (Franklin, 1964: 200–201). This allocation of public funds "for ostensibly private charitable and educational ventures, coupling public and private resources, donations, tax monies, earned income, and voluntarism in order to maintain public services" arose out of the specific circumstances of the eighteenth-century colonies, where the reach of government, tax income, and surplus cash all were limited (McCarthy, 2003: 21).

Franklin's interest in scientific inquiry began long before he proposed the American Philosophical Society in 1743. The Library Company's early acquisitions included books and reference works on scientific subjects. Joseph Breintnall, an original Junto member and secretary of the Library Company, shared his curiosity about natural philosophy with Franklin. The Library Company obtained an air pump and other scientific instruments from London, hosted itinerant lecturers who spoke about scientific subjects, and Company subscribers, headed by Franklin, conducted the electrical experiments of 1747 and 1748 that established his fame as a scientist (Frick, Grimm). "Franklin deliberately chose to work in natural science," argues Joyce Chaplin, "a decision intended to make himself part of a cosmopolitan, enlightened culture, one that impressed him at an early age as encompassing everything America did not" (2006: 5). His interest in science also grew out of a specific attitude towards the production and dissemination of knowledge. It had to be "useful," that is, practical rather than metaphysical, and could be tested by experiment. In the context of describing some of his scientific observations Franklin asked rhetorically, "what signifies Philosophy that does not apply to some Use?" (BF to Mary Stevenson, November?, 1760; PBF, 9: 251). In Frank Kelleter's view, Franklin's focus on usefulness grew out of the peculiar status of the colonies: "to say that a certain idea might be true, but not very useful, takes on a special meaning and urgency in a diversified frontier and settlement culture. Franklin explicitly searched for religious and political institutions that were suitable and necessary for the highly improbable formation of a post-classical, post-European republic in faraway provinces" (2008: 84). With usefulness as a primary concern "knowledge was best advanced," according to David D. Hall, "by allowing a certain liberty or openness of inquiry. Not only, therefore, did learnedness become more in evidence in mid-eighteenth-century America, it also involved a new ethos and ... new sites of cultural production." Knowledge derived from experiment proved useful to the public in "forming virtuous citizens and in leading to 'improvement.'" Thus the Library Company and the Philosophical Society helped to institutionalize Franklin's "sense of collaborative possibilities" (D.D. Hall, 2000: 412, 416, 419).

The foundation of the American Philosophical Society, patterned after the Royal Society of London, was part of Franklin's plan to turn Philadelphia into a central node in the republic of letters. In his "Proposal for Promoting Useful Knowledge" he described it as "the City nearest the Centre of the Continent-Colonies," ideally located to support a learned society connecting the colonies and Europe (PBF, 2: 381). The botanist John Bartram had first proposed a society that connected the "most ingenious and curious men" in the English colonies in 1737, continued to exchange ideas about such an institution with Franklin, and closely collaborated with him in its creation (Bridenbaugh, 1977: 81). The Philosophical Society, however, did not live up to Franklin's hopes. Two years after its inception he concluded that the members "are very idle Gentlemen; they will take no Pains" (BF to Cadwalader Colden, August 15, 1745; PBF, 3: 36). The Library Company remained the center of scientific activity in the colonies before Franklin left for England in 1757. Leo Lemay describes the failure of the Philosophical Society (before its reconstitution in 1768) as a consequence of Franklin's success as a scientist – he devoted all his available time to his electrical experiments – as well as his ambition. It led him to pick the Royal Society's

Philosophical Transactions to publish a notice announcing the results of his experiments rather than starting a natural-philosophy journal in Philadelphia, as originally contemplated to publicize the work of members of the Philosophical Society (Leemay, 2006b: 498–499).

The renown Franklin derived from the London publication of his *Experiments and Observations on Electricity* (1751) all over Europe, however, gained him the Royal Society's Copley Medal for the advancement of scientific knowledge in 1753 as well as entry into the republic of letters as a citizen of equal standing with British and continental savants, as "its most important British colonial member" (Chaplin, 2006: 116). Given the republic's cosmopolitan and elitist character, Franklin's earlier and largely local civic activities and scientific publications, such as the astrological calculations in *Poor Richard's Almanac*, would not have given him access. "This was the central paradox of knowledge as people in Franklin's era conceived of it," emphasizes Joyce Chaplin, "knowledge was sociable and collaborative, but not everyone could contribute to it" (2006: 55). Thus Franklin's fame as a natural philosopher grew out of a gradually widening circle of correspondents in other colonies and especially in Europe. It "depended entirely on European approbation. He was absolutely right to look to Europe for validation. Anglo-America could not yet support the elaborate culture of learning necessary for natural philosophy" (133). All along Europe, and London in particular, had been essential to fostering his interest in natural philosophy and supporting his scientific work. London had given Franklin a patron, Peter Collinson, who selected books for the Library Company and provided information concerning books and scientific matters, his electrical equipment, and validated his work by publishing the *Experiments*.

Franklin retired from active involvement in his printing business in 1748, at a time when his main focus shifted from building civic institutions, where by mid-century no project was imaginable without his participation, to holding office at the local, colonial, and imperial levels. (He already had been appointed clerk of the Pennsylvania Assembly and postmaster of Philadelphia in 1736–1737.) For Franklin this shift constituted primarily a move from one dimension of public service to another, as these different types of service existed on a continuum for him, but the transition from civic leader to elected official and imperial officeholder nonetheless constituted a departure from his prior efforts of constructing civil society. Edmund Morgan and Gordon Wood interpret the redirection of Franklin's primary attention from civil society to government, following the cessation of privateering attacks in the summer of 1748, as his acknowledgment that at this point he could provide the best service to the community by going into government. Though his scientific discoveries delighted him, Franklin weighed "Philosophical Amusements" against public service. In a 1750 letter he placed service to the commonwealth over having the time for further intensive scientific experiments (BF to Cadwalader Colden,

October 11, 1750, PBF, 4: 67–68). Franklin retained his interest in science, and obtained additional instruments from England, but "the Publick now considering me a Man of Leisure, laid hold of me for their purposes; every Part of our Civil Government, and almost at the same time, imposing some duty on me." Election as a city councilman occurred in 1748, followed by appointment as justice of the peace a year later, election as alderman and assemblyman in 1751, and appointment as joint deputy postmaster-general in 1753. He was pleased with his regular reelection and reappointment to these offices, acknowledging, in Wood's estimation, that "that was where true greatness and lasting fame could be best achieved" (Franklin, 1964: 196–197; G.S. Wood, 2004: 67). Doing so also forced Franklin to recognize, as Morgan emphasizes, that his intention to serve the colonial public – and his clear understanding of what needed to be done – ran against British imperial policy that placed the interests of the metropolis first (E.S. Morgan, 2002: 28–29, 71–75).

While Morgan and Wood see Franklin abandoning science in favor of public service, Joyce Chaplin sees a direct connection between them, a transposition of renown in the republic of letters into public office and political influence. Franklin's scientific accomplishments and the resultant public recognition paved the way for his becoming a politician and statesman – doing science and doing politics and diplomacy were distinct, yet intertwined aspects of his public career, and led to the paradoxical situation that his scientific fame "made him unable to continue working in the area that had made him famous" (2006: 117). "He became a statesman because he had done science. And he was able to do so because, in the eighteenth century, science became part of public culture. ... Franklin's contemporaries recognized that this had been his route to prominence. A famous tag proposed that Franklin had snatched lightning from the sky and the scepter from the tyrants – in that order" (5, see 137). And in serving the empire he could help to facilitate the advancement of science and the expansion of the republic of letters. When he applied for the deputy postmastership he told Peter Collinson that Philadelphia would be the ideal location for the office, not Virginia, as heretofore, since it was "the Center of the Continent Colonies, and having constant Communication with the West India Islands" (BF to PC, May 21, 1751; PBF, 4: 135).

It is now impossible to read Franklin's efforts to create a civic infrastructure in Philadelphia as anything other than the blueprint for all future philanthropic efforts in the United States. "Franklin's career," states Kathleen McCarthy, "illustrates the ways in which the scaffolding for American civil society was built over the course of the eighteenth century, including early examples of the ways in which associations built social capital among men of middling means, public-private partnerships, market activities, and a broadened mandate for social advocacy" (2003: 14). His civic activism in the eighteenth century has become a touchstone for exhortations to civic involvement in the twenty-first century. Introducing her study of Franklin's "political philosophy" Lorraine Smith Pangle announces that he "is and has always been the most American of Americans. ... [A]t the heart of his political vision is a view of democratic citizenship, a rich and subtle understanding of the habits and qualities of heart and mind that need to be fostered in order to sustain liberty" and "republican self-government," in particular coherent concepts of citizenship and civic virtue. "In the face of the growing atomization, polarization, and intolerance of contemporary civil society" Franklin's "healthy democratic vision is uniquely suited as an antidote for some of our worst civic woes" (2007: 1, 3, 5).

Both Pangle and Walter Isaacson turn to Alexis de Tocqueville, who does not reference Franklin in his discussion of voluntary associations in *Democracy in America*, to place him at the core of their understanding of the genesis of American civil society. Effectively, Tocqueville's observations make Franklin's civic activism readable as "a quintessentially American solution to the social problems that beset every society" (Pangle, 2007: 95, see 94–98). (Here Pangle and Isaacson replicate Tocqueville's misconception of the spread of nineteenth-century voluntary associations: he vastly underestimated their presence and importance in France and Great Britain, which led him to believe that they were a distinctly American phenomenon and a key to understanding American society.) When Tocqueville concluded that "Americans of all ages, all conditions, and all minds are constantly joining together in groups," he pinpointed the impulse perfected by Franklin: According to Isaacson his "organizational fervor and galvanizing personality made him the most influential force" in implanting a penchant for concerted action as "an enduring part of American life" (2003: 102; Tocqueville, 2004: 595). Whereas Tocqueville perceived a conflict between individualistic and communitarian tendencies, Franklin joined them together seamlessly. "The frontier attracted barn-raising pioneers who were ruggedly individualistic as well as fiercely supportive of their community. Franklin was the epitome of this admixture of self-reliance and civic involvement, and what he exemplified became part of the American character." Franklin also allows Isaacson to calibrate the appropriate degree of governmental involvement in society and economy. With reference to the matching grant Franklin negotiated for the Pennsylvania Hospital, Isaacson notes that "Franklin showed how government and private initiative could be woven together, which remains to this day a very American approach. He believed in volunteerism and limited government, but also that there was a legitimate role for government in fostering the common good. By working through public-private partnerships, he felt, governments could have the best impact while avoiding the imposition of too much authority from above." Isaacson calls this "an American political philosophy" (2003: 102–103, 148).

This account of Franklin's civic endeavors has followed the major contributions on the subject in emphasizing the disinterested and altruistic

Franklin and, perhaps unavoidably, downplaying the entrepreneurial, self-promoting, and self-mythologizing aspects of his life and public image – even though his own advancement and the civic improvement of Philadelphia were interrelated, as he clearly understood and the Franklin scholarship properly accounts for. With the maxim "doing well by doing good" in mind, we have focused on Franklin "doing good" more so than on his "doing well." One task of future work on Franklin's life and career ought to be a fuller accounting of the interaction between self-interest and civic-mindedness within the context of associating and institution-building in colonial Philadelphia (for a close examination of this context see Roney, 2008). Such work needs to chart the impact of Franklin's associational ventures, on his own life but especially on that of other men. Despite his ongoing concern with improving the prospects of aspirational middling sorts, Franklin slowly but steadily rose in Philadelphia society, a process not the least attributable to his championing of civic causes. Arguably, his retirement from business in 1748 – thus dissociating himself from manual labor – constituted a claim to gentility. A comprehensive analysis of the surviving membership data would help us to understand what impact joining one of Franklin's associations had on the lives of the other members.

Related to questions about the influence of associational activities on individual members are questions about the influence of associations on the development of Philadelphia. The sociology of voluntary action has always been interested in processes of inclusion and exclusion, in understanding how the separation between members and non-members changed the interaction between city dwellers. As the number of associations in colonial Philadelphia grew, how did the evolving networks of interlocking membership influence the social structure of the city? Since the city corporation made virtually no effort to shape the development of Philadelphia, it opened a wide space for the efforts of civic institutions to propose solutions for the problems of a quickly growing city. A systematic comparison with other colonial cities would flesh out Jessica Chopin Roney's contention that the specific circumstances of hands-off governance in Philadelphia offered unique opportunities for the flourishing of civic institutions and their leaders, and thus for Franklin's ascent (2008: 347–348). With an unresponsive city government, and a Pennsylvania Assembly equally disengaged from the concerns of Philadelphia residents, the city's voluntary associations provided their members with a framework to think not only about civic but also about political means to address the shortcomings of the local and colonial governments – they opened the door to the political activism of a growing number of the city's men. Lastly, some of the recent work on early-national civil society narrates its evolution as a contest between conflicting notions concerning the legitimate purposes and forms of association (see, for example, Neem, 2008). We know of Thomas Penn's opposition to the militia association, but the Franklin literature does not attempt to establish other instances of antagonism towards his ventures, aside from personal animosity towards him, or to account for the absence of such opposition. Pursuing this perspective would lead to a fuller picture of Franklin's associational world as well as eighteenth-century Philadelphia.

Note

1 Labaree, Leonard W. *et al.*, eds. (1959–). *The Papers of Benjamin Franklin*. 39 vols to date. New Haven, CT: Yale University Press. Hereafter referred to as PBF.

Further Reading

Chaplin, Joyce (2006). *The First Scientific American: Benjamin Franklin and the Pursuit of Genius*. New York, NY.

Frasca, Ralph (2006). *Benjamin Franklin's Printing Network: Disseminating Virtue in Early America*. Columbia, SC.

Green, James N., and Stallybrass Peter (2006). *Benjamin Franklin: Writer and Printer*. Newcastle, DE.

Houston, Alan (2008). *Benjamin Franklin and the Politics of Improvement*. New Haven, CT.

Lambert, Frank (1994). *"Pedlar in Divinity": George Whitefield and the Great Awakening, 1737–1770*. Princeton, NJ.

Larson, David M. (1986). "Benevolent persuasion: The art of Benjamin Franklin's philanthropic papers," *Pennsylvania Magazine of History and Biography* 110: 195–217.

Lemay, J.A. Leo, ed. (1993). *Reappraising Benjamin Franklin: A Bicentennial Perspective*. Newark, DE.

McCarthy, Kathleen (2003). *American Creed: Philanthropy and the Rise of Civil Society, 1700–1865*. Chicago, IL.

Morgan, Edmund (2002). *Benjamin Franklin*. New Haven, CT.

Roney, Jessica C. (2010). "'Ready to act in defiance of Government': Colonial Philadelphia voluntary culture and the defense association of 1747–1748," *Early American Studies* 8: 358–385.

Van Horne, John C. (1993). "Collective benevolence and the common good in Franklin's philanthropy" in Lemay, ed (1993).

Warner, Michael (1990). *Letters of the Republic: Publication and the Public Sphere in Eighteenth Century America*. Cambridge, MA: 73–96.

Wolf, Edwin 2nd, and Hayes Kevin J. (2006). *The Library of Benjamin Franklin*. Philadelphia, PA.

Zuckerman, Michael (1993). "Doing good while doing well: benevolence and self-interest in Franklin's *Autobiography*," in Lemay, ed (1993).

Chapter Eighteen

EMPIRE AND NATION

Eliga H. Gould

If we had to choose the founder who best exemplifies what we think of today as the American character, many of us would choose Benjamin Franklin. Charming, folksy, and urbane, blessed in old age with wealth and influence that he earned – despite relatively humble origins – through a combination of good fortune and hard work, Franklin is accessible in ways that the other founders are not. Franklin's *Autobiography*, first published four years after its author's death in 1790, was (and is) especially important in this regard. Telling the story of Franklin's escape from his brother's print shop in Boston, of his early career as a sojourner in London and a printer in Philadelphia, and of his growing prominence, first in Pennsylvania but eventually throughout Europe, Franklin's account of his own life earned him a lasting reputation as a man who achieved things in America that would have been impossible had he lived somewhere else. In a sense, Franklin was the republic's first self-made man (Lemay, 1986a: 349–360). What could be more American than that?

Before Franklin became the quintessential American, however, he was the quintessential British American. Despite the decade and a half that he spent in the service of the American republic, Franklin devoted most of his life to serving the British Empire. Not only was the empire where he first made his mark as a public figure, but until his public humiliation before the Privy Council in early 1774, he was one of the foremost exemplars of British patriotism in America, attempting to form Britain's North American colonies into a more centralized union at the Albany Congress in 1754, helping raise troops and supplies for the British war effort during the Seven Years' War, working during the 1760s to replace the Penn family's proprietorship

A Companion to Benjamin Franklin, First Edition. Edited by David Waldstreicher.
© 2011 Blackwell Publishing Ltd. Published 2011 by Blackwell Publishing Ltd.

in Pennsylvania with a royally appointed governor, and striving – long after most other Americans had given up hope – to find a solution to the intractable confrontation between Parliament and the colonies. Upon returning to Philadelphia in 1775, Franklin cast his lot with Congress and the supporters of American independence. Doing so required him to sever ties to some of his closest friends, prominent among them his Loyalist son William. It does not require much imagination to suppose that under slightly different circumstances, Franklin, too, might have sided with the king (G.S. Wood, 2004: 153–164).

In the literature on Franklin's life and times, this part of his story is also well-known, yet it is easy to forget just how central British America was to Franklin's self-identification as an American. Although he renounced his allegiance to George III when he signed the Declaration of Independence, the nation that Franklin envisioned after 1776 remained, in many ways, a republican version of the empire that he had wanted British America to be: libertarian in the rights that it guaranteed its citizens, federal in the relations that it encouraged among its constituent parts, and expansionist in its attitudes toward its neighbors. As a subject of the British Empire no less than as a citizen of the United States, Franklin believed that the only way that such an empire could endure was as an "empire of liberty," and he was a steadfast proponent of the idea that the free-born subjects and citizens of this extended nation – for that is what he thought the British Empire and American republic both were – were entitled to the same body of rights and privileges, no matter where they lived. For all these reasons, Franklin remained, at base, what Benedict Anderson calls a "creole nationalist" (B. Anderson, 2006: 61). Even as his disillusionment with Britain mounted and he became increasingly Americanized, Franklin continued to use categories of analysis that he had perfected as a dedicated servant and would-be reformer of the British Empire (G.S. Wood, 2004).[1] That he did so has a great deal to tell us about the man himself, about the British Empire that he served and admired and, ultimately, about the republic that he helped found in its place.

18.1 Trade and Empire

Franklin was certainly not the only founder to start out as a British patriot. Because he was seventy when he signed the Declaration of Independence, making him by far the oldest man to do so, his relationship to Britain differed from that of the other founders in two important respects. First, his formative exposure to British politics and culture came not during the mid-century Anglo-French wars for empire, as was the case with most of the revolution's leaders, but during the quarter century of peace and prosperity that followed the end of the European wars against Louis XIV in

1713. Reaching adulthood during the consumer revolution that took hold in Britain and America during the 1720s and 1730s, Franklin initially experienced the empire as a place of opportunity for a poor, ambitious boy seeking to make his way in the world (Breen, 1986, 1988). While America was especially fortunate in this regard, Franklin had no doubt that the colonies owed their thriving condition to what he called the British Atlantic's "glorious market" (Houston, 2004: 216). Franklin was himself a conspicuous beneficiary of this empire of goods, learning how to write essays from a volume of Addison and Steele's *Spectator*, cultivating ties to people throughout the empire to become the best-known printer and newspaper editor in the colonies, and using his tradesman's knack for self-promotion to broadcast the results of his electricity experiments before audiences in Britain and Europe (Lemay, 2000). In the years before the revolution, few Americans had more compelling reasons to be grateful subjects of the British Empire.

This experience ensured that Franklin never viewed trade as an abstraction in the way that some of the other founders, notably Thomas Jefferson and James Madison, did. Although Franklin was not above lamenting the effects of "foreign luxuries and needless manufactures" on contemporary manners, he believed that in a dispersed, far-flung nation like the British Empire, commerce was the only thing that could hold its various parts together (Houston, 2004: 219). He also thought that most people fulfilled their obligations to society not by participating in the formal political and military institutions of government but by pursuing their own interests and activities through the free exchange of goods and ideas. In this vein, Franklin predicted in *Observations Concerning the Increase of Mankind* (1751) that America's population would double in 25 years. The reason had nothing to do with Britain's vaunted naval power or the colonies' military prowess but was instead a result of America's economic advantages and the relatively young age at which English settlers married. "What an accession of power to the *British* Empire by sea as well as land," he wrote: "What [an] increase of trade and navigation!" (Houston, 2004: 220). One way to read the *Autobiography* is as a parable meant to illustrate the virtues that a young man needed need to make his mark in the empire's competitive, market-driven arena. Predictably, Franklin's advice was not to spend too much time in the contemplation of abstract truths or the quest for perfection. However desirable such pursuits might be for a man of leisure, Franklin assured his readers that they were of little use to the master printer who had to "mix with the world and ... receive people of business at their own hours" (Houston, 2004: 74). Frugality, hard work, and tough-minded pragmatism: such were the individual qualities on which personal wealth depended, and such, Franklin believed, were the qualities that made for national greatness.

This early exposure to Britain's commercial empire also left a lasting mark on how Franklin thought about the British government. Although never an uncritical admirer, Franklin believed that Britain had an indispensible role to play in safeguarding the commercial and maritime rights of British subjects in the colonies, and he thought that it was in America's interest to respect and uphold that role. Called to testify against the Stamp Act in the House of Commons in 1766, he readily conceded that the "sea is yours." Because the Royal Navy maintained the "safety of navigation" throughout the empire and kept the oceans "clear of pirates," it was only natural that Parliament would have a "right to some toll or duty on merchandizes carried through that part of your dominions" (Almon, 1971: 73). While this was rhetorically expedient, it was also something that Franklin believed. Into the early 1770s, he continued to think of the crown in particular as a bulwark of liberty in America, and he assumed that the gravest threats to American rights were as likely to come from petty officeholders and assemblies in the colonies as they were from British ministers in London. Significantly, his first brush with the authorities was with the Massachusetts assembly, which threw his brother James Franklin in jail in 1722 for publishing a piece in the *New-England Courant* that suggested that the colony was being deliberately slow in helping the Royal Navy fight piracy (Lemay, 2000). Nearly fifty years later, as Franklin worked the levers of power in Britain to turn Pennsylvania into a royal colony, his views were apparently unchanged (G.S. Wood, 2004: 124). Although there could be no guarantees, he remained far more comfortable than many Americans with the idea that the imperial rights of the British government and the rights of the king's subjects in America were compatible.

The second thing that set Franklin apart, one also related to when he was born, was that he achieved far more success as an imperial politician and British public servant than any other founder. As the king's deputy postmaster general for North America, which he held from 1753 until his dismissal in 1774, Franklin oversaw the only non-military British institution in America whose jurisdiction included all of the mainland colonies. During the controversies of the 1760s and early 1770s over parliamentary taxation, Franklin used franking privileges that allowed him to send and receive letters free of charge to propagandize against Parliament's reforms, endorsing the covers of letters with the words "B. FREE Franklin" (Lemay, 2000). However, as a royal officeholder, he also approached many imperial questions as an insider. During the opening phase of the Seven Years' War, Franklin made his influence felt in a variety of areas, organizing Pennsylvania's western defenses against the French and Indians, helping with logistics during Major General Edward Braddock's ill-fated expedition against Fort Duquesne (modern Pittsburgh), and attending the Albany Congress, where he submitted a prescient proposal for colonial union. In each of these capacities, he acted the part of the king's loyal servant. This was even true of his prospective union, which the Albany Congress adopted with minor revisions in 1754. Although the plan is often seen as foreshadowing the united colonial response to the Stamp Act a decade later – and sometimes the union that Congress formed in 1776 – the assemblies of the respective colonies uniformly rejected it, claiming, in Franklin's words, that it "allowed too much prerogative" (Houston, 2004: 255). Insofar as Franklin's union had any impact at the time, it was to lend its author's voice to that of other well-placed British observers and officials who thought that all was not as it should be with Britain's empire in the western Atlantic. For many, including in some regards Franklin, the solution was to tighten the reigns of empire (Gould, 2000: 66–68).

The high-point of Franklin's career as a British imperialist came during his mission to London as agent for Pennsylvania between 1757 and 1762. Like many Americans, Franklin found the English to be woefully ignorant of how things worked in the colonies. Shortly after his arrival, Lord Granville, president of the Privy Council, informed him that royal instructions to governors were the "law of the land" in the colonies, even when they clashed with the wishes of the assemblies, and Franklin eventually took to writing pieces on America to educate readers of the London and provincial press (Lemay, 2000; Houston, 2004: 139). At the same time, though, he added a number of Britain's leading public figures to his circle of acquaintances during these years, attending London clubs with Joseph Priestley and Richard Price, becoming friends with the Anglo-Scottish printer (and future member of Parliament) William Strahan, and visiting Scotland, where he met David Hume, Adam Smith, and Lord Kames. In 1760, he intervened in the British debate over peace talks with France, advocating for the retention of Canada in his longest and most influential pamphlet, *The Interest of Great Britain Considered*, and he scored an important victory as Pennsylvania agent when the Privy Council overturned a Board of Trade ruling that prohibited the assembly from taxing land owned by the Penns (Lemay, 2000). As was true of the Scots whose company he found so congenial, Franklin had no trouble wearing more than one hat. Although he never forgot that he was a colonist from Pennsylvania, he had every reason to think of himself as a Briton too.

Based on these two formative experiences – first as a successful tradesman in Philadelphia, then as a man of affairs within the empire – Franklin came to believe that Britain and the colonies constituted a single nation. In the anonymously published *Interest of Great Britain Considered*, which Franklin wrote using the persona of a native Briton, he insisted that the North American colonies were too disunited to threaten Britain's imperial supremacy, and he reminded British readers that trade with America had already enriched the western ports of Scotland and England. Ultimately, however, the question of how to reconcile British and American interests was moot because Britons everywhere belonged to the same political "body." In the event of a war to protect foreign markets for English manufacturing, no one would describe the contest as being merely for "the weavers of

Yorkshire, ... the cutlers of *Sheffield*, or the button-makers of *Birmingham*"; such a war, wrote Franklin, would quite properly be considered a "national" war. The same was true of British America. Because of the increasing tempo of commerce, Britain's maritime empire was a far more unified polity than many of its land-based rivals in Europe, and its far-flung parts were knit together more closely than its European core had been a century and a half before. Thus Franklin wrote:

> While our strength at sea continues, the banks of the *Ohio* ... are nearer to *London*, than the remote parts of *France* and *Spain* to their respective capitals; and much nearer than *Connaught* and *Ulster* were in the days of Queen *Elizabeth*. No body foretells the dissolution of the Russian monarchy from its extent, yet I will venture to say, the eastern parts of it are already much more inaccessible from *Petersburgh*, than the country on the *Mississippi* is from *London*.

Because the British Empire was a fluid and interconnected web, the interests of Great Britain and the colonies were the same – or so it seemed to the empire's preeminent American (Franklin, 1760: 20, 41).

The result was an imperial vision where the human propensity to go forth and multiply – or, as Franklin the political economist might have said, to settle, trade, and marry – worked to foster both expansion and unity. Often, the unity that Franklin had in mind was racial as well as commercial. In the 1751 *Observations*, which Franklin appended to several pamphlets that appeared during the Seven Years' War, he warned that America's heavy reliance on African slavery and its openness to immigrants from Europe – especially "swarthy" Germans – threatened to "darken its people" at a moment when the natural increase of British settlers was tending to make "this side of our globe reflect a brighter light" (Houston, 2004: 221). Following the 1763 massacre of Christian Indians by the Scots-Irish Paxton Boys, Franklin used equally loaded terms to describe the "freckled red-haired men, women, and children" who were coming to the middle colonies in such numbers (Franklin, 1764: 13). "Why should *Pennsylvania*, founded by the *English*, become a colony of *Aliens*?" he asked (Houston, 2004: 221). Eventually, Franklin's criticism of slavery would become part of a larger list of grievances against Britain, which he claimed was largely responsible for the African slave trade (Waldstreicher, 2004: 181). In remarks on the landmark *Somerset* case of 1772, which held that slavery was "odious" and could only be supported by positive law that England lacked, he lambasted "pharisaical Britain" for the self-satisfaction with which it freed one slave in London while allowing its merchants to condemn "many hundreds of thousands" to slavery in America (Houston, 2004: 294). He also became an increasingly public supporter of the antislavery movement in Pennsylvania and the United States, helping draft the first remonstrance to Congress shortly before his death in 1790. Even as his humanitarian sensibilities evolved and matured, however, Franklin never formally disavowed the racial terms that informed his thinking about the empire's demography (Houston, 2004: xxxvii).[2]

No less important, though Franklin never abandoned his optimism about America's long-term prospects. In the closing sentence of the original version of the *Observations*, Franklin seemed to back off his racially based criticism of the slave trade, writing, somewhat casually, that "perhaps I am partial to the complexion of my country, for such kind of partiality is natural to mankind." For the most part, he thought that the forces of demographic and economic growth were beyond Britain's ability to control, and he had no doubt that the British Empire had been a conspicuous beneficiary of their elemental and uncontrollable power. "We have been here but little more than 100 years," wrote Franklin of the colonies' brief history in 1751, "and yet the force of our privateers in the late war ... was greater both in men and guns than that of the whole *British* navy in Queen *Elizabeth's* time" (Houston, 2004: 220–221). When he returned to Pennsylvania in 1762, the sense of British patriotism in America that Franklin himself exemplified had never been stronger, and he was at the height of his powers. He was the most famous American in the empire, to say nothing of Europe. Anything that enhanced the colonies' reputation in the eyes of the metropolitan public was bound to enhance his own, and anything that served Britain's interests in America seemed to be in his interest as well. Although he had compelling personal reasons to say what he did about the British Empire, there was little to suggest that he was not saying what he believed.

18.2 The American Revolution

In the event, the British Empire was about to change in ways that Franklin found impossible to accept. For Franklin, as for no other founder, the American Revolution was a bitter civil war. In part, this was because so many of his friends, including his longtime political ally in Pennsylvania Joseph Galloway and his son William, who was governor of New Jersey in 1776, sided with the king (G.S. Wood, 2004: 160–163). Although he was on a ship from England when the opening shots were fired at Lexington and Concord, Franklin also viewed Britain's resort to force as a stunning betrayal. In the colonial plan of confederation that he unsuccessfully urged Congress to adopt in July 1775, he made reconciliation conditional on the British government's willingness to make reparations "for the injury done to Boston by shutting up its port; for the burning of Charlestown [during the battle of Bunker Hill]; and for the expence of this unjust war" (Houston, 2004: 315–316). During Britain's last-ditch attempt to forestall the French alliance in 1778, Franklin said essentially the same thing to the British spy and double agent Paul Wentworth when the two met in Paris. While welcoming what amounted to an unofficial British peace overture and conceding that if they were reunited, "Britain and America [could] be the greatest empire on earth," Franklin spent most of the interview lecturing the hapless Wentworth about the suffering that Britain had inflicted on his country. At one point, he even spoke of "Englishmen as barbarous!" (Gould, 2012). Whatever attraction the empire had once held, the course of events effectively destroyed the vision of a greater British nation that had been so central to Franklin's self-identity.

Nonetheless, Franklin found it impossible to sever all ties, let alone break habits formed by decades of faithful service to the British crown and empire. When asked during his testimony in 1766 before the House of Commons to describe American views of Britain, he responded unequivocally: "The best in the world" (Almon, 1971: 67). Although he never doubted where his ultimate allegiance was – or ought to be – Franklin believed to the end of his life that the split with Britain was, on some level, regrettable, and he continued to think that there should have been a way to prevent it. In 1789, just over a year before he died, he wrote that if the Albany union, "or something like it," had been adopted in 1754, the "separation of the colonies from the Mother Country might not so soon have happened, nor the mischiefs suffered on both sides have occurred." Continuing, he explained that had Britain's colonies been able to defend themselves, there would have been no need to send a British army to secure the North American frontier, no pretense for Parliament to tax the colonists to pay for its support, and no basis for the quarrel that cost so much blood and treasure. In short, "the different parts of the empire might have remained in peace and union" (Houston, 2004: 255). For a man who had played a leading role in the America Revolution, signing the Declaration of Independence, negotiating the Treaty of Paris that ended the war with Britain, and serving in the convention that drafted the United States Constitution, it was an extraordinary thing to say.

This residual affection for the British Empire inevitably colored how Franklin thought about the American republic. First of all, Franklin believed that the United States was the rightful heir and successor to all of Britain's North American empire as confirmed by the peace that ended the Seven Years' War in 1763. In the Model Treaty of 1776, which Franklin helped John Adams write as a guide for Congress's relations with foreign governments, this capacious union was held to include not only the thirteen colonies that declared independence from Britain but also Canada, Nova Scotia, Newfoundland, East and West Florida, and Bermuda (Stagg, 2009: 14). Elsewhere, Franklin went still further, adding the Bahamas to the list of prospective American states during negotiations with Lord Howe after the fall of New York in 1776 and including Ireland and the West Indies in the colonial articles of confederation that he proposed in 1775 (PBF: 22,

120–125, 630–632).[3] Franklin also served on the commission that Congress dispatched in March 1776 to persuade Quebec's French inhabitants to join the thirteen colonies in their resistance to Parliament, and he repeatedly pressed both France and Britain to recognize the union's claims on Canada during his years as American ambassador in Paris. To everyone's surprise, including Comte de Vergennes, who had no wish to see "the new republic [become] mistress of the entire continent," he nearly succeeded, securing a tentative British agreement in 1782 to cede most of what later became the province of Ontario (Perkins, 1993: 38). Had the agreement held up, there would have been little to prevent the upstart republic from eventually succeeding to the rest of the North American empire that Franklin had spent so much of his life working to bring into being.

In embracing this expansionist vision of the union, Franklin was indirectly giving voice to the related hope that the United States would be Britain's successor in terms of the opportunities that were available to ordinary Americans. As Franklin made clear in the *Observations* of 1751, the main reason for the colonies' prosperity and demographic growth was the abundance of land. Because real estate was so plentiful and cheap, a "labouring man" in British America found it relatively easy to plant a farm and start a family, and he and his wife had every reason to believe that their children would eventually be able to provide for themselves in the same way (Houston, 2004: 216). The passage of time did nothing to alter these views. In a paper written before he left France in 1785, Franklin described America as a land of vacant forests and "fertile soil full of wood" where industrious immigrants faced little difficulty becoming land-owning settlers. By allowing artisans to avoid low-wage work and leave "trades for agriculture," the abundance of cheap land also made America more egalitarian than the densely settled countries of Europe. As long as land remained available on such liberal terms – which meant continuing to expand the union's borders – Franklin believe that America would be a nation where what someone did mattered more than who he or she was. Never one to let the truth get in the way of a good story, Franklin even claimed that most Americans liked to think that they were descended from "ploughmen, smiths, carpenters, turners, weavers, tanners, or even shoemakers"; this, apparently, was preferable to having ancestors who were "gentlemen, doing nothing of value" (Houston, 2004: 342–345).

Franklin's *Autobiography* underscored the legacy of economic opportunity that he hoped British America would bequeath to the United States. Although he wrote the first part in 1771 and the rest during the 1780s, the narrative stops with his mission to London in 1757. In a letter that appeared in the published version, Lord Shelburne's Anglo-American secretary Benjamin Vaughan laid out the work's central purpose, which was to set an example to "your vast and rising country" (Houston, 2004: 62). Everything in the story that Franklin told occurs before the revolution began and involves a man who was a loyal and steadfast subject of the British Empire, yet he believed that the lessons that he had learned as a youth in colonial Boston were equally applicable to the citizens of the new republic. Writing in a letter to Vaughan in 1784 about the American market for luxury goods, Franklin described a nation where the circulation of people and goods created the same individual and collective opportunities that they had for subjects of the British Empire:

> In our commercial towns upon the seacoast, fortunes will occasionally be made. Some of those who grow rich, will be prudent, live within bounds, and preserve what they have gained for their posterity. Others fond of showing their wealth, will be extravagant and ruin themselves. Laws cannot prevent this; and perhaps it is not always an evil to the public .... A vain silly fellows builds a fine house, furnishes it richly, lives in it expensively, and in [a] few years ruins himself, but the masons, carpenters, smiths and other honest tradesmen have been by his employ assisted in maintaining and raising their families, the farmer has been paid for his labour and encouraged, and the estate is now in better hands. (Houston, 2004: 350)

Because they were no longer British subjects, Americans were now the primary beneficiaries of this freewheeling market in ways that they had not been before 1776. Otherwise, there was little to distinguish what Franklin had to say about the United States from what he had once said about the American colonies.

The third area where Franklin's understanding of the British Empire influenced his thinking about the American union was in matters of constitutional government. By his own admission, Franklin had fewer problems with the concentration of power than most Americans. The plan of union that he presented to the Albany Congress in 1754 was, among other things, an attempt to entrust colonial defense to a handful of knowledgeable experts – "men of good abilities for business and men of reputation for integrity," as Franklin wrote in remarks on the scheme. Although he was an early critic of the idea of parliamentary taxation in America, Franklin also believed during the 1750s that Parliament alone had the authority to overcome the colonies' petty rivalries and enact such a union (Franklin, 1779: 88, 97; G.S. Wood, 2004: 72–78). Twenty years later, he still thought this way. In the plan of confederation that he wrote for the united colonies in 1775, Franklin proposed to give Congress powers that, in some ways, exceeded what the federal government enjoyed under the Constitution of 1787, and they were far greater than those allowed by the Articles of Confederation in 1777 (Lemay, 2000). Significantly, in describing the Constitutional Convention to an English friend in 1787, Franklin likened the delegates to "what the French call *une assemblée des notables*, a convention composed of ... the principal people from the several states of our confederation" (G.S. Wood, 2004: 216). In each case, the goal was to give elected and appointed officials enough power to put the good of the whole ahead of their own "selfish views" and to encourage Americans to think of themselves as "members of the same body" (Franklin, 1779: 89, 91). Before the American Revolution, this was how Franklin had understood the constitutional role of the British crown and Parliament within the British Empire, and it was how he continued to think about Congress and the American union.

Despite his royalist views and support for a strong union, Franklin recognized early on that the only way to realize those goals was through federalism. Here again, some of his most important statements involved the structure of the British Empire. In his testimony before the House of Commons in 1766, Franklin reminded his interlocutors that Britain's empire was an empire not of force but of liberty and freely given consent. Until the Stamp Act changed these feelings, Americans "submitted willingly to the government of the crown":

> Numerous as the people are in the several old provinces, they cost you nothing in forts, citadels, garrisons or armies, to keep them in subjection. They were governed by this country at the expense only of a little pen, ink and paper. They were led by a thread. (Almon, 1971: 67)

This insight was obviously meant to appeal to a Parliament looking for ways to reduce the costs of imperial defense, but it eventually formed the basis for a distinctively "American theory of empire" whereby the colonies were bound to Britain as "states" with same rights under the British crown as the kingdoms of Ireland and Scotland before the union of 1707, including the exclusive right to tax themselves (Gould, 2000: 123). Although Franklin was by no means the only American to embrace the new theory, he played a key role during the late 1760s and 1770s in popularizing it in Britain and the colonies (G.S. Wood, 2004: 120–124). In so doing, he indirectly helped prepare the way for the loose-knit commonwealth that Britain's settler empire in Canada, Australia, and New Zealand became during the nineteenth century, and his ideas were crucial for the development of American constitutional thought, both before and after the Constitutional Convention of 1787 (Greene, 1986; Gould, 1999: 476–489). As with everything else that Franklin did, it was sometimes hard to tell where his service to British America ended and his obligations to the United States took over.

During the last fifteen years of his life, Franklin distinguished himself as a forthright and committed patriot. Although his years of residence in London exposed him to allegations of being a closet Loyalist, he became one of most radical founders, presiding over the constitutional convention that gave Pennsylvania the most democratic legislature in the union in 1776 and condemning the use of property qualifications for the right to vote and hold office in deliberations over the United States Constitution in 1787

(Lemay, 2000). In 1782, when Lord Shelburne, George III's newly-appointed prime minister, made one last attempt at reconciliation by offering the American states commonwealth status within the empire, Franklin was categorical in his rejection, accusing the government of attempting to create an Anglo-American universal monarchy. All Europe, he wrote, would see in such an over-mighty empire a threat to their own "national independence," and making a separate peace with Britain would be a gross betrayal of the American treaty with France. Yet Franklin never ceased to think of the American republic in British American terms. Significantly, in his exchange with Shelburne, Franklin conceded that the United States might eventually acquire Britain's "imperial stability," at which point Americans might also "commence tyrants over our subjects, insulters of neighboring states, and ... despisers of political, friendly, and relative alliances" (Franklin, 1782: 23–25). Although Americans were now citizens of a union with its own history and traditions, they were still lineal descendants of the empire that they had just defeated. Who was to say what other parts of Britain's history they would eventually replicate?

18.3 American Icon

In many ways, Franklin's most enduring contribution to the United States – certainly his most famous role – was to personify the values that Americans believed were essential to the republic's success. He was able to do this, at least in part, because his reputation as a British American was already so great. Following the London publication of his *Experiments and Observations on Electricity* (1751), Franklin vaulted to fame as the "modern Prometheus," as the German philosopher Immanuel Kant wrote in 1756 (Chaplin, 2006; Delbourgo, 2006: 3). Although he could not have done this without mastering the terms and methods used by *literati* in Europe, admirers everywhere came to see his spectacular rise as evidence of the "New World's capacity to produce an untutored genius" (G.S. Wood, 2004: 65). During the 1750s, Harvard, Yale, and William and Mary all recognized his achievements with honorary degrees. During his first mission to Britain, the Universities of St Andrews in Scotland and Oxford added to these honors by awarding him doctorates, and he was elected a member of the Royal Society in 1753 and, eventually, an associate of the French *Académie royale des sciences*. By the time that Franklin landed in France in late 1776, the self-educated son of a Boston tallow chandler and soap maker had long since metamorphosed into the international celebrity universally known as Dr Franklin. "What say you to your friend and brother philosopher Franklin," wrote Edmund Burke in 1775, "who at upwards of seventy years of age, quits the study of the laws of nature in order to give laws to new commonwealths .... Few things more extraordinary have happened in the history of mankind" (Lemay, 2000).

The nine years that Franklin spent in Paris strengthened and refined his image as a provincial man of letters. From the outset, Franklin was lionized by French society. Mindful of Pennsylvania's reputation as a land of plain-spoken Quakers, the septuagenarian ambassador generally went without a wig, and he often wore homespun. In an act of sartorial self-parody that would have been ridiculed had it happened in Philadelphia, he even sat for a portrait wearing a fur cap. The result was one of the most successful propaganda campaigns ever. While he was in Paris, Franklin's visage became a stock feature of French prints and engravings – as well as hats, canes, snuff boxes, watches, clocks, rings, chinaware, and anything else that could be embellished with his image. Doyennes of the Parisian salons vied to see who could throw the most lavish parties and entertainments, while statesmen wrote poems in his honor (Palmer, 1959–1964: 1, 251–252). In a famous encounter at the French Academy in 1778, weeks after the signing of the Franco-American treaty, he and Voltaire embraced and kissed to loud acclaim. The ever-critical John Adams, on hand to witness the event, wrote: "Oh! it was enchanting to see Solon and Sophocles embracing!" (L.H. Butterfield, 1961: 4, 81). At times, the adulation seemed to catch even Franklin by surprise. "Figure me," he wrote his English friend Emma Thompson, "very plainly dress'd, wearing my thin grey straight hair, that peeps out under my only coiffeur, a fine fur cap, which comes down my forehead almost to my spectacles. Think how this must appear among the powder'd heads of Paris" (Lemay, 2000). Having spent his adult life acquiring the trappings of cosmopolitan gentility, Franklin achieved his last and greatest triumph as an exemplar of common virtue.

This, of course, is the Franklin that generations of readers would come to know from the *Autobiography*. By the time that the narrative ends in the 1750s, the author's meteoric rise was well underway; however, the main focus is on Franklin's life as a curious and adventurous boy in Boston, as an ambitious printer in Philadelphia, and as an aspiring scientist, inventor, and citizen of the European Atlantic's republic of letters. During the 1790s, this Franklin became a symbol of the middling and artisanal values associated with the new Democratic Republican party – a "brother mechanic," as New York's Society of Mechanics and Tradesmen called him in an Independence Day toast in 1795 – and in the twenty-two editions that appeared between 1794 and 1828, Franklin's life story served to illustrate the virtues of industriousness and entrepreneurialism that Americans were coming to see as the revolution's crowning achievement (G.S. Wood, 2004: 235–236, 239). Never one to let a profitable marketing opportunity pass, Franklin surely would have welcomed this development had he lived to see it. Yet given his penchant for irony and love of deflating well-worn myths and comfortable assumptions, it is an equally certain bet that Franklin would have found it hard to resist noting that the circumstances that made his remarkable life possible were as British as they were American. This would have come as no surprise to those who knew him while he was alive, and it is a part of Benjamin Franklin's story that is worth remembering today.

Notes

1 Although Gordon Wood places more emphasis on Franklin's post-1776 identification with Europe and France, the argument here follows his contention that Franklin's role as American symbol masked a deeper and more complicated set of attitudes.
2 The final two paragraphs of *Observations*, where the quoted passages about the African slave trade, the immigration of "swarthy" Germans and the need to "brighten" America appear, were omitted from versions published after 1755 (Houston, 2004: 221, n3).
3 Labaree, Leonard W. *et al.*, eds. (1959–). *The Papers of Benjamin Franklin*. 39 vols to date. New Haven, CT: Yale University Press. Hereafter referred to as PBF.

Further Reading

Aldridge, A.O. (1949). "Franklin as demographer," *Journal of Economic History* 9: 25–44.
Anderson, D. (1997). *The Radical Enlightenments of Benjamin Franklin*. Baltimore, MD.
Clark, C.E. (1993). *The Public Prints: The Newspaper in Anglo-American Culture, 1665–1740*. New York, NY.
Hanna, W.S. (1964). *Benjamin Franklin and Pennsylvania Politics*. Stanford, CA.
Houston, A. (2008). *Benjamin Franklin and the Politics of Improvement*. New Haven, NJ.
Lambert, F. (1993). "Subscribing for profits and piety: The friendship of Benjamin Franklin and George Whitefield," *William and Mary Quarterly* 3rd ser 50: 529–554.
Lemay, J.A.L. (2005–). *The Life of Benjamin Franklin*, 3 vols. Philadelphia, PA.
McCoy, D.R. (1978). "Benjamin Franklin's vision of a republican political economy for America," *William and Mary Quarterly* 3rd ser 35: 605–628.
Pangle, L.S. (2007). *The Political Philosophy of Benjamin Franklin*. Baltimore, MD.
Rossiter, C. (1952). "The political theory of Benjamin Franklin," *Pennsylvania Magazine of History and Biography* 76: 259–293.

Chapter Nineteen

Franklin's Pictorial Representations of British America

Lester C. Olson

During Benjamin Franklin's lifetime, visual messages circulated on almost every extant medium in British America, Britain, and France. Throughout the eighteenth century, partisans sought to influence their contemporaries' beliefs and actions with symbolic images. As messages calculated to persuade other people, such visual rhetoric was distributed throughout the British Empire and beyond it on countless mundane objects and highly refined art in public and private life. Symbolic designs appeared on metal and paper currency, medals, paintings, statues, architectural elements, flags, drums, powder horns, illuminated displays, imprinted textiles, housewares, carved furniture, and, above all, illustrations which circulated in magazines, pamphlets, almanacs, newspapers, and broadsides. Sometimes displayed exclusively among intimate friends in the home, other times ubiquitous in public life among all ranks of people, symbolic images were employed by partisans to express and advocate political commitments throughout the Revolutionary era.

Throughout Franklin's lifetime, portraits and statues were commissioned and displayed prominently in praise of leaders who had defended British America's interests, while portraits and statues of other opprobrious individuals were removed from public forums and destroyed. A medal featuring Franklin's portrait illustrates only one such example honoring his leadership while he was a plenipotentiary ambassador in France (Figure 19.1). Engraved, etched, and woodcut illustrations circulated as frontispieces and satirical prints inside pamphlets, magazines, and almanacs or, in other cases, as mastheads on major newspapers, where they recurred week after week. While newspapers and paper currency were the predominant means of visual

A Companion to Benjamin Franklin, First Edition. Edited by David Waldstreicher.
© 2011 Blackwell Publishing Ltd. Published 2011 by Blackwell Publishing Ltd.

Figure 19.1 "The Franklin Medal," 1784. Medium: silver, bronze or brass medal, maker: Augustin Dupré, size: 1 3/4" diameter. Photograph courtesy of the American Philosophical Society.

rhetoric in British America, broadsides were the most pervasive form in which allegorical prints circulated in Britain, where the golden age of caricature was developing in the aftermath of William Hogarth's widely admired engravings. Images of British America represented as one body politic were distributed widely during the decades before the American revolution, not only through art objects, currency, and reading materials, but also through objects displayed or used on a daily basis in the home: commemorative medals, imprinted textiles, and housewares, such as creamware, porcelain, or china pitchers, plates, and bowls.

Franklin was typical of eighteenth-century polemicists in his recognition of visual rhetoric as a powerful means for influencing others' beliefs and actions. My book, *Benjamin Franklin's Vision of American Community* (L.C. Olson, 2004), focused on the pictorial images that he designed to represent the British colonies that became the United States, because, as I was conducting the research for my earlier book concerning eighteenth-century communication, I noticed how varied and how influential

Figure 19.2 "JOIN, or DIE," *Pennsylvania Gazette*, May 9, 1754, p. 2, col. 2. maker: [Benjamin Franklin], publisher: Benjamin Franklin and David Hall, medium: newspaper, 2 7/8" × 2". Photograph courtesy of the Library of Congress.

Franklin's pictorial designs were in his world (L.C. Olson, *Emblems*, 1991). He invented at least one such image to represent British America during each decade from the 1750s to the 1780s. In 1754, "JOIN, or DIE" represented the colonies as a segmented snake in a woodcut designed to promote unity among the British colonies during the French and Indian War (Figure 19.2). A decade later, in 1766, "MAGNA *Britannia: her Colonies* REDUC'D" portrayed the colonies as the severed arms and legs of Britannia in a political cartoon designed to advocate imperial unity during the Stamp Act controversy (Figure 19.3). In 1776, "WE ARE ONE" designated the United States as thirteen interlinked rings on the Continental currency to suggest unity among the States during the initial war years (Figure 19.4). Finally, in 1783, *Libertas Americana* depicted the United States as the infant Hercules strangling two serpents on a commemorative medal issued near the Revolution's conclusion (Figure 19.5). Each of Franklin's designs circulated internationally during the Revolutionary era. No other American colonist's pictorial representations designating the emerging nation as one body politic were more original or influential in their time than those by Franklin. So for many years now, I have been studying Franklin's role as a pictorial

Figure 19.3 MAGNA Britannia: her Colonies REDUC'D," Benjamin Franklin, [circa 1766]. medium: print, size: 4 1/8" × 5 7/8". Photograph courtesy of The Library Company of Philadelphia.

propagandist as a consequence of my earlier fascination with eighteenth-century communication, especially the role of visual images in rhetoric and politics.

I realized that these four pictorial representations of British America were connected by more than their similar subject of the British American colonial community. All can be classified as belonging to the same general kind of visual rhetoric based on three particular features that they shared: (1) a pictorial representation, (2) a motto in the vernacular or Latin, and (3) a resulting moral or lesson. As visual rhetoric, they were derived from an aesthetic tradition of emblems and devices which had spanned centuries in Europe and Britain. Although many varied and sometimes subtle distinctions were drawn between emblems and devices before the eighteenth century (D.S. Russell, 1985), in Franklin's lifetime some individuals used the terms "emblem" and "device" interchangeably or in the combination "emblematical device." Under a pseudonym, "Clericus" outlined essential features that emblems and devices had in common: "An emblematical

Figure 19.4 "One Sixth of a Dollar," 1776. publisher: [David] Hall and [William] Sellers, medium: colonial currency, size: 3 1/4" × 2 1/2". Photograph courtesy the Library of Congress, Thatcher Collection.

Figure 19.5 *Libertas Americana*, proposed and commissioned by Benjamin Franklin, executed by Augustin Dupré, 1783. Photograph courtesy of the British Museum, Department of Coins and Medals. © The Trustees of the British Museum.

device, when rightly formed, is said to consist of two parts, a *body* and a *mind*, neither of which is compleat or intelligible, without the aid of the other. The figure is called the *body*, the motto the *mind*."[1] These comments, published initially in the *Pennsylvania Gazette* in 1775, and reprinted in the *Pennsylvania Magazine* later that year, neither specified whether a human, animal, plant, or architectural form could be used for "the figure" or pictorial element of the design, nor did they mention whether the motto should be in Latin, a foreign language, or the vernacular. This article by "Clericus" has sometimes been attributed to Franklin (E.P. Newman, 1983: 2272–2273; Lemay, 1986b: 122–124). But the attribution is uncertain, however, simply because Franklin never used the expression, "emblematical device," in any of his other known prose.

Franklin's comments about and use of emblems and devices reveal that he did not distinguish between them based on either the subject matter depicted in the pictorial image or the language of the motto, as did some earlier authorities on such messages during the sixteenth and seventeenth centuries in France. Historically, one commonplace distinction was that devices conveyed particular ideas in Latin to the learned, whereas emblems were for ideas applicable to everyone and were expressed in the vernacular. Nor did he adhere to the common practice of distinguishing as "emblems" those pictorial messages that employed representations of the human form, verses "devices," which did not. In these respects, he was typical of most American colonists in apparently using both terms interchangeably (Sommer, 1961).

Whether the mottos of Franklin's pictorial representations were in Latin or the vernacular was rhetorically consequential because of the messages' accessibility to various audiences. But his choices of language did not necessarily reveal his political commitments, such as a "democratic" impulse, as has sometimes been claimed (Lemay, 1987: 473, 475, 494), because his use of Latin mottos recurred regularly throughout his entire lifetime. He used them in his emblems and devices for the Associator flags in 1747, for the Continental currency in 1775, again for the various medals commissioned to honor military victories during the Revolution, and yet again for *Libertas Americana* in 1783. This lifelong pattern of using Latin mottos makes it unlikely that he sought fundamentally to make emblems and devices "democratic," especially since he never explicitly identified himself as having such political commitments. His use of Latin or the vernacular depended, above all, on rhetorical considerations of the audience and their generic expectations for the particular type of message. Such considerations may have taken priority over adhering to familiar conventions distinguishing emblems or devices.

Franklin's language choice may have depended on a combination of factors, including not only the conventions for a specific medium, such as the honorary medals, but also the principal audience's level of education. "JOIN, or DIE" and "WE ARE ONE" were both widely distributed among Americans of all backgrounds, the former in newspapers such as the

Pennsylvania Gazette in 1754, the latter on the Continental currency's fractional notes in 1776; both had vernacular mottos. In contrast, toward the end of his career, *Libertas Americana*, was the title of the commemorative medal that he presented in 1783 to prominent political figures in France and the United States: King Louis XVI, Queen Marie Antoinette, the ministers in the French court, and the president and the representatives in the American Congress. Franklin used Latin in this instance, because most of these leaders would have had the classical education necessary to comprehend the message. One notable problem with this hypothesis about adjusting to audiences, however, is that Latin mottos accompanied the designs on the Continental currency that circulated widely among the American people in 1775. The same is the case for the emission of paper money the following year in 1776 with the exception of Franklin's fractional note design ("WE ARE ONE") and the forty-dollar bill printed in English. Perhaps the use of Latin on the rest of the currency reflected the committee's deliberations, not Franklin's preferences.

The choice of Latin for a motto also had rhetorical ramifications for an author's persona. Franklin was aware of this, judging from a humorous commentary in *The New-England Courant* during 1723, when it was published under Benjamin Franklin's editorship instead of his older brother James's. The *Courant* commented, "Gentle Readers, we design never to let a Paper pass without a Latin Motto if we can possibly pick one up, which carries a Charm in it to the Vulgar, and the learned admire the pleasure of Construing. We should have obliged the World with a Greek scrap or two, but the Printer has no Types, and therefore we intreat the candid Reader not to impute the defect to our Ignorance, for our Doctor can say all the Greek Letters by heart" (*Papers*, 1: 50). Franklin's contemporaries certainly regarded the use of Latin for the mottos as a means to make an author appear well educated.

Although Franklin's experience with the production of emblems and devices was extensive, it is the four pictorial representations depicting British America that are the most important of his designs for understanding his emerging nationalism between the early 1750s and mid-1780s, because, in varied ways, they envisioned the British colonies as one body politic. These four images, as elements in Franklin's communication about the nature of colonial union, are a vehicle to explore his evolving vision of British America, and they also reflected and promoted changes in American culture throughout the Revolutionary era. These images, designed with American audiences in mind, are useful indices of transformations in American culture, because partisans appropriated, subverted, and transformed them for a range of ends, oftentimes to blunt their political import. In addition, they reveal changes in Franklin's vision of a British American community, because in every instance he modified the depictions of unity among those disparate colonies that became the United States.

Even though Franklin directed all of the pictorial images to Americans, he also directed most of them to audiences in Britain and at least one to a French audience. Franklin was a representative in the Pennsylvania Assembly in 1754, a colonial agent in Britain at London in 1765–1766, a representative in the Continental Congress at Philadelphia in 1776, and the United States' plenipotentiary ambassador to France in 1783, when he lived in Paris. At these moments, roughly a decade apart, his political and social roles as an American colonist differed significantly. In 1754 and again in 1776, for example, he was well situated as a representative in Pennsylvania to participate directly in the formation of colonial policies. But in 1766 and again in 1783, he was located on the periphery of the forums for exercising political power and social privilege – first the British Parliament and, subsequently, the French ministry.

Each of the pictorial images representing the British colonies in America were details in much broader campaigns. Because the meanings of these images were shaped not only by the palpable form of the messages but also by the points of view of the audiences and by the political circumstances surrounding their distribution, it was necessary for me to interpret these images in light of the ephemeral, rhetorical understandings and public address of the period. Every one of the pictorial compositions had an enduring but changing significance throughout the Revolutionary era, as contemporary partisans appropriated them for a range of reasons and uses in Britain, France, America, Holland, Germany, Spain, Italy, and elsewhere as far away as China.

Although each image portraying a British American community took on a life of its own internationally at the time, each was admittedly a small part of Franklin's extraordinary life. In fact, the pictorial images were of such slight importance as details in his life that even Franklin's best biographers ordinarily mention only one or two of them – typically the most famous of the images, "JOIN, or DIE", but seldom many others. Even Carl Van Doren, who set the standard for subsequent biographies with his Pulitzer Prize winning *Benjamin Franklin* (Van Doren, 1938), mentioned only three of them, omitting as he did the designs for the Continental paper currency in 1776. But small details though these visual images certainly were in Franklin's life, I have argued that careful attention to them throws into high relief fundamental changes in Franklin's sensibility concerning British America, especially his political commitments as he changed from being an American Whig to a republican (L.C. Olson, 2004). In short, the pictorial rhetoric indices these basic changes in Franklin's politics.

In attempting to synthesize the rhetorical usage of each of the pictorial images, I have employed a classical vocabulary for organizing both the analysis of the message's role in its time and the analysis of the major appeals to the principal audiences during the Revolutionary era. The classical terms for types of persuasive messages in civic forums – deliberative, judicial, and ceremonial rhetoric – were salient genres during the eighteenth century, especially among political leaders who ordinarily had the benefit of a classical education. As such, these genres are useful for organizing an interpretation of the visual rhetoric in these specific forums during that time. Well-educated, economically privileged, and politically powerful men in eighteenth-century patriarchal British and American colonial cultures would have been familiar with these types of persuasive discourse in public life, corresponding as they did to highly visible, public activities in the legislatures, the courts, and ceremonial occasions. Dating back historically to classical Greece, the types of persuasive speeches in these forums were identified and detailed in treatises on rhetoric, especially Aristotle's *Rhetoric*. Each type of public speech had corresponding commonplace lines of public argument (or *topoi*) which recurred in appeals to specific audiences for consensus on the decisions concerning the expediency or inexpediency of future policies, the justice or injustice of past deeds, or the current praiseworthiness or blameworthiness of individuals or institutions. Early writers on emblems and devices drew explicitly on classical treatises on rhetoric to develop their commentaries about these varieties of visual arts.

At the same time, I employed these classical terms for kinds of discourse under certain strictures, such as an emphatic recognition that they were not adequate for understanding broad, popular forms of participation in the rhetorical life of the community. Those without political power and economic privilege often resorted to types of rhetorical appeals in various mundane objects, such as textiles and housewares, as well as popular forums, such as public demonstrations featuring effigies, illuminated displays, and symbolic processions. Such people often relied on metaphor and allegory, as I argued at length in my earlier book, *Emblems of American Community in the Revolutionary Era* (L.C. Olson, 1991), because these were relatively indirect but nonetheless robust means to assert their views. So the utility of the classical terms is ultimately circumscribed, not only through emphatic strictures on their use in relation to specific types of decision making in certain public forums, but also through a conscious broadening of the forms of rhetorical appeal through an examination of common objects used for persuasion in public life: paper money, military flags, textile designs, medals, terra cotta plaques, housewares, and the like.

I argued the thesis that the differences among Franklin's pictorial representations of British America as one body politic reflected his complex process of rejecting Britain's constitutional monarchy and ultimately endorsing republicanism as a form of government in the United States. Initially, he veered toward increasing the monarch's power in British America before he repudiated that political system altogether and embraced republicanism. This transformation resulted from his active engagement with diverse, intercultural influences and his dramatically changing political circumstances. The portrait of Franklin emerging from my book on his visual rhetoric is that of a man whose capacity to reconsider his own most fundamental beliefs resulted in his dramatically changed political commitments over the decades. Franklin's visual rhetoric indices these basic changes in his political commitments. It would be impossible in a brief essay to detail those changes with the care and attention to detail that they deserve, but I would like to try in what follows to give you a general sketch of the broad outlines.

Franklin first published the design of the segmented snake, "JOIN, or DIE," in the *Pennsylvania Gazette* on May 9, 1754 (Figure 19.2). This was the earliest known pictorial representation of a colonial union produced by a British colonist in America. The image of the segmented snake in the *Gazette* consisted of eight sections or parts. The head represented New England, and each of the seven remaining parts corresponded to a single colony, which was identified by its initial letter or letters. The arrangement of the seven remaining parts corresponded from head to tail to the sequence of colonies from north to south: New York, New Jersey, Pennsylvania, Maryland, Virginia, North Carolina, and South Carolina. The image omitted Delaware and Georgia, probably because Delaware shared the same Governor as Pennsylvania and because Georgia, a recently developed colony, "could contribute nothing to common security" (Newbold, 1955: 32).

Franklin's *Gazette* initially circulated "JOIN, or DIE" to represent the united British colonies in America shortly before the Albany Congress, which was scheduled to convene that summer in response to the beginning of the French and Indian War, known in Britain as the Seven Years War (A. Matthews, 1908). In 1754, "JOIN, or DIE" promoted a political policy of unity among the American colonies to be formalized at the upcoming Albany Congress. As such, in classical terms of persuasion, it was a deliberative message which employed commonplaces concerning the consequences of enacting or rejecting policies as expedient or inexpedient. Specifically, the image of the segmented snake suggested to the colonists that their political situation was weakened by the divisions among the British colonies. Only through unification could the parts of the snake survive. In addition, the image promoted identifications among the colonies based on opposition to a shared enemy, the French and their Indian allies. "JOIN, or DIE" was distinctive among Franklin's major pictorial representations of colonial America in that it depicted the body politic as a lower order of animal.

To Franklin, the snake device was not initially a symbol of protest or rebellion within the British Empire. Instead, it dramatically symbolized the need for well-orchestrated action against an outside threat. The British Empire in America could only be protected by the well-coordinated military action by several of the colonies. So there was nothing invidious about what the image implied for the colonies' relationship to Britain in 1754. Indeed, the image complied with the general wishes of the British government's

Board of Trade. The image was widely reproduced in other newspapers at the time, such as the *New-York Gazette,* the *New-York Mercury,* the *Boston Gazette,* and the *Boston Weekly News-Letter,* to promote colony union. In subsequent years after the Coercive Acts of 1774, it recurred in similar designs on various newspaper mastheads, including the *New-York Journal,* the *Massachusetts Spy,* and the *Pennsylvania Journal,* where these mastheads had a confrontational use within the British Empire to object to recent laws.

Franklin's engraving, "MAGNA *Britannia: her Colonies* REDUC'd," likewise had an enduring significance throughout the American Revolution and it proved immensely popular among those critical of the British government's American policies (Figure 19.3). Originally printed at the end of 1765 or the beginning of 1766, "MAGNA *Britannia*" was distributed by him in England and America on note cards. During the subsequent decade of dissent, various illustrators reproduced the engraving in modified forms in America, France, England and Holland. An enlarged broadside was printed anonymously at Philadelphia. There were at least two British versions. One of these by M. [Matthew or Mary] Darly tried to reverse the rhetoric's implications of self destructiveness by attributing it to "her enemies." There was, moreover, at least one French version and a Dutch version as well. The idea of the American colonies as the limbs of a self-destructive empire had recurring relevance throughout the imperial dispute (Wolf, 1955).

These illustrations succinctly dramatized a way of viewing the colonies and their relationship to Britain. The colonies were parts, or limbs, of Britannia. The separateness of the colonies, not only from England but also from each other, was emphasized by labeling Britannia's four severed limbs "Virg," "Pennsyl-," "New York" and "New Eng." These colonial parts were subordinate to Britain, since the colonies constituted the extremities while Britain was the head and torso. Yet, because together they formed one body, the print underscored the interdependence of the colonies and England. The print identified the cause of one with the cause of the other. Finally, internal divisiveness within the empire, especially the use of force to subjugate the colonies, became the equivalent of suicide for the empire.

In addition to visualizing some of Franklin's most vital appeals to the Parliament, "MAGNA *Britannia*" constituted a significant shift among his pictorial representations of the united American colonies, because the emblem was a marked departure from his earlier image of America, "JOIN, or DIE," which had only recently been used by radicals to object to British taxation by featuring the snake device on the masthead of the *Constitutional Courant.* The newspaper came to the attention of the British public through several newspaper accounts and Parliamentarians discussed its ramifications in detail (L.C. Olson, 1987). In fact, it was reproduced as the first document in a publication for Parliament detailing the colonists' resistance to the new

JOIN OR DIE.

COPY

OF

The Constitutional

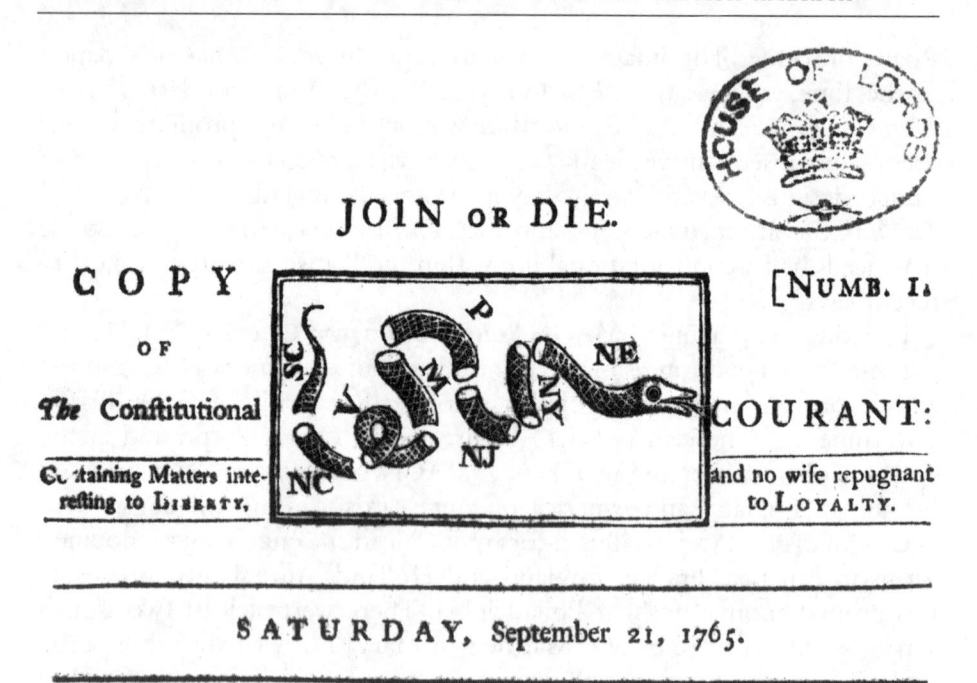

Containing Matters interesting to Liberty,

NC | SC | V | M | P | NY | NE
NJ

[NUMB. I.

COURANT:

and no wife repugnant to LOYALTY.

SATURDAY, September 21, 1765.

Figure 19.6 "JOIN, or DIE," from "Copies & Extracts of Several Newspapers, printed in New England, Sept.-Nov. 1765, and referred to in Gov. Bernard's letters (108 pp.)," masthead (p. 3), February 1766. Parliamentary Archives, London.

law (Figure 19.6). Despite Franklin's efforts tacitly repudiating his own earlier visual rhetoric in its more recent radical usage, the snake device took on a life of its own in American politics: Loyalists sought to connect the image with the biblical traditions wherein the serpent represented guile, deceit, and treachery, while Patriots countered those efforts by associating the image with eternity, vigilance, and prudence. Toward the Revolution's conclusion, Franklin was once again associated with the snake's image when Joseph Duplessis's portrait of him featured a rattlesnake's image carved on the gilt wooden frame.

There is an historical irony in that "JOIN, or DIE" remains the most commonplace image for depicting Franklin's emerging nationalism, yet in 1766 he not only repudiated its radical meanings indirectly through the production of "MAGNA *Britannia*," but also, after the war, actively sought in 1783 to promote an entirely different image of the United States as a youthful god, the infant Hercules. "JOIN, or DIE" was distinctive among Franklin's major pictorial representations of colonial America in that it depicted the unity as a lower order of animal, whose segmented body dramatized the need in 1754 for union among the colonies for defense of the British Empire from the French in North America. Yet, in later years during 1768–70, Franklin continued to allude to British America as various types of animals in his verbal depictions of the colonies to dramatize their treatment by the British government (e.g., *Papers*, 15: 66–67, 187–188; 17: 3). His movement away from such animal representations for the British colonies was not linear, but rather circumstantial and shifting in that the verbal imagery resurfaced even after he had deliberately employed human forms to represent the empire in "MAGNA *Britannia*" in 1766. After the initial distribution of "JOIN, or DIE" in 1754, Franklin's role as colonial agent in London during the conclusion of the French and Indian War impressed upon him that the British government benefitted in terms of political control over America from the colonies' disunion, however much it left the colonists vulnerable to attacks by the French and Indians. Franklin's recognition of this was emphatic. Yet, despite misgivings, he remained a loyal American Whig, who supported the Constitutional monarchy of Britain as the finest government known to humankind.

"MAGNA *Britannia*" represented a significant shift in Franklin's pictorial representations during 1766, by implicitly repudiating any desire on the part of the Americans to separate from the British Constitutional monarchy. The image of Britannia with its long, deeply entrenched history and symbolism in British society dramatized this fundamental political commitment. Yet, the depiction of the woman's dismembered body stressed that she was a victim of unspecified adversaries. Although the body politic was depicted as a human, and therefore possessing greater stature than the earlier depiction of colonial America as a snake, the image of Britannia was nonetheless that of a woman, whose subordination within patriarchal British and American cultures was certain. As such, she could plead with the men in government to change their behavior, but her future depended on their dispensations and pleasure. Like the colonists in America, she was a subordinated being whose future depended on actions taken by dominant men in British government, however much those men professed to idealize her virtues. Above all, the image represented Franklin's movement toward closer connection with the Constitutional monarchy, a political commitment which in his view was sufficiently deep that he preferred a royal colonial government to the proprietary system in Pennsylvania at least until 1765. Even after the Stamp Act, he could propose means for closer union between America and Britain.

"WE ARE ONE", in turn, repudiated the Constitutional monarchy altogether during 1775–1776, representing Franklin's complete and utter rejection of the British government in the aftermath of the Stamp Act, the Townshend Duties, the Boston Massacre, and the Coercive Acts. The design for "WE ARE ONE" on the fractional notes of the Continental currency circulated in large quantities throughout British America (E.P. Newman, 1966, 1983; McBride, 1979). It consisted of thirteen interlinked rings arranged in the form of a circle around a radiant center

(Figure 19.4). Each of the thirteen interlinked rings was inscribed with either the full name or the abbreviation of a colony arranged in geographical order clockwise from north to south. Inserted at the center of this large, circular pattern were two, small, concentric circles with "WE ARE ONE" inscribed within the center circle and "AMERICAN CONGRESS" imprinted within the outer circle. This language affirmed an oxymoron – a plural was a singular – and it identified the Congress as the authority sanctioning the paper currency. The rhetorical figure of an oxymoron, so central to the rhetorical appeal of this message, endeavored to call into being a condition of colonial union that had not, in fact, existed. It was a rhetorical appeal that endeavored to constitute a unified American audience in the British colonies that subsequently became the United States.

The organization of "WE ARE ONE" amplified equality among the distinct colonial governments in Congress, because each colony had equal size and stature as a link within the circle. Despite this symbolic image implying equal status among colony governments, Franklin recognized at least two underlying bases for his own convictions that some colonial governments should have more power in the Congress than others: the sheer number of individuals within each colonial government and the amount of economic support which each government was prepared to contribute to the mutual cause (*Papers*, 22: 572–574). Even so, he depicted egalitarianism among the distinct colonial governments in Congress, by portraying them as thirteen rings of equal size and by using geographical considerations as the principal underlying the sequence: the abbreviations within the rings began with New Hampshire at twelve o'clock and proceeded clockwise from north to south. The participation of every colonial government in Congress was vital to the continuity of the circle, just as the diverse American citizens' active acceptance of the Congress affected its authority, legitimacy, and power.

Franklin underscored the underlying legislative basis for unity and the sanctioning authority, whose political and military power gave credit to the paper money, by inserting the words, "American Congress," in the center of the design. Americans placed confidence in the paper money as a medium of exchange to the extent that they had confidence in the Congress's power to support it. Circulating along with the currency among Americans were tightly intertwined factors concerning the Congress's legitimacy and authority, as well as the Congress's need for evidence of Americans' support in the context of the Loyalists' innumerable protests, the ongoing military battles with Britain, and international diplomacy. Depending not only on trade but also on victories and defeats during the Revolutionary War, the fluctuating economic value of the Continental currency impinged on the Congress's ability to finance the conflict.

Like Franklin's other images representing British America, "WE ARE ONE" was widely distributed throughout the colonies and abroad. The image on the factional notes was reproduced on an immense variety of mundane objects, ranging from military flags, metal coins, state paper currency, newspaper mastheads, frames on portraits, clothing buttons, and carpeting to various housewares employed in daily use such as pitchers, bowls, and plates. The symbolic design was ubiquitous in public life throughout British America and beyond. Yet, unlike the other pictorial representations of British America initiated by Franklin, few contemporaneous poems were written concerning the design's meanings, presumably because the design was an even smaller detail during the war preparations than had been the two earlier images in their relatively circumspect conflicts. That the Congress's American supporters were less expressive about the persuasive potential of the various currency's designs, worrying as many of them did instead about its depreciating worth, may have indicated the effectiveness of the designs as propaganda: the currency was almost unnoticed as such by those in rebellion.

The most powerful indicators of the pictorial rhetoric's significance came from the Congress's adversaries, most emphatically from the American Loyalists such as Joseph Stansbury, who ridiculed and redefined several elements of the design in an attempt to appropriate it to the Congress's detriment. There were also British newspaper accounts detailing the American citizens' rejection of the Continental paper currency as evidence of the Americans' disunited state. For instance, in one poem Stansbury defined the image of thirteen interlinked rings such that they constituted the chains of bondage, slavery, or imprisonment represented by the Congress's power:

> But the last fashion'd Money
>   we all must commend,
> Where a Circle of Rings
>   join in Rings without end,
> Each Ring is a State,
>   and (the Motto explains)
> They all are a Congress –
>   a Congress in Chains![2]

This reversal of the meanings for the image on "WE ARE ONE" suggested that the design foreshadowed the delegates' imprisonment, presumably for violating British laws forbidding the production of paper money, among other offenses. By depicting the interlinked rings as chains, Stansbury redefined the design's meanings and, more importantly, challenged the Congress's legitimacy by depicting its transactions as illegal. The verse challenged the credibility of the constitutive rhetoric by enacting disunity among British Americans and by displaying attitudes underscoring the impossibility of amity among them.

Above all, Franklin's "WE ARE ONE" exhorted the Americans to unify – to constitute a new government in the ongoing war with the British military forces. Colonists could demonstrate their commitment to this unity simply by using the paper money to finance the war. At the same moment that the Americans did so, they tacitly recognized, affirmed, or acquiesced to the Congress's legitimacy as the authority sanctioning the paper money. Yet the Congress's legitimacy was much in doubt among Americans, especially because of the Loyalists' criticism of it. This was a substantial opposition in that about a third of the colonists were Loyalists, while perhaps another third were neutral on the proposition of independence from Britain. Among the Loyalists' extensive writings in newspapers and pamphlets were numerous poetic verses condemning the Congress's paper money as a worthless sham by criminals.

Depicted as a chain, Franklin represented the relationship among the United States as a federation. These rings were a mechanical device, lacking as they did the vital tissues and living connections among states, which were separate yet interconnected states for the purposes of military defense. The image coincided with the Congress's institution of the Articles of Confederation, its unanimous decision to issue paper money despite British law forbidding it, and a unanimous decision to place George Washington at the head of the military.

Finally, in 1782–83, *Libertas Americana* represented the birth of a new nation depicted, above all, as a unified whole transcending and integrating the parts into an organic, living entity (Zigrosser, 1957; Schleiner, 1976–1977). Depicted as infant Hercules, the United States's stature as a youthful, male god exceeded that of any of the earlier organic representations of colonial America as either a lower order of animal or a woman. The classical heritage associated with the imagery of Hercules made an emphatic allusion to a republican system of government. The medal's depiction in *Libertas Americana* suggested the youthful vitality and strength of a classical god. Where Franklin had, at the outset, depicted the colonies as a snake, it was now Britain's armies that were the two snakes being strangled in the infant Hercules's grip. Depicted as a pouncing leopard, it was now Britain, not America, that had the stature of a lower order of animal locked in moral combat with a heroic god embodying national independence and the republican government in the United States. France embodied in Minerva shielded him from the unscrupulous attack.

Libertas Americana became recognized internationally as an expression of the United States's gratitude to France for economic, diplomatic, and military assistance during the American Revolution (Figure 19.5). The gratitude that Franklin expressed with *Libertas Americana* was not simply a gesture of appreciation for the past support from France nor merely a means to display the civic virtue of the United States. Above all, his expression of gratitude was a pragmatic, diplomatic move designed to help strengthen the United States's relationship with France in the interest of future national security (L.C. Olson, 1990). At the same time, his distribution of the medal suggested to other European nations that initiating diplomatic relations with the United States was acceptable to France, the most powerful nation on the western European continent. He intimated that establishing a timely alliance now with the United States could create a debt of gratitude that would be of economic and political value in the future.

Franklin designed *Libertas Americana* primarily to influence the beliefs and actions of those in the centers of political power in France and the United States. In his role as the United States's plenipotentiary ambassador to France, he presented originals of *Libertas Americana* to the most powerful figures in France and the United States. The image subsequently circulated on a variety of pictorial works including broadsides, terra cotta plaques, and textile designs. On one broadside version by Jean-Baptiste Bradel in 1784, the leopard's hide was featured to complete the narrative action portrayed in the pictorial design from the medal.

The act of striking the commemorative medal was in itself symbolically significant, even though this was a common practice at the time among more established nations. By the act of striking the medal, Franklin depicted the United States conducting itself as a member of the community of nations. The commemorative medal was designed to praise those qualities of the United States and France which would be esteemed in the community of nations: for the United States, the medal depicted courage, military skill, and youthful potential for greatness; for France, the medal portrayed generosity, loyalty to an ally, and benign concern for an emerging nation. Franklin sought to design *Libertas Americana* so that it appealed to the interests of the distinct, principal audiences in the United States and France, whose cultural points of view placed different demands on its design and interpretation. Equally important, he employed the design to commemorate past military victories and, by doing so, he urged future political actions in a diplomatic situation charged with ambiguity and tension. Notable national figures in France and the United States were able to interpret the medal differently than Franklin originally had planned, because of the design's allegorical structure and the changing political circumstances during the period between his proposal for the medal and its formal presentation. Partisans nonetheless subverted the design's importance. For instance, one of the prohibited publications in France objected to the treatment of Loyalists and the cost of the war by observing that the infant's cradle was soaked in blood and that it would be difficult to find a more costly cradle.

In Franklin's estimation, the birth of the nation was best portrayed as the infant Hercules, whose youth, courage, industry, promise, and strength boded well for the new nation's character. Franklin himself identified closely with most of these qualities, and he sought to inculcate them in his grandson, whom he once described as an "Infant Hercules." Years earlier, during June 1775 on the eve of the American Revolution, Franklin described his grandchild, William Bache, in a letter to his sister, Jane Mecom, as "the strongest and stoutest Child of his Age that I have seen: He seems an Infant Hercules" (*Papers*, 22: 67). In 1782, by using the image of the infant Hercules on the design for *Libertas Americana* – the medal that Franklin consciously designed to represent a new nation and the emblem that he worked most assiduously to distribute internationally as a symbol designating the United States – the aging grandfather may have identified his own descendants' lives, strength, and future with the birth, character, and promise of the new nation. Devised less than a decade before Franklin's death, the emblem of the infant Hercules on *Libertas Americana* was his legacy to the United States embodied as a powerful youth with a legendary life.

Notes

1 *Pennsylvania Gazette*, September 20, 1775, p. 1, col. 1. *Pennsylvania Magazine* 1 (December 1775): 561.
2 "R.R." [Joseph Stansbury], "The History of Peru & c.," in *Loyalist Rhapsodes*, series 8D, no. 90, reel 49, Peter Force Collection, Manuscripts Division, Library of Congress.

Further Reading

Lemay, J.A. Leo (1987). "The American aesthetic of Franklin's visual creations," *Pennsylvania Magazine of History and Biography* 111: 465–499.

Matthews, Albert (1908). "The snake devices, 1754–1776, and the *constitutional courant*, 1765," *Publications of the Colonial Society of Massachusetts* 11: 409–453.

Olson, Lester C. (1990). "Benjamin Franklin's commemorative medal, *Libertas Americana*: A study in rhetorical iconology," *Quarterly Journal of Speech* 76: 23–45.

Olson, Lester C. (1991). *Emblems of American Community in the Revolutionary Era: A Study in Rhetorical Iconology*. Washington, DC.

Olson, Lester C. (2004). *Benjamin Franklin's Vision of American Community: A Study in Rhetorical Iconology*. Columbia, SC.

Part IV

Franklin and the Categories of Inquiry

Chapter Twenty

AMERICAN LITERATURE AND AMERICAN STUDIES

Edward Cahill

"If you would not be forgotten, as soon as you are dead and rotten," Poor Richard intoned in 1738, "either write things worth reading, or do things worth the writing" (Lemay, 1987: 1208). But despite Franklin's distinction between memorable composition and memorable action, in the long, diverse, often contested history of Franklin criticism in American literary studies and American studies, the achievements of the historical man have consistently informed, when they have not distorted, our understanding of the achievements of the writer. Franklin scholarship in the late nineteenth and early twentieth centuries often took as its starting point the question of his place in the pantheon of Founding Fathers, his greatness as an American and as a man of letters, and his status as a representative of American society and values. Although such questions have long ceased to motivate scholars with the same urgency, and in large part have been repudiated as naïve and exclusionary, Franklin's historical importance as a celebrated American – printer, scientist, diplomat, and revolutionary – and his identification with the nation continue to lend cultural significance to and generate critical interest in his writings. But such significance and interest has not always inspired close reading. During much of the twentieth century, judgments of Franklin's writings – his *Autobiography*, essays, maxims, bagatelles – were constrained by post-Romantic definitions of the literary, and scholars often slighted them as inartistic or merely practical or casual. Franklin scholars today no longer concern themselves with adjudicating his genius as an author or admiring his talents as a stylist. Still, sustained attention to the actual language and rhetorical intricacy of his texts is only a development of the past fifty years. Perhaps more than with any other early American author,

A Companion to Benjamin Franklin, First Edition. Edited by David Waldstreicher.
© 2011 Blackwell Publishing Ltd. Published 2011 by Blackwell Publishing Ltd.

studies of Franklin's writing have typically emphasized the extra-textual significance of his representativeness, his ability both to stand for and to illuminate the essential nature of colonial British-American society, the rise of eighteenth-century print and commerce, the origins of the American Revolution and – even still – the enigma of "American" identity. Indeed, despite the concerted work of scholars in identifying and editing Franklin's vast, far-flung body of work on a prodigious range of topics, we continue to privilege his *Autobiography*, his "masterwork" of self-representation, repeatedly mining its historical richness and representational complexity while paying relatively little attention to his others writings. In short, in nearly a century and a half of scholarly attention to Franklin's work as an author, and across a shifting array of methodologies, our understanding of who he was, what he did, and what it symbolized looms large over our study of what he wrote.

Yet from the beginning both Franklin the man and Franklin the author have also been consistently perceived as evasive and equivocal, intriguing us with precisely the kind of ideological, rhetorical, and textual mysteries that propel our historical and critical investigations. Early Franklin scholars, facing the disorder of his uncollected papers and the seemingly insuperable variety of his interests, strove to discover the "true Franklin" – or at least the truth of his "many sides." Mid-century scholars, too, searched for an authentic Franklin – as well as the authentic national culture he was purported to represent – amid the convolution of his multiple poses. And since the 1960s, scholars we have continued to seek an understanding of the construction of these poses, to get to the bottom of Franklin's enigmatic rhetoric, and to elucidate the paradoxes of his self-representation. The historical relevance of his life and the engaging intimacy of his address, it seems, have long provoked our desire to know the man and his work *essentially*, even as his career and writing appear to challenge the very idea of essence.

If the weight of Franklin's outsized historical presence and our belief in his elusiveness have shaped literary scholarship on his writing, however, so too has his evolving role within the academic institution of American literary studies in the United States. Since its founding, it has embraced Franklin as a central object of inquiry, offering to each generation of scholars not only a rich life history and canon of writing but also numerous sources of professional affirmation. In the late nineteenth century, many discovered in Franklin a productive figure of literary history; if he was thought to be "less literary" than Emerson, Longfellow, or Howells, his writing nevertheless provided an abundant source of historicist inquiry whose empirical rigor promised to buttress the fragile identity of a fledgling discipline. By the mid-twentieth century, the plodding regimes of literary history made way for the bracing conceptuality of American studies, whose interest in Franklin served to name and debate the moral and social values thought necessary to a newly dominant global super-power. Yet even as studies of Franklin have since shifted from considerations of his "character" and "representativeness" to the rhetorical, theoretical, and cultural analyses of the late twentieth century and beyond, their focus on textuality, representation, and political discourse has discovered in Franklin's "complexity" – and in the technical expertise necessary to explain it – a renewed sense of disciplinary authority, a welcome locus of critical seriousness in the face of the declining cultural capital of literary study and the marginalized status of early American literature within the field of literary studies. In other words, scholars through the years have discovered in Franklin's writing widely divergent forms of literary and cultural knowledge in response to the ever-changing demands of institutional knowledge production.

Perhaps because of these pressures of Franklin's iconic past and our evolving institutional present, the history of Franklin criticism is lively and compelling. If it indicates varying attitudes toward morality and textual specificity, it realizes a long-held belief that Franklin – both as a man and as a writer – is capacious enough to serve our most pressing critical interests. Thus, I mean here to survey this history in terms not only of its varied approaches and claims but also of the shifting intentions and underlying motivations that appear to drive them. Given the limitations of space and the enormous number of published works on Franklin since the 1880s, I have not endeavored to be comprehensive. Rather I aim to chart an illuminating trajectory of focus, from a commitment to the broadly conceived question of Franklin's life, moral character, and their ideological implications to an emphasis on the construction of his various masks and personae, the continuities and discontinuities of his rhetoric, and their function in the context of eighteenth-century Anglo-American culture, politics, and print. This trajectory – from representativeness to representation – is not quite linear and earlier assumptions, questions, and approaches linger tenaciously in later scholarship. But it allows us to see with some clarity the *longue durée* of Franklin and his writing in American literary and cultural studies.

20.1 Early Assessments: Celebration and Ambivalence

Although biographical accounts of Franklin have appeared steadily since his death in 1790, the first sustained critical accounts of his life as an author began with the vogue of literary history and the development of academic literary study in the late nineteenth century. As cultural authority gradually shifted from editors and men of letters to historians and scholars, Franklin emerged as a major, if uncertain, figure in the story of American literature. With the exception of focused studies such as John Bach McMaster's *Benjamin Franklin as a Man of Letters* (1887) and William Cabell Bruce's *Benjamin Franklin Self-Revealed* (1917), literary assessments of Franklin appeared in comprehensive surveys of American literature in which he stands as a key preliminary moment in a broader historical development that finds its fulfillment in nineteenth-century romanticism and realism. Such works as Charles Richardson's *American Literature, 1607–1885* (1895) and Bliss Perry's *The American Mind* (1912) are emphatically nationalist in tone, aiming to define a fertile tradition of vernacular authorship that would match the economic and political power of an increasingly industrialized and ambitious state. In responding implicitly to concerns about the tenuous status of U.S. culture abroad and the effects of mass immigration on cultural unity at home, they discover emblematic value in Franklin's virtuous entrepreneurship, his scientific fame, and his significance as a founder. Thus, Franklin emerges in these histories as a man representative of both colonial American culture and an emergent American modernity. Brander Matthews, for example, figures him as a moral source of the growth and prosperity of the American colonies in the eighteenth century, the development of nationhood, and the formation of the American character: "If the typical American is shrewd, industrious, and thrifty, it is due in a measure to the counsel and the example of Benjamin Franklin" (1896: 22). Likewise, Stuart Sherman's *Cambridge History of American Literature* calls Franklin "the first great Yankee with all the strong lineaments of the type: hardness, shrewdness, ingenuity, practical sense, frugality, industry, self-reliance" (1917: 90).

Such pronouncements generally avoided careful attention to the range and specificity of Franklin's writing and its rhetoric – although the work of Moses Coit Tyler (1878) is a notable exception. But they also understood such writing as merely one aspect of Franklin's life, considerations of which were typically subordinated to fact-laden summaries of his biography and its cultural significance. Thus faintly inspired by the publication of Albert Smyth's *The Writings of Benjamin Franklin* (1905–1907), Sherman concludes that Franklin "deserves his large place in our literary history not so much by virtue of his writings, which had little immediate influence upon *belles-lettres*, as by virtue of his acts and ideas, which helped liberate and liberalize American" (Sherman, 1917: 92). Indeed, the inherent conflict between the broad appeal of Franklin's democratic identity and elite academic evaluations of his life and work is manifest in a persistent tension between liberal admiration for his writing and conservative aesthetic appraisals of it as literature. Scholars routinely admired his self-taught literacy, noted his literary versatility, and applauded his rhetorical gifts. But they also reflexively and explicitly rejected the notion of Franklin's "greatness" as an author. Fred Lewis Patee, for example, holds that Franklin "was only incidentally a man of letters" (1896: 58); and for Paul Leicester Ford, "he was never a literary man in the true and common meaning of the term" (1899: 261). Such assessments repeatedly note Franklin's lack of literary or artistic ambition, the instrumental or hurried nature of his writings, and his supposed lack of influence on later American writers. Even McMaster, the first to approach

Franklin solely as a "man of letters," admits that he "founded no school of literature. He gave no impetus to letters. He put his name on no great work of history, of poetry, of fiction." But these claims are largely bound by assumptions that anachronistically link literary greatness with a disinterested aesthetics, struggle to accept the literariness of such genres as the autobiography, the political essay, and the almanac, and privilege both New England and nineteenth-century authors. As McMaster notes with unusual circumspection, "Till after his day, no such thing as American literature existed. To place him with Irving, Bryant, Cooper, Prescott, and the host of great men that came after him is impossible. There is no common ground of comparison" (1887: 272).

Early literary historians felt themselves on safer ground when they celebrated the excellence of Franklin's writing style and the cultural significance of the *Autobiography* and *Poor Richard*. Franklin's prose, they concur, is above all marked by its clarity and simplicity, what Tyler calls "the pure English of the best writers and of the best talkers" (1897: 365). Most accounts also note Franklin's talent for figuration, humor, and common sense. According to Julian Hawthorne and William Leonard Lemmon, he was "the first American to cultivate the art of literary phrasing" (1891: 16–17). McMaster lauds his "great brevity, great clearness, great force, good-humor, apt stories, pointed allusions, hard common sense, and a wonderful show of knowledge of the practical art of living" (1887: 277). Sherman calls his style uniquely "flexible" and defined by "omnipresent vitality" (1917: 108–109). Although many such claims are offered as unsupported, uncontestable generalizations, statements of fact to be collected with the rest of Franklin's diverse history, others focus their assessments more narrowly on the *Autobiography* and *Poor Richard*. Patee admires the former's "perfect simplicity, its frankness, and its seemingly unconscious revelations of character and motive" (1896: 60–61). Hawthorne and Lemmon see in the latter an author who "can detect analogies in things outwardly diverse, and bind the universe together with cords of sympathy and understanding" (1891: 16–17). Franklin's texts are neither art nor written by an artist, these scholars insist, but rather are exemplary of good American writing and good American sense.

This general limiting of inquiry to Franklin's two most character-driven texts not only reinforced the disciplinary emphasis on exemplariness but led scholars toward what would become the enduring question of his moral character. Many defined his representativeness in purely positive terms by praising "his kindly human sympathy and his shrewd Yankee insight" (Hawthorne and Lemmon, 1891: 17) or by calling him "the best example of a self-made man that history affords" (Patee, 1896: 60). But others understood Franklin's character in terms of what it lacked. Perry identifies in him "the essential disorderliness of the American mind ... reckless of precedent, self-taught, splendidly alive" (1912: 220–221). Beers finds that

Franklin is "Clear rather than subtle, without ideality or romance or fineness of emotion or poetic lift" (1899: 36–37). Such judgments were sometimes informed by explicit moral contrasts with Jonathan Edwards, which would grow sharper in the twentieth century. But they also combined with claims of Franklin's limited literary talent to frame an emerging debate about the limitations of his character and their implications for his representativeness. Some critics, that is, connect his lack of "poetic genius" to a lack of the "instinct of reverence," as well as "grace and taste" (Hawthorne and Lemmon, 1891: 19) or lament that "what lay outside of common sense he did not see" (Matthews, 1896: 36). Most invidiously, Van Wyck Brooks sees Franklin's writing as an example of a "low brow" attitude of mind, a "catch-penny opportunism" that extends to "contemporary business life" (1915: 9–10). To be sure, such views were far from unanimous. Bruce wholly rejects Franklin's reputation as "the father of a penurious, cheese-paring philosophy," observing that "almost every reproach attached to Franklin is attributable to the candor of the *Autobiography*" (1917: 17); and other critics more neutrally championed Franklin's "many-sided" nature as an alternative to strict moral classifications. But the terms had been set for a decades-long debate about moral character that bound Franklin closely to the characters he had created.

20.2 Mid-TwentiethCentury Debates: Character and Representativeness

D.H. Lawrence's famous critique of Franklin's spiritual limitations in *Studies in Classic American Literature* (1923) was thus preceded by earlier ones, including Max Weber's, whose energetic reductionism in *The Protestant Ethic and the Spirit of Capitalism* (1920) offered a pattern for Lawrence's laser-like intensity. But the latter's portrait of Franklin as "cunning," moved by "perfectibility" and "policy," and trapped in a "barbed wire corral" of morality helped to define the question of his exemplariness for a new generation of scholars whose larger aim was to derive a national identity from the diverse material of national culture (Lawrence, 1923: 9, 14). Writing in support of Lawrence's view, Charles Angoff's *Literary History of the American People* insists that Franklin "represented the least praiseworthy qualities of the inhabitants of the New World: miserliness, fanatical practicality, and lack of interest in what are usually known as spiritual things" (1931: 296). He roundly dismisses the *Autobiography* as lacking in "grace of expression, charm of personality, and intellectual flight"; but his larger point is both personal and political: Franklin had a "cheap and shabby soul," and the "vulgarity he spread is still with us" (Angoff, 1931: 302, 309–310). Such disparaging claims, however, were answered by a host of critics, who rejected not only Franklin's superficial morality but also the superficial methodology that discerned it. For Vernon Parrington, the diverse aspects of Franklin's life and writing revealed him to be no moral skinflint but a champion of middle-class virtue, a proponent of "agrarian democracy" and a "self-made democrat" who embodied a "rising class and a new social ideal" (1927: 165). Franklin was a member of the anti-Proprietary party in Pennsylvania, Parrington observes, a critic of British corruption, a progenitor of the labor theory of value, a disinterested social reformer, and a precocious federationist. Gladys Meyer (1941) likewise figures Franklin as a representative of American liberalism, one whose personal social, economic, and intellectual upward mobility parallels that of eighteenth-century Philadelphia. Although Robert E. Spiller agrees with Lawrence that a "large part of the American character lay in him as in a seed," he suggests that in such disparaging analyses the "prudential part of Poor Richard's counsel has been mistaken for the whole of Franklin's wisdom" (Spiller, 1948: 107). Using a far broader archive, Spiller alternatively finds Franklin to be a brilliant man of letters, an indefatigable polymath, a social genius, an unsurpassed diplomat, and a gifted humorist. That is, he was, as Carl Van Doren famously asserts, neither cunningly shallow nor reducible to caricature but a "harmonious human multitude" (1938: 782).

Franklin certainly appeared to liberal advantage next to Jonathan Edwards, the representative eighteenth-century Puritan, against whom he continued to be contrasted. For Parrington, Franklin's life has a "singularly dramatic fitness" compared with the tragic "anachronism" of Edwards's (1927: 164). In Spiller's *Cycle of American Literature*, Edwards is "the symbol of religious fervor of Puritanism at its purest," Franklin "the symbol of Enlightenment" (1955: 12). By the early 1960s, however, with Edwards's reputation largely rehabilitated by Perry Miller, the contrast became less biased toward Franklin and less starkly dichotomous. Miller agrees that history "has been dramatized by a series of pairs of personalities, contemporaneous and contrasting." But if Edwards and Franklin were the "preeminently eloquent linked antagonists in American culture," together they also "realize a potentiality ... concealed beneath the supposed unity" of New England Puritanism (P. Miller, 1962: 83). Despite their profound differences, that is, Miller saw a shared inheritance in their commitment to the plain style, the instrumentality of writing, the ethics of order and disinterestedness, and the personal abnegation inherent in their self-representation. Thus, because the contrast between Franklin and Edwards (and Cotton Mather) would thereafter evolve into the more enduring question of Franklin's Puritan influences, Miller's formulation – and the exemplary historicist practice that produced it – brought nuance to the character debates even as it signaled their demise.

These debates perhaps reached their apex in 1955 with the publication of Charles L. Sanford's essay collection, *Benjamin Franklin and the American Character*, whose description as "readings selected by the Department of

American Studies, Amherst College" advertised the growing institutional prestige of that emerging discipline and its investment in Franklin as a living embodiment of national values. Acknowledging that "for better or worse, rightly or wrongly, Benjamin Franklin has been identified with the American national character," Sanford juxtaposes arguments that view Franklin either negatively "the patron saint of material success" or as positively as "a rallying point for defenders of the American 'way of life'" (Sanford, 1955: v). Thus, for example, whereas Herbert W. Schneider, the Puritan scholar, emphasizes Franklin's "instrumental values" (Schneider, 1955: 78), I. Bernard Cohen, a historian of science, sees the expression of an "empirical temper" (1955: 83). Franklin's many-sided representativeness no doubt rewarded the energized historicism and holistic interdisciplinarity of American studies. Yet it also inspired a tendency toward transhistorical imperatives. This is surely implicit in analyses invested in the perennial "question of his quality as genius and hero" (V.W. Crane, 1954: 205). Even more explicitly, Meyer (1941) looks to Franklin for a model of liberalism that endures into the twentieth century; Cohen asserts that "Franklin has a meaning for the twentieth century which will reward our exploration and which is the means of his worth and enduring fame" (1953: 36); and with a sincerity that might appear hyperbolic by contemporary scholarly standards, Sanford himself inquires: "Can the example of Franklin help us to find the imagination, the sympathy, and the will necessary to control our vast technological machine for human ends?" (1955: viii). Sanford's question perhaps asks Franklin to bear a far heavier ethical burden on behalf of his "posterity" than he ever expressed in the *Autobiography*. But it also suggests the significant degree to which claims about Franklin's character and representativeness were fueled – directly and unabashedly – by the paradigmatic desire in American studies to "probe for the fundamental meaning of America," both past and present (Wise, 1979: 307).

If the interpretive limits of this approach are suggested by such lofty ambitions, however, the future direction of Franklin studies was nevertheless signaled by Sanford's volume, which contained his own analysis of the *Autobiography* as a moral quest narrative, a kind of secular *Pilgrim's Progress*. By reading Franklin's text as a literary invention, Sanford presented its first sustained rhetorical treatment. To be sure, scholars had been publishing philological accounts of *Poor Richard*, "Silence Dogood," and the satires since the early 1940s; and by the early 1960s significant monographs by Richard Amacher (1963) and Bruce Granger (1964) would historicize Franklin as an authentic man of letters, oppose earlier stereotypes, and delineate the remarkable diversity of his work. But at the same time, in response to the methodological claims of the New Criticism, as well as two major milestones in textual editing – the appearance of Max Farrand's "Parallel Text Edition" of the *Autobiography* (1949a) and the comprehensive Yale-based *Papers of Benjamin Franklin* (Labaree *et al.*, 1959–) – scholars also began to turn their focus to the formal structures of Franklin's writing, particularly the *Autobiography*. Thus, Walter Shear argues that its style derives from the "indefinite spatial extension" of the narrator, whose search for his "true interest" invests "the surface of the book with the moving symmetry of an ideological pattern" (1962: 73, 75). Amacher insists on its "organic unity," which he sees as the product of a "carefully patterned long and short design" and "the variety and the continuity of the main parts" (Amacher, 1963: 48–49). In an especially influential essay, David Levin holds that Franklin "*actually creates himself as a character*," and that his use of humor and candor and his tendency to represent himself as "more naïve, and practically more materialistic" than he really is make the text artistically "deceptive" and easily misinterpreted by "careless" readers (1964: 259, 273). By assuming and scrutinizing the complexity of Franklin's rhetoric, then, these readings turned the focus of criticism from moral character to literary characterization or from representativeness to representation.

20.3 Later Twentieth-Century Innovations: Rhetoric and Representation

Scholars of the 1960s and 1970s often pointedly rejected the assumptions and conclusions of the character debates – their moral oppositions (Connor, 1965), extra-literary focus (J. Griffith, 1971), and presentism (Sappenfield, 1973; Lemay, 1976a) – as if they represented an oppressive intellectual burden whose removal would liberate new resources of critical energy. The virtual explosion of work on Franklin after 1970, however, comes in response to a wider array of forces. National bicentennial celebrations in 1976 and 1987, as well as that of Franklin's death in 1990, reflected a renewed cultural interest in our national origins and yielded a steady stream of essay collections aimed at defining the state of Franklin scholarship (Lemay, 1976; Barbour, 1979; Buxbaum, 1987; Lemay, 1993; Oberg and Stout, 1993; Balestra and Sampietro, 1993). Such productivity, of course, was only possible because of the growing institutional prestige of early American literary studies, which was marked by the founding of the journal *Early American Literature* in 1966, as well as a sharp increase in the training and hiring of specialists by English and American studies departments. In the 1970s, the tightening of both the academic job market and tenure requirements, rather than reducing the number of publications, increased it and quickened the pace of scholarly innovation. If Franklinists – and early Americanists in general – felt the influence of critical theory and its methodological possibilities somewhat belatedly, the advent of post-structuralism, psychoanalytic theory, the new historicism, and public sphere theory ultimately provided generative vocabularies for explaining the historical and rhetorical richness of Franklin's work. Thus, Franklin scholarship from the 1960s to the 1990s and beyond signals a range of collective aspirations: improved intellectual status for members of a minor sub-field; cultural relevance to students, funders, and other significant publics increasingly doubtful of the value of literary study; and perhaps even an affirming image of tradition and stability in the ever-changing institution of the academy. But it also evinces an especially lively conversation about Franklin, his writing, and the culture of the Anglo-American eighteenth-century and the early Republic.

The textual turn in Franklin studies produced what would become a series of compelling readings of the *Autobiography* and, as a result, a narrowing of interpretive focus. Scholars of this period consistently emphasized the construction of Franklin's narrator-persona; the "literary device" of the letter to the son; the iconic image of Franklin's entrance into Philadelphia; differences between the four parts of the text; the significance of the James and Vaughan letters; the status of Franklin's scheme to achieve moral perfection; his understanding of the relation between virtue and appearance; and the "artful" and "planned" or "chaotic" and "spontaneous" nature of the *Autobiography*'s composition, all of which would become mainstays of critical analysis for years to come. But the best work of the period also began to articulate an understanding of Franklin's persona as more provisional, performative, and parodic than the character debates had held him to be. John William Ward explores Franklin's dynamic conception of virtue, as well as his "capacity to respond to the situation in which he found himself and to play the expected role" (1969: 133). Even more incisively, John F. Lynen argues that "prudence and virtue" are continuous in the *Autobiography* (1969: 122). Because Franklin's skepticism leads him to "conceive value as an experiential event rather than a lump sum," he argues, we must approach his role-playing as dramatic artistry rather than as instrumental morality or shallow cynicism (1969: 134, 141). Other work examines the text's "self-parody" (Sappenfield, 1973), "cunning craftsmanship" (Zall, 1976), and constitutive conflict between individualism and exemplariness (Spengemann, 1980). If such readings of the *Autobiography* discerned new levels of complexity, however, they did so at a certain cost. Although sporadic discussions of Franklin's almanacs (Nichols, 1976), *The Way to Wealth* (Gallagher, 1973), his letters to the English press (Granger, 1976), and "The Speech of Miss Polly Baker" (Lemay, 1976) paid similar attention to their rhetorical construction, in general the focus on the *Autobiography* witnessed the declining critical significance of *Poor Richard* and diverted attention from an otherwise expanding Franklin canon. In much the same way, a critical preoccupation with parts 1 and 2 of the *Autobiography* revealed an increasingly detailed picture of Franklin's self-representation even as it narrowed the range of his themes and formal tendencies.

At the same time, however, historicist scholarship explored the breadth of Franklin's interests in an effort to transcend the stereotypes of the past.

Paul W. Connor aims to put Franklin "back in the eighteenth century," where amid "the Newtonians, neoclassicists, satirists, and natural philosophers, he is intellectually at home and intelligible" (1965: 222). Alfred O. Aldridge reads his life through the lenses of eighteenth-century French intellectual culture (1957) and transatlantic natural philosophy (1965), and surveys the scope of his religious engagements, concluding that he "applied the experimental method to his attempt to unravel the secrets of divinity and morality" (1965: 6). In fact, the most pressing historical questions of this period concerned Franklin's views on religion and Puritan influences on his writing. Although nearly all scholars agreed on the insufficiency of earlier contrasts with Edwards and Mather, the search for specificity and subtlety led them to field-changing developments. Rejecting Parrington's claim that "the Calvinism in which he was bred left not the slightest trace upon him" (1927: 167), Phyllis Franklin (1969) connects the *Autobiography* to works-based Calvinism and Puritan ideas of the calling and the commonwealth. Other critics see in Franklin and Puritan writers common attempts to foreground the struggle to "gain control of the causes of virtue" (Shea, 1968: 101); discover the "perfect adjustment of momentary experience and external being" (Lynen, 1969: 91); advocate conversion as a solution to the problem of human imperfection (Parker, 1976); and articulate middle-class values of prudence (Gilmore, 1977). Some, like Campbell Tatham (1971) and Norman S. Fiering (1978), seek to reinscribe distinctions between Franklin and Puritanism in terms of virtue, piety, belief, and grace. But the most forward-looking work pursues questions of religion as questions of representation. Philip D. Beidler, for example, reads the *Autobiography* against what he calls "an awareness of the immense practical power of [printed] expression coupled with an anxious distrust of such power," in this way discovering the contradictions of Franklin's print personality in the contrary assumptions of didactic Christian autobiography (1982: 257). When such expression is most effective, Mitchell Breitweiser argues of Franklin and Mather, it seeks to construct a unifying representative personality in print, a purified and disciplined form of modern self-representation that is also the product of "systematic self-masking" (1984: 3–4, 17). In other words, Beidler and Breitweiser suggest Franklin's Puritan influences must be understood in the context of the print cultures and literate political collectives that made his self-representation possible.

These arguments assume the rhetorical intention rather than the historical reality of Franklin's representativeness. But they also point to an emerging conception of ideology in Franklin criticism of the 1970s and 1980s that apprehends Anglo-American civil society as distinct from religion, economics, and the power of the state and enabled by republican ideas of virtue and the representational norms of the eighteenth-century "republic of letters." Thus, for example, Melvin H. Buxbaum argues that the *Autobiography* constitutes Franklin's attempt to manage America's reputation for virtue, as well as his own, during the unrest of the Revolutionary era (1975: 5, 10). Sacvan Bercovitch, too, sees Franklin's text as exemplary of what he calls "auto-American-biography," a form whose representation of "corporate selfhood" at once "recapitulates the nation's past and predicates its future" (1975: 234, 143). Such formulations of Franklin's self-representation rely, to a greater or lesser extent, on the growing influence of several major intellectual trends in social and political history and literary criticism. The work of J.G.A. Pocock, Bernard Bailyn, and Gordon Wood alerted scholars to the amalgam of seventeenth-century commonwealth theory and classical civic humanism known as republicanism, whose principles often shaped the form and content of eighteenth-century American expression. Media studies and the History of the Book illuminated the significance of print commerce, printed textuality, literacy, and belletrism to literary culture and authorship. Finally, novel theoretical understandings of selfhood revealed print identities to be neither natural nor unmediated but rather constructed within diverse cultural frameworks and subject to a multitude of conflicting interests, both public and private. These new paradigms combined to lead Franklin scholarship toward two different but closely related approaches, both of which have yielded original and challenging understandings of Franklin's linguistic self-fashioning.

In the first approach, psychoanalytic theories of identity informed new interpretations of the relationship between selfhood, rhetoric, and the constitution of political power. In an early, groundbreaking psychoanalytic treatment of the *Autobiography*, Richard Bushman argues that attention to the structures of infant identity-formation discovers an emblematic rhetorical pattern in Franklin's text involving strategies of "compensatory skill" and "withdrawal" in the negotiation of self-interest and authority (1966: 231). Some of the work that followed was, however, decidedly divorced from history. John Griffith, for example, understands Franklin's rhetorical contradictions not as deception or hypocrisy but as the effect of a keen awareness of the "social processes" by which identity and self-awareness are formed (1976: 124, 129); and Ada Van Gastel (1990) traces his persistent sublimation of sexual desires into acts of literacy and public self-representation. Yet the most influential analyses combined psychoanalytic with historicist inquiry to uncover the unconscious structures of rhetoric and politics in Franklin's writing. Thus, Hugh Dawson explores the oedipal conflict expressed in Franklin's "psychologically crucial self-measurement" against his father, many father figures, and "real and symbolic children" in terms of the filial metaphors of the revolution and post-war era (Dawson, 1979: 19). More broadly, Jay Fliegelman sees such conflicts as a response to the "new antipatriarchal ideology" of the eighteenth century and Franklin as a "prodigal son" whose youthful rebellion and advancement prefigure American colonial resistance and exemplify the possibilities of self-making in a "limitless and inconstant world" (1982: 106, 112). Likewise, Ormond

Seavey's comprehensive "psychohistory" reveals in Franklin's life and writing a persistent struggle between conflicting "identity needs" for "acknowledgment and independence" and – like Bushman – a pattern of "withdrawal from hostilities," even as it exemplifies an affirmative "mode of consciousness, which the *Autobiography* makes available for imitation" (1988: 5, 114). But the consideration of Franklin's conflicted identity and its significance for American national identity received its keenest treatment in Christopher Looby's "historicized psychoanalysis," which understands Franklin's "accession to language" and "the nation's self-constitution in language" in terms of both a rebellion against and a reconstitution of patriarchal order (1993: 100).

Looby's sense of Franklin's repressive and divided textual self and its relation to a fragile and uncertain national polity, however, derives in part from the assumptions of the second approach scholars took in the late twentieth century, which emphasized the dynamic representational capacities of printed texts in the eighteenth-century public sphere. In a prescient early analysis, Lewis P. Simpson uses "Silence Dogood," "An Apology for Printers," and *Poor Richard* to consider Franklin's role in the "Third Realm" of print culture and his discovery that printing "opened to the person of talent and ambition a self-education in letters and learning." But where Simpson explores Franklin's investment in the "identity of author and reader" and a rhetorical "strategy of intimacy" (Simpson, 1976: 8–9), Albert Furtwangler (1979) considers his less intimate forms of address – elusiveness, censoriousness, satire – and his discovery of the impersonal power of print anonymity, which, Furtwangler insists, Franklin modeled on Joseph Addison's *Spectator*. Such power was understood to be particularly useful during the unsteady years of the early republic. As Robert A. Ferguson (1986) argues, Franklin's rhetoric of control, avoidance of discord, tendency toward accommodation, and production of unanimity was emblematic of a more general tendency in the writing of the founders, despite his singular use of humor, hoax, and irony to achieve such rhetorical ends. The fluid movement between private and public selfhood that such writing required, however, was also seen to be particularly complex and demanding of theorization. Thus, Joseph Fichtelberg, invoking Roland Barthes's notion of the "constant loss" that occurs in any articulation of self, finds that by modeling the "calculated transformations" involved in producing a public persona Franklin's *Autobiography* teaches readers to "regard life itself as a composing process" (1988: 203); and Myra Jehlen, exploring the text's rhetoric of virtue and appearance, explains that "the space that separates them is precisely the theater of morality" in which the political drama of "private character and public persona" is staged (1990: 513). These ideas are perhaps most fully realized in Michael Warner's influential treatment of Franklin in terms of "republican print ideology." Citing Jürgen Habermas's account of the eighteenth-century bourgeois public sphere (which understood *The Spectator* as an exemplary form of printed expression), Warner examines Franklin's self-identification with republican print culture and its valorization of rational, disinterested, generalized subjecthood and negative, impersonal authority, concluding that the logic of his writing and career is identical with "the logic of representation" (1990: 96).

Like much scholarship in early American studies of the late 1980s and early 1990s, this criticism took the rise of U.S. nationhood as its chief frame of reference and republicanism as its primary ideological paradigm. It saw in both Franklin's political writing and in his prominent roles in the colonial crisis, the Revolution, and even the Constitutional Convention the work of a national figure, a committed republican, and a thoroughgoing Federalist. Likewise, it understood the *Autobiography* – particularly the nationalizing elements of parts 2 and 3 – as narrating "the reflexive relationship that existed between his career and the opportunities presented by his homeland" and thereby constructing a reproducible model of virtuous citizenship (Ziff, 1991: 85). In other words, it continued to see Franklin as a representative American. At times, to be sure, scholars considered the challenges of such representativeness, the difficulty, for example, of reconciling Franklin's pro-British imperialism and anti-revolutionary impulses with his "allegorical relation" to a "nation founded in revolution" (Looby, 1993: 127–128). But in general, as they turned their focus to the political, social, and cultural contexts of eighteenth-century America, they discovered in Franklin a key witness to its most important political forms and print traditions. Thus, these interpretations revealed Franklin to be a new kind of representative figure, no longer an archetype of moral character but rather one of rhetorical assumptions, processes, and performances. In doing so, they also offered new ways of explaining the strange, often compelling, sometimes discomfiting paradoxes of Franklin's writing – the persistent gaps between its simplicity and irony, self-assertion and self-effacement, immanence and abstraction – which have long intrigued his readers.

20.4 Recent Developments and Future Directions

The past fifteen years have seen an enormous number of new historical studies of Franklin, mostly biographical, many for the popular press, exploring the gamut of Franklin's many sides, from his experiments with electricity to his diplomatic adventures in France. With similar energy and prolificacy, literary studies and American studies have continued to explore his writing in the contexts of Revolutionary politics, rhetorical selfhood, and the print public sphere. But in response to an increasingly diverse university and global culture, it has also begun to place him in the less explored contexts of social class, economics, gender, race, and colonialism. Undoubtedly, these advances are still preliminary and have come with some resistance. Until the twenty-first century, Franklin scholarship seemed immune to many of the decentralizing forces that had been changing early American studies for over a decade and slow to perceive the now widely accepted reality that his American culture was never an integrated whole. Indeed, for all his manifest capaciousness, Franklin has too often been perceived, however unconsciously, as offering a kind of respite from such forces, his singular authority and centrality blinding scholars to the full breadth of his interests and experiences, particularly those that did not imply a consistent American identity. Recently, however, Franklin criticism has been more centrifugal than centripetal. Rather than turning inward on his larger-than-life identity and merely confirming his representativeness, that is, it is turning outward toward the diversity of eighteenth-century Anglo-American culture and, following Looby, questioning the limits of his representativeness. Franklin's writing is now being explored in terms of the transnational, non-elite, non-white worlds he knew intimately. Aided by the Library of America's convenient and extensive volume of Franklin's *Writings* (Lemay, 1987) and the interdisciplinary procedures of Atlantic studies and material culture studies, such new perspectives have interested scholars in texts other than the *Autobiography* and inspired inventive new ways of reading it; but they have also brought to bear a range of new objects – from cities and houses to paper currency and slave advertisements – on the continuing project of reading Franklin and his life.

Perhaps the most pervasive tendency in recent work has been an effort to augment or challenge Warner's thesis about Franklin's relation to print culture. One vein of critique has argued for a less efficacious notion of printed textuality. Grantland Rice (1997), following Beidler, insists on Franklin's sense of its instability, its tendency not only to advance the fortunes of authors and ideas but also to threaten or devalue them. Likewise, Michael Drexler examines Franklin's awareness of print not as autonomous but as merely "part of a system" of public communication, as well as his recognition of the "unpredictable or unwanted and dangerous directions" its expressions can take (1998: 62). Both Rice and Drexler, for example, note the inability of Poor Richard's maxims to sway the crowd in *The Way to Wealth* and the *Autobiography*'s account of the diminished popularity of the revivalist George Whitefield after he publishes his theological principles. Such readings demonstrate that, if Franklin's life is organized around a fundamental identification with print, his understanding of print's specific deployments is as multidimensional as the politics in which they intervene. Thus, scholars have also emphasized the degree to which Franklin sees printed texts not in terms of public print rationality but rather the ineluctable force of private interest. By reading Franklin's writing in the context of the rising but unstable commodity culture of the eighteenth century, Rice identifies a key tension between "the recession of the individual subject" in the "rationalized social realm" of the public sphere and the "corresponding rise of the fiercely individualistic public personality" within the market for printed texts (1997: 48–49). Similarly, Betsy Erkkila (2000) explores his tendency to focus on bodily desire, its potential for excess, and the moral imperative of its disciplining; Jennifer J. Baker (2005) observes that, after Franklin's retirement, the *Autobiography*'s notions of both personal and national credit are specifically dependent upon the reputations of individuals – particularly Franklin's own – rather than depersonalized abstractions or objectified selves; and Nancy Glazener (2008) discovers in Franklin's writing the "interest-bearing self" of secular civil society, which challenges neat distinctions between private identity and public rationality. These studies have brought useful nuance and qualification to the easily caricatured idea of republican print ideology, but they have also directed our attention to less noticed aspects of Franklin's writing and its often impressively coherent patterns of rhetoric.

Scholars have also recently attempted to see beyond the fictions of social equality inherent in both the print public sphere and republican ideology by exploring the class dynamics of Franklin's writing. In emphasizing that print is never a "neutral medium of exchange," Drexler explores Franklin's use of it as an instrument of social control, particularly the ways in which print "coordinated" action outside of the elite confines of print culture (1998: 58). In a similar vein, Paul Downes (2002) considers Franklin's rhetorical strategies of anonymity, self-effacement, and concealment as essential elements of the anxious subjectivity of a post-monarchical republican culture. Of course, Franklin has long been associated with the economic upward mobility of America and its "rising people," and the notion continues to retain its appeal. By locating the *Autobiography* within a tradition of texts promoting the promise America held for European emigrants, for example, J.A. Leo Lemay (1986) and Carla Mulford and Nian-Sheng Huang (2009a) see in Franklin's portrait of virtue and industry rewarded the "definitive formulation" of "American Dream" (Lemay, 1986a: 351). But less transhistorical accounts place Franklin in more specific, dynamic, and conflicted socioeconomic contexts. David Waldstreicher describes Franklin as a tradesman whose success depends not only on the exploitation of "people as capital" but also a profound understanding of the contingencies of freedom and unfreedom in colonial America (2004: 88). A number of scholars have addressed the question of Franklin's own murky class status: his ambiguous and "awkward" transition from mechanic to gentleman (G.S. Wood, 2004); the literary dimensions of that transition as expressed in his writings on affluence and the building and furnishing of his Market Street house (Cahill, 2008); his awareness of the instability and "ethical potential" of European modes of polite sociability (Chaves, 2007); and his enduring identification with his working class origins (S.P. Newman, 2009). In what is perhaps the most provocative reading of Franklin's class politics to date, Ed White (2006) refocuses our attention on his neglected mid-century writings, as well as the "public Business" of part 3 of the

Autobiography. In this way, its representations of sectarian politics and public boosterism emerge as the "social tactic" of a "petty bourgeois" (180) – which, for White, is obscured by the organic narrative of individualism and sincerity in parts 1 and 2 – and Franklin, as an advocate of urban federalism bent on the political domination and economic manipulation of rural democrats. Overall, these analyses define Franklin as neither exceptional nor representative but more thoroughly immersed in the diverse economic transformations of colonial British America than earlier studies have held him to be.

If White (2006) relocates Franklin beyond urban spaces and our critical focus beyond the federalist biases of conventional interpretations, other scholars – following Warner's (2000) suggestion that Franklin's Englishness is too often ignored – have traced his cultural influences and interests across the diversity of the Atlantic world and away from a narrowly American identity. To be sure, mid-century historians, such as Cohen, Aldridge, and Verner Crane, routinely placed him in British and French contexts and linked him to leading Enlightenment thinkers like Newton and Locke. But more recent efforts at transatlanticism have discerned less linear and predictable currents of cultural exchange. Douglas Anderson demonstrates that Franklin's intellectual "apprenticeship" as a reader of Shaftesbury, Mandeville, and other English writers informed not only his radical ideas about religion, science, economics, and politics but also taught him the rhetorical strategies of satire and the psychological "potential of character" (1997: 12). In similar ways, Colleen E. Terrell (2003) explores Franklin's engagement with European discourses of mechanism and their moral implications; Christina Lupton (2007) traces his mature experiments with English literary style and its linguistic performance of sincerity; and Nick Wrightson (2010) examines the mutuality of his Atlantic natural philosophy and book-trade exchange networks. But other accounts have located Franklin in the Atlantic world of commerce, slavery, and empire. Waldstreicher (2004) finds him at home in the culture of slavery, defending its prerogatives, evading its contradictions, and inhabiting its rhetorical guises, despite his renowned egalitarianism and belated antislavery politics. From a different perspective, Sean Goudie (2006) sees Franklin as a "creole nationalist" whose American identity is grounded in anxious "paracolonial" attitudes about the West Indies and circum-Atlantic trade. Both studies not only reveal how much Franklin was engaged in the theories and practices of empire, but they also expand our range of reference by devoting serious attention to such little-read texts as "Observations on the Increase of Mankind" (1755) and *Interest of Great Britain Considered* (1760).

This brief discussion of recent Franklin criticism admittedly leaves out a number of important studies, including Michael Zuckerman's on Franklin's benevolence (1993b); Lester C. Olson's on his political emblems (2004), James Green and Peter Stallybrass's on his work as a printer (2006), and

Lemay's three-volume unfinished biography (2006, 2008). But it also suggests some of the directions that future scholarship might take. Accounts of the volatility and interestedness of print indicate an approach to Franklin's writing that assumes its complex imbrications of privacy and publicity. For example, White's view of Franklin as a savvy social negotiator transcends readings of him as either a wily entrepreneur or as a disinterested public man and invites further discussions of his place in the unruly colonial nexus of economics, politics, and religion. In the same way, Erkilla's analysis of embodied desire and Waldstreicher's discussion of women, consumption, and domestic labor in Franklin's writing point the way to future work on his representations of "busy bodies" and the persistent connections he makes between sex, gender, pleasure, reproduction, population, politics, and print. But work on Franklin and class also suggests that, despite his long-cherished identity as a self-made man, the cultural structures and narrative representations of economic and social mobility in his eighteenth-century world – of labor and leisure, risk and reward, ambition and anxiety, wealth and poverty, ascendance and failure – remain underspecified. Finally, Waldstreicher's and Goudie's studies indicate the importance of connecting Franklin to the racial and imperial contexts that his identity as a liberal and rational Philadelphia printer seems to evade, and they remind us that relatively little work has been done on his representations of Native Americans, Pennsylvania Germans, western settlement, trade, war, emigration, and travel.

Most of these recent studies have given us a Franklin who is less sentimentalized and geographically confined by unitary identities than in the past. Along with analyses of Franklin's image in American cultural history by Huang (1994) and Mulford (1999), it teaches us that the best scholarship avoids capitulating to the historical and mythological density of his fame and its powerful authority. But it also points us to the large number of texts in the Franklin canon – over 225 in *Writings*, excluding his letters – many of which remain underappreciated, even more than two centuries after his death. More attention to this diversity promises not only to assist us in the still evolving process of reconstructing the many sides of Franklin the historical man, but it should also encourage us to read across his body of work in order to discern the deep formal patterns of rhetoric, imagery, and vocality that continue to distinguish Franklin the writer.

Further Reading

Huang, Nian-Sheng (1994). *Benjamin Franklin in American Thought and Culture, 1790–1990*. Canton, MA.

Lemay, J.A. Leo (1967). "Franklin and the Autobiography: An Essay on Recent Scholarship," *Eighteenth-Century Studies* 1: 185–211.

Maddox, Lucy, ed. (1999). *Locating American Studies: The Evolution of a Discipline*. Baltimore, MD.

Mulford, Carla (1999). "Figuring Benjamin Franklin in American Cultural Memory," *New England Quarterly* 72(3): 415–443.

Sanford, Charles, ed. (1955). *Benjamin Franklin and the American Character*. Boston, MA.

Stokes, Claudia (2006). *Writers in Retrospect: The Rise of American Literary History, 1875–1910*. Chapel Hill, NC.

Chapter Twenty-one

BENJAMIN FRANKLIN'S MATERIAL CULTURES

Megan E. Walsh

In June 1779, Benjamin Franklin wrote a letter to his daughter Sarah Bache, in which he mentioned that he was beginning to notice a trend. The overabundance of "pictures, busts, and prints, (of which copies upon copies are spread every where)," Franklin wrote, "have made your father's face as well known as that of the moon" (June 3, 1779, PBF, 29: 613).[1] Appearing in a huge variety of traditional and popular media, portraits of Franklin followed him wherever he went in France, Britain, and the United States. In an age when copying artworks was a frequent and even expected practice, it is no wonder that representations of Franklin showed up on canvas, paper, dishware, medallions, jewelry, watches, fabrics snuffboxes, and elsewhere. Far from finding the attention unsettling, Franklin delighted in the production of his image, and he frequently commissioned copies in order to give them to his friends, family, and acquaintances.

The identities that accompanied that famous face were as varied as the media on which its representation could be found. Since the first time he appeared in a portrait likely painted by Robert Feke in the first half of the eighteenth century, Franklin has been depicted as an embodiment of his many interests and occupations. Sometimes Franklin was seen as the man of science, the inventor of lightning rods, and famous flyer of kites. At other times, he was depicted as the unparalleled American politician, contrite before the Privy Council, attending peace negotiations, or quarreling with Pennsylvanian leaders. Other times, he was the great civic improver, encouraging his fellow Pennsylvanians to adopt his useful programs for fire prevention, sewage drainage, and other such plans. Or he was represented as the genius inventor of devices for making everyday life easier, crafting useful

A Companion to Benjamin Franklin, First Edition. Edited by David Waldstreicher.
© 2011 Blackwell Publishing Ltd. Published 2011 by Blackwell Publishing Ltd.

designs such as the Franklin stove and his library chair with folding steps. On many occasions he was the humble Philadelphia printer, churning out copies of the *Pennsylvania Gazette* and *Poor Richard's Almanack*, and spending late nights at his desk and press. In taking a significant interest in his image as a scientist, inventor, statesman, businessman, writer, and printer during his lifetime, Franklin influenced how his contemporaries saw him and laid the groundwork for the array of images that have been created since then.

By the time he died in 1790, Franklin had had become the subject of a vast archive of artistic representations consigned to the hands of descendants, friends, institutions, and complete strangers. But he also left a sizeable trove of other material artifacts, ranging from important scientific inventions to household furnishings. The objects that he invented, owned, and gave and received as gifts remain a central part of Franklin's identity and are a key to understanding the moment in which he lived. The many cultures of materiality in which Franklin participated paralleled and informed his many personal, social, scientific, artistic, and political networks. Not only did Franklin live, work, and write in a material eighteenth-century world, he was also a producer and shaper of that world.

Even though Franklin wrote extensively about the objects he invented, collected, and sent as gifts, studies have only recently begun to approach Franklin's relationship to material objects with a significant and sustained critical and theoretical interest. Scholars have long considered Franklin's engagement with political culture, but have recently come to embrace more diverse areas of study, giving significant attention to the issues of economic disparity, race, and gender that were central to Franklin's life. In doing so, these studies have necessarily had to rely on a more varied set of evidence in order to inform their narratives, and have increasingly incorporated understudied material archives as sources for crucial pieces of evidence. Work on Deborah Franklin, for example, mines the letters, account entries, and other documents she produced. Because this collection is relatively small compared with that of her husband, however, historians have turned to material sources such as household furniture, fabric and cloth, and other kinds of non-textual evidence often used to understand how eighteenth-century women lived (Fry, 2003; Conger, 2009). Likewise, recent attention to Franklin's relationship to the theories and practices of slavery has demanded a turn to new kinds of evidence as scholars like David Waldstreicher (2004) have looked at indenture papers, slave auction advertisements, and newspaper runaway notices in order to generate more accurate descriptions of Franklin's relationships with enslaved people. As more attention is paid to those early Americans who lived outside the boundaries of traditional written accounts and who produced little or no writing themselves, scholars have increasingly turned to broader and more material archives that better represent the many people whose lives intersected with Franklin's.

In their attentiveness to understudied archives, new kinds of Franklin scholarship have followed changing methodological approaches offered by the relatively new field of material culture studies. Initially a subject of study covered almost exclusively by archeologists, historians of folklore and folklife, and collectors of antiques, areas of inquiry labeled "material culture" became a focus of scholarly attention in the 1980s, a development indebted to publications on the role of commodities by Arjun Appadurai (1986) and Igor Kopytoff (1986), studies on the fetish by Emily Apter and William Pietz (1985, 1993) and Ann Rosalind Jones and Peter Stallybrass (2000), and finally, literary scholarship such as Bill Brown's notion of thing theory (2003). In the field of early American studies, scholars such as Richard Bushman (1992), Robert Blair St George (1988, 1998), Ann Smart Martin (1993, 1997), Laura Rigal (1998), Laurel Thatcher Ulrich (2001), T.H. Breen (2004), and John Styles and Amanda Vickery (2006) have argued for a sustained concentration on the ways objects – dishes, tables, chairs, fences, houses, and other daily possessions – operated and conveyed meaning through a language of signs and symbols. Many recent accounts of early American material culture, moreover, have effectively challenged notions that Americans' interest in consumer goods was a late nineteenth-century development, and have shown the need for more studies of the economic and social uses of objects during the "Consumer Revolution," a period that roughly mirrors that of the American Revolution. In doing so, these studies have begun to trace the links between material production, commercial exchange, and gift culture in the colonial and early national period and the tremendous political, social, economic, and cultural changes taking place at the same time.

Recent work in material culture studies has also redefined ways of encountering and categorizing a wide range of cultural productions by arguing that material objects operate within networks of meaning. Jules Prown (2001), for example, has argued that works of fine art, just as their decorative art counterparts, are best analyzed as objects with unique characteristics that inhere in the physical traits of the artwork. The physical properties of a painting, in this view, are as central to understanding a painting's meaning as the image it depicts. This shift in thinking about different kinds of material objects has had an especially large impact on the ways scholars have studied visual culture and has breathed new life into materials such as etchings, engravings, prints, and other reproduced images that until recently were often seen as purely derivative because they were produced to copy graphic elements of paintings and other fine arts. Such images are now frequently treated as unique cultural objects as scholars investigate the elements associated with their creation (through copperplate engraving, coloring, and other forms of reproduction) and their use (by examining fading, tearing, and marking by individual owners). This change in categorizing visual arts has shifted the modes of analysis away from traditional discussions about taste and provenance as objects are positioned within networks of production, consumption, and appreciation.

In a similar vein, recent work in the field of museum studies has also challenged the ways we understand material objects, generating new debates about how individuals approach things from the past. Studies such as those by Richard Handler and Eric Gable (1997) as well as Alan Wallach (1998), for example, have asked scholars to rethink how fine arts, decorative arts, and other artifacts are presented to the public as well as how they operate within underlying political and cultural arguments that museums and other exhibitions inevitably make. Exhibits have gradually come to display objects in more critical and more historically accurate ways. Overall, recent attention to material culture in fields as diverse as archeology, art history, history, literary criticism, museum studies, and sociology have led to the development of a more methodologically rigorous set of standards for the study of artworks and other objects.

Following the approaches developed by the field of material culture studies as well as recent interest in material archives as sources of information for those living in Franklin's satellite, scholars and curators have begun to organize exhibits that collect Franklin's material culture artifacts, including scientific technologies, popular portraits, and personal belongings. The most comprehensive of these, the Benjamin Franklin Tercentenary exhibit "Benjamin Franklin: In Search of a Better World," first present in 2006 in Philadelphia, provided visitors with a chance to see the largest number of Franklin objects ever assembled in one place and continues to share these through a traveling exhibition. Rather than only focusing on Franklin's political and scientific careers for which he his most known, the tercentenary exhibit places Franklin's interest in material culture at its center. The display includes a variety of items from Franklin's home, his scientific instrument collection, family heirlooms, and an assortment of objects that represented Franklin's likeness, all of which were created during his lifetime and around the time of his death.

Despite the huge number of material culture objects with which Franklin came into contact, however, a large number of them remain scattered. Many of the objects we now associate with Franklin were public goods – like the lightning rod, Franklin stove, four-paned street lamp, and firefighting equipment – which were used by many individuals and became embedded in eighteenth-century culture as a whole. Another reason objects associated with Franklin have been dispersed is because Franklin scattered them himself. A frequent giver of gifts and longtime resident of three different countries, Franklin's possessions are now often found in private collections. Moreover, Franklin's home was demolished in 1812 and many of its exact contents remain a mystery. While Franklin wrote a will before his death in 1790, leaving his household possessions to his daughter and her husband, those objects were scattered once the house no longer existed.

In an effort to collect and organize the objects that do remain and that have been found, the tercentenary curators created the Franklin Artifacts database. An electronic catalogue with images hosted and administered by the Phillips Museum of Art at Franklin and Marshall College, the database records over 300 objects from 90 public and private collections. This digital archive offers the most comprehensive collection of Franklin objects and is an especially useful resource for tracing the developments in material culture over Franklin's lifetime.

Some of the most recognizable objects we now associate with Franklin came out of the period in which he first found international fame with the results of his experiments on electricity. While other scientists had long known of the existence of electrical current and that static electricity could be made on glass, Franklin began experiments to test for positive and negative charges. In 1746 Franklin, Ebenezer Kinnersley, Thomas Hopkinson, and Philip Syng, Jr conducted tests by following directions in the British popular periodical *The Gentleman's Magazine* and using an apparatus sent to them by Peter Collinson, a Fellow of the Royal Society in London. Franklin wrote about the results, sending his letters to Collinson, who in turn published them as *Experiments and Observations on Electricity made at Philadelphia in America by Mr. Benjamin Franklin* in 1751. In the spring or summer of 1752 Franklin undertook his famed kite and key experiment with his son William. At the same time that Franklin was working on electricity, Thomas-François Dalibard was directing a similar experiment in France based on his reading of Franklin's *Experiments and Observations*. The successful and nearly simultaneous completion of experiments that verified his hypotheses that clouds contain electricity and that lightning is only an electrical discharge secured Franklin's position as a leading scientific mind.

Finding almost immediate fame with the publication of his findings, Franklin continued his experiments and in the process developed the lightning rod, his first major contribution to eighteenth-century scientific material culture. He attached one to his own home, placing a chime in the middle of it so that he could hear and record any time that lightning struck. Given the success of his findings, Franklin advised readers of *Poor Richard's Almanack* to attach rods of iron with brass wire affixed to the tips to the tallest parts of their houses and other structures, making sure the grounded end of each contraption was sunk several feet into the earth and that the highest parts extended several feet above the top of roofs (*Poor Richard Improved* 1753; PBF, 4: 408–409). In spite of the rods' success in preventing lightning strikes and fires, Franklin faced opposition from some religious thinkers who felt the rods were an interference with the will of God. Nevertheless, Franklin prevailed, and after colonial astronomer David Rittenhouse discovered that the lightning rods put up in Philadelphia had achieved their purpose by significantly reducing the number of lightning strikes in the city, the invention became a commonplace and Franklin was celebrated by leading Americans as well as European thinkers and heads of state. In 1753, the Royal Society awarded Franklin its prestigious Copley Gold Medal, and three years later he was elected Fellow. In France, Franklin received the prestigious status of "foreign associate" in 1772 from the Académie Royale des Sciences (Krider, 2005). It was the lightening rod, the most material incarnation of his ideas about electricity, which served as the ticket of admission for his entrance to Britain and France's elite scientific societies and paved the way for Franklin's later diplomatic connections.

Franklin continued to find fame with his other scientific inventions, especially the Franklin stove. First describing it in his 1744 pamphlet *An Account of the New Invented Pennsylvanian Fire-Places*, Franklin's fireplace was designed to reduce the amount of wood fuel needed to heat a home. Relying on the efficiency of convection as well as the conducting capabilities of metal, Franklin's design was for a free-standing metal stove. The first prototypes were cast by Franklin's neighbor Robert Grace, who had also paid for the publication of the pamphlet that detailed the construction and use of the fireplace. While it was not initially popular, others improved on Franklin and Grace's design to such success that by the end of the century such stoves were in regular use and nearly all were referred to as Franklin stoves. Despite the name, however, Franklin's fireplace was derived from an earlier model invented by Nicolas Gauger and described in detail in his *Le Mécanique du Feu* (1709), a work acknowledged in Franklin and Grace's pamphlet. The front plate design of some early Franklin and Grace models, which featured the image of a sun in the form of a human face with two banners on either side, hints at the fireplace's antecedent. On the left, the banner reads "ALTER," and on the left, "IDEM," or "Another the same," a phrase that suggests shared thought and imitation, rather than unassisted genius. The textual motto included in the stove's visual design, the scientific insights about convection heat, and the networks of pamphlets on such inventions evidence Franklin's participation in a transatlantic network of ideas and friendship shaped by material culture.

Perhaps his most famous invention, Franklin's bifocal eyeglasses, further attest to Franklin as a collaborative thinker. Franklin frequently wore his "Double Spectacles," but even though he regularly proclaimed their usefulness, he never claimed to have invented them. In 1785, for example, he declared to his friend George Whatley that he was "happy in the Invention of Double Spectacles," wording that implied involvement with their creation but that did not claim credit (May 23, 1785; FDE).[2] It is more likely that bifocals were the result of joint efforts by Franklin, the London optician and instrument maker Peter Dollond, and the artists Joshua Reynolds and Benjamin West, both of whom were known to have begun wearing bifocals around the time that Franklin did (Levene, 1972). Just as with the lightning rod and the stove, Franklin's relationships with leading optical thinkers were developed through and around a material object.

Unsurprisingly, the assortment of Franklin's other inventions like the odometer, catheter, glass armonica, and swimming fins were developed within existing networks of ideas about distance, medicine, and music. Some, like Franklin's "Long Arm," seemed to speak directly to issues well beyond the scope of their immediate use value. Conceived to help him reach books from the highest of his library shelves, Franklin's mechanical prosthesis allowed him mobility even while he battled gout. As David Waldstreicher (2002) has argued, Franklin's lengthy description of his "Long Arm" fits within common metaphors linking amputation and diseases affecting the limbs to political disunity and a lack of self-sufficiency. Even though Franklin's persona as an inventor was the leading one of his lifetime, Franklin always found ways in his writings to connect his material productions to the larger issues of the day.

Perhaps because his scientific persona was the one for which he was initially known, the very first visual representations of Franklin were those that depicted him with the tools of his scientific trade. Mason Chamberlain's celebrated 1762 portrait pictured Franklin seated as his desk with symbolic evidence of his scientific mastery. One of the most widely reproduced of the early portraits of Franklin, and one of Franklin's favorite images of himself, the portrait visually capitalized on Franklin's fame as the inventor of lightning rods and his continued success with advances in electricity. In the portrait, Franklin wears a brown-violet suit, holds a pen and paper, and looks off to the distance. Over his right shoulder is pictured the lightening rod with chimes that he designed for his home and over his left shoulder is an open window showing lightning striking rods on several buildings. A house and a church, both without rods, are depicted in a state of demolition resulting from lightning. Commissioned originally by Franklin's friend Philip Ludwell III, the portrait pleased Franklin more than any other before, and in 1763 Franklin and his son William placed an order with the engraver Edward Fisher to produce at least one hundred mezzotint copies of the Chamberlin portrait to give as gifts by both father and son. Franklin sent one to Thomas Francois Dalibard, the French scientist who had conducted experiments with electricity the same year Franklin had. In his accompanying letter, Franklin explained that the mezzotint image would serve as his substitute, writing "As I cannot soon again enjoy the Happiness of being personally in your Company, permit my Shadow to pay my Respects to you" (September 22, 1769; PBF, 16: 206).

As Franklin's popularity grew and he became an international statesman, the visual representations of him changed to reflect those new personas. While Chamberlin had painted Franklin as man of science, French artist Charles Nicolas Cochin depicted him as American rustic abroad, dramatizing Franklin's role as ambassador from North America. The portrait, which pictured Franklin as a caricature of New World simplicity complete with spectacles, homespun garb, stringy shoulder-length hair, and a fur cap, became immensely popular throughout Europe and the new United States. As R. Jackson Wilson has explained, Cochin's image subtly complicated his representation by showing Franklin peering out towards the viewer from around the frames of his glasses to suggest Franklin's "keenness of sight" and investment in "seeing or being seen" in a particular way (Wilson, 1989: 41). Perhaps because of its calculated depiction of simultaneous naiveté and canniness, an engraving of the portrait by Augustin de Saint Aubin, first advertised on June 16, 1777 in the *Journal de Paris*, made the rounds of European society. Just as the Chamberlin portrait served as the model for a number of reproductions, several paintings that appeared shortly after the widespread release of the Saint Aubin print featured Franklin in a fur cap with spectacles. Famed American painter John Trumbull, for example, acknowledged the French popular artwork for his 1778 painting of Franklin, noting the image in his portrait list as "Head of Dr. Franklin – a fur cap – from a French print" (Sellers, 1962: 231). Long after the Saint Aubin print was released, drawings, paintings, engravings, and etchings of Franklin in spectacles and fur cap continued to abound.

As images of Franklin changed as his identities shifted, Franklin became increasingly more interested in how his image was presented in public. He wrote to family and friends asking what they thought of his various portraits and communicating his numerous opinions about artistic merit and aesthetic success. Engravings of the Chamberlin portrait, for example, became so popular and the painting so widely known, that its reproductions provided Franklin with amusement, and in some cases, irritation. Franklin took a keen interest in a version of the image that was published as a frontispiece engraving for a 1773 French edition of Franklin's *Observations on Electricity*, noting how it had changed a number of qualities of the original representation. He wrote derisively in 1773, "tho' a Copy of that by Chamberlin" the French frontispiece "has got so French a Countenance, that you would take me for one of that lively Nation" (September 1, 1773; PBF, 20: 384).

Perhaps because he knew that his likeness might change as images were reproduced from existing reproductions, Franklin sometimes directed artists to make particular copies of earlier artworks. A portrait of Franklin with a bust of Isaac Newton first painted by British artist Benjamin Martin in 1766, for example, was reproduced numerous times at Franklin's behest. Unlike the Chamberlin portrait, the Martin portrait was usually copied by other artists in oil on canvas, a choice of medium that limited the image's circulation because of its lengthy production time and the expense of its materials. Franklin even left one version to the Supreme Executive Council of Pennsylvania in his 1789 will, further suggesting how Franklin made visual representations of himself central to his life and to the political sphere he helped develop. By the end of his lifetime, Franklin had become the subject of a huge number of painted portraits, including works by Chamberlin, as well as those by famed artists Louis Carrogis de Carmontelle, Joseph Siffred Duplessis, Jean Baptiste Greuze, Benjamin Martin, David Martin, Charles Willson Peale, Charles Philippe Amédée Vanloo, Benjamin West, and Benjamin Wilson, many of which commented on Franklin's status as a leading scientific mind (Sellers, 1962; Craven, 1993; E.G. Miles, 1993).

Like other eighteenth-century men of wealth, Franklin hoped to cement personal and professional relationships with the help of portraits. Numerous scholars have explored the extent to which early Americans used visual culture objects to reinforce their social, political, and economic status and to have material proof of their achievements. As Margaretta Lovell has shown, relationships between patrons, artists, and family members are apparent in the repeated poses and motifs present throughout eighteenth-century portraiture. The development of a painting was often collaborative, as sitters instructed artists to paint them in particular settings or with certain family members, household objects, or iconographic motifs. In order to reference existing conventions or popular styles, artists frequently copied elements of established works, often relying on cheaply produced engravings of famous works (Lovell, 2005). As Brandon Brame Fortune and Deborah J. Warner have explained, men like Franklin traded portraits and portrait prints with each other to maintain circuits of friendship and the exchange of scientific ideas. Just as with Franklin's mention of the Gauger fireplace in his pamphlet and use of the "Alter idem" motto on the stove, as well as with his portrait gift to fellow electrical scientist Dalibard, portraits served as "material evidence of the value of correspondence and exchange within the growing transatlantic scientific community" (Fortune and Warner, 1999: 114–115). The circulation of Franklin portraits evidences the rich development of Franklin's visual representation in his lifetime as well as with his engagement with the production of his image as it existed within the culture in which he lived.

Franklin wrote at length about his formal portraits, but he was also concerned with much less highbrow, less aesthetic pictorial representations. Even though Franklin took control of his image, both professional and amateur artists took liberties, often depicting Franklin in unforgiving ways. A wide variety of political cartoons depict Franklin in caricature in an effort to critique his positions within Pennsylvania politics and especially within the context of the heated debates of the 1760s. Other artists imagined not Franklin's political problems, but instead his social transgressions. On a trip to London as a young man, Philadelphia painter Charles Willson Peale, for example, sketched a small drawing of Franklin in his diary. The sketch shows a seated Franklin kissing a woman on his lap, suggesting that on his initial meeting with Franklin, Peale was left with one leading impression of the famous gentleman. Examples of such unflattering images of Franklin abounded, and while some were widely disseminated, others, like Peale's, remained confined to the pages of diaries and other less public forms.

Graphic representations of Franklin were the most frequently reproduced, but artists also crafted likenesses of Franklin in three dimensions. Created by Jean Jacques Caffiéri in 1777, the first widely exhibited bust of Franklin featured the thinker in marble. Described by Franklin's friends and family as the most accurate representation ever made of him, the Caffiéri bust was produced after long sittings with its subject. Franklin favored the image so much that it was the only bust that he ever purchased, although many others were given to him as gifts. While the Caffiéri bust was the first to attract much attention from Franklin and contemporaries, the bust created only a year later by Jean-Antoine Houdon was more celebrated. First crafted out of terra cotta and then produced in marble, the Houdon bust was widely thought to capture Franklin's likeness as well as his personality by mobilizing new techniques in shaping the eyeballs to look up and away rather than steadfastly forward as was traditional. Created at the same time that Houdon was making busts of Rousseau, Moliére, and Voltaire, the Franklin likeness seems not to have been sculpted from life, since no records indicate that Houdon had anything more than a brief encounter with Franklin before exhibiting the bust. Nevertheless, so taken were Franklin's contemporaries with the sculpture, that Thomas Jefferson and George Washington commissioned their own busts from Houdon. Both the Caffiéri and Houdon busts were copied extensively in Franklin's lifetime, and continued to be reproduced throughout the nineteenth and early twentieth centuries.

Classical busts of Franklin were popular, but so too were less elite, three-dimensional representations. Artists and craftspeople such as Charles Gabriel Sauvage, François Marie Suzanne, and Ralph Wood produced small figurines of Franklin in materials such as porcelain, terra cotta, and bronze. Known less for their lifelike representations of their subjects than for their ubiquity, these small statues capitalized on the trend for decorative figurines. Other craftspeople produced three-dimensional likenesses in more popular media such as wax and wood. One French maker, perhaps following Houdon's sculptural grouping, produced a tableau of Franklin, Rousseau, and Voltaire as wax dolls with removable wigs, seated in an outdoor setting with a black child and a white child, and placed inside a glass box. Commissioned to produce a likeness of Franklin to hang in a bookseller's shop in New Haven, American artist William Rush carved a wooden likeness of Franklin in the late 1780s. Some scholars have even suggested that Franklin's likeness, like those of other leaders, may have taken the form of a ship's masthead, although no definitive version of such an object has yet been found. Relief sculptures by Isaac Gosset, William Hackwood, Jean Baptiste Nini, Josiah Wedgwood, and the Manufacture Nationale de Sèvres were also popular and sold well. The most famed reliefs were those created by Wedgwood in his Etruria factory in Staffordshire, United Kingdom, which produced a series of medallions ranging in size from small cameos to large wall plaques. Metal artists such as Jean François Bernier and

Augustin Dupré also crafted popular medallions of Franklin, and unlike many terra cotta or porcelain reliefs, often included Latin mottos and classical imagery on the reverse sides. Popular during his lifetime and after, relief cameos and medallions could be found in the possession of many American, British, and French people of upper-class status living at the turn of the nineteenth century.

As Franklin's image became increasingly sought after, makers began adding it to a wide variety of decorative furnishings and other similar media. One of the most popular images to be reproduced in material media was the Saint Aubin portrait print with its fur cap and spectacles, variations of which appeared on personal objects as diverse as textiles, snuffboxes, and porcelain dishware. As with the Houdon exhibition of busts and the anonymously created wax figurine tableaux, luxury goods sometimes depicted Franklin with Voltaire and Rousseau. A late eighteenth- or early nineteenth-century French-made snuffbox made of horn, wood, a colored engraving, and glass, depicts Franklin with the two other thinkers under the motto "Le Flambeau de l'Univers" (The Light of the Universe). Franklin was also commonly pictured with George Washington, especially in the years after their deaths at the end of the century. One textile pattern called "The Apotheosis of Washington and Franklin," for example, features a complicated and finely detailed allegorical design, and was transferred using copperplate printing with sepia, brown, or red ink on bleached cotton fabric. Likely the most widely employed medium on which a derivative of the Saint Aubin image appeared was as a transfer piece used on a series of cream-color earthenware bowls and other dishware manufactured in England. Probably produced by the Wedgwood company, the transfer print dishes features the image on both exterior and interior surfaces. One bowl exhumed in an archeological site in Philadelphia shows considerable wear, suggesting that the dishes were used in spite of possible damage to Franklin's image. So many of the dishes exist it is impossible to accurately trace all of their provenances, but examples have been found in collections and archeological sites in Britain, France, as well as in the United States, further evidence that the vogue for Franklin merchandise was a thoroughly transatlantic affair. Franklin's fashionable circles dined on dinnerware depicting America's biggest international celebrity, an image created by a French artist most likely when Franklin was in France, and manufactured into an object by English earthenware companies. From France to England to America and back again, the circulation of the Saint Aubin portrait print evidences a need to understand images of Franklin within many geographic, cultural, and material contexts.

Perhaps unsurprisingly, Franklin frequently made reference to the Saint Aubin image in his writing. In one particularly telling exchange in the winter of 1777, just a few short months before the Cochin print appeared, Franklin sent a telling letter from Paris to his friend Emma

Thompson in London. In it, he asked that his geographically distant friend imagine his appearance:

> Figure me in your mind as jolly as formerly, and as strong and hearty, only a few Years older, very plainly dress'd, wearing my thin grey strait Hair, that peeps out under my only Coiffure, a fine Fur Cap, which comes down my Forehead almost to my Spectacles. (PBF, February 8, 1777; 23: 298)

A textual version of the image that was on the verge of inundating European media, Franklin's description of himself to Thompson attests to the level of Franklin's investment with his visual representation. Likely suspecting the image that he had commissioned and which he hoped would convey his status as a humble American and learned philosopher would become immensely popular, Franklin practiced its effectiveness by deploying its textual corollary in his letter. He added further intimacy to an already intimate letter by implying that a description of his aged appearance and his lack of obvious fashion sense were a form of personal revelation.

Franklin might have found the new media on which his image appeared a delightful innovation in portrait custom, since he was interested in the decorative arts even from the outset of his career. Writing under the pseudonym "Anthony Afterwit" in a 1732 piece for the *Pennsylvania Gazette*, for example, Franklin satirized a growing desire among colonial Americans for luxury consumer goods. Anthony Afterwit, an "honest Tradesman" who claims to have been fooled by his wife's father into thinking her wealthier than she is, takes action once he realizes that his wife's "Strong Inclination to be a *Gentlewoman*" is draining his finances. While she is away on a two-week visit "to see a Relation," Afterwit enacts some "surprising Revolutions" by removing all of his wife's expensive possessions and replacing them with more affordable alternatives. He "dispos'd of the Tea-Table, and put a Spinning Wheel in its Place," while "The stately Clock I have transform'd into an Hour-Glass," jokingly suggesting that the new furnishings are more aesthetically pleasing and more tasteful than the original objects. The Spinning Wheel "looks very pretty" and the Hour-Glass is cast as an important "Ornament ... to the Room," Afterwit declares. Pitting useful furnishings against their imported luxury counterparts, Franklin used the Afterwit piece to critique refinement, finding it a particular fault among colonial women like Mrs Afterwit.

Franklin wrote publically about material objects, chiding fictional figures such as Mrs Afterwit for purchasing too much luxury, but privately, Franklin wrote a great deal about his interest in luxury commodities. Scholars have noted the extent to which Franklin discussed the details of his home with his wife, sister, and daughter (Roach, 1960; Dorman, 1969; Lopez, 1981; Talbott, 2005b). During his thirty years in England and France, Franklin frequently shipped silver, kitchen utensils, fabrics, desks, chairs, candle snuffers, wallpaper, glassware, jewelry, portraits, ceramics, mirrors, and countless other items to his family. Much of Franklin's correspondence was filled with directions on how best to decorate the prominent three-story, ten-room brick house set in a large courtyard off Philadelphia's Market Street that Franklin had commissioned from Philadelphia builders Robert Smith and Samuel Rhoads in 1762. Franklin worried endlessly about the minutest details, writing to Deborah at length about the house's "blue room," anxious that it might be "too blue, the Wood being of the same Color with the Paper" (June 22, 1767; PBF, 14: 194–195). Franklin was so fond of the luxuries his new life afforded that he even adopted a coat of arms – a pair of lions' heads, two doves, a dolphin, pike's head, and two olive branches – to adorn silverware such as a tankard by New Jersey silversmith Elias Boudinot. The letters and gifts Franklin sent to Philadelphia testify to his interest in an increasingly genteel style of living that was manifested through material goods and that, ironically, became increasingly more available to him the further he was from home.

Other scholars, such as Edward Cahill, have suggested that Franklin's interest in material culture signifies a "psychological ambivalence with which he faced the ethics of pleasure, luxury, status, and socioeconomic self-transformation" (Cahill, 2008: 31). Franklin lived during a moment in which republican citizenship meant disavowing one's personal interests, came from a part of the world heavily influenced by Quakers and their beliefs about simple living, and wrote in the wake of his own publications advocating frugality and austerity. Because he was able to buy – and significantly not use – the lavish furnishings he purchased for his Philadelphia home, according to Cahill, Franklin was able to profess a simple lifestyle while at the same time indulging in the rich consumer culture in which his successes enabled him to participate.

Franklin's *Autobiography* distilled the complicated relationship he had with material possessions, often directing readers to think of the international man of science and politics in more domestic registers. The longest and most literary of Franklin's writings, his *Autobiography* provides an account of Franklin's life in the form of a letter to his son William. Suggesting that the events of his life might be "fit to be imitated" (1990: 43), Franklin explained how he came to leave his family in Boston, set himself up as a printer in Philadelphia, and embark on a number of projects for civic and political improvement in Pennsylvania. Franklin's account of his rise from "Poverty and Obscurity" to "a State of Affluence and some Degree of Reputation" (43) has often been read as a manual on self-improvement and entrepreneurial capitalist success and on how to juggle the competing interests of extreme personal wealth with a self-professed strict adherence to values of humility and frugality. Writing at the start of the twentieth century, critics took Franklin at face value, generally assuming that strictly he followed his lessons on frugal living without succumbing to the kinds of lifestyles his success would have allowed. Max Weber, for example, explained, "the *summum bonum* ... the earning of more and more money, combined with the strict avoidance of all spontaneous enjoyment of life ... is thought of ... as an end in itself" (2009: 25). Similarly, D.H. Lawrence criticized Franklin's apparently excessive commitment to money, an ascetic lifestyle, and lack of humor, calling him "Doctor Franklin. Snuff-coloured little man!", "Sound, satisfied Ben!" (Lawrence, 1923: 24–25). While Weber's and Lawrence's arguments have been challenged in the last one hundred years, their assessment that Franklin's *Autobiography* hinges on his ability to present individual capitalist success that simultaneously dismisses an interest in luxury still often persists.

The *Autobiography* provided Franklin with a way of writing about his values of thrift and humility, and as a result often turns on a number of moments in which material objects become the focus. In particular, Franklin's growing stores of luxury household goods always enter the narrative through the actions of others; expensive chinaware and silver were first purchased by his wife Deborah, not Franklin. Franklin explained (1990: 65):

> Being call'd one Morning to Breakfast, I found it in a China Bowl with a Spoon of Silver. They had been bought for me without my Knowledge by my Wife, and had cost her the enormous Sum of three and twenty Shillings, for which she had no other Excuse or Apology to make, but that she thought her Husband deserv'd a Silver Spoon and China Bowl as well as any of his Neighbours.

Franklin dodges the responsibility of having purchased luxury goods by blaming them on his wife's desire to compete their neighbors' levels of refinement. The only point in the *Autobiography* at which Franklin discussed delighting in material goods is framed as a lesson. Franklin learns that displaying wealth can cause ill-will and he vows not to do it again. On his first return to Boston after finding work in Philadelphia, Franklin visits his brother (and former apprentice master) at his shop. Franklin explained that his brother James "receiv'd me not very frankly, look'd me all over, and turn'd to his Work again" because he "was better dress'd than ever while in [James's] Service, having a genteel new Suit from Head to foot, [and] a Watch." To impress James's workers the youthful Franklin "produc'd a handful of Silver and spread it before them," and then gives the men the "Opportunity of letting them see my Watch" (*Autobiography*, 1990: 24). Learning that the behavior does not put him on good terms with his family, Franklin vowed not to exhibit the material signifiers of his newfound gentility again.

Moreover, Franklin went out of his way to frame the narrative around distinctly unrefined material goods in order to illustrate his thriftiness and work ethic. In one of the most cited passages in the *Autobiography*, Franklin explained (1990: 54):

> In order to secure my Credit and Character as a Tradesman, I took care not only to be in Reality Industrious and frugal, but to avoid all Appearances of the Contrary. I drest plainly; I was seen at no Places of idle Diversion; I never went out a-fishing or shooting; a Book, indeed, sometimes debauch'd me from my Work; but that was seldom, snug, and gave no Scandal: and to show that I was not above my Business, I sometimes brought home the Paper I purchas'd at the Stores, thro' the Streets on a Wheelbarrow.

Franklin's statement about image management suggests that appearance mattered as much, if not more, than the reality of personal behavior. And Franklin imparted the lesson about being a visibly hard worker in this passage, crucially, through his reference to a material object. A symbol of Franklin's artisan background, Franklin relied on the wheelbarrow to signify hard work and the accessibility of success. It is worth noting that elsewhere in the *Autobiography* Franklin downplayed references to his artisan roots, referring, for example, to the Leather Apron Club by its later name Junto, suggesting that one's artisan identity was best deployed only at key moments and only to generate a certain image.

Franklin also made use of household furniture to chart his rise to wealth. He underscored his characters' relatively impoverished lifestyles by noting that they used stools rather than more expensive and genteel chairs. In recalling his family reading the Bible "thro' the Reign of Queen Mary," for example, Franklin described how his ancestors decided to "conceal and secure it ... with Tapes under and within the Frame of a Joint Stool." Franklin's "Great Great Grandfather" was able to read the book aloud to his family when "he turn'd up the Joint Stool upon his Knees, turning over the Leaves then under the Tapes" (1990: 4). Similarly, when he recounted his visit to a Catholic hermit woman in London, Franklin described her meager furniture: "a Matras, a Table with a Crucifix and Book, a Stool" (1990: 38). And when Franklin recalled sitting at the table for mealtimes with his family as a boy, he did not note any furniture at all, an omission that suggests that Franklin's boyhood home was like many other working-class homes in colonial America. Franklin's home very likely lacked furniture designated only for seating, forcing residents and guests to take their meals seated on the floor or on a bed. Frequently overlooked as an essential part of Franklin's mythmaking abilities in the *Autobiography*, material culture objects such as wheelbarrows and stools provided symbols that signified class and his uncomfortable relationship to his newfound wealth.

The *Autobiography* also reminds us that Franklin was first and foremost a printer, even though he retired from that position as a relatively young man. Franklin referenced the vocabulary of printing as he noted that his life's mistakes were errata, the printers' term for error. So central was printing to his life that no other material objects would have been more a part of Franklin's life as a young man than the ink balls, ink stands, composing sticks, type trays, and printing presses with which he worked. Franklin was involved in the development of print in colonial America from the outset, working with and helping to establish shops throughout the colonies, competing with other Philadelphia printers Andrew Bradford and Samuel Keimer, and becoming friends with London printer and publisher William Strahan. In fact, Franklin's first trip abroad was to London to acquire printing equipment with which to establish his own shop in Philadelphia under the patronage of Governor Keith. While Keith's promises fell through, Franklin spent eighteen months in London improving his printing knowledge and skills, and returned to eventually set up shop with former fellow apprentice Hugh Meredith. Even though Franklin retired from his own printing house in Philadelphia, leaving the business in the hands of his partner David Hall, Franklin nevertheless maintained an active interest in the dissemination and circulation of print in early America for the rest of his life.

Recent scholarship on the history of the book and print culture has reinvigorated debates about the need to consider the material nature of printed texts. Scholars such as Michael Warner (1990), James N. Green and Peter Stallybrass (2006), Trish Loughran (2007), and David D. Hall and Hugh Amory (2007) have argued that in colonial America the material conditions surrounding the production of texts mattered significantly for their contents. In Franklin's America, almost all books were imported, but a culture of domestically printed newspapers and pamphlets flourished. The size and thickness of the paper, the color of the ink, the styles of binding or folding, the quality of the typesetting, and countless other conditions affected how readers, fluent in a language of the material qualities of print, engaged with words in the colonial period. The material conditions of the blank forms, newspapers, almanacs, pamphlets, broadsides, and books that Franklin printed are central to how we understand his relationship to culture.

Perhaps as no other text could, Franklin's *Autobiography* signals the extent to which the material conditions of print are central to how we read eighteenth-century texts. Written in four parts as a manuscript over a period of nineteen years, Franklin's *Autobiography* is famously fragmented. Even though he only produced it as a manuscript, Franklin drafted the *Autobiography* with printing techniques in mind, writing on sheets of paper folded into columns that left plenty of space blank for corrections or possibly even printers' directions. Its existence as a complete, printed monograph is an invention of nineteenth-century printers and his grandson William Temple Franklin's decision to finally print all of the parts in one complete version in 1818. Moreover, early English editions of the *Autobiography* were often English translations of French translations of portions of

Franklin's manuscript, many of which included large sections of text supplied by various editors and sometimes passed off as Franklin's writing. Even as new editions became available, many editors merely made changes to earlier editions rather than returning to the manuscript. The first full copy of the *Autobiography* to accurately reproduce the four-part manuscript written by Franklin was edited by J.A. Leo Lemay and P.M. Zall and published in 1981. As modern readers who encounter the *Autobiography* as a single bound book, we tend to miss the material conditions through which it came to exist that way. What is more, as readers of the recently digitized *Papers of Benjamin Franklin* at Yale University, we tend to think of Franklin's works as a complete, coherent body as we skip over the realities of dispersal, pseudonymous writing, and print production that existed in Franklin's lifetime.

Even though the *Autobiography* is Franklin's most imaginative and fanciful work, it is also the cultural object that should remind us to consider Franklin's world and the furnishings, inventions, portraits, and writings of which it was comprised. Just as with Franklin's identities, the material culture objects with which he was associated proliferated into countless iterations in a network around him. Investigating the connections between the overlapping cultures of scientific invention, artistic representation, household decoration, and personal and public writing helps us better understand Franklin's personal investment with material objects and shows us new ways of analyzing his writing and his place in American history. Franklin consistently sought to control his image, to instruct his family and friends on what to do with gifts, to recommend the use and sale of some invention or another, and above all, to stress that material objects, like texts, always existed within a web of shifting cultural codes and symbols.

Notes

1 Labaree, Leonard W. *et al.*, eds. (1959–). *The Papers of Benjamin Franklin*. 39 vols to date. New Haven, CT: Yale University Press. Hereafter referred to as PBF.
2 Franklin, Benjamin (2006). *The Papers of Benjamin Franklin: Digital Edition*. Los Altos, CA. Available at: http://franklinpapers.org/franklin/. Hereafter referred to as FDE.

Further Reading

Cahill, Edward (2008). "Benjamin Franklin's Interiors," *Early American Studies* 6: 27–58.
Fortune, Brandon Brame, and Warner Deborah J. (1999). *Franklin And His Friends: Portraying the Man of Science in Eighteenth-Century America*. Washington, DC.

Green, James N., and Stallybrass, Peter (2006). *Benjamin Franklin: Writer and Printer*. New Castle, DE.

Lemay, J.A. Leo, ed. (1993). *Reappraising Benjamin Franklin: A Bicentennial Perspective*. Newark, DE.

Sellers, Charles Coleman (1962). *Benjamin Franklin in Portraiture*. New Haven, CT.

Talbott, Paige, ed. (2005). *Benjamin Franklin: In Search of a Better World.* New Haven, CT.

Chapter Twenty-two

BENJAMIN FRANKLIN AND POLITICAL THEORY

Jerry Weinberger

One could argue that there's no such thing as a "Franklinian" political theory. Just think how oddly the term rings on our ears. Not so for "Hobbesian," or "Machiavellian," or "Aristotelian." From these thinkers we have long and formal treatises on politics, each accounting for the origins and kinds and order of political regimes, the nature of law and justice, and so forth. The same is true, although perhaps to a lesser extent, for the other American founders, who wrote enough to make the terms "Madisonian" or "Jeffersonian" seem clear enough, even though they are contested, as is all political theory, in the halls of academe (without "revision," what would professors have to do?).

There is no Franklin treatise on politics. And Franklin's *writings* on politics were always pamphlets addressing some pressing and discrete matter of colonial or revolutionary politics, including religious politics. Franklin in London was by 1770 the paid agent of Pennsylvania, Georgia, New Jersey, and Massachusetts, which is almost as much as to say that he was, among other things, a hired propagandist for these colonies in the lead-up to the imperial crisis. For that reason alone, it makes it difficult to take what he wrote as serious political thought, not to mention "political philosophy" (more about that later). Moreover, the great bulk of Franklin writings consist of short articles (some anonymous and pseudonymous) from his newspaper, the *Pennsylvania Gazette*, letters by the barrel-full, bagatelles, more than a few short literary hoaxes, and even a dialogue featuring Socrates and a blockhead, appropriately named Crito. And then there's the fact that Franklin's most famous and enduring work is the *Autobiography*, the story

---

A Companion to Benjamin Franklin, First Edition. Edited by David Waldstreicher.
© 2011 Blackwell Publishing Ltd. Published 2011 by Blackwell Publishing Ltd.

of his rise from obscurity and relative poverty to being the most famous American (at least abroad) of his time: "The First American."

So it is no wonder that Franklin has been the scholarly object primarily of American historians, intellectual historians, and scholars of English literature, and of course popular biographers. Books and articles on his "political theory" are relatively few, and most of those are recent, by which I mean the last twenty-five years or so. Moreover, in the long course of Franklin scholarship and criticism there is a persistent opinion that Franklin has little of theoretical importance to tell us, or better, that what he does tell us about America, to the extent that it is true, is something of which we should be ashamed.

From the American transcendentalists to such anti-bourgeois thinkers as Max Weber and D.H. Lawrence, and as late as Alasdair MacIntyre's *After Virtue*, Franklin comes across as the epitome of America materialism and utilitarianism (MacIntyre, 1981: 181–186, 198–199). To hear Lawrence describe Franklin, he was a flat-headed Babbitt whose sole mission in life was making money and stunting the souls of those who read his newspaper and *Poor Richard's Almanack*. Said Lawrence of Franklin: "unlovely, snuff-colored little ideal, or automaton, of a pattern American. The pattern American, this dry, moral, utilitarian little democrat, has done more to ruin the old Europe than any Russian nihilist" (Sanford, 1955: 64). To Weber, Franklin was the embodiment of the secularized Protestant Ethic, for which material prosperity was both a calling and a sign of divine favor (Weber, 1958: 48–56, 64–65). By these accounts, there is no need to read Franklin; everything he said and did can be explained by the critique of bourgeois capitalism. And so Weber read almost nothing of Franklin, and, while Lawrence read more, he did so with an ear deaf to the dead-pan humor and irony of Franklin's literary style.

It was almost inevitable, therefore, that a much more nuanced view of Franklin began to emerge in the 1960s. Intellectual historians began to see a Franklin who was deeply engaged in the intellectual currents of the Enlightenment, including such figures as Anthony Collins, Shaftesbury, Bacon, Hobbes, Locke, Milton, Mandeville, Hutcheson, and Trenchard and Gordon of *Cato's Letters*. Critics came to appreciate the ironic charm of the *Autobiography*, indeed installing it in the pantheon of the great products of American letters. This new Franklin, however, emerged as a many-sided mystery. The classic version of this mystery was presented in John William Ward's 1963 essay "Who Was Benjamin Franklin?." According to Ward Lawrence was led astray because he did not see the Franklin manifold: Franklin "contained in his own character so many divergent aspects that each observer can make the mistake of seeing one aspect as all and celebrate or despise Franklin accordingly." Ward said that Franklin meditated deeply on the nature of pride and sin, and that he gets under our skins, because while we admire him "at the same time we are uneasy with the man who wears so many masks that we are never sure who is there behind them. Yet it is this very difficulty of deciding whether we admire Franklin or suspect him, that makes his character an archetype for our national experience" (Ward, 1963: 542, 553).

A year later David Levin argued that the *Autobiography* is a great work of art characterized by "humorous self-criticism," in which Franklin "deliberately appearing to be more simple than he is ... draws our attention away from the books he has read." Though a clear representative of the Enlightenment, Franklin is deceptively simple and a man who hides himself (Levin, 1964: 272–275). This new trope, of Franklin's elusive many-sidedness, has lasted down through Gordon Wood's 2004 *The Americanization of Benjamin Franklin*, where we are told that Franklin was a "man of many masks" and thus not easy to know (2004: 13–15).

Now all this Franklin rehabilitation did little to establish him as a serious political theorist, much less one on a par with the likes of Hobbes or Locke. In fact, it made matters worse, because instead of producing just one, predictable Franklin, the new scholarship produced too many unpredictable ones. For political theory it does not matter all that much *who* Thomas Hobbes or John Locke were, in the sense of what went on silently in their heads. We have their treatises and we can read what they say and agree or disagree. But with Franklin, the question of what he thought and who he was "internally" have become closely intertwined, in large part because the new scholarship was correct to see the centrality of the *Autobiography* for the whole of Franklin's thought, and to sense a powerful elusiveness and irony in almost everything that Franklin wrote. The new scholarship was right to sense that for Franklin, there was a deep sense that the personal is political; and that makes getting at his political theory a difficult task, especially since he held his personal cards so closely to his chest.

***

While Franklin, and what he says about life and politics, have pretty much been owned by literary scholars and American and intellectual historians, a few scholars of political theory have turned their sights on Ben. Since 1965, the following work, by scholars of politics or political thought, has appeared: Paul W. Conner's *Poor Richard's Politics: Benjamin Franklin and His New American Order* (1965); Ralph L. Ketcham's *Benjamin Franklin* (1966); Ralph Lerner's "Franklin Spectator" in his 1979 *The Thinking Revolutionary*, and "Dr. Janus" in J.A. Leo Lemay's 1993 *Reappraising Benjamin Franklin*, and "Franklin's Double Take on Rights" in his 2009 *Playing The Fool: Subversive Laughter in Troubled Times*. Between 1993 and 2006, Steven Forde published a string of articles and book chapters: "Benjamin Franklin's *Autobiography* and the Education of America" (1992), "Ben Franklin, Hero" (1999), "Benjamin Franklin and the Theory of the Social Compact" (2003), "Benjamin Franklin: An American Model and a

Model American" (2003), "Benjamin Franklin's 'Machiavellian' Civic Virtue" (2006). This writer's *Benjamin Franklin Unmasked: On the Unity of His Moral, Religious, and Political Thought* came out in 2005 and was reissued in paperback in 2008. Lorraine Pangle's *The Political Philosophy of Benjamin Franklin* appeared in 2007, and Alan Houston's *Benjamin Franklin and the Politics of Improvement* hit the shelves in 2008.

Not a lot, in the course of almost half a century. Nevertheless, there is enough to allow one remarkable thing to stand out: Most of these works and their authors (including me for truth in reporting) hale to one degree or another from the interpretive school of Leo Strauss. Of the seven scholars on the list, four are Straussians. And of the thirteen items listed (books, periodical articles, and book chapters) ten are by them. Any way you look at these facts, it is a remarkable imbalance.

Strauss to my knowledge wrote nothing about and never taught a course on Benjamin Franklin. But two of Strauss's favorite writers of fiction were Jane Austen and Dashiell Hammett, a taste that bespeaks attraction at once to the grace of polite sociability and to hardboiled and gritty but morally straight-shooting realism, surely both Franklin virtues. That by itself could perhaps explain the attraction of Franklin to adherents of Strauss' school. But a more powerful attraction is surely the fact, widely recognized in the new scholarly *establishment*, that Franklin's writing is ironic, in fact downright slippery: said Gordon Wood, in Franklin's "personal writings ... his assuming different personas and rolls makes it difficult to know how to read him" (2004: 14).

Perhaps the most powerful attraction to Straussians is the fact that Franklin presented himself, *as a model for others*, by way of an artful account of his life. In this sense Franklin placed himself in the tradition of Plato, Xenophon, Augustine, and Rousseau, who philosophized by creating a written spectacle of a life: Socrates's in the cases of Plato and Xenophon, and their own in the cases of Augustine and Rousseau. How, indeed, could scholars who expect irony and indirectness in great writers, and who read with care, long resist the charms of Franklin's *Autobiography*, not to mention the vast array of his other playful writings?

There is another remarkable fact about this list. Almost without exception, the intellectual and American historians and the literary scholars not on it ignore everything written by the Straussians. As does Alan Houston, a political scientist, who is largely (but not completely) influenced by the "so-called Cambridge School" that "insist[s] that the full meaning of a text could not be captured unless it was located in a meticulously constructed historical context," the most important parts of which are "the major and minor texts circulating at that time. The history of political thought is the history of political discourse. Only by paying attention to how contemporaries used language is it possible to grasp 'the point of the original intellectual enterprise'" (Houston, 2008: 19).

"Insisting" seems rather an unscholarly thing to do. And by this account, were one to write in two hundred years the history of political thought scholarship of our time, one would have to conclude that the historians and literary scholars, and those political scientists influenced by them, dogmatically hummed, fingers in the ears, whenever a Straussian said anything about Franklin in one of their minor texts. If historians read only what their kind writes, it is an indictment of the habits of their craft. But for a political scientist like Houston, who won the American Political Science Association Leo Strauss Award for his Ph.D. thesis on Algernon Sydney, to write a book on Franklin, with nary a nod to Ralph Lerner, Steven Forde, Lorraine Pangle, or me, is a disturbing surprise. So where is the "discourse"? Or perhaps, on second thought, the surprise is like Renault's at Rick's in *Casablanca*.

But let us move on. All of the recent work on Franklin's political thought is pretty good stuff, give or take varying degrees of sparkle. Of course it is not hard to write interestingly about Franklin, who without doubt belongs in the pantheon of great American writers. He was, in addition, one of the greatest humorists in our history, although some of it was until well into the twentieth century considered too vulgar and obscene to be given the light of day. Said Albert Henry Smyth, editor of the 1905 edition of the *Writings of Benjamin Franklin*: "Unfortunately, it is impossible without offence to quote many of his briefer paragraphs. We may track him through thirty years of the Gazette by the smudgy trail he leaves behind him. ... As is said of Angelo in the play, 'I am sorry one so learned and wise, should slip so grossly'" (1907: 171).

Smyth was not exaggerating. A careful reading of Franklin's *Old Mistress Apologue* reveals a reflection on sex and marriage that in its materialistic obscenity puts Mercutio to shame, and Franklin wrote a letter to James Read (a relative of his wife Deborah) in which he joked that the door to the imitation of Jesus is a woman's vagina (see Weinberger, 2005: 67–68, 101–107, 128–131). And there's lots of stuff like this, not to mention public attacks on the Philadelphia Presbyterian establishment that completely belie the picture of tolerance Franklin paints of himself in the *Autobiography*.

That Franklin could write such raunchy and cutting pieces and at the same time pen the *Autobiography* and *The Way to Wealth* has led to a problem in Franklin scholarship across the board. Ward got it right when he implied that Franklin observers often pick and choose according to the axes they grind. Franklin makes this easy, because he is such a slippery customer and fibber. John Adams (no Franklin admirer but also no dope) complained about the chameleon Franklin on matters of religion: "The Catholics thought him almost a Catholic. The Church of England claimed him as one of them. The Presbyterians thought him half a Presbyterian, and the Friends believed him a wet Quaker." Adams claimed he wasn't fooled, and reported that Franklin had no religion at all and that in Paris "all the atheists, deists, and libertines, as well as the philosophers and ladies, are in his train, another Voltaire, and thence" (1856, 1: 661).

There is something of the Franklin-as-a-mirror problem in the works on the list, although taken together they disclose a Franklin who makes sense on his own. In general, Straussians who study American political thought believe in and approve of American Exceptionalism. So their studies tend to see Franklin, especially the Franklin that emerges from the *Autobiography*, as a contributing model of the unique American character. But that is exactly what Franklin wanted us to think, which is why he inserted, between parts one and two of the *Autobiography*, the hyperbolic letters from Abel James and Benjamin Vaughn, praising him as the moral model (right up there with the Bible) for Americans to come. Said Vaughn: "all that has happened to you is also connected with the detail of the manners and situation of a rising people; and in this respect I do not think that the writings of Caesar and Tacitus can be more interesting to a true judge of human nature and society" (Lemay, 1987: 1373–1379). Whatever else we are to make of the bombast, there is no doubt that one cannot get a handle on Franklin without taking with at least some seriousness his claim to be the model, if not the first, American.

The Straussians also bring to the table their tropic distinction between the ancients and the moderns. This is especially central to Forde's "Benjamin Franklin's *Autobiography* and the Education of America" and "Benjamin Franklin's 'Machiavellian' Civic Virtue" and to Lorraine Pangle's *The Political Philosophy of Benjamin Franklin*. In an over-simplifying nutshell, the ancient modern divide is marked by Machiavelli's turn from the high road of classical political thought, with its imagined republics and concern for nobility and moral virtue, to the real world of effectual truth: what human beings are and not what we wish them to be. This moral realism was mated with a turn from speculative metaphysics to empirical modern science and the project to conquer nature, and both turns were used for a relentless attack on the Kingdom of Darkness, by which Hobbes meant Christianity. The Straussians tend to have at least one foot on the classical side of the divide, more on that later, but in general it is fair to say that their work on Franklin aims to find his place in the Enlightenment turn to modernity.

As sort of a "Cambridge School" man, Houston too comes at Franklin with some tropic conceptual baggage: the divide between the Locke-liberal side of our republic and its "classical republican" opposite (the latter being a *conflation* of the ancients and the moderns), rooted in the thinking of a Machiavelli who isn't Machiavellian and James Harrington's 1656 *Commonwealth of Oceana*. For the liberal side, a republic is founded on individual self-interest and the natural right to private property. For the classical side, a republic is founded on yeoman independence and virtuous dedication to the common good. Houston takes on the task of locating Franklin's place on this ideological divide.

It is a stretch to call Ralph Ketcham's book recent, but he is Professor Emeritus of History, Public Affairs, and Political Science at the Maxwell School at Syracuse and a well-known scholar of political thought. So, looking for political science scholars of political thought who had written on Franklin, it made sense to make the stretch back to 1966. By that time, the universities were clouded in tear gas, and critical theory and deconstruction were making their way along with Nietzsche and Heidegger. Twenty years before the late Alan Bloom's *The Closing of the American Mind*, Ketcham was worried about his students' moral relativism, and he brought that concern to his study of Franklin's political thought.

The late Paul W. Conner's book was not just temporally first; it was to the best of my knowledge the first book by a social scientist to present Franklin as having a coherent political theory, and this against a background scholarly consensus that Franklin's political thinking was a jumble of pragmatic bits and pieces. And like Ketcham, Conner had an ax to grind related to the turbulence of his time.

***

Many of the themes of the late Paul W. Conner's book are treated elsewhere in this volume, so I will not dwell too long. The book had its problems. There is too much psychology for my taste, for instance the claim that Franklin pursued the dames of Paris because of "a latent yearning for a wife more genteel and witty" than Deborah (Conner, 1965: 215). And it is often just too much over the top on its topics. But Conner was on to something new and important about Franklin, however much in the end it eluded a firm grasp.

Conner starts out with a lament about the fragmented and "Forsaken Franklin," which is partly Franklin's fault because he wrote no political treatise, and partly the fault of a political science profession that, with a few exceptions, had ignored him. Of those nonpolitical scientists who had at that time written about Franklin, Conner does not have much nice to say. Of Clinton Rossiter's view that Franklin was "a lovable old democrat" (Conner's words), Conner calls it "a Parson Weems with footnotes" (5). One reviewer of this book, the late Edward Handler, was mightily offended by this crack (1966: 285). Conner could have been more respectful, but he did have a good point: that while Franklin was most certainly an egalitarian, he was too much of a political fixer, indeed a social technician, to be a partisan of any political form.

Conner understood, as few did at the time, that Franklin's political thought and project were too broad to be wedged into the familiar categories of conventional scholarship. And so he was right to argue in the body of this book that Franklin's politics and political thinking coherently reflected the Enlightenment promise of a rational new order: "a bright, moral edifice to be built on earth." Conner's book takes seriously, and examines in some detail, the grand scale of Franklin's concept of what we might call the empire of modernity: decidedly Anglo-American (stretching from Great Britain to the whole of north America) and altogether rational and humane and organically whole, as bound by egalitarian civility and benevolent scientific progress.

The grand social vision Conner ascribes to Franklin sounds just like the society depicted in Sir Francis Bacon's *New Atlantis*. This should come as no surprise, since Franklin was such a keen reader, admirer and follower of Bacon. Conner was absolutely right to sniff out Franklin's Baconianism, even if his two references to Bacon have nothing to do with Bacon's project for the scientific conquest of nature. Conner was also right to sniff something fishy about Franklin – a gap between his theory and his practice – although what this gap might reveal is left for us as a mystery (1965: 212). Even so, thought Conner, what is clear in Franklin's progressive theory is lost to us today. Why so? Because the alienating and disintegrative force of modern capitalism has left us as blind to the promise of a "new order" as we are blind to the "unity in Franklin's design" (224). This sounds more like Mario Savio than it does like Francis Bacon. It is certain that Franklin, who sometimes quipped about his soul's return in a new body, would not have liked Conner's crack that it would be more at home in 1965 Moscow than Philadelphia. And Conner might have been kinder to Rossiter, had he known that the great historian would just five years later commit suicide as Cornell University was shaken by student revolution.

***

Ralph Ketcham's book was part of the Washington Square Press Great American Thinkers Series. The books in this series were intended for general readers and undergraduates looking for introductions. As such, it is not exactly academic, lacking as it does any scholarly apparatus, and it does not at any point dwell on problems or dig too deeply into interesting issues. It is in general, a breezy sweep across the usual Franklin preoccupations (pretty much as they show up in the *Autobiography*, as far as it goes): boyhood moral training; early reading; skepticism and heterodoxy in religion; science; politics in Pennsylvania; empire and revolution; the art of congeniality; international relations; religion; and a concluding summary discussion of the "public philosophy of a sage."

As a primer, there was not a lot in this survey that was not available elsewhere at its time. But it is nevertheless as charming as it is helpful to its audience, and it makes a very serious and (to the best of my knowledge) novel observation about Franklin. Ketcham starts out by noting that Franklin's reputation took a drubbing with the twentieth-century rise of "positivism in philosophy, behaviorism in social science, relativism in ethics, obscurantism in literature, and specialization in all fields of knowledge." The resulting Franklin was, to "sophisticated students of

American political thought," quaint or superficial and irrelevant, on the one hand, or a pernicious fraud, on the other. This dreary slide was reversed with the magisterial, 1938 Carl Van Dorn biography and the publication, still ongoing, of the Franklin *Papers*. Acclaim for Franklin was renewed and he emerged not as a priggish "thrift monger" or "crusading skeptic," but as "marvelously harmonious and interesting human being" (Ketcham, 1966: vii–viii). Now this judgment did not jibe with the emerging and now canonical view of the manifold and mysterious Franklin. But Ketcham did have a sense that with Franklin there really is something decidedly problematic.

Ketcham, advances an early version of what soon emerged in neoconservative Daniel Bell's (1976) *Cultural Contradictions of Capitalism*: The traditional bourgeois virtues, including especially religion, produced the leisure and freedom that undermine those very virtues. Modern capitalism thus lives on and squanders its essential "moral capital," and one sign of this was surely the drugged out hippies cavorting in the California woods, fornicating and living on wild berries.

Franklin was of course the farthest thing possible from Jimmy Hendrix. But in his concluding chapter on "the public philosophy of a sage," Ketcham ends with a cranky if accurate complaint that in our time of everything-is-relative modernity "college sophomores, applauded by their teachers, commonly go though a phase of doubting everything and finding old assurances hopelessly outmoded and themselves adrift in a meaningless void". He then follows this comment by noting that Franklin would have been sympathetic, since he was "the first American pragmatist," even though he carelessly bought in to the Enlightenment and rationalist faith in inevitable progress in morality and social understanding. In other words, as a model for Americans there is something a bit wrong with Benjamin Franklin(1966: 198–199).

Ketcham starts out being glad that Franklin is neither a thrift monger nor a crusading skeptic. But in the end and about the most important questions, Ketcham comes close to D.H Lawrence in leveling at Franklin the charge of complaisant superficiality. In Ketcham's telling in his early chapter on skepticism and orthodoxy (32–54), Franklin's Puritan upbringing at the hands of his father, as well as the stern morality of his literary model *The Spectator*, cushioned his Enlightenment discovery of deism and utilitarianism. As a consequence there was no abrupt and traumatic, skeptical "conversion experience," and so Franklin avoided an extreme and fanatical outlook and remained moderate and easy and balanced. Now I do not think this telling remotely reflects the *Autobiography*, and to the extent that it does there is scant attention to the actual text. But that is beside the point.

In his penultimate chapter on religion (163–184), Ketcham describes Franklin as "almost flippant" in his attitude to orthodox Christianity (in a letter to Ezra Stiles written when Franklin had one foot in the grave). He was, says Ketcham, a conventional deist, "eclectic, not always consistent, and sometimes neglectful of dilemmas" (176–179). This shallowness in matters of faith allowed Franklin easy reconciliation of his intellectual skepticism and the generous humanitarianism produced by his childhood training and his adult experience. All this is, to Ketcham, pretty thin spiritual gruel.

In discussing Franklin's famous 1757 letter to an anonymous friend about to attack the doctrine of particular providence, Ketcham notes that Franklin says that his friend did not get his own fine standards and moral habits from his "application of the system of natural ethics" and that Franklin "guessed" that those standards and habits came from the author's "religious education" (182–184). Actually, Franklin does not say this at all.

He says rather: "You yourself may find it easy to live a virtuous life without the assistance afforded by religion; you having a clear perception of the advantages of virtue and the disadvantages of vice, and possessing a strength of resolution sufficient to enable you to resist common temptations." And then after saying most people cannot do this, he adds "and perhaps you are indebted to her originally, that is to your religious education, for the habits of virtue upon which you now justly value yourself" (Lemay, 1987: 748–749). All this is much more tentative than Ketcham reports it. Moreover, Franklin's warning that the author is about to unchain the tiger of nonbelief concerns not the *author* becoming bad, but rather the odium and mortification he could suffer from the enemies his treatise will produce, or from those made bad by it. The clear implication is that the latter might believe it and be corrupted and steal the author's horse. But the former will not believe it and will hate the author for generating more horse thieves.

But never mind the text. Ketcham then says that what goes for Franklin's interlocutor goes for Franklin himself. Franklin's skeptical tiger had been constrained by his father's moral education and correction of his youthful indiscretions, and his lack of reflection on this fact accounts for his proposal to chain the tiger in others by way of "such a superficial scheme as his art of virtue." And then comes the kicker:

> Put another way, Franklin lived all of his moral life on the dividends from the large stock of moral capital his father had drawn from his religious faith. Though Benjamin Franklin retained a large measure of the profits (virtue) he cut himself off from his father's supplying bank. Was it wise to suppose the flow of dividends would continue for generations to come? Also, he seemed to think most other men had passions and impulses no more ungovernable than his own subdued and directed ones. The porous sands of overconfidence in human nature and oversimplification of social problems which critics have seen under Franklin's thought may have been deposited there by his failure to see the full implications of his own close connection with the great value-causing institutions of his native land. (Ketcham, 1966: 183)

In summing up Franklin's spiritual life, Ketcham concludes that Franklin was just unable or unwilling to "partake of deep spiritual experience." It is true that Franklin wasn't the flat-head derided by Lawrence, but to Ketcham "it is true that vast and wondrous realms of human experience were untouched by Franklin, and would remain febrile and impoverished if all genius was challenged as his was" (1966: 184). If we add all this up, there's a direct line from the skeptical, heterodox Franklin as the model American to the moral bank gone bust in the mid-twentieth century.

And something even bigger is implied in all this: it is not so much Franklin's religious heterodoxy that bothers Ketcham (though it bothers him a lot). It is the fact of Franklin's Enlightenment-induced optimism, and likewise-induced *dogmatism* about the stupidity of orthodox faith. In the concluding chapter, Ketcham notes that Franklin "was confident of this progress because he was sure his age had discovered the eternal verities – natural rights – of enlightened politics. Though he and his contemporaries took natural rights too much for granted to have spent much time trying to define them, they would have agreed that they included ... " and then follows a list of some rights (199). I think Ketcham is flat wrong about Franklin on religion and natural rights (more on this later). But he does have a point about Enlightenment dogmatism on matters of religious faith. This is especially troubling as we witness the Heidegger-led assault on Enlightenment rationalism, accompanied by his claim that "only a God can save us." Ketcham might agree with Heidegger on this last point. But I doubt that Ketcham has the same God and religion in mind.

***

In 1979 and 1993, Ralph Lerner published two tiny gems respectively entitled "Franklin Spectator" (Lerner, 1979: 41–59) and "Dr. Janus" (Lerner, 1993: 415–424). The brief scope of these pieces belies their enormous importance. In "Franklin Spectator," Lerner made a point that no one to my knowledge ever had. However much Franklin claimed in the *Autobiography* to have intended "only 'to relate facts, and not to make apologies for them,' he is, in truth, doing much more – and much less. The *Autobiography* is an open book, but the same cannot quite be said for either the author or the subject" (Lerner, 1979: 54). That part of Lerner's point was not particularly new, since the elusive Franklin manifold had been current since Ward.

But the main and closing point of the essay was for me a Franklin revelation: It is that Franklin in the *Autobiography* "require[s] that we read his book, that we permit some of its episodes to impress themselves upon our memories, that we expose ourselves to its coherent point of view" (1979: 58–59). In other words, if we read *seriously* what Franklin wrote, we can discover a whole Franklin, not just discordant parts; we can discover a "coherent point" of view.

Moreover, and just as important if not more, Franklin does not just pose as a *model* for his readers. As no less "ardent a fisher for souls as the Preacher Whitefield," Franklin differs from the Reverend in "persuad[ing] from a distance. His audience must be disabused of older notions, shown the way to earthly satisfactions, and confirmed in their resolution." In doing this, "Franklin proceeds by charming us into looking at the world in his way. If, in the end, his charms work and we are persuaded, it is owing to his own powerful example. *By showing us how he looks at others, Franklin teaches us how to look at ourselves.*" (The emphasis is mine.) Franklin displays to his readers his self-examination, with the aim of inducing one of their own. One does not ape Ben Franklin, one engages with him in conversational self-discovery and disclosure.

In "Dr. Janus," Lerner began by repeating his point that Franklin encourages no "slavish imitation of any model" (416–417). Indeed, his relationship with his readers is mediated by "artifice and concealment." Lerner spells this out first by commenting on the twists and turns and reversals in Bacon's anonymous 1732 essay "On Simplicity" (417–418). The most impressive twist is Franklin's comment that "they are pretenders only, to policy and business, who have recourse to cunning and the little chicaneries thereof: for cunning is but the ape of wisdom, as sheepishness is of modesty, impudence of courage, and pedantry of learning. – Cunning, says my Lord Bacon, is a sinister or crooked wisdom, and dissimulation but a faint kind of policy; for it asks a strong wit and a strong heart, to know when to tell truth and to do it; therefore they are the weaker sort of politicians, that are the greatest dissemblers."

Lerner makes it clear that Franklin quotes Bacon accurately and approvingly, and on its face the quote means that the issue of simplicity and cunning is to know when to lie. But the reference to Bacon is brilliantly double, since it combines into one sentence the opening lines of *two* of Bacon's essays: "Of Cunning" and "Of Simulation and Dissimulation." Reading these essays together shows not only that the issue of sincerity is knowing when to lie, but that the maxim applies both in matters of state and the common good *and also* to matters of life in general. It is hard not to conclude that Bacon explains more fully what Franklin refers to as "policy and business."

Lerner says that Franklin's sleights of hand are not just for their own sakes, but are rather means to "an education Franklin thinks worth administering" (422). Franklin enlists good works in the service of vanity and to produce self-determination in his pupils. And then the crucial point: "With the near-disappearance of a God whose wonder-working providence is there for all to see, Benjamin Franklin's trainees have to depend on their own good intentions, their own good works, and their concern for their own good names. What they hear from Franklin is unlikely to stir darker thoughts or deeper doubts about this human providence. Nor is what they hear from

Franklin likely to make him more transparent to their understandings, given the complexity or remoteness of his mind ... Indeed, the very reasons that impel Franklin to conceal the dangers in his program necessitate in turn further concealments." And so Franklin remains guarded and covert. There is a whole and coherent Benjamin Franklin, but he's so elusive because at the heart there is a problem: a "danger" that has something to do with "the near disappearance" of a providential God.

***

Steven Forde's pieces on Franklin are all models of scholarship and writing and not to be missed by anyone interested in Franklin's political thought. His chapter, "Benjamin Franklin's 'Machiavellian' Civic Virtue" (Forde, 2006: 143–165) situates Franklin in the legacy of Machiavelli's turn against classical teleology and moral perfectionism and Christianity. It is true that Machiavelli focused on war and martial virtue, but his successors, especially the likes of Francis Bacon, Marchamont Nedham, and John Locke, had by Franklin's day turned Machiavelli's anti-utopian realism to the ends of "commerce, wealth, and creature comforts" (143). Machiavelli's attack on Christianity was replaced by arguments for toleration, and, once skewered by Machiavelli, universal Christian charity was replaced by civility and humanitarianism, all summed up in Bacon's recommendation that the human mind be turned from the contemplation of the "cosmos" to the conquest of nature for the relief of man's estate.

Franklin was a denizen of this Anglo-mediated Machiavellian world, as we can see first in his tough-minded, power-and-interest-dominated *realpolitik* in the *Canada Pamphlet* of 1760, where Franklin argued for imperial annexation of all of Canada after the Seven Years War, and his tough negotiations with England at the end of the Revolutionary War. In the pamphlet, Franklin argued that advantages gained in the course of the war might increase the scope of American "rights," and he took no account of the views of the Canadians (146–147). His negotiations with England, especially his insistence that there be no American border east of the Mississippi, were determined by his keen understanding of the "underlying American strength" (147). Franklin never says outright that might makes right, but he sure does imply as much, and acted on it too.

Franklin's conception of modern science was Machiavellian too, since it rejected teleology and "the cosmos" and discovered truth about nature from utility and then applied that truth to the conquest of nature. Franklin was also Machiavellian in matters of morality, albeit with an English twist. Like Machiavelli, Franklin's virtues are means to conquer fortune, although for Franklin that conquest is the domestication of nature by productive labor and commerce (157–160). In place of the classical obsession with perfecting the soul, for Franklin sociability (getting along and going along) and self-reliance forge the connection between the individual and the common good. Without Machiavelli, Machiavelli's domestication, in the person of Old Ben, would not have been possible. What a charming essay this is; it's a wonder that Professor Houston, influenced as he is by "The Machiavellian Moment," seems not to know that it exists.

The essays on Franklin as a "hero" (Forde, 1999) and American "model" (Forde, 2003a) and the social compact (Forde, 2003b) are just as good. In these brief essays, Forde illuminates Franklin's pragmatic antipathy to abstract political theory, especially to the doctrines of the original social compact and natural rights as foundations of legitimate government. Franklin's take on politics was, in Forde's term, "teleological" in the sense that the ends of political life – equality, happiness and material prosperity – determine political means (concrete political arrangements). Moreover, Franklin was preoccupied throughout his life with the mores of democratic citizenship: It is one thing to have institutions but quite another to maintain them, and the latter requires equal citizens first to cultivate self-reliance and then to care about the public good. But politics also requires leadership, which is a problem in an egalitarian society where standing out and standing forth can engender vanity and resentment among those who hold leaders to be no better than them. In these pieces the most charming of Forde's points concern Franklin as the model of a democratic leader: Franklin teaches how to lead without seeming to, a small but necessary chicanery in the service of egalitarian politics.

But Forde's most important essay, at least for me, was his first: "Benjamin Franklin's *Autobiography* and the Education of America" (1992: 357–368) published just months before Lerner's "Dr. Janus" appeared. Forde showed that Franklin's thinking contains "a surprisingly subtle and multi-layered moral teaching" that is not subject to the charge of crass materialism (357). Franklin bursts the balloon of moral perfectionism, especially as it appeared in Christianity and heroic classical virtue, in order to fashion a morality appropriate to a democratic and egalitarian people. Despite its origin in the low principle of utility, that morality nevertheless aims at realistic virtues, moderation, and high-minded democratic public service. Franklin likewise subordinates the pursuit of wealth to higher goods such as sincerity and justice, for all men, and for science and philosophy, for himself (359).

There is, nevertheless, a puzzle in Franklin's moral doctrine: on the one hand the *Autobiography* "tries to inspire its readers with a sincere devotion to virtue." But on the other hand, "Franklin's own devotion as portrayed at points in the work has to be described as casual at best" (359). By this he means especially the extent to which Franklin excused his own "errata" by appealing to various necessities, such as his youth or the difficulty of governing his passions. And to this must be added the fact that the virtues Franklin touts are "hardly models of moral strictness." Forde here mentions Franklin's definition of "chastity" as the rare use of "Venery but for health or offspring; never to dullness, weakness, or the injury of your own or another's peace or reputation" and his recommendation of such "virtues" as "silence, order and cleanliness," which would not have been mentioned by "most earlier moralists."

The answer to this puzzle is not simply that Franklin was trying to describe a virtue available to every man, although that's certainly part of the story. Rather, Franklin's remarkable moral indulgence can be traced primarily to his intention to "combat the kind of moralism that had been characteristic of earlier traditions, particularly those of Puritan America. The moral code Franklin wants to replace them with, however, is somewhat elusive." Still, we can get some purchase on the matter, by considering Franklin's "distinctive notion of *reasonableness*," which "is a pragmatic and skeptical *bon sens*, which, among other things acts as a brake on speculative reason" and related forms of intolerance and zealotry (360). In general, as Forde spells it out, this reasonableness consisted of a down-to-earth and realistic assessment of, and accommodation to, what human nature compels us to do. And ultimately, this reasonableness led Franklin to "strong convictions about certain of the goods of life." While Franklin's experiential approach to morality smacks of pragmatism, Franklin "remains closer to the Socratic approach" than to pragmatism because Franklin regarded his "convictions or principles to be objective, not radically bound to his own experience."

Thus there are two sources of Franklin's "indulgent or forgiving" moral outlook: His utilitarianism, which sees virtue as a means to happiness and the social good, and which Franklin opposed to the "deontological" approach (strict perfectionism or moralism) he rejected; and his own experience that "persuaded him that much more of human nature can be indulged than earlier moralists had thought." For Franklin, "there can be nothing more natural than for there to be a happy coincidence of [pretty easy] virtue and utility and nothing more ill conceived than to propose a radical separation of the two" (362–363). The product of this moral nonchalance was Franklin's preoccupation with the art of sociability. What matters for our own happiness is mediated by how we affect others, and this boils down to getting them to do what we want them to do without stirring their pride and vanity. Especially in public matters, this involves using pride and vanity against themselves. Franklin does not simply equate pride and vanity, however, since he is willing to call his own legitimate pride vanity if it will help turn the vanity of others to public goods (363–366).

Forde closes by noting that Franklin, in both the *Autobiography* and his real life, cultivated "a peculiar mixture of intimacy and distance, transparency and concealment. But Franklin's irony, if Socratic in spirit, is not Socratic in extent" (366). That's because Franklin was a democrat, and so he "cannot, for all his irony, be portrayed as an esoteric elitist in the classical sense." In most respects, says Forde, Franklin "makes himself and his views completely known to his readers," and in the *Autobiography* he sets out deliberately to portray himself as "a model American, imitable by all of his fellow countrymen." But there is one thing for sure that he does conceal, which is his manifest superiority to the average man. And so, "in the end the *Autobiography* gives us a hero who is more ordinary than Franklin himself really was."

***

Combined especially with Lerner's two beautiful and provocative essays, Forde's remarkable first essay made it clear, at least to me, that Franklin was not just the "First American," but a possibly serious *thinker* about the human condition. First, Lerner's powerful suggestion that Franklin's elusiveness was associated with a "danger" involving the "near disappearance of a providential god" just can not be taken lightly, especially since Franklin was so obvious in his skepticism about the doctrines of Christianity and yet preached in his public rhetoric and sometimes declared in private letters his belief in divine particular providence. Perhaps, I wondered, the danger of which Franklin was aware went beyond the confines of Franklin's proclaimed, particular-providence "deism." And then for all of its brilliance and attention to detail, something bothered me about Forde's resolution of the central contradiction in Franklin's moral thought: that he wants to inspire his readers to a "sincere devotion to virtue" and at the same time explains the extenuating circumstances excusing his own lapses from that devotion. The whole idea of easy-going "devotion" seemed close to paradoxical. Still, perhaps Franklin's intention was as Forde describes: Franklin's naturalistic opposition to traditional "deontological" moralism.

But I started to doubt this explanation when I thought about this academic term "deontological." The term takes morality as some pretty heady theoretical stuff: the morality of a philosophical monk in a cell or spelled out by Kant in massive and hard-to-read treatises. It seemed to me rather that what Forde was talking about, and on his telling what Franklin thus opposed, was the commonsense morality of my counselor (no professor was he) at Boy Scout camp: "What if everybody did that" (categorical imperative!) and "do the right thing because it's right, not because it'll get you something you want; and so never tell a lie because a Boy Scout is honest (deontological perfectionism!)." It occurred to me that this is hardly the morality of some heroic and aristocratic bygone age, or Puritanism, or some airy school of moral "philosophy"; it is the basic principle of what any ten year old learns from an unlearned and well-meaning teacher. Indeed, it is the basic intuition behind aristocratic nobility, Puritanism, Kantianism, and the Boy Scout law: a morally right thing occurs when one subordinates one's interests to those of others.

That intuition is rooted in morality as such, no matter what its form (and if one could probe could be shown to lurk in utilitarianism as well: why, for instance, should the few defer to the utility of the many?). Machiavelli betrays his knowledge of this timeless moral fact when he argues in *The Prince* (Ch. 16) that a prince cannot be generous *virtuously* since, if he is, *it won't be seen* and the prince will wind up with a smaller purse but a reputation for being cheap. Moreover, it seemed to me that this common moral intuition is, in real life, flatly inconsistent with Forde's claim, on behalf of Franklin, "that there is a happy coincidence of virtue and utility and nothing more ill conceived than to propose a radical separation between the two." It is also inconsistent with Franklin's "nothing is useful that is not honest," because a Boy Scout tells the truth *no matter what*. And of course Franklin did not believe this honesty nonsense for a second and, it seemed to me, was stupid if he really thought he could convince any serious reader of the lie.

In the end, it just seemed to me that when we respect Franklin as a model of public service, which he wanted his democratic readers to do, we admire him for subordinating his preferred activities (science and philosophy) to the public good, to the interests of others. This is exactly what most recent scholarship of every stripe does. If Franklin really thought moral virtue (the humble Boy Scout law) and utility to be the same, then it seemed to me he either knew nothing of practical life, which is preposterous, or he was posing a real problem for the basic, universal intuition at the heart of moral virtue, however that virtue is otherwise understood. These puzzles, about the near disappearance of a providential god and moral virtue, convinced me that it might be worthwhile to study and then write about Ben Franklin, which I wound up doing for ten uninterrupted years.

My *Benjamin Franklin Unmasked: On the Unity of His Moral, Religious, and Political Thought* came out in 2005 and was reissued in paperback in 2008. I cannot of course assess here my own work, so I will just comment that those who liked it loved it and those who did not loathed it. I will briefly describe how I came to my approach and what the book is about. On reading Franklin as intensely as I could, and reading I think just about all of the relevant literature at the time, I concluded that Franklin's *Autobiography* was, among many other things, an account of Franklin's encounter not just with the Enlightenment, but with the Enlightenment's sinister side – the danger remarked on by Ralph Lerner. The story was, after all, about a good and well-raised boy who just happened to be a genius and who by the age of nineteen had read more widely in the literature of the West, including the Enlightenment greats, than most university professors have today. But from his Enlightenment reading he suffered a moral and religious fall, and became the model Benjamin Franklin only after self-reflection and a return to morality and religion. The *Autobiography* was thus a kind of cautionary tale about the downside of the likes of Bacon and Hobbes and Locke.

But one day while engaged in my umpteenth reading of the *Autobiography*, I discovered something that caused me to drop the book on the floor. It seemed clear enough that the narrative frame of the *Autobiography* is the saga of fall and self-redemption, albeit tempered by Franklin's pervasive light-heartedness and irony. At the low point of the fall, says Franklin, he wrote his pamphlet *A Dissertation on Liberty and Necessity, Pleasure and Pain*. It was an error on his part, he says in the *Autobiography*, because by denying free will, particular providence, and the distinction between virtue and vice, its doctrine corrupted his friends who then harmed him. The *Dissertation* had "an ill tendency," as he said of it in a letter to his friend Benjamin Vaughn. Amazingly, in that letter of 1779 Franklin tells Vaughn that he burned the copies of the *Dissertation*. There is not a peep about this in the *Autobiography*, even though Franklin is careful there, with one telling exception, to describe the rectification of his errors.

On the day I dropped the book, I was reading part two of the *Autobiography* where Franklin recapitulates his spiritual life before going on to talk about his rise in business and politics and science. There I read to my astonishment: he "never doubted, for instance, the existence of the Deity, that he made the world, and governed it by his providence; that the most acceptable service of God was the doing good to man; that our souls are immortal; and that all crime will be punished and virtue rewarded here or hereafter ..." (Lemay, 1987: 1382). In other words, the fundamental narrative frame of the *Autobiography* is good boy who becomes Enlightenment bad boy who denies particular providence and the distinction between vice and virtue, but then redeems himself and returns to morality and particular providence; but Franklin *always* believed in particular providence and the distinction between vice and virtue.

The fundamental story in the *Autobiography* is rived by a fundamental contradiction. The narrative frame and the part-two spiritual summary cannot both be true, and as I thought, the contradiction cannot be dismissed as a slip on Franklin's part: Who, I asked myself, could forget such a spiritual experience as falling from belief to unbelief and then experiencing self-redemption? It would be preposterous to say this of Homer Simpson, much less Benjamin Franklin. So I had to come to the *Autobiography* with fresh eyes especially on the lookout for contradictions, things that did not make sense, and sleights of hand. I came to see that the *Autobiography* has layers of irony that have to be peeled away. And Franklin does not just *say* what he wants his careful readers to discover. He rather provokes them, with things that at first do not add up, to think them through on their own. I came also to see that the *Autobiography* is the roadmap of Franklin's intellectual and spiritual journey: in it he tells us where to find the most important of his writings in this regard, and when one pairs these writings with the *Autobiography* a remarkable picture emerges. I concluded that Franklin's skepticism was "even more radical and more thoughtfully grounded than the one the scholarship [and Franklin too] says he rejected" (Weinberger, 2005: xiii). I also concluded that he was a freethinking critic of Enlightenment freethinking.

To come to these conclusions, I devote two chapters ("The *Autobiography*: A Comic Moral Saga?" and "The *Autobiography*: Or Just a Pack of Lies?") to unraveling the ironic structure of the *Autobiography*, starting from the fundamental contradiction lodged in its narrative frame. I conclude that the weight of the evidence as it emerges from the contradictions and twists and turns in the story tells against Franklin's story about his Enlightenment fall and subsequent moral and then religious redemption. The evidence is not conclusive at this point in my account, but we cannot honestly avoid following up its disturbing indications.

I turn next to Franklin's humor in two chapters entitled "The Philosophical Wag" and "Shameless Ben." Franklin's humor is, as I commented above, often obscene and scatological, and it is filled with bizarre and nut-ball characters and jokes that spiral from the ridiculous to the disturbing and back again to the ridiculous. He makes fun of enthusiastic believers; dogmatic rationalists; two normal men, condemned to death for theft, zapped like experimental mice by the shock of unexpected reprieve; divine and human justice; and smelly little boys who become bad by small attempts to be good. In the course of all this, some of our most cherished intuitions about morality and progress take a real drubbing.

Moreover, Franklin's humor is shameless: there is nothing he does not make fun of to some degree: the family and his wife, the American Revolution, natural science, the Freemasons, himself, divine providence, and Jesus. As I put it at the end of "Shameless Ben": "if Franklin's humor is philosophical and not simply the product of an irrepressible jokester, then in going all the way up [to the heavens] it also goes all the way down to the grounds of political seriousness. Franklin's humor leads us to doubtful thinking about those issues the political man cannot take lightly or mock, and cannot really doubt, either" (Weinberger, 2005: 134). This conclusion then leads to a problem: What are we to make of Franklin's "lifelong involvement in political life"?

Next comes a long chapter called "The Metaphysical Follies." In this I consider Franklin's "metaphysical" writings: *The Dissertation on Liberty and Necessity, Pleasure and Pain*; *Articles of Belief and Acts of Religion*; and *On the Providence of God in the Government of the World*. It is a long story, but the upshot is that in these writings Franklin was ridiculing both particular providence and the theoretical pretensions and moral assumptions of deism: the *Articles of Belief*, for instance, is an upside down "defense" of providence on the grounds of Hobbes's argument against the possibilities of "powers invisible" and miracles (165–166). My argument in this chapter is that the traditional scholarship has been vexed on the exact nature of Franklin's skepticism because it conflates the deductive and "metaphysical" skepticism of the *Dissertation* with the conversational Socratic refutations that got the young Franklin run out of Boston by the good people of the town who decried his being an "infidel" or "atheist" (142).

The next chapter is called "Dialectics and the Critique of Morality." Here I return to the *Autobiography* to follow up Franklin's clues about what Franklin's Socratic refutations were all about. The upshot is that Franklin leads us to see that it is not possible coherently to maintain the distinction between moral virtue and prudence, however much our common intuitions tell us that we can (176–182). Franklin elaborates this issue in two earlier pieces he wrote and identifies in the *Autobiography*: an essay entitled "That Self-Denial is Not the Essence of Virtue," and a charming Socratic dialogue (starring none other than Socrates and a dimwit named Crito) entitled "A Man of Sense"; and the 1732 essay "On Simplicity". I finish the chapter by hazarding some conclusions about Franklin's path of thinking: that path led him to see that the Enlightenment thinkers could not settle the question of particular providence and miracles. Franklin argues that the better path is attention to what lurks right under our noses, so he considers the coherence of the idea that we human beings could ever deserve the rewards and punishments that people hope providence will supply. Having decided that the whole idea makes no internal sense, Franklin became convinced, as far as reason could allow, that divine providence was not for him (199–205).

The final two chapters treat Franklin's understanding of the human good once we see the world as it is and not as our moral vanity wants it to be. In "The Political Principles of the Good Life" I discuss Franklin's understanding of happiness in contrast to Hobbes and Locke, the virtues that it makes sense to cultivate and the goods they can supply, Franklin's take on anger, his stance toward Sir Francis Bacon's project for the conquest of nature (for it!), his abiding egalitarianism, his skepticism about natural rights (226–234), his complete pragmatism on the matter of political forms, and his profound sense of the limits of progress. And most important for my story, I argue that there is no tension between Franklin's religious and moral skepticism and his long political career. First, Franklin never gave up philosophy for politics: his Craven street house in London was as much a laboratory as the office of a political agent, and he did not *start* the *Autobiography* until 1771. And second, Franklin engaged in politics "only because it was among the things he most liked, and what Franklin liked, Franklin did" (225).

In the last chapter, "The Political Project of the Good Life," I consider the particular projects that occupied Franklin's political career. "These projects reflect his political principles and his philosophical understanding of life in general. Therefore, they reflect at once the forward-looking projecting of Franklin's Baconianism and the deep skepticism with which he viewed the ... Enlightenment." In this general context, I treat "the modern political empire, toward the end of his life the question of slavery, and through the course of his life the practical circumstances of modern religion" (254). In my brief conclusion, "Will the Real Ben Franklin Please Stand

Up," I sum up, and tell a final story about Franklin's understanding of the difference between the ties of moral obligation and the ties of the human heart (290–292).

That's what I do in *Benjamin Franklin Unmasked*. If the reader wonders if I've succeeded, there's only one way to find out.

***

Lorraine Smith Pangle's interesting and lively *The Political Philosophy of Benjamin Franklin* came out in 2007. It is a rich and ambitious book, and the chapter "The Economic Basis of Liberty" is the best discussion of this topic that I know. Now in titles sometimes lie tales: Straussians tend to use the term "political philosophy" rather than "political thought," with the intention of distinguishing between serious reflections on timeless problems and political argument that, to be understood, must be situated in a particular and contingent historical context. Pangle thus treats Franklin as a philosopher, albeit with serious reservations associated with Franklin's participation in the project of modernity. Here's the Straussian ancient-modern divide again, and to locate Franklin on that divide Pangle engages in a running comparison of Franklin to Socrates (on the really big questions). This is to my mind an interesting and fruitful way to think about Franklin, although as it stands in this book non-Straussians will have a hard time recognizing the Greek, and Straussians will have to take Pangle's word on the matter since references to the Platonic dialogues and Xenophon are so few and cursory as to reveal little of how Pangle came to her take on Socrates.

At any rate, the essential point of the book, at least as I see it, is made in the last chapter ("The Ultimate Questions") although it governs the argument from the beginning (Pangle, 2007: 185–223). The stage is set by comments of John Adams and the Abbé Flamarens that Franklin had no religion "at all." Of this Pangle says that in France Franklin was known as a "virtual atheist." How no religion "at all" can count as "virtual" atheism is a mystery to me, but it is the lead-in for what follows: "But if he was indeed a virtual atheist, how should we understand this 'virtual'? From the perspective of a serious man of faith there is little to choose between the impious half-believer and the unbeliever; both are abominable. But from the perspective of Socrates, the difference between one who wholly rejects the existence of a providential god and one who harbors secret hopes of his existence is fundamental." The issue, says Pangle, is not whether Franklin was often impious. Nor is it whether he was "a perfect atheist in the sense of being a materialist." Like most of the Enlightenment skeptics, she says, Franklin believed in some kind of divine creator. (How Pangle knows this, or how it is based in the texts, she does not say.) The "real question" for Pangle is whether his "faith went any further" (206).

And for Pangle, indeed it seems to have gone: We should not be "surprised" when "the famously irreverent Franklin gives evidence of drifting back into piety in his old age" (211). Commenting on this evidence (more about it later), Pangle says (213–214):

> These signs of a return to piety are not conclusive, but they are suggestive and intriguing; in a certain way they are even in character. The thoughts Franklin expresses would have been comforting to an old man, especially one who had never held a grudge against God, unlike Aristophanes, Machiavelli, Voltaire, Thomas Paine, and other radical skeptics. Franklin had his quarrels with the established church and especially with its depiction of God as jealous and vengeful, but nowhere did he express the thought that the existence of a providential god as such would be bad news for humanity as fatal to human dignity. Nor did he ever claim absolute certainty for his religious views. And such a drift back to piety would be perfectly natural: it would be hard to withstand the temptation to hope for an afterlife unless one saw God as hostile, or unless one had spent a lifetime probing and scouring one's moral hopes and confusions and forcefully keeping death before one's eyes, as Socrates did.

Then to continue: "For all Franklin's endless curiosity, there is a lack of gravity to his thinking, an absence of the urgent, incessant habit of connecting immediate questions with eternal ones and seeking in every new fact evidence for the truth about where we stand as human beings and what the fate of our souls is. It is the absence of this impulse, which Pascal shared so deeply with Socrates, that leaves Franklin open to his most penetrating critics."

In this respect, Franklin, despite being free of the anti-theological ire of Hobbes, Bacon, and Spinoza, is still a typical Enlightenment figure in "turning away from the problem of death and addressing ourselves to soluble problems" (220). Pangle for a while leaves it open as to whether Socratic depth or Franklin lightness is closer to the truth of the human condition, but in the end she tilts toward the ancients: "Classical rationalism teaches us always to confront its rivals and consider whether they might not after all be right: the contest between reason and revelation is always alive in Socrates' conversations, and Socratic philosophy never for a moment stops struggling to justify its own audacious activity" (222).

Conventional readers of Plato will be surprised to find in Socrates an atheist with no "secret hopes" for the existence of a providential god. But that's beside Pangle's point, which is that Franklin, along with the rest of the Enlightenment, skated on thin theoretical ice when it came to the problem of religion and the grounds of rationalism itself. Why so? Because "for Franklin these contests [between reason and revelation] are not compelling, and the superiority of rationalism in its peculiar modern variant is treated as self-evident." Franklin, says Pangle, "could not take seriously the idea that traditional Christianity might be true. As it gave but middling guidance for this life, how could one put any stock in the fabulous claims that it made about the next" (194)? Given this dogmatic rationalist faith, suggests Pangle, should we be surprised to see an aging Franklin succumb to an equivalent faith in a life after death?

All this is as interesting and lively and provocative as one might hope for in an academic study of old Ben. The problem, to my mind, is that Pangle's argument could be better grounded on Franklin's texts. The great observation of Ralph Lerner was that Franklin's most important pieces are literary gems, complex wholes that with their twists and turns undermine themselves and point the reader to self-examination. Pangle does not read the Franklin texts with their character as artful wholes in mind, but rather picks and chooses willy-nilly from them, and I think this weakens the story she wants to tell.

To start with the obvious, Pangle asserts confidently: "Franklin could not take seriously the idea that traditional Christianity might be true." But even though she refers to Franklin's pseudonymous 1730 "Letter of a Drum" and the next-day response from "Philoclerus" (Lemay, 1987: 145–151) in order to emphasize Franklin's utilitarian defense of religion, she flatly ignores the argument, proffered by Philoclerus (a.k.a. Ben Franklin), that eviscerates Hobbes's and the classical Enlightenment's case against the possibility of miracles. The intellectual historians and American literature scholars, who shill for Franklin as a typical Enlightenment "deist," shut their eyes to these two complex, powerful, and extraordinary pieces. And so it is all the more surprising that Pangle does so as well. Nobody familiar with Franklin's familiarity with Hobbes should miss the power of this shot across the Enlightenment's skeptical bow.

In a similar vein, Pangle asserts early on that "Franklin saw nothing deeply puzzling in justice and the other virtues that Socrates was forever asking about; it never occurred to him that wisdom was to be gained by listening carefully to and pondering the self-contradictions within ordinary moral opinion. But it is possible that Franklin saw almost instinctively the deeper lessons that Socrates labored to discover" (Pangle, 2007: 12). A corollary of this bald assertion is another: that Franklin never considers whether "honesty is really good for itself, apart from all consequences, as Kant thinks, or whether it is good only as a means to further ends, and, if the latter, why it would be rational to abandon honesty in exceptional cases when a very great cost would be incurred by upholding it" (52–53).

This latter judgment follows on Pangle's description of Franklin's "pile of disparate reasonings," regarding the utility of honesty and the shame of dishonesty discovered. This pile is assembled by Pangle, not Franklin, and includes bits from the 1730 "Lying Shopkeepers," a snippet from the 1758 *Poor Richard Improved*, and another snippet (one sentence) from the 1758 "Letter of Father Abraham to his Beloved Son." Now, to snatch a single line from the "Letter of Father Abraham to his Beloved Son" is to inflict interpretive mayhem on a brilliant, multifaceted (and scatological) essay that forces the reader to reflect on virtue and vice and the impossibility of guilt and responsibility, and the near-impossibility of knowing what is right in matters of moral choice. No one, after a careful reading of "Father Abraham," (especially its scatological aspects) could conclude with Pangle that "wisdom is not for Franklin the core of virtue in the Socratic sense [whatever this murky phrase means], since knowing what is right seems easy to Franklin and applying it seems the difficult part; yet wisdom does have an important place, as we shall see" (73–74).

Even more surprising, there is not a peep in this book about two of Franklin's most interesting essays that treat both justice and honesty: the rich and provocative "Speech of Miss Polly Baker" and Franklin's complicated, Baconian, and self-undermining (a trait of Bacon's *Essays*, by the way) 1732 "On Simplicity." The former makes our heads spin as we reflect on conundrums of divine and human justice; the latter makes it clear that "doing no hurtful deceit" means knowing when to lie in both public *and* private matters.

Now let us move to the less obvious. In her account of Franklin's spiritual and intellectual journey as depicted in the *Autobiography*, Pangle says that the contradiction between the saga of fall and redemption and the claim always to have believed in particular providence "is useless" for her consideration of Franklin and God because Franklin "did openly doubt the immortality of the soul and the existence of heaven and hell in the *Dissertation on Liberty and Necessity*" (204–205). Pangle is here a bit careless with the text of the *Dissertation*: the words "heaven" and "hell" do not even *occur* in it, and Franklin comments that the ancient concept of "Ilizium" is an "idle fable" not because it could not exist, but because its promise of "uninterrupted ease and happiness" rests on ignorance of the relationship between pleasure and pain (Lemay, 1987: 68–69). Worse still, Franklin did *not* openly doubt the immortality of the soul in the *Dissertation*: quite to the contrary, in an argument that scooped Daniel Dennett's *Consciousness Explained*, he distinguished between a possibly immortal soul (well, Dennett would not buy that part) and the mortal brain-meat that contains the memories, constituting the self, on which the soul reflects. Were a departed soul to be re-embodied, it would have no memories of where it had been before: it would have to go through the process, along with the brain, of getting itself a self. (Unless, per Dennett and even possibly the far-sighted Franklin, the self could be downloaded before death and then uploaded to newly "ensouled" piece of meat.) Now it is true that openly denying the immortality of the *self* will disappoint or even shock those who agree with Franklin that the soul could be immortal. The point here is that Franklin's moves in the *Dissertation* are far more complex and subtle than Pangle describes.

But aside from this casualness with the text, one has to ask how it can be useless for anyone interested in Franklin to be indifferent to the fundamental contradiction that shatters the unity of Franklin's narrative frame in the *Autobiography*. The contradiction raises a host of dilemmas that Pangle sweeps under the rug. At the very least, the contradiction could well mean that when he wrote the *Dissertation* he did not believe (for whatever reason) the doctrine he defends in it. Why on earth, then, did he write it? And the issue clearly is not that he said some shocking things in the *Dissertation*; he did. The issue is that with the contradiction, the entire saga of religious and moral fall and redemption is cast into doubt, and to work though that doubt we have read the *Autobiography* and the writings to which Franklin points us to in that work as wholes, and with care.

I think we see here the excessive weight of the ancients-versus-moderns schema: Modern rationalism, as opposed to its classical counterpart, was dogmatic on the questions of morality and religion, and as a result its foundations are weak and its devotees subject to variants of the religious enthusiasm they labored to uproot. So on the religious side of the story, Franklin's skepticism was dogmatic and thus, abetted by "secret hopes," in the end he fell prey to faith. And on the moral side, Franklin came to understand the "most important error" of the *Dissertation* to be "the illogical inference from the denial of radical freedom [whatever that is] to the denial of any meaningful distinction between vice and virtue." But the breezy utilitarian morality he then accepted was insufficiently grounded to prevent his possible harboring of "a lingering belief that the highest thing of all is generous sacrifice" (Pangle, 2007: 63, 67, 148, 169).

But why, one has to ask again, would Franklin have fallen into this most important error if in fact he always believed in particular providence? That problem just cannot be made to go away. Moreover, Pangle's account of Franklin's most important error is based, again, on some careless reading of the text. Of the *Dissertation*, Pangle argues that Franklin is right to note that if all human action is motivated by the desire to avoid pain, "there can be no disinterested action and no claims of merit on that basis." "But it does not follow," she argues, "that there can be no vice and no virtue. There can still be stupidity, cowardice, laziness, and failures of self-control that prevent one from attaining what happiness is available; there can still be cruelty that brings no one any benefit, and steadfastness and kindness that bring good things for oneself and others whose happiness is intertwined with one's own" (58–59).

Let us forget about the fact that in the many pieces Pangle ignores Franklin leads us to see that the vices and virtues Pangle lists are conditions, much like having a cold or being able to run fast, for which it is absurd to praise or blame the victim or the winner for having. But we could figure much of this out from a careful reading of the *Dissertation* itself. Pangle makes it seem that the *Dissertation* is fixed on denying "any meaningful distinction between virtue and vice." If that's true, why do the words "virtue" and "vice" occur *but once each* in the *Dissertation*, and only in a final summary line that says that "Prop. VIII in SECT I [is] again demonstrated"? In that Proposition, and in the entire preceding whole, Franklin's concern is with "merit" and "demerit" in creatures, or "evil" and "deserving" (Lemay, 1987: 62, 70). In other words, Franklin is clearly raising the issue not of all virtue and vice, but *moral* virtue and *moral* vice. And the clear assumption here is that we praise ("merit") and blame ("demerit") (or God rewards or punishes) moral virtue and moral vice, with the former requiring a sacrifice of our interests and the latter being a preference for our interests over those of others. Let's say one overcomes one's laziness, which is a vice. Why should I praise you morally (or God reward you) for doing what is good for you? That's part of what Franklin is talking about in the *Dissertation*.

Now it is true that in both sections of the *Dissertation*, Franklin really does say that all's well with the world even though it includes "pain, sickness, want, theft, murder, etc." In that case there really is no distinction between *all* vice and virtue (being honest or being a crook, being lazy and being industrious). But the stupidity of this view is demonstrated in the hilarious second section where Franklin claims that "the monarch is not more happy than the slave, nor the beggar more miserable than Croesus" (Lemay, 1987: 66). It takes a pretty stuffy reader not to see the comedy in Franklin's Panglossian idiocy; and Franklin warns us to take it all with a huge grain of salt with the fundamental contradiction in the *Autobiography* that makes us wonder why he wrote the *Dissertation* in the first place. It is highly unlikely that Franklin ever believed there was "no meaningful distinction between vice and virtue" and any scholar who attributed such a view to the mature Franklin, as Pangle says one does, would have to be blind to the distinction between *moral* virtue and vice, on the one hand, and the goods that any sensible person would wish for himself, on the other.

So what are we to make of the ultimate claims: that Franklin softened on faith and yearned, albeit unbeknownst to himself, for morality as noble sacrifice. Here again, I do not think the textual evidence bears the weight. The moral softening is the lesser issue in Pangle's book. But it is important nevertheless because it bears out her claim that Franklin spent no time "on the question that Socrates wrestled with for so long, the question of whether the many virtues people honor or should honor are one and the same. Behind this question is the question of whether virtue is reducible to prudence or whether it ever requires a sacrifice of prudent self interest" (Pangle, 2007: 67). But Franklin does wrestle with this question (or better, entices his reader to do so on her own) in the many pieces Pangle ignores, and especially in the crucial section of the *Autobiography* where Franklin describes his move from one form of Socratic irony to another. Pangle glances at this section in a short paragraph that ignores its amazingly complex moves, in order to conclude that Franklin "seems to be hedging, almost willing to grant that souls are governed by inner necessities that do not leave them free to be more sensible than they are, and yet still not prepared to rule out some modicum of freedom that he never explains." This conclusion seems a bit murky to me.

At any rate, Pangle's evidence for Franklin's secret love of the noble is on the thin side. The first problem is that most of it comes from Franklin's polemical political writings in London and Paris. Here we have a problem about which anyone writing about Franklin as a philosopher should be wary: Franklin was a paid propagandist abroad and an unpaid one at home, and I think it is very difficult, or at best purely speculative, to derived philosophical conclusions from the rhetoric of the polemical moment. Even more difficult is concluding about how Franklin actually felt (i.e., furious, "smolderingly" angry, indignant, etc.) when composing his polemics (140, 147). (This is a real problem for the likes of Gordon Wood and Robert Middlekauff, who make a big deal of Franklin's supposed anger on the basis of his polemical writing. If you are interested, I have addressed the flimsiness of their evidence in *Benjamin Franklin Unmasked*, pp. 314–318.)

Pangle seems to recognize this problem, because she concludes in favor of Franklin's yearning for nobility with a speculative question on two occasions, and in another presents the conclusion (that Franklin cared "enormously" "that the cause [the Revolution] he was advancing was just, that it was the cause of freedom, and that it could be – and he hoped ultimately would be – embraced as the cause of all mankind") as something she "believes" (148, 164–169). I'm certainly prepared to believe this, but not on the evidence as presented. And if it is true, why, one wonders, did Franklin write and publish in 1782 a grotesque hoax about an intercepted cargo of scalps from the British-allied Indians to the King, and add to that a pathetic letter from the Indian chief bemoaning to George their expulsion from their country by the Americans who have "also got great sharp claws" (Lemay, 1987: 956–964)? And what of his 1783 letter to Sir Joseph Banks, on the treaty with England, in which Franklin bemoaned the terrible waste the war involved (Lemay, 1987: 1073–1074)?

Pangle is more positive on the question of Franklin's late-life religious softening. She bases her suspicions on the fact that Franklin's remarks on God in his last decade "have a new ring of earnestness" and are connected to "expressions of righteous indignation" and "the somber awareness of the approach of death" (Pangle, 2007: 211). Again, the evidence could be a lot better. First of all, Franklin was capable of summoning up expressions of righteous indignation throughout his rhetorical career: perhaps the most over the top is the hysterical moral rant in his 1764 *Narrative of the Late Massacres*, the high dudgeon of which gets ignored when Pangle touches on this piece briefly in another context. (In a letter to John Fathergill in London that same year, Franklin discussed the affair in an entirely cool manner and even used the occasion to crack a joke at his own expense.) And depending on his correspondent, Franklin was on and off on the issue of divine providence from the beginning of his life to the end (Lemay, 1987: 540–558, 802–805; Pangle, 2007: 180).

Pangle cites a 1782 letter to James Hutton about an Indian massacre permitted by King George, in which Franklin professed his "comfortable belief" in divine providence where the wicked will get their comeuppance (2007: 211–212). Fine; but again, Franklin professed a belief in providence on again and off again throughout his life, and 1782 was the same year he wrote the outrageous scalp hoax: if there's a final reckoning, the Americans have as much to fear as George. And it was just about three years after Franklin's hilarious blasphemy against general providence, sent to the Abbé Morrelet, in which the elbow is described as providentially constructed for the guzzling of wine (Lemay, 1987: 939–942).

The next bit of evidence is a 1784 letter to William Strahan in which Franklin attributes the success of the revolution to justice and divine providence and remarks to Strahan that had he ever been an atheist he would now believe in God (Pangle, 2007: 212). Fine; but against this is the 1777 (granted, some years earlier) report in Arthur Lee's diary about Franklin on the "miracle of the revolution." "He told me," wrote Lee, "the manner in which the whole of this business had been conducted, was such a miracle in human affairs, that if he had not been in the midst of it, and seen all the movements, he could not have comprehended how it was effected." In other words, it looked like a miracle, but it was not. It was, as Lee writes Franklin said, "a deliberate system" (PBF, 25: 100–102).[1]

A 1785 letter to George Whatley "On Annihilation and Bifocals," in which Franklin argues among other things for God's conservation of matter, such that Franklin cannot imagine the "annihilation of souls" or think that God "would suffer the daily waste of millions of minds ready made that already exist, and put himself to the continual trouble of making new ones," says Pangle, "may or may not have been simply playful" (2007: 212–213). Aside from the fact that the distinction between matter and souls and minds reminds obviously of the Dennett-like argument in the *Dissertation*, this piece is more than playful. It is mostly a scream and breezy from beginning to end, and Franklin ends the part on souls with a shopworn bit from his "Old Printer's Epitaph" and the beginning of the *Autobiography*: "Thus finding myself to exist in the world, I believe I shall, in some shape or other [someone else's body?] always exist; and with all the inconveniences human life is liable to, I shall not object to a new edition of mine; hoping, however, that the errata of the last may be corrected" (Lemay, 1987: 1104–1110). This epitaph shard will prove to be important evidence *against* taking this soul stuff seriously, and we'll get back to it later on.

But Franklin follows up the soul comments with a side-splitting account of the extraordinary increase in French foundlings. The reason, Franklin says a French surgeon assured him, is that the women of Paris "*n'ont point de tetons.*" Observation, says Franklin, made him see some truth in the fact that "they have nothing more there ... than I [the doctor] have upon the back of my hand." Concludes Franklin: "possibly nature, finding they made no use of Bubbies, has left off giving them any." The snippet about souls is hard to take seriously on its face; the broader context of Franklin's raunchy jocularity in the whole piece makes this a slim reed on which to hang a late-life conversion to divine providence.

Franklin's god-watches-sparrows speech on prayer, which Pangle also cites, was a ploy to calm down the disintegrating Constitutional Convention, and it is no easier to take seriously than the letter to Whatley; even Alan Houston has his doubts (2007: 213; Houston, 2008: 198–199). At the end, Pangle pulls her punch and then takes another jab: the signs of a return to piety are not conclusive, she says, "but they are suggestive and intriguing; in a certain way they are even in character." And then we get the conclusion, cited above, that for a dogmatic skeptic, like Franklin and unlike Socrates, "a drift back to piety would be perfectly natural" (213–214). I doubt it, and the evidence marshaled for it in this book is too thin to bear its weight.

Pangle is correct to doubt Franklin's conventional deistic profession of faith in the near-deathbed letter Franklin wrote to his old friend Ezra Stiles, but just a few pages later she says of that letter: "Is it perhaps no accident that he expresses such strong faith both in a God who rewards everyone according to his merits and in a heaven that no one deserves? Is it not likely that, suffused with both gratitude and hope, he might have failed to see the contradiction" (205–206, 213)?

For Franklin not to have seen this contradiction would require that he had slipped into senility. But he had not; the later piece on the slave trade, written when he was wracked by pain and doped on opium, is as tight and clear and self-undermining as can be. Actually, in the letter to Stiles, Franklin included a sarcastic, 1753 letter to John Huey (which Pangle notes in another context but, surprisingly, does not connect with the letter to Stiles) that makes this contradiction *much more explicit* (Lemay, 1987: 475–477, 1178–1180; Pangle, 2007: 210). Together, these two letters gave Stiles all he needed to see the contradictions inherent in the notion of divine justice, if he had a mind to do; but he did not and so Franklin consoled him with his usual profession of faith.

Now aside from matter of the evidence, there is another big problem with suggesting that Franklin was tempted by or overcome by the hope for another life in heaven or anywhere else. It is related to the comical 1785 letter to Whatley. Franklin bandied about his "printers epitaph" through most of his life. However, a glance at Franklin's wills discloses that he included it in none of them, although the will of June 1750 exudes the usual pieties conventional in wills at the time. But in the will of July 17, 1788, done after Franklin had written to Madame Brillon that he was soon to die and have his curiosity satisfied in another world (that other well-used trope), was absolutely *devoid* of these conventional pieties. And more important, in the codicil of June 23, 1789, done after Franklin had been reminded of his future by a long spell of excruciating gout, says very clearly that his tombstone will have *just his name* on it, along with Deborah's (Smyth, 1907, 10: 493–510; PBF, 3: 480–482; Lemay, 1987: 1178–1180; 475–477; Brillon April 19, 1788, FDE).[2] So much for the printer's epitaph, and this when Franklin was staring into the maw. Why, one surely has to wonder, if Franklin had even a teeny bit hoped for life after death, would he have taken such care, and stuck with it to the end, *not* to have the famous epitaph on his stone?

***

When I checked the index and realized Alan Houston had not engaged (or even mentioned) the writings surveyed here, I expected to be irritated by his *Benjamin Franklin and the Politics of Progress*. Some quick reflection on Benjamin Franklin took care of the problem: If I could ask him what he thinks about the matter, he'd surely advise that it is Houston who's poorer for having ignored all this interesting stuff (assuming of course Franklin's thumbs-up). That's true. But that said, I was pleased nevertheless to find some interesting and useful things in this book.

Houston describes his approach as being like "a geologist, drilling into his political thought from five different locations. Each chapter begins with a specific text or problem, and then traces the seams of ideas and practices that are connected to it" (Houston, 2008: 118–121). The five "locations" are: Commerce, Association, Population, Union, and Slavery. These wells do not all produce gushers: The chapter on slavery is perfunctory and adds nothing that cannot be found elsewhere; and it gives four-word short shrift to David Waldstreicher's essential *Runaway America: Benjamin Franklin, Slavery, and the American Revolution*. We are told in a footnote that it is "a provocative revisionist account" (200–216, 199n. 3). The chapter on association is skimpy as well, with little that's new (65–105). One interesting point on this score, however, is Houston's observation that Franklin's understanding of voluntary association was "a potent challenge to the shibboleths of classical republicanism" (63, 89). For Franklin, the motor of association and civic virtue was commercial interest and its aim was to foster equality, not social hierarchy as one finds in the writing of James Harrington.

More fruitful are the chapters on commerce, population, and union (which is not to say they are crammed with new stuff). Most interesting in the chapter on commerce are Houston's comments, in his section called "The Politics of Money," on Franklin's take on the "political determinants of economic development" and the conventionality, and hence contestability, of any regime of property rights (41–52). And Houston's related discussion of the importance of book credit in a cash-starved colonial economy provides interesting context for thinking about the Franklin so despised by D.H. Lawrence. Book credit stood in for cash, and one's book credit was determined by one's reputation for paying one's bills. This led me to a new take on Franklin's fussy description of his work habits and concern for his reputation, and ambivalence about luxury, in the *Autobiography*. It is not that Franklin really *was* a prig, but that under the conditions of the colonial economy and commercial society it was functionally necessary that he look like one.

The chapter on population has to my mind the most interesting section in the book (106–146). Most of the chapter is conventional old material, and though it begins with the far-fetched (indeed laughable to anyone familiar with Polly) claim that the "The Speech of Miss Polly Baker" addressed "a serious topic: the relationship between population growth and the public good," there is no doubt that Franklin was long concerned with "political arithmetic" (106–108). And I, for one, did not know about the possible later effects of his basic discovery that population grows up to but cannot exceed the limits of subsistence, although for Franklin this did not mean that those limits cannot be extended indefinitely by progress in natural science (140–146). It is common knowledge that it wound up on the first page of the (1803) second edition of Thomas Robert Malthus' "Essay on the Principle of Population." Wrote Malthus: the greatest obstacle to human happiness is "the constant tendency in all animated life to increase beyond the nourishment prepared for it. It is observed by Dr. Franklin, that there is no bound to the prolific nature of plants or animals, but what is made by their crowding and interfering with each other's means of subsistence … This is incontrovertibly true" (142–143).

Again, it is not news that Franklin influenced Malthus; it is there for all to see in Malthus, and Walter Isaacson, for instance, mentions the fact in his breezy, popular Franklin biography. Nor is it news that Malthus influenced Darwin in coming to the principle of natural selection under conditions of the struggle for biological existence. What I did not know, however, was that Darwin's grandfather, Erasmus, "an early evolutionist," had been a friend of Franklin's in London and "fellow member" of the Lunar Society. Moreover, Darwin's father Robert, "studied medicine in Paris in the early 1780s, where he often saw Franklin. As a boy, Charles was treated to stories of Franklin's 'wit' and 'affection'" (144).

Houston notes that Darwin read and liked Franklin's *Autobiography*, but that there is no evidence that he read any of Franklin's scientific works, especially the *Observations concerning the Increase of Mankind, Peopling of Countries, etc*. But he then comments that the crucial paragraph of Darwin's Notebook D, which is "'the first formulation of natural selection,'" begins with Malthus' statement of "the relationship of population and subsistence." It reads as follows: "population in increase in at geometrical ratio in FAR SHORTER TIME THAN 25 YEARS – yet not until the one sentence of Malthus no one clearly perceived the great check amongst men." Houston notes that the distinction between geometrical and arithmetical growth was original to Malthus, but the "core idea – 'There is … no bound to the prolific nature of plants or animals, but what is made by their crowding and interfering with each other's means of subsistence' – was Franklin's. So, too, was the claim that the natural rate of increase for humans, visible in North America, was twenty-five years" (144). Wow, lightning rods and bifocals and, perhaps by unintended influence, a piece of the theory of evolution! It's delicious and worth the price of admission.

The chapter on union is not chocked with new observations, but it does make an interesting case for Franklin's having anticipated later American constitutional developments. The Albany Plan of Union reflected Franklin's concern to foster colonial cooperation, especially on matters of defense, without having to resort to the top-down centralization of French imperial rule (167). Franklin opposed partial unions, because they would be "more susceptible to partial passions and interests because they magnify the power of their constituent members. New York, one-thirteenth of a general union, would be one-third or one-fourth of a partial union." Thus in anticipation of Madison in Federalist 10, for Franklin "the grand scale of a continental union, frightening to many, is its greatest asset" (168). Franklin was for American bigness, and though no *partisan* of private property he expected the union to be commercial and based on interests and given to free trade; in these respects, he was no friend of classical republicanism.

But then neither, says Houston, was Franklin a believer in the natural right to private property. He is thus "virtually invisible" in the conceptual contest between those who think America is based on Lockean liberalism and those who hope for a return the classical republican origins "crushed by the liberal Constitution of 1787" (219–221). Because he does not quite fit in the frameworks of this contest, "we have assumed that there was little to be said about Franklin's political thought." Well, maybe: but only if we believe that Houston's book is the only recent study that has resisted this assumption. It is not. One is tempted to ask Houston *why* Franklin did not think natural property rights exist. Don't hold your breath until he gives us the reason.

***

There is one thing with which all the authors surveyed in this essay agree: Benjamin Franklin was a very complicated thinker and perhaps an even more complicated man. While he wrote no formal treatise on politics, his thinking is so broad and dispersed in so many literary genres and so often tongue-in-cheek as to function like a mirror. It is thus easy for scholars to approach him as Adams said the Catholics, Anglicans, Presbyterians, and Friends did: either fooled by his poses or finding the Franklin they want to find. In general, the works surveyed in this essay avoid that trap and rather illuminate gracefully the many aspects of Franklin's take on politics and modernity.

Taken together, these works show that Franklin's political thought as a whole reflects the complex course of the Enlightenment as it was first confidently embodied in America and then, in the second half of the twentieth century, became less sure of its promise and foundations. Conner and Ketcham bring to Franklin the two sides (secular versus faithful) of the nascent American culture war that emerged from the tear-gassed campuses. Forde unearths the contradictions in Franklin's all-too-modern morality, and Lerner has Franklin warn us of the death of God: who would have thought that Franklin foreshadowed Friedrich Nietzsche? Pangle sees in Franklin the creaky foundations of the modern view that politics can be founded on reason alone. And Houston reminds us that one such as Franklin could have doubts about natural right. There are few studies of Benjamin Franklin by scholars of political theory. But let me humbly suggest that the works surveyed here disclose a Franklin with much to tell us about the monumental questions of our time.

Notes

1 Labaree, Leonard W. *et al.*, eds. (1959–). *The Papers of Benjamin Franklin.* 39 vols to date. New Haven, CT: Yale University Press. Hereafter referred to as PBF.
2 Franklin, Benjamin (2006). *The Papers of Benjamin Franklin: Digital Edition.* Los Altos, CA. Available at: http://franklinpapers.org/franklin/Hereafter referred to as FDE.

Further Reading

Aldridge, Alfred Owen (1967). *Benjamin Franklin and Nature's God.* Durham, NC.
Anderson, Douglas (1997). *The Radical Enlightenments of Benjamin Franklin.* Baltimore, MD.
Buxbaum, Melvin H. (1975). *Benjamin Franklin and the Zealous Presbyterians.* University Park, PA.
Campbell, James (1999). *Recovering Benjamin Franklin: An Exploration of a Life of Science and Service.* Chicago, IL.
Stourzh, Gerald (1969). *Benjamin Franklin and American Foreign Policy.* Chicago, IL.

Chapter Twenty-three

BENJAMIN FRANKLIN AND INTERNATIONAL RELATIONS

Leonard J. Sadosky

Benjamin Franklin played an influential role in shaping the international relations of the provinces of British North America within and without the British Empire and he played a definitive role in guiding the international relations of the United States of America during the American Revolution. As a printer and leading citizen of Philadelphia, Pennsylvania, Franklin mobilized his adopted home city for war during the War of Austrian Succession. As a printer, he provided reportage and perspective on Pennsylvania's relations with its American Indian neighbors. As a colonial agent, Franklin guided the evolution of the American colonies' relationship with the British metropolis, other colonies, and foreign powers. As a member of the Continental Congress, Franklin played a leading role in pushing the decision for independence, and then became the United States' leading minister to the Court of Versailles and the government of France. Franklin was the leading American diplomat in Europe during the Revolution, helping to engineer the Treaty of Alliance with France, the Peace of Paris with Great Britain, and the initial commercial treaties between the United States and other European states. As much as any American during the colonial and Revolutionary eras, Benjamin Franklin played a crucial role in defining how the independent United States would engage the wider world.

23.1 Overview

The scholarly discussion of Franklin's engagement with the arena of international relations has paralleled changes in interpretation of early American foreign relations as a whole. Scholars have shifted from seeing

A Companion to Benjamin Franklin, First Edition. Edited by David Waldstreicher.
© 2011 Blackwell Publishing Ltd. Published 2011 by Blackwell Publishing Ltd.

Franklin's activities as a statesman and a diplomat as expressions of an inherent American exceptionalism to attempting to understand Franklin's thoughts and actions concerning Pennsylvania's external relations, colonial Indian relations, the structure of the British Empire, American independence, and the French Alliance in light of their intercolonial, transatlantic, and other contemporary contexts. The interpretive shift has been generally away from depicting Franklin as an idealist seeking to alter a corrupt world of international politics in light of both Enlightenment and American exceptionalist principles and towards understanding Franklin as a more of a foreign policy realist. The most recent scholarship has attempted to reconcile these two interpretive trends, realism and idealism, seeing Franklin as a student of a transatlantic world of political thought and practice, who deployed his knowledge and understanding of this world to further a particular goal – that of American independence – in which he heartily believed. In short, historians of Franklin's conduct and thinking about international relations have seen a productive tension between idealism and realism, while increasingly downplaying the importance, if not outright disregarding any American exceptionalism (DeConde, 1983).

The first professional early American diplomatic historians – most notably, Samuel Flagg Bemis – saw the diplomats of the American Revolution as embracing a vision of diplomatic thought and practice that was part and parcel of the revolution itself. Revolutionary diplomats saw their work as an extension of the revolutionary political project of republicanism. They rejected the diplomatic practice of the old regime as monarchical and corrupt and wanted no part of the Machiavellian calculus of the balance of power. The Plan of Treaties, or Model Treaty, that Congress had put forward in September 1776 (of which John Adams was the primary author), envisioned an ideal of American interaction with the international system where the United States would seek out commercial treaties with the various European powers rooted in principles of free trade and commercial reciprocity but avoid political treaties. This early professional historical vision of revolutionary diplomacy emphasized not only how revolutionary American diplomats eschewed the political calculus of the old regime but also its inherent corruption. Bemis in particular emphasized the virtue of the American diplomats during the revolution, including Franklin. Bemis's diplomatic histories were explicitly nationalist in focus and wove an account of American virtue and exceptionalism into the story of the early American international relations (Bemis, 1957). The generation of historians who followed Bemis began to problematize this nationalist account. For Felix Gilbert and Gerald Stourzh, any discussion of revolutionary American international relations, and the diplomacy of Franklin in particular, had to deal with the fact that the United States contracted the Treaty of Alliance with France and then made a generous peace treaty with Great Britain without consulting France – Franklin and his colleagues played the game of old regime diplomacy successfully. Gilbert and Stourzh both identified an inherent tension in early American diplomacy between foreign policy idealism and foreign policy realism. Stourzh's study of Franklin, *Benjamin Franklin and American Foreign Policy* saw this tension as a creative one – Franklin was motivated by Enlightenment ideas of diplomacy rooted in the Law of Nations and believed in a vision in which nations conducted business guided by morality, but at the same time Franklin believed in American independence and would, realistically, do what needed to be done to assure the achievement of that goal (Gilbert, 1961; Stourzh, 1969).

The tension between idealism and realism was the pivot around which most the debates over the interpretation of early American diplomatic history revolved for the next four decades, with historians increasingly downplaying American exceptionalism and as a consequence also emphasizing realism in lieu of idealism. Historians working with Franklin and international relations have been most congenial to the hybrid interpretation first put forward by Stourzh of Franklin being an idealistic realist when it came to dealing with the French and the British and also imagining the place of the United States in the wider world. This interpretation of Franklin has been expanded upon, rather than overturned in recent years. Jonathan Dull's now standard history of the international relations of the American Revolution, *A Diplomatic History of the American Revolution*, offered a realist reading of the diplomacy of the revolution from not only the American perspective, but also the French, British, and Spanish, as well as the Dutch and Russian. Dull (1985), as one of the editors of the *Papers of Benjamin Franklin*, profited from an extensive knowledge of Franklin and saw Franklin operating with a framework of idealistic realism similar to that of Stourzh.

Beyond the field of diplomatic history, the interpretive and investigatory transformation wrought by the rise of Atlantic history caused historians to reassess Franklin. He was now seen as a denizen of the British Empire and his diplomatic thought and practice were understood in light of the continuous acts of cultural and political negotiation most Atlantic peoples found themselves involved in throughout the eighteenth century. Both Edmund S. Morgan's and Gordon S. Wood's biographies dealt with Franklin in this manner. In both accounts, Franklin is notable, but not unique, in having an identity defined by his membership in a British North American society. Franklin "becomes American" in Morgan's telling and undergoes a process of "Americanization" in Wood's biography, when as a colonial agent and diplomat, he dealt with the ruptures wrought by the imperial crisis and was forced to confront what being an American meant and how the United States would survive as he undertook his duties as a statesman and a diplomat. For Morgan and Wood, Franklin did not seek to make the world like America as much as the wider realm of international relations forced him to define what America is. Additionally, Franklin's role in shaping international relations while a Philadelphia printer and active participant in the intercolonial and transatlantic public sphere has been put in deeper perspective by scholars studying British imperial history and the history of American Indian relations. Franklin's printing of numerous Indian treaties has garnered new scrutiny in light of an increased knowledge of Pennsylvania's eighteenth-century Indian relations by historians such as James Merrell and Jane Merritt and the collection and annotation of a new edition of Franklin's Indian treaties edited by Susan Kalter. Timothy Shannon's in-depth study of the Albany Congress of 1754 illuminated Franklin's role in a conference that brought together Indian nations, colonial governors, and imperial agents (Shannon, 2000; Kalter, 2006). The maturation of diplomatic history, in concert with the emergence and growth of Atlantic and American Indian history, and the recalibration of imperial history have all allowed historians to chart the depth of ways in which Benjamin Franklin shaped eighteenth-century international relations generally and those of the United States in particular.

23.2 Colonial Pennsylvania's International Relations

As both a private citizen and an officer in colonial government, Benjamin Franklin directly and indirectly shaped the international relations of his adopted home colony of Pennsylvania and the British Empire as a whole. As the printer of the *Pennsylvania Gazette*, Franklin had printed numerous accounts relating to all aspects of international relations, including Pennsylvania's negotiations and treaties with its American Indian neighbors. As an advocate, Franklin first entered the public discussion of international relations during the War of Austrian Succession, as he pushed for Pennsylvania to organize a militia to defend the province in the event of a French attack. After the War, Franklin retired from his printing business, and was elected to the Pennsylvania assembly. Franklin's partner David Hall continued to print Indian treaties as well as other accounts, commentaries, and treatises regarding Pennsylvania's and British North America's international relations. Discussions in the public sphere, along with Franklin's observations of colonial and imperial government, led him to attend the Albany Congress of 1754 and put forward a detailed Plan of Union that was designed to strengthen the British American colonies in the event of a future war. Franklin's spirited advocacy and his awareness of the world beyond the borders of his home colony, was one of many factors informing his ultimate appointment as a colonial agent for Pennsylvania in 1757.

Franklin's first sustained engagement with issues involving international relations occurred in 1747, during the War of Austrian Succession, known in the North American colonies as King George's War. Unlike the Seven Years War that followed it, the American theater of the War of Austrian

Succession was confined largely to the borderlands between New England and Canada and naval operations in the West Indies. This war found Great Britain fighting both France and Spain, and while neither Pennsylvania nor most of British North America feared a major invasion, an attack by sea by an enemy naval force or by enemy privateers was a possibility. When French and Spanish privateers were sighted in Delaware Bay in July 1747, Pennsylvanians became worried. Anxiety increased when rumors arrived from the West Indies that French privateers were planning to sack Philadelphia. These increased fears that Philadelphia might find itself the target of an attack spurred Franklin to action (Stourzh, 1969).

In response to the fears that Philadelphia and Pennsylvania might suffer an attack during the War of Austrian Succession, Franklin publicly proposed that the willing citizens of both the city and the province organize themselves into a voluntary militia. This was a controversial motion given that Pennsylvania had been created by its founder, William Penn, in large part as a home for Quakers, who embraced pacifism as part of their religious creed. While Pennsylvania had become home to a diverse body of British and continental European settlers, Quakers continued to hold enough power in the provincial assembly to thwart efforts at mobilization, in accordance with their pacifist beliefs. Franklin wrote and published a pamphlet entitled, *Plain Truth, or, Serious Considerations on the Present State of the City of Philadelphia, and Province of Pennsylvania*, in which he made the public case for forming a militia company in order to defend the city and province. In *Plain Truth*, Franklin challenged both wealthy merchants who were disinclined to provide the funding for a militia, the Quakers who emphasized their personal rights of conscience over the wellbeing of the community, and all citizens to come together to support the common good in the face of a crisis caused from beyond Pennsylvania's borders. *Plain Truth* pointed to dangers to Pennsylvania not only from the ocean, but also from French-allied Indians on the borderlands. Franklin's pamphlet saw the province in a truly international context facing threats of violence and invasion from all quarters. Franklin's solution to the crisis – a voluntary association – was modeled on the earlier associations, such as the Library Company of Philadelphia, that had shaped public life in the city during the previous decade, and that Franklin had been the major impetus behind. *Plain Truth* proved to be the spur to the formation of the voluntary militia known as the Association. While Philadelphia was not attacked during the final year of the war, Franklin's lobbying proved instrumental in transforming his home province's stance during an international crisis. *Plain Truth* and the formation of the association were Franklin's first serious and sustained public engagement with issues of international relations (Stourzh, 1969).

The following year witnessed not only the conclusion of War of Austrian Succession, but also saw Franklin take on David Hall as a partner in his printing business. With Hall engaged in the day-to-day running of Franklin's business, Franklin formally retired as a printer, and began to play a fuller role in Philadelphia's and Pennsylvania's public life. Franklin was elected to the Pennsylvania assembly in 1752, and chosen in 1757 to represent the colony as its agent in London. Franklin's years in public life between his retirement from printing and the beginning of his agency in London saw him regularly engaged with issues of international relations. As it was in 1747, the colony's major preoccupation in terms of international relations was the fear that it could suffer invasion or attack in the event of a new war with France. In response to an essay written by New Yorker Archibald Kennedy and printed by Franklin's friend, New York printer James Parker, Franklin endorsed a plan for a defensive union among the colonies. As a New Yorker, Kennedy had called for incorporating the Iroquois Six Nations into the union. Franklin did not take issue with this, but did feel that negotiations for any union would be delicate, requiring "ambassadors" from each colony to come together to forge any agreement. When Franklin joined other colonial representatives at a treaty conference with the Six Nations in Albany in the summer of 1754, he seized on the opportunity to promote the vision he and others had been gestating for several years (Stourzh, 1969; Shannon, 2000).

The Albany Plan of Union that emerged from the Albany Congress of 1754 was shaped in large part by Franklin's thinking and initiative. Derived in the immediate aftermath of an Indian treaty conference and attempting to provide a framework for unified colonial action in the face a new impending war with France, the Albany Plan of Union marked a further evolution in Franklin's engagement with the issues of British North America's international relations. Franklin had composed a list of ideas for an intercolonial union, known as *Short Hints towards a Scheme for Uniting the Northern Colonies*, which he circulated to the delegates at the Albany Congress. Whereas Franklin had agreed with Kennedy's desire for a colonial defensive union in 1751, by the time of the Albany Congress he had a much comprehensive vision for a colonial union – he now wanted a colonial "Grand Council" and "Governor-General" to organize colonial policy not only for defense, but also for making treaties with the Indian nations and for organizing western settlement. The union would not simply be an ad-hoc alliance, but a permanent organization sanctioned by an act of Parliament. Delegates at Albany came not only from New York and Pennsylvania, but also from Massachusetts, New Hampshire, Rhode Island, Connecticut, and Maryland. The Congress was intended to provide a forum for the represented colonies to renew their ties by treaty to the Iroquois Six Nations. It was Franklin who pushed the Congress to go beyond this initial task and discuss coordinating defensive activities should a war with France break out and then to discuss a permanent structure of union. *Short Hints* was Franklin's starting point for these discussions. The Congress ultimately proposed a Plan of Union that would have incorporated not only the seven colonies present, but also Virginia, Delaware, North Carolina, and South Carolina – the Union would have included all of British North America except for Nova Scotia and Georgia. Ultimately, none of the colonies, including Franklin's Pennsylvania, approved the Union, nor did Parliament. The questions of intercolonial cooperation and coordination, as well as the colonists relations with their Indian neighbors, did not disappear, however, and they remained flashpoints for discussion and disagreement among colonial and metropolitan authorities through the Seven Years War (Stourzh, 1969).

The initial skirmishes in what would become the Seven Years War (known in the colonies as the French and Indian War) had already occurred at the time of the Albany Congress. A small detachment of Virginia militia under Colonel George Washington had surprised a small group of French troops near the Forks of the Ohio River (territory claimed by both Virginia and Pennsylvania). After a Delaware Indian allied with the Virginians had killed a French officer during negotiations, the French garrison from Fort Duquesne (modern Pittsburgh) had surrounded Washington's smaller force and won his surrender. The incident caused tensions between the French and British that had been simmering for years to boil over and the British dispatched an expeditionary force under General Edward Braddock to castigate the French forces in the American interior (F. Anderson, 2000). Although his plan for an intercolonial union had come to naught, Franklin played a leading role in ensuring that Pennsylvania supported the British war effort. Franklin made sure that advertisements soliciting wagons, horses, and other materiel were printed and circulated, and he personally guaranteed eventual repayment to ensure that Pennsylvania farmers contributed horses and wagons to support Braddock's forces. Franklin also got the Assembly to approve a militia bill that created a provincial militia similar to the Association of 1747, except that was approved by the government. Franklin was appointed a colonel and supervised the construction of forts in the Pennsylvania backcountry during the late winter of 1756. As a leading member of the Assembly, Franklin played an important role in mobilizing Pennsylvania for war (Isaacson, 2003).

23.3 Franklin's Colonial Agency and International Relations

Franklin was appointed by the Pennsylvania Assembly in February 1757 as its agent to travel to England. The Assembly's major concern was the relationship between the colony and its proprietors – William Penn's sons Thomas Penn and Richard Penn. The Seven Years War, and the financial demands imposed by supplying Braddock's army, creating a militia, and generally preparing the colony for war strained the colony's budget. The crisis pushed to a head a long-standing dispute between the Assembly and the Penn family, namely that the lands and property held by the proprietors were exempt from taxation. Franklin's primary goal was to negotiate more freedom for the assembly to legislate and to tax. Franklin would eventually come to support making Pennsylvania a Crown colony, so that its governor would be appointed directly by the king and ministry, rather than the proprietors. While Franklin's negotiations with the Penn brothers were unsuccessful, the years of his first stint as a colonial agent (1757–1762) saw his understanding of Pennsylvania's and British North America's international relations begin to shift. Where Franklin, when living and operating in America, had imagined little difference between the British American and British metropolitan perspectives on the world, both his time in London as an agent and the events of the Seven Years War had caused him to begin to perceive differences between metropolitan and colonial interests (E.S. Morgan, 2002; Isaacson, 2003).

In the aftermath of the decisive British victories over French forces at Quebec in 1759 and Montreal in 1760, the British public began to expect an ultimate British victory. The looming question for the British government, which became a heated topic for discussion in the public sphere, was the ultimate structure of the peace agreement. Most observers believed that in order to secure peace with France, Britain would not able to retain all of the territories it had captured. Commentators fixated on which possession should be returned to France – Canada or the Caribbean island of Guadeloupe. Over sixty pamphlets appeared before the final peace treaty in 1763 considering both sides of the question. Franklin entered the debate with a 1760 pamphlet he published anonymously entitled *The Interest of Great Britain Considered with Regard to Her Colonies and the Acquisitions of Canada and Guadaloupe* [sic]. Studying Franklin's writing in context of the larger debate, Gerald Stourzh believes that the *Interest of Great Britain Considered* marked a crucial point in the development of Franklin's thinking on international relations. At this moment, he both began to perceive the relationship between the colonies and the metropolis differently than metropolitan writers; Franklin saw the security and prosperity of British North America as essential to the health of the Empire as a whole, and was willing to put that concern ahead of questions of international law and the law of nations (Stourzh, 1969).

The sharpest challenge to the vision of international relations that Franklin put forward in his 1760 pamphlet can be found in the writings William Burke, a cousin of Edmund Burke, as well in the writings of other anonymous authors who forcefully opposed the retention of Canada. For Franklin and others who wished to retain Canada, the justification of their position was obvious – it was a matter of security. Retaining Canada in British hands prevented future territorial rivalries and thus would prevent future wars. Burke did not disagree with this reasoning, but felt that choosing to keep a territory merely for reasons of security was a base, political motive. The British Empire was supposed to be an empire devoted to the promotion of commerce and the augmentation of wealth, not simply the agglomeration of territory.

Guadeloupe promised the most immediate and sure wealth; it was the more logical choice. At the same time, to Burke, justifying acquire a territory in the name of security seemed like a dangerous principle. It presupposed that a people could not live in peace with their neighbors – one could justify an endless stream of conquests in the name of security. This was contrary to principles of the law of nations, which aimed for a vision of positive peace. Finally, Great Britain had not gone to war with the express purpose of conquering Canada, therefore, its acquisition was not "an original right." The concern over security had evolved later. Franklin had taken issue with all of this. He did not concede Burke's distinction between right and security. Indeed, Franklin argued that the quest for security on the part of a state could justify taking new and heretofore unimagined courses that presented themselves, because the dynamics between states evolved and changed. Franklin pointed to examples from recent European history, and drew a different contrast between conquest for security, which were justifiable and conquests for mere ambition, which were not. In describing this interpretation, Stourzh sees Franklin as more of a realist than an idealist – he was seeking to articulate an intellectual ground on which to base a structure for future British North American security, rather than accommodate British American society to an inflexible set of norms. Franklin adopted this position in large part because he saw colonial American society as dynamic and growing – the ongoing growth of the colonial population he had described in his 1751 essay *Observations on the Increase of Mankind* compelled the colonies' expansion. Without the removal of the French presence from North America, future conflict between the British and French colonists would be a guarantee (Stourzh, 1969).

Franklin's years as a colonial agent pose a challenge for the historian considering his identity and thinking on international relations. While modern biographers of Franklin, particularly Edmund Morgan and Gordon Wood, portray Franklin's years in England as the time when he came closest to conforming to the habits and perspectives of metropolitan Britons, his writings and actions as an agent and political commentator reveal an adherence to a British American perspective. Charged with advocating for the colonial view, Franklin tended to perceive the international controversies and challenges that the British Empire confronted in that light. The debate over the peace settlement of the Seven Years War was the most obvious case. Franklin also began to challenge many of the pillars of mercantilist political economy and, of course, defended the colonists' belief, early in the imperial crisis, of the distinction between internal and external taxes.

Franklin saw colonial British America as dynamic and growing, and his views on international relations were conditioned by that. He defended policies that would protect American security, foster American commerce, and preserve the American colonies' position within the British Empire (Stourzh, 1969; E.S. Morgan, 2002; G.S. Wood, 2004).

23.4 Franklin's Revolutionary Diplomacy

Franklin's belief that the British Empire was the best vehicle to further the position of the American colonies in the realm of international relations was one of the factors that made him a relative latecomer to the American revolutionary movement, but it was this understanding of the international system that made him one of the new United States' most important diplomatic thinkers and agents. Franklin would be one of the first revolutionaries to consider the international implication of the revolutionary movement during the summer of 1775; he would take the lead in reaching out to potential European friends in the winter of 1775–1776, would play a role in formulating the foreign policy of the newly independent United States, and then, famously, take charge of American diplomacy during the revolution as one of the ministers to the Court of Versailles and the government of French King Louis XVI. Franklin would play the leading role among the American ministers of securing the 1778 Treaty of Alliance with France. Franklin would then play a major role in negotiating the final peace treaty with Great Britain to end the Revolutionary War and secure British recognition of American independence, implicitly violating the terms of the alliance he had helped negotiate. Before he leaving France for America in 1784, he would help put American diplomacy in Europe on a sound footing that his successors, John Adams and Thomas Jefferson, would build upon.

Franklin returned from England and his second stint as a colonial agent on May 5, 1775, and was appointed the next day as one of Pennsylvania's delegates to the Second Continental Congress. When the Congress opened on May 10, Franklin was regarded with suspicion by some, having spent all but two years since 1757 in England and having spent most the Imperial Crisis attempting to mediate the two sides of the controversy. In the aftermath of the battles at Lexington and Concord and then Bunker Hill, Franklin was appalled at the aggressive conduct of Thomas Gage and the North Ministry, although he publicly spent the summer of 1775 occupying a middle position between delegates leaning towards independence and those pushing for reconciliation. Franklin's knowledge of international relations informed his prescriptions for resolving the crisis. In July, Franklin composed a series of draft articles of confederation for Congress to consider. His draft articles specifically called for the possibility of bringing in

Canada, the Caribbean, and even Ireland into the American cause, as well as cultivating new and deeper alliances with the Indian nations to the west. Franklin saw that the international system, providing the possibility for breaking up the British Empire, could provide leverage for the American cause in wringing concession from the North Ministry and King George III. Franklin's articles were not approved, but discussions of reaching out for foreign assistance and opening American ports to foreign commerce became more frequent among the delegates to Congress and their constituents in the autumn of 1775 and even more in the wake of George III's October declaration that the colonies were in open rebellion, and the December 1775 Prohibitory Act, through which Parliament closed all the American colonies to any commerce (Sadosky, 2009).

With the British king and Parliament treating the American colonies as a rebel power, Congress formally reached out to the international system for assistance, and Franklin was a major part of the initiative. He was a member of the Committee of Secret Correspondence, created on November 29, 1775. The committee was charged with reaching out to potential friends of the American cause in Britain, Ireland, and the European continent. Franklin immediate sent a letter to the committee's Dutch correspondent, Charles-Guillaume-Frédéric Dumas, thanking him for a gift of Vattel's *Law of Nations*, describing the American situation in glowing terms, and asking him for any intelligence on which European powers would be disposed to assist the Congress and the American colonies in their resistance to the measures of Great Britain. In addition to contacting Dumas, the Committee reached out to the remaining colonial agents in London; only Virginian Arthur Lee returned the Congress's attempts at communication. Lee would become the Congress's first agent in Europe, paving the way for Silas Deane and then Franklin himself to follow. The committee dispatched Deane in March 1776 to France in an attempt to open communication with the French government and to contract for supplies for the Continental Army. The Americans were reaching out into the international system, engaging in acts of diplomacy, and by the summer of 1776 were doing most of the things an independent nation did, short of actually declaring this independence itself (Dull, 1985; Sadosky, 2009).

The international implications of the Declaration of Independence have been a subject relatively ignored by most scholars until David Armitage's study of the question, *The Declaration of Independence: A Global History* appeared in 2007. Armitage argued that one of the Declaration's primary purposes was to serve as what practitioners of international law call a general manifesto – a statement of principles justifying a course of action in the international realm. Franklin's role in drafting the Declaration was, of course, editorial, but as the movement towards the final Declaration unfolded, Franklin and the Committee of Secret Correspondence continued to expand its ambit of action, dispatching William Bingham to the

West Indies in early June to acquire war materiel and to gather intelligence. After the Declaration was issued, Franklin continued to be occupied with the business of the Committee of Secret Correspondence and was part of the congressional committee that engaged in the response to British general William Howe's call for negotiation in September 1776. At the same time, Franklin was a member of the committee that drafted the Plan of Treaties, or Model Treaty, which Congress agreed to on September 24, 1776. Although largely the work of John Adams, Franklin's thinking was congruent with that of Adams as to the contents of the plan. In short, the Plan of Treaties was the blueprint for the types of treaty the United States hoped to negotiate with France and the other European powers. Adams had borrowed the structure and language of the treaty plan from the texts of other eighteenth-century French treaties. In terms of structure, Franklin and Adams were not acting as American exceptionalists, they were attempting to conform American diplomacy to the existing forms of the European system. At the same time, the Plan of Treaties called for the United States to pursue only commercial ties with other European powers, and to eschew political alliances. As a statement of principles, the Plan of Treaties was revolutionary. Franklin still adhered to the view that he articulated in his writings from the 1750s forward, that the American population and strength was growing over the long term, that America had a different set of ultimate interests than Europe, but that given the bulk of the American population would remain agriculturalists for the foreseeable future, the best footing on which to base the European–American relationship was a commercial one. Americans would exchange agricultural products and raw materials for European manufactures and luxury goods (Stourzh, 1969; Sadosky, 2009).

Franklin would use the Plan of Treaties as the starting point for negotiations with France when he arrived there at the end of 1776. That Franklin would play a role in leading the negotiations himself was confirmed two days after the approval of the Plan of Treaties, when congress appointed him, Deane, and Thomas Jefferson to serve as ministers to France. Jefferson declined his appointment and was replaced by Arthur Lee, but Franklin began preparations to depart, and left for France at the end of October, arriving at port in Auray on December 3, and ultimately making his way to Paris within two and half weeks. Franklin would quickly become the leading minister among the three-man team of himself, Deane, and Lee. In retrospect, Franklin's performance as a diplomat at the Court of Versailles and a *philosophe* in the salons of Paris, make it difficult to imagine any other contemporary American filling his role. Historians have not only debated the nature of Franklin's diplomatic performance in France, but also pointed out that he might not have been the most natural choice for the role. Jonathan Dull, an editor of the *Papers of Benjamin Franklin* and diplomatic historian, has rightly pointed out that Franklin was aged 70 at the time of his appointment, and both the ocean crossing and the energy required by his diplomatic duties were taxing. Franklin's health was constantly challenged throughout his stay in France. The formal and informal demands of a court diplomat in old regime France were not manual labor, but they were not slight. Franklin was constantly challenged throughout the course of embassy to France (Dull, 1982, 1983).

Historians' discussion of Franklin's diplomacy in France revolved around two issues – roughly, style and substance. In terms of style, historians often discuss Franklin's "unofficial diplomacy" in the salons of Paris, in his house at Passy, and in the wider public sphere of France and continental Europe, where Franklin and his fellow American diplomats sought to turn public opinion towards the American cause. The question of style also refers specifically to Franklin's negotiating style and the tactics he used to get the results he wanted from French foreign minister Comte de Vergennes and King Louis XVI, and then ultimately from Lord Shelburne and Richard Oswald, when negotiating the peace treaty with Great Britain. The substance of Franklin's diplomacy is also a subject of great concern – historians debate the extent to which Franklin's diplomatic and political positions reflect his vision of a rising America and its particular place in the transatlantic political economy. Historians also debate the extent to which Franklin sought to promulgate a new international order that diminished the role of the balance of power or whether he was a realist who sought to manipulate the existing diplomatic system to America's advantage (Dull, 1983).

Franklin's style of diplomacy was no doubt a large factor in his success. Franklin's fame from his publications and his scientific experiments made him an instant celebrity in France. He was invited to numerous dinners and parties and was a presence in salons. Everywhere Franklin traveled, he not only represented the American cause but also embodied it. He altered his style of dress to be plain and donned a fur cap on occasions. The public presentations were, Jonathan Dull cautions, less outward lobbying for the American cause than they were acts that reinforced what elite Parisians believed or wanted to believe about Americans and the American cause. More serious lobbying occurred in the press, where Franklin and the other ministers published essays that argued for the necessity and righteousness of the American cause, and also described a political and economic vision where France and America could coexist beneficially. At the same time, Franklin's style of negotiating was a product of his years as a colonial agent. Where Franklin had once pressed hard in negotiations with his counterparts, in France he remained reserved, never pushing Vergennes too hard. Although it took over a year before the French agreed to the Treaties of Alliance and Commerce in February 1778, Franklin's waiting game ultimately paid off (Dull, 1982).

The question of whether Franklin was primarily a diplomatic realist manipulating the European balance of power to America's ends or was an idealist who hoped to transform the way nations interacted with each other is a more difficult question. Beginning with Stourzh's study, most subsequent diplomatic historians, including Jonathan Dull and Alexande DeConde, have come down on the former side, with only Bemis's old work and Richard Morris's narrative of the Treaty of Paris negotiations proffering notions of idealism and exceptionalism (Bemis, 1957; Morris, 1965; Dull, 1982, 1983, 1985; DeConde, 1983). There is much to commend the realist view. Up until Vergennes concluded the final negotiations with the Americans, Franklin continued to have semi-secret meetings with British agents, including one of Lord North's spies, Paul Wentworth. Rather than seriously contemplate reunion with Britain, Franklin was attempting to get the French to conclude the treaties faster. The Treaty of Alliance itself was a departure from the idealistic vision of the Plan of Treaties – America had obtained a commercial treaty that opened French and American ports to each other's commerce, but at the cost of an old regime-style political alliance. And Franklin famously played the Machiavellian game of diplomacy in concluding peace with Britain. The alliance required that France and the United States conclude peace together, but Franklin and the American commissioners negotiated with the British government on their own during the course of 1782, leaving France to fight the war on its own through the end of 1782 and most of 1783. Although Franklin did push against his partners John Jay and John Adams, when they refused to allow Vergennes to be informed of the status of their peace negotiations, he did not push all that hard. Little idealism and little signs of American exceptionalism shine through Franklin's conduct of the Paris peace negotiations. The consistency is with Franklin's earlier vision of a rising and growing American nation that needed access to western lands and the power to negotiate openings of foreign markets for its produce. Franklin believed America had a separate and distinct destiny, but was willing to use all the tools at his disposal within the framework of old regime diplomacy to preserve American independence and give the United States the space to grow (Stourzh, 1969; Dull, 1982).

The Treaty of Paris, which ended the Revolutionary War, was agreed to preliminary form in November 1782 and finally concluded in September 1783. It was not Franklin's work alone, but the product of negotiations between British commissioner Richard Oswald and Franklin, John Adams, and John Jay. Henry Laurens had also been appointed as an American commissioner, but had been captured at sea by the British, held in the Tower of London, and did not make his way to Paris until the negotiations were nearly concluded. The commissioners secured beneficial terms for the United States: British recognition of American independence, a western boundary at the Mississippi River, and American access to the fisheries off the Canadian Maritimes, mostly in exchange for promises on both sides that they would endeavor to see the restitution of the seized property of the combatants. Peace did not end Franklin's diplomatic endeavors. He, along with John Adams and Thomas Jefferson, who arrived in France in the summer of 1784, had been granted commissions by Congress to negotiate commercial treaties with the other powers in Europe. Franklin had concluded one such treaty, with diplomatic representatives from Sweden, before Jefferson's arrival, and another one with Prussia after Jefferson reached. By 1785, approaching eighty years of age, Franklin was determined to return to America. Jefferson was appointed as minister to France to relieve Franklin, and he left for America on July 12, 1785.

Franklin's final years in the United States, from his arrival in September 1785 to his death in April 1790, were not without his involvement in the issues relating to international relations. Obviously, Franklin's participation in the Philadelphia Convention of 1787, and his signature on and support of the Federal Constitution implicate him in the creation of the new American federal government. As first Frederick W. Marks (1973) and then David Hendrickson (2003) argued the constitution was, among many things, an instrument designed to concentrate diplomatic and military power and give the United States the ability to engage the international system with more success than it had under the Articles of Confederation (Sadosky, 2009). As Doron Ben-Atar's study (2004) of industrial espionage and intellectual piracy reminds readers, Franklin was an early advocate for America's acquisition of foreign technology. Franklin continued to advocate for this in the 1780s and contemporaries such as Tench Coxe and Alexander Hamilton followed Franklin's lead in advocating for the vigorous acquisition of foreign technology to bolster America's standing and competitiveness in the international order. Although problematic on many levels, Franklin's public stance against African slavery and the slave trade was part of a larger transatlantic movement that would bear fruit and begin to transform the international order in the early nineteenth century, when first Britain (1807) and then the United States (1808) outlawed the Atlantic slave trade (Isaacson, 2003).

Franklin's legacy in international relations is a mixed one. Unlike many of his contemporaries, such as Thomas Jefferson, he was not a passionate advocate of an idealistic world governed by the law of nations. His idealism, such as it was, was reserved for informing his advocacy for the interests of his colony, then British North America as a whole, and then of the United States. In terms of international relations, Franklin's modern academic biographers, Edmund S. Morgan and Gordon Wood, are right to see a man who became American. He advocated passionately for American interests in the international arena, and then as a diplomat, used guile, skill, and reserve to effect the most beneficial outcomes he could for his nation. In the realm of international relations, Benjamin Franklin was a realist and a nationalist.

Further Reading

Anderson, Fred (2000). *The Crucible of War: The Seven Years' War and the Fate of Empire in British North America, 1754–1766.* New York, NY.

Bemis, Samuel Flagg (1957). *The Diplomacy of the American Revolution.* Bloomington, IN.

DeConde, Alexander (1983). "Historians, the war for independence, and the persistence of the exceptionalist ideal," *International History Review* 5: 399–430.

Dull, Jonathan R. (1982). "Franklin the diplomat: The French mission," *Transactions of the American Philosophical Society* 72: 1–76.

Dull, Jonathan R. (1983). "Benjamin Franklin and the nature of American diplomacy," *International History Review* 5: 346–363.

Dull, Jonathan R. (1985). *A Diplomatic History of the American Revolution.* New Haven, CT.

Hendrickson, David (2003). *Peace Pact: The Lost World of the American Founding.* Lawrence, KS.

Isaacson, Walter (2003). *Benjamin Franklin: An American Life.* New York, NY: Simon and Schuster.

Kalter, Susan (2006). *Benjamin Franklin, Pennsylvania, and the First Nations: The Treaties of 1736–62.* Urbana, IL.

Morris, Richard B. (1965). *The Peacemakers: The Great Powers and American Independence.* New York, NY.

Sadosky, Leonard (2009). *Revolutionary Negotiations: Indians, Empires, and Diplomats in the Founding of America.* Charlottesville, VA.

Shannon, Timothy (2000). *Indians and Colonists at the Crossroads of Empire: The Albany Congress of 1754.* Ithaca, NY.

Stourzh, Gerald (1969). *Benjamin Franklin and American Foreign Policy.* Chicago, IL.

Wood, Gordon S. (2004). *The Americanization of Benjamin Franklin.* New York, NY.

Chapter Twenty-four

Benjamin Franklin in Memory and Popular Culture

Andrew M. Schocket

From his death in 1790 to today, Benjamin Franklin has played a unique role in American memory and popular culture. Of all the heroes and villains in the nation's founding pantheon, Benjamin Franklin has been the one least often remembered as a remote, lifeless statue. George Washington endures as the indomitable leader, John Adams as the prickly bulldog, Thomas Jefferson as the inveterate dreamer, James Madison as the cold political intellect, Benedict Arnold as the talented traitor, Alexander Hamilton the urban financier, and George III as the insensitive tyrant. There they are, much as they have been, carved in granite. But Franklin? He contributed no less than they did as individuals to the nation's political founding, and much more to its cultural, scientific, technological, and institutional founding, as a printer, essayist, diplomat, scientist, inventor, satirist, politician, and civic patron. But that is the point. Because of Franklin's versatility, his social mobility, his cosmopolitanism, and his long career, Franklin is unique among those whom the nineteenth-century Americans called their "founding fathers." Although the image of each of them has changed and the estimation of them (with the exception of Washington) fluctuated over the years, reflecting new political and cultural realities, perhaps the memory of Franklin has been perhaps the most fluid, for several reasons. Franklin's role in the revolution helped describe him but never wholly defined him. Alone among the founding cohort, he had already accomplished a grand and celebrated life's work before the revolution, allowing multiple avenues for future generations to follow in their consideration of him. Franklin's having grown up poor and continuing to sympathize with common working people, while also engaging in elite politics and cultural

A Companion to Benjamin Franklin, First Edition. Edited by David Waldstreicher.
© 2011 Blackwell Publishing Ltd. Published 2011 by Blackwell Publishing Ltd.

work (which, in the eighteenth century, included scientific experimentation), allowed room for different memories of him not only according how values changed over time but also among people of different social status. And Franklin's personality – his wit and his manner with women – allowed for him to be perceived as more humanly accessible than the other "great" men of his cohort.

Franklin's somewhat accidental status as by far the revolution's oldest major figure resulted in a curiously mixed American reaction to his death on April 17, 1790. A few recent historians have puzzled over what they have called the muted reaction to Franklin's death, as least in America. When the news reached France in June, the Comte de Mirabeau immediately eulogized Franklin, the National Assembly supported Mirabeau's official resolution of mourning, and the Commune of Paris soon followed suit. The official American response, at least at the national level, was far less enthusiastic. Although James Madison successfully sponsored a resolution of mourning in the federal House of Representatives, Charles Carroll's parallel measure in the Senate was tabled. And even one of the institutions Franklin helped to found, the American Philosophical Society (APS), did little better. Not until about a year after his death did the APS finally get around to having one of its members, William Smith, deliver an official eulogy. That gesture, too, was at best ironic, given that Smith had been one of Franklin's most stalwart political detractors for many years, and Smith himself even wondered aloud in the course of his eulogy whether he was the most appropriate person to honor Franklin. Historians have generally attributed this weak official reaction to the association between Franklin and France in the public mind, especially in light of the French Revolution, which would become such a mark of disapproval once it turned bloody. But as of the spring of 1790, before Louis XVI's execution and the Reign of Terror, American opinion had not yet fallen strongly against its French revolutionary counterparts.

Rather, we might chalk it up to domestic politics. Although the incomparable George Washington would be immediately canonized when he died in 1799, both Thomas Jefferson's and John Adams's reputation benefited from their dying in 1826, many years after their partisan days were over, and thus giving time for their most passionate opponents to soften or die out. On the other hand, Franklin had much more recently been the subject of considerable controversy – a circumstance that Alexander Hamilton's admirers could later appreciate, given Hamilton's sudden death while he, too, was not far removed from political controversy. With over two centuries' hindsight, the muted American reaction to Franklin's passing might seem bizarre. After all, his diplomacy in France had exceeded any reasonable expectations: he had been the prime mover in obtaining recognition and funding for a hatchling republic from the proudest and most indebted monarchy in Europe, and he had been a key figure in peace terms so beneficial that both the English and the French marveled at the deal the Americans had wangled from them. However, notwithstanding the results, which were far better than anyone else of his generation would likely have achieved, in the decade before his death Franklin's methods had been called into question, even by – rather, especially by – other members of the diplomatic team, Arthur Lee and John Adams. Meanwhile, his political stance as a mature conciliator among various political factions had resulted in none of them claiming his as their own. He had attended the Constitutional Convention and approved of its product, thus alienating him from anti-federalists, but he was not a passionate federalist, either. During the convention, he had supported structures similar to the Pennsylvania constitution then in force, including frequent direct elections of the executive and even of judges. That stance had put him at odds with the federalists in Pennsylvania, who too were pushing hard for a new, more conservative state constitution. And the last movement that he championed, the abolition of slavery, did not do much to increase his popularity in a Congress dominated by slaveholders. But we should not let the Congress's tepid response to Franklin's represent the totality of American mourning: the federal congress was composed primarily of federalists concerned about the nature of the precedent they would set concerning federal commemorations of individual citizens and never greatly enamored of Franklin's egalitarian political instincts.

The broader popular reaction to Franklin's death was swift and deep, especially in Franklin's beloved Philadelphia. On April 21, four days after his death, Philadelphia held proportionally the largest funeral ever in the City of Brotherly Love, with as many as 20,000 people attending, nearly forty per cent of the nation's largest city's entire population. Clergy of Jewish and all Christian denominations led the procession, followed by Franklin's body. His pallbearers included the top men of Pennsylvania and Philadelphia, and represented the broad range of his activities and associations over the course of his lifetime. Pennsylvania president Thomas Mifflin, Pennsylvania chief justice Thomas McKean, U.S. Senator from Pennsylvania William Bingham, and Bank of North America president Thomas Willing's presence testified to the mark Franklin had made on national politics. Like Franklin, Samuel Powell had parlayed local artisan activities into a considerable fortune – in Powell's case, what in the eighteenth century was called carpentry but what we would call contracting and developing. Rounding out the group was polymath David Rittenhouse – a clockmaker, instrument maker, mathematician, and inventor who was a member of the APS and who eventually ran the U.S. Mint. Then, after Franklin family members, walked the Pennsylvania Executive Council, its General Assembly, its Supreme Court, the city's lawyers, the city's elected officials, the city's printers, members of the APS, members of the College of Physicians, members of the Sons of Cincinnati, and then the University of Pennsylvania, trailed by, as the newspapers reported, "sundry other societies, together with a numerous and respectable body of citizens."[1] These proceedings were reported and repeated as newspapers in the United States, Britain, and France waxed lyrical about Franklin's virtues as a scientist and civic innovator.

Among the men whom one might consider among the founding fraternity, Franklin had already secured his place as one of whom they thought the public perceived as the two indispensable founders of the nation. At least it seemed that way to John Adams, who only two weeks before Franklin died sarcastically lamented that the revolution would be falsely remembered so that "the essence of the whole will be that Dr Franklins electrical Rod smote the earth, and out sprung General Washington. That Franklin electrised him with his rod and thenceforward these two conducted all the policy, negotiation, legislation, and War."[2] Thought Adams and Thomas Jefferson agreed on very little at the time, in this they concurred. On hearing of Franklin's passing, Jefferson proposed to George Washington that the members of the executive branch wear mourning clothes for two months. Ever concerned with precedent, Washington rejected Jefferson's plea: Better not to mourn anyone officially lest the president get drawn into deciding who should be mourned and who not. For Jefferson, though, "the world had drawn so broad a line between [Washington] & Dr. Franklin, on the one side, and the residue of mankind, on the other, that we might wear mourning for them, and the question still remain new & undecided as to all others."[3] Still, Franklin's time and association with France did not help his reputation over the course of the 1790s, as the Americans' shock over what they perceived as the excesses of the French Revolution and the Quasi-War with France led to denigration of anything having a gallic tinge.

In the early nineteenth century, however, the publication of Franklin's memoir greatly shifted people's perceptions of him to ones that were perfectly in harmony with the new tunes of the early republic. The political passions and rivalries that resulted in the muted reaction to Franklin's death faded as passions cooled, different issues came to the fore, and Franklin's rivals followed his exit of the political scene. Franklin had not initially expected to write a work as a public manual for self-improvement and paean to America's possibilities for social mobility. He had set to write it in a moment of defeat and reflection, to re-gather himself, in an act both to shape his own memory for himself and for his son William, only later revising it for broader readership after the two men's estrangement. However, the version that we know as definitive did not appear in print for many years: Temple Franklin was Franklin's literary executor, and clearly did not take his grandfather's messages about discipline to heart, squandering twenty years before publishing an official edition. But as early as 1792, a French version was published in Paris, which then soon appeared in

London and then in America in re-translation – that is, from Franklin's original to the French and back to English. Even in that inelegant initial English form, the book became a publishing success on both sides of the Atlantic.

When Franklin had set down to write, he had referred to his written recollections as a memoir, but by the 1810s, it became the great archetype of a new genre perfectly fitting American culture. His was the first and in many ways the best of early American republic autobiographies, but far from the only one: autobiography was perhaps the most prevalent genre of published American book in the early decades of the nineteenth century. Here was a departure from memoir: the autobiography told a tale of individual striving rather than a series of picaresque adventures (though it might do that as well). The combination of cheaper paper, a growing population, increased literacy, wider book distribution networks, and eventually changes in printing technology provided for an explosion in the quantity of all sorts of books in the early republic, but especially in the writing, publishing, and reading of autobiographies. Those autobiographies tended to come in one of two flavors: on the one hand, the bitter tales of paupers, captives, slaves, and criminals, and on the other, sweet stories of hard-earned success. Historian Joyce Appleby analyzed hundreds of the sweeter variety written in the decades after independence by Americans who had grown up as U.S. citizens rather than as British subjects. She found several common patterns. Writers had egalitarian outlooks. Instead of recording in a passive tone and writing what happened to them, they wrote actively, as authors of both their biographies and their destinies. They believed in the possibilities of improving society. They were joiners, that is, they were civically active, participating in a great range of associations and organizations. They were sentimental in that they married for love and had deep emotional and often conflicted commitments to their children. Franklin's autobiography, of course, exhibited all these traits, and, given its widespread appearance in the 1790s, might well have been the template for many of them, thus becoming the genre's great exemplar.

Nonetheless, as several scholars have noted, for American intellectuals the 1790s Franklin remains less of a personage for admiration than a subject of disdain. Nian-Sheng Huang attributed this disapproval of Franklin to disapprobation of his character. Both Arthur Lee and especially John Adams had been greatly critical of Franklin's conduct in France. In the decades after Franklin's death, Adams continued to begrudgingly acknowledge Franklin's scientific achievements while demeaning his diplomatic and political ones. When as a seventeen year old, Franklin had fled Boston, he had brought his Puritan work discipline with him, as evidenced by his sayings in Poor Richard's almanac and by the virtues he listed in his autobiography. But he had left behind the Puritan desire for severe judgment of oneself and others. Not so John Adams. An appalled Adams perceived Franklin's flirting, socializing, and willingness to play the games of diplomacy as then practiced in Europe as both frivolous and intentional insincerity, all traits near the bottom of what Adams's list of desirable qualities would have been, had he written them down in Franklin style. Accordingly, Adams and many of the early writers of the revolution looked askance at Franklin as a revolutionary leader. This was especially true in the half century after independence, when character was the lens through which elite Americans looked at and wanted to project their revolutionary leaders and thus their models of republican citizenry. Furthermore, this view of insincerity lasted, not only in the Adams' clan, but also more broadly in many biographies and accounts of the revolutionary period. Ironically, more literary figures were critical of Franklin precisely because they took his words perhaps too literally. In an age in which first romanticism and then transcendentalism became the dominant modes of elite American literature and in which Franklin's *Way of Wealth* and *Autobiography* showed a practical man little interested in emotion, aesthetics, or spirituality, Franklin's literary critics dismissed him as a pied piper of the money-grubbing, literal-minded coarseness that for them pervaded American society – a thread that would wend its way into the twentieth century through the writings of Thoreau, Melville, Henry Adams, and D.H. Lawrence. Especially among the northeastern elite, Franklin's reputation remained at a low for the first half of the nineteenth century.

Uniquely among the founders, Franklin's personae as artisan printer, author, and self-made man ensured that he would be remembered by the common people differently from the way he was by the elite. To some extent, Franklin made sure of that himself. In his will, Franklin dedicated part of his considerable estate to establishing funds in Boston and Philadelphia that could be lent to local tradesmen, funds that continued to be dispensed well into the twentieth century. Print workers in particular claimed him as their patron saint. Notably, the people who worked the presses latched onto Franklin's heritage no less than those owned them. There is some evidence that Franklin may have silently approved of a strike of print workers in Philadelphia in 1786, and an organization primarily of the men who participated in the strike formed a "Franklin Society," which began meeting before Franklin's death and continued well into the 1790s. Although there are no surviving written sources directly implicating Franklin in support of print workers, given how small a fraternity it was in the early republic, word spread diffusing them of his sympathetic stance would certainly have been inspiring. Print workers organized the Franklin Typographical Society of Journeymen Printers in New York in 1799, eventually followed by a Franklin Typographical Society in Boston and more societies in other cities. These were benevolent associations – that is, partly social fraternities but most importantly functioning as self-funded insurance institutions. Here workingmen could follow Franklin's example of forming civic associations as well as following in his footsteps by setting type. Although played down in the many hagiographies of Franklin for much of the nineteenth century, the memory of Franklin as someone who had worked with his hands made him unique among the founders and particularly attractive to printers' organizations, especially those that would eventually function as unions. As the city counterpoint to Jefferson, that farmers' champion, and the strivers' answer to Paine, the radical idol, Franklin would be adopted by white, urban tradesmen as the founder who had actually worked with his own hands.

Press owners and their well-to-do peers better appreciated and celebrated Franklin's entrepreneurial acumen. In many cities, by the 1830s associations of printers began feting his birthday as the focus of their yearly gatherings. The toasting of Franklin and celebration of his life became rituals that cemented printers' commonalities despite their competition with each other and their political and ethnic differences. They could thereby tie themselves into the founding of the nation through their association with one of its most illustrious figures. For printers Franklin was the founder who kept on giving, in ways that further ensured Franklin's exposure to new generations of readers. Just as Franklin's *Autobiography* was reprinted over a hundred times, thus testifying to its continued ability to generate revenue for printers, the many editions of his *Way to Wealth* and the various iterations of *Poor Richard's Almanack* provided steady revenue throughout the nineteenth century. These books held little attraction for the elite, except perhaps in their serving as examples to others further down the social ladder. The *Way to Wealth* by title and content and Franklin's *Autobiography* were unabashed paeans to wealth accumulation and hard work as values in and of themselves. As Allan Kulikoff has noted, the primary appeal here lay among not laborers, for whom "wealth" was probably not a realistic expectation, but rather among ambitious middle-class readers as a guidebook for and an endorsement of their strivings in the marketplace and in civic life.

Franklin's character or stature as a revolutionary and as an exemplary American spread geographically as the nation grew. Perhaps no greater evidence of this remains than the number of places named after him from the revolution onwards. Place names (state, county, municipal, and streets) followed a few general patterns: In Ohio, for example, as in other states, places were often named after Native American monikers for local geography or people (Wapakoneta and Ottawa), celebrating events and places at the time associated with democracy (Lima, Delphos), in recognition of places left behind (North Baltimore and Bowling Green), and for contemporary or historical national heroes (Fremont and Franklin). Franklin was also one of only three revolutionary figures whose names graced a state (the other two were Washington and Jefferson). However, like Jefferson's ill-fated namesake, Franklin's was stillborn: Carved out of what was then western North Carolina in 1785, the State of Franklin lasted only a couple of years before being reabsorbed. But from the 1790s onward, citizens in nearly every state would name places after him. Today, nearly half the states – twenty three – have a county or parish bearing his name (there is also a Franklin county in Idaho not named after Benjamin), trailing only Washington (thirty) and Jefferson (twenty five). Most of these counties are east of the Mississippi and were established before the Civil War, that is, during the same period when Franklin's reputation suffered most among novelists and historians but when more plebeian New Englanders were migrating west in large numbers. The same is true of municipalities, with at least forty six named after Franklin, liberally sprinkled throughout the union, but again mostly established in the first half of the nineteenth century and again the majority east of the Mississippi – intriguingly, half a dozen of them being small towns in Wisconsin. Hundreds of towns showed their patriotism and affinity for the founders by naming streets after the revolutionary heroes, and in those places, Franklin was nearly invariably included as worthy of recognition. In this way, Franklin's memory has became, and still is, part of the daily landscape for a large proportion of Americans.

If Americans were not looking around to find Franklin, they could touch him by reaching into their wallets or their pockets. Regardless of what appeared to be a federal snubbing at Franklin's death, the federal government soon produced tacit, tangible evidence of Franklin's inclusion in the founding myth already being generated. As Carla Mulford has detailed, the U.S. Mint, a federal agency, issued some of the first Franklin medals. Thus began of a flood of medals and tokens portraying Franklin to be given as tokens or used as awards for a variety of purposes. Meanwhile, Franklin's appearance on hundreds of banknotes showed the degree to which bankers, and, they hoped, their customers associated the man with frugality, industry, and respectability. From the 1780s through 1865, banks rather than the federal government printed money. Although the first and second Bank of the United States worked as the banker of the federal government, and some states had analogous institutions, nearly all banks were primarily run as businesses to supply credit and to generate dividends for their stockholders. The vast majority of them were also incorporated by specific acts of legislature by the state in which they operated, and while many were in big cities, by the 1830s most counties could boast at least one local bank or, in a few states, a branch of a major state bank. By 1820, there were over 260 banks; by 1840, over 700; and in 1860, over 1,300. In their desire to distinguish themselves from their considerable competition, to project an image of patriotism and stolidity, and to stay one step ahead of counterfeiters, the banks printed thousands of notes. As antiquarian John Muscalus later catalogued, Franklin appeared on at least 400 of those notes. Muscalus organized his listing by state rather than by date; nonetheless, his data show that bankers across the country, especially in the east and old northwest, believed that including an image of Franklin on their notes would bring positive associations in the mind of the public, especially at a time when banks constantly strove to show that they were indeed solid and solvent institutions.

Further pushing Franklin irrevocably into the popular pantheon of American founders, Americans could also find Franklin in their mail, as another federal agency implicitly made Franklin an official national icon. As with printing, writing, and science, the postal system was yet another area of endeavor in which Franklin's participation in the nation's founding meshed with his other activities to enhance both in the public mind. Franklin's postal experience began with his being appointed postmaster of Philadelphia in 1737; from 1753 to 1774 he served as joint postmaster general for the colonies, introducing innovations such as the penny post, having riders carry mail not only by day but also by night, allowing all newspapers to go through the mail, and measuring distances between post offices. In July 1775, he was appointed first postmaster of the United States, a post he held until his mission to France led to his replacement. The United States Postal System adopted Franklin as its own founding father. Despite the protestations otherwise, as an independent nation the United States continued to look to Britain for institutional precedent for much of the nineteenth century, and in 1840 the British postal system introduced the first postage stamp, referred to as the "penny black" for its cost and color, and, as was the style with coinage, the stamp bore Queen Victoria's profile. The stamps were soon issued in red rather than black, for the very practical reason that black cancellations stood out better against the red background. In 1847, the United States followed suit. Having no monarch, and wanting to avoid the monarchical undertones of issuing stamps with the sitting president, the postal service decided that the first stamps it would issue would show the likenesses of two men beyond reproach: Washington, foremost among the nation's founders; and Franklin, founder of the post office, in red and in green. Franklin has since appeared on more stamps than any other person besides Washington.

Meanwhile, by molding Franklin into the apotheosis of the American self-made man, his many nineteenth-century hagiographers put their versions of his life story to nationalistic work. Indeed, by the nation's centennial Franklin had already begun to become in popular writing the first true American, exhibiting all the traits that admiring and aspiring writers wanted to project over the nation. Beginning with works such as Mason Locke Weems's *Life of Benjamin Franklin* in 1818 to the writings of Amos Taylor, Robert Thomas, Silas Felton, Samuel Griswold Goodrich, and more than a score of others stretching through the 1800s, chronicles of Franklin's life appearing in books for adults, readers for children, in serials, in trade journals, and in newspaper columns, all testifying qualities that marked him as worth emulating in order to be properly socialized into American society. Carla Mulford has argued that these highly stylized and highly complimentary chronicles of Franklin's life were intended to serve as instructive examples to children, to men on the make, and to immigrants as a way of molding them into American citizens. Between Franklin's *Way to Wealth* and the *Autobiography*, on the one hand, and homilies from Franklin's life (most based on his life, some not) on the other hand, popular writers crafted a Franklin who was less a man and more an idealized statue. As with other founders, this Franklin was male and Anglo-Saxon. He was a proponent of liberty, or, more precisely, national liberty, although Franklin's late-in-life embracement of the abolition of slavery was soft-pedaled or entirely elided. He was practical, thus fulfilling the American gendered self-image in comparison with effeminate Europeans. Franklin's hand in establishing so many civic institutions in Philadelphia became an ideal civic model for men in towns, with cities springing up all over the west as they struggled to establish civic societies amid spectacular population growth and with little state or federal help. Weems's Washington might have been useful for teaching children to be honest, but Washington's service as a general did not provide transferable examples for everyday living. By contrast, the Franklin that Franklin (in his *Autobiography*), Weem, and other writers profiled became the blueprint for the American man. Horatio Alger's novels delighted generations of schoolboys, but it was Franklin whom men such as Andrew Carnegie would credit as inspiring them to achieve the American dream.

At the turn of the twentieth century, a confluence of factors in popular American culture led to a transformation in Franklin portrayals from one of the overachieving Franklin to one closer to the one we would find familiar, the avuncular Franklin. Film, music, radio, and the rise of celebrity culture gave Americans the illusion that they were closer to illustrious figures. The content remained largely the same in terms of trumpeting his rise from escaped apprentice to master printer, his scientific and technological achievements, and his role in the nation's founding. The clearest index to this transformation can be measured in two ways, one nomenclatural and the other sartorial. First, sometime no later than the 1870s, the illustrious "Dr" or "Benjamin" Franklin started being referred to as the personable, approachable "Ben" Franklin. That other historical figures underwent the same phenomenon demonstrates how pervasive was the urge to humanize previously untouchable figures: Thomas Jefferson became "Tom," as did Thomas Paine, notwithstanding a complete lack of evidence that either went by such a nickname. Before then, most mentions of "Ben" had been in reference to him as a boy, although not all – one of the first steamboats on the Ohio River was christened *Ben Franklin*. Nonetheless, increasingly, and in more formal settings, the use of "Ben" rather than "Dr" or "Benjamin" narrowed the distance between Franklin and early twentieth-century Americans. Also, whether in pictures or in prose, more and more, Franklin appeared wearing what became his signature accessory, the fur cap. As we know, Franklin's adoption of a fur cap in public occurred during his mission to France, when he found the French people's delighted reaction to it both amusing and useful. Painted soon after his arrival France, Charles Nicholas Cochin's portrait of Franklin as engraved by Augustine Saint Aubin, which pictured Franklin in a formless fur cap looking out from behind glasses, grew in popularity in comparison with other more formal portraits. Even in print, Franklin was being described more and more as wearing a fur cap, even in passages recounting his life before his French adventures.

In conjunction with this broader trend of informality and of the examination of politicians' and celebrities' personal lives and foibles came increased attention to Franklin's relationships with women. Several phenomena helped usher in this watershed for Franklin's memory. Although there had been White House whisperings and scandals before (Jefferson had been accused – accurately, as we now know – of fathering children with slave Sally Hemings, and Jackson's cabinet had been embroiled in the Eaton affair), the 1884 presidential race, in which Grover Cleveland publicly took responsibility for fathering an illegitimate child, marked a departure from previous national campaigns in its examination of a candidate's personal life. The yellow press, eager to drum up sales, was less reluctant than previous generations of newspapers to find sensational stories. For the first time, some individuals would be famous just for being famous: celebrities. In addition, new evidence concerning Franklin had come to light, and historians were willing to make more it. The publication of Abigail Adams's correspondence in 1841 first made available to the public her disgust for what she interpreted as Madame Helvétius's shocking behavior and seeming physical affection for Franklin, a passage that in the 1880s and 1890s multiple biographers took to quoting. Perhaps the most popular longer biography of Franklin at the time, Paul Leicester Ford's *The Many-Sided Franklin* (1899a), dedicated an entire chapter, "Franklin's relations with the fair sex," to Franklin and his dealings with women. Though they made clear that William Franklin was born before Franklin's common-law marriage to Deborah Read, turn-of-the-century biographers generally remained within the bounds of polite conjecture about Franklin's sex life given their late-Victorian audience and that their subject was still a revered founding father. Furthermore, rather than being critical of Franklin's abandoning his wife in Philadelphia during his long sojourns in England, they blamed her entirely for the separation, as she was claiming that she was reluctant to make the transatlantic crossing and surely would not have been as happily sociable as her husband. Nonetheless, the suggestion of Franklin as a sexual man, even if cloaked or slyly denied, further made him accessible as a human to Americans in comparison with the ever-distant Washington.

Throughout the twentieth century, Franklin continued to serve as an upstanding model of hard work, of saving, and of honesty at all points of the economic spectrum. If, as Calvin Coolidge averred in 1925, "the chief business of the American people is business," Franklin could fulfill a new role as a useful exemplar for government as well as commercial ventures and the clientele that they hoped to attract. In 1914, the U.S. Mint placed Franklin's image on the hundred dollar bill, thus assuring that the few Americans who could afford one would see his likeness. Both Edward Butler and Rupert H. Johnson valued what they perceived as Franklin's image of frugality, honesty, and prudence. The former hoped to attract common people to his "Ben Franklin" chain of Main Street five-and-dime stores that the Butler Brothers mail-order company launched in 1927. Johnson was a Wall Street mainstay who in 1947 labeled his new investment firm Franklin Templeton and chose "BEN" as his stock-ticker symbol. Associating with Franklin certainly did not hurt either business, as Ben Franklin eventually included nearly 2,000 franchises and Franklin Resources (Franklin Templeton's corporate parent) has continued to attract investors and survive stock-market shocks. Certainly neither soured Franklin's reputation for Hyrum R. Smith, who in 1984 sold the first "Franklin Planner," an organizational system named to evoke Franklin's steady habits and his penchant for carrying around a notebook. Sales eventually skyrocketed when Stephen Covey made the planners the basis of the best-selling *The Seven Habits of Highly Effective People* in 1989. Even more taken with Franklin, in 2000 Ellen Rohr founded "Benjamin Franklin, the Punctual Plumber," a plumbing services franchise company that, as Allan Kulikoff has noted, seeks to emulate Franklin in name (it calls its franchiser arm "the Junto") and in spirit (Rohr has a portrait of Franklin in her office, and channels him sometimes by modeling her conduct after how she believes he would act).

The diffusion of Franklin's memory through nearly the entire range of media – popular and elite, commercial and governmental – accelerated over the course of the twentieth century, accentuating earlier trends of greater informality, greater interest in Franklin's personality, highlighting his interactions with women, and underlining his versatility and success in a wide range of endeavors. Interestingly, in the age of the self-help book, Franklin's *Autobiography* draws modest attention in terms of how Franklin is portrayed, while his ingenuity has been more widely emphasized. All of these elements have come together in various combinations in the many fictionalizations of Franklin that have appeared on the page. As with many historical figures, Franklin's recent fictional life threatens to outshine his historical one. He has been a peripheral figure in fictional novels on board a ship on his way to be a diplomat to France and in London political intrigues regarding letters sent to the colonies, among others. But his most extensive set of fictional adventures for adults comes courtesy of the mystery genre. The most notable of these have been set in London rather than in Philadelphia, perhaps because of the legacy of Sherlock Holmes or perhaps because the imperial capital provides more possibilities for dark alleys, crime syndicates, and rain and fog. Donald Zochert's *Murder in the*

Hellfire Club (1978) has a reserved Franklin using his wits to track down a killer of devotees of a debauched sex group. Beginning in the late 1980s, historical fiction writer Robert Lee Hall launched a series of "Benjamin Franklin Mysteries," in which his fur-cap-wearing sleuth tracks down culprits with his fictional illegitimate son, Nick Handy. Both authors made sure to employ Franklin's expertise with electricity in a central dramatic element at a crucial moment. The use of Franklin in the detective genre suggests three particular elements in how writers and their readers imagine Franklin. First is the degree to which Franklin has become associated with science and experimentation. Franklin's application of practical logic is necessary to any would-be detective. Secondly, Franklin must interact with people at all social levels, which is plausible because of readers' knowledge of his having been an apprentice, a business owner, and eventually a diplomat. Finally, Franklin is remembered as being interested in women, whether for flirting or more physical interaction.

That interest in women has been the most signal development in changing perceptions of Franklin over the past half-century. Academics have always gone to great lengths to argue that Franklin's flirtations were just that, and that he did not have sexual relations with any of the many women with whom he had very forward correspondence and conversation. And yet, the popular perception is that Franklin undoubtedly had many sexual dalliances. The image of Franklin as practical, versatile, and interested in women has become even more exaggerated on stage and on the screen than it has been on the page – as has the notion that much of Franklin's conversation consisted of Poor Richard's maxims. This persona pervades both high-minded productions as well as more standard popular fare. The moderately successful 1964 Broadway musical *Ben Franklin in Paris*, starring Robert Preston in the title role, had Franklin dropping *bon mots* – some of Franklin's original words and others clearly of more recent vintage to suit early 1960s American musical theater – and successfully pursuing his diplomatic ends by wooing a courtier who has the ear of Louis XVI. Howard Da Silva played Franklin in the hit 1969 Broadway musical and 1972 movie *1776* as the resident wise man and cheery dispenser of maxims and jokes. The *Washington Post* celebrated the 200th anniversary of his death in 1990 with an article detailing the loves of what its headline called "the founding flirt." More recent portrayals have been no different. In HBO's 2008 lavishly-funded *John Adams* miniseries, actor Tom Wilkinson plays Franklin as one part wise man, one part wisecracker, and one part Lothario. Portrayed in a very unflattering light – the miniseries does, after all, offer an Adams-eye view of the world – Franklin offers suggestive puns, and Madame Helvétius on first meeting Abigail Adams immediately volunteers that Franklin has proposed marriage to her several times, to which Abigail remarks, "an inconvenience to Mrs Franklin, surely." It is an odd choice for the scriptwriters, given their protestations of historical accuracy and

Deborah Franklin's death over a decade before the reputed scene takes place, unless they were trying to demonstrate what they considered as Franklin's infidelity.

These interpretations go beyond productions showing Franklin in eighteenth-century context, demonstrating just how deeply the impression has stuck. In a February 2000 episode of the intentionally anachronistic and campy television adventure-comedy *Jack of All Trades*, set in 1801 on a fictional island in the East Indies, title character Jack Stiles and his sidekick Amelia rescue a kidnapped Ben Franklin, who seems at least as interested in Amelia's décolletage as he is in the electric submarine she has invented to spring him from the ship where he is being held. Seven years later, the popular sitcom *The Office* aired an episode entitled "Ben Franklin." In a loony effort to ensure gender equality, office supervisor Michael Scott decides that to justify hiring a female stripper for an in-office bachelor party, another male stripper must be brought in too for a bridal party. But to thwart Michael, office worker Jim Halpert instead calls the "Scholastic Speakers of Pennsylvania" and orders a Franklin impersonator. This conceit works both because the show takes place outside of Philadelphia and because, when he appears, the women can plausibly think of Franklin as not only a historical figure but also one with a sexual persona. And when the ersatz Franklin talks about his inventions, the women hone in on other matters. "Do you have girlfriends in Paris, a lot of them?" Pam asks, to which Franklin answers, "That is a gray area of my life." She persists by asking him whether he wears "boxers, briefs, or pantaloons," to which he replies, "You're very saucy." And later in the episode, Franklin approaches Pam in a plainly lascivious tone.

Not surprisingly, Franklin's sexuality has been a subject of considerable fodder for the greatest media sink of all matters sexual, the internet. Much of it is laughable, and meant to be. One series of comic animated shorts on Youtube, "Sy Waxer: Time Traveler," features an episode titled "Ben Franklin Sex Tapes." Set in 2810, the title character goes back in time to give Franklin a belt to facilitate time-travel so that Franklin can rewrite the Bill of Rights. Instead, he becomes "our pounding father," the inventor of the sex tape, a specimen of which features Franklin, mercifully offscreen, with various famous women from U.S. history.[4] On the urbandictionary.com website, the phrase "Ben Franklin" is defined in various ways, most notably as someone eager to have sex with any partner.[5] The "uncyclopedia.com," a parody of Wikipedia, includes a number of fake Franklin quotations categorized by topic ("Franklin on Economics," "Franklin on War," "Franklin on God," etc.); the lengthy list of "Franklin on Sex" quotations begins with, "Yes please!" and ends with "I am required by law to let you know, I am a registered sex offender ...," with various wittier but less printable ones in between.[6] Other offerings meant to be more serious indicate the degree to which many people do perceive Franklin to have been very sexually active. Some of it is inspired by Franklin's own "Advice to a Young Man on the Choice of a Mistress" (1745). Notably, the interest in Franklin's sexual life crosses contemporary gender boundaries, with "Advice" being quoted or linked to in online venues attracting and catering mostly to men, e.g., bodybuilding.com.[7] One discussion board specifically dedicated to women's discussions about sex and sexual relationships (though not sexually explicit) includes the text of "Advice," and many discussants clearly assumed that Franklin had many sexual relationships. A typical post rhetorically asked "was he not infamous for debauching his Young serving wenches?"[8] One site intended to combat the deification of American political figures goes too far in the other direction, making the wild claim that "Visitors would often arrive to find Ben Franklin having sex with a parlor maid."[9] Multiple Amazon.com customers' reviews of the *John Adams* miniseries refer to Franklin's sexual activity as a given.

This is not to say that every depiction of Franklin begins and ends with sexuality. More than Washington or Jefferson, the image of Franklin as versatile, ingenious, and industrious– as well as, more recently, a rediscovery of his opposition to slavery – has also made him a favorite subject for children on the page and on the screen. Kids have been treated to many fictional takes on a logical, cheerful, good-humored, and patient Ben Franklin. None has been more longer-lived and broadly read than writer and artist Robert Lawson's 1939 *Ben and Me*, which has gone through dozens of printings, and in 2005, under the theme of "Freedom," it was one of fifteen books selected by the National Endowment for the Humanities as part of its annual "We the People" program to distribute exemplary American children's books to public libraries. Coming on the heels of the success of Lawson's *Revere and I*, a tale of the collaboration between Paul Revere and his horse, *Ben and Me* features a mouse name Amos who is the real brains behind a well meaning and industrious but also bumbling Franklin. Lawson's Franklin wears his fur cap all the time from 1745 onward. Disney's 1953, twenty-minute animated adaptation of *Ben and Me* for the big screen focused primarily on the mouse behind the man, but, like the 1954 Warner Brothers animated short *Yankee Doodle Bugs*, it emphasizes Franklin's kite experiment. Ingenuity and experimentation are central to many of the children's books concerning Franklin, both non-fiction and historical fiction, treating his activities as printer, inventor, founding father, and even as mathematician, such as in Frank Murphy's *Ben Franklin and the Magic Squares* (2001). Franklin's range of accomplishments was the prime reason that television producer Kevin O'Donnell specifically chose Franklin as the central adult in the 2002, 40-part PBS animated series *Liberty's Kids*. Voiced by Walter Cronkite, here a gentle, wise, and avuncular Franklin is celebrated for his contributions to science, to the postal service, to Philadelphia, to music (in his invention of the glass harmonica) as well as to the cause of the American Revolution.

Over the past decade, the memory of Franklin like others of his cohort has been rejuvenated in what *Newsweek* reporter Evan Thomas dubbed in 2001 "founders chic," launched by David McCullouch's massive and million-selling biography *John Adams*. The thirst for new treatments of the founding generation can be attributed to disillusion with current politicians combined with the more comforting delusion that these founding politicians were more pure of heart and wiser than today's variety, especially among conservatives looking to the national founding for contemporary political and cultural authority. Although Evans actually only mentioned Franklin in passing in that article – typically, relating an anecdote about one of Franklin's quips – bestselling books and ratings-garnering documentaries about Washington, Jefferson, Adams, and Franklin, together and separately, have re-catapulted Franklin into the national consciousness again in the context of his "founding brothers," as the title of Joseph Ellis's 2000 prizewinning account called them. In November 2002, PBS aired its lavish, three-part documentary *Benjamin Franklin*, billed with the tagline "An Extraordinary Life, An Electric Mind." The miniseries frames Franklin as a man born only fifteen years after the Salem witch trials but dying on the edge of modernity, and being responsible as much as anyone for America's transformation from a world of superstition and tradition to one of reason, innovation, and meritocracy. The A&E network followed in 2004 with an installment in its biography franchise with *Benjamin Franklin: Citizen of the World*. Scholars H.W. Brands, Edmund Morgan, and David Waldstreicher have produced notable biographies of Franklin aimed at non-scholarly audiences. Morgan's was on the *New York Times* bestseller list already in 2003 when former *Time* manager editor and CNN executive Walter Isaacson's *Benjamin Franklin: An American Life* appeared and surpassed it, selling over a half-million copies in less than a year. Helping launch Isaacson's book, *Time* dedicated its July 7, 2003 issue to, as its cover blared, "The Amazing Adventures of Ben Franklin." Edited editions of his quotations and wisdom still pour forth and sell, from serious efforts like a Library of America editions of his writings (first printed in 1987, reprinted in 1997, and still selling well) to the continually brisk-selling *Fart Proudly: Writings of Benjamin Franklin You Never Learned in School*. As a topic of individual interest, Franklin continues to fascinate.

Franklin's newfound "founders chic" popularity stems from more than a fascination with his many achievements and with his droll personality (if it was indeed droll): In a multicultural age, Franklin's late-in-life opposition to slavery puts him in what is perceived as favorable light compared with fellow founders who went to the grave as slaveholders. As David Waldstreicher writes in his essay in this volume, Franklin contributed little to the actual ending of slavery and only advocated abolition once he no longer happened to have slaves, and even that in Pennsylvania, which had already enacted a gradual abolition law. The early twenty-first century is not the first time

Franklin's abolitionist credentials have been touted. Some nineteenth-century abolitionists, too, claimed him as one of their own. Frederick Douglass counted Franklin among other founders such as Washington and Jefferson as recognizing slavery's evils. But as in so many other ways, not all abolitionists agreed with this. Prominent New York abolitionist Lewis Tappan publicly claimed Franklin as a distant relative and identified with him as a fellow self-made man, but cited the constitution in denying that anyone of the founding generation was truly dedicated to instant and universal abolition. Within a few decades that part of his legacy had been forgotten: Carl Van Doren's Pulitzer prize-winning 1938 biography mentions Franklin's abolitionism only once in passing. In the past decade however, in contrast to Washington's failure to release his slaves while he was alive and the overwhelming evidence scholar Annette Gordon-Reed uncovered demonstrating Thomas Jefferson's longtime sexual relationship with slave Sally Hemings, Franklin's having been president of the Pennsylvania Society for the Promoting the Abolition of Slavery has been seized upon as a way to further lionize him. The desire to paint a racially egalitarian Franklin appears most on screen, especially on PBS, which includes multiculturalism as one of its programming tenets. Thus, although *Liberty's Kids* opens in 1773, its free black character Moses had sought out Franklin to work for because of Franklin's reputation as opposing slavery, and its *Benjamin Franklin* documentary considers abolition to be Franklin's "last crusade," an odd image for a man wearied with age and gout that nonetheless portrays him as an admirable model for contemporary Americans.

The range of ways in which institutions continue to memorialize, honor, or claim Franklin testify to the ways that American memory of him reflects a conception of the man as multifaceted, as well how an association with Franklin has been and is perceived as gaining purchase on cultural legitimacy. Businesses are not the only organizations to claim Franklin in one way or another. Least surprisingly, the Philadelphia institutions that he had a hand in founding continuing to carry on their projection of Franklin's legacy, especially the American Philosophical Society, the Library Company of Philadelphia, and the University of Pennsylvania, each of which continues to include Franklin images, statues, and memorabilia in its public and physical presences. But more interesting is the multiplicity of other groups that have adopted Franklin for his honor and their own. Promoting and legitimizing their various pursuits, Americans have inducted Franklin into no fewer than a dozen halls of fame. Some of these are well-established institutions, such as the International Swimming Hall of Fame, the Insurance Hall of Fame, the U.S. Chess Hall of Fame, and the World Kite Museum Hall of Fame. Some are lesser known (the Cooperative Hall of Fame) while others either are grasping at straws – the web only "Self-Publishing Hall of Fame" – or are of the tongue-in-cheek variety, like the Geek Hall of Fame, which appears to exist solely for the purpose of selling colorful T-shirts and mugs of historical figures. Still more people and groups find Franklin's name recognition useful for other purposes. In 1979, psychological researchers coined the "Ben Franklin effect" based on the Franklin quotation, "He that has once done you a Kindness will be more ready to do you another, than he whom you yourself have obliged." The phenomena is that someone who has done someone a favor is more likely to do that person another favor than the other person is to do the first person a favor, and the same goes for negative behavior. Given children's familiarity with Franklin, the federal government has enlisted Franklin to serve as the host of its internet site "Ben's Guide to the U.S. Government for Kids" to inform children about the workings of federal agencies.

Franklin not only continues to be remembered deeply, in terms of continually being a subject of books, documentaries, television shows, and movies, but also broadly across most sectors of the American population, and that interest shows no sign of abating soon. A recent survey of 2,000 U.S. high school students and 2,000 American-born adults asked them to list the ten most famous Americans, not including presidents and their wives. Franklin appeared on thirty seven per cent of the adults' lists – more than any other figure, and one of only two from the eighteenth century (the other being Betsy Ross). Furthermore, although the lists of respondents diverged somewhat by race, Franklin was the only white person among the five most-often named people among both white and black adults. And while high school students reported a somewhat different pantheon than adults, they did not do so at the expense of Franklin. Lest anyone fear that he will slip out of the public mind, Franklin was fifth on the students' lists, appearing on twenty-nine per cent of them, and was the only one whose primary accomplishments came before the mid-nineteenth century. That results not only from the specific books and movies dedicated to him, but also from the way his name and face have dissolved through American culture in ways that have become so familiar as to seem naturalized. He makes cameo appearances on *The Simpsons* and *The Colbert Report*. Movie and television characters bear his name, like Benjamin Franklin Pierce of *M*A*S*H* on the big and small screen and Benjamin Franklin Gates of the recent *National Treasure* blockbuster movie franchise. People refer to one hundred dollar bills as "benjamins" and "ben franklins" in slang and in crime movies and novels. Billboards showing his likeness and celebrating his ingenuity grace some of the nation's highways as part of a public service campaign to promote values in American life. He graces the walls of school classrooms, some of which are in the thousands of American public schools named after him. Just as he loved gadgets and media, they love him: as of June, 2010, there were twenty-one iPod apps featuring Franklin, more than half of them e-books of his autobiography, a few of them e-books about him, but also collections of quotations and one focusing on his of virtues. Franklin remains an icon firmly planted in the national consciousness.

The grand 2006 commemorations of the 300th anniversary of Franklin's birth, and the way it was celebrated suggests that Walter Isaacson is not alone in asserting that Franklin, or at least how we remember him, is a man for our time. In 2005, Congress authorized the Department of the Interior to release funds to Philadelphia's Franklin Institute to spruce up the Benjamin Franklin National Memorial in that city in preparation for the big event. There were celebrations and speeches in Philadelphia and by the many surviving institutions in which he had a hand. Franklin and Marshall College (named for him, of course) and the Phillips Museum of Art collaborated on a website of resources dedicated to the great array of extant artifacts that Franklin used or possessed and publicizing the traveling exhibition of many of those artifacts. Social observer and columnist David Brooks, looking out over the service-industry ex-urban sprawl at the turn of the twenty-first century and considering Franklin's zest for practical innovation, talent for making a buck, and lack of existential introspection, suggested that "if office parks and the people in them do indeed set the tone for American life over the next century, then we're going to have to regard Benjamin Franklin as the real father of our country."[10] Where the next century will take Franklin's memory may be beyond the reckoning of historians, but as this look at Franklin's memory indicates, they are not the only ones guiding themselves by looking into their rear-view mirrors.

Notes

1 Anonymous (1874). *American Historical Record* 3(25), 13–15.
2 John Adams to Benjamin Rush, April 4, 1790.
3 Thomas Jefferson to Benjamin Rush, "Letter," October 4, 1803. Available at: http://memory.loc.gov/cgi-bin/query/r?ammem/mtj:@field(DOCID+@lit(tj100017)).
4 *Sy Waxer: Time Traveler–Ben Franklin Sex Tapes*, 2008. Available at: http://www.youtube.com/watch?v=ft1B2j7bimA&feature=youtube_gdata
5 "Ben Franklin," *Urban Dictionary*, n.d. Available at: http://www.urbandictionary.com/define.php?term=ben+franklin.
6 "Unquotable: Benjamin Franklin," *Uncyclopedia*, n.d. Available at: http://uncyclopedia.wikia.com/wiki/Unquotable:Benjamin_Franklin.
7 "Benjamin Franklin, Advice to a Young Man on the Choice of a Mistress (1745)," *Bodybuilding.com*, January 26, 2009. Available at: http://forum.bodybuilding.com/showthread.php?t=113690521.
8 "Benjamin Franklin, Advice to a Young Man on the Choice of a Mistress (1745)," *Tribes Forum: Ask a Sexy Woman Anything*, February 11, 2008. Available at: http://askasexywomananything.tribe.net.
9 Tony Banks, "American History XXX," *American History*, 2001. Available at: http://www.loompanics.com/Articles/AmericanHistory.html.
10 David Brooks, "Our Founding Yuppie; Ben Franklin's America," *The Weekly Standard*, October 23, 2000.

Further Reading

Bernstein, R.B. (2009). *The Founding Fathers Reconsidered*, 1st edn. New York, NY: Oxford University Press.

Bodzin, Eugene Saul (1969). *The American Popular Image of Benjamin Franklin, 1790–1868*. Ph.D. dissertation, University of Wisconsin, Madison, WI.

Kammen, Michael G. (1978). *A Season of Youth: The American Revolution and the Historical Imagination*, 1st edn. New York, NY: Knopf.

Mulford, Carla, and Huang, Nian-Sheng (2008). "Benjamin Franklin and the American dream," in *The Cambridge Companion to Benjamin Franklin*, ed. Mulford, Carla. New York, NY: Cambridge University Press, pp. 145–158.

Schocket, Andrew M. (2010). "Little founders on the small screen: Interpreting a multicultural American revolution for children's television," *Journal of American Studies* 45: 145–163.

Thomas, Evan. (2001). "Founders chic: Live from Philadelphia," *Newsweek* July 9.

Waldstreicher, David (2002). "Founders chic as culture war," *Radical History Review* 84: 185–194.

Bibliography

Adams, John (1850–1856). *The Works of John Adams, Second President of the United States*, C.F. Adams, ed., 10 vols. Boston, MA.

Adams, John (1790). *Letter to Benjamin Rush*, April 4. Adams to Rush. April 4, 1790 in Alexander Biddle ed. *Old Family Letters*. Philadephia (1892), p. 55.

Agamben, Giorgio (2005). *State of Exception*. Translated by Kevin Attell. Chicago, IL.

Aldridge, Alfred Owen (1957). *Franklin and his French Contemporaries*. New York, NY.

Aldridge, Alfred Owen (1962). "Benjamin Franklin and the *Pennsylvania Gazette*," *Proceedings of the American Philosophical Society* 106: 77–81.

Aldridge, Alfred Owen (1965). *Benjamin Franklin: Philosopher & Man*. Philadelphia, PA.

Aldridge, Alfred Owen (1967a). *Benjamin Franklin and Nature's God*. Durham, NC.

Aldridge, Alfred Owen (1967b). "Form and substance in Franklin's autobiography," in Ghodes, ed. (1967).

Aldridge, Alfred Owen (1972). "Polly Baker and Boccaccio," *Annali Instituto Universitario Orientale* 14: 5–18.

Aldridge, Alfred Owen (2004). "Feeling or fooling in Benjamin Franklin's 'The Elysian Fields'," *Early American Literature* 39: 121–128.

Almon, J., ed. (1971). *A Collection of Papers Relative to the Dispute between Great Britain and America, 1764–1775*. New York, NY.

Amacher, Richard E. (1962). *Benjamin Franklin*. New York, NY.

Amory, H. and Hall, D.D., eds (2000). *A History of the Book in America*, vol. 1. *The Colonial Book in the Atlantic World*. Cambridge, England.

Anderson, B. (1991). *Imagined Communities: Reflections on the Origin and Spread of Nationalism*, 2nd edn. London.

A Companion to Benjamin Franklin, First Edition. Edited by David Waldstreicher.
© 2011 Blackwell Publishing Ltd. Published 2011 by Blackwell Publishing Ltd.

Anderson, B. (2006). *Imagined Communities: Reflections on the Origin and Spread of Nationalism*, 3rd edn. New York, NY.
Anderson, D. (1997). *The Radical Enlightenments of Benjamin Franklin.* Baltimore, MD.
Anderson, D.A. (1983). "The Origins of the Press Clause," *UCLA Law Review* 30: 455–541.
Anderson, Fred (2000). *Crucible of War: The Seven Years' War and the Fate of Empire in British North America, 1754–1766.* New York, NY.
Andrews, William, ed. (1990). *Journeys in New Worlds: Early American Women's Narratives.* Madison, WI.
Angoff, Charles (1931). *A Literary History of the American People.* New York, NY.
Anonymous (1874). *American Historical Record* 3(25), 13–15.
Anonymous (1939). *Dr. Benj. Franklin and the Ladies: Being Various Letters, Essays, Satires to and about the Fair Sex.* Mount Vernon, NY.
Appadurai, Arjun, ed. (1986). *The Social Life of Things: Commodities in Cultural Perspective.* New York, NY.
Appleby, Joyce Oldham (2000). *Inheriting the Revolution: The First Generation of Americans.* Cambridge, MA.
Appleby, Joyce (2001). "The vexed story of capitalism told by American historians," *Journal of the Early Republic* 31: 1–18.
Appleby, Joyce (2009). *The Relentless Revolution: A History of Capitalism.* New York, NY.
Apter, Emily and Pietz, William (1993). *Fetishism as Cultural Discourse.* Ithaca, NY.
Arendt, Hannah (1959). *The Human Condition.* Chicago, IL.
Armitage, David (2007). *The Declaration of Independence: A Global History.* Cambridge, MA.
Augst, T. and Carpenter, K. eds (2007). *Institutions of Reading: The Social Life of Libraries in the United States.* Amherst, MA.
Baetier, Katherine (2003). "Benjamin Franklin's daughter," *Metropolitan Museum Journal* 38: 160–181.
Bailyn, Bernard (1967). *The Ideological Origins of the American Revolution.* Cambridge, MA.
Bailyn, Bernard (1968). *The Origins of American Politics.* New York, NY.
Bailyn, Bernard (1974). *The Ordeal of Thomas Hutchinson.* Cambridge, MA.
Bailyn, Bernard (2000). "Slavery and population growth in colonial New England," in Peter Temin ed. *Engines of Enterprise: Am Economic History of New England.* Cambridge, MA, pp. 253–260.
Bailyn, Bernard (2003). *To Begin the World Anew: The Genius and Ambiguities of the American Founders.* New York, NY.
Baker, Ira L. (1977). "Elizabeth Timothy: America's first woman editor," *Journalism Quarterly* 54: 280–285.
Baker, Jennifer Jordan (2000). "Benjamin Franklin's *Autobiography* and the credibility of personality," *Early American Literature* 35: 274–294.
Baker, Jennifer Jordan (2005). *Securing the Commonwealth.* Baltimore, MD.

Baldasty, G.J. (1976). "Toward an understanding of the first amendment: Boston newspapers, 1782–1791," *Journalism History* 3: 25–30, 32.
Baldwin, Ida H. (1941). "His mother's kindred," *Americana* 35: 7–32, 276–318, 497–551, 673–735.
Balestra, Gianfranca and Sampietro, Luigi, eds (1993). *Benjamin Franklin: An American Genius*. Rome.
Bancroft, George. (1875). *The History of the United States*. Boston, MA.
Banks, Tony (2001). "American history XXX," *American History*. Available at: http://www.loompanics.com/Articles/AmericanHistory.html.
Barbour, Brian M., ed. (1979). *Benjamin Franklin: A Collection of Critical Essays*. Englewood Cliffs, NJ.
Barbour, Hugh and Frost J. William (1988). *The Quakers*. Westport, CT.
Barnes, T.W. (1884). *Memoir of Thurlow Weed*. Boston, MA.
Barry, Jonathan and Brooks, Christopher, eds (1994). *The Middling Sort of People: Culture, Society, and Politics in England, 1550–1800*. New York, NY.
Bauman, Richard (1983). *Let Your Words be Few. Symbolism of Speaking and Silence among Seventeenth-Century Quakers*. Cambridge, England.
Beard, C.A. (1913). *An Economic Interpretation of the Constitution of the United States*. New York, NY.
Becker, Carl L. (1931). "Benjamin Franklin," in *Dictionary of American Biography* 3: 144.
Beers, Henry Augustin (1899). *Initial Studies in American Letters*. Cleveland, OH.
Beidler, Philip D. (1981–1982). "The 'Author' of Franklin's autobiography," *Early American Literature* 16(3): 257–269.
Bell, Daniel. (1976). *The Cultural Contradictions of Capitalism*. New York, NY: Basic Books.
Bell, Whitfield J. (1956). "'All clear sunshine:' New letters of Franklin and Mary Stevenson Hewson," *Proceedings of the American Philosophical Society* 100: 521–536.
Bellah, R.N., Madsen, Richard, Sullivan, William M., Swidler, Ann and Tipton Stephen M. (1985). *Habits of the Heart: Individualism and Commitment in American Life*. New York, NY.
Bemis, Samuel Flagg (1957). *The Diplomacy of the American Revolution*. Bloomington, IN.
"Ben Franklin." *Urban Dictionary*, n.d. Available at: http://www.urbandictionary.com/define.php?term=ben+franklin.
Ben-Atar, Doron S. (1998). "Nationalism, neo-mercantilism, and diplomacy: Rethinking the Franklin mission," *Diplomatic History* 22: 101–114.
Ben-Atar, Doron S. (2004). *Trade Secrets: Intellectual Piracy and the Origins of American Industrial Power*. New Haven, CT.
Bender, Thomas, ed. (1993). *The Antislavery Debate*. Berkeley, CA.
"Benjamin Franklin, advice to a young man on the choice of a mistress (1745)," *Tribes Forum: Ask a Sexy Woman Anything*, February 11, 2008. Available at: http://askasexywomananything.tribe.net/thread/fb1cbad5–58a9–4fff-9235–60efa9c8be07.

"Benjamin Franklin, advice to a young man on the choice of a mistress (1745)," *Bodybuilding.com*, January 26, 2009. Available at: http://forum.bodybuilding.com/showthread.php?t=113690521.

Bercovitch, Sacvan (1975). *Puritan Origins of the American Self.* New Haven, CT.

Bercovitch, Sacvan, ed. (1986). *Reconstructing American Literary History.* Cambridge, MA.

Bessel, Richard, Rendall, Jane and Guyatt, Nicholas, eds. (2010). *War, Empire and Slavery, 1770–1830.* Houndmills, England.

Bezis-Selfa, John (2004). *American Crucible: Adventurers, Ironworkers, and the Struggle to Forge an Industrious Revolution.* Ithaca, NY.

Bigelow, J., ed. (1868). *Autobiography of Benjamin Franklin: Edited from His Manuscript, with Notes and an Introduction.* London.

Biggs, E. Power (1957). "Benjamin Franklin and the Armonica," *Daedalus* 86: 3, 231–241.

Blackburn, Robin (1997). *The Making of New World Slavery, 1492–1800.* London.

Bleyer, W.G. (1927). *Main Currents in the History of American Journalism.* Boston, MA.

Bloch, Ruth A. (1993). "Women, love and virtue in the thought of Edwards and Franklin," in B.B. Oberg and H.S. Stout, eds (1993), pp. 134–151.

Block, Seymour Stanton (1975). *Benjamin Franklin: His Wit, Wisdom and Women.* New York, NY.

Blumin, Stuart (1989). *The Emergence of the Middle Class: Social Experience in the American City, 1760–1900.* New York, NY.

Bond, Donovan H. and McLeod W. Reynolds, eds (1977). *Newsletters to Newspapers: Eighteenth-Century Journalism.* Morgantown, WV.

Bonomi, Patricia U. (1986). *Under the Cope of Heaven: Religion, Society, and Politics in Colonial America.* New York, NY.

Borsay, Peter. (1989). *The English Urban Renaissance: Culture and Society in the Provincial Town, 1660–1770.* Oxford.

Bosco, R.A. (1987). "'He that best understands the world, least likes it': The dark side of Benjamin Franklin," *Pennsylvania Magazine of History & Biography* 111: 525–554.

Botein, S. (1975). "'Meer mechanics' and an open press: The business and political strategies of colonial American printers," *Perspectives in American History* 9: 127–225.

Boudreau, G. (1996). "'Highly valuable and extensively useful': Community and readership among the eighteenth-century Philadelphia middling sort," *Pennsylvania History* 63: 302–329.

Boudreau, G. (2002). "'Done by a tradesman': Franklin's educational proposals and the culture of eighteenth-century Philadelphia," *Pennsylvania History* 69: 524–557.

Boudreau, G. (2007). "Solving the mystery of the Junto's missing member: John Jones, shoemaker," *Pennsylvania Magazine of History and Biography* 131(3): 307–317.

Boyd, Julian P., ed. (1938). *Indian Treaties Printed by Benjamin Franklin, 1736–1762.* Philadelphia, PA.

Braddock, Alan C. and Irmscher Christoph, eds (2009). *A Keener Perception: Ecocritical Studies in American Art History*. Tuscaloosa, AL.
Braithwaite, William C. (1912). *The Beginnings of Quakerism*. London.
Braithwaite, William C. (1919). *The Second Period of Quakerism*. London.
Brands, H.W. (2000). *The First American: The Life and Times of Benjamin Franklin*. New York, NY.
Breen, T.H. (1986). "An empire of goods: The anglicization of colonial America, 1690–1776," *Journal of British Studies* 25: 467–499.
Breen, T.H. (1988). "Baubles of Britain: The American and consumer revolutions of the eighteenth century," *Past and Present* 119: 73–104.
Breen, T.H. (1997). "Ideology and nationalism on the eve of the American revolution: Revisions *once more* in need of revising," *Journal of American History* 413–439.
Breen, T.H. (2004). *The Marketplace of Revolution: How Consumer Politics Shaped American Independence*. New York, NY.
Breitweiser, Mitchell (1984). *Cotton Mather and Benjamin Franklin: The Price of Representative Personality*. Cambridge, England.
Brenton, J.J., ed. (1850). *Voices from the Press: A Collection of Sketches, Essays, and Poems by Practical Printers*. New York, NY.
Bridenbaugh, C. (1977). "Philosophy put to use: Voluntary associations for propagating the enlightenment in Philadelphia, 1727–1776," *Pennsylvania Magazine of History and Biography* 110: 70–88.
Bronner, Edwin B. (1986). "Quaker discipline and order, 1680–1720: Philadelphia yearly meeting and London yearly meeting," in Dunn and Dunn, eds, (1986), pp. 323–335.
Brooke, J.L. (2004). "Consent, civil society, and the public sphere in the age of revolution and the early American republic," in Pasley, Robertson, and Waldstreicher, eds (2004), pp. 207–250.
Brooks, David (2000). "Our founding yuppie; Ben Franklin's America," *Weekly Standard* October 23. Available at: http://0-www.lexisnexis.com.maurice.bgsu.edu/us/lnacademic/frame.do?reloadEntirePage=true&rand=1276610233101&returnToKey=20_T9554576873&parent=docview&target=results_listview_resultsNav&tokenKey=rsh-20.794036.6659332757.
Brooks, Van Wyck (1915). *America's Coming of Age*. New York, NY.
Brown, Bill (2003). *A Sense of Things: The Object Matter of American Literature*. Chicago, IL.
Brown, Bill, ed. (2004). *Things*. Chicago, IL.
Brown, Charles Brockden (1798; 1991). *Wieland and the Memoirs of Carwin the Biloquist*. New York, NY.
Brown, Christopher L. (2002). "The politics of slavery," in David Armitage and Michael J. Braddick eds., *The British Atlantic World, 1500–1800*. New York, NY, pp. 214–232.
Brown, Christopher Leslie (2006). *Moral Capital: Foundations of British Abolitionism*. Chapel Hill, NC.
Brown, R.D. (1990). *Knowledge is Power: The Diffusion of Information in Early America, 1700–1865*. New York, NY.
Bruce, William Cabell (1917). *Benjamin Franklin Self-Revealed: A Biographical and Critical Study Based Mainly on His Own Writings*. New York, NY.

Bryant, W.C. (1873). *Orations and Addresses.* New York, NY.
Bryant, W.C., and Gay, S.H. (1881). *A Popular History of the United States,* 4 vols. New York, NY.
Buckingham, J.T. (1852). *Specimens of Newspaper Literature: With Personal Memoirs, Anecdotes, and Reminiscences,* 2 vols. Boston, MA.
Buel, Richard, Jr (1998). *In Irons: Britain's Naval Supremacy and the American Revolutionary Economy.* New Haven, CT.
Bullock, S.C. (1996). *Revolutionary Brotherhood: Freemasonry and the Transformation of the American Social Order, 1730–1840.* Chapel Hill, NC.
Burlingame, Roger (1967). *Benjamin Franklin: Envoy Extraordinary.* Newyork, NY: Coward-McCann, Inc.
Bush, Sargent Jr, ed. (1990). "The journal of Madam Knight," in Andrews, ed. (1990), pp. 67–116.
Bushman, Richard (1966). "On the uses of psychology: Conflict and conciliation in Benjamin Franklin," *History and Theory* 5(3): 225–240.
Bushman, Richard (1985). *King and People in Provincial Massachusetts.* Chapel Hill, NC.
Bushman, Richard (1992). *The Refinement of America: Persons, Cities, Houses.* New York, NY: Knopf.
Buskirk, S.W., Harestad A.S., Raphael M.G., and Powell R.A., eds (1994). *Martens, Sables, and Fishers, Biology and Conservation.* Ithaca, NY.
Butterfield, K. (2009). "A common law of membership: Expulsion, regulation, and civil society in the early republic," *Pennsylvania Magazine of History and Biography* 133: 255–275.
Butterfield, L.H., ed. (1951). *Letters of Benjamin Rush,* 2 vols. Princeton, NJ.
Butterfield, L.H., ed. (1961). *Diary and Autobiography of John Adams,* 4 vols. Cambridge, MA.
Butterfield, L.H., ed. (1963). *The Adams Family Correspondence,* vol. 1. Cambridge, MA: Harvard University Press.
Buxbaum, Melvin H. (1975). *Benjamin Franklin and the Zealous Presbyterians.* University Park, PA.
Buxbaum, Melvin H., ed. (1987). *Critical Essays on Benjamin Franklin.* Boston, MA.
Cahill, Edward (2008). "Benjamin Franklin's Interiors," *Early American Studies* 6: 27–58.
Calloway, Colin (2006). *The Scratch of a Pen: 1763 and the Transformation of North America.* New York, NY.
Campbell, James (1999). *Recovering Benjamin Franklin. An Exploration of a Life of Science and Service.* Chicago, IL.
Canny, Nicholas and Pagden, Anthony, eds (1987). *Colonial Identities in the Atlantic World.* Princeton, NJ.
Capp, B.S. (1979). *Astrology and the Popular Press: English Almanacs, 1500–1800.* London.
Carey, J.W. (1989). *Communication as Culture: Essays on Media and Society.* Boston, MA.
Carey, Lewis (1928). *Franklin's Economic Views.* New York, NY.
Carp, B.L. (2007). *Rebels Rising: Cities and the American Revolution.* New York, NY.

Carr, William G. (1990). *The Oldest Delegate: Franklin in the Constitutional Convention*. Newark, DE.
Carson, Cary, Hofman, Ronald, and Albert, Peter J., eds (1994). *Of Consuming Interests: The Style of Life in the Eighteenth Century*. Charlottesville, VA.
Carton, Evan (2002). "What feels an American? Evident selves and alienable emotions in the new man's world," in Millette and Travis, eds (2002), pp. 23–43.
Chafee, Z. Jr (1941). *Free Speech in the United States*. Cambridge, MA.
Chamberlin, B.F. and Brown, C.J., eds (1982). *The First Amendment Reconsidered: New Perspectives on the Meaning of Freedom of Speech and Press*. New York, NY.
Chambers, Sarah C. and Norling, Lisa (2008). "Choosing to Be a Subject: Loyalist Women in the Revolutionary Atlantic World," *Gender and History* 20: 39–62.
Chaplin, J.E. (2006). *The First Scientific American: Benjamin Franklin and the Pursuit of Genius*. New York, NY.
Chartier, R. (1994). *The Order of Books: Readers, Authors, and Libraries in Europe Between the Fourteenth and Eighteenth Centuries*. Stanford, CA.
Chase, A. (1996). "Ben and me: The Disney version," *Left History* 4: 2.
Chastellux, Marquis de (1787). *Travels in North America*, 2 vols. London.
Chaves, Joseph (2007). "Polite mentors and Franklin's 'Exquisite Pleasure': Sociability, prophylaxis, and dependence in the *Autobiography*," *Early American Literature* 42: 555–571.
Clark, C.E. (1994). *The Public Prints: The Newspaper in Anglo-American Culture, 1665–1740*. New York, NY.
Clark, C.E. (2000). "Early American journalism: News and opinion in the popular press," in Amory and Hall, eds (2000), pp. 347–366.
Clark, C.E., and Wetherell, C. (1989). "The measure of maturity: The *Pennsylvania Gazette*, 1728–1765," *William and Mary Quarterly*, 3rd series, 46: 279–303.
Clark, P. (2000). *British Clubs and Societies, 1580–1800: The Origins of an Associational World*. New York, NY.
Clark, Ronald (1983). *Benjamin Franklin: A Biography*. New York, NY.
Clark, William Bell (1932). *Lambert Wickes, Sea Raider and Diplomat: The Story of a Naval Captain of the Revolution*. New Haven, CT.
Clark, William Bell (1956). *Ben Franklin's Privateers: A Naval Epic of the American Revolution*. Baton Rouge, LA.
Clay, C.M. (1872). "Introduction," in Reavis, ed. (1872), pp. ix–xi.
Cobbett, W., ed. (1813). *Parliamentary History of England*, vol. 16. London.
Cohen, B. (1955). "The Empirical Temper," in Sanford, ed., (1955), 83–93.
Cohen, I. Bernard (1941). *Benjamin Franklin's Experiments; a New Edition of Franklin's Experiments and Observations on Electricity*. Cambridge, MA.
Cohen, I. Bernard (1953). *Benjamin Franklin: His Contribution to the American Tradition*. New York, NY.
Cohen, I. Bernard (1956). *Franklin and Newton: An Inquiry into Speculative Newtonian Experimental Science and Franklin's Work in Electricity as an Example Thereof*. Philadelphia, PA.
Cohen, I. Bernard (1990). *Benjamin Franklin's Science*. Cambridge, MA.
Cohen, I. Bernard (1995). *Science and the Founding Fathers*. New York, NY.
Colley, Linda (1992). *Britons: Forging the Nation*. New Haven, CT.

Conger, Vivian Bruce (2009). " 'There is a graite odds between a mans being at home and a broad': Deborah Read Franklin and the eighteenth-century home," *Gender and History* 21: 592–607.

Conger, Vivian Bruce (2010). "Deborah Read Franklin and Sally Franklin Bache: An intergenerational exploration into the gendered nature of politics, consumer culture and the household." Paper Delivered at the Annual Meeting of the Pennsylvania Historical Association.

Conner, Paul W. (1965). *Poor Richard's Politicks: Benjamin Franklin and his New American Order*. New York, NY.

Cook, E.C. (1912). *Literary Influences in Colonial Newspapers, 1704–1750*. New York, NY.

Cook, E.C. (1917). "Colonial newspapers and magazines, 1704–1775," in Trent, Erskine, Sherman, and Van Doren, eds (1971), pp. 111–123.

Copeland, D.A. (1997). *Colonial American Newspapers: Character and Content*. Newark, DE.

Copeland, D.A. (2006). *The Idea of a Free Press: The Enlightenment and Its Unruly Legacy*. Evanston, Il.

Cotter, John L., Roberts, Daniel G. and Parrington, Michael. (1995). *The Buried Past: An Archaeological History of Philadelphia*. Philadelphia, PA.

Cowell, John M. (1884). "The family of Deborah Franklin: Notes," *Pennsylvania Magazine of History and Biography* 8: 403–407.

Crane, Elaine F., ed. (1991). *The Diary of Elizabeth Drinker*. Boston, MA.

Crane, Verner W. (1934). "Benjamin Franklin and the Stamp Act," *Transactions of the Colonial Society of Massachusetts* 32: 56–77.

Crane, Verner W. (1936). *Benjamin Franklin – Englishman and American*. Baltimore, MD.

Crane, Verner W. (1949). "Review of *The Restoration of a 'Fair Copy'*," *Modern Philology* 47: 127–134.

Crane, Verner W. ed. (1950), *Benjamin Franklin's Letters to the Press, 1758–1775*. Chapel Hill, NC.

Crane, Verner W. (1954). *Benjamin Franklin and a Rising People*. Boston, MA.

Craven, Wayne (1993). "The American and British portraits of Benjamin Franklin," in Lemay, ed. (1993), pp. 247–271.

Crowley, John E. (1993). *The Privileges of Independence: Neomercantilism and the American Revolution*. Baltimore, MD.

Currey, Cecil B. (1968). *Road to Revolution: Benjamin Franklin in England, 1765–1775*. New York, NY.

Currey, Cecil B. (1978). *Road to Revolution: Benjamin Franklin in England, 1765–1775*, 2nd edn. Gloucester, MA.

Dallett, Francis James (1960). "Dr. Franklin's in-laws," *Pennsylvania Magazine of History and Biography* 21: 297–302.

Daniels, Bruce C., ed. (1986). *Power and Status: Officeholding in Colonial America*. Middletown, CT: Wesleyan University Press.

Darnton, Robert (1967). *Mesmerism and the End of the Enlightenment in France*. Cambridge, MA.

Daunton, Martin and Halpern, Rick, eds. (1999) *Empire and Others: British Encounters with Indigenous Peoples, 1500–1800*. Philadelphia, PA.

Davies, Adrian (2000). *The Quakers In English Society, 1655–1725*. New York, NY.

Dawson, Hugh (1977–1978). "Franklin's 'Memoirs' in 1784: The design of the *Autobiography*, Parts I and II ...," *Early American Literature* 12: 286–291.

Dawson, Hugh (1979–1980). "Fathers and Sons: Franklin's 'Memoirs' as Myth and Metaphor," *Early American Literature* 14: 269–292.

Debates and Proceedings in the Congress, 1st Cong., 2nd sess. (1834). Washington DC.

DeConde, Alexander (1983). "Historians, the war for independence, and the persistence of the exceptionalist ideal," *International History Review* 5: 399–430.

Delbourgo, J. (2006). *A Most Amazing Scene of Wonders: Electricity and Enlightenment in Early America*. Cambridge, MA.

deTernant, Andrew (1928). "Marianne and Cecilia Davies and Benjamin Franklin," *Notes and Queries* 155: 14.

Dorfman, Joseph (1971). "Benjamin Franklin, economic statesman" in Sparks, ed. (1971).

Dorman, Charles (1969). "*The Furnishings of Franklin Court, 1765–1790: A Preliminary Study*." Report prepared for Independence National Historical Park. Philadelphia, PA.

Downes, Paul (2002). *Democracy, Revolution and Monarchism in Early American Literature*. Cambridge, England: Cambridge University Press.

Draper, T. (1996). *A Struggle for Power: The American Revolution*. New York, NY.

Dray, P. (2005). *Stealing God's Thunder: Benjamin Franklin's Lightning Rod and the Invention of America*. New York, NY.

Drescher, Seymour (2002). *The Mighty Experiment: Free Labor versus Slavery in British Emancipation*. New York, NY.

Drexler, Michael (1998). "Managing the Public: Strategic Publication in Franklin and Whitman," *Modern Language Studies* 28(2): 55–67.

Duane, William (1848). "Sarah Bache," in Ellet, ed. (1848), pp. 332–345.

Dull, Jonathan R. (1975). *The French Navy and American Independence: A Study of Arms and Diplomacy, 1774–1787*. Princeton, NJ.

Dull, Jonathan R. (1982). "Franklin the diplomat: The French mission," *Transactions of the American Philosophical Society* 72: 1–76.

Dull, Jonathan R. (1983). "Benjamin Franklin and the nature of American diplomacy," *International History Review* 5: 346–363.

Dull, Jonathan R. (1985). *A Diplomatic History of the American Revolution*. New Haven, CT.

Dull, Jonathan R. (2005). *The French Navy and the Seven Years' War*. Lincoln, NE.

Dull, Jonathan R. (2010). *Benjamin Franklin and the American Revolution*. Lincoln, NE.

Dunn, Elizabeth E. (1987). "From a bold youth to a reflective sage: A reevaluation of Benjamin Franklin's religion," *Pennsylvania Magazine of History and Biography* 111: 501–524.

Dunn, Mary Maples (1967). *William Penn. Politics and Conscience*. Princeton, NJ.

Dunn, Richard S. and Dunn, Mary Maples, eds (1981–1987). *The Papers of William Penn*, 1–5 vols. Philadelphia, PA.

Dunn, Richard S. and Dunn, Mary Maples, eds (1986). *The World of William Penn*. Philadelphia, PA.

Earle, Peter (1989). *The Making of the English Middle Class: Business, Society and Family Life in London, 1660–1730.* Berkeley, CA.

Egnal, M. (1988). *A Mighty Empire: The Origins of the American Revolution.* Ithaca, NY.

Ehrenberg, J. (1999). *Civil Society: The Critical History of an Idea.* New York, NY.

Eisenstadt, P. (1998). "Almanacs and the disenchantment of early America," *Pennsylvania History* 65: 143–169.

Elias, Robert H., and Finch, Eugene D., eds (1982). *Letters of Thomas Atwood Digges (1742–1821).* Columbia, SC.

Eliot, Thomas D. (1924). "The Relations Between Adam Smith and Benjamin Franklin Before 1776," *Political Science Quarterly* 39: 67–96.

Ellet, Elizabeth, ed. (1848). *The Women of the American Revolution.* New York, NY

Ellis, Joseph J. (2000). *Founding Brothers: The Revolutionary Generation.* New York, NY.

Ellis, M. (2006). *Eighteenth-Century Coffee-House Culture.* London.

Elsenaar, Arthur and Remko Scha (2002). "Electric body manipulations as performance art: A historical perspective," *Leonardo Music Journal* 12: 17–28.

Eltis, David (1999). "Slavery and freedom in the early modern world," in Engerman, ed. (1999), pp. 25–49.

Emery, M., Emery, E., and Roberts, N.L. (2000). *The Press and America: An Interpretive History of the Mass Media,* 7th edn. Boston, MA.

Endy, Melvin B. Jr (1973). *William Penn and Early Quakerism.* Princeton, NJ.

Endy, Melvin B. Jr (1986). "Puritanism, Spiritualism and quakerism: An historiographical essay," in Dunn and Dunn, eds (1986), pp. 281–301.

Engerman, Stanley L., ed. (1999). *Terms of Labor: Slavery, Serfdom, and Free Labor.* Stanford, CA.

Erkkila, Betsy (2000). "Franklin and the revolutionary body," *English Literary History* 67(3): 717–741.

Eve, Sallie (1773). *Diary.* Special Collections Department, William R. Perkins Library, Duke University.

Fabian, Ann (2000). *The Unvarnished Truth: Personal Narratives in Nineteenth-Century America.* Berkeley, CA.

Farrand, Max, ed. (1949). *Benjamin Franklin's Memoirs: A Parallel Text Edition.* Berkeley, CA.

Fay, Bernard (1928). "His Excellency Mr. Franklin: The last loves of the first American," *Forum* 79: 321–324.

Fay, Bernard (1929). *Franklin: The Apostle of Modern Times.* Boston, MA: Little Brown and Company.

Felks, Madeleine (1969). "New England Amazon: The life and times of Sarah Knight: Traveler, business woman, teacher of Benjamin Franklin," *New-England Galaxy* 10: 16–22.

Ferguson, Robert A. (1986). "'We Hold These Truths': Strategies of control in the literature of the founders," in Bercovitch, ed. (1986).

Ferguson, Robert A. (1997). *The American Enlightenment, 1750–1820.* Cambridge, MA.

Fichtelberg, Joseph (1988). "The Complex Image: Text and reader in the autobiography of Benjamin Franklin," *Early American Literature* 23(2): 202–216.

Fiering, Norman S. (1978). "Benjamin Franklin and the way to virtue," *American Quarterly* 30: 199–223.

Finger, Stanley (2006). *Doctor Franklin's Medicine.* Philadelphia, PA.

Finkelman, Paul (2001). *Slavery and the Founders,* 2nd edn. Armonk, NY.

Fisher, Sydney George (1898). *The True Benjamin Franklin.* Philadelphia, PA.

Fliegelman, Jay (1982). *Prodigals and Pilgrims: The American Revolution Against Patriarchal Authority.* New York, NY.

Fliegelman, Jay (1993). *Declaring Independence: Jefferson, Natural Language, and the Culture of Performance.* Stanford, CA: Stanford University Press.

"Floundering Father." *Jack of All Trades,* January 31, 2000. Available at: http://www.hulu.com/watch/3221/jack-of-all-trades-the-floundering-father.

Folkerts, J., Teeter, D.W. Jr, and Caudill, E. (2009). *Voices of a Nation: A History of Mass Media in the United States,* 5th edn. Boston, MA.

Follett, F. (1847). *History of the Press of Western New-York; Prepared at the Request of a Committee, Together with the Proceedings of the Printers' Festival, Held on the 141st Anniversary of the Birth-Day of Franklin.* Rochester, NY.

Foner, Eric (1976). *Tom Paine and Revolutionary America.* New York, NY.

Ford, Paul Leicester (1899a). *The Many-Sided Franklin.* New York, NY.

Ford, Paul Leicester (1899b). "Franklin's relations with the fair sex," *Century Magazine* 58: 410–427.

Ford, Paul Leicester (1889c). *Who Was the Mother of Benjamin Franklin's Son?* New York, NY.

Forde, S. (1992). "Benjamin Franklin's autobiography and the education of America," *American Political Science Review* 86: 357–368.

Forde, S. (1999). "Ben Franklin, hero," in McNamara, ed. (1999), pp. 39–58.

Forde, S. (2003a). "Benjamin Franklin: An American model and a model American," in Frost and Kikkenga, eds (2003), pp. 80–92.

Forde, S. (2003b). "Benjamin Franklin and the theory of the social compact," in Pestritto and West, eds (2003), pp. 255–276.

Forde, S. (2006). "Benjamin Franklin's 'Machiavellian' civic virtue," in Rahe, ed. (2006), pp. 143–165.

Fortune, Brandon Brame and Warner, Deborah J. (1999). *Franklin And His Friends: Portraying the Man of Science in Eighteenth-Century America.* Washington DC.

Foucault, Michel (1965). *Madness and Civilization: A History of Insanity in the Age of Reason.* Translated by Richard Howard. New York, NY.

Foucault, Michel *Power/Knowledge: Selected interviews and Other Writings, 1972–1977,* ed. Colin Gordon. Translated by Colin Gordon, Leo Marshall, John Mepham, and Kate Soper. New York, NY.

Franklin, Benjamin (1760). *The Interest of Great Britain Considered, with Regard to Her Colonies, and the Acquisitions of Canada and Guadaloupe. To Which Are Added, Observations Concerning the Increase of Mankind, Peopling of Countries, &c.,* London.

Franklin, Benjamin (1905–1907). "A preface to the speech of Joseph Galloway," in Smyth, ed. (1905–1907), IV: 346.

Franklin, Benjamin (1764). *A Narrative of the Late Massacres, in Lancaster County, of a Number of Indians, Friends of This Province*. Philadelphia, PA.

Franklin, Benjamin (1779). *Political, Miscellaneous, and Philosophical Pieces*, ed. Vaughan, B. London.

Franklin, Benjamin (1782). *Two Letters from Dr. Franklin, to the Earl of Shelburne*. London.

Franklin, Benjamin (1949a). *Benjamin Franklin's Memoirs: Parallel Text Edition*, ed. Max Farrand. Berkeley, CA.

Franklin, Benjamin (1949b). *Benjamin Franklin's Memoirs: The Restoration of a "Fair Copy."* ed. Max Farrand. Berkeley, CA.

Franklin, Benjamin (1964). *The Autobiography of Benjamin Franklin*, eds, Leonard W. Labaree, Ralph L. Ketcham, Helen C. Boatfield, and Helene H. Fineman. New Haven, CT.

Franklin, Benjamin (1981). *The Autobiography of Benjamin Franklin: A Genetic Text*, eds, J.A. Leo Lemay and P.M. Zall. Knoxville, TN.

Franklin, Benjamin (1982). *The Autobiography and Other Writings*, ed. Peter Shaw. New York, NY.

Franklin, Benjamin (1986a). *The Autobiography and Other Writings*, ed. Kenneth Silverman. New York, NY.

Franklin, Benjamin (1986b). *Benjamin Franklin's Autobiography: An Authoritative Text*. J.A. Leo Lemay and P.M. Zall, eds. New York, NY.

Franklin, Benjamin (1987a). *Autobiography* in *Writings*. Lemay, J.A. Leo, ed. New York, NY.

Franklin, Benjamin (1987b). *Writings*. J.A. Leo Lemay, ed. New York, NY.

Franklin, Benjamin (1990). *The Autobiography*. New York, NY.

Franklin, Benjamin (2006). *The Papers of Benjamin Franklin: Digital Edition*. Los Altos, CA. Available at: http://franklinpapers.org/franklin/.

Franklin, Phyllis (1969). *Show Thyself a Man: A Comparison of Benjamin Franklin and Cotton Mather*. Hague: Mouton.

Frasca, R. (1988). "Benjamin Franklin's printing network," *American Journalism* 5: 60–72.

Frasca, R. (1996). "'The glorious publick virtue so predominant in our rising country': Benjamin Franklin's printing network during the revolutionary era," *American Journalism* 13: 21–37.

Frasca, R. (2006a). *Benjamin Franklin's Printing Network: Disseminating Virtue in Early America*. Columbia, MO.

Frasca, R. (2006b). "'The partners wife at Caroline having succeeded, was encourag'd to engage in others,' The genesis of Benjamin Franklin's printing network," *Southern Studies* 13: 1–23.

Frick, G.F. (1994). "The library company of Philadelphia: America's first philosophical society," in Hutchins, ed. (1994), pp. 181–200.

Frost, D. and Kikkenga, J., eds (2003). *History of American Political Thought*. Lexington, KY.

Fruchtman, Jack (1991). "Common Sense," in Jack P. Greene and J.H. Pole eds. (1991). *The Blackwell Companion to the American Revolution*. Cambridge, MA, pp. 254–257.

Fry, Jennifer Reed (2003). "'Extraordinary freedom and great humility': A reinterpretation of Deborah Franklin," *Pennsylvania Magazine of History and Biography* 127: 167–196.
Furet, Francois (1984). *In the Workshop of History*. Chicago, IL.
Furtwangler, Albert (1979). "Franklin's apprenticeship and the spectator," *New England Quarterly* 52(3): 377–396.
Gallagher, Edward J. (1973). "The rhetorical strategy of Franklin's 'Way to Wealth'," *Eighteenth-Century Studies* 6: 475–485.
Gannon, B.A. (1998), "The lord is a man of war, the god of love and peace: The association debate, 1747–1748," *Pennsylvania History* 65: 46–61.
Garrett, Matthew (2008). "Benjamin Franklin's Mother," Paper presented at the McNeil Center for Early American Studies.
Gaustad, E.S. (2006). *Benjamin Franklin*. New York, NY.
Ghodes, Clarence, ed. (1967). *Essays on American Literature in Honor of Jay B. Hubbell*. Durham, NC.
Gilbert, Felix (1961). *To the Farewell Address: Ideas of Early American Foreign Policy*. Princeton, NJ.
Gilmore, Michael T. (1977). *The Middle Way: Puritanism and Ideology in American Romantic Fiction*. New Brunswick, NJ.
Gipson, Lawrence Henry (1937–1970). *The British Empire before the American Revolution*, 14 vols. New York, NY.
Gipson, Lawrence Henry (1954). *The Coming of the Revolution, 1763–1775*. New York, NY.
Glazener, Nancy (2008). "Benjamin Franklin and the limits of secular civil society," *American Literature* 80(2): 203–231.
Goldman, Aaron "Our founding flirt; cuddlesome Ben Franklin, the randy rebel with a cause," *The Washington Post*, n.d. Available at: http://www.lexisnexis.com.maurice.bgsu.edu/us/lnacademic/frame.do?reloadEntirePage=true&rand=1276612655361&returnToKey=20_T9555093131&parent=docview&target=results_listview_resultsNav&tokenKey=rsh-20.465836.4987963095.
Goudie, Sean (2006). *Creole America: The West Indies and the Formation of Literature and Culture in the New Republic*. Philadelphia, PA.
Gould, E.H. (1999). "A virtual nation: Greater Britain and the imperial legacy of the American revolution," *American Historical Review* 104: 476–489.
Gould, E.H. (2000). *The Persistence of Empire: British Political Culture in the Age of the American Revolution*. Chapel Hill, NC.
Gould, E.H. (2011). *An Unfinished Peace: The American Revolution and the Legal Transformation of the European Atlantic*. Cambridge, MA.
Gould, E.H. and Onuf, Peter S., eds. (2005). *Empire and Nation: The American Revolution in the Atlantic World*. Baltimore, MD.
Granger, Bruce Ingham (1964). *Benjamin Franklin: An American Man of Letters*. Ithaca, NY.
Granger, Bruce (1976). "Franklin as Press Agent in England," in Lemay, ed., (1976a), 21–32.
Greeley, H. (1864). "Self-made men," in Parton, ed. (1864), pp. 677–679.

Green, J.N. (2000). "English books and printing in the age of Franklin," in Amory and Hall, eds (2000), pp. 248–298.

Green, J.N. (2005). "Benjamin Franklin, printer," in Talbott, ed. (2005a), pp.55–90.

Green, J.N. (2007). "Subscription libraries and commercial circulating libraries in colonial Philadelphia and New York," in Augst and Carpenter, eds (2007), pp. 53–71.

Green, James N. and Stallybrass, Peter (2006). *Benjamin Franklin: Writer and Printer*. New Castle, DE.

Greene, Jack P. (1973). "An uneasy connection: An analysis of the preconditions of the American revolution," in Kurtz and Hutson, eds (1973), pp. 132–180.

Greene, Jack P. (1976). "The alienation of Benjamin Franklin, British American," *Journal of the Royal Society for the Encouragement of the Arts, Manufactures, and Commerce* 124: 52–73.

Greene, Jack P. (1986). *Peripheries and Center: Constitutional Development in the Extended Polities of the British Empire and the United States, 1607–1788*. Athens, GA.

Greene, Jack P. (1992a). "All men are created equal: Some reflections on the character of the American revolution," in Greene, ed. (1992c), pp. 236–267.

Greene, Jack P. (1992b). "A fortuitous convergence: Culture, circumstance, and contingency in the emergence of the American nation," in Greene, ed. (1992c), pp. 290–309.

Greene, Jack P. (1992c). *Imperatives, Behaviors, and Identities: Essays in Early American Cultural History*. Charlottesville, VA.

Greene, Jack P. (1995a). "The alienation of Benjamin Franklin, British American," in Greene, ed. (1995c), pp. 247–284.

Greene, Jack P. (1995b). "Pride, prejudice, and jealousy: Benjamin Franklin's explanation for the American revolution," in Greene, ed. (1995c), pp. 18–47.

Greene, Jack P., ed. (1995c). *Understanding the American Revolution: Issues and Actors*. Charlottesville, VA.

Griffith, John (1971). "The rhetoric of Franklin's autobiography," *Criticism: A Quarterly for Literature and the Arts* 13: 77–94.

Griffith, John (1976). "Franklin's sanity and the man behind the masks" in Lemay, ed. (1976a), pp. 123–138.

Griffith, S.F. (1992). "'Order, discipline, and a few cannon': Benjamin Franklin, the association, and the rhetoric of boosterism," *Pennsylvania Magazine of History and Biography* 116: 131–155.

Grimm, D.F. (1956). "Franklin's scientific institution," *Pennsylvania History* 23: 437–462.

Gromin, S.S. (2007). *Everyday Nature: Knowledge of the Natural World in Colonial New York*. New Brunswick, NJ.

Gustafson, Bruce (1987). "The music of Madam Brillon: A unified manuscript collection from Benjamin Franklin's circle," *Notes* 2nd ser., 43: 522–548.

Guyatt, Nicholas (2007). *Providence and the Invention of the United States, 1607–1876*. New York, NY.

Habermas, J. (1989). *The Structural Transformation of the Public Sphere: An Inquiry into a Category of Bourgeois Society*. Translated by T. Burger. Cambridge, MA.

Hadlak, Heather (2000). "Sonorous bodies: Women and the glass harmonica," *Journal of the Musicological Society* 53: 507–542.
Hall, David D. (1979). "The world of print and collective mentality in seventeenth-century New England," in Higham and Conklin, eds (1979), pp. 166–180.
Hall, David D. (1996). *Cultures of Print: Essays in the History of the Book.* Amherst, MA.
Hall, David D. (2000). "Learned culture in the eighteenth century," in Amory, Hugh and David D. Hall, eds. *A History of the Book in America*, vol. 1. *The Colonial Book in the Atlantic World.* New York, NY, pp. 411–433.
Hall, Max (1990 [1960]). *Benjamin Franklin and Polly Baker: The History of a Literary Deception.* Pittsburgh, PA.
Hall, Robert Lee (1988). *Benjamin Franklin Takes the Case: The American Agent Investigates Murder in the Dark Byways of London.* New York, NY.
Hallock, Thomas (2009). "Drawn from nature: Vivification in the botanic art of William Bartram" in Braddock and Imscher, eds (2009).
Handler, E. (1966). "Review of Conner (1965)," *New England Quarterly* 39: 284–286.
Handler, Richard and Gable, Eric (1997). *The New History in an Old Museum: Creating the Past at Colonial Williamsburg.* Durham, NC.
Hanna, W.S. (1964). *Benjamin Franklin and Pennsylvania Politics.* Stanford, CA.
Hardie, James (1805). *The New Universal Biographical Dictionary and American Remembrancer*, vol. 2. New York, NY, pp. 386–410.
Harper, Stephen C. (2004). Delawares and Pennsylvanians after the walking purchase, in Pencak and Richter, eds (2004), pp. 167–179.
Harper, Stephen C. (2006). *Promised Land: Penn's Holy Experiment, The Walking Purchase, and the Dispossession of the Delawares, 1600–1763.* Bethlehem, PA.
Harris, M. (2005). Civil society in post-revolutionary America, in Gould and Onuf, eds (2005), pp. 197–216.
Harris, Sharon M. (1995a). Hannah Webster Foster's *The Coquette:* Critiquing Franklin's America, in Harris, ed. (1995b), pp. 1–22.
Harris, Sharon M., ed. (1995b). *Redefining the Political Novel: American Women Writers, 1797–1901.* Knoxville, TN.
Hart, Charles Henry (1911). "Who was the mother of Franklin's son? An inquiry demonstrating that she was Deborah Read, wife of Benjamin Franklin," *Pennsylvania Magazine of History and Biography* 35: 308–314.
Hawke, David Freeman (1976). *Franklin.* New York, NY.
Hawthorne, Nathaniel (1851). *True Stories From History and Biography.* Boston, MA.
Hawthorne, Julian and Lemmon, William Leonard (1891). *American Literature.* Boston, MA.
Heilbron, J.L. (1979). *Electricity in the Seventeenth and Eighteenth Centuries: A Study of Early Modern Physics.* Berkeley, CA: University of California Press.
Heilbron, J.L. (2007). "Benjamin Franklin in Europe: Electrician, academician, politician," *Notes and Records of the Royal Society* 61:3, 353–373.
Hendrickson, David (2003). *Peace Pact: The Lost World of the American Founding.* Lawrence, KS.

Henry, Susan (1977). "Ann Franklin: Rhode Island's woman printer," in Bond and McLeod, eds (1977).
Herskowitz, Leo and Meyer, Isidore S., eds (1968). *Letters of the Franks Family (1733–1748), Studies in American Jewish History 5.* Waltham, MA, p. 47.
Higham, J. and Conkin, P., eds (1979). *New Directions in American Intellectual History.* Baltimore, MD.
Hill, Melvyn A. (1979). *Hannah Arendt, The Recovery of the Public World.* New York, NY.
Hochschild, Adam (2005). *Bury the Chains: Prophets and Rebels in the Fight to Free an Empire's Slaves.* New York, NY.
Hodgson, Dennis (1991). "Benjamin Franklin on population: From policy to theory," *Population and Development Review* 17: 639–661.
Hoefnagel, Dick (1989). "Benjamin Franklin and 'The Stol'n Kiss'," *Dartmouth College Library Bulletin* 30: (November).
Holmes, David L. (2006). *The Faiths of the Founding Fathers.* New York, NY.
Home, Henry, Lord Kames (1774). *Sketches of the History of Man,* 2 vols. Edinburgh.
Horkheimer, Max and Theodor, Adorno (1972). *Dialectic of Enlightenment.* Translated by John Cumming. New York, NY.
Horle, Craig W., Foster, Joseph S. and Wolfe Laurie M., eds (1997–2005). *Lawmaking and Legislators in Pennsylvania. A Biographical Dictionary,* 3 vols. Philadelphia, PA.
Horrocks, T.A. (2006). "Poor Richard's offspring: Benjamin Franklin's influence on the almanac trade in America," *Harvard Library Bulletin* 17(1/2): 41–46.
Houston, Alan, ed. (2004). *Franklin: The Autobiography and Other Writings on Politics, Economics, and Virtue.* Cambridge, MA.
Houston, Alan (2008). *Benjamin Franklin and the Politics of Improvement.* New Haven, CT.
Howe, Daniel Walker (1997). *Making the American Self: Jonathan Edwards to Abraham Lincoln.* Cambridge, MA.
Huang, Nian-Sheng (1994). *Benjamin Franklin in American Thought and Culture, 1790–1990.* Philadelphia, PA.
Huang, Nian-Sheng (2000). *Franklin's Father Josiah: Life of a Colonial Boston Tallow Chandler, 1657–1745.* Philadelphia, PA.
Huang, Nian-Sheng and Mulford, Carla (2009). "Benjamin Franklin and the American dream," in Mulford, ed., (2009a), 145–158.
Hudson, F. (1873). *Journalism in the United States, from 1690 to 1872.* New York, NY.
Hume, David (1753). Of national characters, in Hume, ed. (1994).
Hume, David (1994). *Political Essays,* ed. Knut Haakonsen. Cambridge, MA.
Hunt, Margaret (1996). *The Middling Sort: Commerce, Gender, and the Family in England, 1660–1750.* Berkeley, CA.
Hutchins, Catherine E., ed. (1994). *Shaping a National Culture: The Philadelphia Experience, 1750–1800.* Wintherthur, DE.
Hutson, James H. (1969). "Benjamin Franklin and Pennsylvania politics, 1751–1755: A reappraisal," *Pennsylvania Magazine of History and Biography* 93: 303–371.
Hutson, James H. (1972). *Pennsylvania Politics, 1756–1770: The Movement for Royal Government and its Consequences.* Princeton, NJ.

Hutson, James H. (1980). *John Adams and the Diplomacy of the American Revolution.* Lexington, KY.
Immerman, Richard H. (2010). *Empire for Liberty: A History of American Imperialism from Benjamin Franklin to Paul Wolfowitz.* Princeton, NJ.
Inikori, Joseph (2002). *Africans and the Industrial Revolution in England: A Study in International Trade and Economic Development.* Cambridge, England.
Isaacson, Walter (2003). *Benjamin Franklin: An American Life,* 1st edn. New York, NY.
Isaacson, Walter (2005). "What Benjamin Franklin means for our times," in Talbott, ed. (2005a), pp. 1–13.
Jacobson, D.L., ed. (1965). *The English Libertarian Heritage.* Indianapolis, IN.
Jefferson, Thomas (1785). *Notes on the State of Virginia.* Paris.
Jefferson, Thomas (1803). *Letter to Benjamin Rush.* "Letter," October 4. Available at: http://memory.loc.gov/cgi-bin/query/r?ammem/mtj:@field(DOCID+@lit(tj100017)).
Jefferson, Thomas (2002). *Notes on the States of Virginia, with Related Documents,* ed. David Waldstreicher. Boston, MA.
Jehlen, Myra (1990). "'Imitate Jesus and Socrates': The making of a good American," *South Atlantic Quarterly* 89(3): 501–524.
Jennings, Francis (1970). "The scandalous Indian policy of William Penn's sons: Deeds and documents of the walking purchase," *Pennsylvania History* 37: 19–39.
Jennings, Francis (1988). *Empire of Fortune: Crowns, Colonies, and Tribes in the Seven Years War in America.* New York, NY.
Jennings, Francis (1996). *Benjamin Franklin, Politician; the Mask and the Man.* New York, NY.
Jensen, M. (1968). *The Founding of a Nation: A History of the American Revolution, 1763–1776.* New York, NY.
Jeppson, Patrice (2006). "Which Benjamin Franklin – yours or mine? Examining responses to a new story from the historical archaeology site of Franklin Court," *Archaeologies* 2(2): 24–51.
John Adams. HBO Video (2008).
Jones, Ann Rosalind and Stallybrass, Peter (2000). "Fetishisms and renaissances," in Mazzio and Trevor, eds. (2000), pp. 21–35.
Jones, Jacqueline (1998). *American Work: Four Centuries of Black and White Labor.* New York, NY.
Jones, Rufus M. (1921). *The Later Periods of Quakerism.* London.
Jordan, Winthrop D. (1968). *White Over Black: American Attitudes Toward the Negro, 1550–1812.* Chapel Hill, NC.
Joy, Neill R. (1998). "Politics and culture: The Dr. Franklin – Dr. Johnson connection, with an analogue," *Prospects* 23: 60–81.
Kalter, Susan, ed. (2006). *Benjamin Franklin, Pennsylvania, & the First Nations: The Treaties of 1736–62.* Urbana, IL.
Kammen, M.G. (1968). *A Rope of Sand: The Colonial Agents, British Politics, and the American Revolution.* Ithaca, NY.
Kamrath, Mark L. and Harris, Sharon M., eds (2005). *Periodical Literature in Eighteenth-Century America.* Knoxville, TN.

Kant, Immanuel (1784). "An answer to the question: 'What is enlightenment?'" *Political Writings*. Translated by N.H. Nisbet, ed. Hans Reiss. Cambridge, England (1970).

Kelleter, F. (2009). "Franklin and the enlightenment," in Mulford, ed. (2009a) pp. 77–90.

Kelley, Mary (2000). "Petitioning with the left hand: Educating women in Benjamin Franklin's America," in Tise, ed. (2000b), pp. 83–102.

Kelly, T. (1966). *Early Public Libraries: A History of Public Libraries in Great Britain before 1850*. London.

Kenny, Kevin (2009). *Peaceable Kingdom Lost: The Paxton Boys and the Destruction of William Penn's Holy Experiment*. New York, NY.

Ketcham, Ralph L. (1963). "Conscience, war, and politics in Pennsylvania, 1755–1757," *William and Mary Quarterly* 3rd ser. 20: 416–439.

Ketcham, Ralph L. (1964). "Benjamin Franklin and William Smith: New light on an old Philadelphia quarrel," *Pennsylvania Magazine of History and Biography* 88: 142–163.

Ketcham, Ralph L. (1966). *Benjamin Franklin*. New York, NY.

Klepp, Susan E. (2009). *Revolutionary Conceptions: Women, Fertility, and Family Limitation in America, 1760–1820*. Chapel Hill, NC.

Klepp, Susan E. and Wulf, Karin, eds (2010). *The Diary of Hannah Callender Sansom: Sense and Sensibility in the Age of the American Revolution*. Ithaca, NY.

Kobre, S. (1960). *The Development of the Colonial Newspaper*. Gloucester, MA.

Kopytoff, Igor (1986). "The cultural biography of things: Commoditization as process," in Appadurai, ed. (1986), pp. 64–91.

Krider, E. Philip (2005). "Benjamin Franklin's Science," in *Benjamin Franklin: In Search of a Better World*, ed. Talbott, pp. 169–197.

Kulikoff, Allan (2004). "Electric Ben: Franklin and popular history," *Journal of The Historical Society* 4: 211–244.

Kulikoff, Allan (2005). "The founding fathers: Best sellers! TV stars! Punctual plumbers!," *Journal of The Historical Society* 5(2): 155–187.

Kurtz, Stephen and Hutson, James H., eds (1973). *Essays on the American Revolution*. New York, NY.

La Courreye Blecki, Catherine and Wulf, Karin A., eds (1997). *Milcah Martha Moore's Book: A Commonplace Book from Revolutionary America*. University Park, PA.

Labaree, Benjamin Woods, Willcox, William, Oberg, Barbara, *et al.*, eds (1959–). *The Papers of Benjamin Franklin*, 39 vols to date. New Haven, CT: Yale University Press.

LaFeber, W. (1972). "Foreign policies of a new nation: Franklin, Madison, and the 'Dream of a new land to fulfill with people in self control'," 1750–1804," in Williams, ed. (1972), pp. 9–37.

Laird, Pamela Walker (2006). *Pull: Networking and Success since Benjamin Franklin*. Cambridge, MA: Harvard University Press.

Lambert, Frank (1993). "Subscribing for profits and piety: The friendship of Benjamin Franklin and George Whtiefield," *William and Mary Quarterly* 3rd ser. 50: 529–555.

Lambert, Frank (1994). *"Pedlar in Divinity": George Whitefield and the Transatlantic Revivals, 1737–1770*. Princeton, NJ.

Landsman, Ned C. (1997). *From colonials to provincials: American thought and culture, 1680–1760*. Ithaca, NY.

Langford, Paul (1989). *A Polite and Commercial People: England, 1727–1783*. Oxford.

Larson, David M. (1975). "Franklin on the nature of man and the possibility of virtue," *Early American Literature* 10: 111–120.

Larson, David M. (1986). "Benevolent persuasion: The art of Benjamin Franklin's philanthropic papers," *Pennsylvania Magazine of History and Biography* 110: 195–217.

Larson, Rebecca (1999). *Daughters of Light. Quaker Women Preaching and Prophesying in the Colonies and Abroad, 1700–1775*. New York, NY

Latour, Bruno (1993). *We Have Never Been Modern*. Translated by Catherine Porter. Cambridge, MA.

Latour, Bruno (2010). *On the Modern Cult of the Factish Gods*. Translated by Heather Maclean and Catherine Porter. Durham, NC.

Laut, Agnes C. (1901). *The Fur Trade of America*. Norwood, MA.

Lawrence, D.H. (1923). *Studies in Classic American Literature*. New York, NY.

Lawrence, D.H. (1964). *Studies in Classic American Literature* [1923]. New York, NY.

Lawrence, D.H. (1984). *The Letters of D.H. Lawrence*, ed. James T. Boulton and Andrew Robertson. Cambridge, MA.

Lawson, Robert (1939). *Ben and Me; a New and Astonishing Life of Benjamin Franklin as Written by His Good Mouse, Amos, Lately Discovered, Edited & Illustrated by Robert Lawson*. Boston, MA.

Leary, Lewis (1948). "Joseph Dennie on Benjamin Franklin," *Pennsylvania Magazine of History and Biography* 72: 240–246.

Lee, J.M. (1917). *History of American Journalism*. Garden City, NY.

Lee, A.R. and Verhoeven, W.M., eds (1996). *Making America / Making American Literature: Franklin to Cooper*. Amsterdam.

Lemay, J.A. Leo (1965). "Franklin's suppressed busy-body," *American Literature* 37: 307–311.

Lemay, J.A. Leo (1967). "Franklin and the *Autobiography*: An essay on recent scholarship," *Eighteenth-Century Studies* 1: 185–211.

Lemay, J.A. Leo, ed. (1976a). *The Oldest Revolutionary: Essays on Benjamin Franklin*. Philadelphia, PA.

Lemay, J.A. Leo (1976b). "The text, rhetorical strategies, and themes of 'The Speech of Miss Polly Baker'," in Lemay, ed. (1976a), pp. 91–120.

Lemay, J.A. Leo (1978). "Benjamin Franklin, Universal Genius," in *The Renaissance Man in the Eighteenth Century: Papers read at a Clark Library Seminar 9 October 1976*. Los Angeles, CA.

Lemay, J.A. Leo (1986a). "Benjamin Franklin and the American Dream," in J.A. Leo Lemay, and P.M. Zall, eds. *Benjamin Franklin's Autobiography: An Authoritative Text, Backgrounds, Criticism*. New York, NY.

Lemay, J.A. Leo (1986b). *The Canon of Benjamin Franklin, 1722–1776*. Newark, DE.

Lemay, J.A. Leo (1987). "The American aesthetic of Franklin's visual creations," *Pennsylvania Magazine of History and Biography* 111: 465–499.

Lemay, J.A. Leo, ed. (1993). *Reappraising Benjamin Franklin: A Bicentennial Perspective*. Newark, DE.

Lemay, J.A. Leo (2000). "Benjamin Franklin," *American National Biography Online*. Available at: http://www.anb.org/articles/01/01-00298.html.

Lemay, J.A. Leo (2001). "An attribution of reflections on courtship and marriage (1746) to Benjamin Franklin," *Papers of the Bibliographic Society of America* 95: 59–96.

Lemay, J.A. Leo (2004). "Deborah Franklin, Lord Loudoun, and Franklin's 'Autobiography'," *Huntington Library Quarterly* 67: 607–621.

Lemay, J.A. Leo (2006a). *The Life of Benjamin Franklin*, vol. 1. *Journalist, 1706–1730*. Philadelphia, PA.

Lemay, J.A. Leo (2006b). *The Life of Benjamin Franklin*, vol. 2. *Printer and Publisher, 1730–1747*. Philadelphia, PA.

Lemay, J.A. Leo (2009). *The Life of Benjamin Franklin*, vol. 3. *Soldier, Staesman, and Politician*. Philadelphia, PA.

Lemay, J.A.L. and Zall, P.M., eds (1981) *The Autobiography of Benjamin Franklin: A Genetic Text*. Knoxville, TN: University of Tennessee Press.

Lemon, J.T. (1972). *The Best Poor Man's Country: A Geographical Study of Early Southeastern Pennsylvania*. Baltimore, MD.

Leonard, T.C. (1999). "Recovering 'Wretched Stuff' and the Franklins' synergy," *New England Quarterly* 72: 444–455.

Lepore, Jill (2010). *The Whites of their Eyes: The Tea Party's Revolution and the Battle over American History*. Princeton, NJ.

Lerat, Christian (1993). "Essay at revisiting Benjamin Franklin as a philogynist," in Balestra and Sampietro, ed. (1993), pp. 99–119.

Lerner, R. (1979). *The Thinking Revolutionary: Principle and Practice in the New Republic*. Ithaca, NY.

Lerner, R. (1993). "Dr. Janus," in Lemay, ed. (1993), pp. 415–424.

Lerner, R. (2009). *Playing the Fool: Subversive Laughter in Troubled Times*. Chicago, IL.

Lessig, L. (2004). *Free Culture: How Big Media Uses Technology and the Law to Lock Down Culture and Control Creativity*. New York, NY.

Levene, John R. (1972). "Benjamin Franklin, F.R.S., Sir Joshua Reynolds, F.R.S., P.R.A., Benjamin West, P.R.A. and the Invention of Bifocals," *Notes and Records of the Royal Society of London* 27: 141–163.

Levin, David (1964). "The autobiography of Benjamin Franklin: The puritan experimenter in life and art," *Yale Review* 53: 258–275.

Levy, Barry (1988). *Quakers and the American Family. British Settlement in the Delaware Valley*. New York, NY.

Levy, Barry (2009). *Town Born: The Political Economy of New England from Its Founding to the Revolution*. Philadelphia, PA.

Levy, L.W. (1960). *Legacy of Suppression: Freedom of Speech and Press in Early American History*. Cambridge, MA.

Levy, L.W. (1985). *Emergence of a Free Press*. New York, NY.

Lewis, Jan (2000). "Sex and the married man: Benjamin Franklin's families," in Tise, ed. (2000b), pp. 67–82.

Liberty's Kids the Complete Series. DVD. Shout! Factory (2002).

Linebaugh, Peter and Marcus Rediker (2000). *The Many-Headed Hydra*. Boston, MA.
Lipowski, Z.I. (1984). "Benjamin Franklin and Princess Czartoryska: An unknown therapeutic encounter," *Pennsylvania History* 51: 167–171.
Lipper, Mark (1980). "Benjamin Franklin's 'Silence Dogood' as an eighteenth century 'Censor Morum'," in Bond and MacLeod, eds (1977), pp. 73–83.
Lokken, Roy N. (1959). *David Lloyd: Colonial Lawmaker*. Seattle, WA.
Looby, Christopher (1993). *Voicing America*. Chicago, IL: University of Chicago Press.
Looby, C. (1996). *Voicing America: Language, Literary Form, and the Origins of the United States*. Chicago, IL.
Lopez, Claude-Anne (1966). *Mon Cher Papa: Franklin and the Ladies of Paris* New Haven, CT.
Lopez, Claude-Anne (1981). *Benjamin Franklin's "Good House": The Story of Franklin Court*. Washington DC.
Lopez, Claude-Anne (2000a). *My Life with Benjamin Franklin*. New Haven, CT.
Lopez, Claude-Anne (2000b). "Three women, three styles: Catherine Ray, Polly Hewson, and Georgiana Shipley" in Tise, ed. (2000b), pp. 52–63.
Lopez, Claude-Anne (2003). "Why he was a babe magnet," *Time*, July 7.
Lopez, Claude-Anne (2004). "Deborah Read Franklin," in *American National Biography Online*, eds, John A. Garraty and Mark C. Carnes
Lopez, Claude-Anne and Herbert, Eugenia W. (1975). *The Private Franklin: The Man and His Family*. New York, NY.
Loughran, Trish (2007). *The Republic in Print: Print Culture in the Age of U.S. Nation Building, 1770–1870*. New York, NY.
Lovell, Margaretta M. (2005). *Art in a Season of Revolution: Painters, Artisans, and Patrons in Early America*. Philadelphia, PA.
Lupton, Christina (2007). "Sincere performances: Franklin, Tillotson, and Steele on the plain style," *Eighteenth-Century Studies* 40(2): 177–192.
Lynd, Staughton (1968). *Intellectual Origins of American Radicalism*. New York, NY.
Lynen, John F. (1969). *The Design of the Present: Essays on Time and Form in American Literature*. New Haven, CT.
Lyons, Clare (2006). *Sex Among the Rabble: An Intimate History of Gender and Power in the Age of Revolution, Philadelphia, 1730–1830*. Chapel Hill, NC: University of North Carolina Press.
Machor, J., and Goldstein, P., eds (2008). *American Reception Study: Reconsiderations and New Directions*. New York, NY.
MacIntyre, A. (1981). *After Virtue*. Notre Dame, IN.
Mack, Phyllis (1992). *Visionary Women. Ecstatic Prophecy in Seventeenth-Century England*. Berkeley, CA.
Maddox, Lucy, ed. (1999). *Locating American Studies: The Evolution of a Discipline*. Baltimore, MD.
Maier, P. (1972). *From Resistance to Revolution: Colonial Radicals and the Development of American Opposition to Britain, 1765–1776*. New York, NY.
Malthus, Thomas Robert (1922). *An Essay on the Principle of Population, 1803*, ed. Donald Winch. Cambridge, England.

Marietta, Jack D. (1984). *The Reformation of American Quakerism, 1748–1783.* Philadelphia, PA.

Marks, Frederick W. (1973). *Independence on Trial: Foreign Affairs and the Making of the Constitution.* Baton Rouge, LA.

Martin, Ann Smart (1993). "Makers, buyers, and users: Consumerism as a material culture framework," *Winterthur Portfolio* 28: 141–157.

Martin, Ann Smart, ed. (1997). *American Material Culture: the Shape of the Field.* Winterthur, DE.

Martin, R.W.T. (1994). "From the 'Free and Open' press to the 'Press of Freedom': Liberalism, republicanism and early American press liberty," *History of Political Thought* 4: 505–534.

Martin, R.W.T. (2001). *The Free and Open Press: The Founding of American Democratic Press Liberty, 1640–1800.* New York, NY.

Marx, Karl (1972). *On America and the Civil War*, ed. Saul K. Padover. New York, NY.

Marx, Karl (1977). *Capital*, vol. 1. Translated by Ben Fowkes. New York, NY.

Matson, Cathy D., ed. (2006). The *Economy of Early America: Historical Perspectives and New Directions.* University Park, PA.

Matthews, Albert (1908). "The snake devices, 1754–1776, and the constitutional courant, 1765," *Publications of the Colonial Society of Massachusetts* 11: 409–453.

Matthews, Albert (1928). "Marianne and Cecilia Davies and Benjamin Franklin," *Notes and Queries* 155: 22, 390–391.

Matthews, Brander (1896). *Introduction to the Study of American Literature.* New York, NY.

May, Henry F. (1976). *The Enlightenment in America.* New York, NY.

Mazzio, Carla and Douglas Trevor, eds (2000). *Historicism, Psychoanalysis and Early Modern Culture.* New York, NY.

McBride, David P. (1979). "Linked rings: Early American unity illustrated," *Numismatist* 92: 2374–2393.

McCarthy, K.D. (2003). *American Creed: Philanthropy and the Rise of Civil Society, 1700–1865.* Chicago, IL.

McConville, Brendan (2006). *The King's Three Faces: The Rise and Fall of Royal America, 1688–1776.* Chapel Hill, NC.

McCoy, Drew R. (1978). "Benjamin Franklin's vision of a republican political economy for America," *William and Mary Quarterly* 3rd ser. 35: 605–628.

McCoy, Drew R. (1980). *The Elusive Republic: Political Economy in Jeffersonian America.* Chapel Hill, NC.

McCusker, John and Menard, Russell (1985). *The Economy of British America, 1607–1789.* Chapel Hill, NC.

McKillop, A.D. (1948). "Some newtonian verses in *Poor Richard*," *New England Quarterly* 21: 383–385.

McLeod, K. (2005). *Freedom of Expression®: Overzealous Copyright Bozos and Other Enemies of Creativity.* New York, NY.

McMahon, A.M. (1992). "'Small matters': Benjamin Franklin, Philadelphia, and the 'Progress of Cities'," *Pennsylvania Magazine of History and Biography* 116: 157–182.

McMaster, John Bach (1887). *Benjamin Franklin as a Man of Letters.* Boston, MA.
McNally, David (1988). *Political Economy and the Rise of Capitalism.* Berkeley, CA.
McNamara, P., ed. (1999). *The Noblest Minds.* Lanham, MD.
Meaders, Daniel E., ed. (1993). *Eighteenth-Century White Slaves: Runaway Notices, vol. 1, Pennsylvania, 1729–1760.* Westport, CT.
Medlin, Dorothy (1977). "Benjamin Franklin and the French language: A letter to Madame Brillon," *French-American Review* 1: 232–239.
Medlin, Dorothy (1980). "Benjamin Franklin's bagetelles for Madam Helvétius: Some biographical and stylistic considerations," *Early American Literature* 15: 42–58.
Menard, Russell (2001). "Capitalism and slavery; Personal reflections on Eric Williams and the reconstruction of early American history," in Shade and Kennedy, eds (2001), pp. 321–331.
Merrell, James H. (1999). *Into the American Woods: Negotiators on the Pennsylvania Frontier.* New York, NY.
Meyer, Donald (1987). "Franklin's religion," in Buxbaum, ed., *Critical Essays on Benjamin Franklin.* Waterville, ME.
Meyer, Gladys (1941). *Free Trade in Ideas: Aspects of American Liberalism Illustrated in Franklin's Philadelphia Career.* New York, NY.
Middlekauff, Robert (1996). *Benjamin Franklin and His Enemies.* Berkeley, CA.
Middleton, Simon (2009). "'Artisans' and the 'Middling Sort' in Gary Nash's eighteenth-century urban America?" *Pennsylvania Magazine of History and Biography* 133: 416–423.
Miles, Ellen G. (1993). *The Portrait in Eighteenth-Century America.* Newark, DE.
Miles, Richard D. (1957). "The American image of Benjamin Franklin," *American Quarterly* 9: 117–143.
Miller, C.W. (1961). "Franklin's poor Richard Almanacs: Their printing and publication," *Studies in Bibliography: Papers of the Bibliographical Society of the University of Virginia* 14: 97–115.
Miller, Jacquelyn C. (1990). "Franklin and friends: Benjamin Franklin's ties to quakers and quakerism," *Pennsylvania History* 57: 318–336.
Miller, Perry (1953). *The New England Mind: From Colony to Province.* Cambridge, MA.
Miller, Perry, ed. (1962). "Benjamin Franklin, 1706–1790; Jonathan Edwards, 1703–1758" in *Major Writers of America*, ed. Perry Miller. New York, NY.
Millette, Shamir and Travis, Jennifer, eds (2002). *Boys Don't Cry? Rethinking Narratives of Masculinity and Emotion in the U.S.* New York, NY.
Minardi, M. (2004). "The Boston inoculation controversy of 1721–1722: An Incident in the History of Race," *William and Mary Quarterly* 3d ser. 61: 47–76.
Mitchell, Trent (1998). "The politics of experiment in the eighteenth century: The pursuit of audience and the manipulation of consensus in the debate over lightning rods," *Eighteenth-Century Studies* 31: 3, 307–331.

Montaigne, Michel de (1943). *Selected Essays.* Translated by and ed. Donald M. Frame. New York, NY.

Moraley, William (2006). *The Infortunate,* eds, Susan E. Klepp and Billy G. Smith, 2nd edn. University Park, PA.

Morgan, David T. (1996). *The Devious Dr. Franklin, Colonial Agent: Benjamin Franklin's Years in London.* Macon, GA.

Morgan, Edmund S. (1991). "Secrets of Benjamin Franklin," *New York Review of Books* 38: January 31.

Morgan, Edmund S. (2002). *Benjamin Franklin.* New Haven, CT.

Morgan, Edmund S. (2005). "The end of his pragmatism," in Talbott, ed. (2005a), pp. 299–315.

Morgan, E.S. and Morgan, H.M. (1962). *The Stamp Act Crisis: Prologue to Revolution,* revised edn. New York, NY.

Morris, Richard B. (1965). *The Peacemakers: The Great Powers and American Independence.* New York, NY.

Morrison, M.A. and Zook, M., eds (2004). *Revolutionary Currents: Nation Building in the Transatlantic World.* Lanham, MD.

Morse, John T. (1889). *Benjamin Franklin.* Boston, MA.

Moss, Roger (2004). *Historic Sacred Places of Philadelphia.* Philadelphia, PA.

Mott, F.L. (1941). *American Journalism: A History of Newspapers in the United States Through 250 Years, 1690–1940.* New York, NY.

Mulford, C. (1996). "Benjamin Franklin and the myths of nationhood," in Lee and Verhoeven, eds (1996), pp. 15–58.

Mulford, C. (1999). "Figuring Benjamin Franklin in American cultural memory," *New England Quarterly* 72: 415–443.

Mulford, C. (2000). "Franklin, women, and American cultural myths," in Tise, ed. (2005a), pp. 103–128.

Mulford, C., ed. (2009a). *The Cambridge Companion to Benjamin Franklin.* New York, NY.

Mulford, C. (2009b). "Introduction," in Mulford, ed. (2009a), pp. 1–10.

Mulford, C. (2009c). Benjamin Franklin, traditions of liberalism, and women's learning in eighteenth-century Philadelphia, in Pollack, ed. (2009a), pp. 100–121.

Muller, Jerry Z. (1993). *Adam Smith in His Time and Ours.* New York, NY.

Murphy, Frank (2001). *Ben Franklin and the Magic Squares.* New York, NY: Random House.

Muscalus, John Anthony (1938). *An Index of State Bank Notes That Illustrate Washington and Franklin.* Bridgeport, PA.

Nash, Gary B. (1968). *Quakers and Politics. Pennsylvania, 1681–1726.* Princeton, NJ.

Nash, Gary B. (1977). "Up from the bottom in Franklin's Philadelphia," *Past and Present* 77: 57–83

Nash, Gary B. (1979). *The Urban Crucible: Social Change, Political Consciousness, and the Origins of the American Revolution.* Cambridge, MA.

Nash, Gary B. (2002). *First City: Philadelphia and the Forging of Historical Memory.* Philadelphia, PA.

Nash, Gary B. (2006a). *The Forgotten Fifth: African Americans in the Age of Revolution.* Cambridge, MA.

Nash, Gary B. (2006b). "Franklin and slavery," *American Philosophical Society Proceedings* 150: 620–637.

Neem, J.N. (2008). *Creating a Nation of Joiners: Democracy and Civil Society in Early National Massachusetts*. Cambridge, MA.

Nerone, J.C. (1987). "The mythology of the Penny Press," *Critical Studies in Mass Communication* 4: 376–404.

Newbold, Robert C. (1955). *The Albany Congress and Plan of Union of 1754*. New York, NY.

Newcomb, Benjamin H. (1972). *Franklin and Galloway: A Political Partnership*. New Haven, CT.

Newcomb, R. (1955). "Franklin's debt to Lord Halifax," *Publications of the Modern Language Association* 70: 535–539.

Newell, Margaret (1998). *From Dependence to Independence: Economic Revolution in Colonial New England*. Ithaca, NY.

Newman, Eric P. (1966). "Continental currency and the Fugio cent: Sources of emblems and mottoes," *Numismatist* 79: 1587–1598.

Newman, Eric P. (1983). "Benjamin Franklin and the chain design," *Numismatist* 96: 2272–2273.

Newman, Simon P. (2003). *Embodied History: The Lives of the Poor in Early Philadelphia*. Philadelphia, PA.

Newman, Simon P. (2009). "Benjamin Franklin and the leather-apron men: The politics of class in eighteenth-century Philadelphia," *Journal of American Studies* 43(2): 161–175.

Nickels, Cameron C. (1976). "Franklin's poor Richard's almanacs: 'The Humblest of his Labours'" in Lemay, ed. (1976a), pp. 77–90.

Nolan, J. Bennett (1936). *General Benjamin Franklin: The Military Career of a Philosopher*. Philadelphia, PA.

Nolan, J. Bennett (1938). *Benjamin Franklin in Scotland and Ireland, 1759 and 1771*. Philadelphia, PA.

Nord, D.P. (2006). "James Carey and journalism history: A remembrance," *Journalism History* 32: 122–127.

Nord, D.P. (2008a). "The history of journalism and the history of the book," in Zelizer, ed. (2008), pp. 162–180.

Nord, D.P. (2008b). "Accuracy or fair play? Complaining about the newspaper in early twentieth-century New York," in Machor, and Goldstein, eds (2008), pp. 233–254.

Norton, Anne (1988). *Reflections on Political Identity*. Baltimore, MD.

Novak, M., ed. (2008). *The Age of Projects*. Toronto.

Novak, W.J. (2001). "The American Law of Association: The legal-political construction of civil society," *Studies in American Political Development* 15: 163–188.

Oberg, Barbara B. and Stout, Harry S., eds (1993). *Benjamin Franklin, Jonathan Edwards and the Representation of American Culture*. New York, NY.

Okoye, F.N. (1980). "Chattel slavery as the nightmare of the American revolutionaries," *William and Mary Quarterly* 3rd ser. 37: 3–28.

Olson, Alison (1993). "The lobbying of London quakers for Pennsylvania friends," *Pennsylvania Magazine of History and Biography* 117: 131–152.

Olson, Lester C. (1987). "Benjamin Franklin's pictorial representations of the british colonies in America: A study in rhetorical iconology," *Quarterly Journal of Speech* 73: 18–42.

Olson, Lester C. (1990). "Benjamin Franklin's commemorative medal, *Libertas Americana*: A study in rhetorical iconology," *Quarterly Journal of Speech* 76: 23–45.

Olson, Lester C. (1991). *Emblems of American Community in the Revolutionary Era: A Study in Rhetorical Iconology.* Washington DC.

Olson, Lester C. (2004). *Benjamin Franklin's Vision of American Community: A Study in Rhetorical Iconology.* Columbia, SC.

Olton, C.S. (1975). *Artisans for Independence: Philadelphia Mechanics and the American Revolution.* Syracuse, NY.

Ott, Katherine, Serlin, David H., and Mihm, Stephen, eds (2002). *Artificial Parts, Practical Lives: Modern Histories of Prosthetics.* New York, NY.

Pace, Antonio (1958). *Benjamin Franklin and Italy. (Memoirs of the American Philosophical Society 47).* Philadelphia, PA.

Palmer, R.R. (1959–1964). *The Age of the Democratic Revolution: A Political History of Europe and America, 1760–1800*, 2 vols. Princeton, NJ.

Pancaldi, Giuliano (2005). *Volta, Science and Culture in the Age of Enlightenment.* Princeton, NJ.

Pangle, Lorraine Smith (2007). *The Political Philosophy of Benjamin Franklin.* Baltimore, MD.

Parker, David A. (1976) "From sound believer to practical preparationist: some puritan harmonies in Franklin's autobiography," in Lemay (1976a), 67–75.

Parrington, Vernon L. (1927). *Main Currents of American Thought: The Colonial Mind, 1620–1800.* New York, NY.

Parton, J. (1855). *Life of Horace Greeley, Editor of the New York Tribune.* New York, NY.

Parton, J. (1864). *Life and Times of Benjamin Franklin.* New York, NY.

Parton, J. (1866). *Life and Times of Benjamin Franklin*, 2 vols. Boston, MA.

Pasley, Jeffrey L., Robertson, Andrew R., and Waldstreicher, David, eds (2004). *Beyond the Founders: New Approaches to the Political History of the Early American Republic.* Chapel Hill, NC.

Patee, Fred Lewis (1896). *A History of American Literature.* Boston, MA.

Payne, G.H. (1920). *History of Journalism in the United States.* New York, NY.

Patterson, Mark R. (1988). *Authority, Autonomy, and Representation in American Literature, 1776–1865.* Princeton, NJ.

Pencak, W. (1992). "Politics and ideology in poor Richard's almanack," *Pennsylvania Magazine of History and Biography* 116: 183–211.

Pencak, W. (2002). "Beginning of a beautiful friendship: Benjamin Franklin, George Whitefield, the 'Dancing School Blockheads,' and a defense of the 'Meaner Sort'," *Proteus* 19(1): 45–50.

Pencak, W. (2007). "Benjamin Franklin: The many faces of an American revolutionary," in Weisberger, Hupchick, and Anderson, eds, *Profiles*, pp. 58–70.

Pencak, William A. and Richter, Daniel K. (2004). *Friends and Enemies in Penn's Woods: Indians, Colonists and the Racial Construction of Pennsylvania.* Philadelphia, PA.

Perelman, Michael (2000). *The Invention of Capitalism: Classical Political Economy and the Secret History of Primitive Accumulation*. Durham, NC.

Perkins, B. (1993). *The Creation of a Republican Empire, 1776–1865*. Cambridge, MA.

Perry, Bliss (1912). *The American Mind*. Boston, MA.

Pestritto, R.J. and West, T.G., eds (2003). *The American Founding and the Social Compact*. Lanham, MD.

Peterson, M.A. (2002). "*The Selling of Joseph*: Bostonians, antislavery, and the protestant international, 1689–1733," *Massachusetts Historical Review* 4: 1–22.

Pietz, William (1985). "The problem of the fetish, I," *RES: Anthropology and Aesthetics* 9: 5–17.

Pollack, John. H., ed. (2009a). *The Good Education of Youth: Worlds of Learning in the Age of Franklin*. Newcastle, DE.

Pollack, John H. (2009b). "Introduction: Worlds of learning in the age of Franklin," in Pollack, ed. (2009a), pp. 2–35.

Poor Robin (1725). Bound volume of almanacs belonging to Princess Sophia, Folger Shakespeare Library, Washington DC.

Porter, Roy (2001). *The Creation of the Modern World: The Untold Story of the British Enlightenment*. New York, NY.

Pratt, Mary Louise (1992). *Imperial Eyes: Travel Writing and Transculturation*. London.

Pray, I. (1855). *Memoirs of James Gordon Bennett and His Times, by a Journalist*. New York, NY.

Preston, Robert (1964). *Ben Franklin in Paris*. Hollywood, CA: Capitol.

Priestley, Joseph (1774–1777). *Experiments and Observations on Different Kinds of Air*, 3 vols. London.

Prince, Sue Ann, ed. (2006). "The princess and the patriot: Ekaterina Dashicova, Benjamin Franklin and the age of enlightenment," *Transactions of the American Philosophical Society* 96: 1–129.

Prown, Jules David (2001). *Art as Evidence: Writings on Art and Material Culture*. New Haven, CT.

Prucha, Francis Paul (1984). *The Great Father: The United States Government and the Indians*, 2 vols. Lincoln, NE.

Rabban, D.M. (1985). "The ahistorical historian: Leonard Levy on freedom of expression in early American history," *Stanford Law Review* 37: 795–856.

Rabban, D.M. (1997). *Free Speech in Its Forgotten Years*. Cambridge, England.

Rahe, P., ed. (2006). *Machiavelli's Liberal Republicanism*. New York, NY.

Raven, J. (2007). "Social libraries and library societies in eighteenth-century North America," in Augst and Carpenter, eds (2007), pp. 24–52.

Reavis, L.U. (1872). *A Representative Life of Horace Greeley, with an Introduction by Cassius M. Clay*. New York, NY.

Reid, W. (1875). "Whitelaw Reid, editor of the 'New York Tribune'," in Wingate, ed. (1875), pp. 25–40.

Reid, W. (1879). *Some Newspaper Tendencies: An Address Delivered before the Editorial Associations of New-York and Ohio*. New York, NY.

Rettig, Jessica (2009). "America's founding playboys: Washington, Franklin and Hamilton," *U.S. News and World Report Online*, Decemder 31, 2009.

Rice, Grantland (1997). *The Transformation of Authorship in America*. Chicago, IL.
Richardson, C.F. (1895). *American Literature, 1607–1885*, vol. 1. *The Development of American Thought*. New York, NY.
Richardson, David (1991). "Slavery, trade, and economic growth in eighteenth-century New England," in Solow, ed. (1991a), pp. 237–264.
Rigal, Laura (1998). *The American Manufactory: Art, Labor, and the World of Things in the Early Republic*. Princeton, NJ.
Riley, Edward M. (1951). "The Deborah Franklin correspondence," *Proceedings of the American Philosophical Society* 95: 239–245.
Riley, Edward M. (1953). "Franklin's home," *Transactions of the American Philosophical Society* 43: 148–160.
Roach, Hannah Benner (1960). "Benjamin Franklin slept here," *Pennsylvania Magazine of History and Biography* 84: 127–174.
Roach, Joseph (1996). *Cities of the Dead: Circum-Atlantic Performance*. New York: Columbia University Press.
Rockman, Seth (2006). "The unfree origins of American capitalism," in Matson, ed. (2006), pp. 3335–3361.
Roelker, William Greene (1948). "The Franklin-Green correspondence," *Proceedings of the American Philosophical Society* 92: 186–193.
Roelker, William Greene, ed. (1949). *Benjamin Franklin and Catherine Ray Greene: Their Correspondence, 1755–1790*. Philadelphia, PA.
Roney, J.C. (2008). "'First movers in every useful undertaking': Formal voluntary associations in Philadelphia, 1725–1775." Ph.D. dissertation. Johns Hopkins University.
Roney, J.C. (2010). "'Ready to act in defiance of government': Colonial Philadelphia voluntary culture and the defense association of 1747–1748," *Early American Studies* 8: 358–385.
Root, Winfred Trexler (1912). *The Relations of Pennsylvania with the British Government, 1696–1765*. New York, NY.
Rorabaugh, W.J. (1986). *The Craft Apprentice: From Franklin to the Machine Age in America*. New York, NY.
Rosemont, Henry P (1981). "Benjamin Franklin and the Philadelphia typographical strikers of 1786," *Labor History* 22: 398–429.
Ross, J.F. (1940). "The character of poor Richard: Its sources and alterations," *Publications of the Modern Language Association* 55: 785–794.
Rossignol, Marie-Jeanne (2010). "Jacques-Pierre Brissot and the fate of Atlantic antislavery during the age of revolutionary wars," in Bessel, ed., pp. 139–156.
Rossiter, Clinton (1953). *Seedtime of the Republic: The Origin of the American Tradition of Political Liberty*. New York, NY.
Rossiter, Clinton. (1956) *The First American Revolution: The American Colonies on the Eve of Independence*. New York, NY.
Royot, Daniel (1993). "Humor and sex: The French connection in Franklin's lovelife," in Balestra and Sampietro, eds (1993), pp. 89–98.
Russell, Daniel S. (1985). *The Emblem and Device in France*. Lexington, KY.
Russell, Phillips (1926). *Benjamin Franklin: The First Civilized American*. New York, NY.

Ryan, M.P. (1999). "Civil society as democratic practice: North American cities during the nineteenth century," *Journal of Interdisciplinary History* 29: 559–584.

Ryerson, R.A. (1978). *The Revolution Is Now Begun: The Radical Committees of Philadelphia, 1765–1776*. Philadelphia, PA.

Sadosky, Leonard (2009). *Revolutionary Negotiations: Indians, Empires, and Diplomats in the Founding of America*. Charlottesville, VA.

Salinger, Sharon (1987). *'To Serve Well and Faithfully': Labor and Indentured Servitude in Pennsylvania, 1682–1800*. New York, NY.

Sanborn, F.B. (1874). "Journalism and journalists," *Atlantic* 34: 55–66.

Sanford, Charles, ed. (1955). *Benjamin Franklin and the American Character*. Boston, MA.

Sappenfield, James A. (1973). *A Sweet Instruction: Franklin's Journalism as a Literary Apprenticeship*. Carbondale, IL.

Schaeper, Thomas J. (1995). *France and America in the Revolutionary Era: The Life of Jacques-Donatien Leray de Chaumont*. Providence, RI.

Schaffer, Simon (1993). "The consuming flame: Electrical showmen and Tory mysticism in the world of goods," in *Consumption and the World of Goods*, eds, John Brewer and Roy Porter. London: Routledge, pp. 488–526.

Schiff, Stacy (2005). *A Great Improvisation: Franklin, France, and the Birth of America*. New York, NY.

Schiff, Stacy (2009). "Franklin in Paris," *American Scholar*.

Schiffer, Michael Brian (2003). *Draw the Lightning Down: Benjamin Franklin and Electrical Technology in the Age of Enlightenment*. Berkeley, CA.

Schleiner, Winfried (1976–1977). "The infant Hercules: Franklin's design for a medal commemorating American liberty," *Eighteenth Century Studies* 10: 235–244.

Schlesinger, A.M. (1922). "The American Revolution," *New Viewpoints in American History*. New York, NY.

Schneider, Herbert (1955). "Ungodly puritans" in Sanford, ed. (1955), pp. 77–83.

Schultz, R. (1993). *The Republic of Labor: Philadelphia Artisans and the Politics of Class, 1720–1830*. New York, NY.

Schwartz, Sally (1987). *"A Mixed Multitude": the Struggle For Toleration in Colonial Pennsylvania*. New York, NY.

Schweitzer, Mary (1987). *Custom and Contract: Household Government and the Economy in Colonial Pennsylvania*. New York, NY.

Seavey, Ormond (1985). "D.H. Lawrence and 'The First Dummy American'," *Georgia Review* 39.

Seavey, Ormond (1987). "Benjamin Franklin and D.H. Lawrence as conflicting modes of consciousness," in Buxbaum, ed. (1987).

Seavey, Ormond (1988). *Becoming Benjamin Franklin: The Autobiography and the Life*. University Park, PA.

Seavey, Ormond (1993). "Benjamin Franklin as imperialist and provincial," in Balestra and Sanpietro, eds (1993), pp. 19–37.

Ségur, Louis-Philippe, comte de Ségur (1824–1826). *Mémoires, ou souvenirs et anecdotes*, 3 vols. Paris.

Sellers, Charles C. (1955). "Jane Mecom's little picture," *Proceedings of the American Philosophical Society* 99: 433–435.
Sellers, Charles C. (1962). *Benjamin Franklin in Portraiture*. New Haven, CT.
Shade, William G. and Kennedy, Michael V., eds (2001). *The World Turned Upside Down: The State of Eighteenth-Century American Studies at the Beginning of the Twenty-First Century*. Bethlehem, PA.
Shannon, Timothy (2000). *Indians and Colonists at the Crossroads of Empire: The Albany Congress of 1754*. Ithaca, NY.
Sharp, Granville (1769). *A Representation of the Injustice and Dangerous Tendency of Tolerating Slavery*. London.
Shaw, M.J. (2007). "Keeping time in the age of Franklin: Almanacs in the Atlantic world," *Printing History* 27: 17–37.
Shaw, Peter (1982). "Introduction," in *Benjamin Franklin, The Autobiography and other Writings*. Peter Shaw, ed. New York, NY.
Shea, Daniel B. (1968). *Spiritual Autobiography in Early America*. Madison, WI.
Shear, Walter (1962). "Franklin's Self-Portrait," *Midwest Quarterly* 4: 71–86.
Shepherd, William Robert (1896). *History of Proprietary Government in Pennsylvania*. New York, NY.
Sherman, Stuart P. (1917). "Franklin" in Trent, Erskine, Sherman, and Van Doren, eds (1917).
Shields, David S. (1997). *Civil Tongues and Polite Letters in British America*. Chapel Hill, NC.
Shields, David S. (2009). "Franklin in the republic of letters," in Mulford, ed. (2009a), pp. 50–62.
Shumway, David R. (1994). *Creating American Civilization: A Genealogy of American Literature as an Academic Discipline*. Minneapolis, MN.
Shy, J. (1976). *A People Numerous and Armed: Reflections on the Military Struggle for American Independence*. Ann Arbor, MI.
Silver, Peter (2008). *Our Savage Neighbors: How Indian War Transformed Early America*. New York, NY.
Simler, L. (1986). "Tenancy in colonial Pennsylvania: The case of Chester County," *William and Mary Quarterly* 3rd ser. 43: 542–569.
Simpson, Lewis P. (1976). "The printer as a man of letters: Franklin and the symbolism of the third realm" in Lemay, ed. (1976a), pp. 3–20.
Skemp, Sheila (1990). *William Franklin: Son of a Patriot, Servant of a King*. New York, NY.
Skemp, Sheila (2000). "Family partnerships: The working wife, honoring Deborah Franklin," in Tise, ed. (2000b), pp. 19–36.
Slessarev, Helga (1966). "Susanne von Bandemer and Benjamin Franklin," *American Notes and Queries* 4: 149–151.
Sloan, Roberta and Moritz, Dennis with O'Connor David (2010). "*First Lady of Philadelphia: The Life and Times of Deborah Franklin*." Unpublished Script, Performances by Sloan.
Sloan, W.D., ed. (2008). *The Media in America: A History*, 7th edn. Northport, AL.
Sloan, W.D. and Williams, J.H. (1994). *The Early American Press, 1690–1783*. Westport, CT.

Smail, John (1994). *The Origins of Middle-Class Culture: Halifax, Yorkshire, 1660–1780.* Ithaca, NY.

Smeall, J.F.S. (1959). "'Miss Polly Baker's speech' 'An American Text'," *North Dakota Quarterly* 27: 78–80.

Smeall, J.F.S. (1960). "The readerships of the Polly Baker texts," *North Dakota Quarterly* 28: 20–29.

Smith, Adam (1976). *An Inquiry into the Nature and Causes of the Wealth of Nations,* in R.H. Campbell and A.S. Skinner, eds. (1976).

Smith, Adam (1982). The theory of moral sentiments, eds, D.D. Raphael and A.L. Macfie. Indiannapolis, IN.

Smith, Billy G. (1981). "The material live of laboring Philadelphians, 1750–1800," *William and Mary Quarterly* 3rd ser. 38: 163–202.

Smith, Billy G. (1984). "Inequality in late colonial Philadelphia: A note on its nature and growth," *William and Mary Quarterly* 3rd ser. 38(4): 629–645.

Smith, Billy G. (1990). *The "Lower Sort": Philadelphia's Laboring People, 1750–1800.* Ithaca, NY.

Smith, Billy G. (2005). "Benjamin Franklin, civic improver," in Talbott, ed. (2005a), pp. 91–123.

Smith, Billy G. and Wojtowicz, Richard, eds (1989). *Blacks who Stole Themselves: Advertisements from the Pennsylvania Gazette, 1728–1790.* University Park, PA.

Smith, J.A. (1988). *Printers and Press Freedom: The Ideology of Early American Journalism.* New York, NY.

Smith, J.A. (1990). *Franklin and Bache: Envisioning the Enlightened Republic.* New York, NY.

Smith, J.A. (1993). "'Infamous Practices': Risk-taking in Franklin's early journalism," in Lemay, ed. (1993), pp. 40–51.

Smith, J.A. (2008). "Franklin, Benjamin," in Vaughn, ed. (2008), pp. 179–181.

Smith, M.A.Y., and Baldasty, G.J. (1979). "Criticism of public officials and government in the new nation," *Journal of Communication Inquiry* 4: 53–74.

Smolenski, J. (2005). "'Incorporated … into a Body Politic': Clubs, print, and the gendering of the civic subject in eighteenth-century Pennsylvania," in Kamrath and Harris, eds (2005), pp. 47–73.

Smolenski, J. (2010). *Friends and Strangers: The Making of a Creole Culture in Colonial Pennsylvania.* Philadelphia, PA.

Smyth, A.H., ed. (1905–1907). *The Writings of Benjamin Franklin,* 10 vols. New York, NY.

Sollers, Werner (1983). "Dr. Benjamin Franklin's celestial telegraph, or indian blessings to gas-lit American drawing rooms," *Social Science Information* 22: 983–1004.

Solow, Barbara L. (1987). "Capitalism and slavery in the exceedingly long run," in Solow and Engerman, eds (1987), pp. 51–77.

Solow, Barbara L., ed. (1991a). *Slavery and the Rise of the Atlantic System.* New York, NY.

Solow, Barbara L. (1991b). "Slavery and colonization," in Solow, ed. (1991a), pp. 21–42.

Solow, Barbara L. and Engerman, Stanley, eds (1987). *British Capitalism and Caribbean Slavery: The Legacy of Eric Williams.* New York, NY.

Somerville, W. (1996). *The Tuesday Club of Annapolis (1745–1756) as Cultural Performance*. Athens, GA.

Sommer, Frank H. (1961). "Emblem and device: The origin of the great seal of the United States," *Art Quarterly* 24: 57–76.

Sosin, J.M. (1965). *Agents and Merchants: British Colonial Policy and the Origins of the American Revolution, 1763–1775*. Lincoln, NE.

Sparks, Jared, ed. (1971). *Essays on General Politics, Commerce, and Political Economy, Being Volume II, Part II of The Works of Benjamin Franklin*. New York, NY.

Spengemann, William C. (1980). *The Forms of Autobiography*. New Haven, CT.

Spiller, Robert, ed. (1948). *Literary History of the United States*, vol I. New York, NY: MacMillan.

Spiller, Robert (1955). *The Cycle of American Literature: An Essay in Historical Criticism*. New York, NY.

St George, Robert Blair, ed. (1988). *Material Life in America, 1600–1860*. Boston, MA.

St George, Robert Blair (1998). *Conversing by Signs: Poetics of Implication in Colonial New England Culture*. Chapel Hill, NC.

St George, Robert B., ed. (2000). *Possible Pasts: Becoming Colonial in Early America*. Ithaca, NY.

Stabile, Susan (2000). "Salons and power in the era of revolution: From literary coteries to epistolary enlightenment," in Tise, ed. (2000b), pp. 129–148.

Stagg, J.C.A. (2009). *Borderlines in Borderlands: James Madison and the Spanish-American Frontier, 1776–1821*. New Haven, CT.

Stallybrass, Peter and White, Allon (1986). *The Politics and Poetics of Transgression*. Ithaca, NY: Cornell University Press.

Starobinski, Jean (1988). *Jean-Jacques Rousseau: Transparency and Obstruction*. Translated by Arthur Goldhammer. Chicago, IL: University of Chicago Press.

Stenhoff, Mark (1999). *Ball Lightning: An Unsolved Problem in Atmospheric Physics*. Hingham, MA.

Stern, Jeremy A. (2006). "Jane Franklin Mecom: A Boston woman in revolutionary times," *Early American Studies* 4: 147–191.

Stifler, James Madison, ed. (1927). *"My Dear Girl": The Correspondence of Benjamin Franklin with Polly Stevenson, Georgiana and Catherine Shipley*. New York, NY.

Stinchcombe, William C. (1969). *The American Revolution and the French Alliance*. Syracuse, NY.

Stokes, Claudia (2006). *Writers in Retrospect: The Rise of American Literary History, 1875–1910*. Chapel Hill, NC.

Stourzh, Gerald (1969). *Benjamin Franklin and American Foreign Policy*, 2nd edn. Chicago, IL.

Stout, Harry S. (1991). *The Divine Dramatist: George Whitefield and the Great Awakening*. Grand Rapids, MI.

Stowell, M.B. (1977). *Early American Almanacs: The Colonial Weekday Bible*. New York, NY.

Streumph, Vernon (1970). "Who was Elizabeth Downes Franklin?" *Pennsylvania Magazine of History and Biography* 94: 533–534.

Styles, John and Vickery, Amanda (2006). *Gender, Taste, and Material Culture in Britain and North America, 1700–1830*. New Haven, CT.

Sutton, Geoffrey (1981). "Electric medicine and mesmerism," *Isis* 72: 3, 375–392.
Sy Waxer: Time Traveler–Ben Franklin Sex Tapes (2008). Available at: http://www.youtube.com/watch?v=ft1B2j7bimA&feature=youtube_gdata.
Talbott, Page, ed. (2005a). *Benjamin Franklin: In Search of a Better World*. New Haven, CT.
Talbott, Page (2005b). "Benjamin Franklin at home," in Talbott, ed. (2005a), pp. 125–162.
Tatham, Campbell (1971). "Benjamin Franklin, Cotton Mather and the outward state," *Early American Literature* 6: 223–233.
Taylor, Alan (2003). "The good father," *The New Republic* 2003: 48–53.
Terrell, Colleen E. (2003). "'Republican Machines': Franklin, Rush, and the manufacture of civic virtue in the early republic," *Early American Studies* 1(2): 100–132.
The Office–Season Three. National Broadcasting Company (NBC) (2007).
Thayer, Theodore. (1953). *Pennsylvania Politics and the Growth of Democracy, 1740–1776*. Harrisburg, PA.
Thomas, I. (1810). *The History of Printing in America*, 2 vols. Worcester, MA.
Thompson, E.P. (1963). *The Making of the English Working Class*. London.
Thompson, E.P. (1991). *Customs in Common*. New York, NY.
Thompson, Peter John (1999). *Rum Punch and Revolution: Taverngoing and Public Life in Eighteenth-Century Philadelphia*. Philadelphia, PA.
Tise, Larry, ed. (2000a). *Benjamin Franklin and Women*. University Park, PA.
Tise, Larry (2000b). "Introduction: Benjamin Franklin and the world of women," in Tise, ed. (2000a), pp. 1–18.
Tise, Larry (2000c) "Liberty and the rights of women: Sarah Franklin's declaration of independence," in Tise, ed. (2000a), pp. 37–50.
Tocqueville, A.D. (2004). *Democracy in America*. Translated by A. Goldhammer. New York, NY.
Tolles, Frederick B. (1948). *Meeting House and Counting House: The Quaker Merchants of Colonial Philadelphia, 1682–1763*. Chapel Hill, NC.
Tomlins, Christopher (2010). *Freedom Bound*. New York, NY.
Tourtellot, A.B. (1977). *Benjamin Franklin, The Shaping of Genius: The Boston Years*. Garden City, NY.
Trent, W.P., Erskine, J., Sherman, S.P, and Van Doren, C., eds (1917). *The Cambridge History of American Literature*, vol. 1. *Colonial and Revolutionary Literature, Early National Literature, Part I*. New York, NY.
Tully, Alan (1972). *Pennsylvania Politics, 1746–1770. The Movement for Royal Government and Its Consequences*. Princeton, NY.
Tully, Alan (1977). *William Penn's Legacy: Politics and Social Structure in Provincial Pennsylvania, 1726–1755*. Baltimore, MD.
Tully, Alan (1982). "Politics and peace testimony in mid-eighteenth-century Pennsylvania," *Canadian Review of American Studies* 13: 159–177.
Tully, Alan (1983). "Ethnicity, religion and politics in early America," *Pennsylvania Magazine of History and Biography* 107: 491–536.
Tully, Alan (1986). "Quaker party and proprietary policies: The dynamics of politics in pre-revolutionary Pennsylvania, 1730–1775," in Daniels, ed. (1986).

Tully, Alan (1994). *Forming American Politics. Ideals, Interests, and Institutions in Colonial New York and Pennsylvania*. Baltimore, MD.

Twain, M. (1875). *Mark Twain's Sketches, New and Old*. Hartford, CT.

Tyler, Moses Coit (1878). *History of American Literature, 1607–1765*. New York, NY.

Tyler, Moses Coit (1897). *Literary History of the American Revolution, 1763–1783*. New York, NY.

Ulrich, Laurel Thatcher (2001). *The Age of Homespun: Objects and Stories in the Creation of an American Myth*. New York, NY.

"Unquotable: Benjamin Franklin." *Uncyclopedia*, n.d. Available at: http://uncyclopedia.wikia.com/wiki/Unquotable:Benjamin_Franklin.

U.S. Congress (1834). *Debates and Proceedings in the Congress of the Untied States*, vol. 2 Washington, DC (1234, February12, 1790).

Van Alstyne, R.W. (1965). *Empire and Independence: The International History of the American Revolution*. New York, NY.

Van Doren, Carl (1938). *Benjamin Franklin*. New York, NY.

Van Doren, Carl (1948). "Benjamin Franklin" in *Literary History of the United States*, vol. 1. Robert E. Spiller, Willard Thorp, Thomas H. Johnson, Henry Seidel Canby, and Richard M.Ludwing, eds. New York, NY.

Van Doren, Carl (1950a). *Jane Mecom: The Favorite Sister of Benjamin Franklin*. New York, NY.

Van Doren, Carl, ed. (1950b). *The Letters of Benjamin Franklin and Jane Mecom*. Princeton, NJ.

Van Gastel, Ada (1990). "Franklin and Freud: Love in the *Autobiography*," *Early American Literature* 25(2): 168–182.

Van Horne, John C. (1993). "Collective benevolence and the common good in Franklin's philanthropy," in Lemay, ed. (1993), pp. 425–440.

Vann, Richard T. (1986). "Quakerism: Made in America?," in Dunn and Dunn, eds (1986), pp. 157–170.

Vaughn, S.L., ed. (2008). *Encyclopedia of American Journalism*. New York, NY.

Wages, Jack D. (1973). "Father Benjamin and the ladies: Chauvinist or champion?" *Proceedings of Conference of College Teachers of English of Texas*, 38–42.

Wahrman, Dror (1995). *Imagining the Middle Class: The Political Representation of Class in Britain, c.1780–1840*. Cambridge, England.

Wahrman, Dror (2004). *Making the Modern Self: Identity and Culture in Eighteenth-Century England*. New Haven, CT.

Waldstreicher, David (1999). "Reading the runaways: Self-fashioning, print culture, and confidence in slavery in the eighteenth century mid-Atlantic," *William and Mary Quarterly* 3rd ser. 56: 243–272.

Waldstreicher, David (2002). "The long arm of Benjamin Franklin," in Ott, Serlin, and Mihm, eds (2002), pp. 300–326.

Waldstreicher, David (2004). *Runaway America: Benjamin Franklin, Slavery, and the American Revolution*. New York, NY.

Waldstreicher, David (2009). *Slavery's Constitution: From Revolution to Ratification*. New York, NY.

Wallace, Anthony F.C. (1999). *Jefferson and the Indians: The Tragic Fate of the First Americans*. Cambridge, MA.

Wallach, Alan (1998). *Exhibiting Contradiction: Essays on the Art Museum in the United States.* Amherst, MA.
Wallerstein, Immanuel (1985). *Historical Capitalism; with Capitalist Civilization,* 2nd edn. London.
Walters, Kerry (1999). *Benjamin Franklin and his Gods.* Urbana, IL.
Walzer, Michael (1973). *The Revolution of the Saints: A Study of the Origins of Radical Politics* New York, NY.
Ward, John William (1963). "Who was Benjamin Franklin?" *American Scholar* 32: 541–553.
Ward, John William (1969). *Red, White, and Blue: Men, Books, and Ideas in American Culture.* New York, NY.
Warner, Michael (1990). *The Letters of the Republic: Publication and the Public Sphere in Eighteenth Century America.* Cambridge, MA.
Warner, Michael (1993). "Savage Franklin," in Balestra and Sanpietro, eds (1993), pp. 85–87.
Warner, Michael (2000). "What's colonial about colonial America?" in St George, ed. (2000).
Weaver, Glenn (1957). "Benjamin Franklin and the Pennsylvania Germans," *William and Mary Quarterly* 3rd ser. 14: 536–559.
Weber, M. (1930). *The Protestant Ethic and the Spirit of Capitalism.* Translated by T. Parsons. New York, NY.
Weber, M. (1958). *The Protestant Ethic and the Spirit of Capitalism.* Translated by T. Parsons. New York, NY.
Weber, Max (2009). *The Protestant Ethic and the Spirit of Capitalism.* Richard Swedberg, ed. New York, NY.
Weddle, Meredith Baldwin (2001). *Walking in the Way of Peace. Quaker Pacifism in the Seventeenth Century.* New York, NY.
Weed, T. (1851). "Mr. Weed to the New York typographical society, Albany, January 12, 1851," in Barnes, ed. (1884), pp. 191–195.
Weinberger, Jerry (2005). *Benjamin Franklin Unmasked: On the Unity of His Moral, Religious and Political Thought.* Lawrence, KS.
Weisberger, R.W., Hupchick, D.P., and Anderson, D.L., eds (2007). *Profiles of Revolutionaries in Atlantic History: 1700–1850.* New York, NY.
Wellenreuther, Herman (1970). "The political dilemma of the Quakers in Pennsylvania, 1681–1748," *Pennsylvania Magazine of History and Biography* 94: 135–172.
Wendel, Thomas (1975). *The Politics of Liberty: A Biography with Readings.* New York, NY.
Wendell, B. (1901). *A Literary History of America.* New York, NY.
West, Thomas G. (1998). *Vindicating the Founders.* Lanham, MD.
Wheeler, Roxann (2000). *The Complexion of Race: Categories of Difference in Eighteenth-Century British Culture.* Philadelphia, PA.
White, Ed (2006). *The Backcountry and the City: Colonization and Conflict in Early America.* Minneapolis, MN.
(1801). "Wieland, or the transformation," *American Review and Literary Journal for the Year 1801.* 1, 333–339.
Williams, Eric (1944). *Capitalism and Slavery.* Chapel Hill, NC.

Williams, Eric (1984). *From Columbus to Castro: The History of the* Carribbean. New York, NY.
Williams, William Appelman (1959). *The Contours of American History*. Cleveland, OH.
Williams, William Appelman (1961). *The Contours of American History*. Cleveland, OH.
Williams, William Appelman, ed. (1972). *From Colony to Empire: Essays in the History of American Foreign Relations*. New York, NY.
Willis, William (1868). "Doctor Franklin, Charles Thompson and Mrs. Logan," *Historical Magazine* 2nd ser. 4: 280–282.
Wilson, R. Jackson (1989). *Figures of Speech: American Writers and the Literary Marketplace, from Benjamin Franklin to Emily Dickinson*. New York, NY.
Winch, Donald (1996). *Riches and Poverty: An Intellectual History of Political Economy in Britain, 1750–1834*. New York, NY.
Wingate, C.F., ed. (1875). *Views and Interviews on Journalism*. New York, NY.
Winkler, L. (1977). "Pennsylvania German astronomy and astrology, Part 14: Benjamin Franklin's almanacs," *Pennsylvania Folklife* 26: 36–43.
Wise, Gene (1979). "'Paradigm dramas' in American Studies: a cultural and institutional history of the movement." *American Quarterly* 31: 293–337.
Wolf, Edwin II. (1955). "Benjamin Franklin's stamp act cartoon," *Proceedings of the American Philosophical Society* 99: 388–96.
Wood, E.M. (2002) *The Origin of Capitalism: A Longer View*. London.
Wood, Gordon S. (1992). *The Radicalism of the American Revolution*. New York, NY.
Wood, Gordon S. (2004). *The Americanization of Benjamin Franklin*. New York, NY.
Wood, Gordon S. (2006). *Revolutionary Characters: What Made the Founders Different*. New York, NY.
Woods, John A. (1967). "The correspondence of Benjamin Rush and Granville Sharp, 1773–1809," *Journal of American Studies* 1: 1–38.
Wright, E. (1986). *Franklin of Philadelphia*. Cambridge, MA.
Wrightson, Nick (2010). "[Those with] Great abilities have not always the best information: How Franklin's transatlantic book-trade and scientific networks interacted, ca. 1730–1757," *Early American Studies* 8(1): 94–119.
Wroth, Lawrence C. (1927–1928). "The Indian treaty as literature," *Yale Review* n.s., 17: 749–766.
Wulf, Karin (2000). *Not All Wives. Women of Colonial Philadelphia*. Ithaca, NY.
Young, Alfred F. (2005). *Masquerade: The Life and Times of Deborah Sampson, Continental Soldier*. New York, NY.
Young, Christopher J. (2001). "Mary K. Goddard: A classical republican in a revolutionary age," *Maryland Historical Magazine* 96: 4–27.
Zall, P.M. (1976). "A portrait of the autobiographer as an old artificer" in Lemay, ed. (1976a), pp. 53–65.
Zall, P.M. (1989). *Franklin's Autobiography: A Model Life*. Boston, MA.
Zelizer, B., ed. (2008). *Explorations in Communication and History*. London.
Ziff, L. (1991). *Writing in the New Nation: Prose, Print, and Politics in the Early United States*. New Haven, CT.

Zigrosser, Carl (1957). "The medallic sketches of Augustin Dupré in American collections," *Proceedings of the American Philosophical Society* 101: 535–550.

Zimmerman, John J. (1960). "Benjamin Franklin and the Quaker party, 1755–1756," *William and Mary Quarterly* 3rd ser. 17: 291–313.

Zochert, Donald (1978). *Murder in the Hellfire Club*, 1st edn. New York, NY.

Zuckerman, M. (1993a). *Almost Chosen People: Oblique Biographies in the American Grain*. Berkeley, CA.

Zuckerman, M. (1993b). "Doing good while doing well: Benevolence and self-interest in Franklin's *Autobiography*," in Lemay, ed. (1993), pp. 441–451.

Index

Academy and Charitable School of Philadelphia *see* University of Pennsylvania
Adams, John 70–71, 73, 75–8, 129, 158, 161
Albany Congress of 1754 42
  Plan of Union (Franklin) 114
Aldridge, Alfred Owen 130, 131, 134–6, 139, 141, 144
Allen, William 108
American Philosophical Society 31
American Revolution 79, 90, 126
Anderson, Douglas 130, 133–4, 143
Andrews, Jedediah 137
Anglicans 106
  Christ Church (Philadelphia) 137
Anglicization 127
Aranda, Count de 76
"Articles of Belief and Acts of Religion" (Franklin) 133–4
Artisans 143, 160 *see also* Printers
"Art of Virtue" (Franklin) 141–2
Assembly *see* Pennsylvania, Assembly

Autobiography of Benjamin Franklin 1, 7, 10, 25–6, 28, 31–2, 66, 78, 89, 107, 133, 137, 141–2, 144

Bache, Benjamin Franklin 68, 71
Bache, Richard 36, 68, 70
Bache, Sarah (Sally) Franklin 35, 68
Bailyn, Bernard 48, 156, 159–61
Bancroft, Edward 73
Barbeu-Dubourg, Jacques 71
Benezet, Anthony 141
Blumin, Stuart 93–5
Bonvouloir, J. 70
Borsay, Peter 93
Boston, Mass. 7–8, 10–12, 16, 26, 28, 38, 60, 155
Boston Tea Party 60, 66, 155, 158
Boylston, Dr. Zabadiel 15, 21
Braddock, Edward 67, 116
Bradford, Andrew 27, 37, 39, 43
Bradford, William 25, 27, 37–8
Brands, H.W. 2, 63, 89, 90
Breen, Timothy H. 61, 149

A Companion to Benjamin Franklin, First Edition. Edited by David Waldstreicher.
© 2011 Blackwell Publishing Ltd. Published 2011 by Blackwell Publishing Ltd.

INDEX

Breintnal, Joseph 30, 37
Brillon, Mme. 75
British Empire 48–9, 54, 55, 72, 73, 79, 86, 114, 118, 120, 151
  Constitution of, 127
Brownell. George 18
Buffon, Comte de 149–50
Bunker Hill, Battle of 158, 159
Bute, Lord 65, 146
Buxbaum, Melvin 137–9

Calvinism 130–131, 135, 137
  New England 130, 142–3
  secular 142
  see also Puritanism
Canada 69
Chaumont, J. 72, 74
Checkley, John 14
Clark, Ronald 2
Class 83–102
  hybridities 96, 100–101
  lower sort 119
  middle class 88–90, 93–7, 99, 100, 149
  middling sorts 113, 119
  working class 93, 95, 97, 99
  upper class 94, 96–9, 100
Clergy *see* Religion
Clubs *see* Voluntary Associations; Junto
Cockpit 58–61, 65, 158
Coercive Acts 60–61, 66
Coleman, William 30, 37, 108
Collins, John 18
Collinson, Peter 40
Conner, Paul W. 48, 54, 151, 153, 160
Constitutional Convention of 1787, 10, 147
  prayer at 135
Constitutionalist Party 78
Constitution of the United States 128, 160
Consumer revolution 34
Continental Army 67, 70, 74

Continental Congress 61, 66, 68–71, 73–5, 77, 147
  Committee of Secret Correspondence 70
  Second 146
  Secret Committee 70
Convicts, transportation of to America 152
Crane, Verner W. 2, 48, 55, 58
Crowley, J. E. 151
Currency *see* Paper money
Currency Act 154
Currey, Cecil 55, 57, 59, 61, 63, 155, 157
Cushing, Thomas 59

Deane, Silas 70–74
Declaration of Independence 67, 70–71
Declaratory Act 55, 155
Deference 39
Defoe, Daniel 19, 142
Deism 130
Denham, Thomas 28–9, 107
Dickinson, John 52, 57, 148, 154
  Letters from a Farmer 154
Digges, Thomas 75
Dingo 20
Dissertation Upon Liberty and Necessity, Pleasure and Pain (Franklin) 131–3, 138
Douglass, Dr. William 14–15
Draper, Theodore 151
Dull, Jonathan R. 2
Dunn, Elizabeth 132, 133, 135, 144

Earle, Peter 93, 99
Education 19
Edwards, Jonathan 143
Egnal, Marc 151, 157
Election of 1764 (Pennsylvania) 119–20
Electricity 41–2
  Kite experiment 41

Empire 147
  see also British Empire
Enlightenment thought 26, 30, 48, 143
Evangelicalism 139–41
  see also Great Awakening

Fable of the Bees (Mandeville) 142
Fay, Bernard 47, 54
Feke, Robert 100, 412
Fisher, Sydney George 48, 63
Fitzherbert, Alleyne 77
Foner, Eric 92–3
Fortune, Brandon Brame 91
Founders 62, 129, 146, 162
Founding Fathers *see* Founders
France 41, 71–8, 100
  aristocracy 72
  Navy 72–3
  Royal Academy of Sciences 72, 74
Franklin, Abiah Folger 7–9, 18, 35, 130
Franklin, Benjamin
  agent for colonies 58, 96, 98, 118, 120
  American identity of 88, 90–91, 126, 156
  and the American Revolution 146–62
  Autobiography (*see Autobiography of Benjamin Franklin*)
  childhood, 7–10, 23–4. 130
  and class 84, 86–92, 94–8, 148
  at Constitutional Convention 147
  diplomacy 72, 98, 123
  economic ideas of 151–2
  as Founding Father 146–7
  and Great Britain 28–30, 46–63, 65, 110, 126, 141, 146, 152
  personality and character 2, 9, 23–4, 47, 51, 61, 65–7, 78–9, 107, 110, 112, 114, 120–121, 128, 147, 161
  politics 1, 42–63, 98, 107–28, 149–65

  as Assemblyman 115–16, 118–20
  political philosophy of 48–50, 123, 126–8, 155
  portraits of 100
  postmastership 96
  printer, 2, 11–13, 36–43, 98, 109, 149, 161
  and Quakers 26–7, 125–7, 140–141
  and religion 10, 121, 129–45
  runaway, 1, 95
  scientist 40–42, 72, 91, 149–50
  shop of, 33–4
  slaves of, 44
  will and testament of 104
  women and (*see* Women)
  writer, 2, 11, 13, 15–18, 23, 111
    personae of (*see* "Silence Dogood" essays; *Poor Richard's Almanack*; Dingo)
  see also individual works
Franklin, Benjamin (the elder) 8, 12
Franklin, Deborah Read Rogers 31–5, 38, 65, 95
Franklin, Francis Folger (Franky) 35, 65
Franklin, James 10–15, 21–3, 138
Franklin, John 12
Franklin, Josiah 7–9, 11–12, 20, 130
Franklin, William 34, 36–7, 50, 54, 68, 71, 74, 76–8. 109, 118, 146
Franklin, William Temple 68, 71, 75, 271, 272, 427, 482
Freedom of the press 160
Freemasons 71–2, 115
  Nine Sisters 71–2
French and Indian War *see* Seven Years' War

Galloway, Joseph 48, 53, 68, 146, 155
Gardner, Nathanael 13, 15
Gender 84

Gentility 90, 100
George III, King 48, 49, 66, 74, 77, 78
Gérard, Conrad-Alexander 72, 73
Germans (Pennsylvanian), 38, 41, 114, 118, 120, 122,
Gipson, Lawrence Henry 151
Godfrey, Thomas 30, 33
Gordon, Patrick 107
Grace, Robert 30, 37
Great Awakening 40
Great Britain *see* British Empire
Greene, Jack P. 60, 151–6, 160
Green, James N. 37
Grenville, George, Lord 53, 54, 65

Hall, David 40–41
Hall, Hugh 20
Hamilton, Andrew 108–10, 115, 121
Hamilton, James 115
Hanna, William S. 52, 54, 56, 60, 156, 157
Hawke, David Freeman 57, 63
Helvétius, Mme. 75
Hemphill, Samuel 40, 136, 144
  Hemphill Affair 136–8, 143
Hillsborough, Lord 57, 58, 157
Holmes, David 142
Holmes, Robert 28
Houston, Alan 142–3
Howe, Sir Richard 61, 69–71
Hughes, John 54, 65
Hume, David 160
Hutcheson, Francis 143
Hutchinson, Thomas 58, 59, 146, 156
  Hutchinson affair 58–61, 65, 157–8
Hutson, James H. 51, 54, 58, 152

Ideology 40, 47
  of American Revolution 158–60
  see also Whig ideology;
    Enlightenment thought;
    Deference; Mercantilism;
    Royalism; Republicanism
Indians 52. 85, 117, 119, 153, 158
  wars 111, 117, 118
Interest of Great Britain Considered, The (Franklin) 152
Isaacson, Walter 2, 47, 57, 89–90, 130, 139

Jay, John 75–7
Jefferson, Thomas 48, 70, 71, 76–7
Jennings, Francis 47, 63
Jensen, Merrill 155
Jesus 145
Jones, John Jr. 30
Journalism 13–14
Junto 30, 37, 41, 96, 101, 134, 143

Kammen, Michael 151
Keimer, Samuel 27–8, 32, 36, 38
Keith, George 106
Keith, Sir William 28–9, 43, 107, 108
King George's War 67, 111, 115
Kinnersley, Ebenezer 41
Knox, William 156–7

Lafayette, Marquis de 159
LaFeber, Walter 151
Lambert, Frank 140
Landsman, Ned 143
Land speculation 54, 58, 98, 156
Langford, Paul 93
Laurens, Henry 75–6
Lawrence, D.H. 129, 142
Lay, Benjamin 141
Lee, Arthur 71, 73
Lemay, J.A. Leo 7, 13–14, 18, 34, 42, 88–90, 109, 130–136, 138, 143–4
Lepore, Jill 1
Leviathan (Hobbes) 142
Libraries 30–31, 39
  see also Library Company of Philadelphia

Library Company of Philadelphia 31, 36–7, 39–40, 43, 97
Lloyd, David 107, 109, 122
Loan office 124
Locke, John 47–8, 134
Logan, James 39–40, 43, 122, 141
London, 28–30, 49, 93–5, 101
Looby, Christopher 159, 161
Lopez, Claude-Anne 25
Loudon, Lord 44
Louisbourg expedition 112
Louis XVI, King 73
Loyalists 77
Lynd, Staughton 160

Mark, Karl
Marxian scholarship 93
Masons *see* Freemasons
Massachusetts 21, 58, 112, 148, 157
  General Court 21, 108
  House of Representatives 59, 157
Mather, Cotton 10, 15–16, 130, 142
  Bonifacius (Essays to Do Good) 15, 130, 142
  Magnalia Christi Americana 15–16
Maugridge, William 30
May, Henry F. 144, 145
McConville, Brendan 50
McCoy, Drew R. 151
McMaster, John Bach 2
Mecom, Jane Franklin 18, 35
Mercantilism 48–9, 151
  Neo-mercantilism 151, 154
Meredith, Hugh 30, 36–7
Meyer, Donald H. 133, 135
Middle class *see* Class
Middlekauff, Robert 51, 61, 63
Militia 31, 105, 111, 116, 123, 126
  association 111, 115–16, 126
  Militia Act (1756) 123–4
Miller, Jacquelyn 141
Miller, Perry 7
Milton, John 133

Ministers *see* Religion, clergy
Molasses Act 154
Morgan, David T. 52–3, 56, 58, 63
Morgan, Edmund S. 2, 47, 51, 55, 57, 59, 62, 133, 137, 154,
Morgan, Helen M. 154
Morris, Robert Hunter 109, 121, 124
Morse, John T. 46, 59
Mulford, Carla 86, 150

Nash, Gary B. 93, 149, 152
Native Americans *see* Indians
Natural philosophy *see* Science
Natural rights 123
Nature and Necessity of a Paper Currency (Franklin) 107
Navigation Acts 105, 330, 331
Neo-mercantilism *see* Mercantilism
Newcomb, Benjamin H. 47, 52, 53, 64
New-England Courant see Newspapers
Newman, Simon P. 99
Newspapers 11–12, 21, 23
  advertisements 20, 39
  American Weekly Mercury 37, 43
  Boston Gazette 12–13
  Boston News-Letter 13, 20
  London Chronicle 153
  New-England Courant 7, 13–15, 21–3
  Pennsylvania Gazette 35–6, 38–9, 43, 108, 137
Newton, Isaac 29
Nonimportation 148
Norris, Isaac Jr. 113, 115, 122, 141
North, Lord 61, 73, 75

Observations Concerning the Increase of Mankind (Franklin) 49. 114, 151
Ohio Country 123, 139
Oliver, Thomas 59

INDEX

Omohundro Institute of Early American History and Culture 84–5
  annual conferences 84–5, 91
"On the Providence of God in the Government of the World" (Franklin) 134–5
Oswald, Richard 76

Paine, Thomas 48, 70, 148
Palmer, Anthony 111
Paper money 39, 107, 115, 154
Parliament 47–50, 52–3, 55–7, 59, 66, 154, 160
  Board of Trade 58, 109, 115, 124
  House of Commons 53, 56, 105, 153
  House of Lords 61
  Privy Council 53, 60, 118
  sovereignty of 156
  see also individual acts of
Parsons, William 30
Paxton Affair 52, 119, 126, 138
Pemberton, Ebenezer Jr. 138
Penn, Hannah Callowhill 28–9, 43, 107, 108
Penn, John 43
Penn, Richard 43
Penn, Thomas 43–4, 51, 52, 54, 58, 65, 78, 108–9, 111, 114–16, 118–20, 127
Penn, William 26–7, 39, 42–3, 104–5, 120, 122
Pennsylvania 104–5, 108–28
  Assembly, 28–9, 38–9, 42, 44, 50–52, 68, 96, 105–6, 109–24, 153
  Charter of Privileges (1701) 105, 109, 111, 122
  Committee of Safety 67
  constitution (1776) 160
  Council 111
  economy 107
  Hospital 31, 42, 113, 115
  political culture 124

proprietors. *see* William Penn, Thomas Penn, Hannah Callowhill Penn
Pennsylvania Gazette see Newspapers
Philadelphia 23, 25–44, 78, 92–5, 101, 106, 110, 139, 147–8
  economy 106
  grid layout of 26
  historiography of 92–4
  religious diversity 27
Philadelphia Contributionship 31
Pitt, William (Lord Camden) 61
Plain Truth (Franklin) 42, 111–12
Poor Richard's Almanack 13–14, 37–8, 43–4, 107, 143
  Bridget Saunders 13–14
  Father Abraham 44
  Richard Saunders 13–14, 44, 143
Potts, Stephen 30
Pownall, Thomas 156–7
Presbyterians 113, 136–9
  evangelical (new side) 139
Print 158, 161
Printers 12, 23, 27–9, 33
  see also individual printers by name
Prisetley, Joseph 65, 129
Privy Council *see* Parliament
Propietary Party 44, 54, 121, 152
Protestantism 47
Puritanism 143–4

Quaker Party 52, 54, 63, 110–113, 115–16, 118, 121–3, 167, 170
Quakers (Society of Friends) 26, 28–9, 37, 43, 104–6, 109, 112–13, 118, 121
  American Quakerism 125–6
  civil Quakerism 124–7
  and war 112–13, 116, 123–4, 127

Race 84–5
Read, Sarah 32–3

Religion 17, 21, 40
　clergy 17, 19, 23, 40, 138
　toleration of 122
　see also Quakers; Great Awakening; Anglicans; Calvinism; Protestantism; Anglicans; Presbyterians; Deism
Republicanism 51, 126–7, 161
Revolutionary War 68–9, 115
Rights 47, 55
Rockinghman, Marquis de (Charles Watson-Wentworth) 75–6
Rogers, John 32, 34–5
Rose, Aquila 27
Rossiter, Clinton 47, 147, 148, 156
Royalism 50–51
　royal government 152
Royal Society 41
Rush, Benjamin 78, 154

Sailors 74
Sartine, Gabriel de 72
Schlesinger, Arthur M., Sr. 158
Schultz, Ronald 93
Science 40–42
Scull, Nicholas 30
Seavey, Ormond 49, 61
Seven Years' War 44, 115–18, 123
Sewall, Samuel 8, 17, 20, 22
　The Selling of Joseph 20
Shaftesbury, Earl of (Anthony Ashley Cooper) 130, 143
Shelburne, Earl of (William Petty) 75–7
"Silence Dogood" essays 15–18
Slavery 20–21. 85
Slaves 44, 85
　Slave rebellion 159
Sloane, Hans 29
Smallpox controversy 14–15, 35
　Inoculation 14–15, 35
Smith, Adam 49
Smith, Billy G. 149
Smith, William 126
Societies see Voluntary associations
Sons of Liberty 157

Massachusetts 157
South Carolina 148
Sovereignty 128
　see also Parliament
Spain 73, 76
Spectator, The (Addison and Steele) 14, 130, 134
"Speech of Miss Polly Baker, The" (Franklin) 144
Spencer, Archibald 41
Spotswood, Alexander 39
Stamp Act 47, 53–7, 65, 66, 146, 154
Steward, Dr. George 14
Stourzh, Gerald 151
Stout, Harry S. 139
Strahan, William 40

Taxes, 54–6, 58, 115, 118–19, 123, 124, 153–4
　see also Stamp Act; Townshend Acts
Temple, John 59
Tercentenary of Franklin's birth 86
Thompson, E.P. 84, 93, 99
Tise, Larry 86
Tourtellot, Arthur B. 7
Townsend Acts, 56–8, 148
Townshend, Charles 55
Treaty of Alliance (1778) 73
Treaty of Amity and Commerce (1778) 73
Treaty of Paris (1783) 146, 158
Tryon, Thomas 10

Union Fire Company 31
University of Pennsylvania 31, 42, 100, 113, 115

Van Alstyne, Richard 155
Van Doren, Carl 2, 54, 57, 63, 88–9, 90
Vergennes, Comte de (Charles Gravier) 70, 72–3, 75–6
Voluntary associations 19, 100, 111
　see also specific organizations

Waldstreicher, David 1, 3, 86, 95, 99, 141, 149, 156
Walking Purchase 43
Walters, Kerry S. 129–37, 140–142, 144
Ward, John William 62
Warner, Deborah Jean 91
Warner, Michael 161
Washington, George 66, 67, 75
Way to Wealth, The (Franklin) 49, 148
Webb, George 30
Wedderburn, Alexander 60–61
Weems, Mason Locke 129
Weinberger, Jerry 132–7
Wendel, Thomas 54
West Indies, 32, 77
Whateley, Thomas 59
Whateley, William 59

Whig historians 52, 53
Whig ideology 13, 47
  see also Republicanism
Whitefield, George 40, 139–41
Whitemarsh, Thomas 38, 96
Wilcox, John 29
Willcox, William 56
Williams, William Appelman 151, 155, 158
Women 18–20, 31–4, 75, 85, 86
  education of 19–20
  see also *individual women*
Wood, Gordon S. 2, 49–52, 57, 59, 63, 89–99, 133, 149, 152. 156, 159, 160
Wright, Esmond 48–9, 50, 52, 89

Ziff, Larzer 156, 161

Erratum Booklet

A Companion to Benjamin Franklin
Edited by David Waldstreicher
ISBN 978-1-4051-9996-4

The index in the printed book is incomplete. This erratum booklet contains the full index. The publisher apologizes for this error.

abolition *see* antislavery
Academy and Charitable School of Philadelphia *see* University of Pennsylvania
Adams, Abigail Smith, 237
Adams, John, 70–1, 73, 75, 76–8, 129, 158, 161, 237, 256, 371, 434, 464, 472, 474, 476, 479, 480, 482, 483–4
Africa, 204, 224, 226–7
see also Sierra Leone
Africans, 184, 197
see also Blacks
Albany Congress of 1754, 42, 165, 167, 169, 271, 362, 466, 468
Plan of Union (Franklin), 114, 168, 189–90, 227, 366, 368, 461, 468–9
Aldridge, Alfred Owen, 130, 131, 134–6, 139, 141, 144, 268, 403, 409
Allen, William, 108
Amacher, Richard, 400, 401
American literature, 260, 263
see also Literary studies
American Philosophical Society, 31, 309, 314, 344, 353–4, 480
American Revolution, 79, 90, 126, 191, 197, 211–12, 214, 235, 360, 365–70, 456, 464, 472–5
see also Revolutionary War
American studies, 400, 406, 407
"Americanus" (Franklin), 227–8
Amherst, Jeffrey, 194
Anderson, Benedict, 360
Anderson, Douglas, 130, 133–4, 143, 310, 351, 409
Andrews, Jedediah, 137
Anglicans, 106
Christ Church (Philadelphia), 137, 248
Anglicization, 127
Angoff, Charles, 398
"Anthony Afterwit" (Franklin), 423
antislavery, 191, 197–9, 201–7, 209, 211–13, 231–3, 240–1, 364, 494–5
British, 197, 205, 231, 234
see also Pennsylvania Abolition Society
"Apology for Printers" (Franklin), 299–300, 405
Appleby, Joyce, 212, 483
Aranda, Count de, 76
Armitage, David, 473
"Art of Virtue" (Franklin), 141–2, 266–7, 272
"Articles of Belief and Acts of Religion" (Franklin), 133–4, 448

INDEX 537

Articles of Confederation, 168, 365, 368, 388, 472
artisans, 143, 160, 367
  see also printers
Assembly *see* Pennsylvania, Assembly
Associates of Dr. Bray, 192–3, 229, 240–1
Autobiography of Benjamin Franklin, 1, 7, 10, 25–6, 28, 31–2, 66, 78, 89, 107, 133, 137, 141–2, 144, 180, 215–16, 220, 242, 245, 255–72, 277–8, 290, 335, 345, 361, 367, 371, 393–4, 397, 402, 405–6, 408–9, 424–8, 430–1, 440–1, 446–7, 448, 454–5, 482–3, 487–8, 490

Bache, Benjamin Franklin, 68, 71
Bache, Richard, 36, 68, 70
Bache, Sarah (Sally) Franklin, 35, 68, 237, 240, 244–5, 249, 250, 412
Bache, William, 390
Bacon, Francis, 437, 441, 453
Bailyn, Bernard, 48, 156, 159–61, 212, 404
Baker, Jennifer Jordan, 408
Bancroft, Edward, 73
Barbeu-Dubourg, Jacques, 71
Barletti, Carlo, 323–4

Beccaria, Giovanni, 313, 314
Beidler, Philip, 403, 408
Bemis, Samuel Flagg, 464, 476
Ben-Atar, Doron, 477
Benezet, Anthony, 141, 197–8, 201, 202, 232
Benjamin Franklin House Museum (London), 245
Bennett, James Gordon, 293, 294
Bercovitch, Sacvan, 404
Bigelow, John, 272
"Blackamore" (Franklin) *see* "Molatto Gentleman, The" (Franklin)
Blacks, 184–5, 191–3, 282–3
Blumin, Stuart, 93, 94–5
Bonvouloir, J., 70
Borsay, Peter, 93
Boston, Mass., 7–8, 10–12, 16, 26, 28, 38, 60, 155
Boston Tea Party, 60, 66, 155, 158
Botein, Stephen, 300–1
Bowdoin, James, 167
Boylston, Dr. Zabadiel, 15, 21
Braddock, Edward, 67, 116, 173, 362
Bradford, Andrew, 27, 37, 39, 43, 166, 278
Bradford, William, 25, 27, 37–8

Brands, H.W., 2, 63, 89, 90
Bray Society *see* Associates of Dr. Bray
Breen, Timothy H., 61, 149
Breintnall, Joseph, 30, 37, 352
Bridenbaugh, Carl, 344
Brietwieser, Mitchell, 266, 268, 403
Brillon, Mme., 75
Brissot, Jacques-Pierre, 183, 203, 207
British Empire, 48–9, 54, 55, 72, 73, 79, 86, 114, 118, 120, 151, 186, 194–6, 224, 228, 231, 233, 359–70, 463–73
  Constitution of, 127
Brooks, David, 497
Brooks, Van Wyck, 398
Brown, Bill, 414
Brown, Charles Brockden, 309–10, 313
Brown, Richard D., 281
Brownell, George, 18
Bruce, William Cabell, 395
Buffon, Comte de, 149–50, 165, 183, 187, 190
Bunker Hill, Battle of, 158, 159
Burke, Edmund, 370
Burke, William, 470–1
Bushman, Richard L., 405, 414

Bute, Lord, 65, 146
Buxbaum, Melvin, 137–8, 139, 403

Cahill, Edward, 424
Calvinism, 130–1, 135, 137
  New England, 130, 142–3
  secular, 142
  see also Puritanism
Cambridge History of American Literature, 296–7, 396
Canada, 69, 188, 366, 367
Canada Pamphlet *see Interest of Great Britain Considered, The* (Franklin)
Canasatego, 168–9, 175–6, 178
capitalism, 211–15, 234–5, 288
"Captivity of William Henry, The" (Franklin), 178
Carey, James W., 301
Carnegie, Andrew, 488
Cato's Letters (Trenchard and Gordon), 279–80, 337
"Causes of the American Discontents" (Franklin), 330–1
Chaplin, Joyce E., 240–1, 310, 339, 349, 353–5
Chaumont, J., 72, 74

INDEX

Checkley, John, 14
citizenship, 183, 187, 443
civil society, 336, 346
Clark, Charles, 301
Clark, Ronald, 2
Clarkson, Thomas, 204
class, 83–102, 219–20, 261, 283, 408–9
   hybridities, 96, 100–1
   lower sort, 119
   middle class, 88–9, 90, 93, 94–5, 96–7, 99, 100, 149, 212, 281
   middling sorts, 113, 119
   upper class, 94, 96, 97–9, 100
   W=working class, 93, 95, 97, 99
clergy *see* Religion
clubs *see* Junto; voluntary associations
Cockpit, 58–61, 65, 158
Coercive Acts, 60–1, 66
Coffin, Kezia Folger, 145
Cohen, I. Bernard, 400, 409
Colden, Cadwallader, 165, 168–9
Coleman, William, 30, 37, 108, 349
Collins, John, 18, 259, 317
Collinson, Peter, 40, 187
Conger, Vivian Bruce, 241
Conner, Paul W., 48, 54, 151, 153, 160, 226, 403, 436–7
Constitution of the United States, 128, 160, 169, 204, 368, 481
Constitutional Convention of 1787, 10, 147, 169, 204, 205
   Franklin's prayer at, 135
Constitutionalist Party, 78
consumer revolution, 34, 414
Continental Army, 67, 70, 74
Continental Congress, 61, 66, 68–71, 73–5, 77, 147, 196, 386–8
   Committee of Secret Correspondence, 70, 473
   Second, 146, 169, 472
"Conversation on the Subject of Slavery" (Franklin), 231–2
   Secret Committee, 70
convicts, transportation of to America, 152, 227, 232
Cook, Elizabeth C., 296–7
Copeland, David, 298
Crane, Verner W., 2, 48, 55, 58, 297, 409
Crowley, J.E., 151
culture, 187
   popular culture, 288, 479–97

currency *see* paper money
Currency Act, 154
Currey, Cecil, 55, 57, 59, 61, 63, 155, 157
Cushing, Thomas, 59

Dalibard, Thomas François, 418, 420
Darwin, Charles, 460
Darwin, Erasmus, 460
Dawson, Hugh, 270, 404
Deane, Silas, 70, 71–4, 473, 474
Declaration of Independence, 67, 70–1, 174, 203, 360, 473–4
Declaratory Act, 55, 155
Deconde, Alexander, 476
deference, 39
Defoe, Daniel, 19, 142, 338
Deism, 130, 445
Denham, Thomas, 28–9, 107
Dennett, Daniel, 453
Dennie, Joseph, 264
Dickinson, John, 52, 57, 148, 154
  Letters from a Farmer, 154
Digges, Thomas, 75
Dingo, 20
diplomacy *see* France; Franklin, Benjamin; Indians; individual treaties

Dissertation Upon Liberty and Necessity, Pleasure and Pain (Franklin), 131–3, 138, 447, 448, 453–5
Douglass, Dr. William, 14–15
Downes, Paul, 408
Draper, Theodore, 151
Drexler, Michael, 407, 408
Dull, Jonathan R., 2, 465, 474–5, 476
Dunn, Elizabeth, 132, 133, 135, 144

Earle, Peter, 93, 99
Easton Treaty of 1758, 166–7, 170–1
education, 19
Edwards, Jonathan, 143, 398, 399, 403
Egnal, Marc, 151, 157
Election of 1764 (Pennsylvania), 119–20, 172
electricity, 41–2, 318–27, 416
  electrocution, 326
  kite experiment, 41
  lightning rod, 416
empire, 147
  see also British Empire
enlightenment, 26, 30, 48, 143, 227, 289, 309–13, 318, 319, 321, 333, 435, 436, 439–40, 447, 449, 450

Erkkila, Betsy, 408, 410
Europe, 311, 370, 474
evangelicalism, 139–41
  see also Great Awakening
Experiments and Observations on Electricity
  (Franklin), 370, 416

Fable of the Bees (Mandeville), 142
Farrand, Max, 272, 400
Fay, Bernard, 47, 54
Ferguson, Robert A., 311, 316, 405
Fichtelberg, Joseph, 405
Fiering, Norman S., 403
Finger, Stanley, 244
Fisher, Edward, 418
Fisher, Sydney George, 48, 63, 238
Fitzherbert, Alleyne, 77
Fliegelman, Jay, 404
Foner, Eric, 92–3
Fontana, Felice, 313–14
Ford, Paul Leicester, 238, 239, 396
Forde, Steven, 432–3, 435, 442–5
Fortune, Brandon Brame, 91, 420
Foucault, Michel, 310
Founders, 62, 129, 146, 162, 165, 237, 359, 479, 494–5

Founding Fathers *see* Founders
France, 41, 71–8, 100, 194, 207, 321, 332–3, 371, 373, 388, 474–7
  aristocracy, 72
  navy, 72–3
  Royal Academy of Sciences, 72, 74, 371
Franklin, Abiah Folger, 7–9, 18, 35, 130, 243
Franklin Academy (Franklin and Marshall
  College), 282
Franklin, Benjamin
  agent for colonies, 58, 96, 98, 118,
    120, 164, 195, 229, 269, 362, 430,
    463, 469–72
  and alcohol, 327
  American identity of, 88, 90–1, 126, 156,
    213, 215, 227, 270, 311, 356, 359,
    393–4, 400, 406, 435
  and the American Revolution, 146–62
  *Autobiography see Autobiography of
    Benjamin Franklin*
  bifocal eyeglasses, 417
  childhood, 7–10, 23–4, 130
  and class, 84, 86–92, 94–8, 148, 191, 212,
    219–20, 283, 408, 410, 426
  at Constitutional Convention, 147, 270
  death, 480, 481–2

Franklin, Benjamin (*cont'd*)
  diplomacy, 72, 98, 123, 164, 172–3, 463–77, 483
  economic ideas of, 151–2
  and education, 341
  film and television about, 491–2, 495, 496
  fireplace, 417
  as Founding Father, 146–7; *see also* Founders
  governor of Pennsylvania, 270
  and Great Britain, 28–30, 46–63, 65, 110, 126, 141, 146, 152, 359–70
  house, 415, 424, 426
  humor, 448
  and Indians, 164–81, 183, 184, 188–91, 193–7, 199–201, 206–8, 282, 327
  journalist, 290–306
  "long arm", 418
  marriage of, 239, 241
  memory of, 179–97
  nationalism of, 183, 215, 227, 360, 477
  in Paris *see* France
  personality and character, 2, 9, 23–4, 47, 51, 61, 65–7, 78–9, 107, 110, 112, 114, 120–1, 128, 147, 161, 359, 394–5, 431, 443–4
  pictorial representations by, 228, 373–90, 420
  politics, 1, 42–63, 98, 107–28, 149–65, 187–8, 286–7, 293–4, 361–3, 380, 409
    as Assemblyman, 115–16, 118–20, 164
    political philosophy of, 48–50, 123, 126, 127–8, 155, 166, 430–62
  portraits of, 100, 384, 389, 412–13, 418, 419–20, 489
  postmastership, 96, 487
  printer, 2, 11–13, 36–43, 98, 109, 149, 161, 165–7, 186, 214, 217–18, 223, 292, 305, 339, 427, 466
  and Quakers, 26–7, 125–7, 140–1
  and religion, 10, 121, 129–45, 178–9, 248, 267, 272, 399, 403, 438–40, 443, 450–2, 457–8
  runaway, 1, 95, 215–16, 220, 249–50
  scientist, 40–2, 72, 91, 149–50, 256, 309–33, 353–5
  sculptures of, 421–2
  shop of, 33–4
  and slavery, 191–3, 197–9, 201–7, 208, 211–35, 364, 413, 477, 481, 494–5
  slaves of, 44, 193, 201

will and testament of, 104
women and, 18–20, 31–4, 75, 85, 86, 185, 222, 237–51, 263, 284, 420, 423, 491–3
writer, 2, 11, 13, 15–18, 23, 111, 255–72, 296–8, 303–5, 393–410, 418, 431, 434; *see also* individual works
Franklin, Benjamin (the elder), 8, 12
Franklin, Deborah Read Rogers, 31–5, 38, 65, 95, 193, 237–43, 247, 248, 263–4, 284–5, 413, 436
Franklin, Francis Folger (Franky), 35, 65, 243
Franklin, James, 10–15, 21–3, 138, 215, 220–1, 277–8, 296, 302, 425
Franklin, John, 12
Franklin, Josiah, 7–9, 11–12, 20, 130
Franklin, William, 34, 36–7, 50, 54, 68, 71, 74, 76–8, 109, 118, 146, 193, 239, 249, 364
Franklin, William Temple, 68, 71, 75, 77, 271, 272, 287, 427, 482
Frasca, Ralph, 298, 302
freedom of the press, 160
Freemasons, 71–2, 115, 342–3
  Nine Sisters, 71–2
French and Indian War *see* Seven Years' War

Fry, Jennefer Reed, 241
fur trade, 173–4, 179, 181, 328–31
Furtwangler, Albert, 405

Galloway, Joseph, 48, 53, 68, 146, 155, 365
Gardner, Nathanael, 13, 15
Garrett, Matthew, 243
gender, 84
gentility, 90, 100
George, 201
George III, King, 48, 49, 66, 74, 77, 78, 174, 473
Georgia, 200, 205
Gérard, Conrad-Alexander, 72, 73
Germans (Pennsylvanian), 38, 41, 114, 118, 120, 122, 185–8, 224, 282, 364
Gilbert, Felix, 464, 465
Gillespie, Elizabeth Duane, 250
Gipson, Lawrence Henry, 151
Glazener, Nancy, 408
Gnadenhutten Massacre, 199–200, 209
Godfrey, Thomas, 30, 33, 276
Gordon, Patrick, 107
Gordon, William, 280
Goudie, Sean, 409
Grace, Robert, 30, 37, 417

Granger, Bruce, 400
Great Awakening, 40, 327
Great Britain *see* British Empire
Greeley, Horace, 264, 290, 292–3
Green, James N., 37, 302, 305–6, 409, 427
Greene, Jack P., 60, 151, 152–3, 154, 155–6, 160
Grenville, George, Lord, 53, 54, 65
Grieve, George, 200
Griffith, John, 404
Griffith, Sally F., 350
Guyatt, Nicholas, 234

Habermas, Jürgen, 281, 311, 336, 405
Hall, David, 40–1, 166, 467
Hall, David D., 353, 427
Hall, Hugh, 20
Hall, Robert Lee, 491
Hamilton, Alexander, 479, 480
Hamilton, Andrew, 108–10, 115, 121
Hamilton, James, 115
Hanna, William S., 52, 54, 56, 60, 156, 157
Harmar, Josiah, 207
Hartley, David, 198, 205, 209, 314
Hawke, David Freeman, 57, 63
Hawthorne, Nathaniel, 238

Heilbron, J.L., 322
Helvétius, Mme., 75
Hemphill, Samuel, 40, 136, 144
  Hemphill Affair, 136–8, 143
Hendrickson, David, 477
Hewson, Mary, 331
Hillsborough, Lord, 57, 58, 157
Hobbes, Thomas, 261, 451
Holmes, David, 142
Holmes, Robert, 28
Houston, Alan, 142–3, 341, 350, 433, 435, 459–61
Howe, Sir Richard, 61, 69–70, 71, 366
Howe, William, 474
Huang, Nian-Shen, 292, 408, 410, 483
Hudson, Frederic, 293–4, 304
Hughes, John, 54, 65
Hume, David, 160, 184, 226–7, 363
Hutcheson, Francis, 143
Hutchinson, Thomas, 58, 59, 146, 156
  Hutchinson affair, 58–61, 65, 157–8
Hutson, James H., 51, 54, 58, 152

ideology, 40, 47, 235, 403
  of American Revolution, 158–60, 235, 280

see also deference; enlightenment; mercantilism; republicanism; royalism; Whig ideology
immigration, 183, 202, 216, 367
imperialism, 183–4
impressment, 227
Indians, 52, 85, 117, 119, 153, 158, 164–81, 184–5, 193–7, 199–201, 206–7, 224
  Conestoga, 172, 194
  Creek, 200
  Delaware, 164, 166, 195, 200
  Iroquois, 164, 166, 168–9, 176, 189, 195, 328
  Miami, 189, 207
  Onondaga, 168, 191
  oratory, 167, 178
  religion, 178
  Shawnee, 164, 166, 195, 200, 207
  Six Nations *see* Indians, Iroquois
  trade with, 188
  treaties with, 165–7, 180, 188, 327, 466; *see also* Albany Congress; Easton Treaty; Lancaster Treaty of 1744; Walking Purchase
  wars, 111, 117, 118, 173, 189, 195, 200–1, 228

see also Franklin, Benjamin
Interest of Great Britain Considered, The (Franklin), 152, 173, 363, 409, 442, 470
Internet, 291, 306
"Invectives Against the Americans" (Franklin), 230
Iroquois Influence Thesis, 168–9
Isaacson, Walter, 2, 47, 57, 89–90, 130, 139, 239, 304–5, 311, 356, 460, 494

Jackson, Andrew, 182
Jackson, James, 205–6
James, Abel, 265–6
Jay, John, 75–6, 77, 476
Jefferson, Thomas, 48, 70, 71, 76–7, 174, 182, 184, 200, 206, 213, 237, 360, 421, 430, 477, 482, 485
Jehlen, Myra, 405
Jennings, Francis, 47, 63
Jensen, Merrill, 155
Jesus, 145
Johnson, Rupert H., 490
Johnson, Samuel, 231, 248
Johnson, Sir William, 195

Jones, John, Jr., 30
journalism, 13–14, 290–306
Junto, 30, 37, 41, 96, 101, 134, 143, 216, 277, 338, 339–41, 343

Kames, Lord (Henry Homes), 183, 184, 363
Kammen, Michael, 151
Kant, Immanuel, 370
Keimer, Samuel, 27–8, 32, 36, 38, 217, 259, 275, 278, 316, 317
Keith, George, 106
Keith, Sir William, 28–9, 43, 107, 108, 339, 427
Kelleter, Frank, 353
Kennedy, Archibald, 168
Ketcham, Ralph, 436, 437–40
King, 193
King George's War, 67, 111, 115, 227, 466
Kinnersley, Ebenezer, 41, 416
Knight, Madame Sarah, 245
Knox, William, 156–7
Kulikoff, Allan, 485, 490

Lafayette, Marquis de, 159
LaFeber, Walter, 151
Lambert, Frank, 140
Lancaster Treaty of 1744, 168, 175
land speculation, 54, 58, 98, 156, 328
Landsman, Ned, 143
Langford, Paul, 93
Larson, David, 346
Latour, Bruno, 310
Laurens, Henry, 75–6, 476
Lawrence, D.H., 129, 142, 259–64, 288, 398, 425, 431, 438
Lay, Benjamin, 141, 241
Le Veillard, Louis-Guillaume, 271, 272
Lee, Arthur, 71, 73, 473, 474
Leeds, Titan, 276, 278
Lemay, J.A. Leo, 7, 13–14, 18, 34, 42, 88–9, 90, 109, 130–6, 138, 143–4, 166, 226, 240, 246, 250–1, 265, 269, 272, 302–4, 353, 408, 410, 428
Leonard, Thomas C., 302
Lepore, Jill, 1
Lerner, Ralph, 433, 434, 440–2, 446, 452
Leviathan (Hobbes), 142
Levin, David, 401, 432
Levy, Leonard, 299–300
Lewis, Jan, 245
liberalism, 461

libraries, 30–1, 39
  see also Library Company of Philadelphia
Library Company of Philadelphia, 31, 36–7, 39–40, 43, 97, 277, 343–4, 347–8, 351, 353
literary studies, 213, 255–72, 296–8, 393–410
Lloyd, David, 107, 109, 122
loan office, 124
Locke, John, 47–8, 134, 338, 435, 442, 461
Logan, James, 39–40, 43, 122, 141, 349
London, 28–30, 49, 93–5, 101, 188
Looby, Christopher, 159, 161, 405, 407
Lopez, Claude-Anne, 25, 245, 247
Loudon, Lord, 44
Loughran, Trish, 427
Louis XVI, King, 73, 289, 475, 480
Louisbourg expedition, 112
Lovell, Margaretta, 420
Loyalists, 77
Lynd, Staughton, 160
Lynen, John F., 402

Machiavelli, Niccolo, 442, 446
MacIntyre, Alasdair, 431

Madison, James, 206, 360, 430, 479
Malthus, Thomas, 460
Mansfield, Lord (William Murray), 233
Marks, Frederick W., 477
Martin, Robert W.T., 300
Marx, Karl, 221
  Marxian scholarship, 93
masons *see* Freemasons
Massachusetts, 21, 58, 112, 148, 157, 275
  General Court, 21, 108
  House of Representatives, 59, 157
material culture, 407, 412–28
Mather, Cotton, 10, 15–16, 130, 142, 266, 268, 338
  Bonifacius (Essays to Do Good), 15, 130, 142, 338
  Magnalia Christi Americana, 15–16
Matthews, Brander, 396
Maugridge, William, 30
May, Henry F., 144, 145
McCarthy, Kathleen, 339, 352, 355
McConville, Brendan, 50
McCoy, Drew R., 151
McMahon, Michael, 345
McMaster, John Bach, 2, 395, 396–7
Mecom, Jane Franklin, 18, 35, 240, 243–4

Menard, Russell, 211
mercantilism, 48–9, 151, 225, 328–9
  neo-mercantilism, 151, 154, 234
merchants, 174, 188, 195, 319
Meredith, Hugh, 30, 36–7, 317, 427
Meyer, Donald H., 133, 135
middle class *see* class
Middlekauff, Robert, 51, 61, 63, 456
Miles, Richard D., 292
Militia, 31, 105, 111, 116, 123, 126, 169, 250, 286, 342, 349–50
  Association, 111, 115–16, 126, 350, 351–2, 467
  Militia Act (1756), 123–4
Miller, Jacquelyn, 141
Miller, Perry, 7, 399
Milton, John, 133
ministers *see* religion, clergy
Model Treaty (1776), 366, 464, 474, 476
Molasses Act, 154
"Molatto Gentleman, The" (Franklin), 191–2, 219, 275
Montaigne, Michel de, 175, 176–7
Moore, Milcah Martha, 246
Moravians, 172, 198–9, 250
Morgan, David T., 52–3, 56, 58, 63

Morgan, Edmund S., 2, 47, 51, 55, 57, 59, 62, 133, 137, 154, 179, 345, 347, 351, 354, 355, 465–6, 471, 477, 494
Morgan, Helen M., 154
Morris, Richard B., 476
Morris, Robert Hunter, 109, 121, 124, 169
Morse, John T., 46, 59
"Mother Country, The" (Franklin), 230–1
Mulford, Carla, 86, 150, 238, 289, 408, 410, 486, 487

Narrative of the Late Massacres (Franklin), 171–2, 456
Nash, Gary B., 93, 149, 152
nationalism *see* Franklin, Benjamin
Native Americans *see* Indians
natural philosophy *see* science
natural rights, 123
Nature and Necessity of a Paper Currency (Franklin), 107
neo-mercantilism *see* mercantilism
New Experiments (Franklin), 320–1, 325
New York, 168
Newcomb, Benjamin H., 47, 52, 53, 64
New-England Courant see newspapers
Newman, Simon P., 99

newspapers, 11–12, 21, 23, 301, 337
  advertisements, 20, 39, 217, 407
  American Weekly Mercury, 37, 43
  Boston Gazette, 12–13
  Boston News-Letter, 13, 20
  London Chronicle, 153, 178, 198
  New-England Courant, 7, 13–15, 21–3, 220, 296–7, 301, 379
  Pennsylvania Gazette, 35–6, 38–9, 43, 108, 137, 166, 191, 217, 227, 250, 276, 298, 302, 345, 378–9
Newton, Isaac, 29, 279
  Newtonian science, 308–12, 317, 321–2
nonimportation, 148
Norris, Isaac, Jr., 113, 115, 122, 141
North, Lord, 61, 73, 75
novel, 271–2

Observations Concerning the Increase of Mankind (Franklin), 49, 114, 151, 179, 184, 192, 212, 224–6, 361, 364–5, 367, 409, 471
Ohio country, 123, 139, 189, 328
"Old Mistress Apologue" (Franklin), 238, 434
Oliver, Thomas, 59

Olson, Lester C., 374–5, 381, 409
Omohundro Institute of Early American History and Culture, 84–5
  annual conferences, 84–5, 91
"On the Providence of God in the Government of the World" (Franklin), 134–5
Oswald, Richard, 76, 475
Othello 193

Paine, Thomas, 48, 70, 148
Palmer, Anthony, 111
Pangle, Lorraine Smith, 356, 433–5, 450–8
paper money, 39, 107, 115, 154, 214, 221, 407, 459
Parliament, 47–8, 49, 50, 52–3, 55–7, 59, 66, 154, 160, 173, 186, 206, 359, 362, 366–8, 473
  Board of Trade, 58, 109, 115, 124, 186, 195, 363, 382–3
  House of Commons, 53, 56, 105, 153, 366
  House of Lords, 61
  Privy Council, 53, 60, 118, 233, 359, 363
  sovereignty of, 156
  see also individual acts
Parrington, Vernon, 399

Parsons, William, 30
Parton, James, 290
Patee, Fred Lewis, 396
Paxton Affair, 52, 119, 126, 138, 171–2, 194, 199
Peale, Charles Willson, 420
Pemberton, Ebenezer, Jr., 138
Pemberton, James, 205
Penn, Hannah Callowhill, 28–9, 43, 107, 108
Penn, John, 43
Penn, Richard, 43, 469
Penn, Thomas, 43–4, 51, 52, 54, 58, 65, 78, 108–9, 111, 114, 115–16, 118–20, 127, 256, 286, 344, 349, 351–2, 357, 469
Penn, William, 26–7, 39, 42–3, 104–5, 120, 122, 171, 185, 189, 279, 280–1, 467
Pennsylvania, 104–5, 108–28, 165, 183, 216, 364–5, 466–9
  Assembly, 28–9, 38–9, 42, 44, 50–1, 52, 68, 96, 105–6, 109–24, 153, 165, 167, 173, 194, 218, 469
  Charter of Privileges (1701), 105, 109, 111, 122
  Constitution (1776), 160, 369, 481
  Council, 111
  diplomacy of, 466–9
  economy, 107
  political culture, 124
  proprietors *see* Penn, Hannah Callowhill; Penn, Thomas; Penn, William
Pennsylvania Abolition Society, 201, 202–3, 204–6
Pennsylvania Committee of Safety, 67
Pennsylvania Gazette see newspapers
Pennsylvania Hospital, 31, 42, 113, 115, 249, 352
Perelman, Michael, 212
Perry, Bliss, 396, 397
Peters, Richard, 256, 347, 349
Philadelphia, 23, 25–44, 78, 92–5, 101, 106, 110, 139, 147–8, 191, 214, 357
  city council, 346
  economy, 106, 188
  grid layout of, 26
  historiography of, 92–4
  religious diversity, 27
Philadephia Contributionship, 31
Pilgrim's Progress (Bunyan), 271
Pitt, William (Lord Camden), 61, 330
Plain Truth (Franklin), 42, 111–12, 224, 349, 467

Pocock, J.G.A., 404
Pontiac's War, 171, 194, 200
Poor Richard's Almanack, 13–14, 37–8, 43–4, 107, 143, 218–19, 222–3, 246, 247, 256, 258, 275–89, 393, 397, 416, 485
  Bridget Saunders, 13–14, 218, 284–5, 286
  Father Abraham, 44, 283, 287–8
  prefaces, 286
  Richard Saunders, 13–14, 44, 143, 218, 222–3, 275, 276, 281, 399, 452–3
population, 460
  see also Observations Concerning the Increase of Mankind
Potts, Stephen, 30
Pownall, Thomas, 156–7
Pratt, Mary Louise, 312
Presbyterians, 113, 136–8, 139, 267, 434
  evangelical (new side), 139
press freedom, 299–300
Price, Richard, 204, 209
Priestley, Joseph, 65, 129, 314–15, 324
Pringle, John, 314, 315–16
print, 158, 161, 218, 302, 405, 407, 410
printers, 12, 23, 27–9, 33, 185, 245, 275, 292, 299–300, 302, 484–5
  see also journalism; individual printers by name
Privy Council *see* Parliament
Proprietary Party, 44, 54, 121, 152, 349
Protestantism, 47
Prown, Jules, 414
Puritanism, 143–4, 261, 399, 403

Quaker Party, 52, 54, 63, 110–13, 115–16, 118, 121–3, 167, 169, 349
Quakers (Society of Friends), 26, 28–9, 37, 43, 104–6, 109, 112–13, 118, 121, 172, 203, 205, 434
  American Quakerism, 125–6
  civil Quakerism, 124–7
  and war, 112–13, 116, 123–4, 127, 349, 467

race, 84–5, 170, 183–8, 192, 197, 208, 215, 219–20, 224–6, 365
Read, Sarah, 32–3, 244
Reid, Whitelaw, 294, 304
religion, 17, 21, 40
  clergy, 17, 19, 23, 40, 138
  toleration of, 122
  see also Anglicans; Calvinism; Deism; Franklin, Benjamin; Great Awakening; Presbyterians; Protestantism; Quakers

"Remarks Concerning the Savages of North-America" (Franklin), 175, 178
republicanism, 51, 126–7, 161, 218, 300, 342, 381, 405–6, 435
Revolutionary War, 68–9, 115, 210, 386
Rice, Grantland, 220, 407
Richardson, Charles, 296, 305, 396
Richardson, Samuel, 271, 279
Richmann, Georg Wilhelm, 322–3
Rigal, Laura, 414
rights, 47, 55
Rittenhouse, David, 416, 481
Roach, Hannah Benner, 244
Rockinghman, Marquis de (Charles Watson-Wentworth), 75–6
Rogers, John, 32, 34–5
Roney, Jessica Chapman, 351
Rose, Aquila, 27
Rossiter, Clinton, 47, 147, 148, 156, 436
Rousseau, Jean-Jacques, 190
Royal African Company, 197
Royal Society, 41, 214, 353–4, 417
royalism, 50–1
  royal government, 152
"Rules By Which a Great Empire May be Reduced to a Small One" (Franklin), 174
Rush, Benjamin, 78, 154

sailors, 74
Sandiford, Ralph, 191
Sanford, Charles L., 399
Sartine, Gabriel de, 72
Schlesinger, Arthur M., Sr., 158, 300
Schneider, Herbert W., 400
Schultz, Ronald, 93
science, 40–2, 308–3, 335
Scull, Nicholas, 30
Seavey, Ormond, 49, 61, 405
servants, 191–2, 214, 216, 222, 227–9, 231
  fugitive, 217, 229
Seven Years' War, 44, 115–18, 123, 170, 173–4, 190, 194, 196, 227, 229, 283, 322, 330, 364, 469–71
Sevier, John, 180, 200
Sewall, Samuel, 8, 17, 20, 22
  The Selling of Joseph, 20
Shaftesbury, Earl of (Anthony Ashley Cooper), 130, 143, 337
Shannon, Timothy, 226, 466

INDEX

Sharp, Granville, 183, 197, 198, 201, 203–4, 209, 231–2
Shaw, Peter, 270
Shea, Daniel, 265
Shear, Walter, 401
Shelburne, Earl of (William Petty), 75–6, 77, 195, 328–9, 370, 475
Sherman, Stuart, 396
Shields, David, 337–8, 343
Shipley, Joseph, 269
Sierra Leone, 204
"Silence Dogood" essays (Franklin), 15–18, 275, 297, 338
Simpson, Lewis P., 405
slavery, 20–1, 85, 183, 197–209, 211–35
slaves, 44, 85, 188, 191–3, 216, 225, 231–3, 364
 fugitive, 189, 191, 225
 slave rebellion, 159
Sloane, Hans, 29
smallpox controversy, 14–15, 35
 inoculation, 14–15, 35
Smith, Adam, 49, 211–12, 235, 342, 363
Smith, Billy G., 149
Smith, Jeffrey A., 299, 300
Smith, William, 126, 348, 480

Smyth, Albert Henry, 297, 396, 434
societies *see* voluntary associations
Somerset v. Steuart, 233, 364
Sons of Liberty, 157
 Massachusetts, 157
South Carolina, 148
sovereignty, 128
 see also Parliament
Spain, 73, 76, 225
Spectator, The (Addison and Steele), 14, 130, 134, 337, 405
"Speech of Miss Polly Baker, The" (Franklin), 144, 222, 453, 460
Spencer, Archibald, 41
Spengemann, William, 265
Spiller, Robert E., 399
Spotswood, Alexander, 39
Stallybrass, Peter, 305–6, 314–15, 409, 427
Stamp Act, 47, 53–6, 57, 65, 66, 146, 154, 172, 173, 195
Stansbury, Joseph, 387
Stevenson, Margaret, 240, 241, 245
Steward, Dr. George, 14
Stourzh, Gerald, 151, 464–5, 470, 471, 476
Stout, Harry S., 139
Strahan, William, 40, 167

Strauss, Leo, 433
Straussians, 433–4, 435, 450

Tathem, Campbell, 403
taxes, 33, 54–6, 58, 115, 118–19, 123, 124, 153–4, 229, 283
  see also Stamp Act; Townshend Acts
Temple, John, 59
Tercentenary of Franklin's birth, 86, 415, 497
Terrell, Colleen E., 409
Thomas, Isaiah, 291, 293
Thompson, E.P., 84, 93, 99
Tise, Larry, 86, 240, 244, 250
Tocqueville, Alexis de, 336, 356
Tourtellot, Arthur B., 7
Townshend Acts, 56–8, 148
Townshend, Charles, 55
treaties *see* Indians
Treaty of Alliance (1778), 73, 463, 475
Treaty of Amity and Commerce (1778), 73, 475
Treaty of Paris (1783), 146, 158, 198, 476
Trenchard, John, 264, 269, 280
Tryon, Thomas, 10
Tyler, Moses Coit, 396

Union Fire Company, 31
University of Pennsylvania, 31, 42, 100, 113, 115, 255, 346, 348

Van Alstyne, Richard, 155
Van Doren, Carl, 2, 54, 57, 63, 88–9, 90, 297, 380, 399, 438, 495
Van Gastel, Ada, 404
Van Horne, John C., 341
Vaughan, Benjamin, 265–7, 268, 270, 271, 367–8, 435
Vergennes, Comte de (Charles Gravier), 70, 72–3, 75–6, 367, 475
Virginia, 205–6, 233
Voltaire, 309, 321
voluntary associations, 19, 100, 111, 282–3, 335–58, 459
  see also specific organizations
Von Haller, Albrecht, 320

Waldstreicher, David, 1, 3, 86, 95, 99, 141, 149, 156, 240, 246, 405, 408, 410, 413, 418, 459, 494
Walking Purchase, 43, 167
Walters, Kerry S., 129–37, 140–2, 144

War of Austrian Succession *see* King George's War
Ward, John William, 62, 402, 431–2
Waring, John, 192
Warner, Deborah Jean, 91, 409, 420
Warner, Michael, 161, 220, 281, 337, 341, 405–6, 407
Washington, George, 66, 67, 75, 180, 421, 479, 480, 482, 487, 488
Watson, William, 318
Way to Wealth, The (Franklin), 49, 148, 277, 283–4, 287–8, 434, 485, 488
Webb, George, 30
Weber, Max, 288, 398, 425, 431
Wedderburn, Alexander, 60–1, 233
Weems, Mason Locke, 129, 487
Weinberger, Jerry, 132–7, 433, 446–50
Weiser, Conrad, 176, 327
Wendel, Thomas, 54
Wendell, Barrett, 296
Wentworth, Paul, 365–6, 476
West Indies, 32, 77, 202, 206, 212, 366, 409, 471
Wetherell, Charles, 301
Whateley, Thomas, 59
Whateley, William, 59

Whig historians, 52, 53
Whig ideology, 13, 47, 280
 see also republicanism
White, Allon, 314–15
White, Ed, 408, 410
Whitefield, George, 40, 139–41, 258, 407
Whitemarsh, Thomas, 38, 96, 277
Wieland (Brown), 308–10, 314, 323
Wilberforce, William, 206
Wilcox, John, 29
Willcox, William, 56
Williams, Eric, 211
Williams, William Appelman, 151, 155, 158, 226
Wilson, R. Jackson, 419
women, 18–20, 31–4, 75, 85, 86, 185, 284, 410
 education of, 19–20
 English, 187, 247
 German, 187, 245, 247
 see also Franklin, Benjamin; individual women
Wood, Gordon, 49–52, 57, 59, 63, 89, 90–9, 133, 149, 152, 156, 159, 160, 212, 240, 310–11, 340, 343, 350, 354, 355, 372, 404, 432, 433, 456, 465–6, 471

Wright, Esmond, 48–9, 50, 52, 89, 338, 340
Wrightson, Nicholas, 409
Wroth, Lawrence C., 166

Zall, P.M., 269, 272, 428
Ziff, Larzer, 156, 161
Zochert, Donald, 491
Zuckerman, Michael, 340, 341, 409

DATE DUE